SPANISH FASHION IN THE AGE *of* VELÁZQUEZ

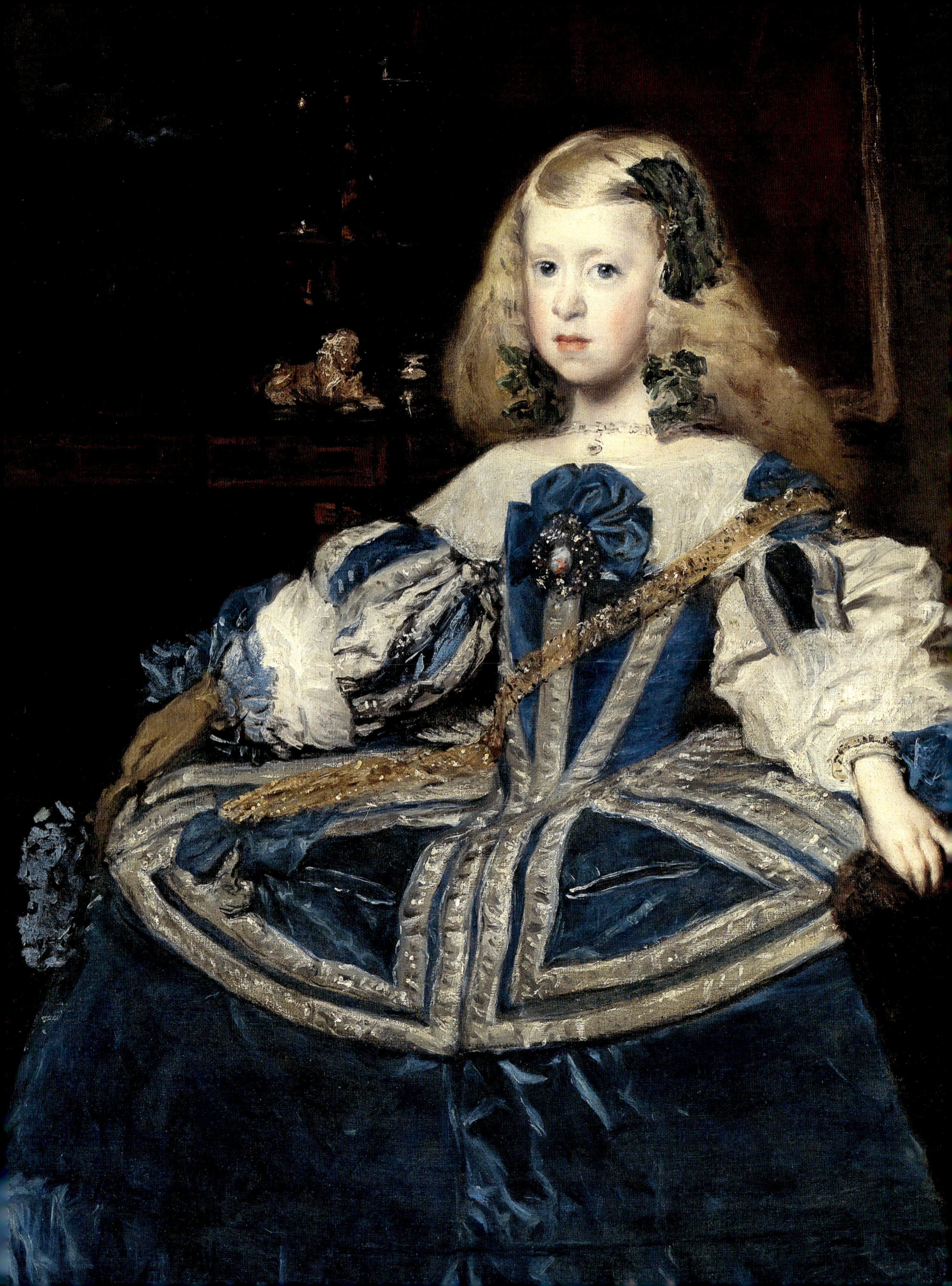

SPANISH FASHION IN THE AGE *of* VELÁZQUEZ

A Tailor at the Court of Philip IV

Amanda Wunder

Yale University Press ~ New Haven and London

This publication is made possible in part from the Barr Ferree Foundation Fund for Publications, Department of Art and Archaeology, Princeton University.

Published with assistance from the Custard Institute for Spanish Art and Culture at the Meadows Museum, SMU.

This book has received the Weiss-Brown Publication Subvention Award from the Newberry Library. The award supports the publication of outstanding works of scholarship that cover European civilization before 1700 in the areas of music, theater, French or Italian Literature, or cultural studies. It is made to commemorate the career of Howard Mayer Brown.

First published by Yale University Press 2024
302 Temple Street, P. O. Box 209040, New Haven CT 06520-9040
47 Bedford Square, London WC1B 3DP
yalebooks.com | yalebooks.co.uk

Library of Congress Control Number: 2022950775

ISBN 978-0-300-24654-4

A catalogue record for this book is available from the British Library

10 9 8 7 6 5 4 3 2 1
2028 2027 2026 2025 2024

Designed by Catherine Bankhurst
Copy edited by Lise Connellan

Printed and bound in Spain by Tallers Gràfics Soler

Front cover: Diego Velázquez, *Queen Mariana of Austria*, 1652 (detail of fig. 27)

Back cover: Unknown Spanish artist, *View of the River Manzanares During the Festival of Saint John the Baptist*, c. 1650–60 (detail of fig. 15)

Front flap: Tailor's shears (see fig. 7)

Frontispiece: Diego Velázquez, *Infanta Margarita in Blue*, 1659 (detail of fig. 151)

FSC www.fsc.org MIX Paper | Supporting responsible forestry FSC® C051148

CONTENTS

Maps

Maps of Spain and Madrid with place names mentioned in the text.

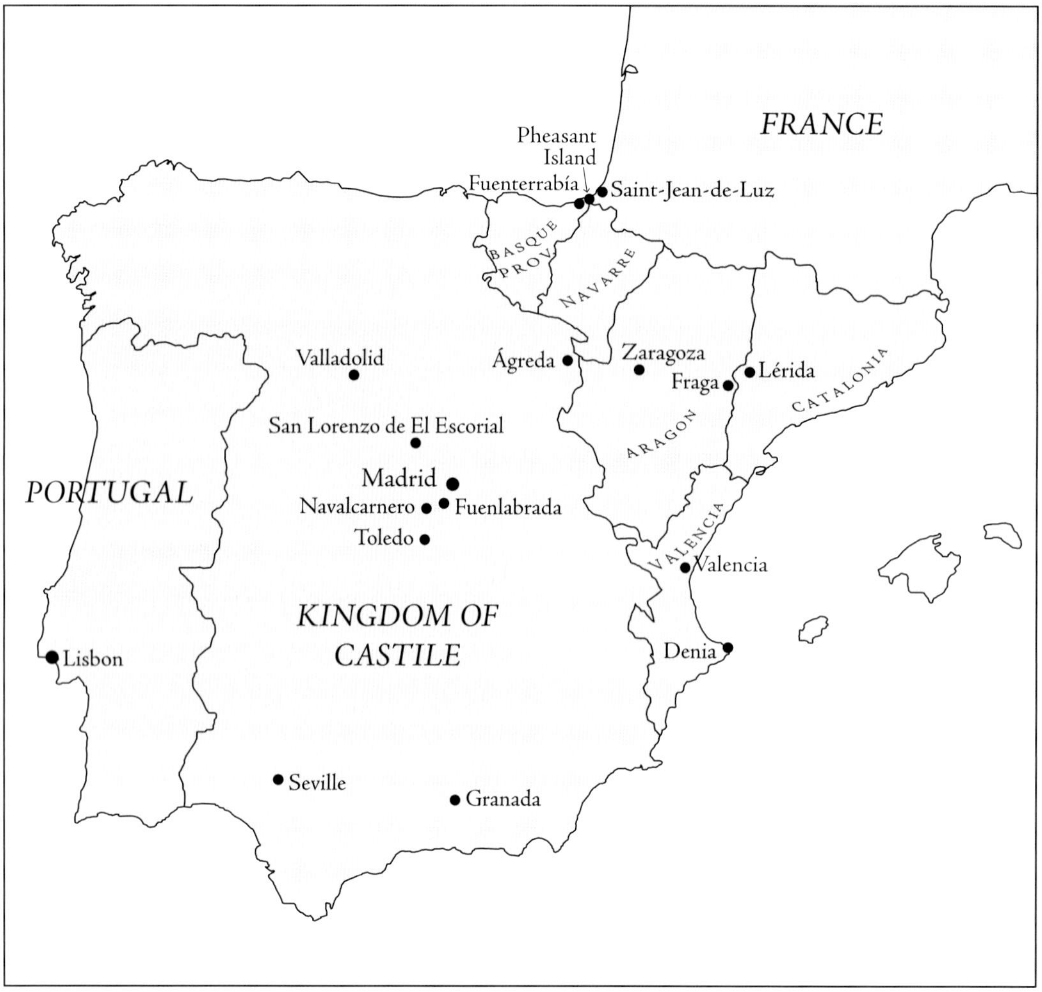

Map 1. Spain during the reign of Philip IV

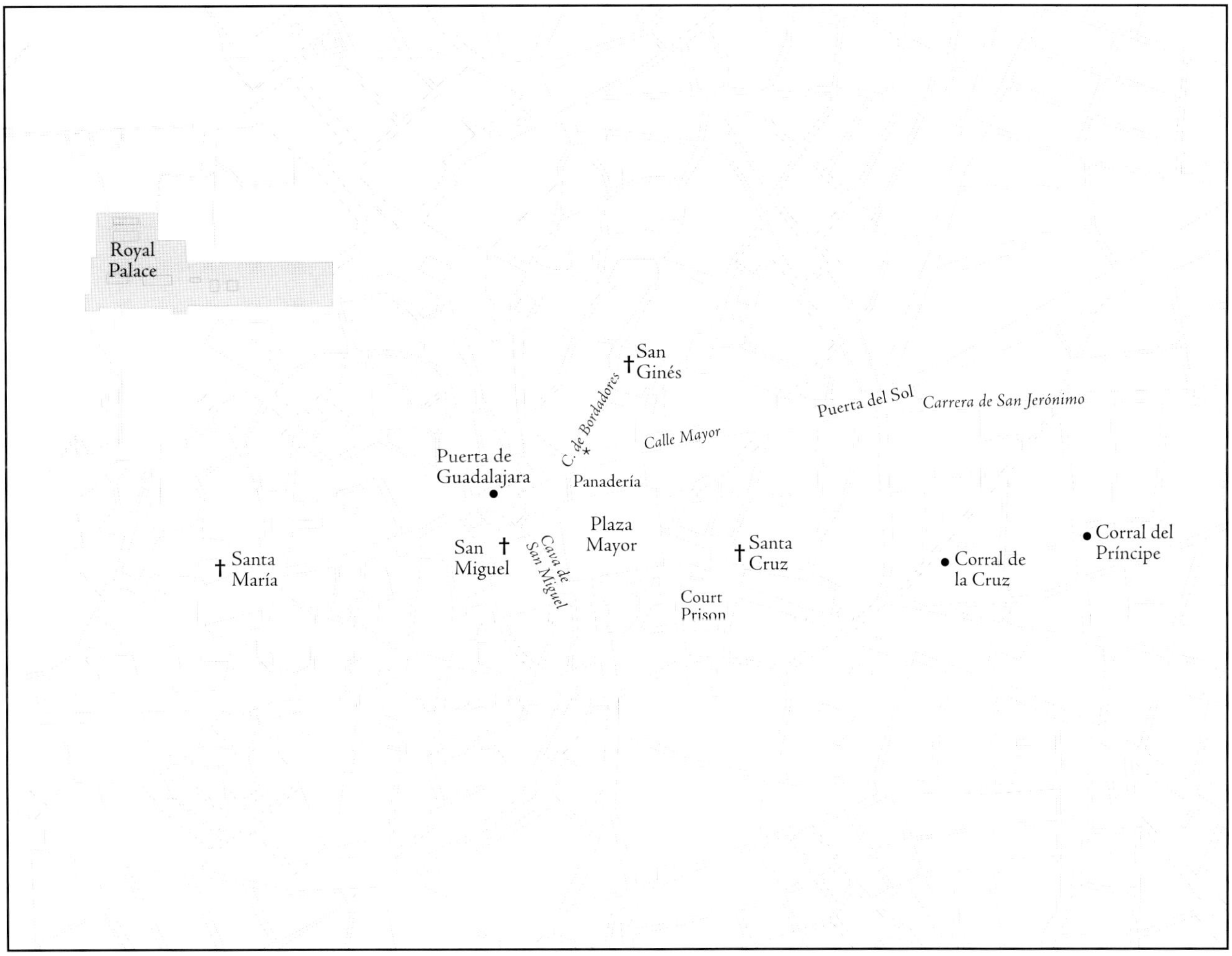

Map 2. Mateo Aguado's Madrid

Family Trees

Names, dates, and occupations (when known) of persons featured in this book.

Family Tree of Mateo Aguado

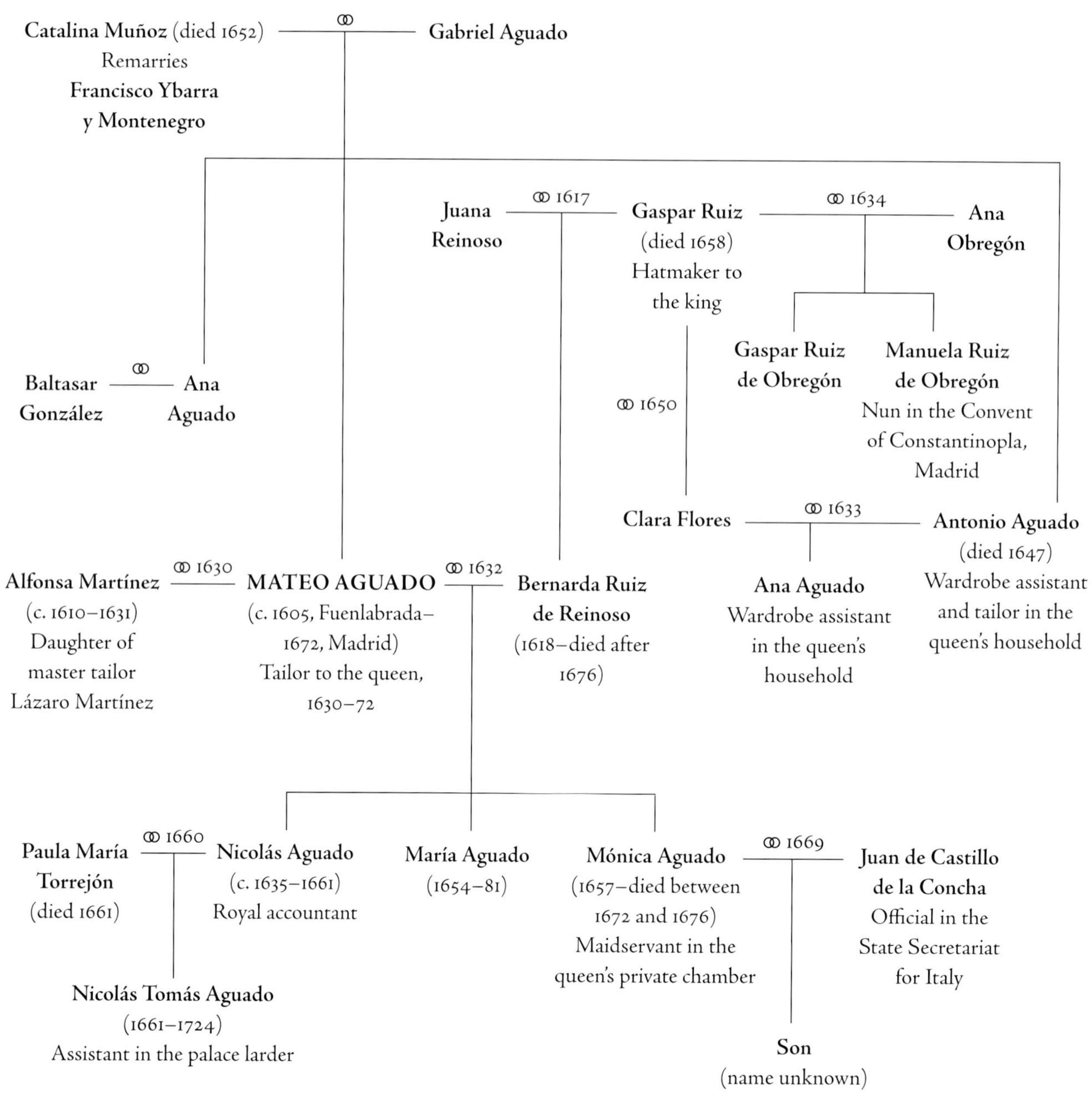

Family Tree of Philip IV

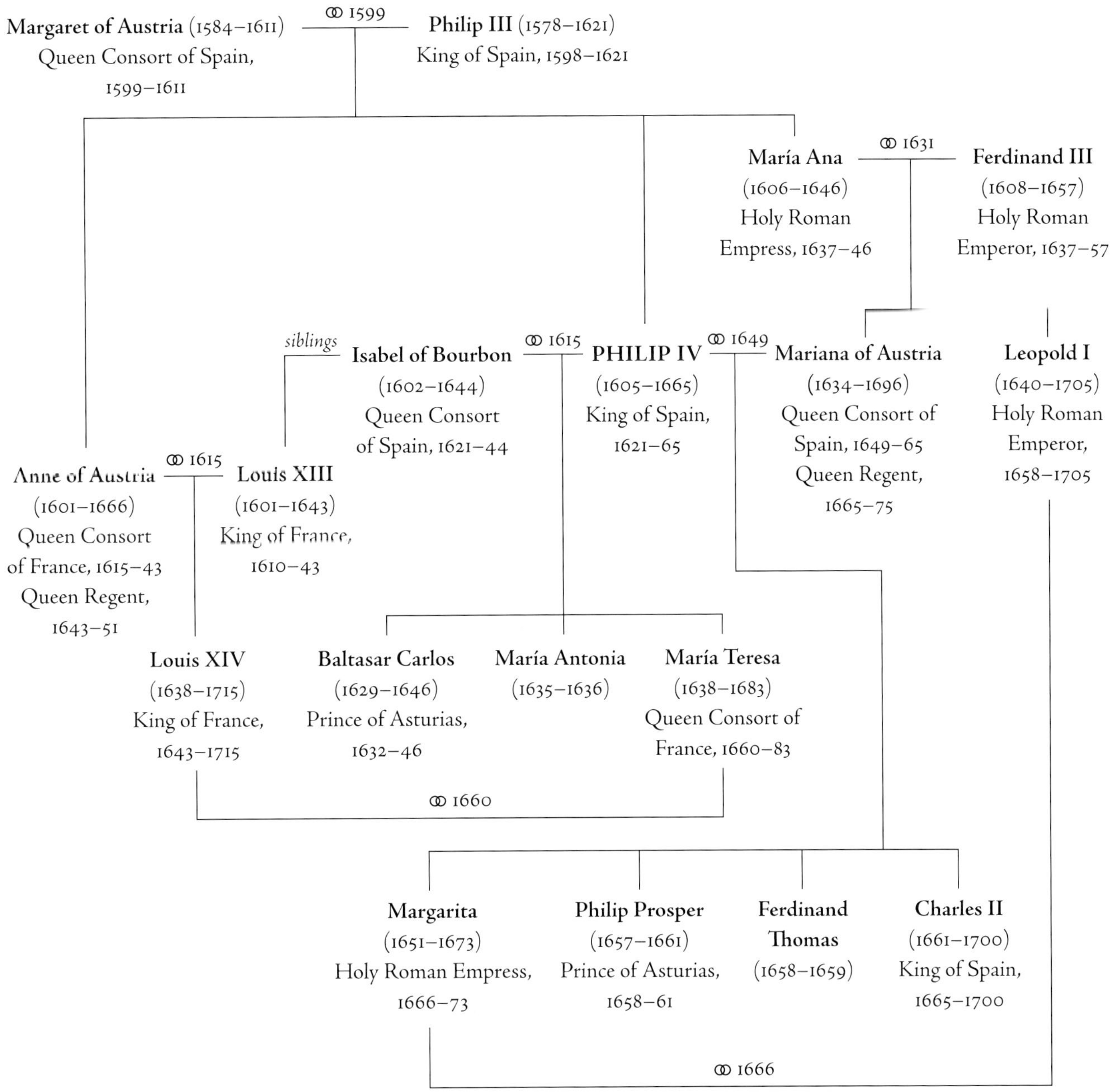

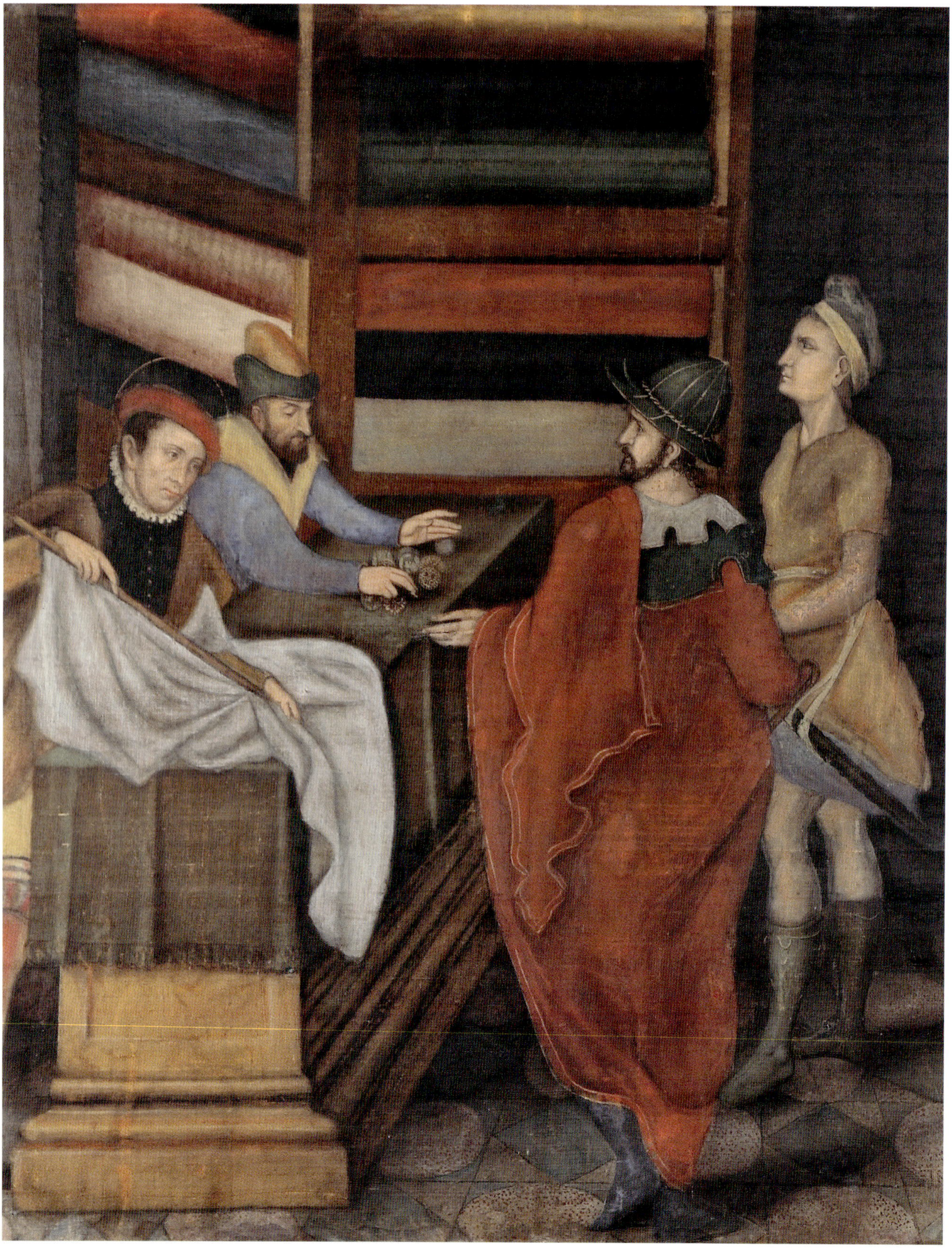

Measurements and Prices

Units of measurement

Fabric was measured by the Castilian *vara* (rod), a linear measurement slightly shorter than one English yard, which was subdivided into *pies* (feet) and *dedos* (fingers).

1 *vara*	=	84 centimeters
1 *pie*	=	28 centimeters
1 *dedo*	=	1.75 centimeters

Silk sewing thread and threads of silver and gold were measured by the *onza*, equal to one ounce today (approximately 28 grams).

Currency

The currency units used in seventeenth-century Spain included, from smallest to largest, *maravedís*, *reales*, and *ducados*, which had the following relative values:

1 *real*	=	34 *maravedís*		
1 *ducado*	=	11 *reales*	=	375 *maravedís*

In this book, all prices have been converted into *reales* to facilitate comparisons.

(facing page) Unknown Spanish artist, *Saint Francis of Assisi, Cloth Merchant* (detail of fig. 39)

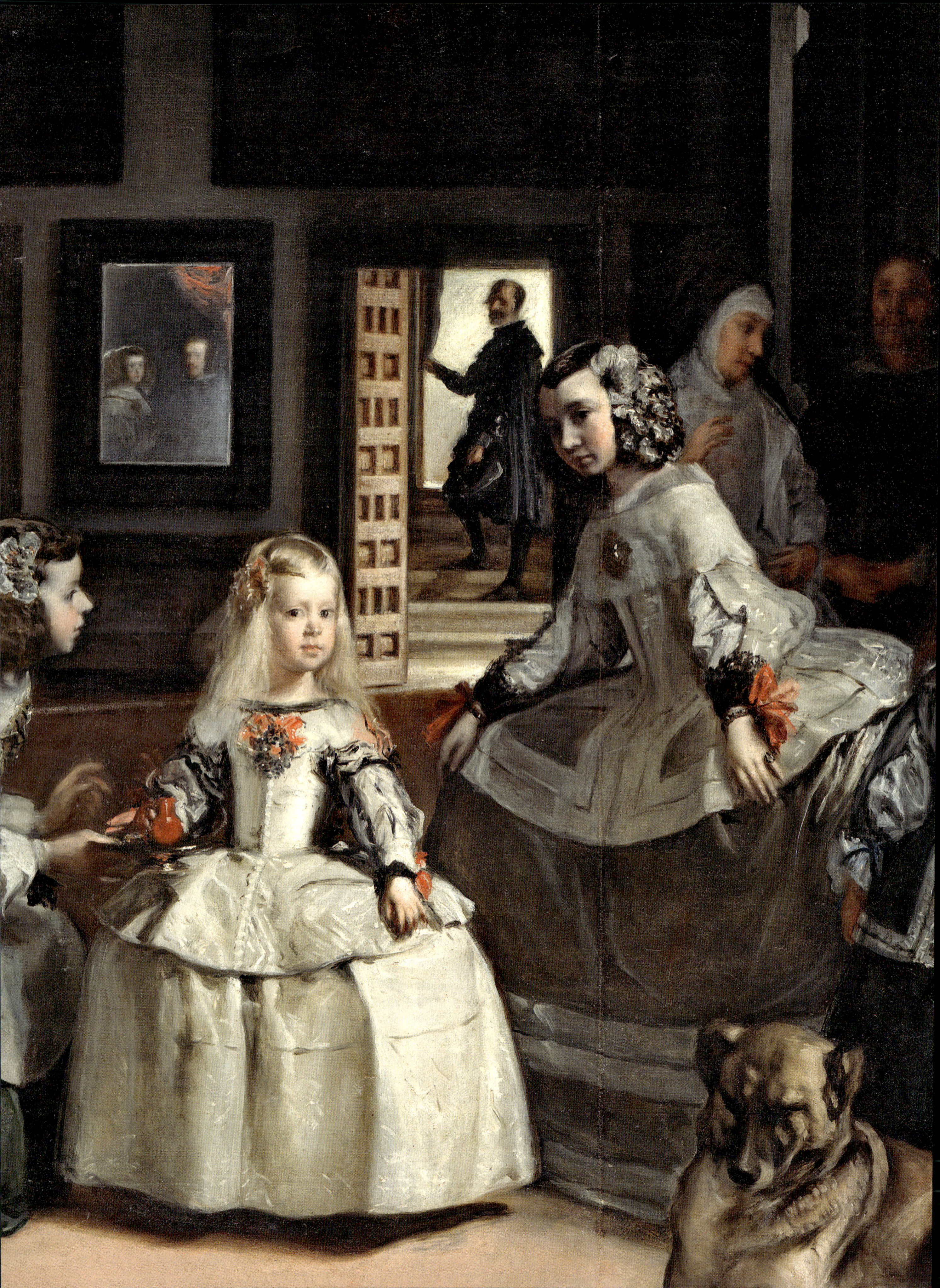

Introduction

Dressing Las Meninas

Diego Velázquez painted *The Family of Philip IV*, known today as *Las Meninas*, on an extra-large canvas made from three lengths of hemp cloth that were stitched together.[1] After the canvas had been primed with gritty earth-toned paint, the painter quickly laid out the composition using a long brush that let him see his work from a distance.[2] The painting features twelve figures, eleven of them human and one canine, with the king's younger daughter, the Infanta Margarita, at the center. The child models the latest courtly fashions, most notably an enormous skirt that is almost as wide as she is tall (fig. 1). She is attended by two *meninas*, as noble maids of honor were called, one of whom kneels within the cage of her hoopskirt to present the infanta with a cup of water (fig. 2). Velázquez presents himself at work, brush and palette in hand, standing in front of a canvas as large as this one. He wears a courtier's tight-fitting suit made from unwashable silk, which was unlikely attire for the activity of painting. The artist first sketched himself looking down at the infanta but changed his mind and shifted the position of his head to gaze directly out at the viewer—or, rather, at the king and queen whose likenesses are reflected in the framed mirror hanging on the back wall of the room. When the work was almost finished, Velázquez daubed thick blobs of white paint on the girls' dresses and jewelry to create sparkling highlights. Like an alchemist turning base metals into gold, he converted the rough hempen canvas and earthy pigments into smooth silks, intricate laces, and glittering silver trimmings. The members of the Spanish royal family and their court who are featured in *Las Meninas* reportedly visited the painter in his studio at the Royal Palace to watch the magic as it happened.[3]

Behind the scenes of *Las Meninas*, a small army of specialized artisans—tailors, hosiers, shoemakers, farthingale-makers, embroiderers, and laundresses, among many others—worked around the clock to craft and care for the elaborate court clothing that was worn by the royalty, ladies-in-waiting, dwarves, and painter in this picture.[4] One of them was Mateo Aguado (c. 1605–1672), head tailor in the queen's household—*sastre de cámara de la reina*—who was responsible for dressing the Infanta Margarita. Appointed tailor to the queen in 1630, Aguado occupied the position for over 40 years in a career that ran parallel to that of his famous colleague Velázquez. The two men surely crossed paths at court, although no documentation has surfaced so far to connect them directly. Both were engaged in the grand project of fashioning the royal image, and Aguado dressed many of Velázquez's portrait sitters: among them, the queens Isabel of Bourbon and Mariana of Austria; royal children Prince Baltasar Carlos, the

1. *(facing page)* Infanta Margarita in *Las Meninas* (detail of fig. 2)

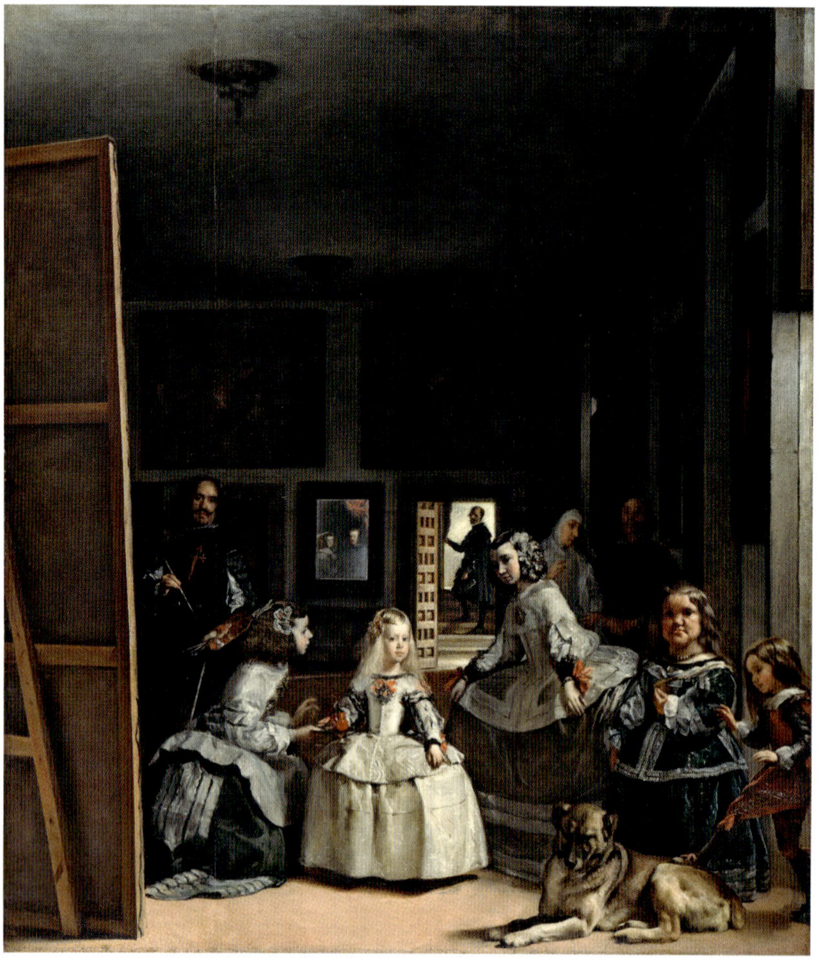

2. Diego Velázquez, *The Family of Philip IV ("Las Meninas")*, 1656. Oil on canvas, 320.5 × 281.5 cm. Museo Nacional del Prado, Madrid

3. *(facing page)* Velázquez's self-portrait in *Las Meninas* (detail of fig. 2)

Infanta María Teresa, and her younger half-sister Margarita; and court dwarves Francisco Lezcano and Nicolasito Pertusato, who prods the king's hunting dog with his toe in *Las Meninas*. Aguado and Velázquez held monopolies over their respective fields at court for decades and reached the heights of their creative powers in the 1650s, around the time that *Las Meninas* was painted. Both men were well rewarded for their many years of service to the court, although Aguado's relatively modest attempts at social climbing were much less successful than those of Velázquez. The painter reached the apex of social advancement toward the end of his life when he was granted membership in the Order of Santiago, a medieval military order named for the patron saint of Spain that only admitted members of the nobility, after a thorough investigation and interventions by the Spanish king and the pope in Rome. The red insignia of Santiago was added by someone else's hand to the breast of Velázquez's self-portrait in *Las Meninas* after his death (fig. 3).

Antonio Palomino predicted in his *Lives of the Eminent Spanish Painters and Sculptors* (1724) that Velázquez had made himself immortal by including his self-portrait in *Las Meninas*.[5] The centuries that

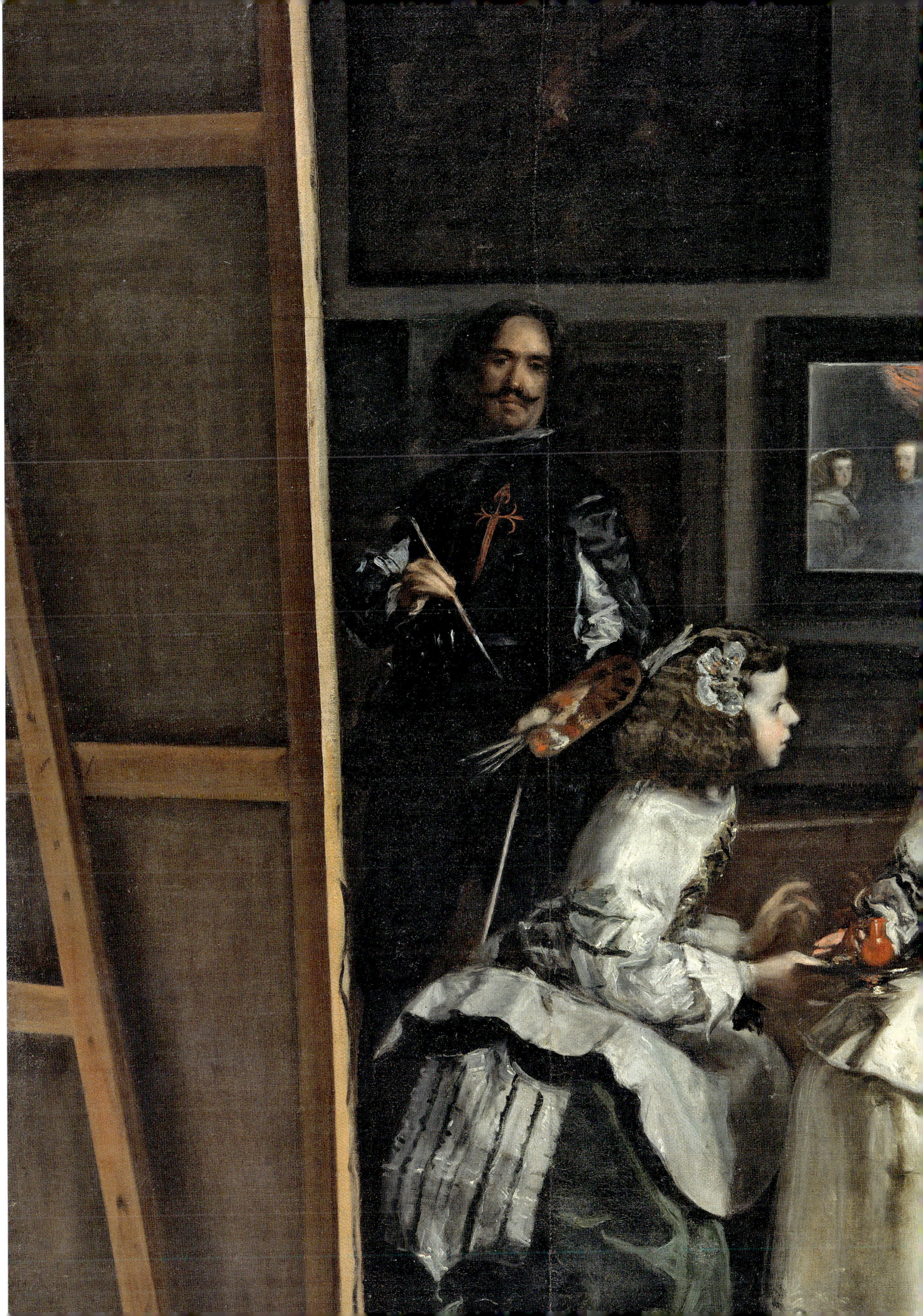

followed proved Palomino correct: Velázquez's fame and reputation rose to eclipse those of his royal patrons, who are remembered today primarily as the painter's subjects, instead of the other way around.[6] Meanwhile, Aguado was almost entirely forgotten.[7] There were no truly famous tailors until the English dress designer Charles Frederick Worth launched the era of the haute couturier in the late nineteenth century and rose to fame by fashioning himself as an artist.[8] While Aguado faded from memory, his work remained in the public eye through its representation in court portraits, especially after the opening of the Prado Museum in Madrid in 1819. Portraits of women dressed by Aguado inspired later generations of artists and dress designers. One was Jean-Philippe Worth (son of Charles Frederick), who recreated the pink and silver dress modeled by the Infanta Margarita in a portrait painted by Velázquez's protégé and successor, Juan Bautista Martínez del Mazo (fig. 4). The "infanta" costume was made for American socialite Kate Brice to wear to the famously decadent Bradley-Martin Ball at the Waldorf Hotel in New York City in 1897 (fig. 5).[9]

Aguado's fall into obscurity is not for lack of historical evidence. The tailor's lengthy career at court is prolifically documented in the General Archive of the Palace, and his personal and domestic life can be reconstructed in detail from notarial records that include a substantial postmortem inventory. Aguado's documentation includes no works of a personal nature to shed light on his inner world, but this is also true of Velázquez. That the painter was remembered while the tailor was forgotten is a product of the system in which they lived and worked. Painting was regarded as the higher art form, and there were deep-seated prejudices

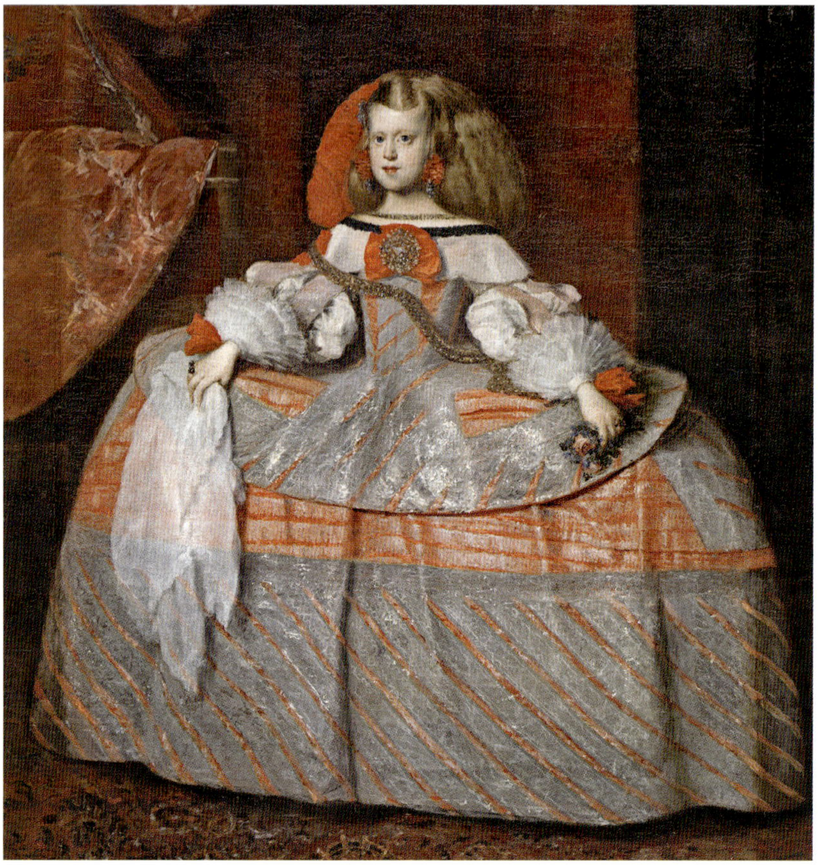

4. Juan Bautista Martínez del Mazo, *Infanta Margarita in Pink and Silver* (detail of fig. 170)

5. *(facing page)* "Infanta" costume by Jean-Philippe Worth for the House of Worth, 1897. White satin bodice and skirt overlaid with rows of organza ribbon and silver lace; organza sleeves with satin bands; machine-made cream lace apron, collar, and cuff edges. Museum of the City of New York

against tailors in the popular culture in the seventeenth century. In the twenty-first century, Madrid's tailors as a collective have been the subject of works of social history, but the things that they made have attracted scant attention.[10] Academic studies and exhibitions have tended to focus on the period immediately preceding Philip IV's reign, when Spanish fashion was at the height of its global influence.[11] Following the example of British dress historian Janet Arnold, whose archival investigations brought to light the work of Queen Elizabeth I's tailor Walter Fyshe, this book seeks to rescue Mateo Aguado from obscurity.[12] By presenting Aguado's life and work in the first full-length study of an individual premodern tailor, the following pages make the case for his inclusion among the major culture-makers at Philip IV's court. In his role as tailor to the queen for over four decades, Aguado was the most important and influential women's dress-designer in the seventeenth-century Spanish world. The goal of this book is to put the tailor back in the picture.[13]

The Art of Tailoring in Early Modern Spain

A tailor was an artisan who "cut out clothes and dresses," as the job was defined by Sebastián de Covarrubias Orozco in the first Castilian dictionary, published in 1611.[14] Throughout early modern Europe, a tailor was identified by his cutting shears: some London tailors signed official documents using a glyph of scissors.[15] In Giovanni Battista Moroni's famous portrait of an unidentified Northern Italian tailor, the elegantly dressed artisan is picking up a pair of shears with his right hand, on the verge of cutting into a piece of black

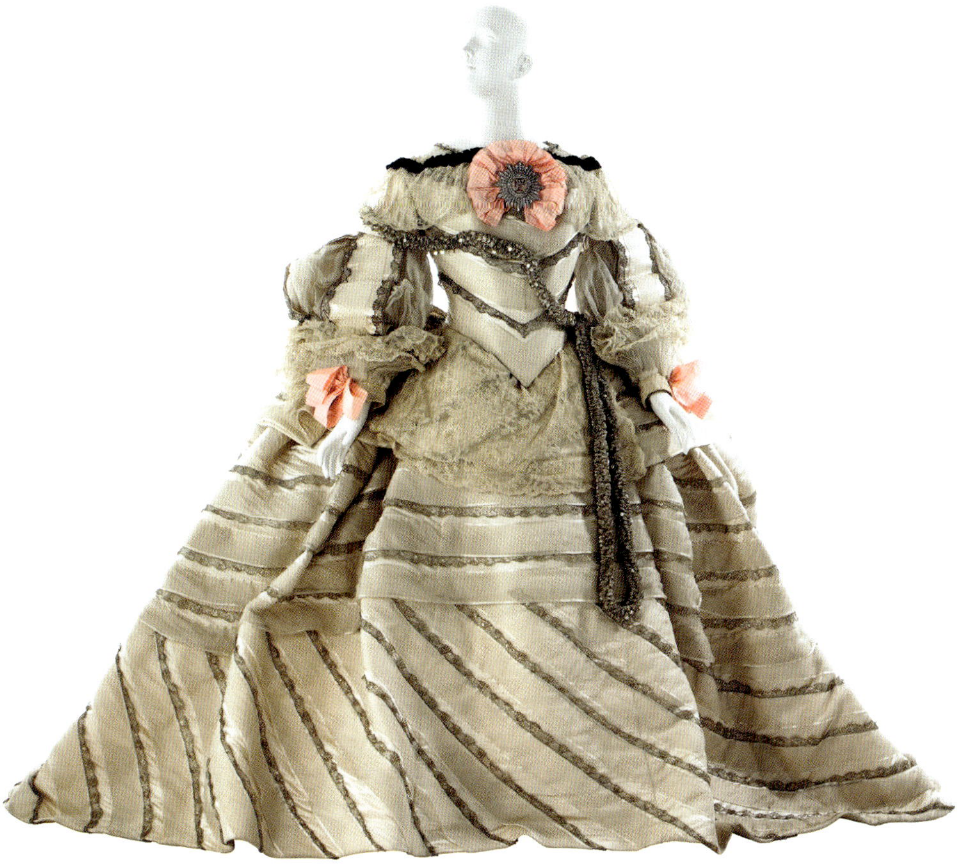

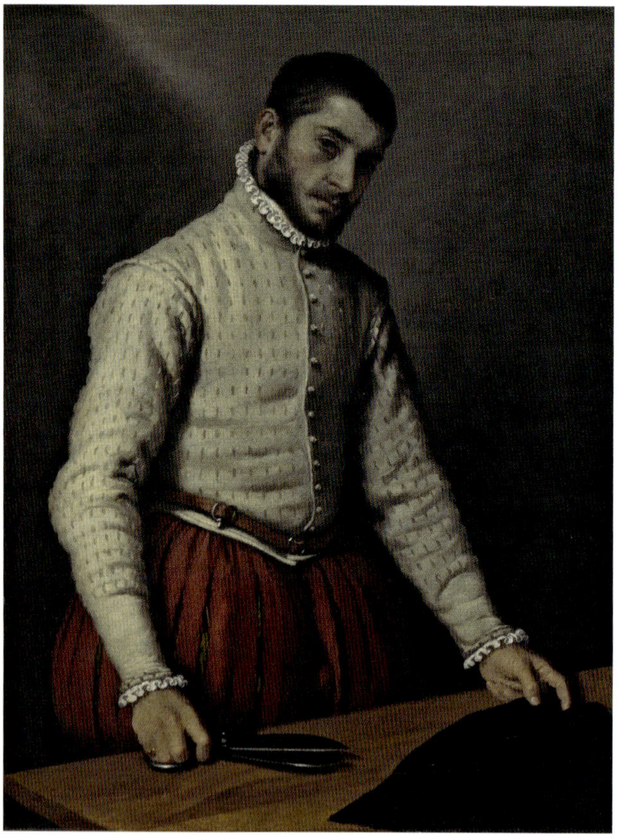

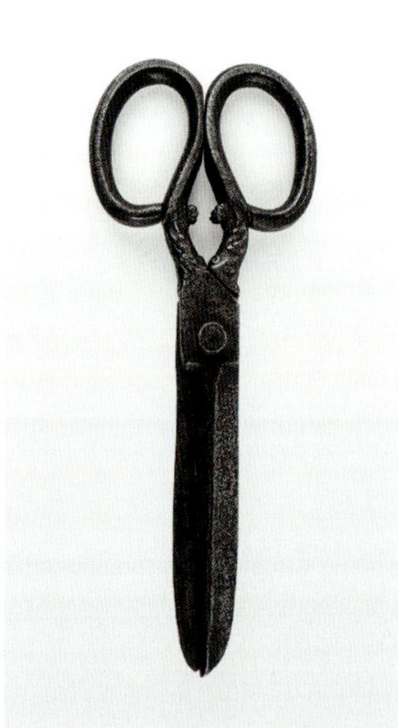

6. *(far left)* Giovanni Battista Moroni, *The Tailor*, 1565–70. Oil on canvas, 99.5 × 77 cm. National Gallery, London

7. *(left)* Scissors, French, 16th century. Iron, 28 cm long, weight 576 grams. MAK–Museum of Applied Arts, Vienna

fabric that has been lightly marked with white cutting lines (fig. 6). A tailor's scissors were a tool of substance: a sixteenth-century pair similar to those used by Moroni's tailor weigh well over half a kilogram (fig. 7).[16] Miguel de Cervantes used the association between tailors and their sizeable shears to comic effect in his play *The Great Sultana* (1615), in which a character masquerading as a tailor boasts, "I'm Spanish and a tailor, with such large scissors that the sun's great tailor doesn't have the like in his sphere."[17] Between 1580 and 1640, a sequence of manuals was published in Spain by master tailors who sought to distance their profession's association with the manual labor of cutting by emphasizing instead their intellectual practice based in geometry.[18] The first of these manuals, the *Book of Geometry, Practice, and Design* (1580, republished in 1589) by the Basque-born master tailor Juan de Alcega, opens with a portrait of the author manipulating the geometer's compass and rule, while his scissors rest on the table in front of him (fig. 8).[19] In another tailoring manual, published in 1617, the Catalan tailor Baltazar Segovia poses with the tools of his trade just like Alcega did, although his fashionable attire has been updated and he wears a significantly larger ruff around his neck (fig. 9).[20]

Tailors and painters were both categorized as *oficiales de manos*—that is, craftsmen who worked with

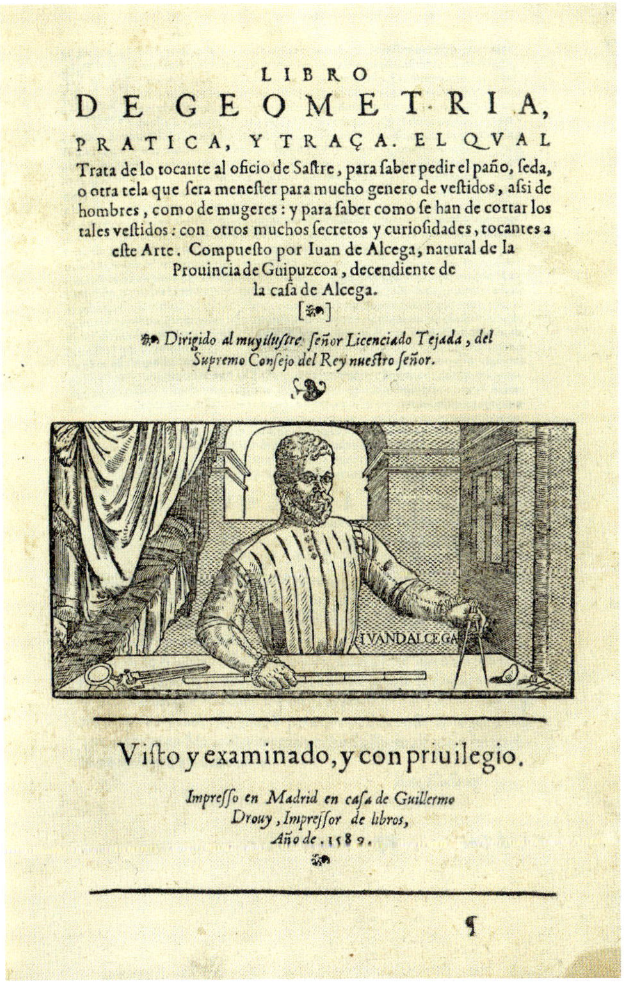

LIBRO
DE GEOMETRIA,
PRATICA, Y TRAÇA. EL QVAL
Trata de lo tocante al oficio de Saſtre, para ſaber pedir el paño, ſeda, o otra tela que ſera meneſter para mucho genero de veſtidos, aſsi de hombres, como de mugeres: y para ſaber como ſe han de cortar los tales veſtidos: con otros muchos ſecretos y curioſidades, tocantes a eſte Arte. Compueſto por Iuan de Alcega, natural de la Prouincia de Guipuzcoa, decendiente de la caſa de Alcega.

Dirigido al muy illuſtre ſeñor Licenciado Tejada, del Supremo Conſejo del Rey nueſtro ſeñor.

Viſto y examinado, y con priuilegio.

Impreſſo en Madrid en caſa de Guillermo Drouy, Impreſſor de libros, Año de. 1589.

¶

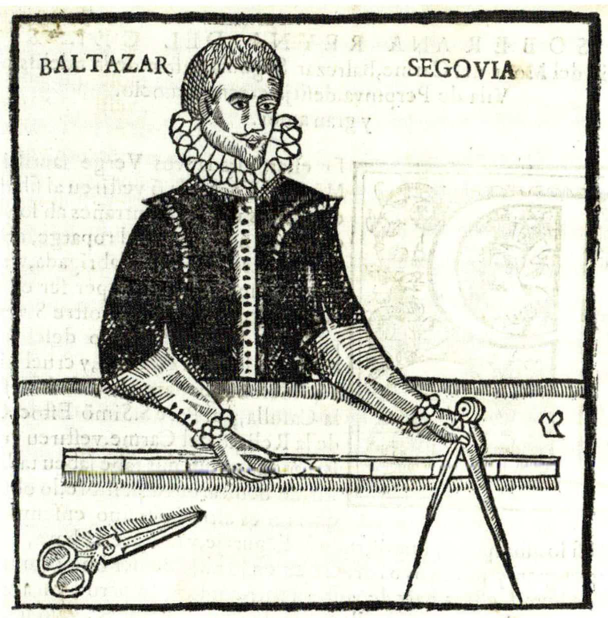

8. *(left)* Author portrait of Juan de Alcega, *Libro de geometria, practica, y traça* (Madrid, 1589). Woodcut, 30 × 21.5 cm. The Metropolitan Museum of Art, New York

9. *(below)* Author portrait of Baltazar Segovia, *Llibre de geometria del offici de sastre* (Barcelona, 1617). Wood engraving, 11.5 × 11.5 cm. Bibliothèque nationale de France, Paris

their hands, along with carpenters, silversmiths, and shoemakers.[21] But there was a hierarchy among *oficiales de manos*, which was outlined by the lawyer Gaspar Gutiérrez de los Ríos, son of a royal tapestry-weaver, in his book of art theory, the *General Notice of the Estimation of the Arts*, in 1600.[22] A mechanical craft came naturally and could be learned in just half an hour, the author explained. In contrast, a mechanical art took time to learn, was governed by certain rules, and required its practitioners to have the use of reason. Cooking to feed oneself was a craft, for example, whereas cooking for a prince was an art. Gutiérrez de los Ríos categorized tailoring as a mechanical art, since it had rules for cutting out different kinds of garments and its practitioners had to master the skill of *tanteo*, which was estimating how much fabric was needed to make a garment. This was a complex calculation that depended on the garment pattern, the size of the client, and the fabric width and design. According to Gutiérrez de los Ríos, tailors had ingenuity—a quality that was also attributed to Velázquez—but they were a step below painters and other practitioners of liberal arts that relied more upon the intellect than the hands and body.[23] More specifically, the liberal arts used drawing for the purpose of imitating nature. According to this system of classification, the arts that were considered liberal included painting, tapestry-weaving, and a type of embroidery called *bordado de matices* that used shaded silks to create human, animal, and vegetal figures—but not embroidery using metal threads to make purely ornamental designs.[24]

Tailors' proprietary ability to estimate fabric inspired distrust among clients, who had to pay for the expensive fabrics and trimmings that tailors used in their made-to-measure garments. "What came first, the lie or the tailor?" quipped court satirist Francisco de Quevedo, drawing on the trope of the dishonest tailor.[25] Stories of cheating tailors abound in early-seventeenth-century Spanish literature. For example, in Carlos García's picaresque novel *Disorderly Greed for the Goods of Others* (1619), a cheating tailor orders a third more wool than he actually needs to make a suit of clothes. When his suspicious client insists on being present for the cutting of the cloth, the sneaky tailor distracts him and steals a valuable remnant.[26] Tailors were also considered suspect because their work brought them into close physical proximity with their female clients. In Cervantes's short story "The Jealous Old Man from Extremadura" (1613), the titular character does not want a tailor to take his young wife's measurements, so he hires a poor woman to serve as a stand-in.[27] The negative reputation of tailors was not unique to Spanish literature: tailors were just as maligned in Shakespeare's England as they were in Cervantes's Spain.[28] Tailors in Spain did, however, suffer from the particular misfortune that the Spanish word for "tailor"—*sastre*—rhymes with "disaster"—*desastre*. This coincidence proved irresistible to many a Golden Age poet.[29]

In light of the tailors' reputation for thievery, the manuals by Alcega and others, which revealed precisely how much material was needed to make various garments from different kinds of fabric, appear to have been designed to rehabilitate tailors' bad reputation by revealing their trade secrets. A skilled tailor had no need to consult the lists of fabric conversions in those books. The author of one such manual, Seville-based master tailor Diego de Freyle, suggested that his book would help tailors' clients "to know if the work they do for them is good or bad."[30] Freyle devoted a chapter of his 1588 book to "gallantry," in which he told tailors how to comport themselves while working in order to distinguish themselves from "lowly craftsmen" and villagers. He advised tailors to avoid making faces or sticking out their tongues when using scissors, "which looks bad to those who are watching and is the ugliest thing that a practitioner of this trade can do." When sewing, Freyle instructed, a tailor had to sit up straight to avoid developing a humpback, and pull the thread away from his face so he would not prick his nose and cheek with the needle.[31] Exquisite manners and careful grooming were especially important for a tailor who had ambitions to work at the court, as Madrid-based author Cristóbal Suárez de Figueroa explained. In order to work with elite clientele, he wrote, a tailor had to be neat and clean, courteous and discreet, unfailingly punctual, and "above all, not stupid."[32]

Cristóbal Suárez de Figueroa was a Spaniard who had spent 16 years in Italy, where tailors were increasingly respected for their creative work as designers in the late sixteenth and early seventeenth centuries.[33] After returning to Spain and settling in

Madrid, Suárez de Figueroa published his *Universal Plaza of All Sciences and Arts* (1615), which was a heavily revised Spanish edition of a popular Italian book of trades. The chapter on tailoring celebrated the state of the profession in the Spanish capital: "Today in Spain this art is practiced with remarkable conscientiousness," he wrote, "because although in times past there were great craftsmen, never before did the style of dress attain the perfection that it has today." Suárez de Figueroa praised the subtle ingenuity of Spanish tailors who were constantly inventing new styles, most of all the tailors at the court in Madrid who were "reforming clothes to modern and better fashion."[34] He admired the excesses of courtly fashions like *mangas de casaca*—tubular sleeves that served no practical function but looked dashing on the dance floor (fig. 10). Excess was the hallmark of courtly fashions during the reign of Philip III, who from the beginning of his kingship purposefully cultivated a "new style of grandeur," as his biographer Gil González Dávila described it (fig. 11).[35]

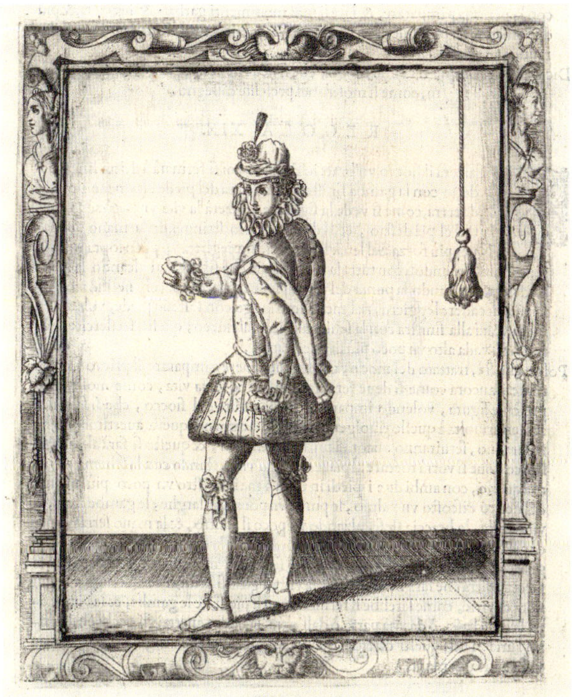

10. Dancing man wearing *mangas de casaca*. Cesare Negri, *Nuove inventioni di balli, opera vaghissima* (Milan, 1604). Engraving, 19.9 × 16 cm. Biblioteca Nacional de España, Madrid

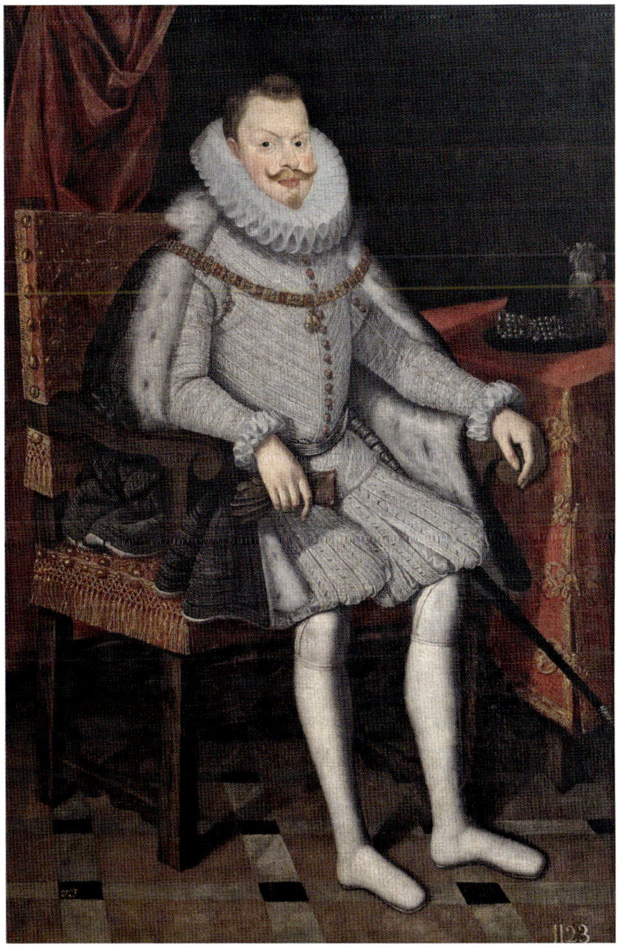

11. *(right)* Bartolomé González, *King Philip III*, c. 1615. Oil on canvas, 160 × 109 cm. Museo Nacional del Prado, Madrid

The next Spanish monarch, Philip IV, had a very different approach, which ushered in a new era for Spanish fashion—and for Spanish tailors.

Spanish Fashion During the Reign of Philip IV (1621–1665)

Before he became king, Philip IV dressed to reflect the grandeur of his father's rule. In a portrait painted prior to his succession, Prince Philip is resplendent in a suit of white silk covered with gold embroidery, a cloak lined in a brocaded silk with silver and gold stripes, and a large ruff trimmed in narrow pointed lace that is set into figures-of-eight (fig. 12). However, as king, Philip IV outlawed every one of these things. In February 1623, significant changes were imposed on Spanish dress as part of a sweeping reform package of 23 Articles of Reformation.[36] The most controversial law forbade men from wearing large, decorated ruffs (women were still permitted to wear them). Fabrics and trimmings made with silver and gold were banned for all but the church and military, and—in the most radical provision of all—dress decoration of any kind was outlawed. The only one of these reforms that had a lasting impact was the ban on the masculine ruff. It was replaced by the *valona*, a flat linen collar that was worn atop a stiff supporter called a *golilla*.[37] The king modeled the new style of collar with a plain black suit in a full-length portrait painted by Diego Velázquez, who had moved to Madrid from his native Seville in 1623 to seek his fortune at the court (fig. 13).[38] In contrast to court portraiture during the reign of Philip III, which meticulously detailed the luxurious fabrics and decorations that communicated grandeur, Velázquez's austere portrait of Philip IV in black projected a new image of reform.[39]

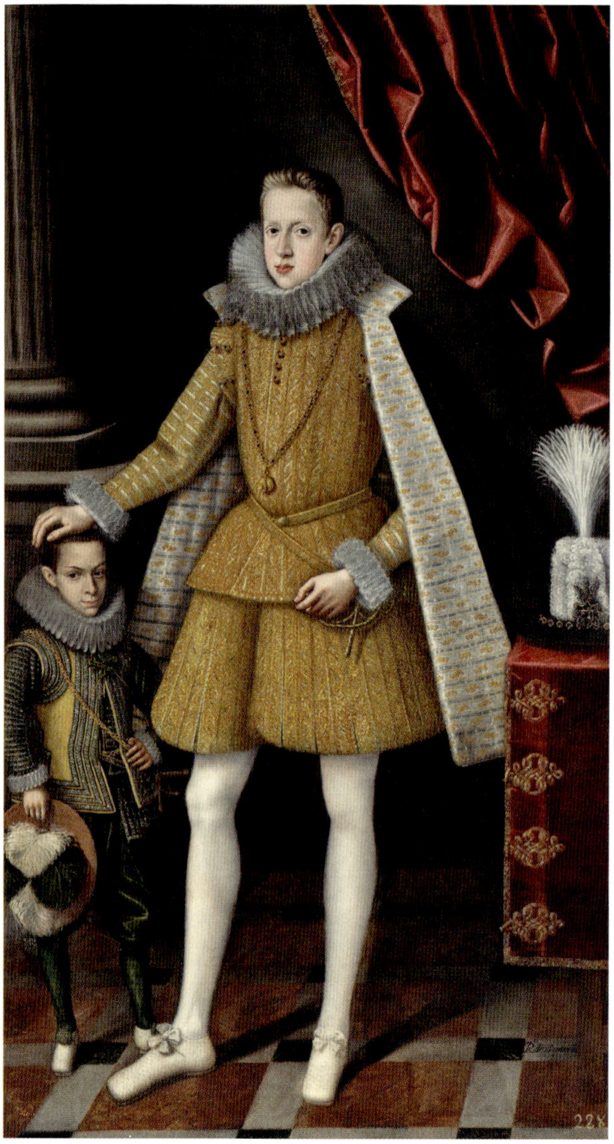

12. Rodrigo de Villandrando, *Prince Philip with Miguel Soplillo*, c. 1620. Oil on canvas, 204 × 110 cm. Museo Nacional del Prado, Madrid

13. *(facing page)* Diego Velázquez, *King Philip IV*, probably 1624. Oil on canvas, 200 × 102.9 cm. The Metropolitan Museum of Art, New York

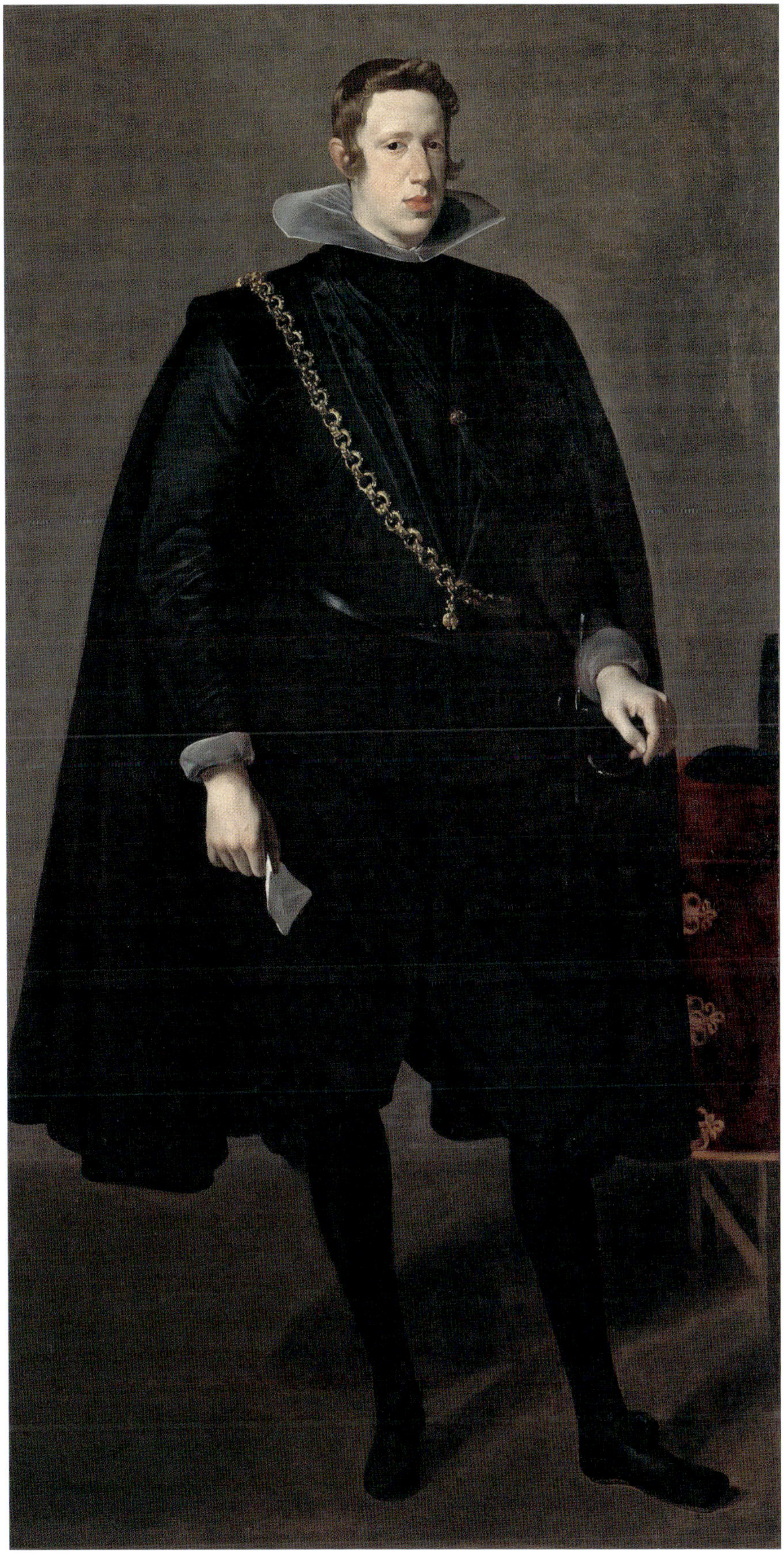

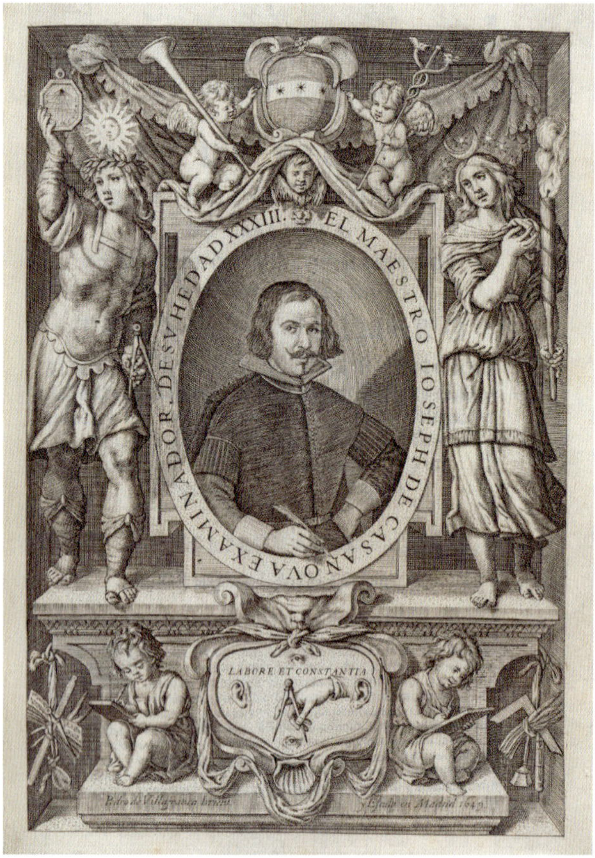

14. Author portrait of José de Casanova by Pedro de Villafranca, *Primera parte del Arte de escrivir todas formas de letras* (Madrid, 1650). Engraving, 31 × 22 cm. The Metropolitan Museum of Art, New York

The king had found the look, and the painter, that would define his reign.

The style of courtly dress that was established for men in the early 1620s remained more or less unchanged, with only minor adjustments, for the rest of Philip IV's reign.[40] Women's courtly fashions began to evolve in the 1630s after Mateo Aguado became the queen's tailor. During Aguado's four decades in office, women's fashions changed continuously, as the chapters in this book describe in detail (for a summary of these developments, see the Chronology of Women's Dress, pp. 214–18). Throughout Philip IV's reign, men's and women's fashions retained the elements of the Spanish style, which was characterized by closely fitted garments worn with support structures made from stiff materials that reshaped the body.[41] The clothes were uncomfortable and restrictive according to José de Casanova, a handwriting expert who complained about the fashions of the day in an off-topic aside in his *Art of Writing* (1650). A man's shoulder-wings—seen in Casanova's author portrait (fig. 14)—made it impossible for him to move his arms, while his legs were "skewered and oppressed" by fragile silk stockings and tight breeches. It was a time, Casanova lamented, when "the clothes are more in charge than the person."[42] Regarding women's fashions, he denounced the *guardainfante*, a farthingale so wide that a woman wearing one filled an entire street, and he expressed dismay over women's immodest low-cut bodices and transparent veils. In a view of Madrid painted in the 1650s, men and women dressed just as Casanova described them frolic along the banks of the Manzanares River on the June 24 feast day of Saint John the Baptist (fig. 15). Amid the dancing and picnicking revelers, the working men and women carrying bundles of laundry are dressed in simple, ragged clothes without the uncomfortable and bulky garments that defined and confined the elites.

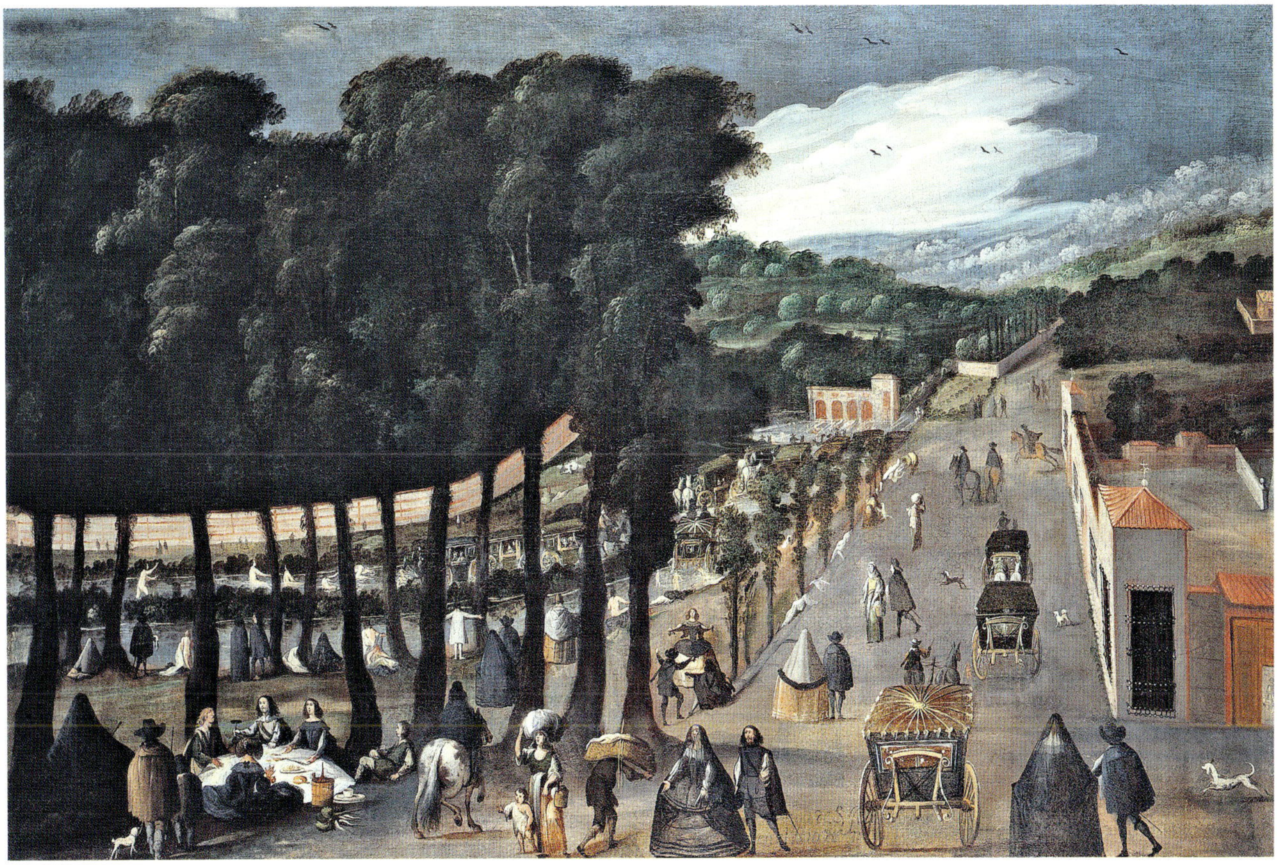

15. Unknown Spanish artist, *View of the River Manzanares During the Festival of Saint John the Baptist*, c. 1650–60. Oil on canvas, 103.8 × 157.5 cm. Abelló Collection, Madrid

Madrid was the fashion capital of the far-flung Spanish Empire, which at this time included Portugal, territories in the Netherlands and Italy (including the cities of Naples and Milan), colonies in North Africa, the Philippines, the Viceroyalties of New Spain (Mexico) and Peru, and islands in the Caribbean and Pacific. The restrictive style of Spanish fashion clearly identified subjects of the Spanish Crown and its allies at a time when other European courts—led by France—were adopting a less structured, more relaxed style of cultivated "negligence," as it was called, in men's and women's dress.[43] In a portrait painted in 1650, Swedish nobleman Nils Nilsson Brahe dresses in French style with a short doublet, richly trimmed in lace, that is undone in the front to show the billowing white shirt underneath (fig. 16). But Brahe had to exchange his French attire for a more buttoned-up Spanish suit in early 1655, when he traveled to Madrid to notify Philip IV

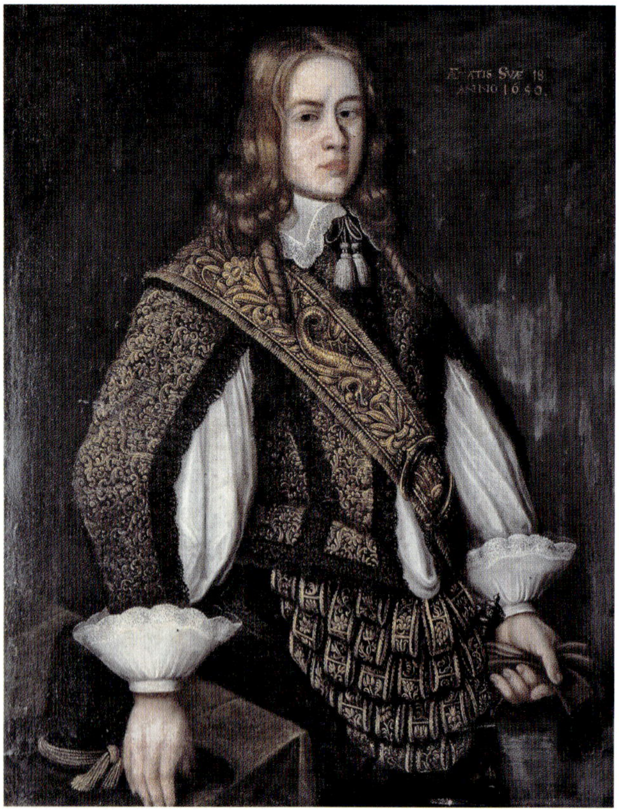

16. Attributed to Jakob Elbfas, *Nils Nilsson Brahe*, 1650. Oil on canvas, 140 × 100 cm. Skokloster Castle, Sweden

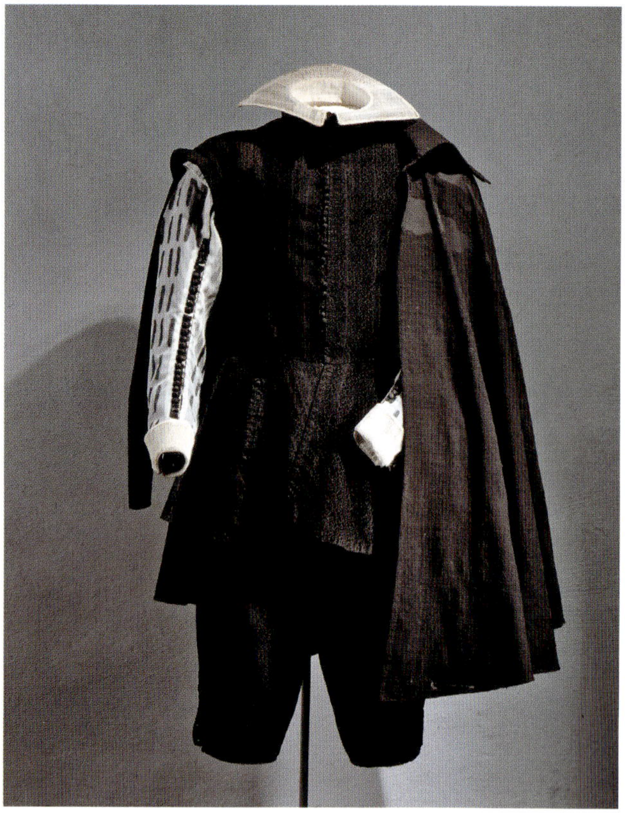

17. Nils Nilsson Brahe's Spanish suit, 1655. Camel hair wool cloak, uncut velvet cassock and breeches, blue silver moiré doublet, linen collar and cuffs. Skokloster Castle, Sweden

that the Swedish Queen Christina had abdicated her throne the previous summer. Brahe commissioned a complete Spanish suit from a Madrid tailor to wear during his audience with Philip IV (fig. 17). "I can hardly appear at court without being dressed in Spanish," he wrote to his uncle back home in Sweden.[44] Philip IV could impose his court's style of dress on foreign guests in Madrid, but Spanish fashion no longer set the pace at the courts of Europe, as it had in the sixteenth century.[45] The differentness of Spanish fashion, which was lampooned in satirical prints and theatrical productions in London and Paris, set Spain apart at a time when the country had more enemies (including France, England, and Portugal) than friends (primarily the Holy Roman Empire, under the rule of the Austrian branch of the house of Habsburg).[46] But even as Spain's influence on European fashion was in decline, Spanish tailoring commanded respect abroad for the quality of its craftsmanship.[47] Precious few examples of seventeenth-century Spanish tailoring have survived the centuries. One rare exception is Nils Brahe's Spanish suit, which he took home with him to Sweden as a memento of his travels to a foreign land—it certainly was not an outfit that he would have worn outside of his diplomatic service in Spain.

In Philip IV's Madrid, the theater and the church were two important venues for displaying, disseminating, and critiquing the latest fashions. Not coincidentally, these were among the few public spaces shared by unmarried men and women. Working classes and elites alike attended performances at open-air public theaters called *corrales* and at the Buen Retiro Palace.[48] In 1659 a French visitor reported seeing merchants and artisans who had abandoned their shops and gone to the theater dressed in capes, swords, and daggers, "everyone calling themselves gentlemen, down to the shoemakers."[49] Crowd-pleasing "cloak and dagger" plays featured the latest fashion trends as central plot devices, and theater companies spent lavishly on costumes.[50] What was worn on stage had widespread impact, and its influence can be found in the queen's wardrobe: in 1630, Queen Isabel of Bourbon wore a dress made from a black, brown, and silver grosgrain (*gorgorán*) called "schism of England"—the name surely derived from the title of a play by Pedro Calderón de la Barca that had been performed for the first time in 1627.[51] Although the play makes no reference to a fabric in such a color combination, it may have been worn during a performance. Like the theaters, Madrid's many churches were well known as places for seeing and showing off the latest fashions and accessories. In Alonso de Castillo Solórzano's picaresque novel, *Teresa de Manzanares* (1632), a woman wears a novel hairpiece to Mass at the Church of La Victoria at the Puerta del Sol, where it is much admired and imitated by the other women.[52] Devotional sculptures of the Virgin Mary, which played an important role in Spanish religious practices, were

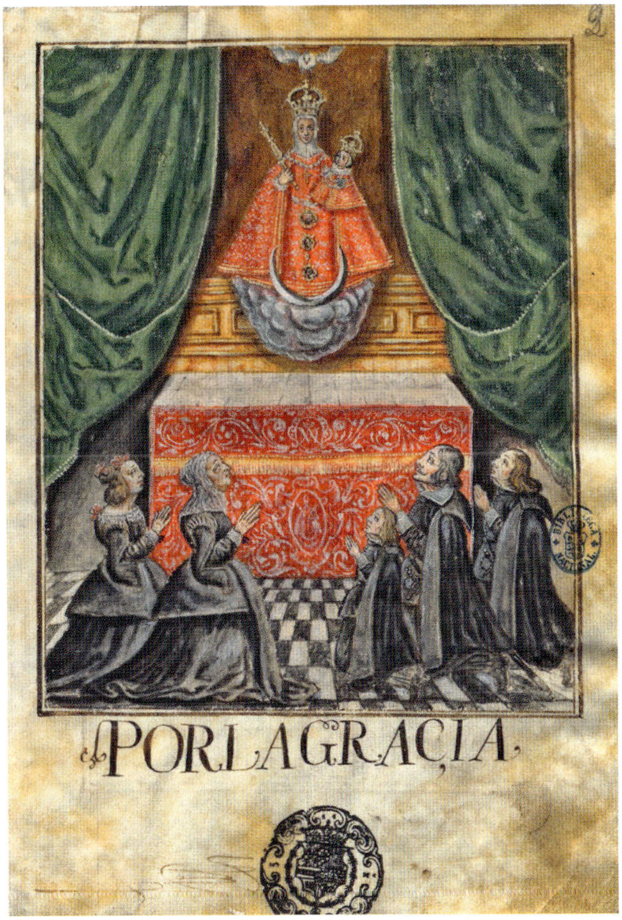

18. *Confirmation of Letters Patent of Nobility of Sebastián de Ortuño and His Sons, Residents of El Espinar*, Valladolid, 1652. Illumination on parchment, 29 × 21 cm. Biblioteca Nacional de España, Madrid

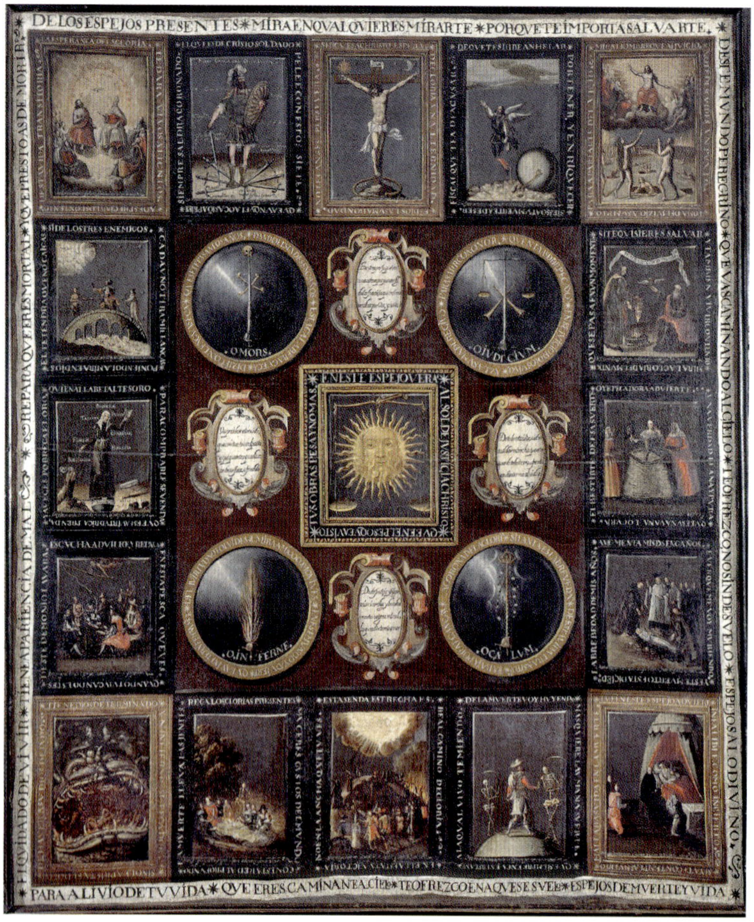

19. Unknown Madrid artist, *Allegory of the Mirror of Death and Life*, c. 1650. Oil on canvas, 214 × 184 cm (with frame). Museo de Burgos

dressed in real clothes made from the most sumptuous fabrics and decorated with trimmings of gold. Richly dressed sculptures of the Virgin and Christ Child are venerated by the family of Sebastián de Ortuño of El Espinar, a town 95 kilometers northwest of Madrid, in his illuminated *cartas ejecutorias*, which were letters patent of nobility (fig. 18).[53] In this important legal document, which proved the family's tax-exempt status, the Ortuños visually reinforce their claim to nobility by demonstrating their Christian piety and by appearing dressed in formal court fashions.

In seventeenth-century Spain, fashion was closely intertwined with religion despite the Catholic Church's long-standing antipathy. As far back as the eighth century, Saint Boniface denounced the "arrogance and pride and wantonness and vanity" of luxurious clothing "sent by Anti-Christ."[54] An unusual mid-seventeenth-century painted *Allegory of the Mirror of Death and Life* presents fashion as a vice that impedes the path to salvation (fig. 19).[55] In one scene, a young woman dressed in the courtly style of the 1650s primps in a mirror that reflects a skeleton back at her. The caption reads: "Look, sinner, heed a truth plain and pure, that it is vain insanity to dress this way" (fig. 20). On the opposite side of the mirror, a woman in a plain, unstructured habit with a rustic rope-belt around her waist, her hair covered by

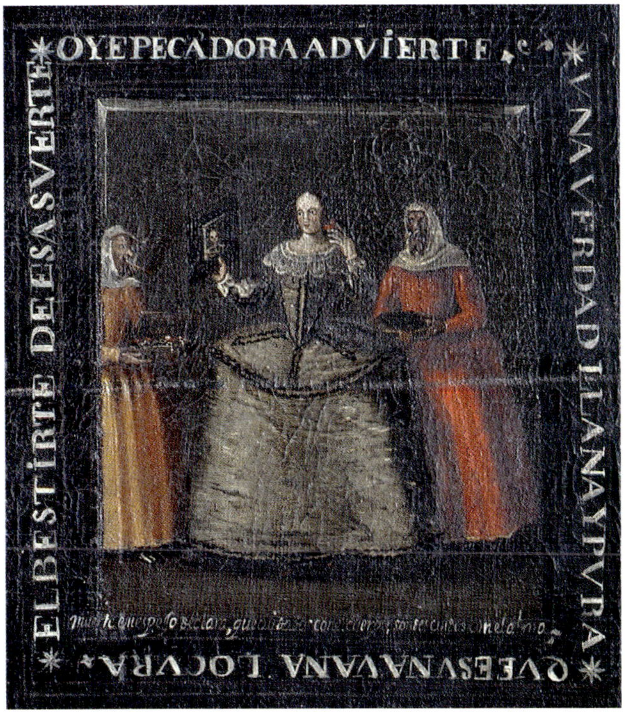

20. "Look, sinner, heed a truth plain and pure, that it is vain insanity to dress this way" (detail of fig. 19)

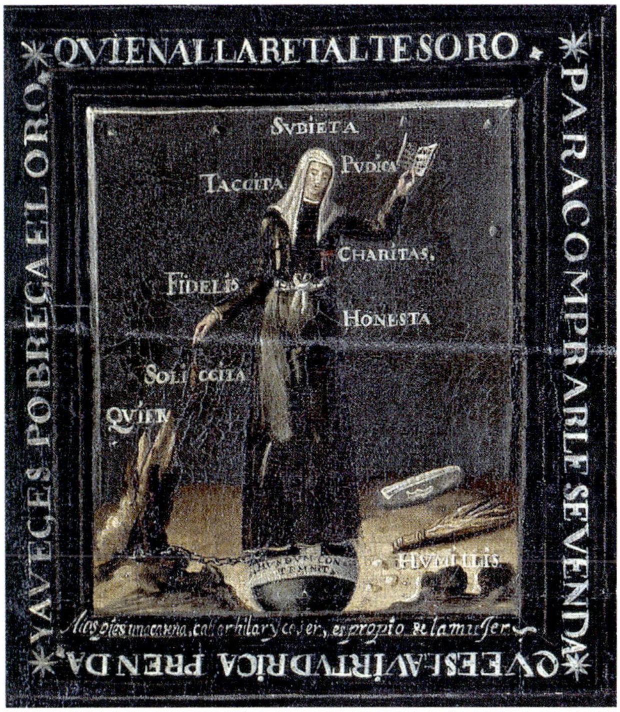

21. "Whoever finds this treasure must sell herself to buy it, since virtue is a rich garment, and sometimes gold is poverty" (detail of fig. 19)

a white headdress, illustrates the concept that "virtue is a rich garment" (fig. 21). A society rife with sins of fashion risked losing divine favor, it was believed, and fashion trends were frequently blamed for causing all sorts of misfortunes, including war, famine, and natural disasters.[56] During Philip IV's reign, influential abbesses, clergymen, and religious zealots pressed the king to reform fashion as a divine solution to Spain's many problems. But even the most zealous reformers acknowledged that only the king could control what the people wore.

The king had the power to issue royal decrees on dress, which were published under the title of *premática* (proclamation) or *pregón* (the proclamation delivered by a crier). Some of these decrees were sumptuary laws that forbade luxuries, while others were dress laws that focused on the cut of garments or how they could be worn.[57] The Enlightenment historian Juan Sempere y Guarinos proclaimed in his *History of Luxury and Sumptuary Laws of Spain* (1788) that "in no other time have more radical provisions been made in Spain to contain luxury than during the reign of Philip IV."[58] Throughout his reign, beginning with the Articles of Reformation in 1623, Philip IV turned to sumptuary laws and dress laws as a political weapon in trying times. Tailors and other artisans suffered the brunt of these laws, which promised harsher penalties to those who made the forbidden goods than to those who wore them. Often capricious in their content and erratic in their enforcement, royal proclamations on dress kept

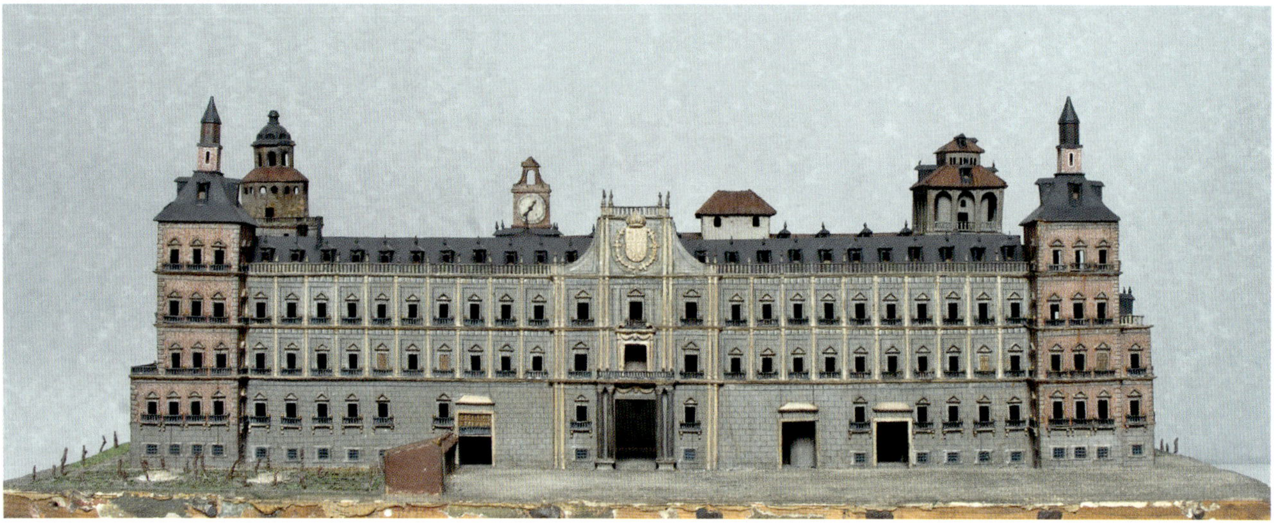

the tailors on their toes. But the laws were only truly effective when they were followed by the royal family: the king's real authority over fashion was exerted through the model of what was worn at court.

The Court Fashion System

The Spanish court was notorious for its formality and ceremony.[59] Every aspect of life, including the production of royal clothing, was governed by rigid bureaucracy. The Royal Palace, located on the westernmost edge of Madrid (see Map 2), was divided physically and bureaucratically into separate households for the king and the queen (fig. 22).[60] Each was governed by its own book of court etiquette. The queen's household, where Mateo Aguado worked, was run by the *camarera mayor*, First Lady of the Bedchamber, who was a woman from the high aristocracy. The royal wardrobe was supervised by a titled nobleman who served as *guardajoyas y ropa*, Keeper of the Jewels and Wardrobe. Household rules required absolute obedience to one's superiors. According to palace etiquette, the queen's tailor was required to be present for the daily ritual of dressing the queen in her private chambers.[61] This made him one of very few men—and even fewer non-noblemen—who were allowed into the queen's inner sanctum. The tailor's official title of *sastre de cámara*—"tailor of the chamber"—reflected the prestige of his office. There could only be one *sastre de cámara*, which was a unique position for an artisan at a court where power derived from physical proximity to the royal persons.

Sumptuously furnished palaces, dignified ceremonies, and retinues of servants and guards guided the public to see royal persons as "human deities" who "ought to be venerated," as royal chronicler Alonso Núñez de Castro wrote in the late 1650s.[62] It is surprising that he left royal dress off of this list, for sumptuous fabrics were fundamental to the public perception of royalty. In Lope de Vega's play *Peribáñez and the Comendador of Ocaña* (1614), a peasant woman is mocked for expressing her belief that royal persons are made "of damask or of velvet," not "of flesh and blood like us."[63] Clothing was especially important for royal women. In addition to projecting royalty, the dress of a queen or infanta reflected her status, which was determined by marriage and reproduction. The

22. *(facing page)* Model of the Royal Palace, Madrid, 17th century. Wood, plaster, and oil paint, 34 × 86 × 25 cm. Museo de Historia de Madrid

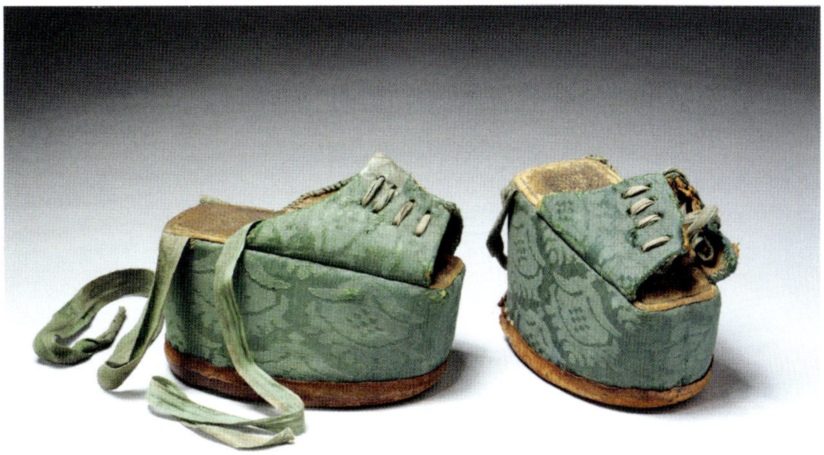

23. Pair of cork-soled *chapines* covered with green silk damask, Spanish, c. 1580–1620. Each 12.5 × 10 × 16 cm. Victoria and Albert Museum, London

dress of an infanta communicated her marriageability to potential suitors. A princess who moved from one royal court to another changed her style of dress to that of her husband's country, especially if the marriage was intended to bring peace between enemy nations. The consummation of that marriage was marked by switching from low-heeled shoes to *chapines*, cork-soled platform shoes that literally showed a woman's elevation with this change in her status: the green damask *chapines* at the Victoria and Albert Museum measure 12.5 centimeters high (fig. 23). A queen who governed as regent required a wardrobe that reflected her power within the confines of accepted gender roles.[64] Widowhood—when a queen gave up sumptuous dress—brought about the most dramatic clothing change of all. Throughout these transitions, it was the responsibility of the queen's tailor to navigate the complex "sartorial politics" of royal women's dress.[65]

The queen's *sastre de cámara* was the first among peers in the elite group of artisans who worked on the royal wardrobe. Other *oficiales de manos* who were involved in dressing the queen included an embroiderer, gold-wire drawer, glover, farthingale-maker, shoemaker, cordmaker, and trimmings-maker. The men and women who filled these positions ran their own workshops staffed with many workers. Most of the work involved in making the royal wardrobe seems to have been done off-site in the artisans' workshops in Madrid's garment district, between the palace and the Plaza Mayor in the center of town. According to the queen's household rules, fabric used to make dresses for the queen and royal children was supposed to be cut under supervision at the *guardajoyas*, the Jewel House on the ground floor of the Royal Palace where valuable textiles were kept along with jewels, porcelain, paintings, and clocks.[66] In practice, this seems to have been done only rarely. Space at the palace was at a premium, and the fact that the king gave Velázquez a workshop and living quarters there was a sign of his extraordinary favor for the painter. Royal artisans, with one foot in the palace and another in the town beyond its walls, occupied a special social position in seventeenth-century Madrid. They were treated like minor celebrities by local chroniclers such as Gerónimo Gascón de Torquemada, who reported when the king's interim tailor was stabbed to death in 1627, and when the daughter of the queen's laundress ran away from a convent (disguised as a laundress) the following year.[67] Neither event was unusual in seventeenth-century Madrid—it was the protagonists' connections to the court that made these incidents newsworthy.

Oficiales de manos employed by the court enjoyed many advantages over other artisans. Some, but not all, of them received annual wages in addition to being paid by the piece for the work that they did. Employees of the court could also receive rations from the royal kitchen, free housing, medical care from court doctors, medicine from the royal pharmacy, and an annual suit of clothes made by the king's or queen's tailor.[68] Royal artisans sought to keep these valuable positions within their families and petitioned for the right to pass their offices on to their heirs. If there was no male heir, a widow or daughter could inherit the position, or subcontract the work to someone else. This was how important positions came to be filled by women, such as Sebastiana de Palacios, who served as the king's embroiderer, and Catalina de Vallejo, the queen's gold-wire drawer.[69] Some *oficiales de manos* at Philip IV's court, such as the furrier Manuel Milor, came from artisan dynasties that had been serving the Crown for as long as there had been Habsburgs on the throne.[70] But the hereditary system did not always work out for the best. Philip IV inherited a uniquely inept tailor, Juan Varela, who was better known for his romantic escapades and fights than for his achievements in the art of tailoring.[71] Varela was eventually fired for pawning fabrics that were intended for the king's wardrobe, but another position was found for him at court as a doorman. It was the perfect position for the derelict tailor, noble courtier Fernando de Borja explained to the king, "for requiring no greater exertion than attending to a door."[72] As Varela's story shows, the Crown had an obligation to look out for its *oficiales de manos*—even the worst of them.

Royal artisans worked at a frenetic pace and produced an enormous volume of work. In 1659, Queen Mariana of Austria's shoemaker, Andrés de Bustamante, made two new pairs of shoes for her and for the Infantas María Teresa and Margarita every week of the year.[73] Aguado created thousands of garments over the course of his 42 years at court, but not a single one of them is known to have survived. The reasons for this will become clear in the chapters of this book. In short, much of royal dress was like the ephemeral architecture that was built for festivals: hastily constructed, it served its purpose, and then it was taken apart. If any of the garments that Aguado designed did survive past the seventeenth century, their rich materials—especially the silver thread used in brocaded silks, embroidery, and lace—were likely picked apart and melted down by future generations. Even in the absence of surviving garments, there are various textual and visual sources that make it possible to reconstruct Aguado's lost body of work.

Reconstructing a Tailor's Lost Work

Extensive records of Mateo Aguado's work for the royal family were kept in accordance with the procedures for ordering new clothes outlined in the rule book for the queen's household.[74] Aguado maintained detailed *cuentas*, which were annual accounts listing each item he made along with a brief description of the garment and its materials, sometimes with additional information about the occasion for which it was made and extra labor involved, and the monetary value of the work.[75] The payment that Aguado requested is noted in the right-hand margin of the page; he was actually paid the smaller amounts on the left (fig. 24). The "moderated" price was determined in an appraisal by two tailors,

24. *(facing page)* Account of Mateo Aguado's work for Queen Isabel, 1630. Archivo General de Palacio, Madrid

Los mrs que se deven a Mateo Aguado sastre del
Rey nro. s.or por las obras que a hecho de su off.o para su Real serv.o
por quenta de hechuras de joias y Ropa desde primero de otubre del año
de seiscientos y [illegible] hasta fin del son los sig.tes

Primeramente hizo unas mangas
redondas de Realbadillo verde y negro
guarnecidas con un galon de oro y Rivete forra
Do1o das en tafetan. valen diez y seis Rs. y ocho — Do18
Rs. — moderadas en diez Rs.

Mas a una basquiña de Realbadillo
Do04 verde y negro. le hizo ruedo y corchetes. — Do08
= vale ocho Rs. = moderado en quatro Rs.

Mas a un manteo de buelta de tafetan
carmesi le hizo entre las abayeras
Do06 y le bolvio a forrar en tafetan. — bale diez — Do1o
y seis Reales = moderado en seis Rs.

Hizo ropa y basquiña de felpa guarnecida
la ropa con un galon de oro
de orilla y los Rivetes de la delantera
guarnecidos con los dos galones. Y en esta
ropa veinte y dos docenas de botones de oro
y la basquiña bastada con ... con
ruedo. Rivete y galon encima. faltriqueras
de damasco — y el jubon de la dha felpa
guarnecido con dos ordenes de ... y ...
por los quartos. sangrias y faldillas
Do15o forrado todo y bastido en tafetan = vale diez — Do22o
y seis ... ducados = moderado en
ciento y cinquenta Rs. — —

Mas hizo un manteo de ... de felpa
carmesi guarnecido con nueve fajas
anchas bordadas de flores de oro y ...
nes que hizo unas bastillas cosidas a
tres puntos. con su ruedo y faltriqueras con
Do77 su Rivete bordado. forrado todo en tafetan. — 0130
vale diez ... ciento y treinta Rs. — Tassado
0241 R en seis ducados — — — 0386 R

one representing Aguado and another appointed by the Crown. Aguado was typically paid about 70 percent of the amount that he requested. The tailor's fee did not include the cost of materials and decorations that were provided by other *oficiales de manos*. After he submitted an annual *cuenta*, Aguado was fortunate if the paperwork was processed within a year; sometimes it took up to four. Documents called *cargos* (charges), which were drawn up based on Aguado's accounts, contain similar information but lack the financial figures.[76] These records are supplemented by the accounts of the royal silk merchants, who recorded minutely detailed information about the various materials that were used in garment construction.[77] The textile and tailoring terms used in the documents appear in parentheses throughout this book and are explained in the Glossary.

Aguado's records supply a vast amount of data about his work, but their terse and formulaic descriptions offer no information about the shape of the garments or how they were worn. This is where court portraits by Velázquez and his workshop provide invaluable evidence. These visual sources also present many challenges.[78] Velázquez's style evolved over the course of his career. Early works are highly finished and offer crisp details of dress, like the darts shaping the white collar around the king's neck in the full-length portrait at the Metropolitan Museum of Art (see fig. 13). Beginning in the 1630s, after a transformative trip to Italy, Velázquez developed his celebrated technique of using quickly applied, short slashes of paint to communicate information about his subjects' dress through "inference rather than detail," as art historian Jonathan Brown put it.[79] Velázquez first applied this technique in *Philip IV in Brown and Silver*, in which the king wears a gala suit of dark brown silk decorated with an indistinguishable tangle of sparkling silver ornaments (fig. 25).[80] There is a key for interpreting Velázquez's brushstrokes in a workshop painting, which appears to have been painted by an artist who was working directly from the garments and accessories in the studio, rather than copying a preexisting portrait by the master (fig. 26).[81] In Velázquez's portrait, it is very difficult to identify the silver decorations on the king's cloak, which have been misinterpreted as tufts of feathers.[82] As the workshop painting makes clear, these are button-and-loop ornaments called *alamares*, which were made from metal thread and appliquéd onto the garment. *Alamares* were applied symmetrically to the king's breeches (*calzones*) and cassock (*ropilla*), although Velázquez eliminated them from the left side of the king's chest (viewer's right), leaving it up to his audience to fill in the missing information. Refusing to get bogged down in the details, Velázquez captured "the *essence* of dress," as dress historian Aileen Ribeiro has described it.[83]

Velázquez's ability to conjure the rich textiles of court clothes came from a deep familiarity bred of personal experience. The painter wore a splendid suit decorated with Milanese silver lace when he accompanied Philip IV to a meeting with Louis XIV of France in 1660, according to Palomino, who wrote that Velázquez "was exceptional in his knowledge of fabrics, for which he had always shown great taste."[84] Velázquez died shortly after that trip, and an inventory was taken of his rooms at the Royal Palace. There were trunks filled with fine garments, including doublets made from watered blue silk, green plush, and cloth of silver, and sets of sleeves with matching gloves embroidered in silver and gold.[85] Velázquez's wardrobe was much richer and more colorful than his self-portraits in the sober black uniform of the courtier suggest. His self-portraits, like his portraits of royal subjects, reflect the culture of the Spanish court, which emphasized decorum above all

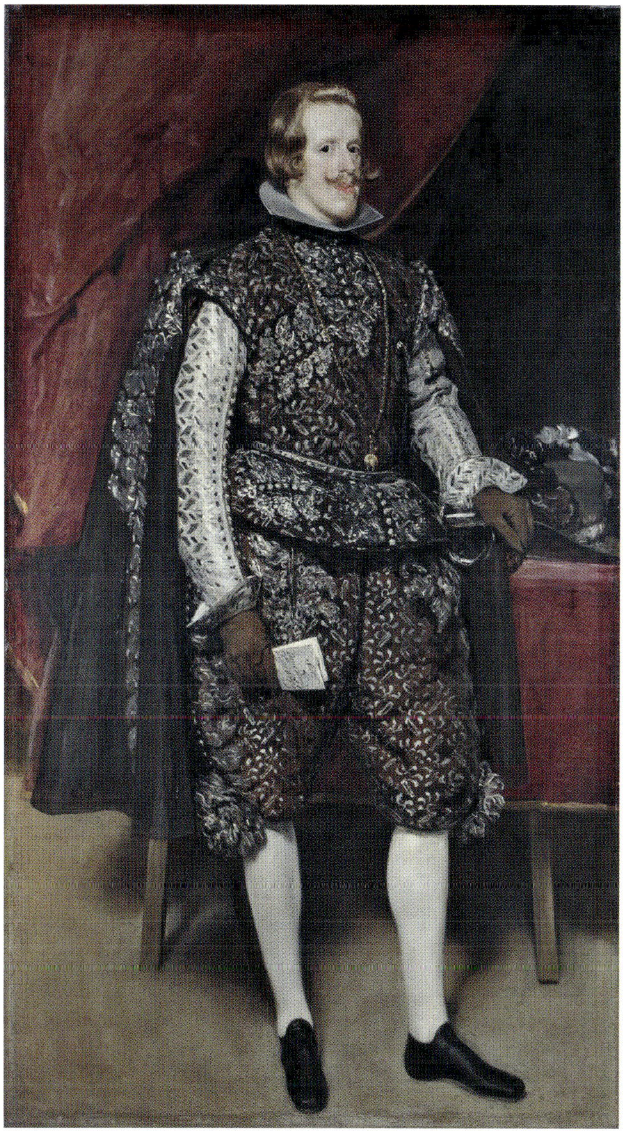

25. Diego Velázquez, *Philip IV in Brown and Silver*, c. 1631–2. Oil on canvas, 195 × 110 cm. National Gallery, London

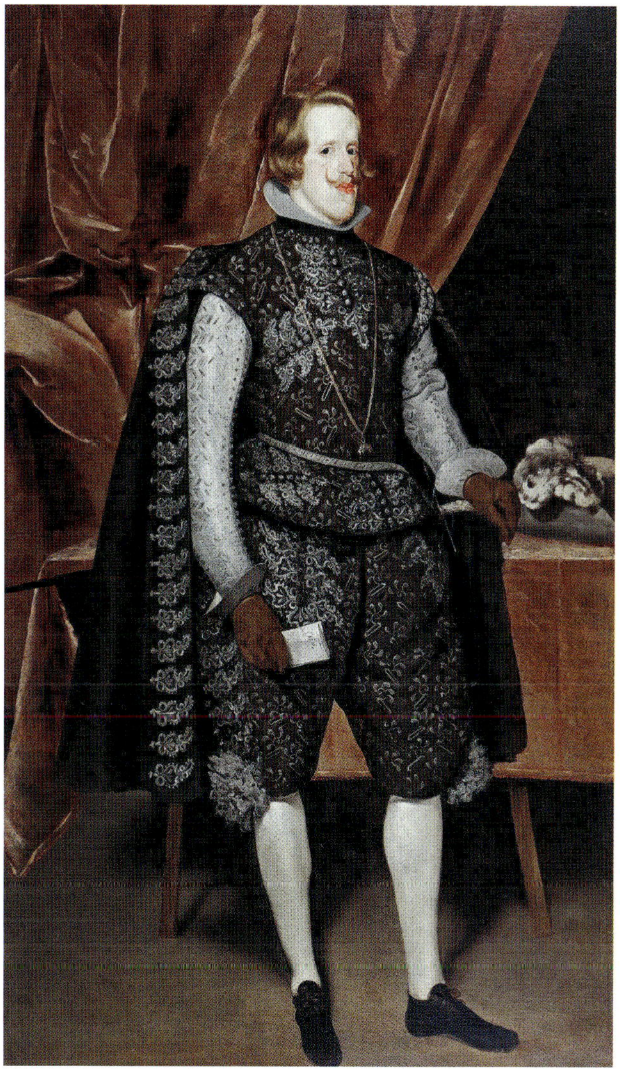

26. Workshop of Velázquez, *Philip IV in Brown and Silver*, c. 1631–2. Oil on canvas, 199.5 × 113 cm. Dorotheum, Vienna

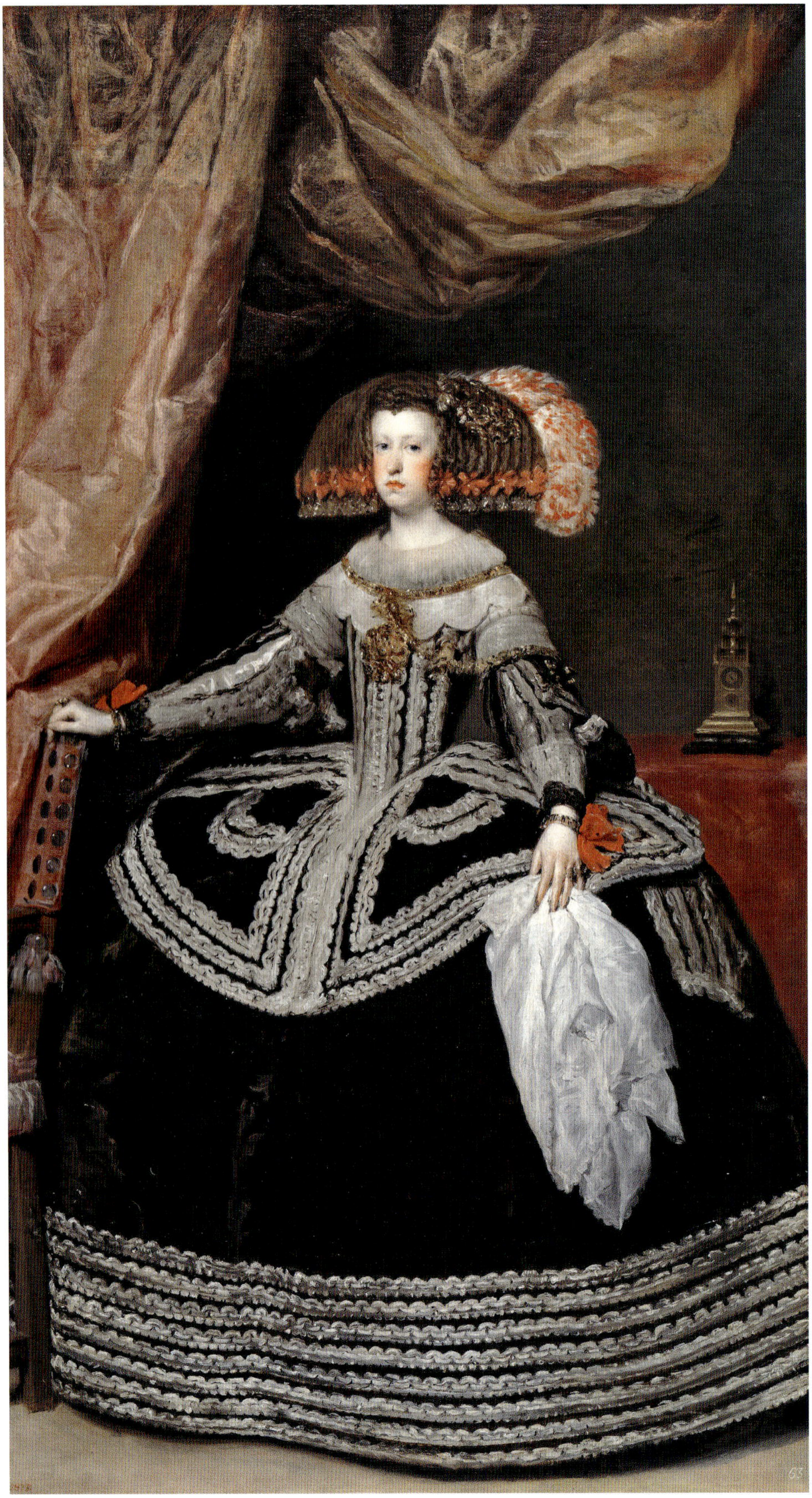

27. Diego Velázquez, *Queen Mariana of Austria ("Mariana in Black and Silver")*, 1652. Oil on canvas, 234.2 × 132 cm. Museo Nacional del Prado, Madrid

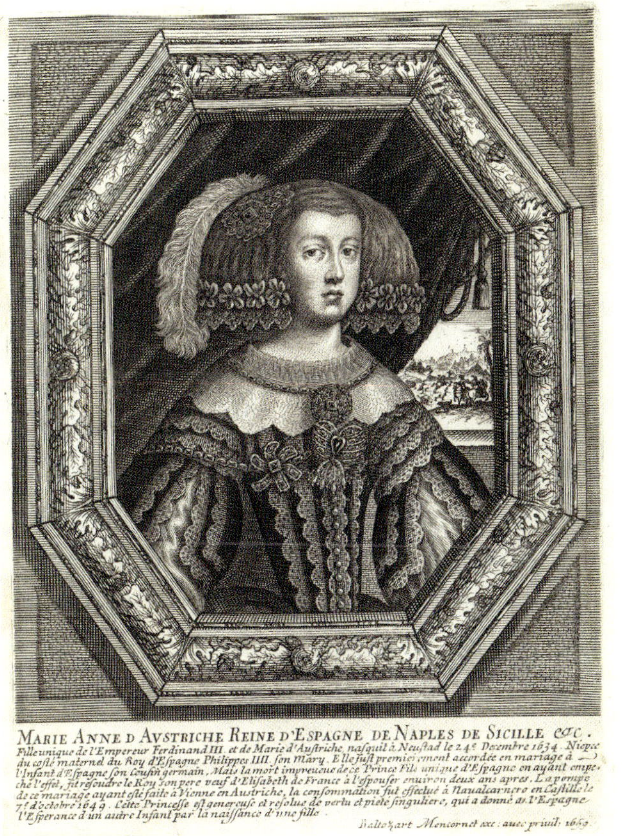

28. Unknown printmaker after Velázquez, *Queen Mariana of Austria*, 1659. Balthasar Moncornet, editor. Etching and engraving, 24.6 × 18.4 cm. Museo Nacional del Prado, Madrid

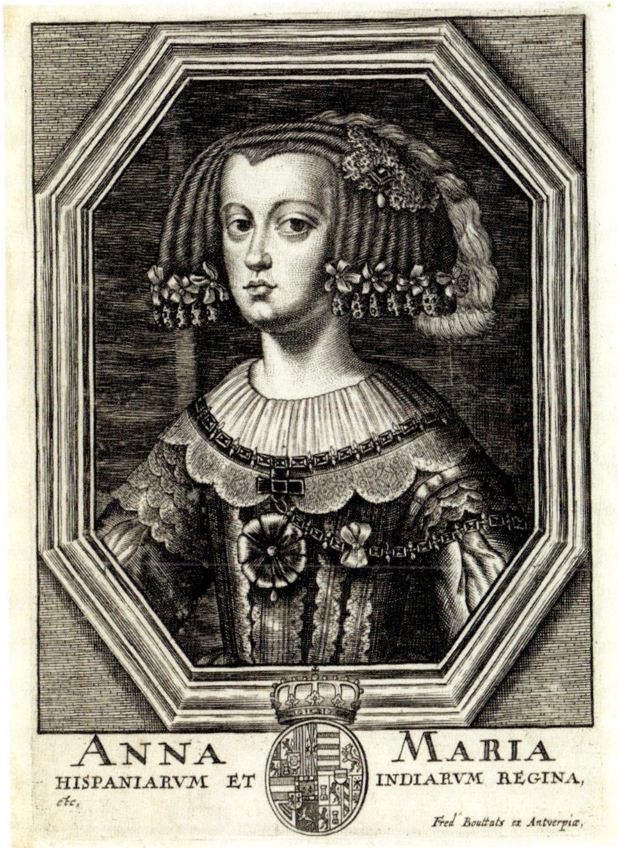

29. Unknown printmaker after Velázquez, *Queen Mariana of Austria*, 1653–76. Frederik Bouttats, editor. Etching and engraving, 17.4 × 12.7 cm. Museo Nacional del Prado, Madrid

else.[86] This presents a striking contrast to the clothing cultures of his contemporaries to the north, such as the Dutch painter Rembrandt, who experimented with berets and vintage costumes in his self-portraits, and Anthony van Dyck, who painted his subjects at the English court with "careless romance."[87] There was nothing careless about dress at the Spanish court or in Spanish court portraiture: in 1633 a portrait that depicted Philip IV wearing green breeches and stockings was confiscated so that the color could be erased and "made decent."[88]

Velázquez enjoyed a monopoly over court portraiture from his appointment in 1623 until his death in 1660. During this time, he produced a fairly small number of royal portraits, which were copied repeatedly by workshop artists.[89] Few and far between, portraits such as *Mariana in Black and Silver* (fig. 27) represent only select moments in the history of fashion at the

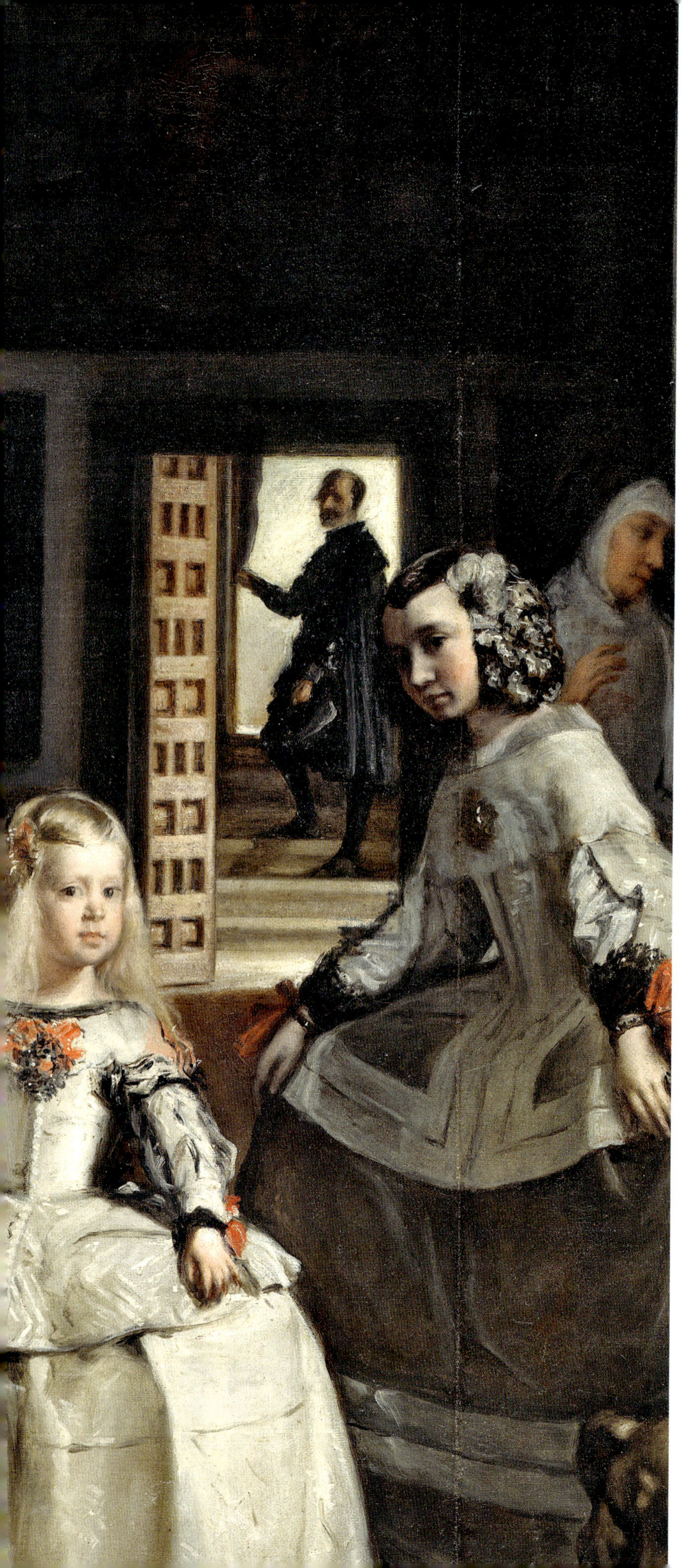

30. José Nieto exits the painter's studio.
Diego Velázquez, *Las Meninas* (detail of fig. 2)

Spanish court during the decades Aguado was active. It is important to acknowledge that many full-length portraits of female subjects were purposefully altered by later generations, who cut off the edges of the paintings to make them three-quarter size—for example, the portraits of Queen Isabel of Bourbon and the Infanta María Teresa at the Kunsthistorisches Museum in Vienna (see figs. 75 and 144). And the passage of time has caused some pigment colors to change: for example, technical analysis has shown that the dark, greenish-black skirt of the kneeling maid of honor in *Las Meninas* was originally a lighter green-blue.[90]

Knowledge about Mateo Aguado's creations circulated internationally through painted portraits by and after Velázquez that were sent to other European courts, and even more widely through printed images. Prints made by two different artists after Velázquez's *Mariana in Black and Silver* suggest that even contemporaries of Velázquez interpreted his brushstrokes differently: the thick silver trimming looks like a scallop-edged lace in one print (fig. 28) and a wavy woven trim layered with ribbon in another (fig. 29). Printed images like these are several steps removed from the garments that Aguado actually made. More reliable information comes from short, unillustrated printed pamphlets called *relaciones* that described royal events such as baptisms, diplomatic visits, and processions. In keeping with the court's focus on fashion, *relaciones* are filled with information about the ceremonial dress that was on display. To write such detailed descriptions, "you very nearly need to be a tailor!" Andrés de Almansa y Mendoza exclaimed in one of his *relaciones*.[91] The descriptions of dress in *relaciones* could be strikingly accurate, as confirmed by comparison to Aguado's records. These pamphlets, which promoted the official palace version of events, sometimes explain the meaning that a particular dress was intended to convey, which makes them extraordinarily valuable sources.

As printed *relaciones* make clear, fashion and politics were inseparable in the Spain of Philip IV. Yet most historical studies of his reign have treated fashion as a frivolous sideshow or ignored it altogether.[92] In this book, fashion reclaims its place at the center of Philip IV's rule. The usual protagonists—the king, his prime ministers, and Diego Velázquez—cede the limelight to Mateo Aguado, his fellow court artisans, and the queens and infantas who were dressed by them. In the background of *Las Meninas*, the figure of José Nieto, usher to the ladies in the queen's household, is framed in the doorway (fig. 30).[93] He pauses on the stairs, on the verge of leaving the room. Following him out the door, we exit the painter's studio and enter Aguado's world.

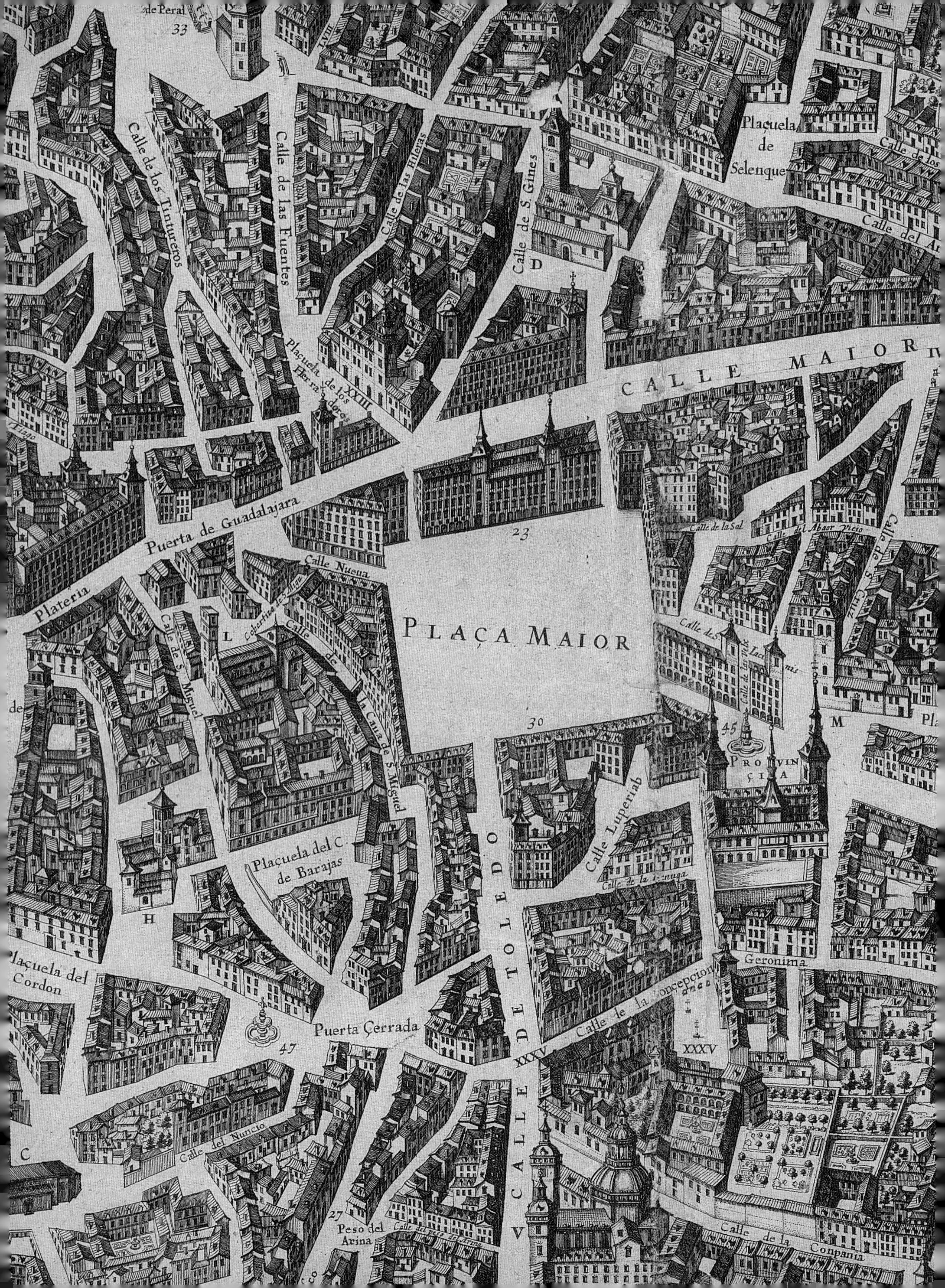
de Peral
33
Calle de los Tintureros
Calle de las Fuentes
Calle de las Hileras
Calle de S. Gines
D
Plaçuela de Selenque
CALLE MAIOR
Plaçuela de los Herradores
XXIII
Puerta de Guadalajara
Plateria
Calle Nueua
23
PLAÇA MAIOR
Calle de la Sal
Calle de S. Miguel
L
Calle de la Caua de S. Miguel
30
45
M
PROVINÇIA
Plaçuela del C de Barajas
H
CALLE DE TOLEDO
Plaçuela del Cordon
Puerta Çerrada
47
Calle de la Concepcion
Geronima
XXXV
XXXV
Calle del Nuncio
C
27
Peso del Arina
V
Calle de la Compania

1. A Tailor in Training

From the Village to the Court, c. 1605–1630

Mateo Aguado was born in Fuenlabrada, a village of thatch-roofed houses with a population of some 1,369 souls, located 19 kilometers southwest of Madrid (see Map 1).[1] The baptism records kept by the village church were destroyed by fire centuries later, but the year of Aguado's birth can be fixed around 1605 thanks to testimony that he delivered as an adult.[2] The surname Aguado, derived from the word *agua*—"water"—was common in Fuenlabrada, where the only landmark of note was an ancient fountain made from pebbles and lime that village elders claimed dated back to the time of the Moors. Fuenlabrada supported a small number of artisans—bakers, shoemakers, carpenters, tanners, tailors, and weavers—who were identified as such in the village tax records. Mateo Aguado likely came to the tailoring trade through his mother, Catalina Galeote Muñoz, who shared the surname Muñoz with a village tailor and two weavers.[3] The Muñozes probably made a coarse cloth called *jerga*, the production of which was a small village industry.[4] Aguado's father, Gabriel, first appears in the tax records as a head-of-household in 1601, without any occupation listed.[5] He most likely supported his family by the sweat of his brow, like most of the village men, who worked as farmers, muleteers, or manual laborers. According to a survey of the village that was taken in 1576, everyone who lived in Fuenlabrada was poor.[6]

When he was about six years old, around the year 1611, Mateo Aguado moved from Fuenlabrada to Madrid.[7] Presumably he was accompanied by his mother, who remarried at some point, along with his brother and sister, Antonio and Ana (see the Family Tree of Mateo Aguado, p. 8). Young Aguado settled in the populous parish of San Ginés to the north of the Plaza Mayor, where he lived for the rest of his life. Aguado's new neighborhood was densely packed with brick buildings that boasted glass windows, iron balconies, and slate roofs, which can be seen in a meticulous bird's-eye view of Madrid by Pedro Teixeira that was "true-to-life, so that one can count the doors and windows of each," as the inscription at the bottom of the map claims (fig. 31).[8] Teixeira's monumental *Topography of the Town of Madrid* captures the Spanish capital as it appeared in the mid-1650s, after four decades of rapid growth, when Aguado was at the peak of his tailoring career at the court (fig. 32). Aguado's first two decades in Madrid are almost entirely undocumented, but he left enough clues in documents recorded later in his life for us to reconstruct, with some speculation, his professional training and induction into the world of the court during an exceptionally dynamic period in the history of Madrid and its fashion industry.

31. *(facing page)* Map of central Madrid, including the Plaza Mayor and the Church of San Ginés (detail; see the complete map in fig. 32). Pedro Teixeira, *Topographia de la Villa de Madrid*, 1656. Biblioteca Nacional de España, Madrid

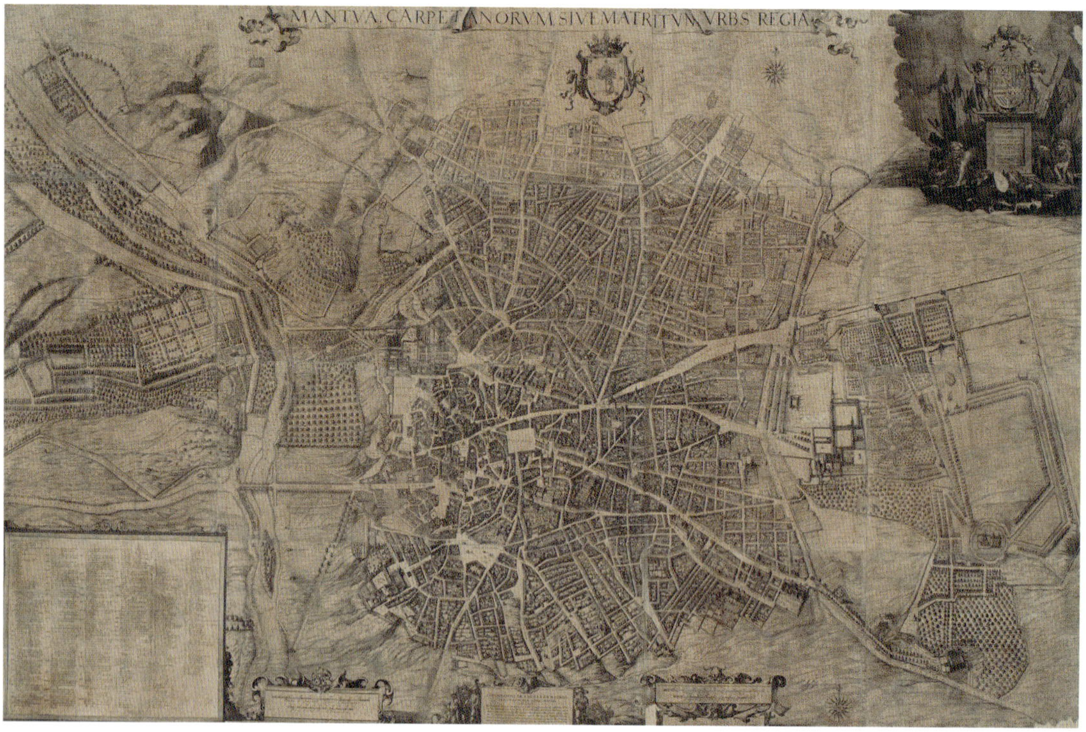

32. Pedro Teixeira, *Topographia de la Villa de Madrid*, 1656. Engraving by Salomon Savery; printed by Jacques van Veerle in Antwerp. 20 folios combined, 178 × 286 cm. Real Biblioteca de Palacio, Madrid (ROLL/109)

Madrid, Fashion Capital

Established as the permanent home of the Spanish court in 1561 by Philip II, early modern Madrid was relatively young and undeveloped compared to other European court cities. The Spanish capital was actually a town, or *villa*, and not a city—that designation required the presence of a bishop and cathedral, which were located in Toledo. Madrid's growth and development were abruptly interrupted in 1601, when Philip III relocated the court to Valladolid at the behest of his *privado*, the royal favorite Francisco de Sandoval y Rojas, 1st Duke of Lerma, who had family interests there. Half of Madrid's residents left, too, and the population dropped from around 90,000 to 45,000. The Madrid town council lured the court back with a large cash donation and a promise to pay for renovations of the old Royal Palace. After the court returned in 1606, Madrid quickly recouped its population losses and grew larger than ever, reaching over 127,000 residents by 1617.[9] The court was a magnet that attracted Spaniards and foreigners from cities and villages near and far—among them the Aguados of Fuenlabrada. Many

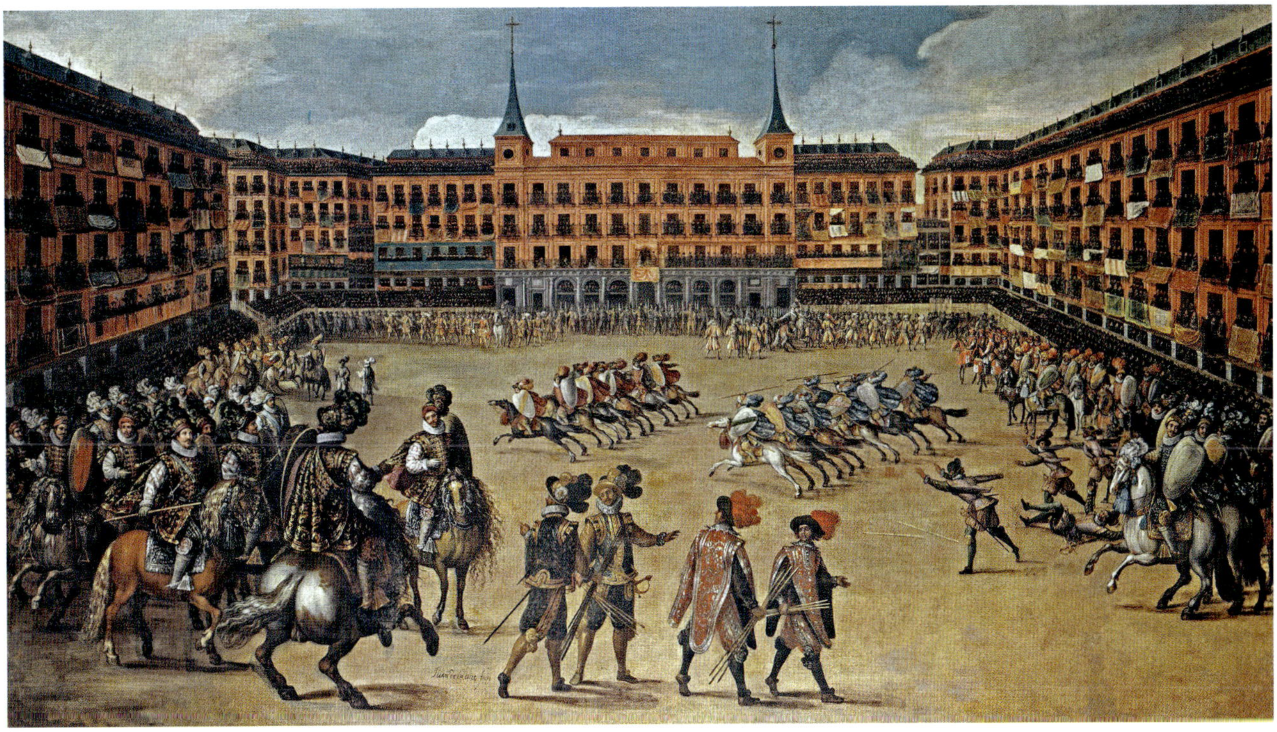

33. Juan de la Corte, *Game of Canes in the Plaza Mayor of Madrid*, 1623. Oil on canvas, 158 × 285 cm. Museo de Historia de Madrid

newcomers, including Mateo and Antonio Aguado, found employment in Madrid's burgeoning fashion industry. With the court back in town, Madrid was again the fashion capital of the Spanish Empire.

Throughout early modern Europe, fashion played an outsized role at the royal courts, where complex garments and a wearer's command over them communicated rank, wealth, and political allegiance. Anyone who desired access to the Spanish king and his court depended on Madrid's tailors. One noble visitor from Aragon in 1657 missed an opportunity to speak with the king while waiting for a local tailor to finish decorating a pair of breeches.[10] Madrid's tailors were called upon to make extravagant finery for men and women to wear to balls, festivals, and masquerades at the Royal Palace. Special costumes were needed for noblemen to wear in jousts, tournaments, and in games of canes during which mounted combatants wore richly decorated tunics and capes inspired by traditional Moorish attire while throwing cane spears at one another in the great town square, the Plaza Mayor (fig. 33).[11] Special-occasion wear was only one aspect of

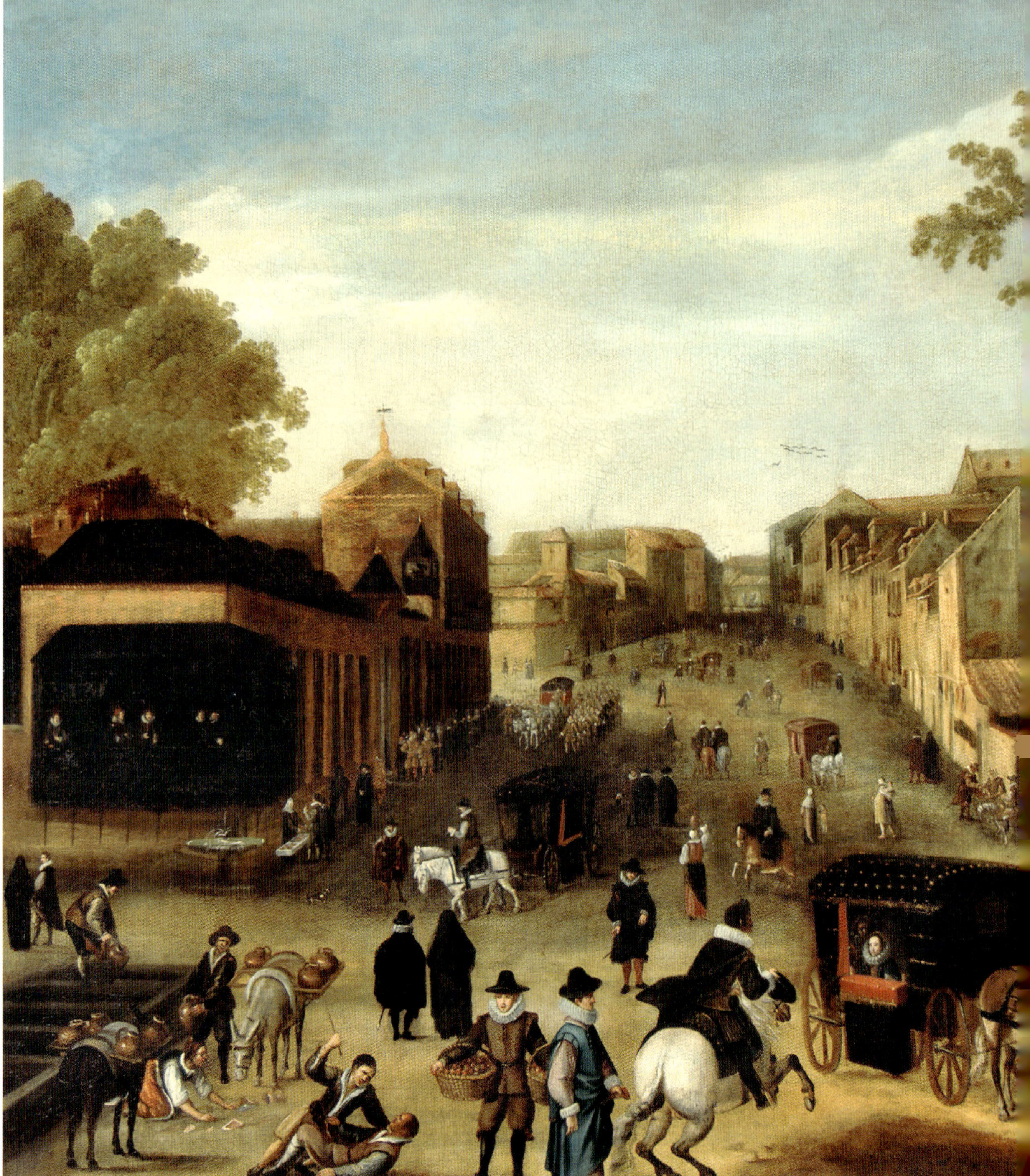

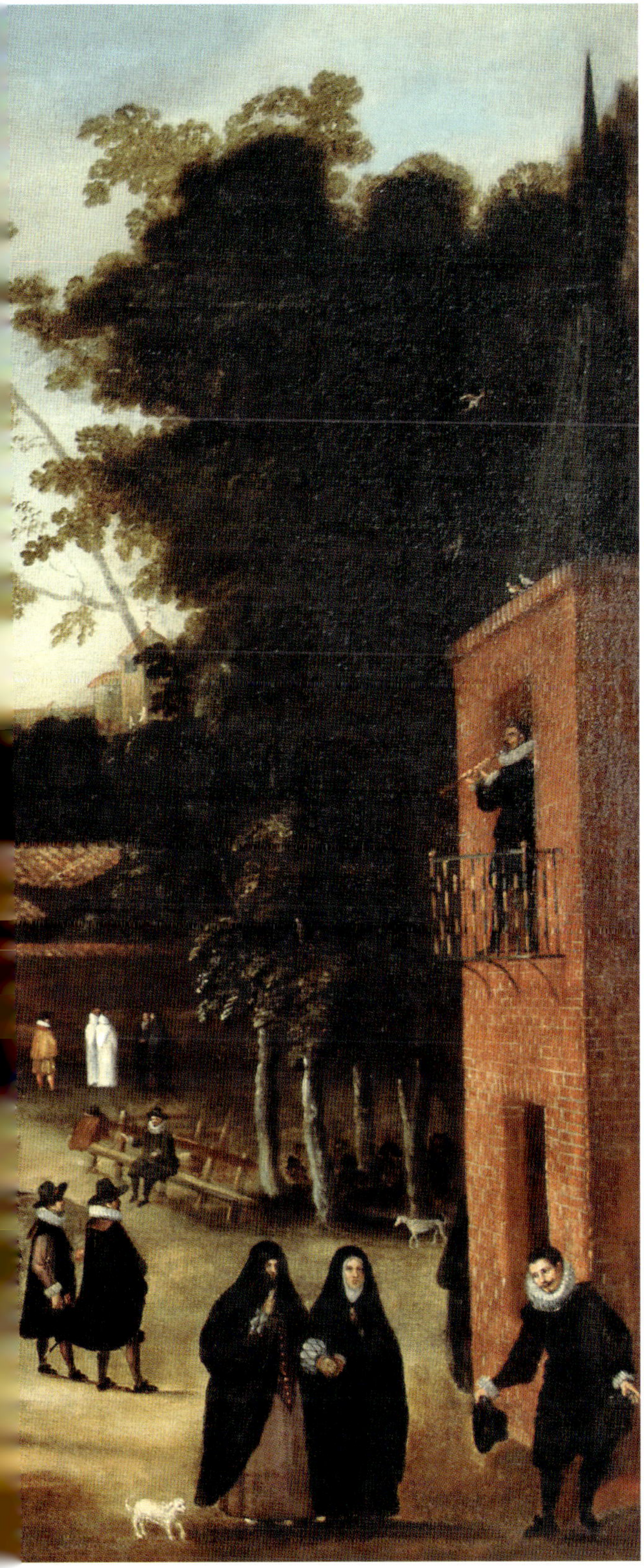

the tailoring trade in Madrid. The return of the court generated an enormous demand for clothing of all kinds and in great quantities: livery for servants, costumes for theater actors and actresses, habits for monks and nuns, vestments for clergymen, uniforms for soldiers, and workaday clothes for everyone else.[12]

Professional tailors were trained to make outerwear (as opposed to underwear) for men and women, secular and ecclesiastical, in silks and woolens. Some tailors specialized in making breeches (*calzones*) or doublets (*jubones*), the latter being especially complex, sculptural garments.[13] Traditional tailoring was done made-to-measure for clients who provided the tailor with the fabric and trimmings for a garment. These materials were worth a great deal more than the labor of the tailor, whose fees for making garments were set by law. A tailor could only charge 6 *reales* to make a cloak (*ferreruelo*), for instance, but the wool for that garment cost 90 to 180 *reales*, depending on the quality of the cloth.[14] The enormous demand for clothing that was created by the court's return set the stage for the rise of ready-to-wear, which posed a threat to traditional tailoring. New-clothes dealers bought fabric in bulk at markets and fairs, bypassing the silk and wool merchants and their fees, and subcontracted tailors to make clothes, which came in sizes small or large.[15]

Tailors belonged to a sprawling network of interconnected trades that worked to dress the fashionable *madrileños* who are pictured promenading in a view of the Carrera de San Jerónimo (fig. 34).[16] *Toqueros* wove fine silk head-coverings that were

34. Unknown Madrid artist, *View of the Carrera de San Jerónimo from the Paseo del Prado*, early 17th century. Oil on canvas, 126 × 177 cm. Fundación Álvaro de Bazán, Madrid

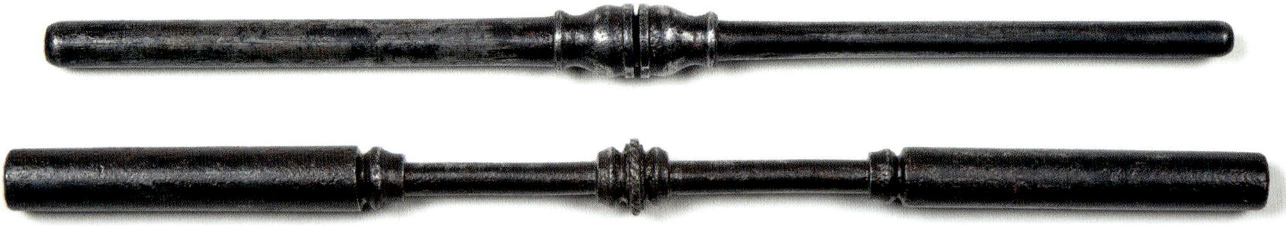

35. Iron rods for shaping ruffs, Spanish, c. 1550–1625. 1 × 25 cm; 1 × 29.5 cm. Museo Nacional de Artes Decorativas, Madrid

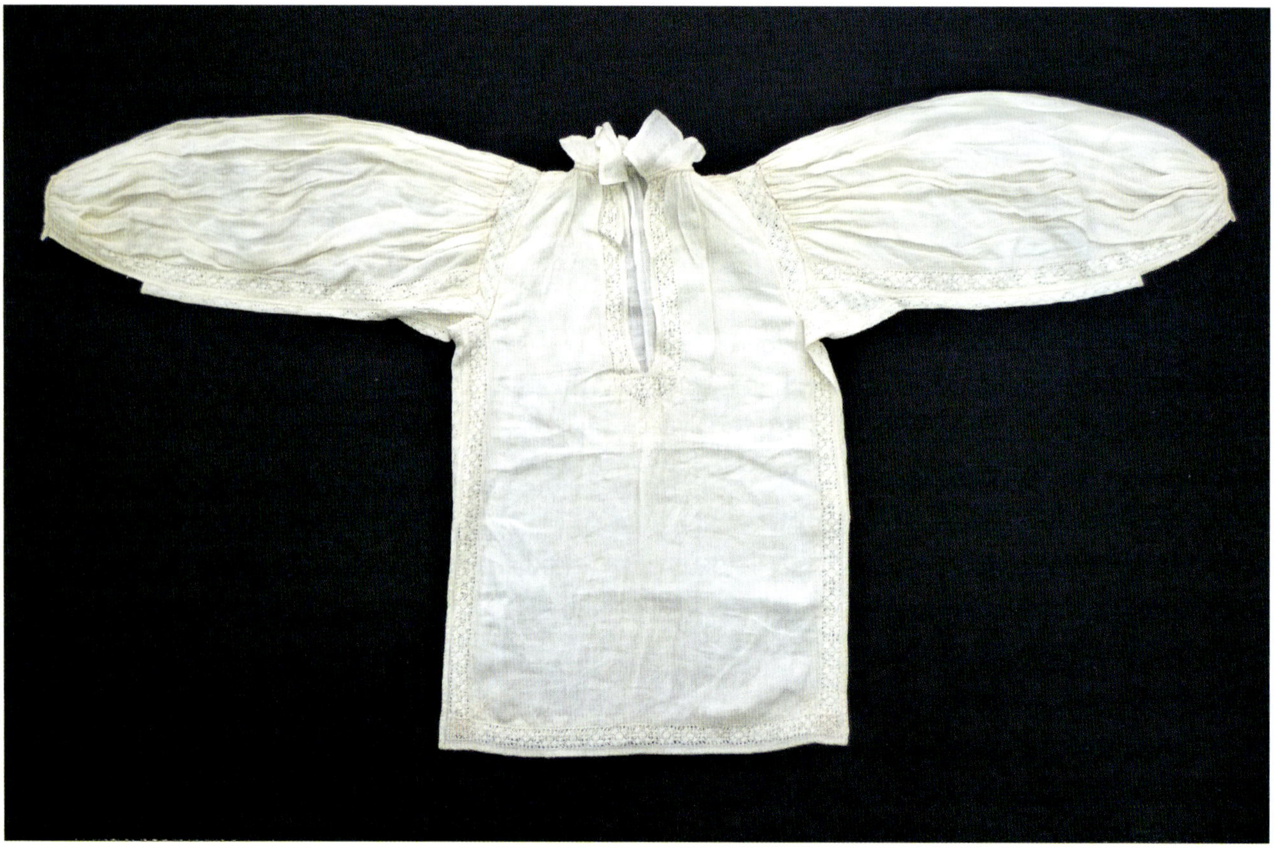

36. Boy's whitework shirt of fine bleached linen with needle lace and bobbin lace insertions, Spanish, 1630–60. Victoria and Albert Museum, London

worn by married women, like the older lady in the right-hand foreground of this view, who accompanies a younger woman wearing an ink-black mantle that she uses to cover most of her face.[17] The gentleman bowing to her wears a linen ruff that has been starched and formed into figures-of-eight by a skilled ruff-setter using heated metal rods (fig. 35). Seamstresses made long linen shirts that men, women, and children of all stations wore beneath their clothing; a child-sized example of the ubiquitous *camisa* is richly but subtly embellished with white silk embroidery and insertions of bobbin lace (fig. 36). Madrid's seamstresses worked with sewing needles made by local *agujeros*. There were also trimmings-makers, cordmakers, shoemakers and *chapines*-makers, weavers, hosiers, embroiderers, farthingale-makers, hatters, glovers (who did double duty as perfumers), leather-dressers, and furriers, among others. Artisans who specialized in used clothes and accessories refurbished and redecorated shoes, hats, and hose before reselling them on the secondhand market.[18] Madrid's embroiderers were especially well-respected, their work considered to be a "very clean art."[19] In a portrait attributed to the court artist Bartolomé González, an embroiderer poses as a maker and consumer of luxury fashions, dressed in a leather jerkin decorated with rich trims, slashed sleeves, and a ruff (fig. 37).

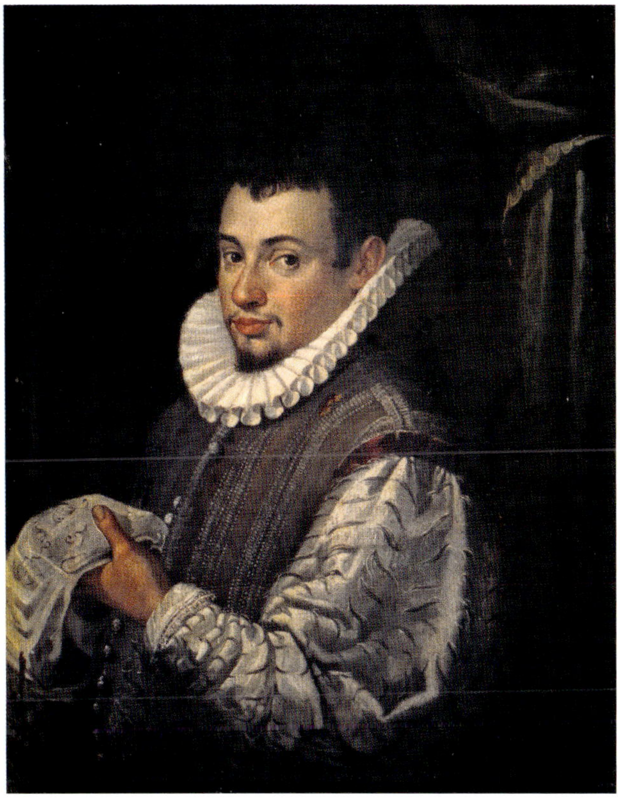

37. Attributed to Bartolomé González, *Portrait of an Embroiderer*, c. 1608–23. Oil on canvas, 81 × 61 cm. Museo Lázaro Galdiano, Madrid

Many trades were organized into guilds, which had been formed in the later sixteenth century after Philip II settled the court in Madrid. Guild bylaws written in 1598 controlled a tailor's progress through the stages of his career, from apprentice to journeyman to master.[20] The guild also provided financial assistance to its poorer members, their widows and orphans, through a devotional confraternity based at the Church of Santa Cruz that members were required to join. The tailors

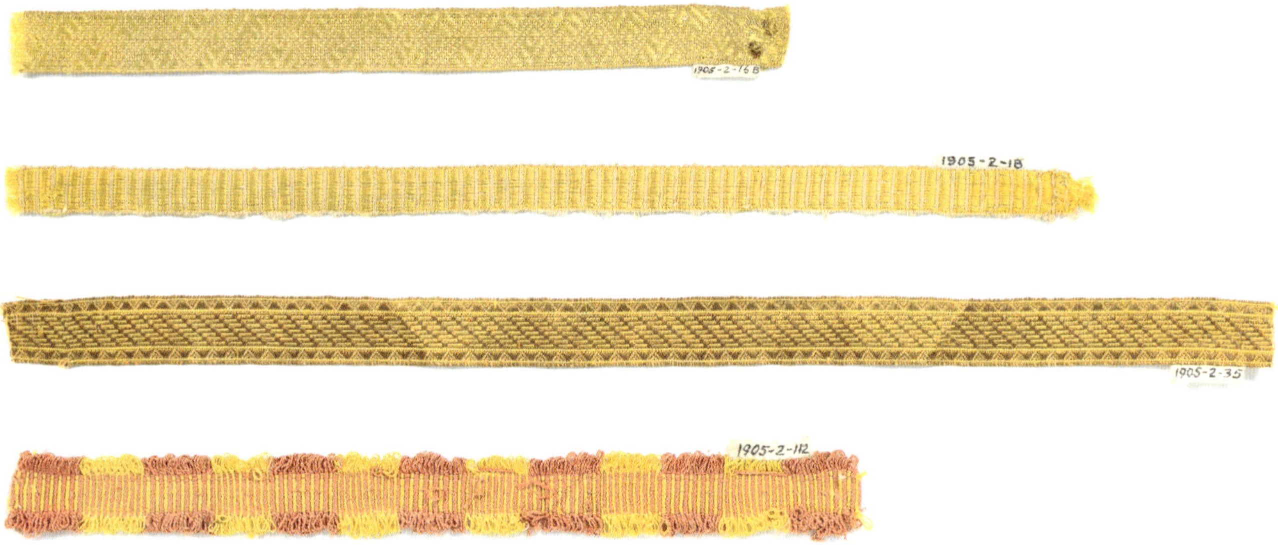

and other craft guilds experienced explosive growth—and consequent growing pains—as they evolved to meet the demands of the town and court in the first two decades of the seventeenth century. This growth is illustrated by the example of the guild of *pasamaneros*, the trimmings-makers who wove galloons, fringes, and other dress decorations from threads of silk, silver, and gold, on small, portable looms (fig. 38). There were 12 master *pasamaneros* in Madrid in 1600, but after the return of the court that number grew tenfold to reach 120 masters in 1618.[21] There is conflicting information available about the number of tailors in Madrid.[22] One list compiled in 1625 named 211 master tailors.[23] Another list taken just two years later named 431 and claimed that the actual number was over 600—and that figure only includes master tailors without counting the larger number of workers on the lower ranks of the tailoring profession.[24]

Many artisans and merchants in the fashion industry resided in the parish of San Ginés, which was Madrid's unofficial garment district and where Mateo Aguado lived.[25] Several doublet-makers named Aguado, perhaps relatives of the Aguados of Fuenlabrada, were also living there in the 1620s.[26] The Church of San Ginés was located at the nexus of three major landmarks: the Royal Palace, the Plaza Mayor, and the Puerta del Sol (see Map 2). The area around the church was one of Madrid's most densely populated neighborhoods, where about one-fifth of the town's residents lived.[27] The parish of San Ginés had a long history as the home of craftsmen who served the nearby Royal Palace. Calle de Bordadores—the street on the western facade of the Church of San Ginés—was named for the royal embroiderers who lived there in the fifteenth century.[28] In the early 1600s, many of Madrid's tailors lived and worked in the parish on the Calle Mayor. The tailors on the Calle Mayor lived just a stone's throw away from the Church of San Miguel, where the guild held important meetings, and the fabric shops at the Puerta de Guadalajara and Plaza Mayor.

38. *(facing page)* Four woven silk trimmings, Spanish, 17th century. 1.5–2.5 cm wide. Cooper Hewitt, Smithsonian Design Museum, New York

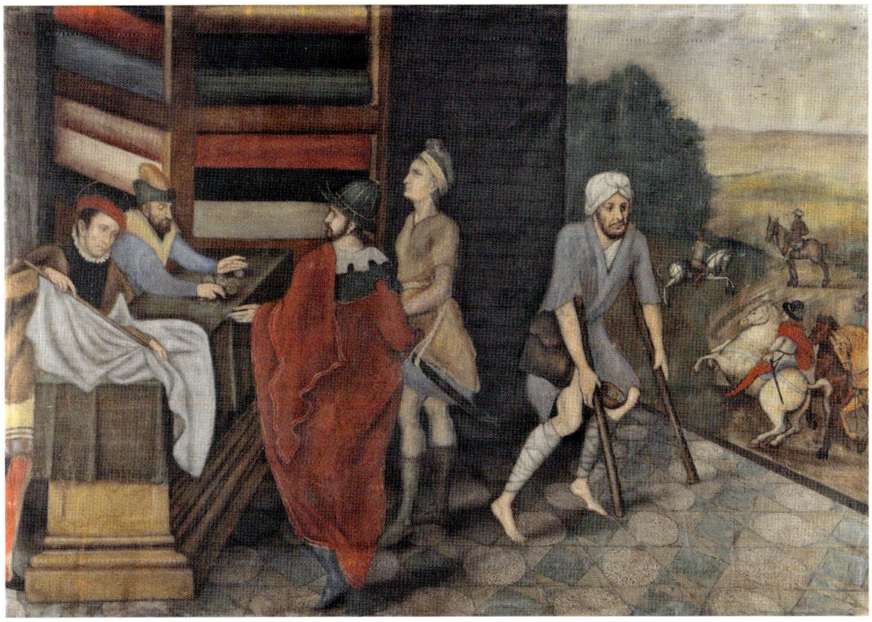

39. Unknown Spanish artist, *Saint Francis of Assisi, Cloth Merchant*, first half of the 17th century. Oil on canvas, 103 × 146 cm. Convent of Las Descalzas Reales, Madrid

Madrid's wool merchants were located on the western side of the Plaza Mayor, where awnings outside the shops protected their merchandise from sun damage.[29] The interiors probably resembled the shop depicted in a seventeenth-century painting of a scene from the life of a medieval saint, Francis of Assisi, who was the son of a wealthy Italian cloth merchant (fig. 39). Bolts of cloth in a variety of colors are displayed on wooden shelves, while the future saint—already marked with a halo but dressed in eye-catching red hose (in sixteenth-century style)—stands behind a tall counter and measures a customer's fabric with a yardstick called a *vara*. (The moral of the painting is that Saint Francis initially ignores the beggar who has entered the shop but later runs out to give him alms.)[30] Madrid's wool merchants primarily sold cloth (*paño*) that was made in Spain, along with some imports from Flanders and France. Prices varied according to thread count, color, and city of origin, with the most expensive variety being the fine black wool woven in Segovia that was known as "24," named for its 2,400 warp threads.[31] Customers went from the wool shops at the Plaza Mayor to the shearmen who worked on the adjacent Cava de San Miguel to have their cloth stretched, shrunk, shaved, and brushed in preparation for cutting by a tailor.[32]

The silk merchants of Madrid were clustered on the section of the Calle Mayor called the Puerta de Guadalajara (the area retained the name of the medieval gate that had been destroyed by fire in 1582). There was a small local silk industry in Madrid based in the neighborhood of Lavapiés, but most of the silk fabric consumed in the Spanish capital came from somewhere else.[33] There were taffetas, brocades, velvets, satins, and cloths of silver and gold (real and imitation) made in Spain's traditional silk-weaving centers of Toledo, Valencia, Seville, and Granada. High-quality silks were imported to Madrid from the Italian silk-manufacturing cities of Naples and Milan—both of which were under Spanish rule at this time—and also from Florence. The same Spanish and Italian cities that provided woven fabrics also supplied the silk thread (*seda*) that was used by Madrid's tailors, embroiderers, cordmakers, and trimmings-makers; the most valuable gold thread was imported from Milan (*oro de Milán*).[34]

Growing up in Madrid's garment district, Mateo Aguado was surrounded by the business of fashion, whose sights and sounds dominated street life at the center of the Spanish capital. The Calle Mayor—Madrid's High Street—was lined with shops selling luxuries, necessities, and accessories. Luxury merchants called *joyeros*—known in English as "milliners"—sold all the latest novelties, including starched ruffs and cuffs, garters, shoe rosettes, silk head-coverings, ribbons, and everything else "related to ladies' finery and dresses."[35] The proprietors of ready-to-wear clothing shops on the Calle Mayor aggressively solicited customers by hanging their colorful wares between the columns of the covered passageways in front of their shops and calling out to passers-by.[36] The Calle Mayor ended at the Puerta del Sol, crossroads of Madrid, where poor widows set up tables to sell used clothes.[37] Just a few minutes' walk south of the Puerta del Sol, Madrid's two commercial theaters, the Corral de la Cruz and the Corral del Príncipe, put on new plays every week with actors and actresses performing on stage using the latest fashion trends to dramatic effect. The crowds going to the theaters to see the latest "cloak and dagger" play by Lope de Vega or Juan Ruiz de Alarcón surely included Aguado by the time he was a young teenager. Aguado acquired an informal but thorough education in the art of fashion while growing up in Madrid's garment district. When he reached his teenage years, it was time for formal training to begin.

From Apprenticeship to Mastery

A tailor spent his entire adolescence working as an apprentice under a master tailor. Aguado's apprenticeship contract has yet to be found, but circumstantial evidence suggests that he may have been apprenticed to master tailor Lázaro Martínez, whose daughter Aguado married in 1630. It was common practice for a master artisan to forge a lasting bond with a favored apprentice through marriage: the painter Diego Velázquez, for instance, married the daughter of his master, Francisco Pacheco. Before Mateo Aguado and Alfonsa Martínez wed, a routine investigation took place to ensure that there were no impediments to their legal marriage. Witnesses from the Martínez family testified that they had known Aguado since the year 1618, when he was about 13 years old.[38] Perhaps Aguado joined the Martínez household as an apprentice at that time; 14 was the average age for a tailor to begin his training.[39] Lázaro Martínez was a master tailor of middling success who rented a home on the Calle Mayor (the most successful tailors owned their homes). When Philip IV called upon Madrid's guilds to make donations to the Crown in 1625 after an English attack on Cádiz, Martínez gave 110 *reales*, which was the average donation from a master tailor.[40] Martínez was unable to sign his name, but his daughter could sign hers.

The conditions of Aguado's apprenticeship must have been similar to those outlined in apprentice contracts that have been found.[41] An apprentice tailor was required to work from sunrise to sunset in his master's shop for 200 to 260 days per year, with the remainder off for holy days.[42] In return, he received food and drink, clean linens, clothes and shoes, and a bed in which to sleep. If an apprentice fell sick, his master was obligated to care for him for up to 15 days (unless the illness was contagious, or a venereal disease). In

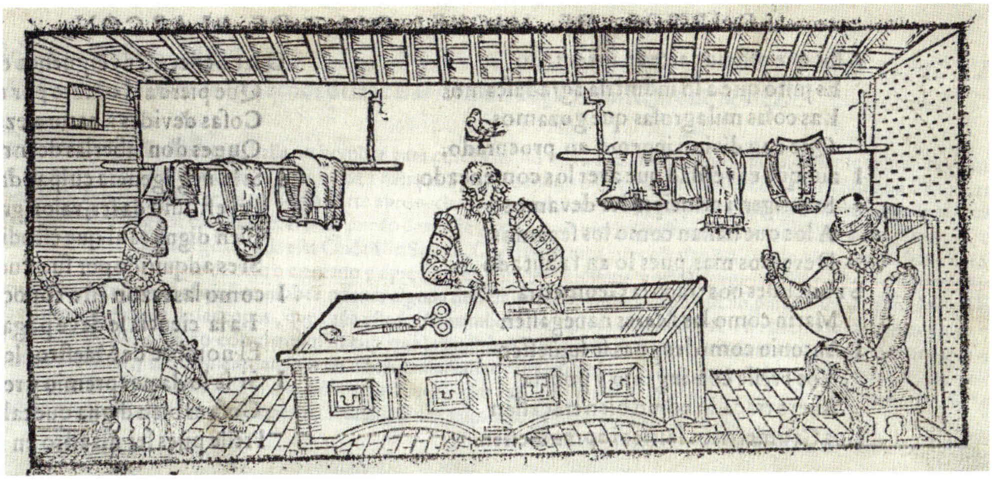

40. A tailor's workshop. Diego de Freyle, *Geometria y traça para el oficio de los sastres* (Seville, 1588). Woodcut, 10 × 29 cm. Folger Shakespeare Library, Washington, DC

the popular imagination, a tailor's apprentice had a miserable existence and was subject to countless indignities: beaten and sworn at, he worked all day only to go to sleep in a filthy, broken bed before waking in the morning to do it all again.[43] A tailor who began his apprenticeship at age 13 finished on average about five years later, which means that Aguado probably completed his around 1623[44]—an eventful year in Madrid that also saw the publication of Philip IV's Articles of Reformation, a surprise visit from the Prince of Wales, and the arrival of Diego Velázquez at the court.

After completing his apprenticeship, a new tailor went to work as a journeyman in a master's workshop, where he was given a day's worth of cut-out garment pieces and trimmings to stitch in exchange for a daily wage. According to the guild rules, only a master tailor who had passed the guild exam was permitted to take on his own commissions and cut out clothes.[45] A late-sixteenth-century woodcut depicting the interior of a Spanish tailor's workshop shows the master tailor standing at his cutting table, compass and rule in hand, while two journeymen sit on low benches, sewing with their work draped over their knees (fig. 40). The amount of daily work that Madrid's journeymen tailors were expected to do rose exponentially after the court's return in 1606, but their wage remained the same. In 1607 the journeymen tailors took the unusual step of going on strike to double their daily wage.[46] Madrid's highest court, the Sala de Alcaldes de Casa y Corte, ruled against the striking journeymen and fixed their wages at 4 *reales*, which was less than their peers earned (journeymen embroiderers earned 5 *reales*, for instance, and hatters earned 6).[47] The court further ruled that journeymen tailors had to work. If they refused, they faced a punishment of exile from Madrid, or rowing in the king's galleys.[48] Forced to work for low daily wages with no control over what he made, the journeyman tailor could only escape his lot by passing the guild exam to become a master.

There were separate exams for tailors who worked in town and at the court. Some tailors took both exams, like the French-born Francisco de la Rocha Burguen, who included his exam certificates in a tailoring manual that he published in 1618.[49] These exams were administered by elected examiners and inspectors who exerted enormous power over their profession. The selection of the examiners was a contentious issue. In 1618 the tailors' guild passed a new rule that privileged its older members by requiring examiners to have been at the level of master tailor for 12 years. A group of young master tailors who called themselves the "modern masters" filed a lawsuit denouncing the "old masters," as they called them. They claimed that the "old masters" were unqualified to examine new tailors, since they did not know how to cut out modern clothes and did not themselves know the "science and practice" that they expected the examinees to demonstrate.[50] The "modern masters" attempted a hostile takeover of the vote for examiners and threatened to "knife" colleagues who did not vote for their candidates.[51] Guild exams were a deadly serious matter: in 1648 a trimmings-maker who failed the exam for *pasamaneros* stabbed the examiner to death.[52]

As described in the guild bylaws, a tailor's exam was a formal ritual process of "complete gravity and rectitude."[53] The examinee presented himself before the guild officials without a cape, hat, or sword—to display his humility—and deposited the exam fee. He was given a choice of making a garment for a man or a woman and then was given his assignment. First, he had to accurately estimate the amount of fabric that the garment required. Then he was tested in his ability to draw the pattern pieces accurately on a piece of cloth. If he passed this test, then the next day the examinee went to the home of the inspector to make his masterpiece, which was evaluated by all the guild officials. If his work was deemed satisfactory, the successful examinee swore an oath that reflected the guild's religious as well as professional functions: to faithfully execute his office, observe the guild ordinances, comply with the rules of the confraternity, and defend the purity of the Virgin. Once he had been sworn in, the examinee joined the elite ranks of the master tailors.

A tailor typically took his exam before age 30, but many journeymen were unable to pay the exam fee and found themselves stuck without any possibility of advancement.[54] There is no evidence to show when, or even if, Mateo Aguado took the master's exam; his name does not appear on the lists of master tailors that were compiled in 1625 and 1627, but both of these lists are known to be incomplete (a tailor named Antonio Aguado, probably Mateo's brother, is named on the second list).[55] The only thing certain about Mateo Aguado's early career is that he began to work for Francisco de Soria, tailor to the queen, sometime in the 1620s.[56] Testimony that Aguado delivered later in life suggests that he first met Soria around 1623, likely about when he was finishing his apprenticeship.[57] Perhaps they met when Aguado took the court guild exam, for which Soria served as an examiner (he was one of the "old masters" named in the lawsuit mentioned above). However it came about, meeting Francisco de Soria was Aguado's lucky break, which opened the door to his career at the court.

In the Old Master's Workshop

In Francisco de Soria's workshop, Aguado learned the art of courtly fashion, and the art of fashioning himself at court, from the master. Originally from Segovia, Soria had decades of experience at the court, where he had served as Queen Margaret of Austria's *sastre de cámara* since March 1, 1601.[58] Soria's work for Queen Margaret was traditional and conservative, steeped in the stiff,

41. *(facing page)* Juan Pantoja de la Cruz, *Queen Margaret of Austria*, 1606. Oil on canvas, 207 × 122 cm. Museo Nacional del Prado, Madrid

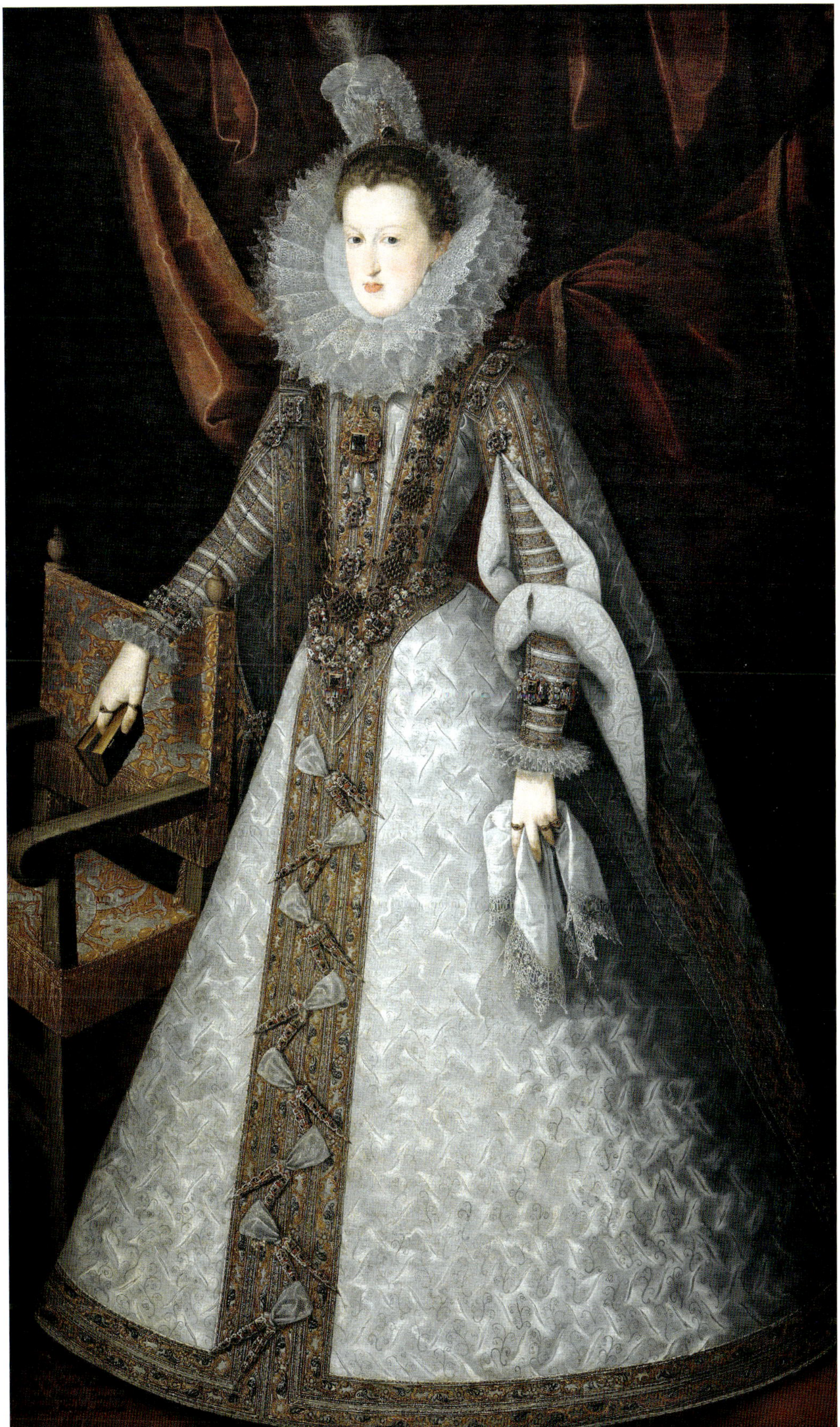

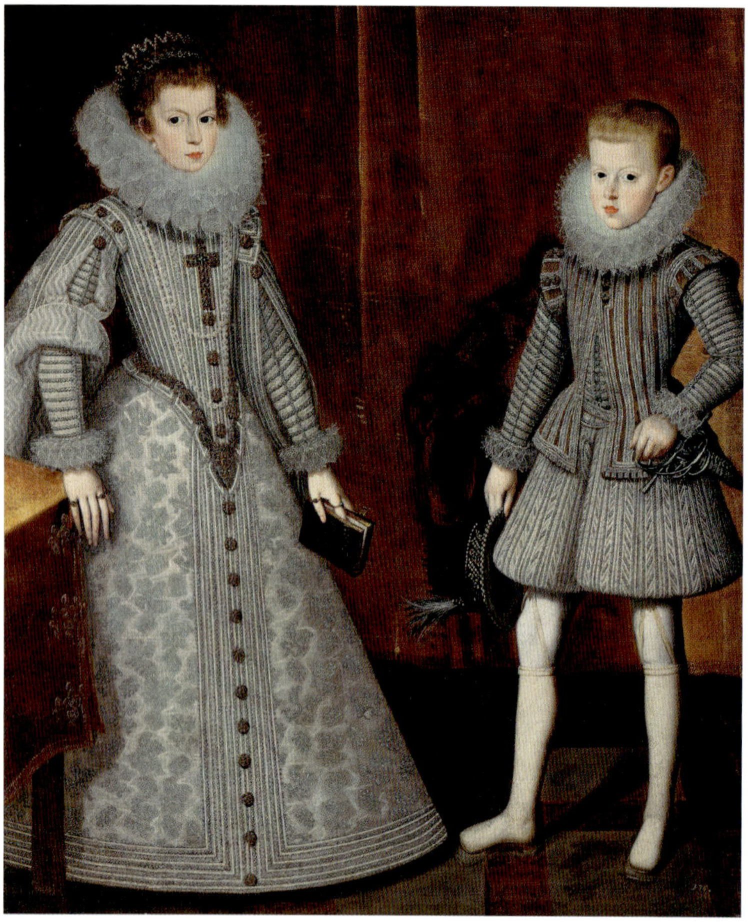

42. Bartolomé González, *Infanta Anne of Austria and Prince Philip*, c. 1612. Oil on canvas, 137 × 118 cm. Kunsthistorisches Museum, Vienna

formal courtly style of the previous century. His dress designs communicated the grandeur of Philip III's reign through luxurious fabrics and decorations that were captured in meticulous detail in court portraits. In a portrait painted by Juan Pantoja de la Cruz in 1606—the year of the court's return to Madrid—Queen Margaret wears a dress made from white satin that has been slashed and pressed with a design of floral sprigs, with one of her long, pointed sleeves (*mangas de punta*) turned up at the hem to show off a sumptuous lining, probably a stamped velvet (fig. 41). The queen's dress is decorated with richly embroidered bands (*fajas*) and beribboned metal aglets (*puntas*). When the queen died in 1611, Soria kept busy with seven royal children to dress, including the future King Philip IV and his sister, Anne of Austria (fig. 42).[59] In 1615 an exchange of princesses took place between Spain and France that was intended to establish a permanent peace between them. The Spanish Infanta Anne of Austria married Louis XIII, king of France, whose sister, Elisabeth of Bourbon, married Prince Philip of Spain (see the Family Tree of Philip IV, p. 9). When Elisabeth arrived in Madrid, it was Soria's job to transform the French princess into a Spanish queen.[60]

A *relación* describing Elisabeth's journey to Madrid reports that the 13-year-old bride came with "many dresses that were very good but in the French style."[61] In a portrait painted a few years earlier, Princess Elisabeth is dressed in the style of the French court with a bodice that was low-cut by Spanish standards, a lace collar worn high behind her neck, and a skirt ruched over a wheel-shaped farthingale (fig. 43). Once in Spain, Elisabeth's name was Hispanicized to Isabel, and the French tailor who had accompanied her was sent home, replaced by Francisco de Soria.[62] During Isabel's first year in Spain, Soria made her a new Spanish wardrobe with dresses in a rainbow of colors—green, blue, pink, white, and one dress with a matching cloak made from silk the color of egg yolk.[63] Soria dressed Isabel through a series of subsequent transitions. In November 1620, when Isabel turned 18 and consummated her marriage to Prince Philip, Soria made her first dress to be worn with *chapines*, the tall cork-soled shoes that marked a married woman's status.[64] Isabel's wardrobe underwent another transition in the spring of 1621, when her husband became king and she was elevated to queen consort. This change in Isabel's status was reflected by the colors of her dresses: the bright colors of previous years were replaced by black, dark gray (*pardo*), and walnut-brown (*noguerado*). A very dark ash color called "rat fur" (*pel de rata*) was briefly popular in the queen's wardrobe in 1627 and 1628.[65]

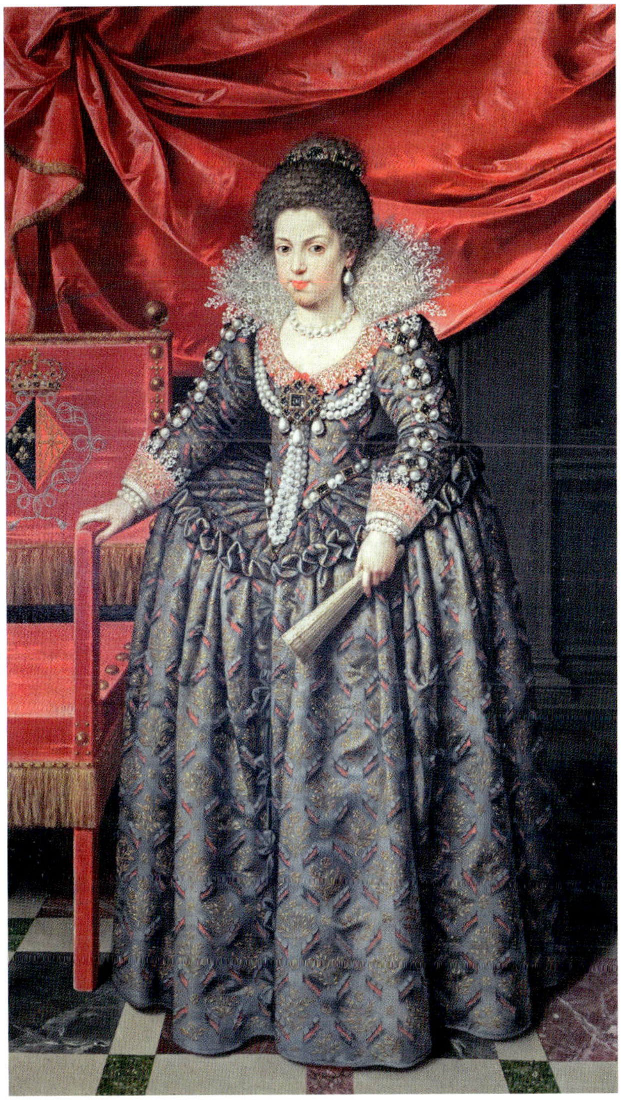

43. Frans Pourbus II, *Elisabeth of Bourbon*, 1611. Oil on canvas, 165 × 103 cm. Palazzo Pitti, Florence

Queen Isabel was Soria's primary royal patron when Aguado joined his workshop in the 1620s. It is unclear what role Aguado played: he may have begun as one of the many journeymen employed by the queen's tailor, or, if he had taken his master's exam, Aguado could have assisted Soria by cutting out fabrics and trims for the

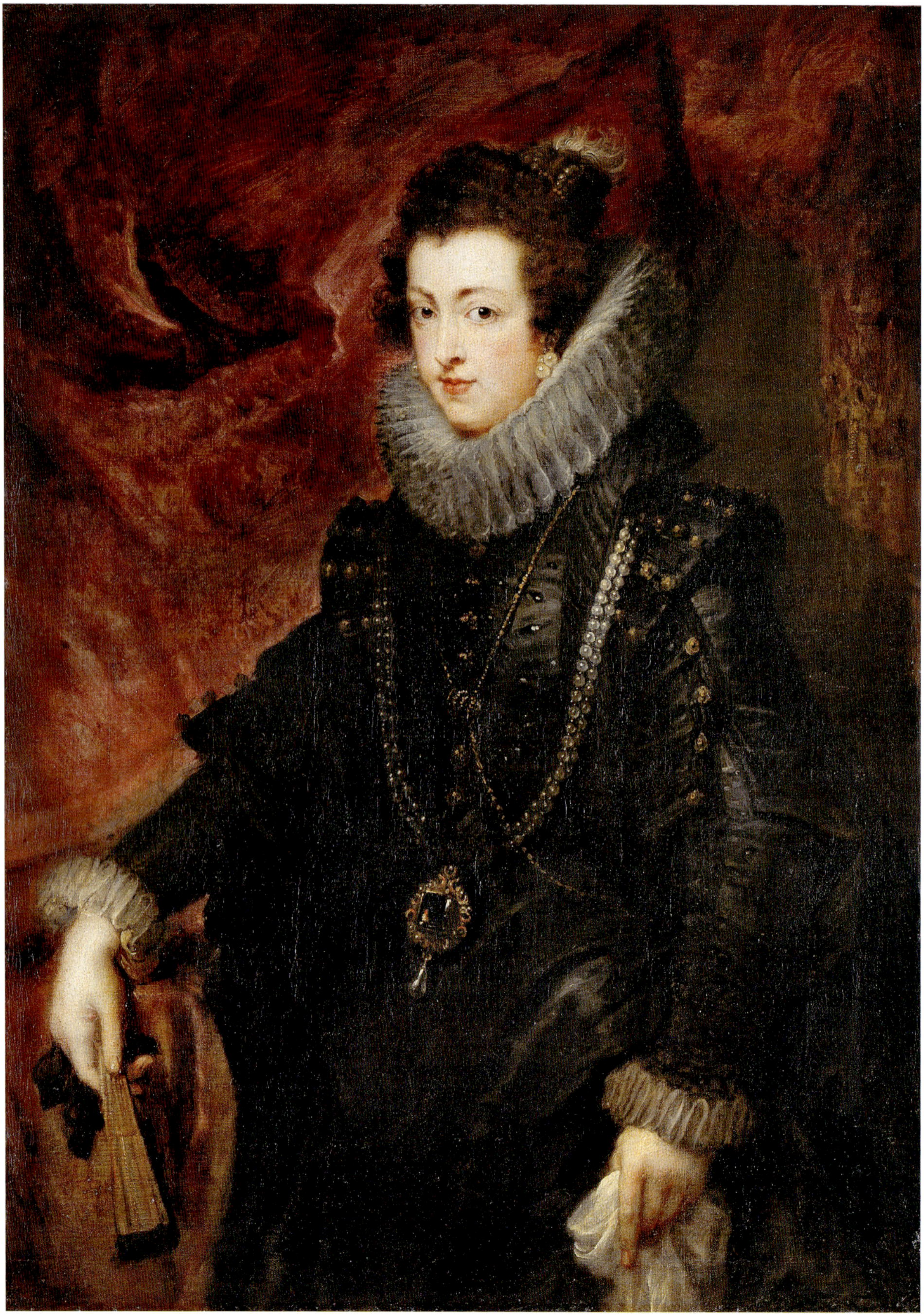

journeymen to sew. Soria's workshop made two different types of dress for the queen: an everyday three-piece *vestido* and a two-piece *saya entera* for special occasions (see the Dress Patterns on pp. 219–20 for details). Other garments (interior, exterior, and informal) were a relatively minor aspect of the workshop's production. In a typical year, Soria's workshop made 22 *vestidos* and 4 *sayas enteras* for the queen. The queen's tailor was paid an average of about 250 *reales* for a dress of either kind, while a special dress could cost over 500 *reales*. By comparison, in 1624, Diego Velázquez was paid 800 *reales* to paint three full-length portraits—one of which was the portrait of Philip IV in black that is now at the Metropolitan Museum of Art in New York (see fig. 13)—which comes to about 267 *reales* per painting.[66] That same year, Soria earned 559 *reales* to make a black taffeta three-piece dress for the queen to wear on the feast day of the Visitation.[67] This was only the tailor's fee and did not include the cost of materials.

The mainstay of the queen's wardrobe was the three-piece dress, which consisted of an over-gown, skirt, and doublet (*ropa*, *basquiña*, and *jubón*). The *vestido* was the ensemble worn most often by the queen, but it appears very rarely in portraits. An exception is a three-quarter-length portrait painted by the Flemish artist Peter Paul Rubens, which depicts Queen Isabel in a black silk three-piece dress of the kind that Soria's workshop was making in the later 1620s (see one version of the portrait in fig. 44).[68] The more subtle details of the dress decoration, which are difficult to read in the painted portrait, are shown more clearly in an engraving made after the original by one of Rubens's pupils (fig. 45). The queen wears her over-gown open at the front to display contrasting facings (*bebederos*) decorated "in harpoon" (*en arpón*), that is, with diagonal stripes of trimming. The stiff wings (*brahones*) that project from the shoulder

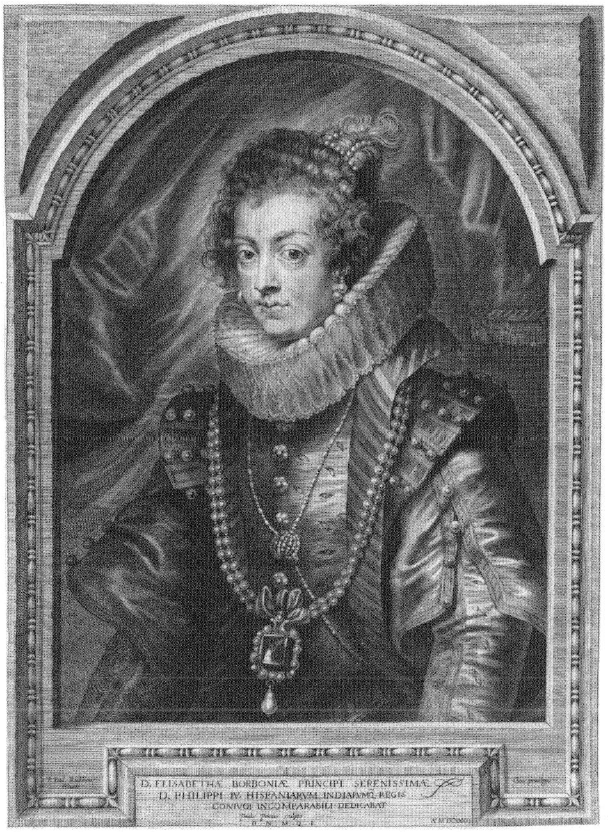

44. (*facing page*) Peter Paul Rubens and Workshop, *Queen Isabel of Bourbon*, 1628–9. Oil on canvas, 112 × 83 cm. The State Hermitage Museum, St. Petersburg

45. (*above*) Paulus Pontius after Peter Paul Rubens, *Queen Isabel of Bourbon*, 1632. Engraving, 45.2 × 33.7 cm. The Metropolitan Museum of Art, New York

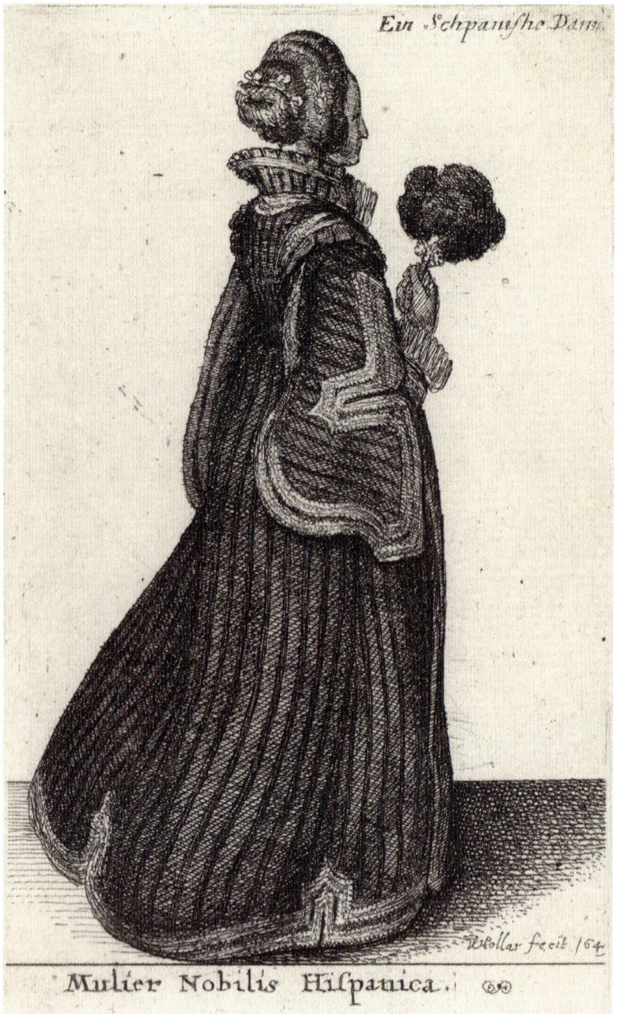

46. Wenceslaus Hollar, *Spanish Noblewoman*, probably 1649. Etching, 9.2 × 5.7 cm. National Gallery of Art, Washington, DC

47. *(facing page)* Workshop of Velázquez, *Isabel of Bourbon* (detail of fig. 65)

of the gown are decorated with black ribbon and gold buttons, as are the round sleeves (*mangas redondas*) that hang below the elbow. An engraving by Wenceslaus Hollar offers a full-length view of such an over-gown, which was a long and loose-fitting garment that had ample space for displaying rows of rich trimmings (fig. 46). In Rubens's portrait of Isabel, the over-gown is pushed back behind her waist to reveal a doublet made from black silk decorated all over with small diagonal cuts (see fig. 44). The doublet has short skirts called *faldillas* and long fitted sleeves (*mangas justas*), which are worn underneath the decorative sleeves of the over-gown.

Most portraits depict Queen Isabel wearing a formal dress known as a *saya entera* (also called a *saya grande*, or simply *saya*) (fig. 47). This was what the queen wore on special occasions such as religious holidays, weddings, and royal birthdays. The upper-body garment, called a *cuera*, was a close-fitting bodice that came to a point at the center front and had short skirts attached at the waist. It was distinguished from a doublet by its shoulder-wings and hanging sleeves, which could be round (like the sleeves of an over-gown), pointed, or tubular. A very rare early-seventeenth-century *cuera* has thick layers of coated linen inside the shoulder-wings, collar, and skirts, which gives them their stiff shapes (fig. 48).[69] The *cuera* could be worn open to reveal contrasting facings and a pair of chest-coverings (*petos* or *petillos*) with matching fitted sleeves (*manguillas*). Requiring only small amounts of fabric, these accessory pieces were made from exceptionally expensive materials. A portrait of Queen Isabel dressed by Soria shows her wearing a formal dress with sleeves and chest-coverings made from a shimmering striped silver fabric, which create the illusion of a doublet but actually required much less material (see fig. 47). The skirt of a *saya entera* was cut longer in the back to form a train (*cola*), which can be

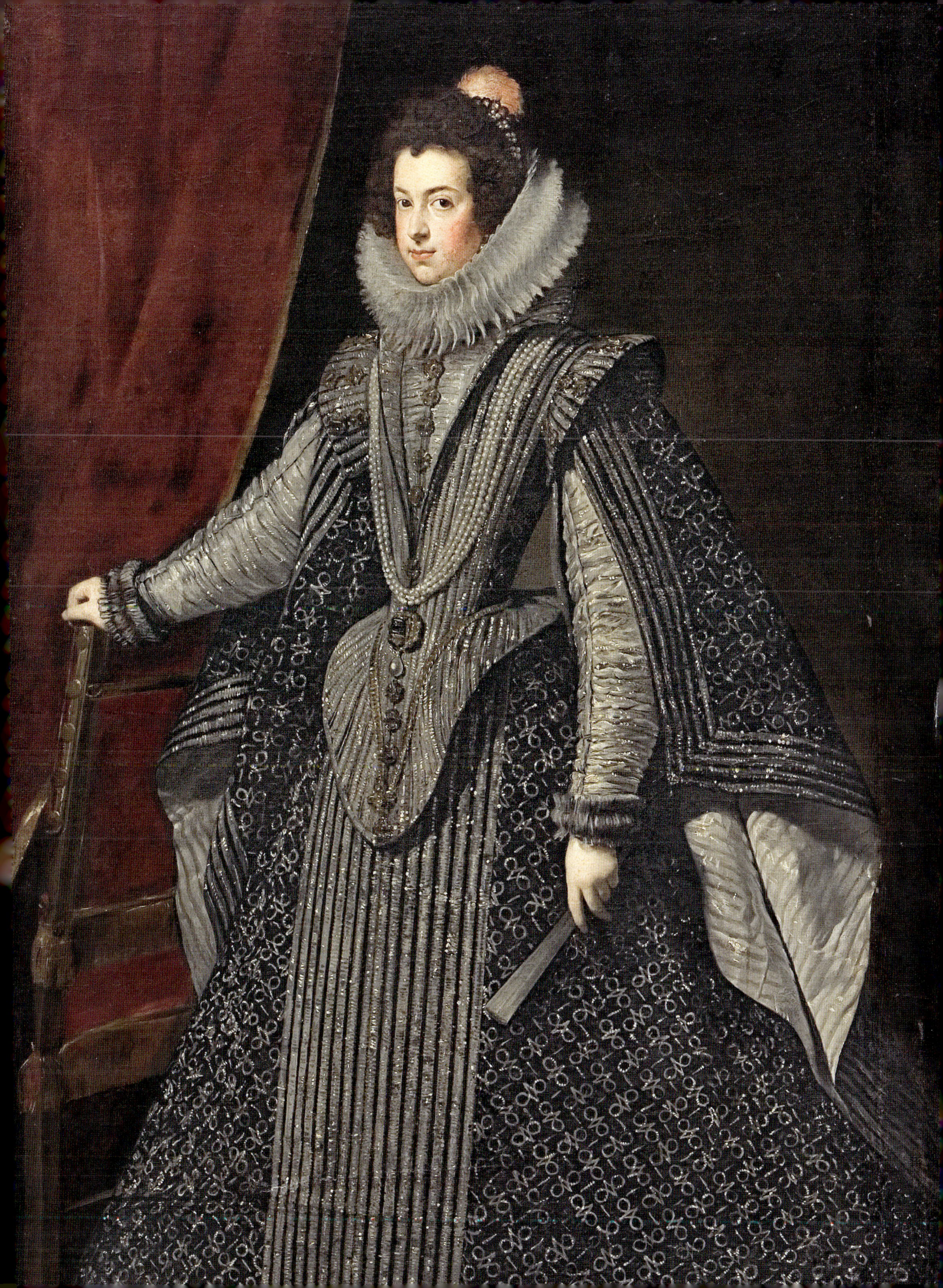

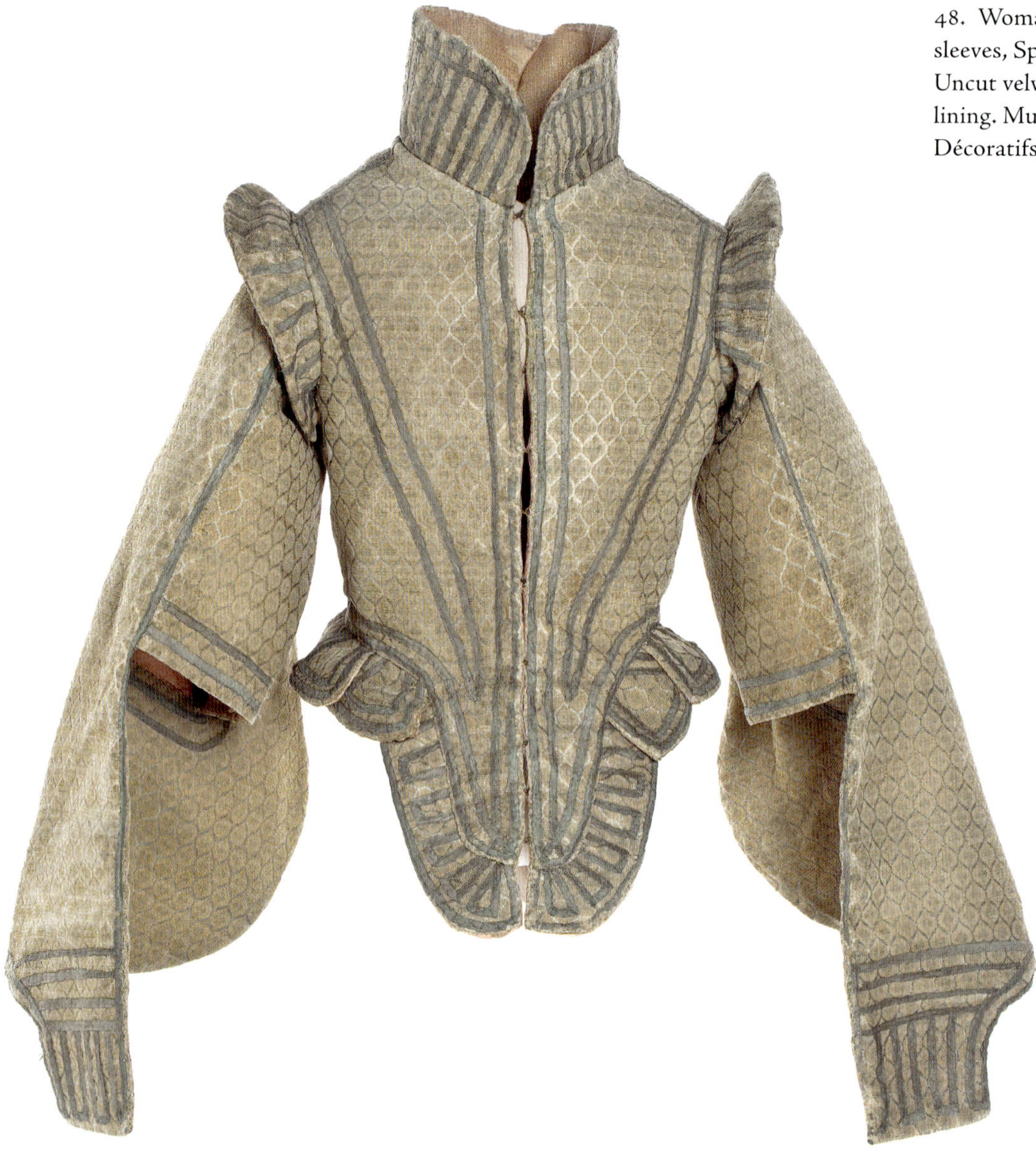

48. Woman's *cuera* with round sleeves, Spanish, c. 1590–1610. Uncut velvet with silk taffeta lining. Musée des Arts Décoratifs, Paris

seen trailing behind Queen Isabel in a view of the royal family in a fantastical palatial setting (fig. 49).[70] With its train and multiple sets of sleeves, a *saya entera* was made from an enormous amount of fabric: the *saya entera* with round sleeves that Francisco de la Rocha Burguen made for his court exam required 15.4 meters of velvet or damask, according to the pattern that he published in his 1618 tailoring manual (fig. 50).[71]

The dresses that Soria's workshop made for the queen were not distinguished by the cut of the garments—pattern layouts for the same styles were published by tailors such as Rocha Burguen for

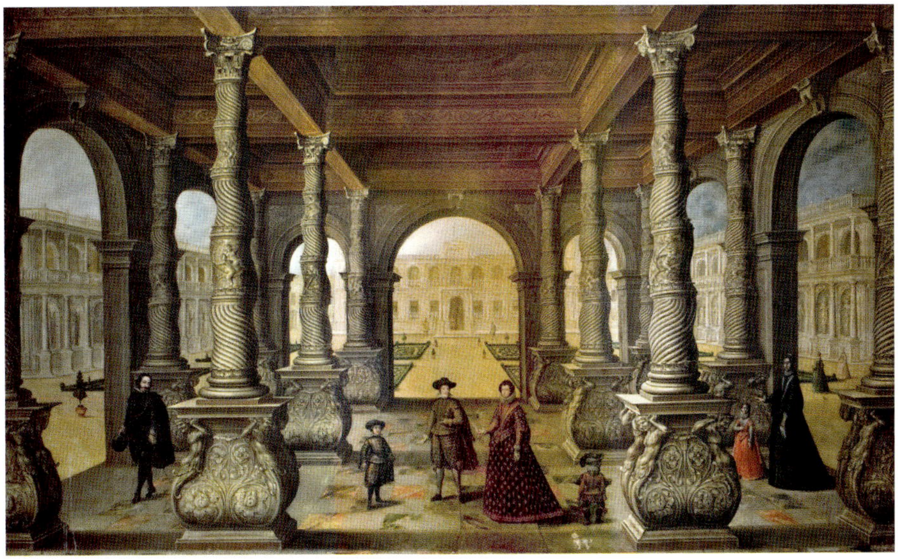

widespread use—but rather by the luxurious fabrics and decorations that were used to make them. The richest fabrics in the queen's wardrobe combined silk with threads of silver or gold. Many of her dresses were made from *espolín,* a silk fabric brocaded with flowers of silver or gold, or both. One such green silk brocaded with metal threads has survived in the form of a chasuble (fig. 51). Shimmering lamé (*lama*) combined colored silk with silver or gold threads that were woven end-to-end. The richest fabric of all was cloth of silver or gold (*tela de plata* or *oro*), which was made predominantly from metal threads; it was extremely rare, even in the queen's wardrobe.

In the 1620s, over two dozen varieties of silk fabric were used to make the queen's dresses. The most common fabric was taffeta (*tafetán*), a lustrous, lightweight ribbed silk with a crisp quality, which was worn in the warmer months. Variants of taffeta called ormuzine (*ormesí*) and camlet (*camelote*) were specially treated to have a rippled, watered effect (*de aguas*). The

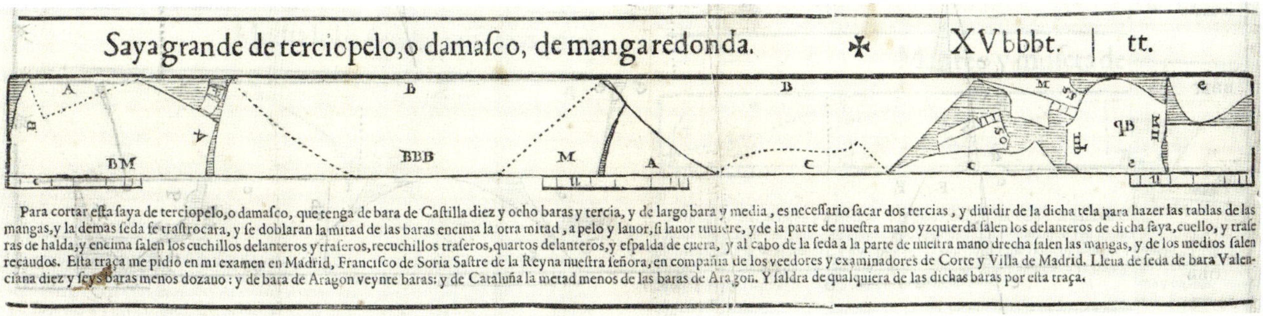

Saya grande de terciopelo, o damafco, de manga redonda. ✠ XVbbbt. | tt.

Para cortar efta faya de terciopelo, o damafco, que tenga de bara de Caftilla diez y ocho baras y tercia, y de largo bara y media, es neceffario facar dos tercias, y diuidir de la dicha tela para hazer las tablas de las mangas, y la demas feda fe traftrocara, y fe doblaran la mitad de las baras encima la otra mitad, a pelo y lauor, fi lauor tuuiere, y de la parte de nueftra mano yzquierda falen los delanteros de dicha faya, cuello, y trafe ras de halda, y encima falen los cuchillos delanteros y traferos, recuchillos traferos, quartos delanteros, y efpalda de cuera, y al cabo de la feda a la parte de nueftra mano drecha falen las mangas, y de los medios falen recaudos. Efta traça me pidio en mi examen en Madrid, Francifco de Soria Saftre de la Reyna nueftra feñora, en compañia de los veedores y examinadores de Corte y Villa de Madrid. Lleua de feda de bara Valenciana diez y feys baras menos dozauo: y de bara de Aragon veynte baras: y de Cataluña la metad menos de las baras de Aragon. Y faldra de qualquiera de las dichas baras por efta traça.

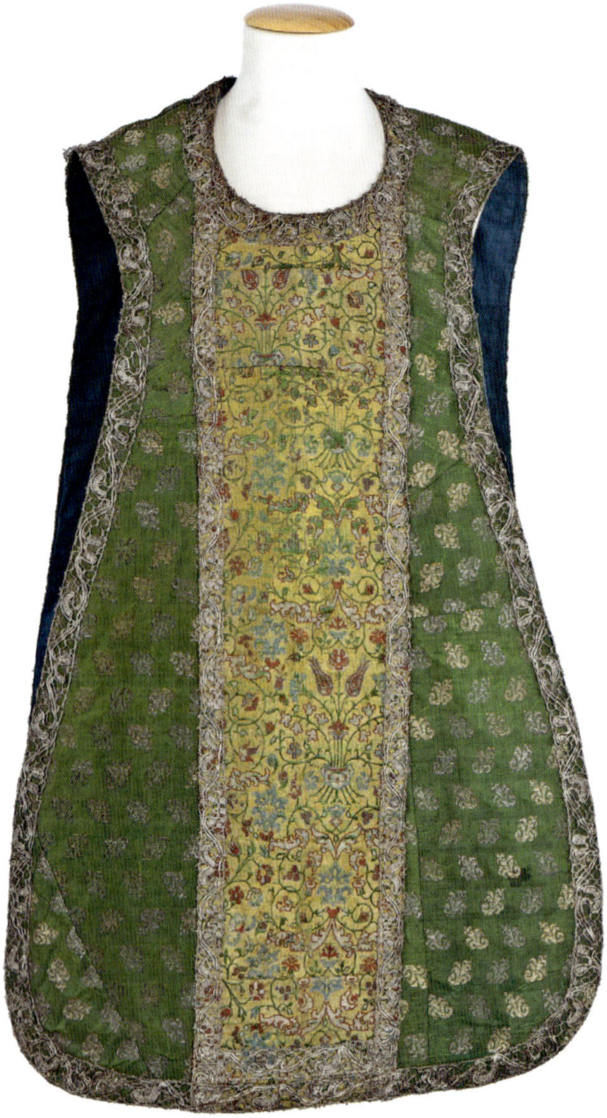

51. Chasuble, Spanish, 17th century. Green silk brocaded with metal thread and yellow silk polychrome brocade, with metal bobbin lace. Museu Tèxtil, Terrassa

second most frequent fabric was satin (*raso*)—a smooth, shiny silk that was used to make trimmings as well as dresses. Satin in all colors was produced domestically in Spain; black satin was imported from Florence, and white satin from China was used for special-occasion garments, such as the dress that the queen wore on the king's birthday in 1627.[72] Wintertime dresses were made from velvet (*terciopelo*), which could be plain, curly, or richly figured with designs (*terciopelo liso*, *terciopelo rizo*, or *terciopelado*). Isabel wears a rich patterned velvet in a portrait painted shortly before she became queen (fig. 52). Fragments of the same fabric reveal the richness of the material, which was created by combining cut and uncut loops of velvet pile on a contrasting satin background (fig. 53).[73] A long-haired velvet called plush (*felpa*) was used to make cold-weather dresses and also to line cloaks, robes, and petticoats.

When plain silks were used to make the queen's dresses, they were decorated with designs that were pricked or pressed onto the fabric by a specialist working in Soria's workshop, or they were sent to the workshop of the queen's embroiderer for decoration (see the 1620s in the Chronology of Women's Dress, pp. 214–15). A skirt panel, which was probably cut down from a woman's garment to dress a religious image, is decorated with the intricate embroidery that was characteristic of the early-seventeenth-century Spanish court (fig. 54).[74] The white satin fabric is embroidered all over with silk thread, cording, and tiny round sequins called *lentejuelas* ("little lentils"). The narrow rows of trimming on the skirt are decorated with zigzag stitching, which also appears in *Isabel of Bourbon in a Velvet Dress* (see fig. 52). Black glass often featured in court embroidery, and it was used in combination with gold to striking effect in the dress that Isabel wore to celebrate King Philip III's entry into Lisbon in 1619 (fig. 55).[75]

The decoration of the queen's dresses involved multiple court artisans with different skills, including an embroiderer, a gold-wire drawer who made metal threads and sequins, and a *cordonero* who twisted silk thread into cords. The queen's tailor effectively served as the designer and project manager, who coordinated the work of these and other specialists to produce the showstopping confections that Isabel wears in the court portraits that were painted in the 1620s. These portraits suggest that Soria had an eye for bold fabric patterns but was less imaginative in his use of trimmings, which are rigidly applied in straight rows, in keeping with traditions of royal dress that had been established in the previous century.

Francisco de Soria built an immensely successful career on a foundation of conservatism and continuity. When Aguado joined his workshop, Soria was at the pinnacle of his profession and was by far the richest tailor in Madrid.[76] He invested his wealth in real estate in the parish of San Ginés, where he rented out apartments to tailors, doublet-makers, embroiderers, doctors, clergymen, and other professionals.[77] Soria and his wife lived in luxury, served by a slave, in a well-furnished home that they owned on the Calle

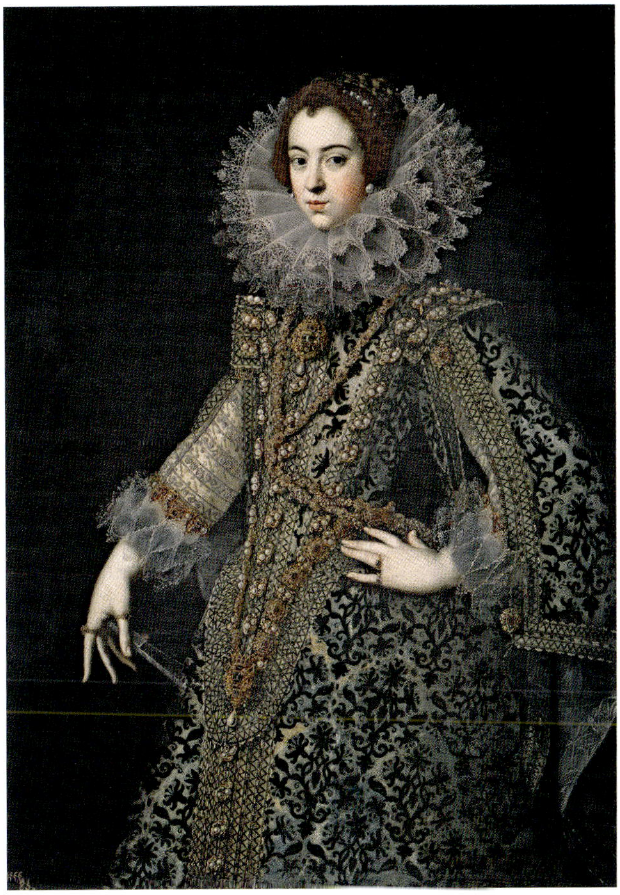

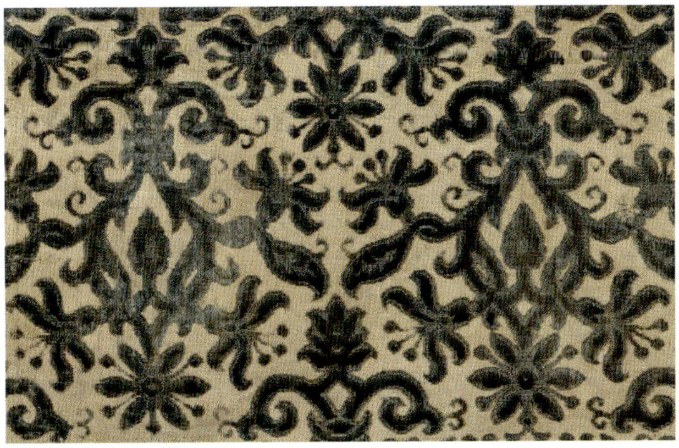

52. *(above right)* Unknown Spanish artist, *Isabel of Bourbon in a Velvet Dress*, c. 1620. Oil on canvas, 126 × 91 cm. Museo Nacional del Prado, Madrid

53. *(right)* Fragment of silk, cut, uncut, and voided velvet against a satin weave foundation (detail), possibly Italian, first quarter of the 17th century. The Art Institute of Chicago

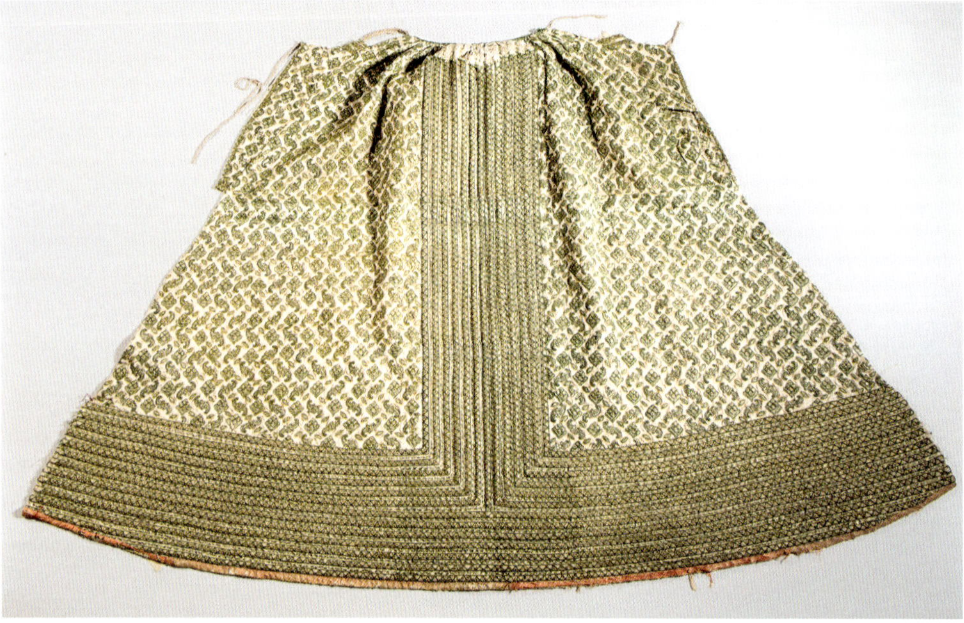

54. Skirt panel of white satin embroidered with green silk and gilded sequins, Spanish, early 17th century. Museo Arqueológico Nacional, Madrid

55. *(facing page)* Rodrigo de Villandrando, *Princess Isabel of Bourbon*, c. 1620. Oil on canvas, 201 × 115 cm. Museo Nacional del Prado, Madrid. (This painting is the companion to *Prince Philip with Miguel Soplillo*, see fig. 12)

Mayor. In a profession that was riven by inequality and generational divisions, Soria was the ultimate old master. He dressed the part with ostentatiously expensive garments and accessories, including a white hat with gold decorations, a kidskin doublet with silver and black striped sleeves, a silk cloak decorated with satin ribbons, and matching sets of gilded swords and daggers.[78] Soria's success showed the material rewards and social prestige that could be had by a *sastre de cámara* in the queen's household. It was an enviable position, and it became available only once in a generation.

Succession

The last garment that Francisco de Soria made for Queen Isabel was a waistcoat (*almilla*) decorated with white lace (*encaje*), which was probably intended as sleepwear.[79] On October 10, 1630, the queen's tailor died—and the office of *sastre de cámara* was vacant for the first time in almost three decades. Soria left behind a fortune of almost 600,000 *reales*, an impressive portfolio of real estate, and a widow, but he had no children to inherit his position in the queen's household.[80] Soria's lack of an heir meant that his successor could be chosen for his qualifications rather than his parentage. When Isabel of Bourbon had arrived at the Spanish court at age 13, she inherited Queen Margaret of Austria's household staff, including Francisco de Soria as her tailor. But by the time of Soria's death in 1630, the queen's status had risen immensely: she had given birth to a baby boy, named Baltasar Carlos, on October 17, 1629, and the child was about to celebrate his first birthday. The queen was in a strong position to exert her own preference to fill the vacancy left by Soria, and there was a large pool of talent from which to select his replacement. She chose Mateo Aguado. On October 14, 1630, the 25-year-old from Fuenlabrada was sworn in as tailor to the queen.[81]

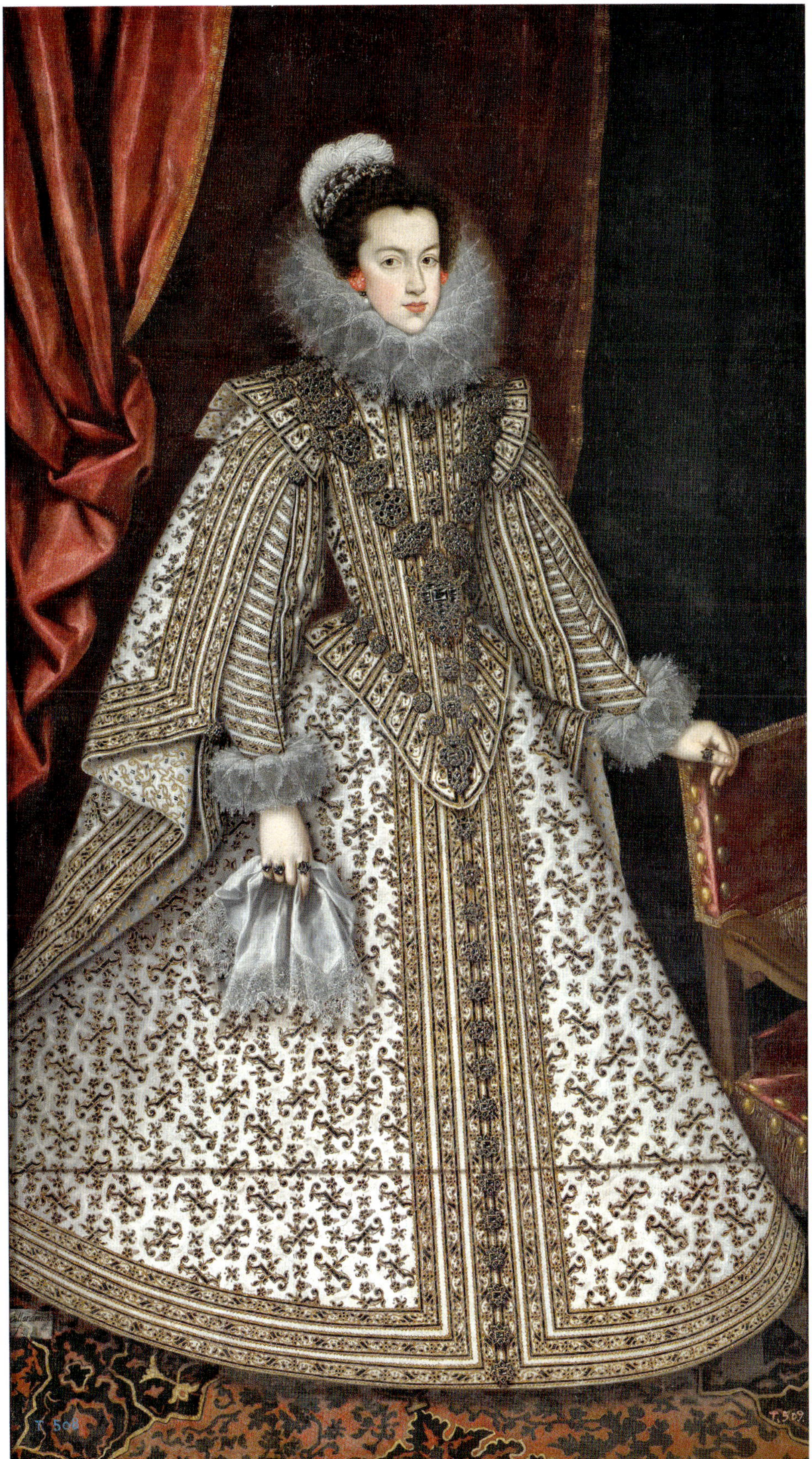

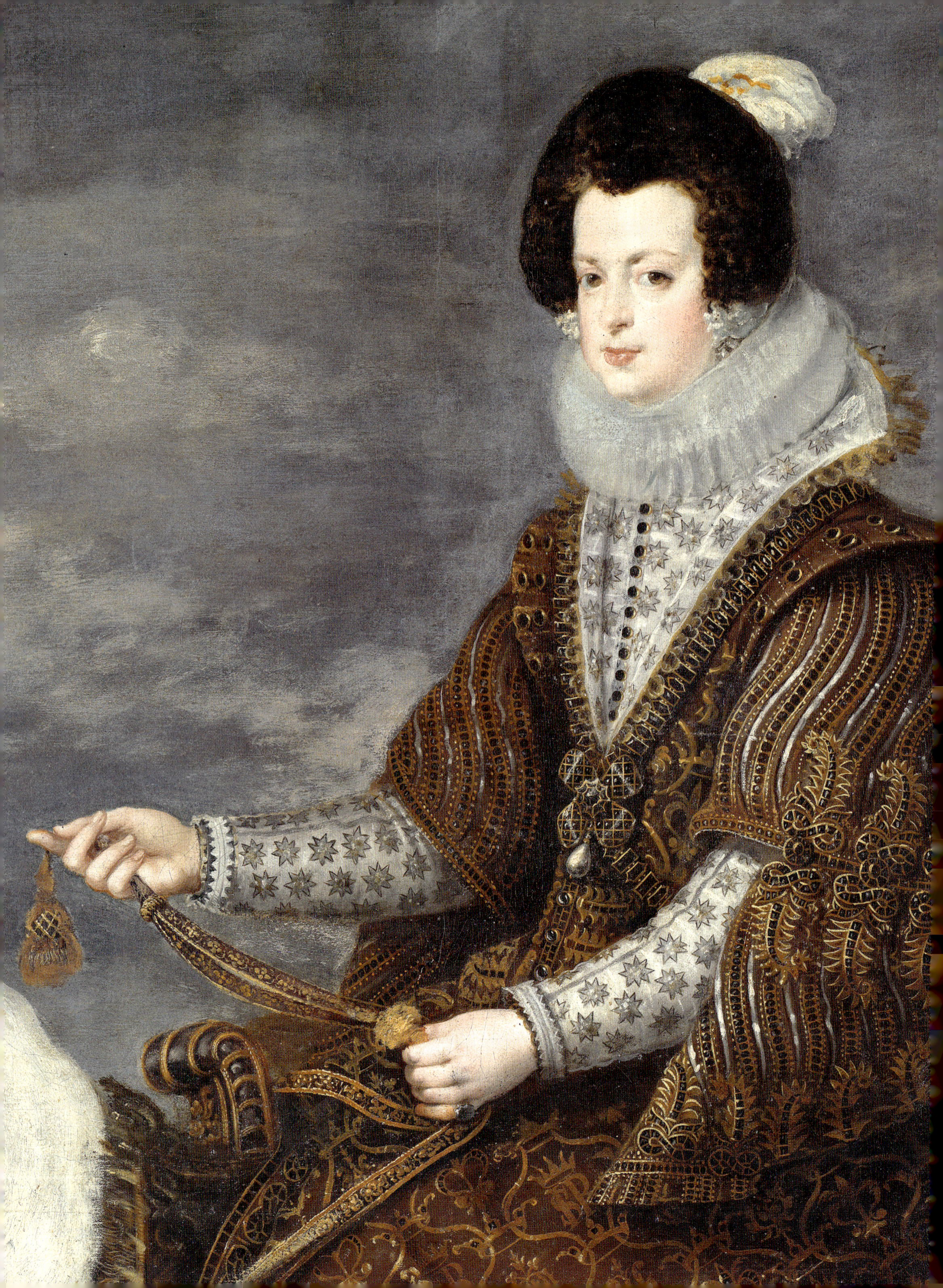

2. The Queen's Tailor

The First Decade, 1630–1639

On October 18, 1630, four days after Mateo Aguado was sworn in as the queen's tailor, marriage banns were posted in the parish church of San Ginés for his marriage to Alfonsa Martínez, the 20-year-old daughter of master tailor Lázaro Martínez.[1] With his new salaried position at court, Aguado was quite a catch. And he needed a wife right away, since only men who were "married and well-regarded" were permitted to enter the queen's private rooms.[2] Guards were posted at the entrance to the queen's quarters, which were arranged around the eastern courtyard of the Royal Palace (no. 4 in fig. 57).[3] The rooms became increasingly private and restricted, culminating in the queen's dressing room and bed chamber. The book of etiquette that governed the queen's household required her *sastre de cámara* to be present for the dressing of the queen but did not specify his role in this daily ritual.[4] The separate components of a dress had to be laced, hooked, or buttoned closed—a doublet alone had five dozen buttonholes—and then accessories such as the collar and cuffs were pinned into place. The tailor knew these garments better than anyone and may have been on hand to make last-minute alterations. The queen's relationship with her tailor was one of the closest physical relationships that she had with anyone, with the exception of the king, with whom she sometimes shared the conjugal bedroom that was located near her dressing room.

Aguado's documented professional life begins in October 1630, which is when he began to keep accounts recording every garment that he made while in the queen's service. These accounts are almost complete for his first decade in office (only the years 1632 and 1633 are missing). Amid repetitive descriptions of garments, fabrics, and trimmings, there are tidbits of information about Aguado's busy new life as a royal tailor and his working relationship with Queen Isabel, who took a keen interest in the making of her wardrobe. Velázquez's portraits of Isabel in the 1630s show notable changes in the queen's style of dress during Aguado's first decade in office. Close study of Aguado's accounts reveals how the queen's wardrobe responded to the major political development of the decade—war with France—and to the physical changes that came from the more intimate events of pregnancy and childbirth.

Making the Queen's Wardrobe

As *sastre de cámara*, Aguado received the same annual wages as Francisco de Soria had before him—about 996 *reales*—but his position came with an obligation to pay

56. *(facing page)* Diego Velázquez and Workshop, *Queen Isabel of Bourbon on Horseback* (detail of fig. 69)

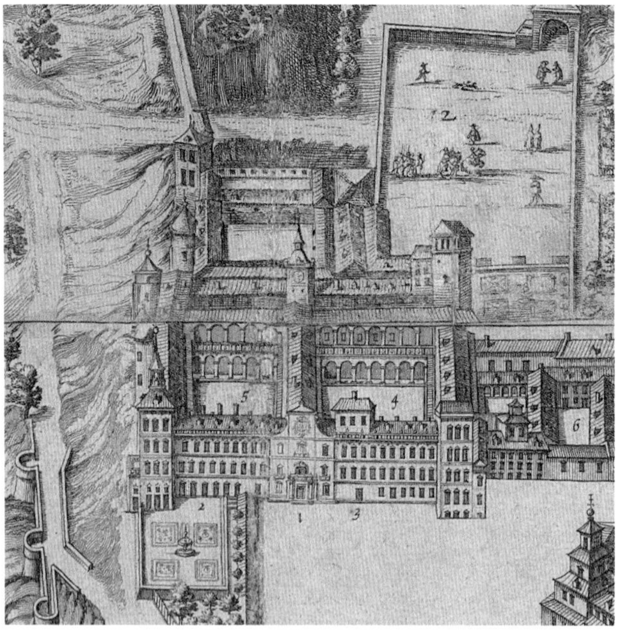

57. The Royal Palace. Pedro Teixeira, *Topographia de la Villa de Madrid* (detail; see the complete map in fig. 32). Biblioteca Nacional de España, Madrid

an even larger annual pension of 1,100 *reales* to Soria's widow, Mariana Núñez, "every year for the rest of her life."[5] Aguado's real income came from the payments he received for the garments that were itemized in his accounts. At the end of 1631, Aguado submitted an account that valued his work for the queen in his first full year on the job at 9,645 *reales*. After the work was appraised, the total was reduced to 6,595 *reales*.[6] That year, he had made 23 new dresses (*vestidos*) for the queen, 2 formal *sayas enteras* with their accessory pieces, a dressing gown (*ropa de levantar*), and several petticoats, waistcoats, and aprons (an apron, called an *avantal*, was a luxurious garment when made for a queen). The amount that Aguado charged to make a garment could vary significantly: the tailor's fee for a three-piece dress ranged from 88 to 550 *reales*. The decorations were a significant factor. Aguado earned less for dresses that were primarily decorated by the embroiderer, and more for dresses that had "very meticulous" decorations made in his workshop.

Very little information is available about Aguado's workshop, which must have been based at his home in the parish of San Ginés. As the guild bylaws noted, it was customary in Madrid for tailors to have their workshops inside their homes, for which they sought out spacious accommodations.[7] Aguado had one longtime employee, a journeyman tailor named Juan Martínez, who began working for him in the early 1630s and remained a valued member of his workshop for over three decades.[8] Perhaps Martínez was a brother or otherwise related to Aguado's wife, Alfonsa Martínez—who died just eight months after their marriage.[9] Aguado had as many as 14 journeymen and up to 50 seamstresses working for him at a time. He also had a *prensador* in his workshop who pricked fabric among other duties, and sometimes he paid a *colchera* to quilt winter garments for him. All of these workers were paid by the tailor, who incorporated these expenses into the amount that he charged for each garment.

Sometimes Aguado charged an extra fee for drawings, especially when he was making the most elaborate and expensive garments.[10] The amount that Aguado was paid for his drawings ranged from 6 *reales* for designing the decorations for a cloak up to 88 *reales* for a dress that the queen was going to wear on the Octave of Corpus Christi. This was a new development: Francisco de Soria had never been paid for drawings (although he may have made them). None of Aguado's drawings has been found, but his accounts indicate that they were designs for dress decorations, which were probably more detailed than surviving tailor sketches from the Medici court (fig. 58).[11] Aguado's drawings

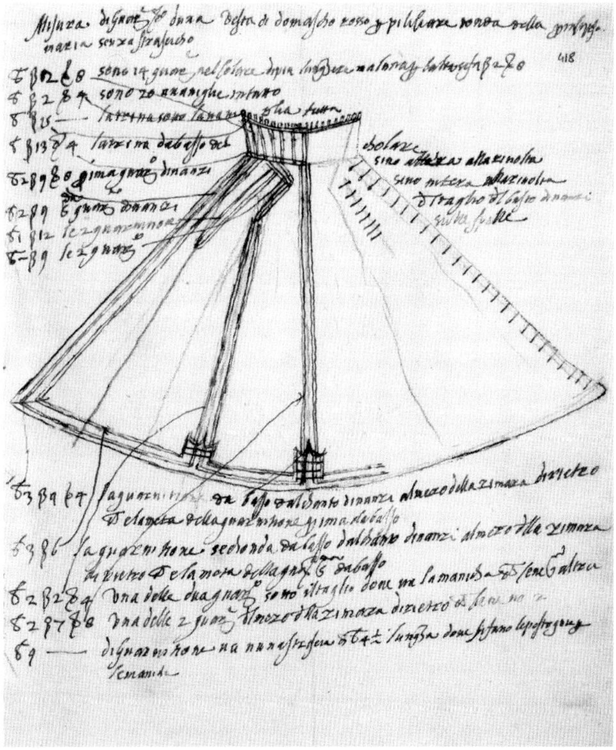

58. Tailor's sketch of a livery robe for the court of Cosimo II de' Medici, Grand Duke of Tuscany, 1593. Archivio di Stato di Firenze, Florence

may have been given to the queen's embroiderer, who was responsible for making many dress decorations, and they could have been damaged or destroyed in the embroiderer's workshop. Aguado's drawings were functional, not artistic: sometimes his charges for drawings were lumped in with his fee for making buttonholes (*ojales*). The tailor's drawings were probably not considered worth keeping once they had served their purpose.[12] Nonetheless, the fact that Aguado was paid to make drawings suggests two things: first, that he was doing something new in the area of dress decorations, and second, that this creative work was valued at the court and considered worthy of compensation.

The most elaborate and expensive dresses that Aguado designed were the ones that the queen wore on major religious holidays. The tailor's busiest season of the year began with the late-winter holidays of Candlemas, the Feast of Saint Blaise, and Carnival, and extended through Holy Week in the spring to reach a climax in early summer with Corpus Christi. This holiday was the fashion event of the year, when the queen was seen by a large and diverse audience.[13] In 1626, for instance, she appeared on a balcony at the Royal Palace to watch the procession of the Host with the king and all the religious and secular institutions of the town and court passing by below her.[14] In 1639, Aguado was paid 1,300 *reales* to make the queen's dress for Corpus Christi, which was the most expensive dress that he ever made for her. The materials for that dress, which was made of black ormuzine and decorated all over with silver ovals and knots, cost 3,504 *reales*.[15]

Aguado often worked overnight on the eve of a major holiday to finish the queen's special outfit. Throughout the year, it was not unusual for the queen's tailor to begin making a garment late in the afternoon or evening—sometimes at 9 or 11 o'clock at night—and to stay up all night with a dozen or more journeymen finishing the garment for the queen to wear the next morning. The inconvenience was reflected in the tailor's fee, and Aguado's accounts are filled with entries noting that a garment had been made "in a hurry" or "in a great hurry," or "staying up all night." In 1636, Aguado and "many journeymen" made a dress for the queen to wear to a wedding in just half a day and one night. Such a garment was very likely to have been made with long stitches that were quick to sew—and would be just as easy to take apart after the garment had been seen in public.

To the Queen's Taste

Queen Isabel was closely involved in the selection of fabrics and decorations for her wardrobe. The silk merchants regularly prepared samples (*muestras*) of fabrics in different colors, sometimes embroidered or decorated with various kinds of trimmings, for the queen to evaluate before a dress was made. Some dress fabrics were specially commissioned to be woven "to Her Majesty's taste" in Madrid or Toledo. These special orders reveal that Queen Isabel's taste leaned towards heavy velvets in dark colors with precious metals, with a particular preference for the combination of black and silver. Some of these rich fabrics were woven by weavers employed by the court, and evidence suggests that the queen kept an eye on their work. In 1635, Isabel stopped production on a blue and gold velvet after only half a *vara* (42 cm) had been woven. Fabric that did not satisfy the queen's taste did not go to waste: the piece of blue and gold velvet was used to cover a pair of *chapines*.[16] This anecdote from the archives suggests that the queen may have been visiting the royal weavers' workshop, just as the king famously watched Velázquez paint in his studio.

In the 1630s, the queen's dresses were predominantly made from plain black silk. The second most common color was walnut-brown, followed by dark gray. Dresses in other colors were relatively rare, and the palette was quite limited. The sober colors in the queen's wardrobe reflected her seriousness of purpose as queen consort and mother of the heir to the throne. Black was especially somber, worn for mourning and also for fulfilling royal duties such as holding audiences; portraits of Philip IV dressed all in black are images of the king at work, as Javier Portús has written.[17] Dark walnut-brown and light tan (*cabellado*) were also considered to be "modest" colors, but they were not as serious as black and were worn on celebratory occasions.[18] Dark gray was "serious and virtuous," according to Fabio Virgilio Cordato, who wrote a treatise in praise of the color *pardo* in 1639.[19] Two-color fabrics, most often black with silver, were common in the queen's wardrobe. Fabrics woven with three colors, one of them always gold, were the rarest and most luxurious silks used to make the queen's dresses. A seventeenth-century cloak made from brown silk brocaded with silver and gold loops demonstrates just how sumptuous these fabrics may have been; this short cloak, in the collection of the Monastery of San Lorenzo de El Escorial, was made to be worn by a priest when going out to administer last rites to the sick (fig. 59).

The dark fabrics used to make the queen's dresses were frequently accented with gold lace and other gold trimmings (see the 1630s in the Chronology of Women's Dress, pp. 215–16). An unidentified noblewoman in a portrait by Velázquez models the popular combination of black accented with gold (fig. 60). She wears a *saya entera* made of a black patterned fabric similar to a fragment of black silk damask (*damasco*), which demonstrates the subtle splendor of these monochrome fabrics (fig. 61). The woman's collar is trimmed with gold bobbin lace, its facings embroidered with gold stars, and she wears a pair of fitted sleeves in shimmering black and gold silk. Queen Isabel's dresses were often decorated with great quantities of buttons—20 to 50 dozen gold buttons or large buttons made from silk thread (*botones de muletilla*). An abundance of gold buttons on a black ensemble was the ultimate sign of social status for men and women, including the members of the Ramírez de la Trapera family, from the southern city of Úbeda, whose group portrait was painted in their letters patent of nobility made in Granada in 1633 (fig. 62). The queen was attentive to the kind of button that Aguado used: on one

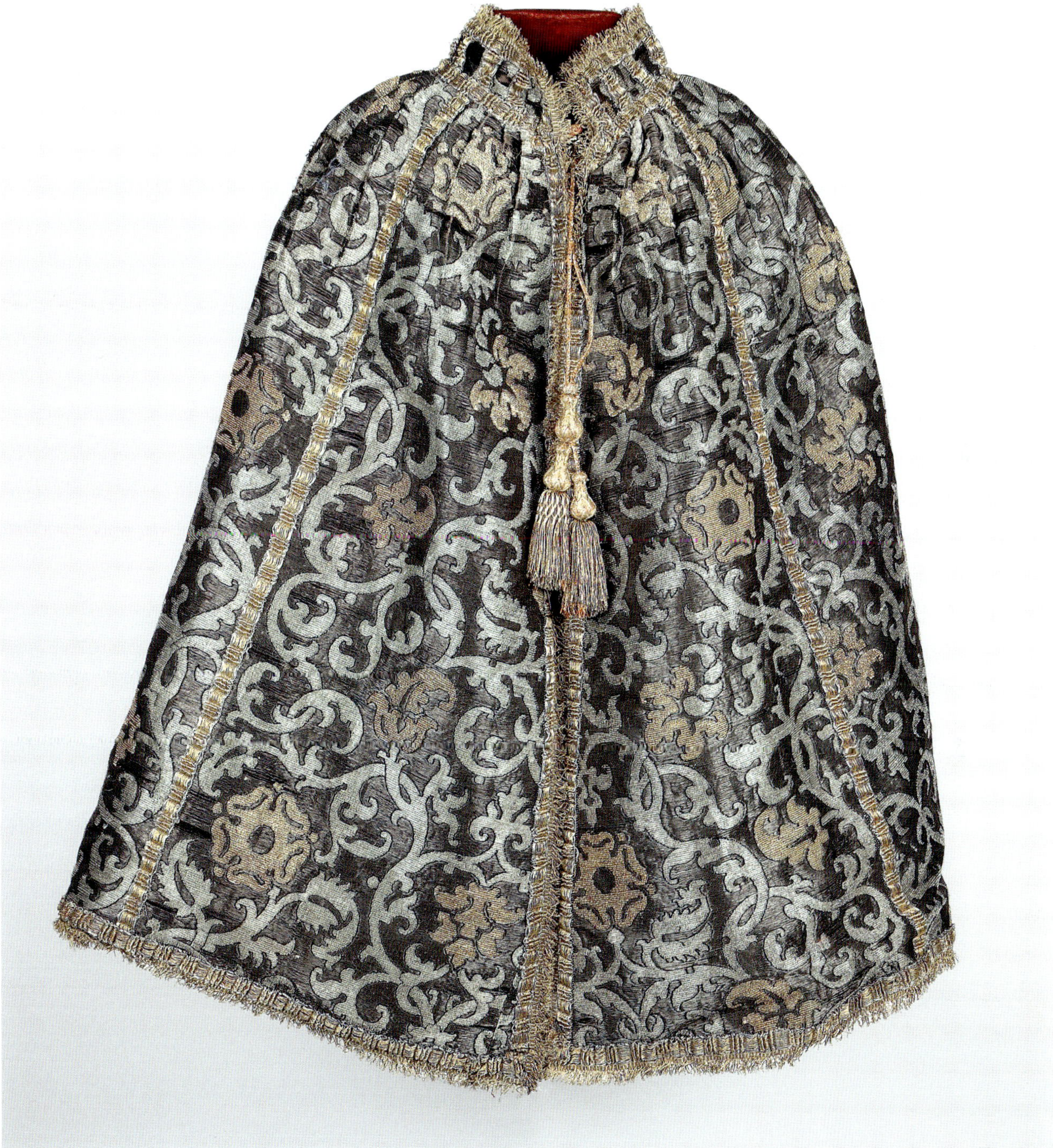

59. Cloak, Spanish, first half of the 17th century. Brown silk brocaded with silver and gold bouclé, trimmed with gold fringe, galloon, cord and tassel. Monastery of San Lorenzo de El Escorial, San Lorenzo

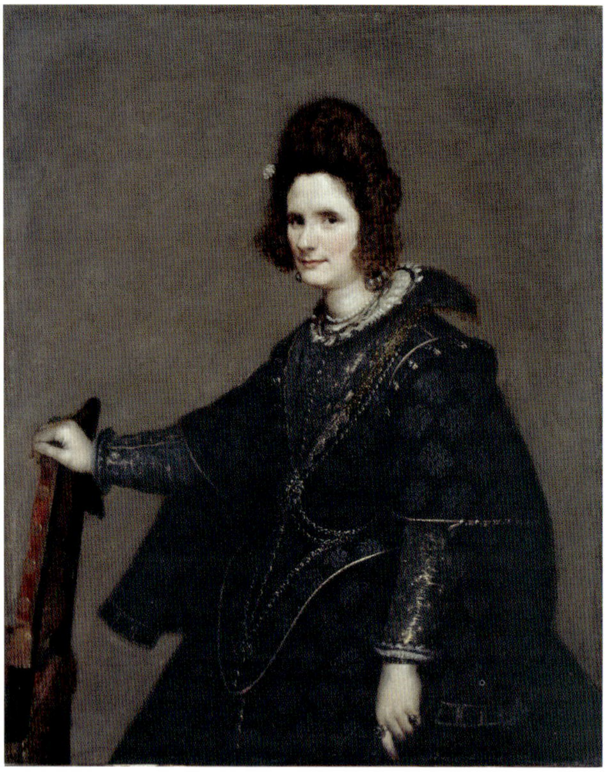

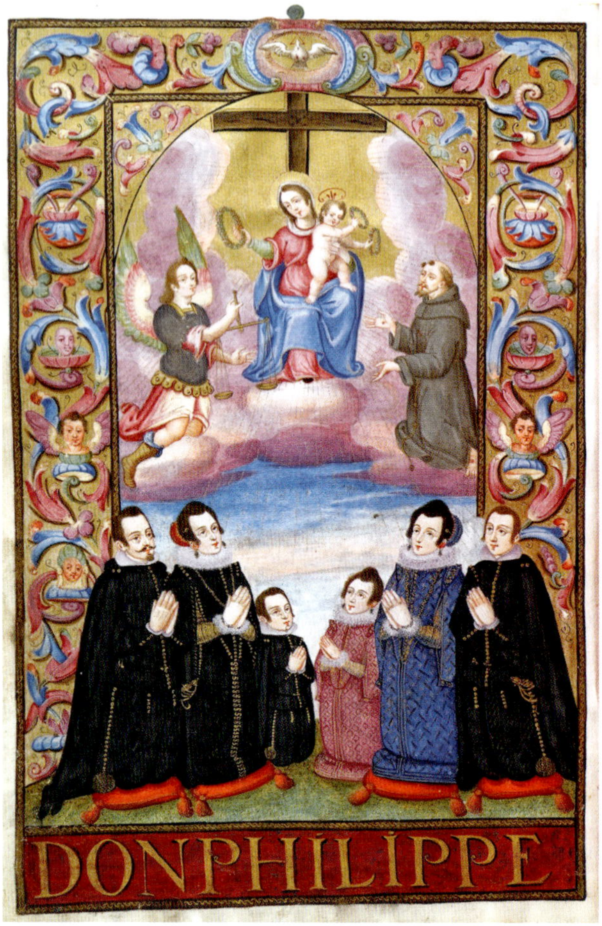

60. *(above left)* Diego Velázquez, *Portrait of a Lady*, c. 1635. Oil on canvas, 123.7 × 101.7 cm. Gemäldegalerie, Berlin

61. *(above right)* Fragment of black silk damask (detail), Italian, 16th–17th century. The Metropolitan Museum of Art, New York

62. *(left)* *Letters Patent of Nobility of Don Francisco y Don Fernando Ramírez de la Trapera, Residents of Úbeda*, Granada, 1633. Illumination on parchment, 30.8 × 21.4 cm. Hispanic Society of America, New York

occasion, she sent a finished dress back to have its 34 dozen buttons replaced because they were not to her taste.[20]

Aguado's accounts record many instances when the queen returned a finished or almost-finished garment with instructions for making changes, usually to its decoration, which could be quite costly and time-consuming. This happened especially frequently in the tailor's first year on the job. In 1631, Queen Isabel returned an over-gown and skirt of silver and black velvet with instructions to replace its black and gold galloon (*galón*) with another trimming. After Aguado had stayed up all night making a brown damask dress, the queen decided that she wanted the fabric to be pricked, which meant that the lining had to be removed and a new taffeta interlining inserted. Aguado had almost completed a dressing gown made from plush in an expensive color called *nácar* (mother-of-pearl), when the queen ordered him to turn the material into a cloak with sleeves (*gabán*) instead.[21] Aguado recorded fewer incidents like these in his accounts for later years, which suggests that the queen and her tailor learned how to work together more efficiently. Several years into their working relationship, as Spain mobilized for war with Isabel's native France, Aguado began introducing more military decorations into the queen's wardrobe. Considering the evidence of Isabel's involvement in the making of her wardrobe, these changes must be seen as a reflection of the queen's own intentions.

Military Decorations at a Time of War

Spanish military men were known for their flamboyant style. Like the church, the military was exempt from sumptuary laws that restricted fabrics and trims made with precious metals. Also like the church, the military expressed its virtue and glory through distinctive and magnificent apparel. The military decorations that served as Aguado's inspiration for the queen's wardrobe in the 1630s were catalogued in a series of 12 epic battle paintings commissioned for the Hall of Realms. This was the throne room of a new palace called the Buen Retiro that Philip IV and his royal favorite, Gaspar de Guzmán, Count-Duke of Olivares, had built on the eastern edge of Madrid in the early 1630s (fig. 63). The battle paintings celebrated Philip IV's military victories

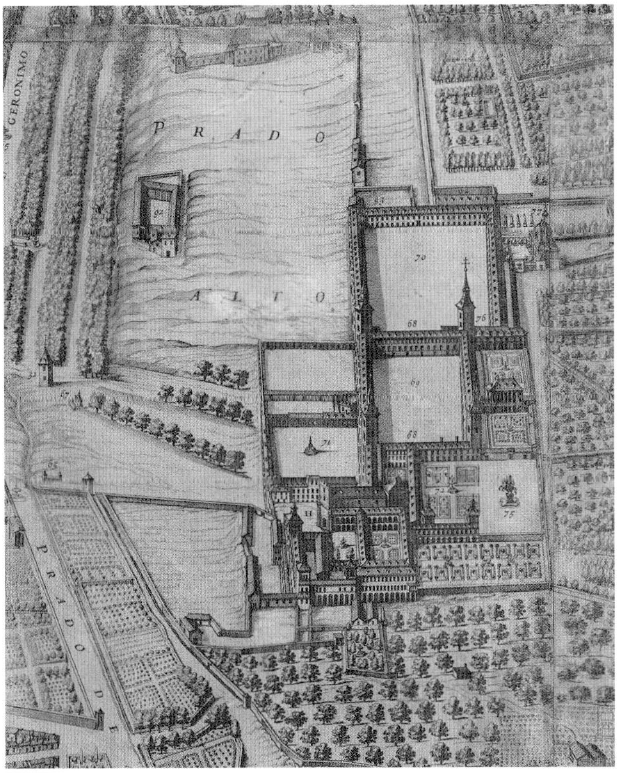

63. The Buen Retiro Palace and Gardens. Pedro Teixeira, *Topographia de la Villa de Madrid* (detail of fig. 32). Real Biblioteca de Palacio, Madrid (ROLL/109)

against Spain's many enemies—including the English, French, Dutch, and Protestant Germans—in theaters of war around the globe.[22] In Félix Castello's *Recapture of Saint Christopher Island*, the officer on the right-hand side, with his brilliant blue sleeves slashed to reveal contrasting yellow fabric underneath, demonstrates why seventeenth-century satirists referred to soldiers as *papagayos*—"parrots" (fig. 64).[23] Hat in hand, the brightly-dressed officer receives orders from the Captain of the Ocean Fleet, whose superior rank is indicated by his red sash trimmed in gold lace, and by the fact that he keeps his richly plumed hat on his head. The aristocratic captain's breeches are a sober gray, but diagonal cuts in the fabric expose a flashy red interlining, and the front pocket openings and side seams are embellished with ornate gold lace buttons. The Hall of Realms battle paintings were commissioned at a time when the drumbeat of war was sounding louder and louder for Spain and France, enemies who had avoided direct conflict since the exchange of princesses that brought Elisabeth (Isabel) of Bourbon to Spain in 1615. The militarization of Spanish culture in the early 1630s that was reflected in the decorative program of the Hall of Realms also influenced Aguado's work for Isabel, whose military-style dress decorations were featured in portraits that were painted for the new palace.

Queen Isabel reportedly did not like to have her portrait painted, but new likenesses of the queen were needed to decorate the Buen Retiro Palace.[24] In January 1631, Velázquez returned to Madrid after a year-and-a-half-long trip to Italy. Sometime after his return, he painted his first portrait of Queen Isabel dressed by Aguado.[25] The new portrait was painted over an older portrait of the queen dressed by Francisco de Soria, a copy of which was sent to Denmark in 1663 and remains in Copenhagen (fig. 65).[26] The style of dress is the

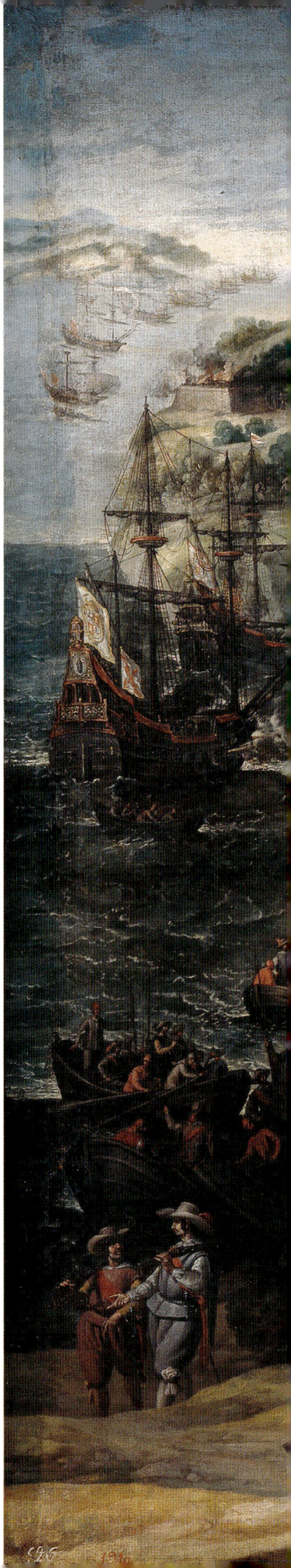

64. Félix Castello, *The Recapture of Saint Christopher Island*, 1634–5. Oil on canvas, 298 × 312 cm. Museo Nacional del Prado, Madrid

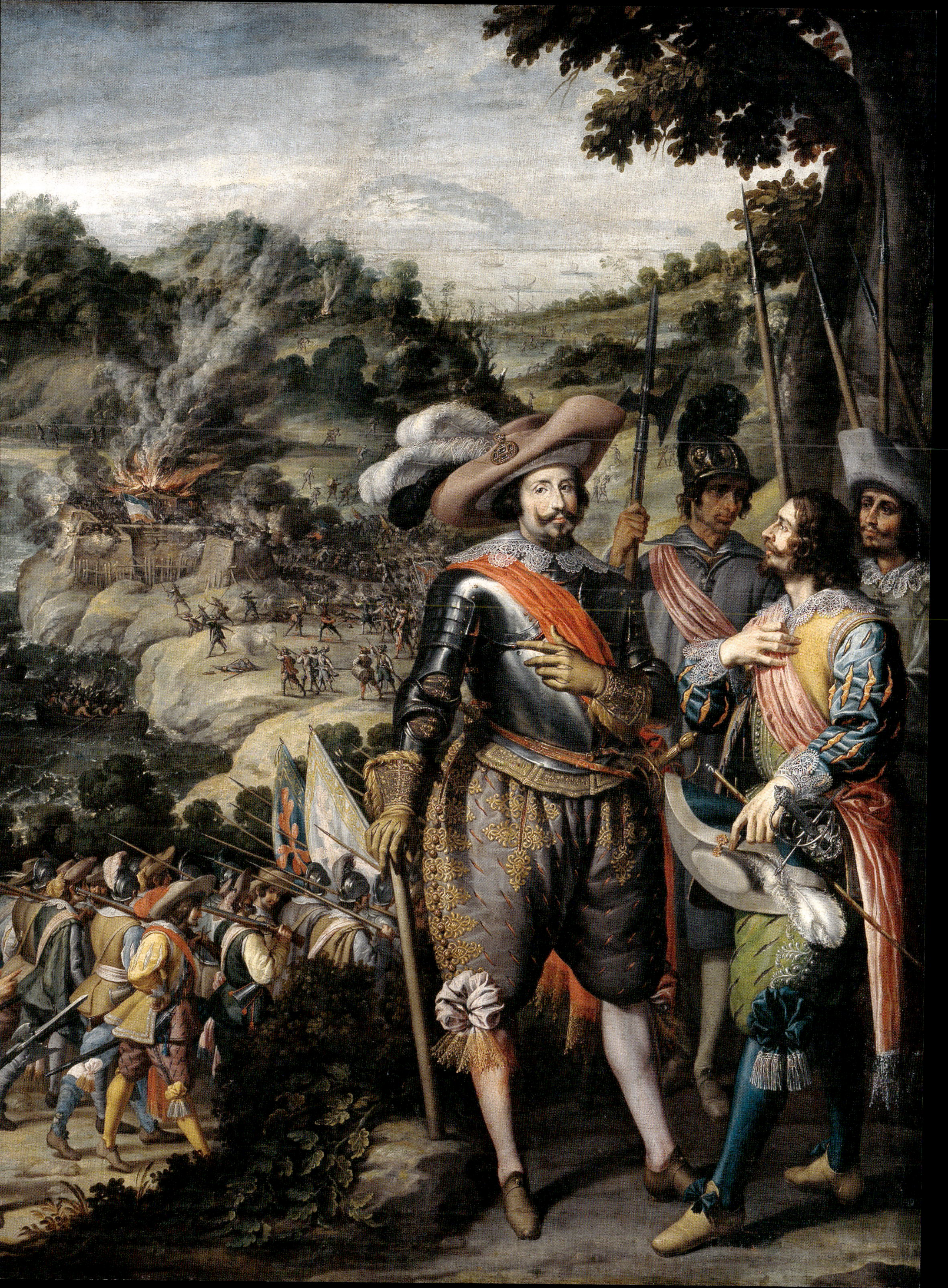

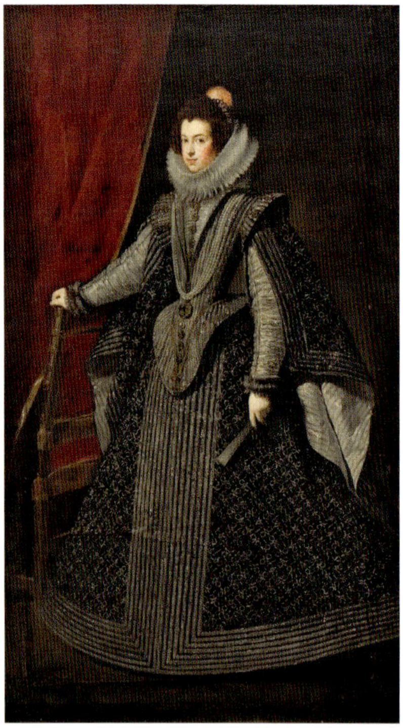

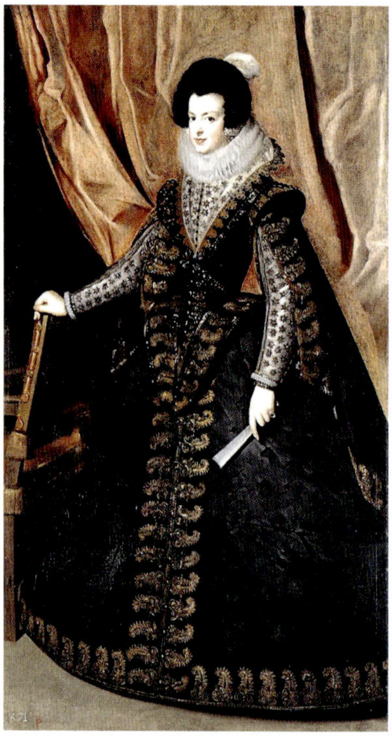

65. *(far left)* Workshop of Velázquez, *Isabel of Bourbon*, 1620s. Oil on canvas, 218 × 127.5 cm. Statens Museum for Kunst/National Gallery of Denmark, Copenhagen

66. *(left)* Attributed to Diego Velázquez, *Isabel of Bourbon*, early 1630s (after 1631). Oil on canvas, 207 × 119 cm. Private Collection

same in both paintings—the queen wears a *saya entera* with pointed sleeves—but the second portrait shows dramatic developments in the queen's dress decorations (fig. 66). The traditional rows of straight trimming that decorate the heavily embroidered dress in the Copenhagen portrait have been replaced with feathery gold ornaments—*alamares*—that stand out against a field of midnight-black.

Alamares, which were known in English as "lace buttons," could serve as functional closures, with a button on one end and a loop on the other, but they were also used for purely decorative purposes on clothing and on furniture. They were a favorite decoration of the military elite, such as Gómez Suárez de Figueroa, 3rd Duke of Feria. The duke was celebrated for his exploits in the Thirty Years' War, which were featured in three of the battle paintings at the Hall of Realms. A portrait painted after the duke's death in Munich in 1634 represents him dressed in half-armor with breeches decorated all over with gold *alamares* (fig. 67). A similar or identical pair of breeches that belonged to the Duke of Feria is preserved at the Army Museum in Toledo, along with a red sash trimmed in gold lace and a partial suit of Italian armor engraved with the duke's personal emblems (fig. 68).

Francisco de Soria had used *alamares* to decorate Queen Isabel's garments, primarily over-gowns and cloaks, in the 1620s, but they became much more prominent, numerous, and varied in Mateo Aguado's work for the queen in the 1630s. Aguado drew *alamares* in various shapes, including plumes, clouds, palms, clubs, and carnations. He also designed *alamares* to decorate furnishings for the queen's household, including bed-hangings, chairs, and table-covers (like the one in the

67. *(right)* Felipe Diriksen, *Gómez Suárez de Figueroa, 3rd Duke of Feria*, 1635. Oil on canvas, 231 × 118 cm. Fundación Casa Ducal de Medinaceli, Seville

68. *(below right)* Breeches of Gómez Suárez de Figueroa, 3rd Duke of Feria, 1615. Museo del Ejército, Toledo

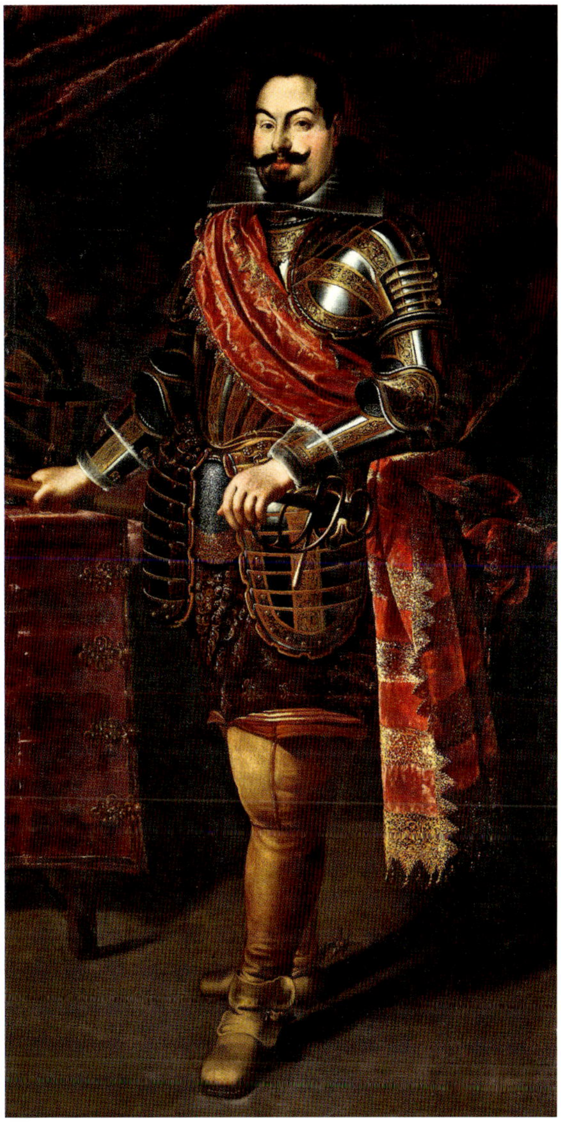

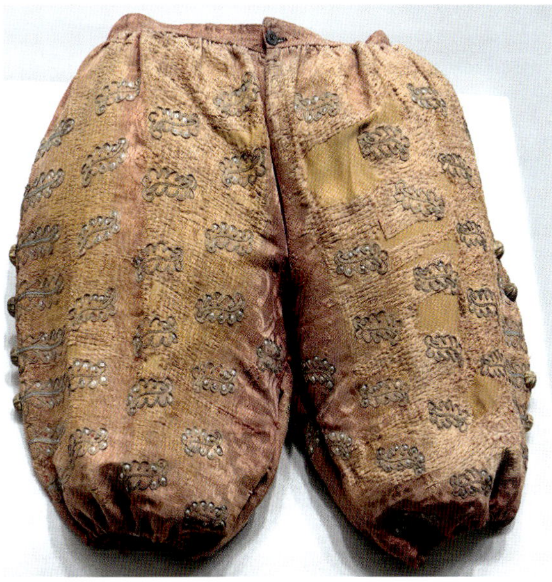

Duke of Feria's portrait, see fig. 67).[27] Aguado's designs were fabricated by the queen's embroiderer, Jerónimo de Negrilla, whose workshop produced them in prodigious quantities: a dress for the queen could have anywhere from 380 to 712 *alamares* applied to it. The embroiderer fashioned these decorative buttons out of narrow trimmings made from black silk, silver, and gold thread, which were sometimes adorned with false jewels or black glass. The *alamares* on the queen's black dress in the portrait for the Buen Retiro are in the shape of plumes (*alamares de penacho*) made from Milanese gold thread and black glass (see fig. 66).

The very same black and gold *alamares* adorn a different dress that Queen Isabel wears in a life-size equestrian portrait that was painted to hang in the throne room, the Hall of Realms, at the Buen Retiro Palace (fig. 69, detail fig. 70).[28] She also wears the same accessory pieces—fitted sleeves, *cuera* facings, and chest-coverings—embroidered with stars in both paintings (see the detail in fig. 56). These were probably based on real garments, according to documentation kept by the queen's silk merchants. On July 2, 1634, the silk merchants supplied 1.05 meters of white satin to make a pair of chest-coverings and decorative bands "embroidered with stars of glass and gold twist." They also provided "little diamonds" for the stars, and gold lace edging for decoration (but they do not mention

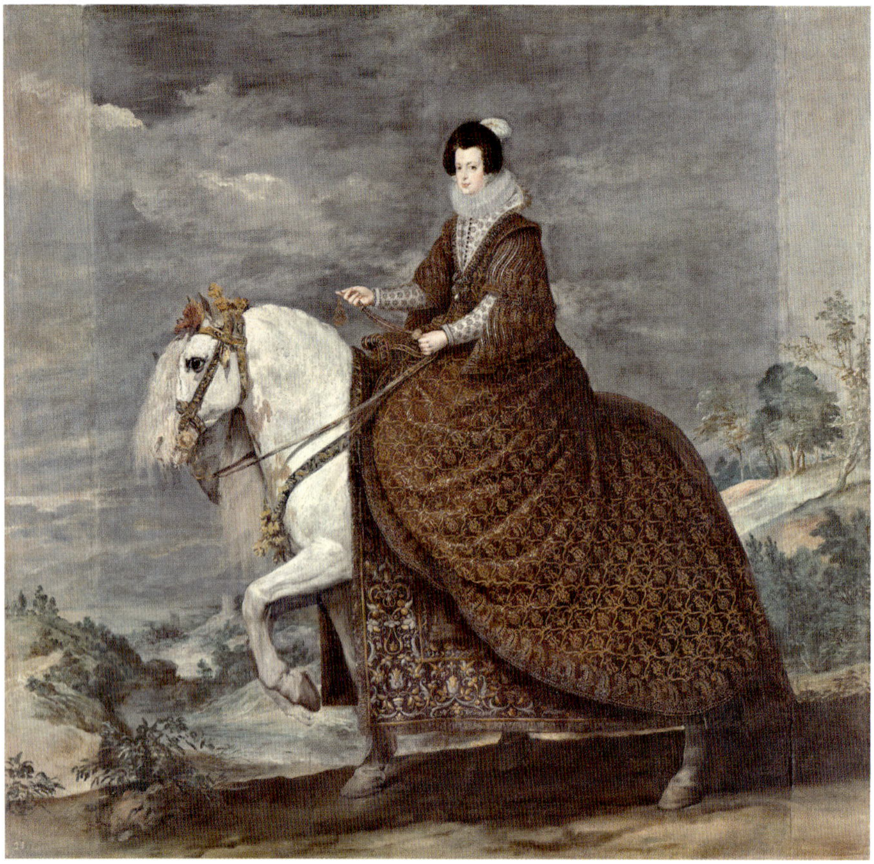

69. Diego Velázquez and Workshop, *Queen Isabel of Bourbon on Horseback*, 1634–5. Oil on canvas, 301 × 314 cm. Museo Nacional del Prado, Madrid

70. *(facing page)* Detail of the *alamares* in fig. 69

matching sleeves).[29] By the next year, some of the diamonds had fallen off the satin chest-coverings, so the silk merchants supplied replacement diamonds and paid a presser to attach them with bitumen.[30] This documentation reveals not only that the star-spangled *petillos* seen in these two portraits of the queen really existed, but also that they were worn and repaired for repeated use.

In March 1635, Queen Isabel visited the recently completed Hall of Realms during a trip to the Buen Retiro that was celebrated with "great galas," according to a letter written by Francisco de Quevedo.[31] It was a major production whenever Philip IV's family left the Royal Palace, even just to go across town, but this was an especially momentous outing as it was the queen's first excursion after giving birth to a girl, María Antonia, on January 17 (the child died of epilepsy shortly before her second birthday in December 1636).[32] By this time, war with France had become imminent. On May 19, 1635, King Louis XIII of France—Isabel of Bourbon's

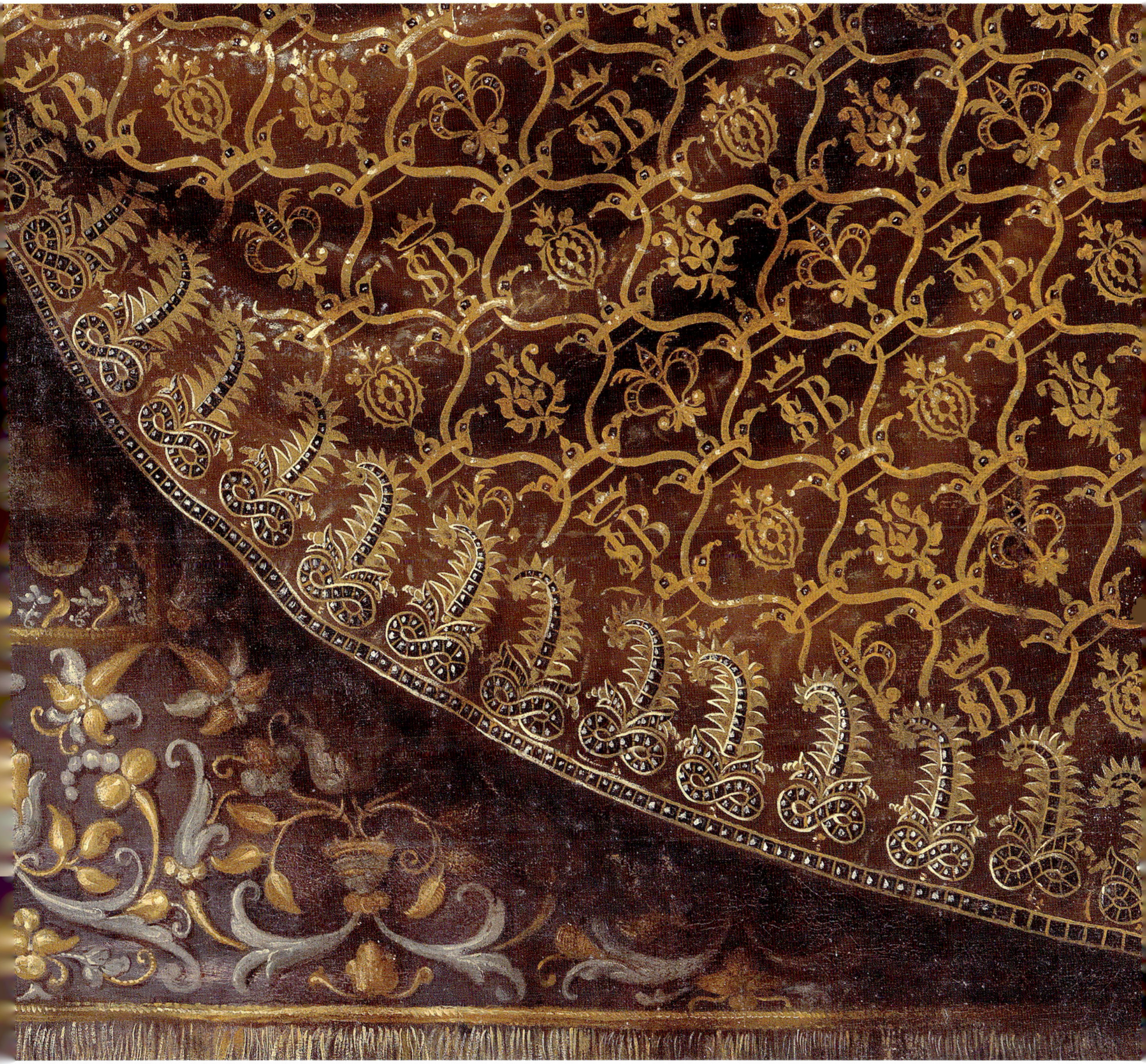

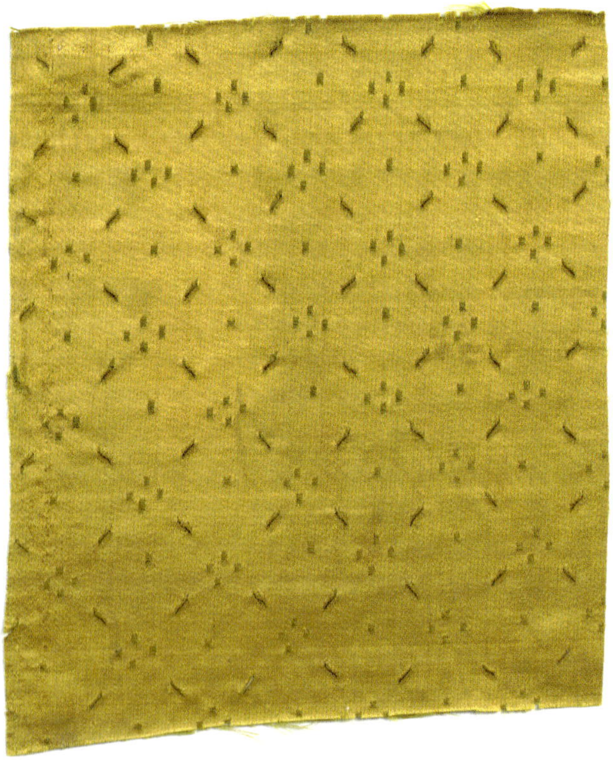

brother—declared war on Spain. This placed Isabel in a very awkward position. Previously, she had acted as a mediator, writing letters urging her mother, Marie de' Medici, and the chief minister of France, Cardinal Richelieu, to keep the peace.[33] With the outbreak of war, Isabel needed to demonstrate her absolute loyalty to Spain. It was precisely at this time, as Spain mobilized for war with France, that Aguado began to add more military details to the queen's dresses with decorative pricking and slashing that were associated with soldierly style.

In Aguado's accounts, the tailor distinguished between two different types of decorative cuts: *picado* (pricked, or pinked) described garments that had small cuts all over the surface of the fabric, while *acuchillado* (slashed) referred to long, vertical slashes in a limited area such as the sleeves.[34] Small cuts had to be made on the diagonal of the fabric, as seen on a fragment of yellow satin, to avoid excessive fraying (fig. 71). Beginning in

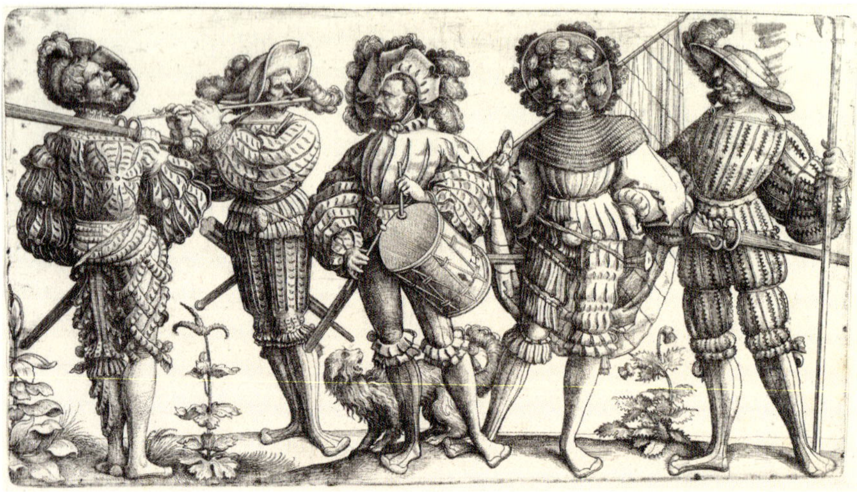

71. *(above left)* Fragment of silk satin with decorative cuts, Italian, 16th century. Cooper Hewitt, Smithsonian Design Museum, New York

72. *(left)* Daniel Hopfer, *Five German Soldiers*, c. 1520–36. Etching, 20 × 37 cm. The Metropolitan Museum of Art, New York

73. *(facing page)* Man's slashed doublet, Spanish, c. 1630. Brown voided velvet, velvet trimming, and linen lining. Museo del Traje, Madrid

1635, Aguado's accounts show an increasing number of dresses for the queen that were pricked. These dresses were made from a dark fabric (black, gray, or brown) with a contrasting interlining (white, blue, or green) that showed through the cuts. In 1636 the queen returned a pricked black satin dress to Aguado with instructions to add a "brilliant" interlining.[35] Until the later 1630s, slashing had only been applied to the round and pointed sleeves of Isabel's over-gowns and *cueras*, but starting around 1636, Aguado began to slash the upper-front of the queen's doublets and their fitted sleeves. This decoration was usually called *acuchillado a lo tudesco*—"slashed in the German style"—in reference to the Landsknechts, German mercenaries who had popularized slashing in the sixteenth century (fig. 72).[36] Because of the length and vertical orientation of slashes, their edges had to be bound in order to maintain the integrity of the garment. A man's patterned velvet doublet made around 1630 has long slashes that are bound in plain velvet (fig. 73). The slashes on the queen's doublets were hemmed and decorated with narrow trims like ribbon or galloon, and each slash was individually lined.

The queen's new militarized look was disseminated abroad through portraits of Queen Isabel wearing a brown dress with slashing on the sleeves and chest that were sent to other European courts.[37] One of these (fig. 74) is a well-documented portrait by Velázquez's workshop that was sent to Charles I of England at Hampton Court in 1639 along with companion portraits of Philip IV and Prince Baltasar Carlos dressed in armor.[38] The queen's dress fabric is decorated with *memorias*—"memories"—interlocking rings that were intended to be a sentimental reminder of something.[39] Aguado made the queen one documented dress from a *tela de memorias*, in 1639, which was a brown silk brocaded with silver rings. The fabric was a gift from Prince Baltasar

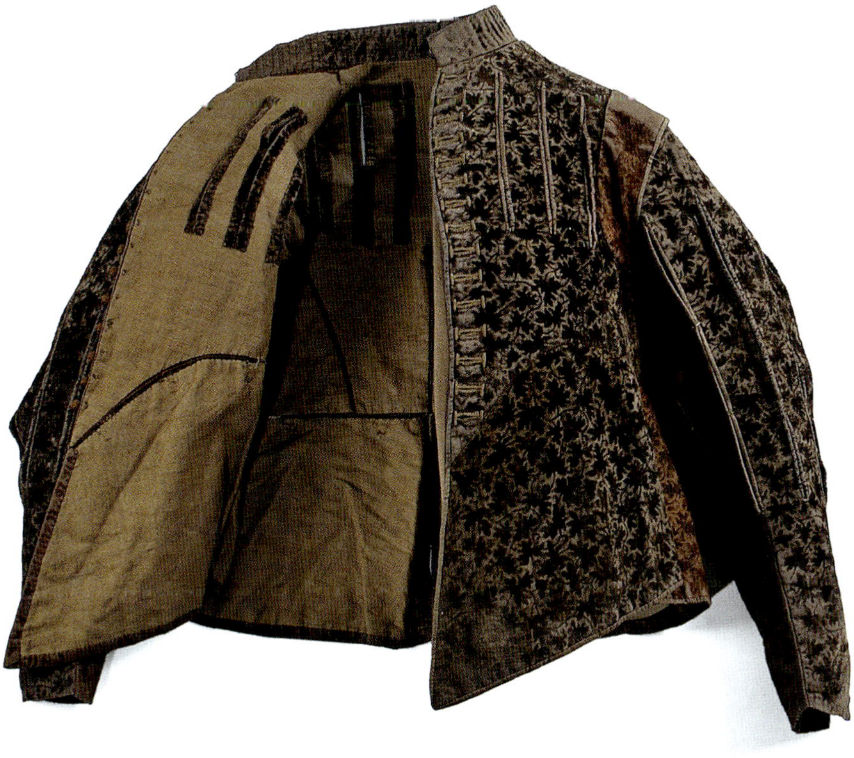

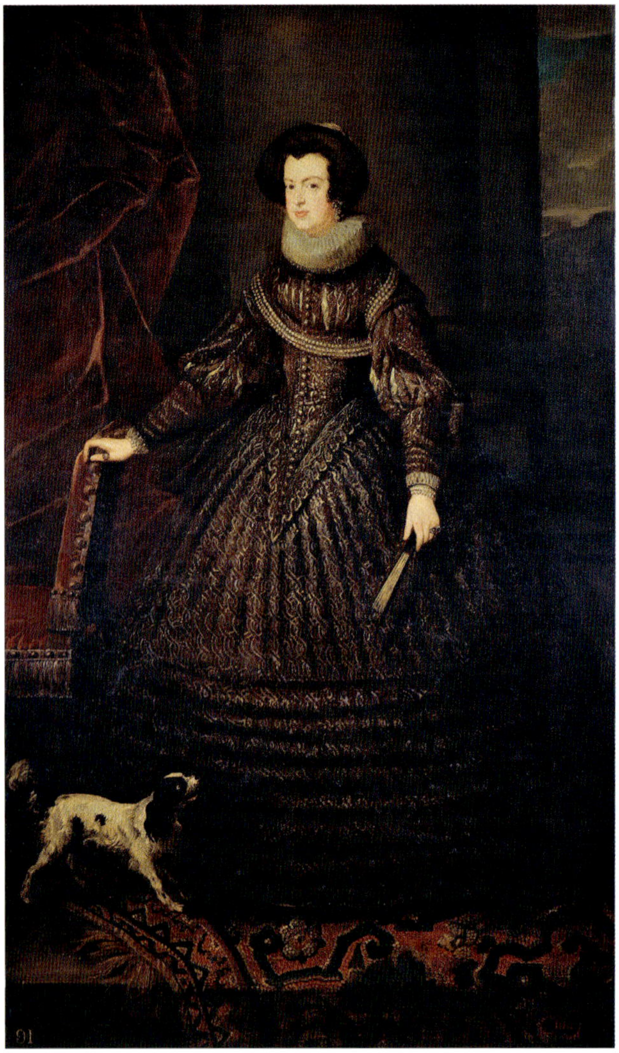

74. Workshop of Velázquez, *Queen Isabel of Bourbon*, c. 1635–8. Oil on canvas, 238.5 × 147.8 cm. Royal Collection Trust, UK

75. *(facing page)* Workshop of Velázquez, *Queen Isabel of Bourbon*, 1630s. Oil on canvas, 132 × 101.5 cm. Kunsthistorisches Museum, Vienna

Carlos to his mother. Aguado stayed up all night making a three-piece dress with a separate train (*cota*) from this special fabric and decorated the ensemble with strips of brown taffeta embroidered with rings in silver wire (*plata pasada*).[40] In the Hampton Court portrait (see fig. 74), the slashes in the queen's bodice and sleeves are lined with contrasting white silk, and the edges of her doublet's short skirts are crenellated like battlements. These decorative features are present, but less prominent, in a version of the portrait that was sent to the imperial court of the Holy Roman Empire at Vienna (fig. 75).[41]

The most striking difference between the portraits sent to the English and imperial courts is the presentation of the skirt, which is pleated around the waist in the former but falls smooth and flat in the latter (the bottom of the skirt in the Vienna portrait was cut off when the portrait, originally full-length, was cut down to three-quarter size). There is nothing in Aguado's accounts to indicate how he was constructing the queen's skirts at this time. Based on what has been learned from comparing versions of *Philip IV in Brown and Silver* by Velázquez and by his workshop (see the Introduction, pp. 34–5), it is likely that the more detailed dress depicted in the Hampton Court portrait (see fig. 74) comes closer to representing the style that Aguado was making for the queen in the late 1630s than the simplified, idealized skirt in the Vienna version (see fig. 75). The smooth surface of that dress emphasizes the bell-like curve of the queen's hip, which marks a departure from the pyramidal shape that had defined courtly women's dress in Spain for over a century. This shift was the product of new developments in the structures hidden underneath Aguado's dresses.

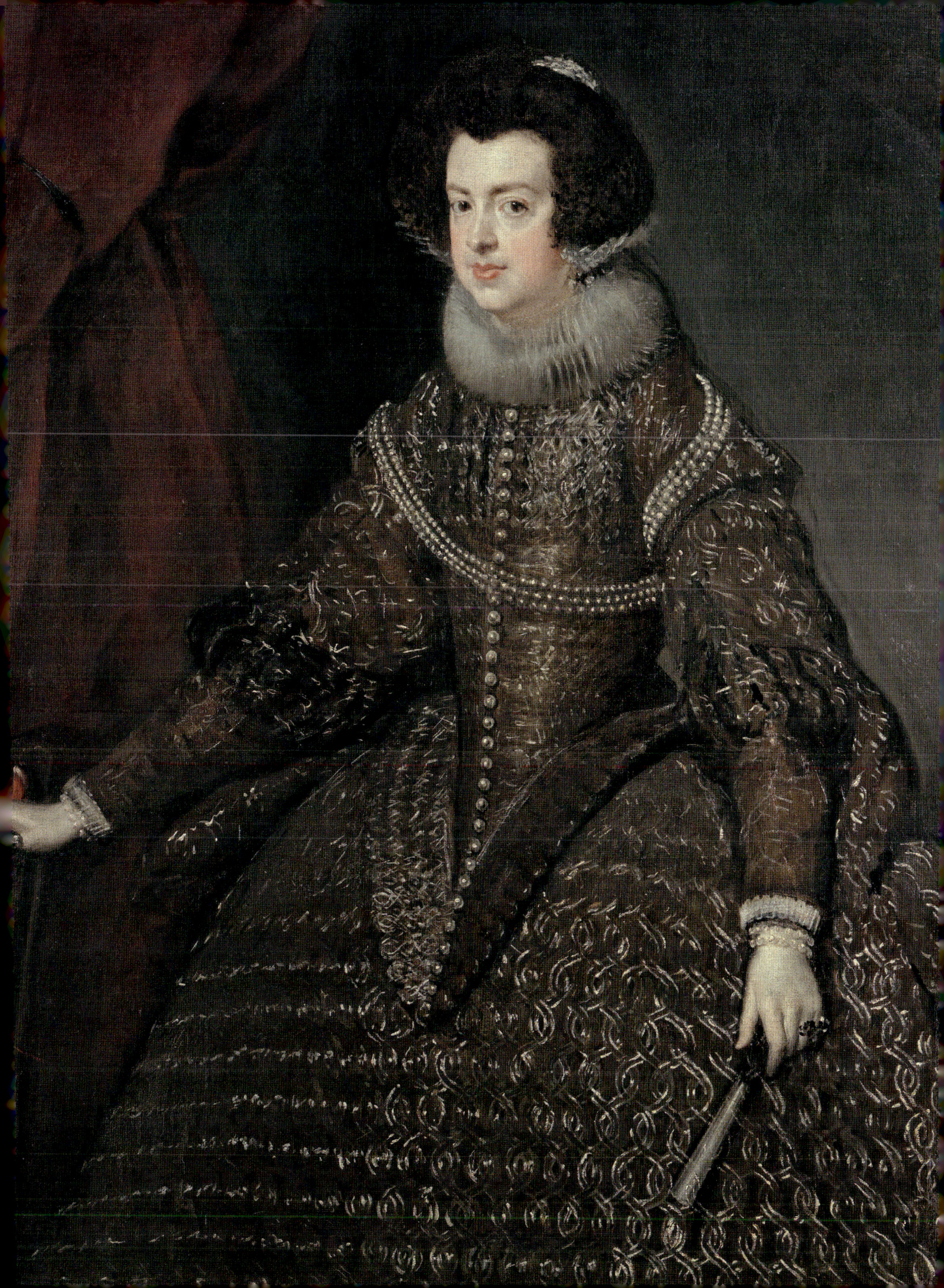

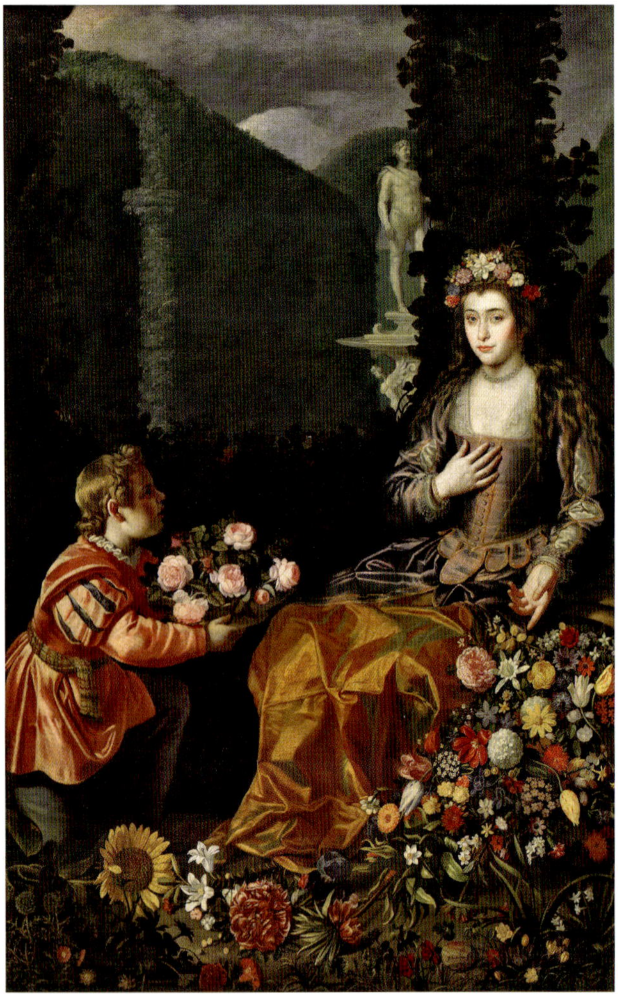

76. Juan van der Hamen y León, *An Offering to Flora*, 1627. Oil on canvas, 216 × 140 cm. Museo Nacional del Prado, Madrid

Architectural Underpinnings

Beneath the decorated surfaces of the queen's dresses lay a scaffolding of rigid undergarments that flattened her chest, cinched her waist, and hid her legs. It was this "architecture," not nature, that gave a woman her proportions, according to the comedic character Tristán in Lope de Vega's play *The Dog in the Manger* (c. 1615). Tristán warns his besotted master that the woman he pines for is not all that she appears to be:

> All is vain architecture;
> as a wise man once said,
> half a woman's beauty is owed
> to the tailors.[42]

Aguado and the queen's farthingale-makers were the architects of her appearance. Their account records, along with those of the silk merchants who supplied their materials, provide detailed insights into the hidden shapewear—corsets, farthingales, and petticoats—that gave the queen her distinctive shape.

The queen wore a boned corset called a *corpiño* over her linen shirt and underneath her doublet. These corsets had little skirts and usually had long sleeves, like the *corpiño* that the goddess Flora wears in a 1627 allegorical painting by court artist Juan van der Hamen y León (fig. 76); Flora's sleeves have openings through which her linen shirt can be seen. The silk merchants provided materials to make two to five *corpiños* per year for the queen in the 1630s, although it is not clear who made the garments, which do not appear in Aguado's accounts. The queen's corsets were made from two layers of double taffeta (*tafetán doble*) with rows of whalebone (*barba de ballena*) in between them, which were decoratively backstitched (*pespuntado*) to hold

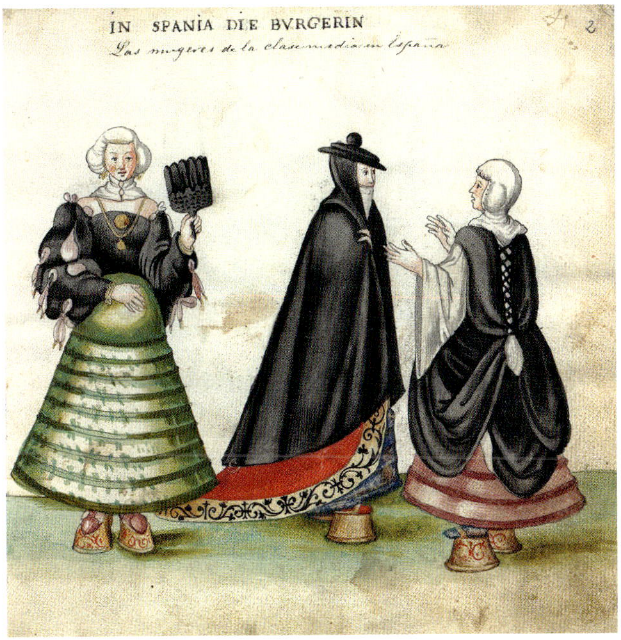

77. Unknown German artist, "Spanish Burgheresses," *Códice Madrazo-Daza*, c. 1547. Pen and gouache on paper, 21 × 20 cm. Biblioteca Nacional de España, Madrid

the layers together and keep the whalebone in place. These intimate garments were almost always made from crimson (*carmesí*) silk and decorated with plaited trimmings made from silver or gold thread (*caracolillos*). The color of the queen's corsets was significant. As the medical doctor Juan Sorapán de Rieros explained in his 1616 treatise *Spanish Medicine*, dark red was more favorable to the human temperament than any other color because of its connection to blood, which was why patients with illnesses of the blood were wrapped in crimson cloth.[43] This belief was not unique to Spain: red was also considered a healthy color in England, where it was recommended for making petticoats.[44] At the Spanish court, crimson was always used to make the queen's gowns for childbirth and was the most common color for her petticoats and farthingales.

Ever since she came to Spain in 1615, Isabel of Bourbon had worn farthingales made by a woman named María Ximénez. The royal farthingale-maker was joined in 1627 by her son Diego López, who took over his mother's appointment at the court in 1638. The farthingales that they made for Queen Isabel were traditional *verdugados*, cone-shaped undergarments that had been worn at the Spanish court since the late fifteenth century, which are clearly illustrated in a German costume book from the 1540s (fig. 77).[45] The *verdugado* was a petticoat with a small hoop slightly below the waist, "below with one wider, and so wider and wider down to the feet, so that it looks exactly like a funnel," as described by the English translator John Stevens in his 1706 English–Spanish dictionary.[46] The *verdugados* that Ximénez and López crafted for the queen in the 1630s were made from crimson double taffeta with hoops of a sturdy grass called *esparto*, which were wrapped in cording and covered with satin or velvet ribbons, with gold trim at the hem. Made with large quantities of silks and precious metal, *verdugados* were expensive garments: the materials cost approximately 560 *reales*, and the hoop-maker's fee added another 80 *reales* to the cost. The royal farthingale-makers produced about three new *verdugados* per year for the queen, and they regularly replaced the hoops and decorations on worn-out or damaged farthingales.[47] These valuable garments were carefully stored in their own custom cases covered with cowhide.[48]

Over her farthingale, the queen wore a petticoat called a *manteo* with a wide, circular hem stiffened by a ring of whalebone or esparto grass.[49] The queen's petticoats were made from lightweight silks for warmer

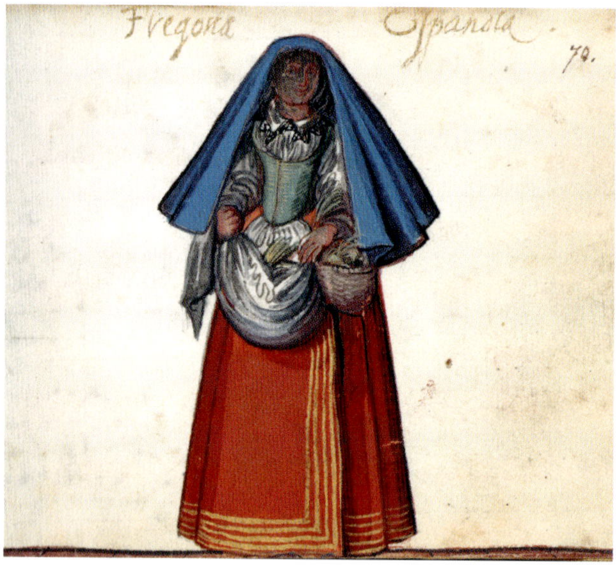

78. "Spanish Scullery-Maid," *Album of Tobias Oelhafen von Schöllenbach*, 1623–5. Illumination on paper, 8 × 10.5 cm. British Library, London

months and baize (*bayeta*) or plush for the winter, and they could be quilted or lined with plush for extra warmth. It was important to keep the lower body warm, for it was believed that cold air entering a woman's skirts chilled the uterus, and that a cold uterus was "totally inept for reproduction."[50] Whatever the season, the queen's petticoats were usually crimson, occasionally mother-of-pearl, and they were decorated with gold lace, galloon, or *alamares*. Aguado made several different kinds of *manteos*, including one version with an attached bodice (*manteo francés*) and another that wrapped around the waist (*manteo de vuelta*).[51] A wrap-around petticoat is worn by a woman identified as a "Spanish scullery-maid" in an illustration in a traveler's scrapbook from the 1620s (fig. 78). This image of a working-class woman, who carries vegetables in her apron, wearing a red petticoat adorned with four rows of gold (or faux gold) trimming, just like the queen, suggests that belief in the power of red as well as the garment style cut across class lines.

In the mid-1630s, all Madrid was abuzz over a new kind of farthingale with an unusual name: the *guardainfante*.[52] A critic of the trend named Alonso Carranza explained that the name of "this diabolical invention" came from France, where unmarried women used the device to conceal that they were with child.[53] The Spanish *guardainfante* was inspired by the wheel-shaped farthingale that had been worn at the French court when Isabel of Bourbon was a girl (see fig. 43). By the 1630s, that style had fallen out of fashion in France, and a slim-hipped, more natural silhouette was favored.[54] The outmoded French farthingale may have been brought to Madrid by traveling theatrical troupes that used it as a costume: male ballet dancers wore padded farthingales, some covered with a skirt and others exposed, in a burlesque performance at the court of Louis XIII in 1625 (fig. 79). In the Spanish version of the 1630s, the French farthingale that extended the width of the hip had hoops suspended from it by broad ribbons (*colonias*).[55] New kinds of petticoats were invented to wear over the *guardainfante*, which were described in detail by another critic, Bartolomé Jiménez Patón. *Enaguas*, made from great quantities of linen or other fabrics pleated at the top and gummed or starched, were worn three or four at a time to increase their bulk. The top-most petticoat, called a *pollera*, had little quilted pillows at the hips.[56]

The first reported appearance of a *guardainfante* in Madrid comes from the theater. The new style of farthingale made its debut on the stage in Madrid in the fall of 1634, in a skit by Luis Quiñones de Benavente called *El guarda-infante*.[57] The next year, the

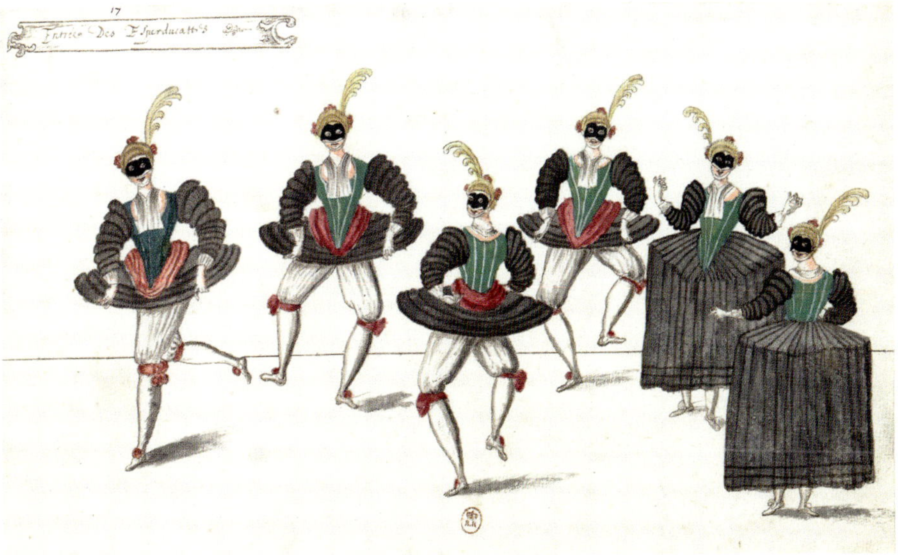

79. Daniel Rabel, ballet costume design for *Les Fées des forêts de Saint-Germain*, 1625. Pen, gouache, and watercolor on paper, 23.6 × 38.8 cm. Bibliothèque nationale de France, Paris

queen's farthingale-makers made the first documented *guardainfante* at court as a gift for a wet-nurse of the Infanta María Antonia. The farthingale-makers were paid only 10 *reales* to make her "a *guardainfante* with four rows" (presumably meaning rows of hoops).[58] This was probably a short, hooped farthingale that did not reach the floor.[59] The first change in Queen Isabel's farthingales is documented in 1638, when Diego López began to made her *verdugados* with "hips and wires."[60] A "hip" (*cadera*) must have been some sort of padding that extended the sides of the farthingale. According to the critic Bartolomé Jiménez Patón, *verdugados* with "hips" were the same thing as a *guardainfante* in all but name.[61] The same year that López made the queen's first "hips," Aguado began to add *maneras* to her skirts; these were vertical openings in the sides of the skirt through which she could insert her hand and adjust the contraption underneath. The documentation suggests that Queen Isabel was somewhat slow to adopt the *guardainfante*, which makes sense considering the controversial fashion's close associations with France at a time when Spain was at war with her native country. But the new style, which was said to hide pregnancies, had potential political advantages for a queen whose popularity depended on her ability to produce heirs to the throne. It was not a bad thing if her inflated skirts gave the impression that she was pregnant.

Pregnancy and Childbirth

Isabel of Bourbon was pregnant approximately every other year from the age of 18, when she and Philip IV consummated their marriage, until her death at age 41. Out of seven live births, only two of her children—Prince Baltasar Carlos and the Infanta María Teresa—lived past the age of two.[62] There are no portraits of Isabel of Bourbon visibly pregnant, although the equestrian portrait at the Hall of Realms may have been painted when she was carrying the Infanta María Antonia (see fig. 69).[63] There is, however, a remarkable portrait of her predecessor, Margaret of Austria, in the final stages of pregnancy (which was made at a moment when pregnancy portraits were also in vogue in England) (fig. 80).[64] The pregnant queen wears a richly decorated three-piece dress and maintains the funnel silhouette of the early seventeenth century despite her protruding belly.[65] The perfect smoothness of her garments probably owed more to artistic invention than it did to a *verdugado*, for Spanish queens assiduously avoided wearing farthingales when they were pregnant, as their tailors' accounts reveal.[66]

Shaping garments were considered to be very dangerous during pregnancy. In his Castilian dictionary of 1611, Sebastián de Covarrubias Orozco wrote that a pregnant woman "must go loose in dress" and denounced those women who ignored this advice and had children born with hunchbacks as a result.[67] Critics of the *guardainfante* claimed that the new style of farthingale could cause miscarriages because the clothes worn over it were so heavy.[68] Aguado's records make plain that Queen Isabel did not wear a farthingale of any kind when she was pregnant: "Her Majesty is pregnant and not wearing a *verdugado*," the tailor noted in 1638.[69] To compensate for the absent farthingale, Aguado reinforced her skirts with linen canvas to maintain their shape. He also widened her bodices in the waist and chest to accommodate her growing belly and bosom. It is unclear what, if anything, the queen wore for a corset when she was pregnant. In 1638, when Isabel was pregnant with María Teresa, *corpiños* with stomachers (*petillos*) were made for her that may have been maternity corsets. A set of maternity stays made in England, which are preserved at Claydon House in Buckinghamshire, have a stomacher and shortened front skirts that could accommodate a growing belly.[70]

The queen's tailor traditionally made her a special gown to wear for giving birth, which was always in crimson silk decorated with gold. As Isabel's pregnancy neared its end in the fall of 1638, Aguado made a crimson damask over-gown and petticoat decorated with 64 meters of gold trimming.[71] A girl named María Teresa was born on September 10. Mother and daughter both survived, and ten days later the silk merchants provided materials to make the queen a new *verdugado*. It was time for Aguado to take in the waistlines on the queen's bodices and prepare her skirts to be worn with the farthingale, as the cycle of pregnancies and alterations resumed its course. With the arrival of María Teresa, the queen's tailor had another member of the royal family to dress. In addition to his demanding schedule of work for the queen, Aguado was responsible for dressing the royal children and making gifts from the queen for her household staff and other recipients. This wide-ranging work, which was a substantial component of Aguado's job, is the subject of the next chapter.

80. *(facing page)* Bartolomé González, *Queen Margaret of Austria with a Child Holding a Golden Marmoset*, c. 1603–9. Oil on canvas, 192 × 120 cm. Kunsthistorisches Museum, Vienna

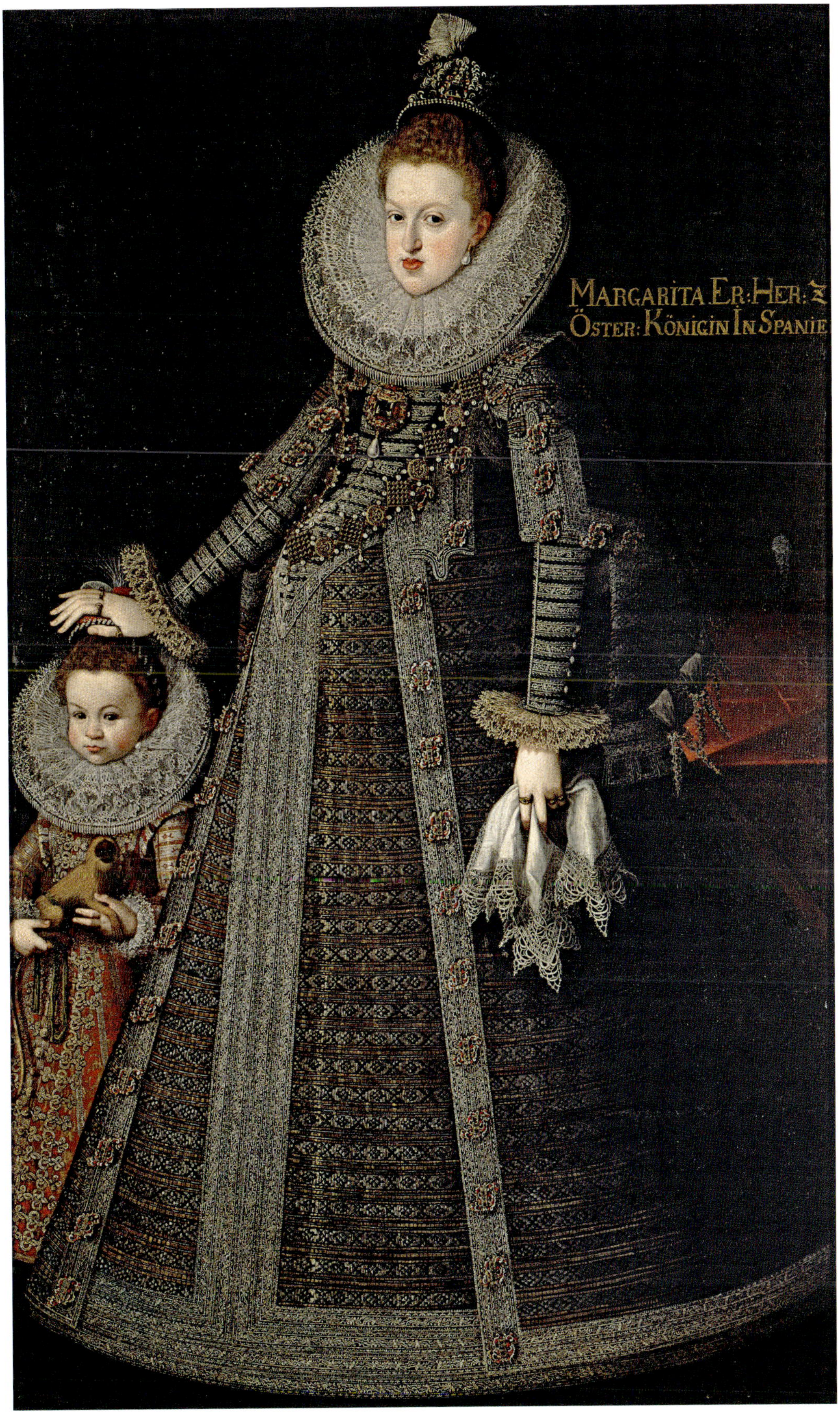
MARGARITA ER: HER: Z
ÖSTER: KÖNIGIN IN SPANIE

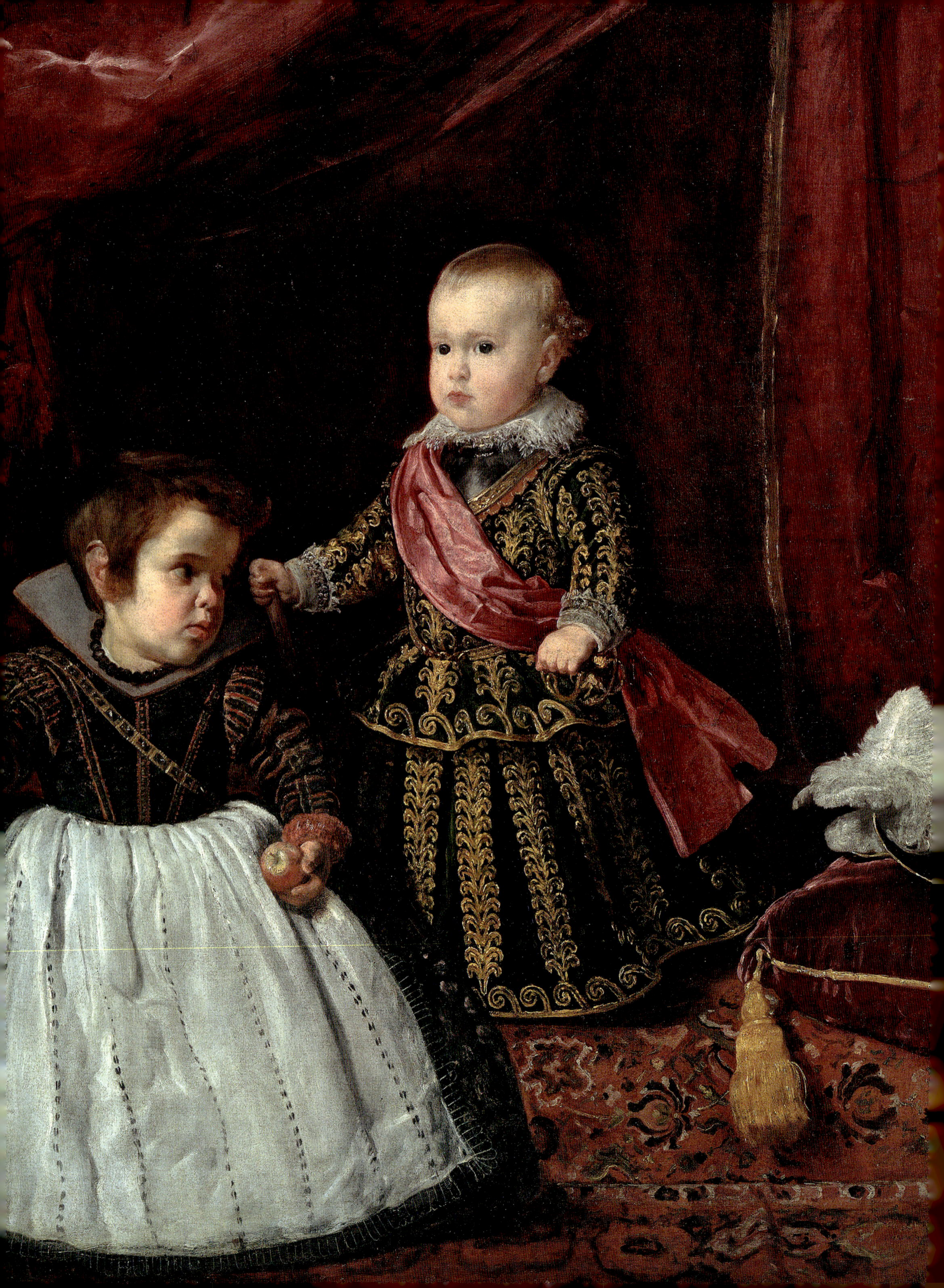

3. Other Responsibilities

Royal Children and Gifts, 1630s

During his first decade in office, Mateo Aguado made clothing for many different people of every age, rank, and gender. He dressed the queen's children like royal treasures, and he made high-quality dresses for their wet-nurses. Every year, he made suits of everyday clothing for staff members in the queen's household, who ranged in rank and status from the sweeper-girl who cleaned the queen's apartments to the noble Keeper of the Wardrobe. When a royal guest visited the Spanish court in 1636, Aguado was responsible for making an ostentatious garment to give as a diplomatic gift. He made several very expensive dresses, including a dress of gray and gold lamé, that Queen Isabel sent as gifts to her sister-in-law María Ana, who had moved to the imperial court in Vienna and become Queen of Hungary (fig. 82).[1] Aguado made clothes from humbler fabrics to give as charitable gifts: for example, outfits of durable woolens (*jerguilla* and *sempiterna*) that were given to a boy being raised at the queen's expense, and a suit made of wool (*paño*) for a Turk who converted to Catholicism.[2] Not all of Aguado's clients were human: sculptures of the Virgin and Christ Child were given real clothes custom-made by the queen's tailor as pious donations. Whomever they were for, the gifts of clothing that Aguado made were part of a courtly exchange of reciprocal favors between the queen and her household staff, her royal peers, and her God.

Aguado itemized his work for the royal children in their own individual accounts, while gifts for royalty were included in his accounts for Queen Isabel. The rest of his work was documented in accounts called *limosnas y mercedes*, "charity and favors." Some years, Aguado earned more for his work on charity and favors than he did making dresses for the queen.[3] The tailor's accounts of this work provide detailed information about the clothing that was worn by a wide range of social types and the ways that fabrics and decorations were used to show rank at the court. They also reveal the important role that clothing played in every aspect of life at the Spanish court, including the politics of succession, diplomatic relations, devotional practices, and the palace economy. The tailor's wide-ranging portfolio of responsibilities positioned him at the very center of the queen's household as the person who knew everybody—and every body.

Dressing the Royal Children: Baltasar Carlos and María Teresa

The clothes that Aguado made for the royal children were small, but the responsibility was large. This was especially true when it came to dressing Baltasar Carlos, born in October 1629 and officially declared heir to the

81. *(facing page)* Diego Velázquez, *Don Baltasar Carlos and an Attendant* (detail of fig. 85)

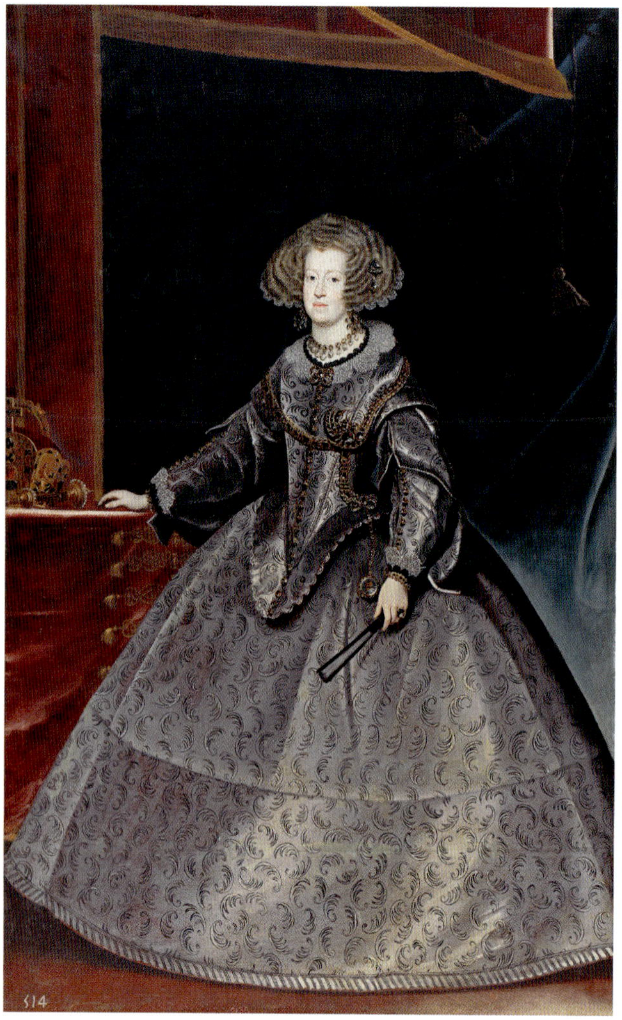

82. Frans Luyckx, *María Ana, Queen of Hungary*, c. 1635. Oil on canvas, 215 × 147 cm. Museo Nacional del Prado, Madrid

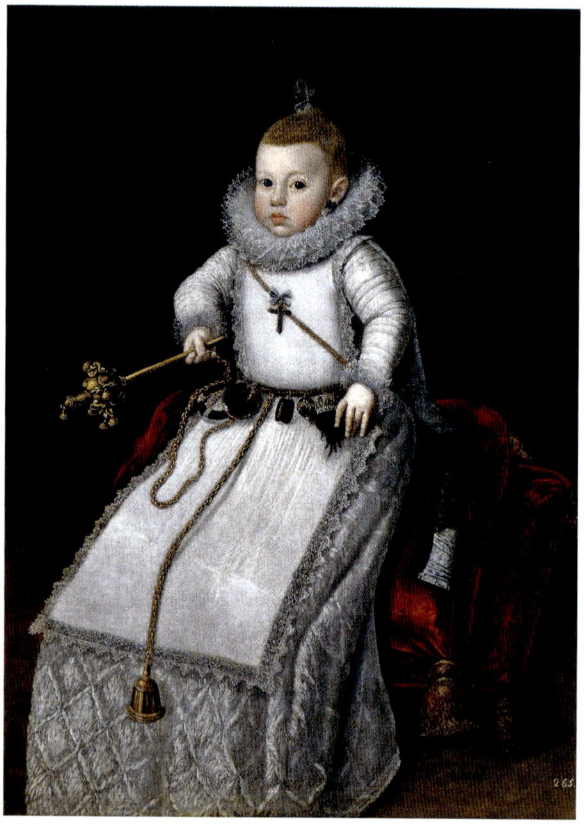

83. Santiago Morán, *Infanta Margarita Francisca, Daughter of Philip III*, c. 1610. Oil on canvas, 100 × 72 cm. Museo Nacional del Prado, Madrid

throne in March 1632. Aguado was on call at all times of day or night to meet the boy's needs. On one occasion, the tailor was summoned at midnight to attach 30 dozen buttons to an outfit for the prince to wear the next morning.[4] Baltasar Carlos also received close attention from Diego Velázquez: beginning when the prince was about two years old, the painter and his workshop produced a series of portraits that recorded the child's growth and his evolving wardrobe. Children's clothes reflected the stages of their development from infancy to childhood to adolescence, which was when they dressed fully like adults.[5] As Aguado's accounts reveal, gender-specific adult garments and accessories were introduced gradually and systematically over a period of years, which

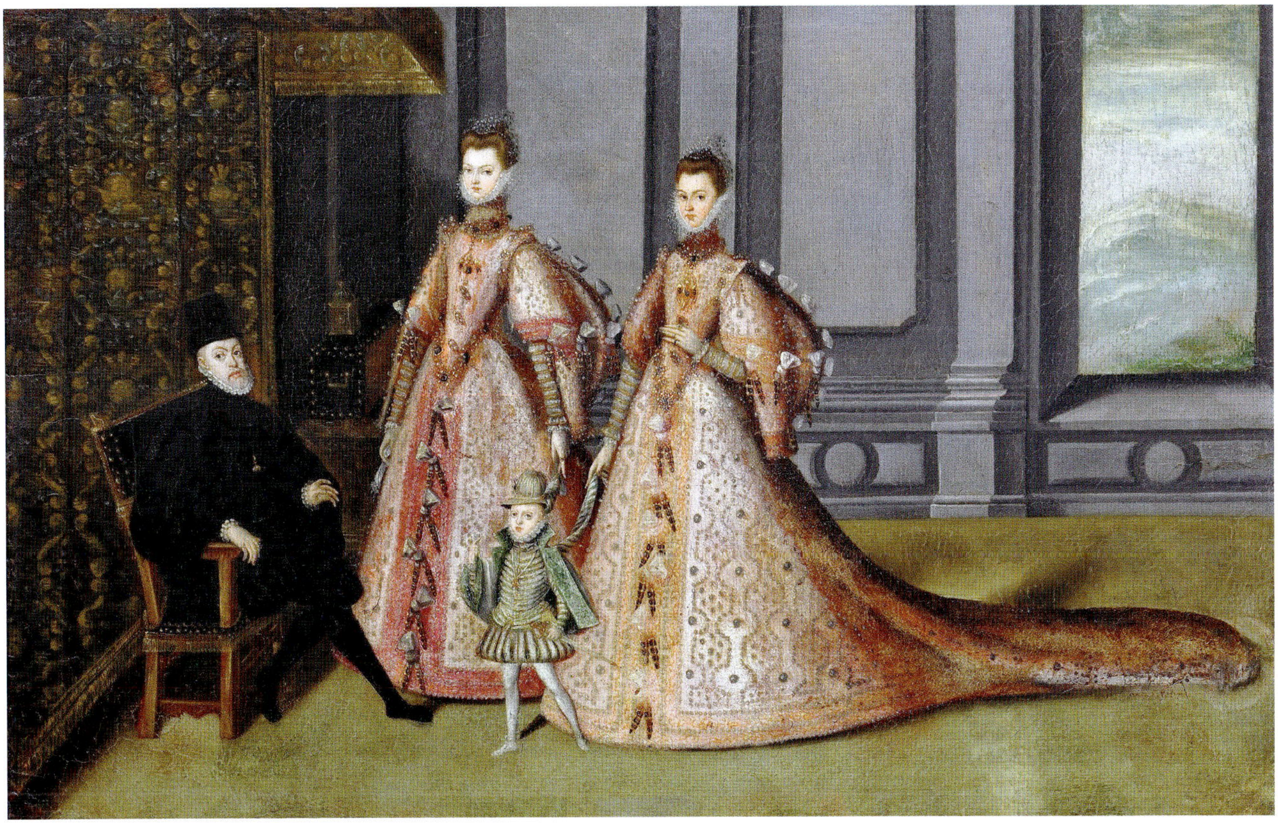

84. Unknown artist, *Philip II and His Children*, c. 1581–4. Oil on panel, 50 × 80 cm. Hispanic Society of America, New York

gave a child time to master each new item and learn to wear it with grace on the road to adulthood.

Clothing for royal children in their first year of life was quite simple. Blankets and garments for babies were made from linen and fine wool, either white or red (the latter considered to be a salubrious color, as discussed in relation to Isabel of Bourbon's undergarments in Chapter 2). Royal newborns were swaddled in *mantillas*, which were little blankets made from white baize or a fine wool dyed scarlet-red (*grana*). On the day of María Teresa's baptism, the infanta was swaddled in a blanket of warm white plush. When it came time to liberate the infanta's arms from swaddling, Aguado made her dresses "with a tail" from Holland cloth (*holanda*), which probably resembled the long dress worn by a daughter of Philip III about three decades earlier (fig. 83).[6] At this early age, silk was used only for special occasions. For toddlers, the tailor made leading strings attached to a harness (*andador de tirantes*) that matched their garments. It was a royal tradition for the elder children of the monarch to hold the leading strings of their younger siblings: María Teresa one day would hold the leading strings of her younger half-sister Margarita, just as Philip II's daughters Isabel Clara Eugenia and Catalina Micaela had led their little brother, the future King Philip III (fig. 84). As toddlers, boys and girls both wore a wrap-skirt (*manteo*), but their upper-body garments were different—a cassock (*ropilla*) with fitted

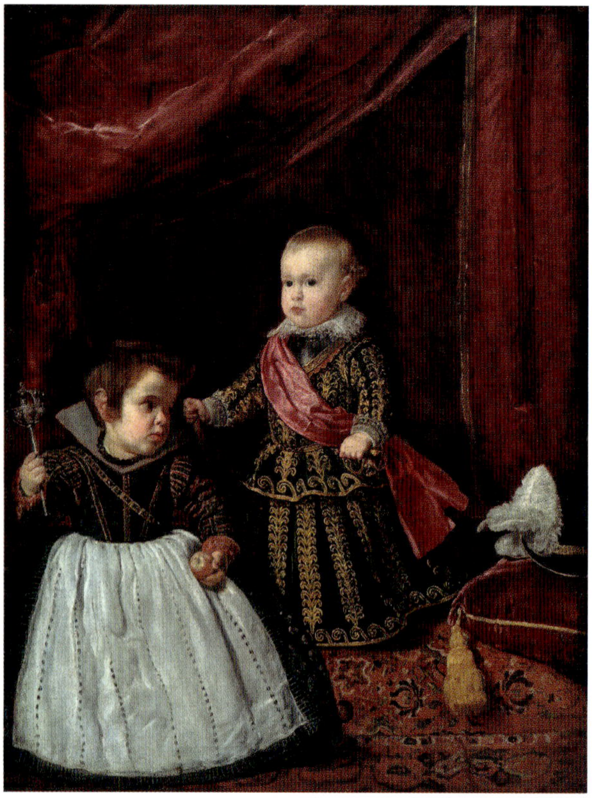

85. Diego Velázquez, *Don Baltasar Carlos and an Attendant*, 1632. Oil on canvas, 128 × 101.9 cm. Museum of Fine Arts, Boston

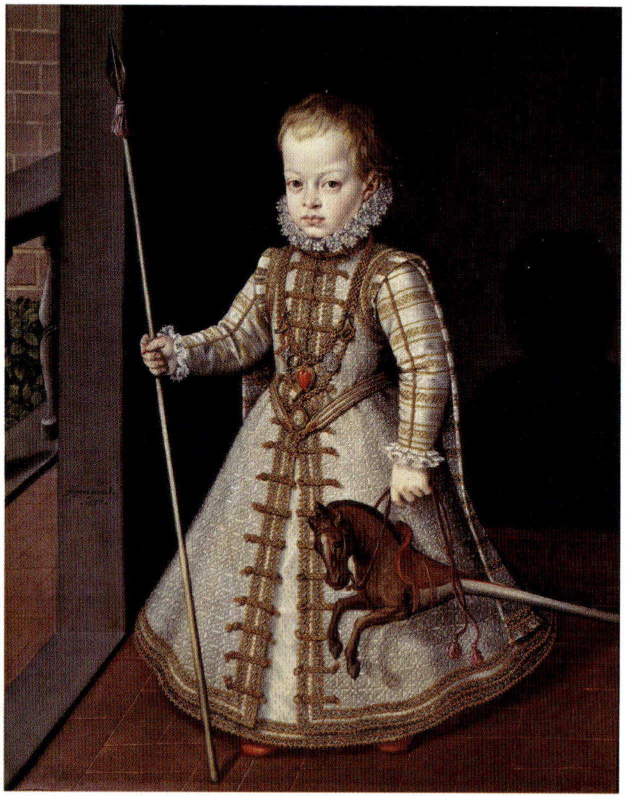

86. Alonso Sánchez Coello, *Infante Diego*, 1577. Oil on canvas, 108 × 88 cm. Liechtenstein, the Princely Collections, Vaduz–Vienna

sleeves and shoulder-wings for Baltasar Carlos, and a "little sack" (*saquito*) with long skirts and sets of fitted and hanging sleeves for María Teresa.

In Velázquez's first portrait of the prince, painted in 1632, Baltasar Carlos wears a skirt and cassock richly decorated with gold trimming, which stands out in contrast to the relatively plain dress of an attendant with dwarfism (fig. 85). Curls of gold trim crawl around the hems of the prince's skirts like little snails; the same gold curls, placed back-to-back, form vertical stacks of flowers that climb up the prince's body. These curvilinear, organic forms demonstrate Aguado's innovative approach to courtly dress decorations in the early 1630s (see the detail in fig. 81). The queen's tailor was frequently paid for drawings of decorations for the prince's clothes, which included *alamares* of various shapes and other ornaments that were made with trimmings of silk, silver, and gold.[7] These expensive decorations were often removed from garments that the young prince had soiled or outgrown and were then reused on new garments. A degree of pragmatism governed the making of royal children's clothes, even for the heir to the throne.

Aguado had to avoid overloading the prince's clothes with heavy ornaments that could impede the child's ability to walk. When the Cortes of Castile swore an oath of allegiance to Baltasar Carlos on March 7, 1632, the decoration on the prince's outfit "was lighter than it was rich, to avoid weighing down and impeding His Highness," according to the official account of the ceremony that Philip IV commissioned from his secretary.[8] On this important occasion, when the two-and-a-half-year-old Baltasar Carlos was formally recognized as heir to the throne, he wore a skirt and *vaquero*, which was a long coat-dress with hanging sleeves.[9] It was a traditional garment that had been worn by the Infante Diego, fourth son of Philip II, over fifty years earlier (fig. 86). For the oath of allegiance ceremony, Baltasar Carlos's *vaquero* was made from crimson plush that was embroidered and trimmed in gold. The prince was led into the Church of San Jerónimo by the garment's hanging sleeves, which were held by his two uncles: the Cardinal-Infante Ferdinand (who was the Archbishop of Toledo) and the Infante Carlos (who was losing his place in the line of succession thanks to this ceremony). Queen Isabel of Bourbon followed behind them wearing an embroidered crimson *saya entera* that, by matching the prince's outfit, called attention to her position as mother of the heir to the throne.[10]

Prince Baltasar Carlos made the transition from a toddler's skirts to a man's breeches sometime before his fifth birthday.[11] Breeching was an important personal milestone in any boy's life, which took on enormous political significance when the boy changing from skirts to breeches was the king-to-be.[12] Aguado did not make the prince's breeches—this specialty garment was made by hosiers called *calceteros*—but the *alamares* that were used to decorate them were surely based on the tailor's designs (fig. 87). Aguado's accounts show that the tailor began to make *golillas*—the collar supporters that were the quintessential accessory worn by Spanish men—for Baltasar Carlos in early 1634, before the prince's fifth birthday. In a portrait that was painted around 1638–9, when he was about ten years old, Baltasar Carlos wears

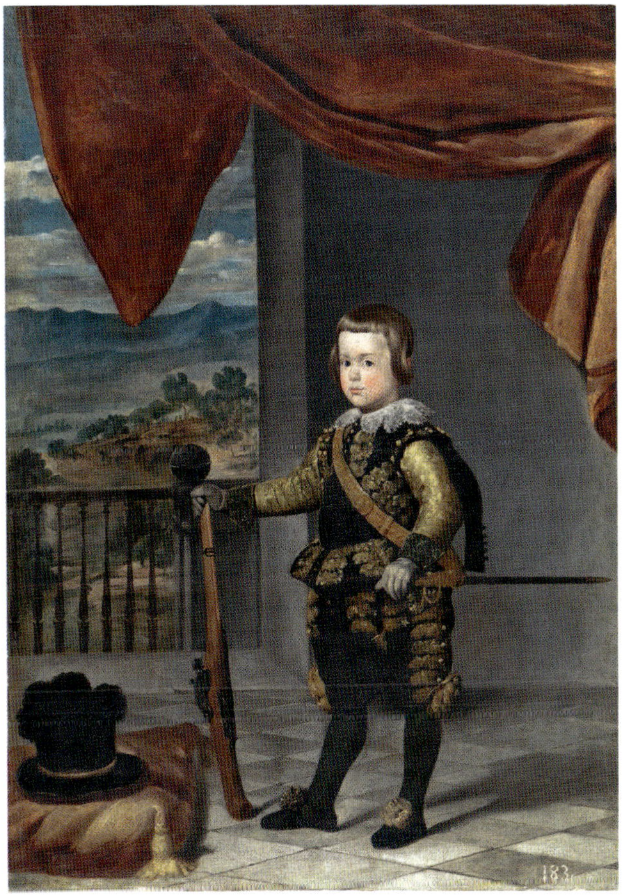

87. Workshop of Velázquez, *Prince Baltasar Carlos*, c. 1636. Oil on canvas, 158 × 113 cm. Museo Nacional del Prado, Madrid

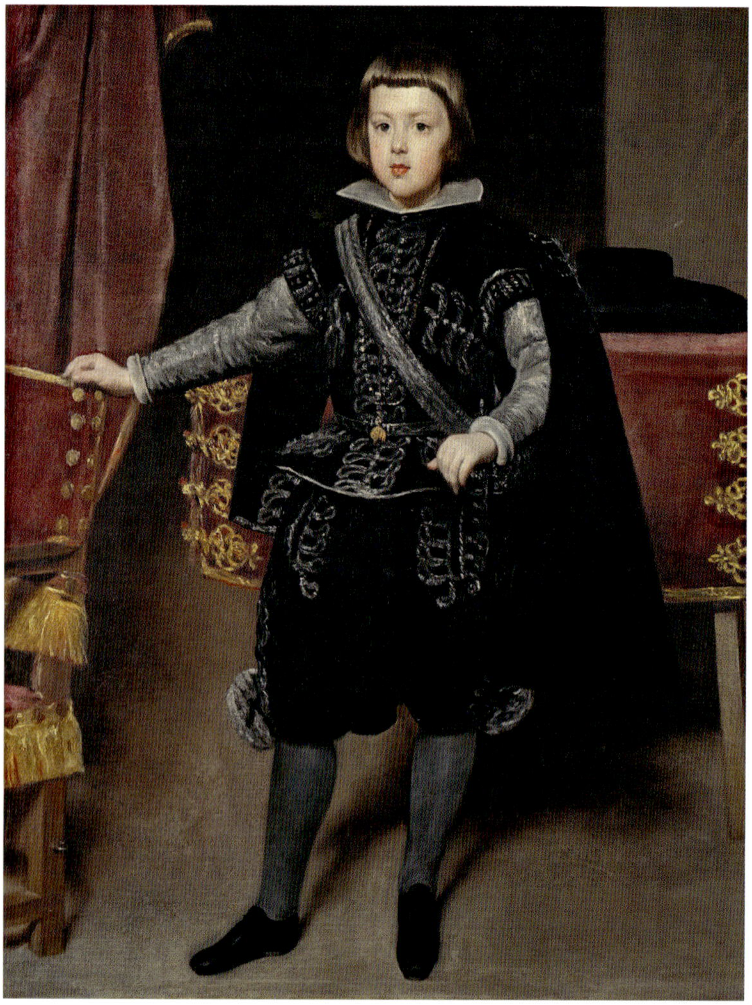

88. Diego Velázquez, *Prince Baltasar Carlos*, 1638–9. Oil on canvas, 130 × 99.5 cm. Kunsthistorisches Museum, Vienna

89. *(facing page)* Unknown Madrid artist, *The Royal Family in the Gardens of the Casa de Campo*, probably early 1640s. Oil on canvas, 115 × 145 cm. Museo de Burgos

a *golilla* beneath a linen collar with a sober black suit decorated with silver *alamares*, a black cloak draped over one shoulder (fig. 88). The rich gold decorations of his early childhood had conveyed Baltasar Carlos's value—and no doubt also helped audiences see and recognize him during public appearances—but as the prince approached adolescence it was time to refashion his image into that of a working royal.

Not everything that Aguado made for the prince was public and political. He also made the prince dress-up clothes, like a four-colored jester outfit and a harlequin costume in yellow linen striped with ribbons in every color.[13] Aguado made uniforms to dress the prince's toy soldiers as the different regiments of the palace guard (the Spanish Guard, German Guard, and Guard of Archers) in jerkins with slashed sleeves and short capes.[14]

During his first decade at court, Aguado also dressed two infantas: María Antonia (born in January 1635, died December 1636) and María Teresa (born in September 1638). Compared to the clothes that he made for the prince, Aguado's work for the Infanta María

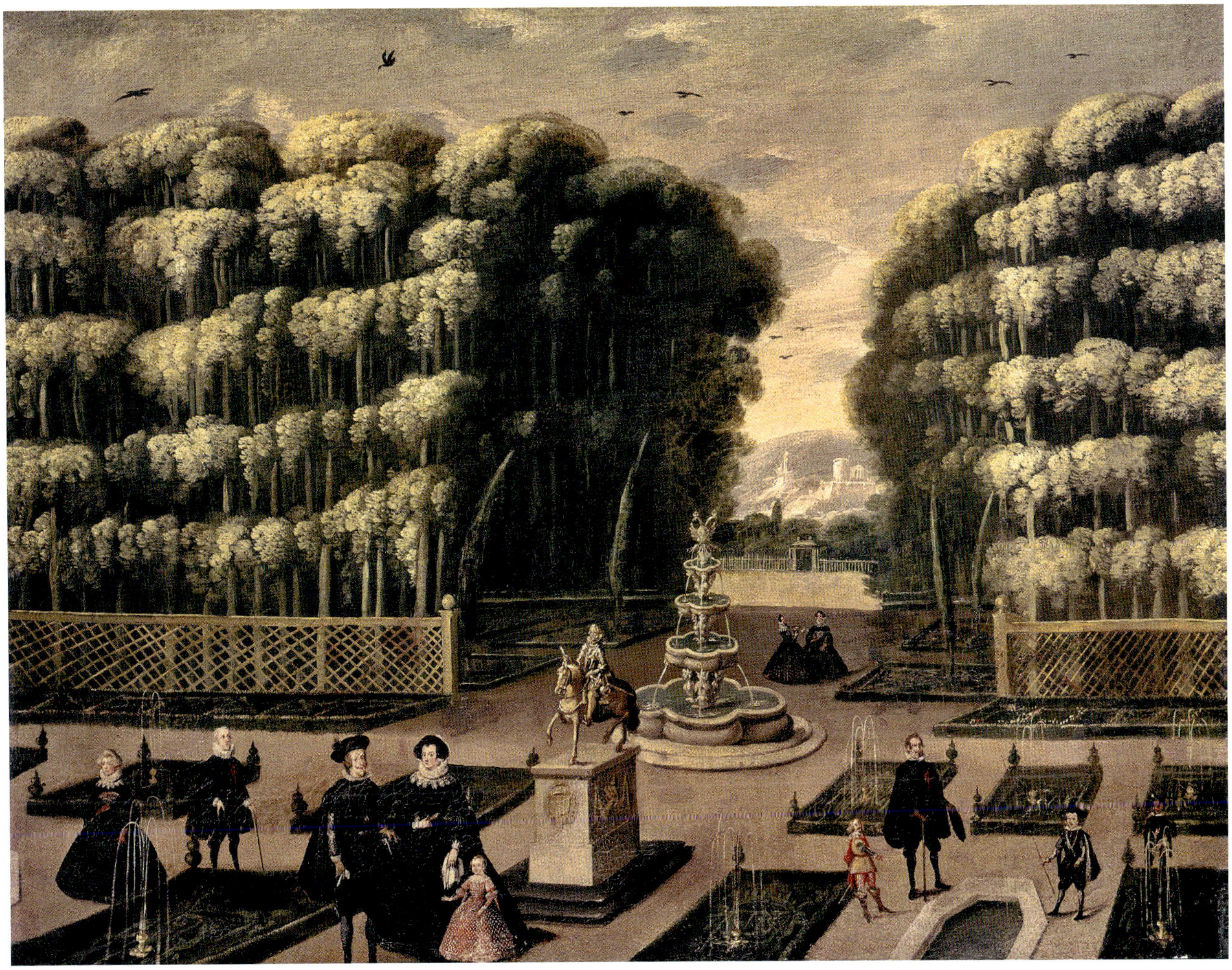

Teresa in the 1630s was relatively undemanding and significantly less remunerative.[15] María Teresa's clothes at this early stage in her life were seen by few: she did not make her first public appearance until she was about four-and-a-half years old.[16] Until then, she was seen almost exclusively by family and staff in the Royal Palace. It was the infanta's governess, Inés de Zúñiga y Velasco, the Countess of Olivares (wife of the royal favorite, the Count-Duke of Olivares), who made decisions about the infanta's clothes. On one occasion, she sent six linen dresses back to Aguado because she was unhappy with their decorations.[17] María Teresa graduated from dresses made of linen to those of silk—satin, damask, taffeta, and velvet—around the age of two. The infanta's silk dresses reflected her mother's taste: Aguado made several from dark brown taffeta decorated in silver or gold trim, with sleeves slashed "in the German style."[18] There are no individual portraits of María Teresa in these early years, but we catch a glimpse of her in a painted view of the royal family strolling in the garden of the Casa de Campo, a royal residence in the countryside just west of Madrid (fig. 89).[19] At her mother's side,

María Teresa is presented as a miniature adult in courtly dress with slashing on her sleeves and bodice, and she carries a closed fan in her left hand (fig. 90). At this young age, the infanta still had much to learn, and new elements of dress—a farthingale, train, corset, and *chapines*—were going to be introduced in the years to come as she prepared to take on a more public role.

A French Fashion Influencer: The Princess of Carignano in Madrid

In November 1636, a blood relation of the French royal family named Marie de Bourbon arrived at the Spanish court for what proved to be a lengthy and controversial visit. A second cousin of Queen Isabel, Marie de Bourbon had come to be known as the Princess of Carignano when she married Thomas of Savoy in 1625. Her husband, who had Spanish and French blood, was a valued ally

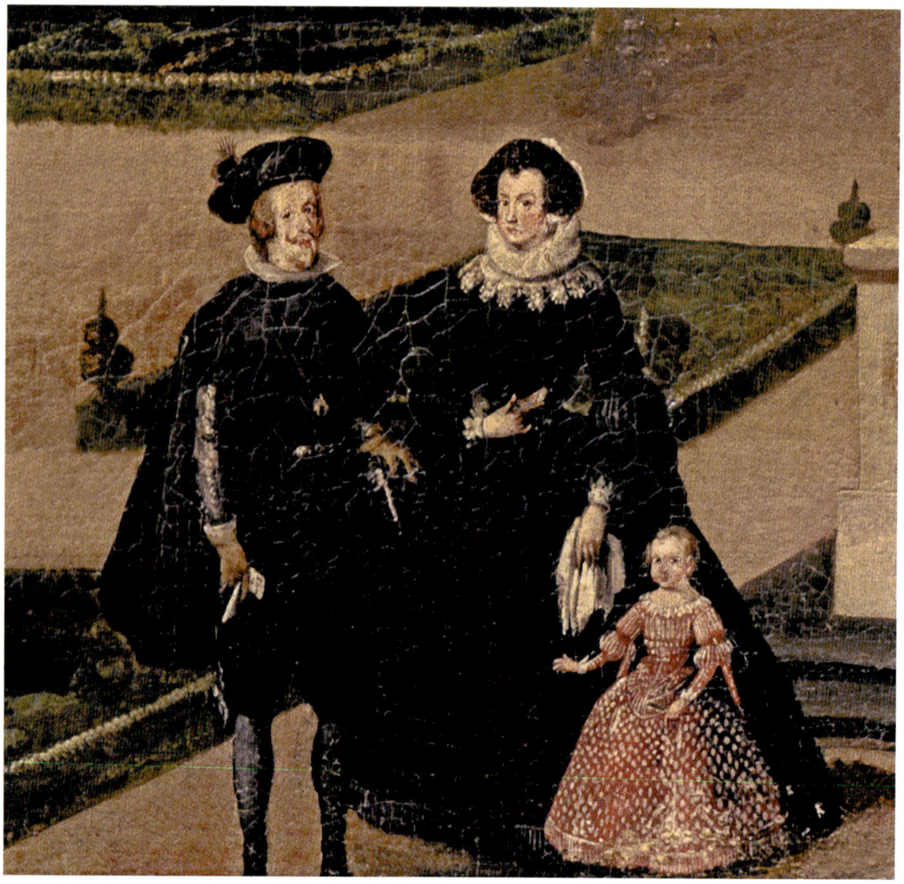

90. Philip IV, Isabel of Bourbon, and María Teresa (detail of fig. 89)

91. *(facing page)* Abraham Bosse, *Youth*, from *The Four Ages of Man* series, 1636. Detail; etching, 26.7 × 32.8 cm. The Metropolitan Museum of Art, New York

of Philip IV but was never fully trusted. The Prince of Carignano was fighting the French in the Netherlands on Spain's behalf when his wife arrived in Madrid with their five children. From the moment the princess entered Madrid on November 27, 1636, her appearance was the subject of public fascination. The princess was described as "very attractive, delicate of body, with two moles on her pale face, which suit her very well; blue eyes, the nose somewhat sharp, everything in good proportion," in an account of her entry into Madrid by Rodrigo Méndez Silva, a Portuguese historian resident at the Spanish court. Less precise about her clothes, Méndez Silva reported only that the princess was "dressed in a brocade the colors of gold and silver" and that her ladies-in-waiting were dressed very richly "*a la francesa*."[20] Courtly dress in France at this moment was characterized by the low-cut bodices and slim skirts worn without farthingales that are depicted in a 1636 etching by the French artist Abraham Bosse, who was the son of a tailor and paid meticulous attention to the details of dress (fig. 91).[21]

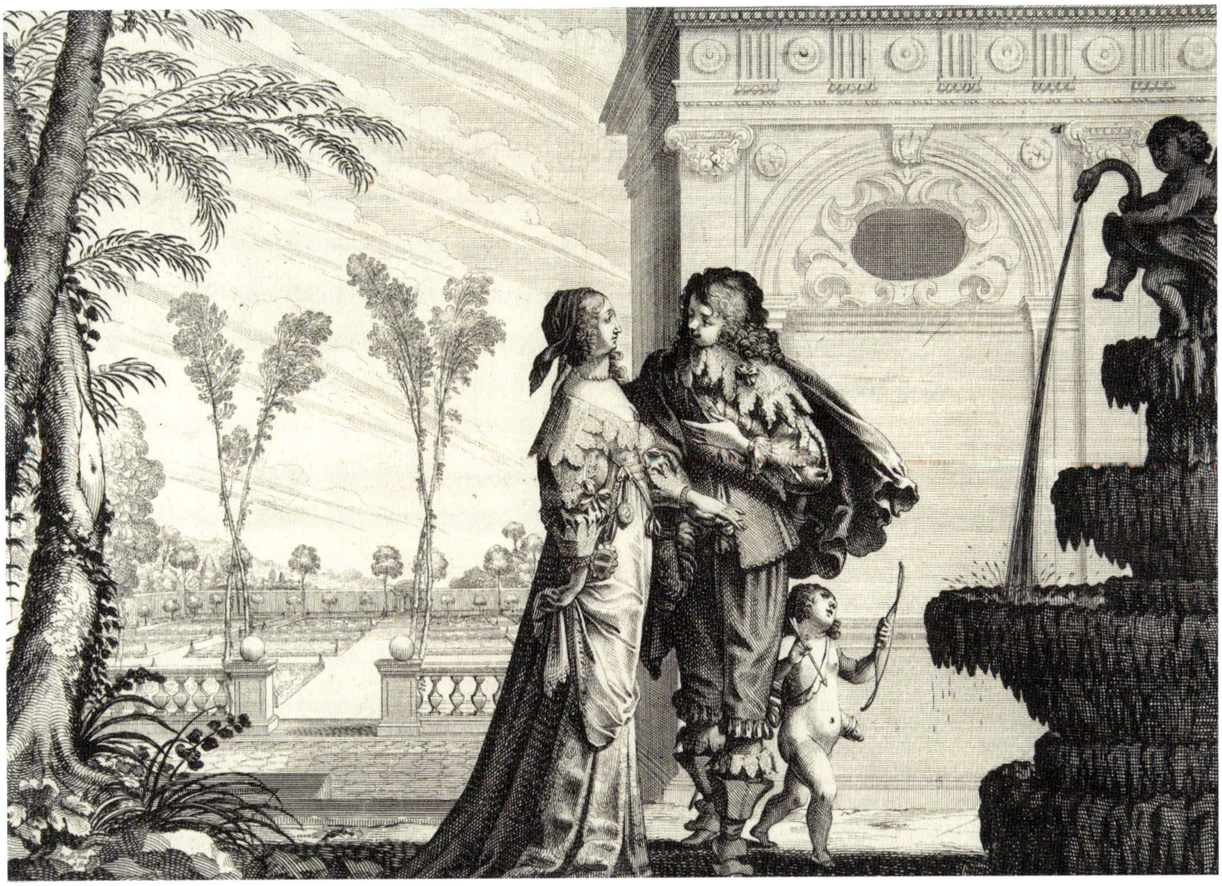

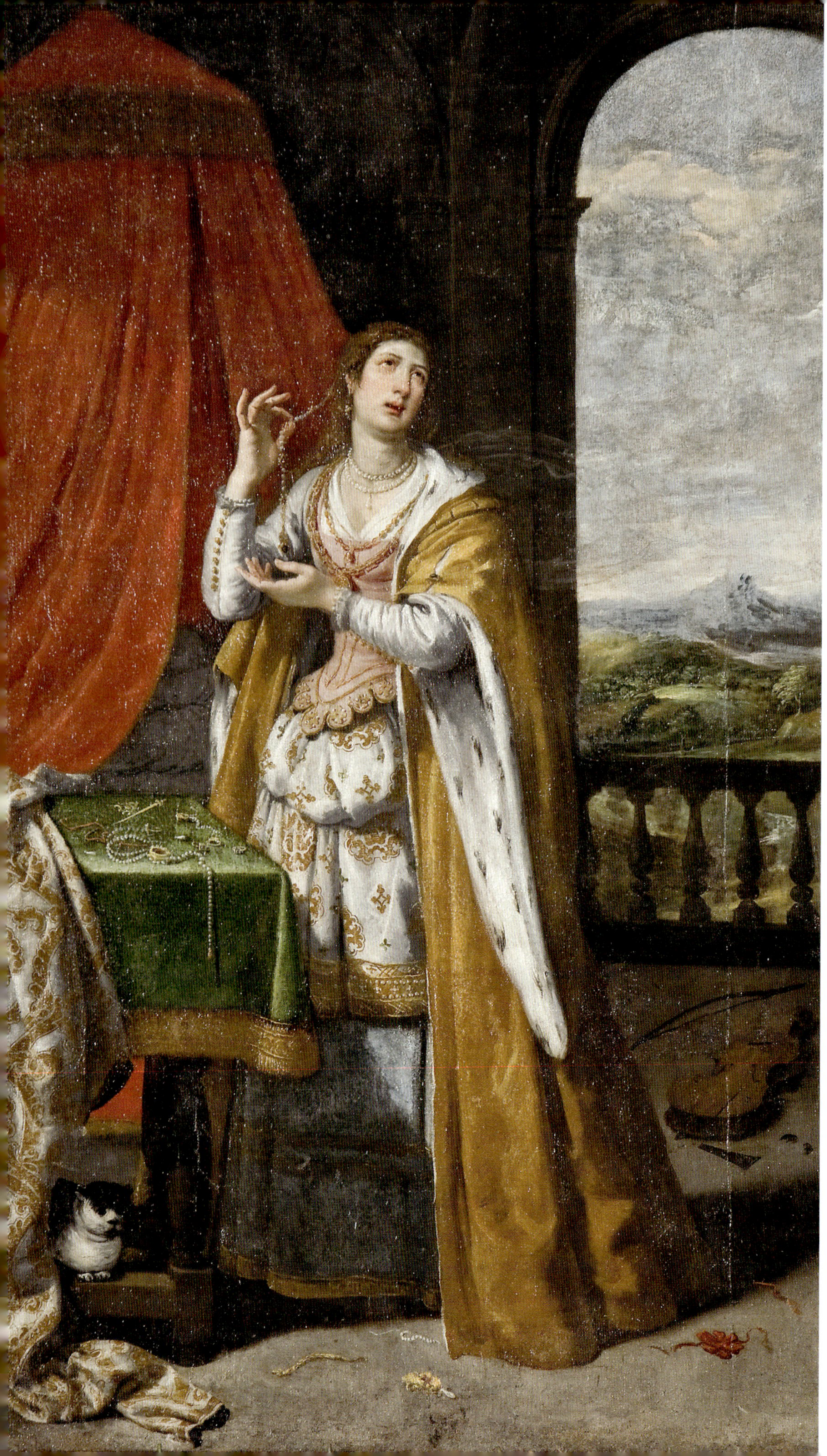

The Princess of Carignano was received in Madrid with all the gala deference that was owed to a royal ally. Her luxurious accommodations in the Treasure House on the grounds of the Royal Palace were richly adorned with tapestries and rugs from the royal collection. On her first night in Madrid, the princess was presented with a dressing gown (*ropa de levantar*) that Aguado had made from chamois-colored lamé (*lama gamuzada*) embroidered with gold and amber (*ámbar*) and decorated with 288 buttons-and-loops.[22] A *ropa de levantar* was a long, loose dressing gown, like the fur-lined gown with pointed sleeves that Mary Magdalene wears over her corset and petticoat in a 1639 altarpiece painting at the Cathedral of La Magdalena in Getafe, in the province of Madrid (fig. 92).[23] This was such a simple, unstructured garment that it took Aguado only three hours to make the Princess of Carignano's gift.[24] A dressing gown made from rich materials was a standard diplomatic present for distinguished guests of the Spanish court: when the Prince of Wales arrived unexpectedly in Madrid to woo the Infanta María Ana in 1623, he was given a *ropa de levantar* scented with ambergris.[25] The robe for the Princess of Carignano only cost 766 *reales* for materials plus 40 *reales* for Aguado's labor, which means that it looked richer than it really was. A printed *relación* described the glittering gift as a sign of the very splendid reception that this royal guest received at the Spanish court.[26]

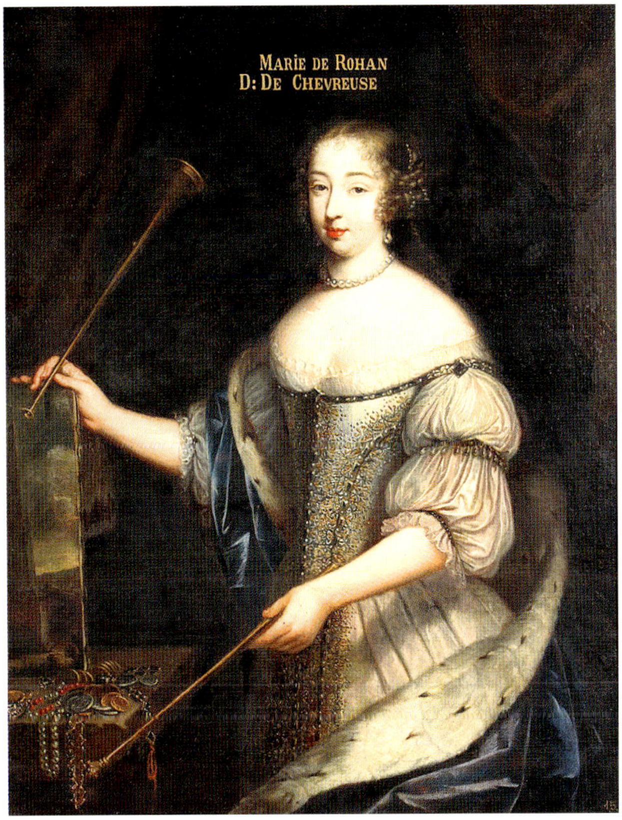

93. Circle of Pierre Mignard, *Marie de Rohan, Duchess of Chevreuse*, mid-17th century. Oil on canvas, 117 × 94 cm. Sychrov Castle, Czech Republic

The Princess of Carignano became a fixture at the court in Madrid in the late 1630s, and local chroniclers reported whenever she appeared with the royal family at Mass, a bullfight, or Corpus Christi festivities, and they took note when she was absent.[27] For nine weeks between December 1637 and February 1638, Madrid hosted a second fashionable Frenchwoman: Marie de Rohan, the Duchess of Chevreuse. The duchess, who was described as "very elegant, bare-breasted, and casual" by one Spanish author, is credited with popularizing the low-cut bodice, called the *escotado*, in Spain.[28] An undated portrait at Sychrov Castle in the Czech Republic portrays the duchess with her trademark décolletage (fig. 93). When the Princess of Carignano and the Duchess of Chevreuse joined the queen to watch a bullfight at the Plaza Mayor, their

92. *(facing page)* Jusepe Leonardo, *Repentant Mary Magdalene Removing Her Jewelry*, 1639. Oil on canvas, 208 × 105 cm. Retablo Mayor, Cathedral of La Magdalena, Getafe

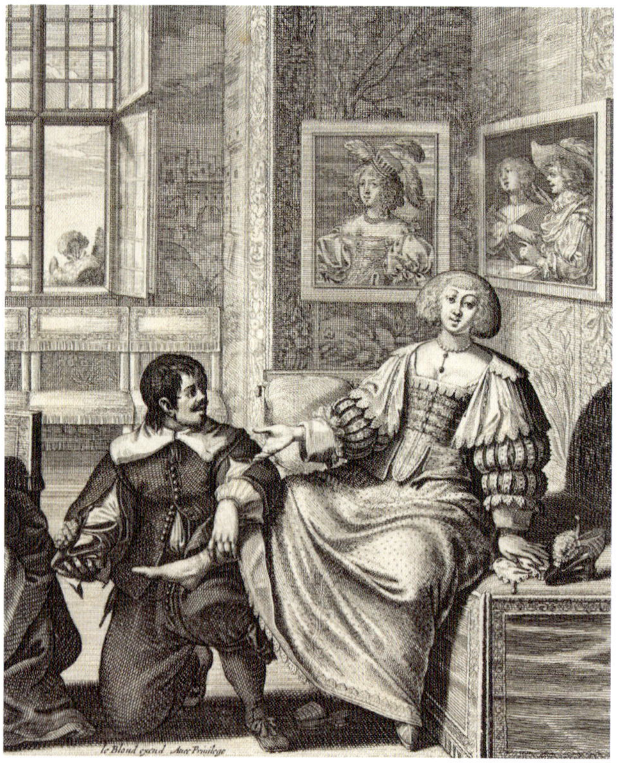

94. Carignano shoe. Abraham Bosse, *The Shoemaker*, from *The Trades* series, c. 1632–3. Detail; etching, 25.3 × 32.7 cm. The Metropolitan Museum of Art, New York

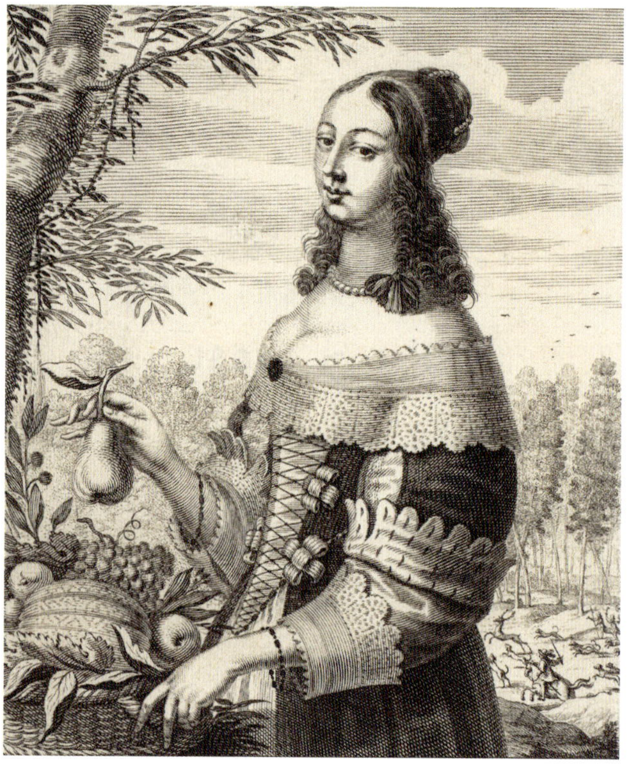

95. Carignano collar. Abraham Bosse, *Earth*, from *The Four Elements* series, 1630. Detail; etching, 14.8 × 10.9 cm. The Metropolitan Museum of Art, New York

appearance was as much of a spectacle as the action in the plaza.[29] Before she left Madrid for England, the Duchess of Chevreuse sat for Velázquez to have her portrait painted "with a French air and dress."[30] The identification of Velázquez's *Lady with a Fan* as the Duchess of Chevreuse is unsupported by the details of dress in that painting, specifically the large skirts of the bodice, which extend over a rounded hip and dip down in the front, which was the fashion a decade after the duchess left Madrid (see Chapter 4, fig. 117).[31]

There are no known portraits of the Princess of Carignano during her years in Spain, and written accounts of her appearance offer very little information about her dress. The most detailed description comes from an anonymous pamphlet describing the baptism of the Infanta María Teresa in October 1638, when all eyes were on the Princess of Carignano, who was serving as the infanta's godmother. At this important event, the princess followed the same playbook that the Prince of Wales had used during his visit to the Spanish court 15 years earlier: during his final public appearance at

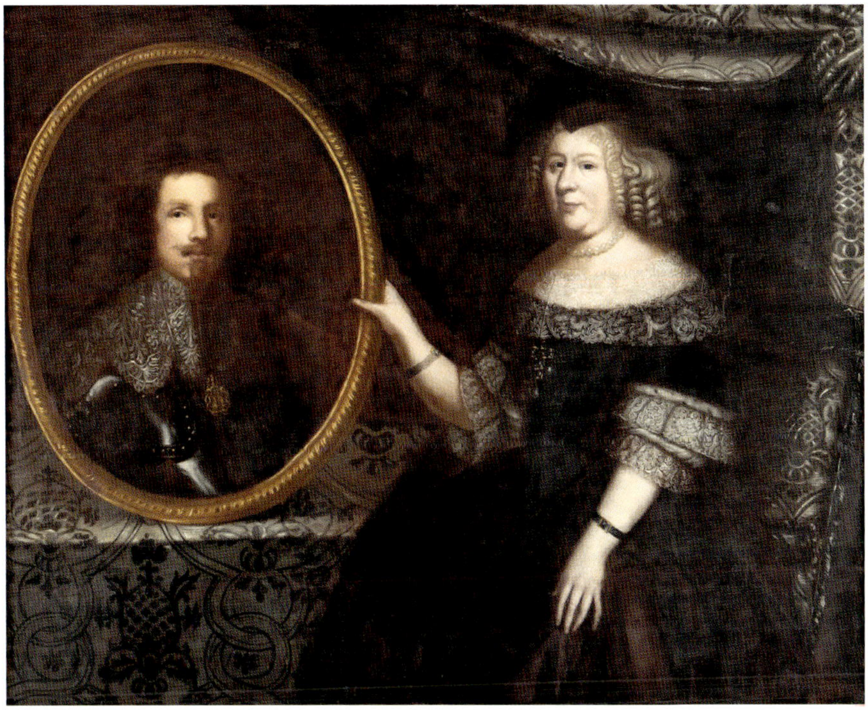

96. Unknown French artist, *Marie de Bourbon, Princess of Carignan, with a Portrait of Her Deceased Husband*, c. 1670. Oil on canvas, 120 × 148 cm. Galleria Sabauda, Turin

a bullfight in the Plaza Mayor on August 21, 1623, the Prince of Wales had appeared in a "suit half in English and half in Spanish," as it was described in one *relación* (whose author neglected to report which half was which).[32] For the infanta's baptism, the Princess of Carignano wore a long dress made from embroidered cloth of silver "*a la francesa*"—presumably this meant a low-cut bodice and slim skirt without a farthingale—combined with pointed sleeves in the Spanish style. The *relación* reported that the princess's hybrid Franco-Spanish attire was universally applauded.[33]

The Princess of Carignano and her Spanish hosts exchanged gifts of clothing during her visit. Philip IV sent a Spanish-style suit to the princess's eldest son,[34] and Isabel of Bourbon gave her two embroidered dresses and an embroidered petticoat (*manteo*).[35] In 1640 the Princess of Carignano reciprocated by giving the queen several rich garments: a dress of silver-on-silver camlet, a petticoat of green and gold watered camlet, and a doublet of black and silver watered lamé. The queen had these gifts altered to suit her own taste. The dress of silver camlet, for instance, was lined with black double taffeta and decorated with black edging.[36] After wearing the dress, the queen had it taken apart and remade in January 1641, with embroidered black gauze (*gasa*) layered over the silver material.[37] Perhaps the queen wished to disguise the princess's gift, for by this time relations were souring between Philip IV and the princess's husband, who was negotiating with the French to secure his claims to inherit territory in

Northern Italy. In September 1642, Thomas of Savoy renounced his Spanish allegiance and went over to the French side.[38] There are no more recorded exchanges of clothing between the Princess of Carignano and Queen Isabel after that date. The princess remained in Spain, effectively a prisoner, until June 1644, when she finally left for France under a cloud of treason.

Following her ignominious departure, the Princess of Carignano's name entered the Spanish lexicon as an adjective to describe feminine French fashions that became popular at the Spanish court in the later 1630s and remained in use decades after. An unusual shoe that is known in English as a "slap-sole shoe" was being called a "Carignano shoe" (*zapato cariñano*) in Madrid by the year 1642.[39] In a print by Bosse with a salacious undertone, a shoemaker fits one of these shapely shoes, which has the toe and heel attached to a flat sole, on a female customer who places her bare foot on his knee (fig. 94).[40] The best-known accessory named for the princess is the "Carignano collar" (*valona cariñana*), as it was being called by 1646, which was a wide band of white fabric or lace worn around the shoulders (fig. 95).[41] Something called a "Carignano hip" (*cadera cariñana*) appears in the royal farthingale-maker's accounts between 1648 and 1650, which was probably some sort of padding added to the side hips of a farthingale.[42] French fashions of the 1630s were slim-hipped, but perhaps the Princess of Carignano wore this apparatus as part of her hybrid diplomatic attire. She wears a dress with a notably wide hip in a portrait that was painted after Thomas of Savoy's death in 1656 (fig. 96). Holding up a likeness of her deceased husband, Marie de Bourbon wears a black widow's peak over her blonde curls and is still wearing her namesake collar, many years after the conclusion of her Spanish adventure.

Pious Donations: Clothes for Devotional Images

In December 1636, just a few weeks after the Princess of Carignano's arrival at the Spanish court, Madrid was struck by heavy rains that flooded a hundred homes. In times of crisis such as this, it was common practice to take a devotional image with a reputation for performing miracles in a procession outdoors to request divine intervention. In an effort to stop the rains of 1636, preparations were made to hold a procession with the Virgin of Almudena. This painted wooden sculpture, which was made around 1500 but was reputed to be much older, was "the most ancient devotional image there is in the Court," according to the royal secretary Gerónimo Gascón de Torquemada (fig. 97).[43] The image was housed in a chapel at the Church of Santa María, located on the Calle Mayor very close to the Royal Palace (see Map 2).[44] "The instant she was taken from her chapel to be adorned and dressed in the Main Chapel," Gascón de Torquemada wrote, "it stopped raining and the sky cleared completely."[45] The royal secretary's account, which claims that the mere intention to dress and adorn the sculpture activated its protective powers, helps to explain the popularity of this religious practice. A 1692 history of the Virgin of Almudena credited the parents of the Count-Duke of Olivares with being the first to dress the sculpture in real clothes and noted that the Olivares family—elevated to a dukedom in 1625—had been richly rewarded with their son's rise to the zenith of political power as Philip IV's royal favorite.[46] At the Spanish court, dressing the Virgin in sumptuous clothes was not only an efficacious religious practice—it was also good politics.

Isabel of Bourbon was well known for her devotion to the Virgin Mary, which endeared the foreign-born queen to her Spanish subjects. Living as she did in an almost constant state of life-threatening pregnancy, Isabel frequently called upon the protective powers of the Virgin. In November 1623, during the final month of her second pregnancy (after her first child had lived only one day), Isabel was carried in a chair to visit the Virgin of Almudena. The queen planned to visit eight more images of the Virgin over the next eight days but gave birth on the third day to a daughter, who lived less than a month.[47] The principal image in the queen's private chapel at the Royal Palace was the "Virgin of the Expectation," a kneeling sculpture of the Virgin Mary in an advanced state of pregnancy.[48] As part of her devotional practice, the queen regularly commissioned her tailor to make clothing to dress the many sculptures of the Virgin and Child that were at the Royal Palace and also to give as pious donations to sacred images at churches and convents in Madrid and further afield.

The clothes that Aguado made for devotional sculptures were usually cut from new fabric and trims and made specially for the images. Aguado used the richest silks, shot through with metal threads and brocaded with silver flowers, and trimmings made from silver and gold. The colors of the fabric were symbolic and tied to specific holy days. The Virgin of Almudena wore purple for Lent, red for Pentecost, and white for Christmas, Easter, and Corpus Christi.[49] Religious sculptures were clothed in courtly garments: the Virgin was dressed in a *saya entera* with a train, and the Baby Jesus wore a *vaquero* with hanging sleeves (like Prince Baltasar Carlos at the oath of allegiance ceremony described earlier in this chapter). The cut of the dresses that Aguado made for images of the Virgin depended on the kind of sculpture to be dressed. For older images such as the Virgin of Almudena, which had carved and painted clothing, Aguado made only the front of a dress, which tied around the neck, and a long mantle that covered the sculpture's back. The

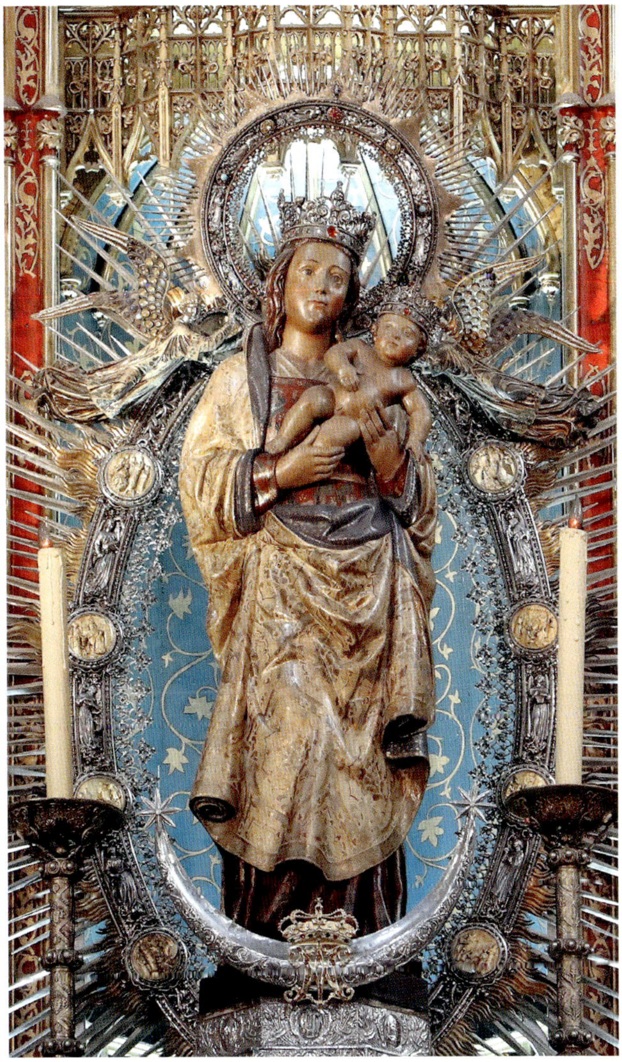

97. Unknown Italian sculptor, *Virgin of Almudena*, c. 1500. Polychromed and gilded pine wood, 158 cm tall. Cathedral of La Almudena, Madrid

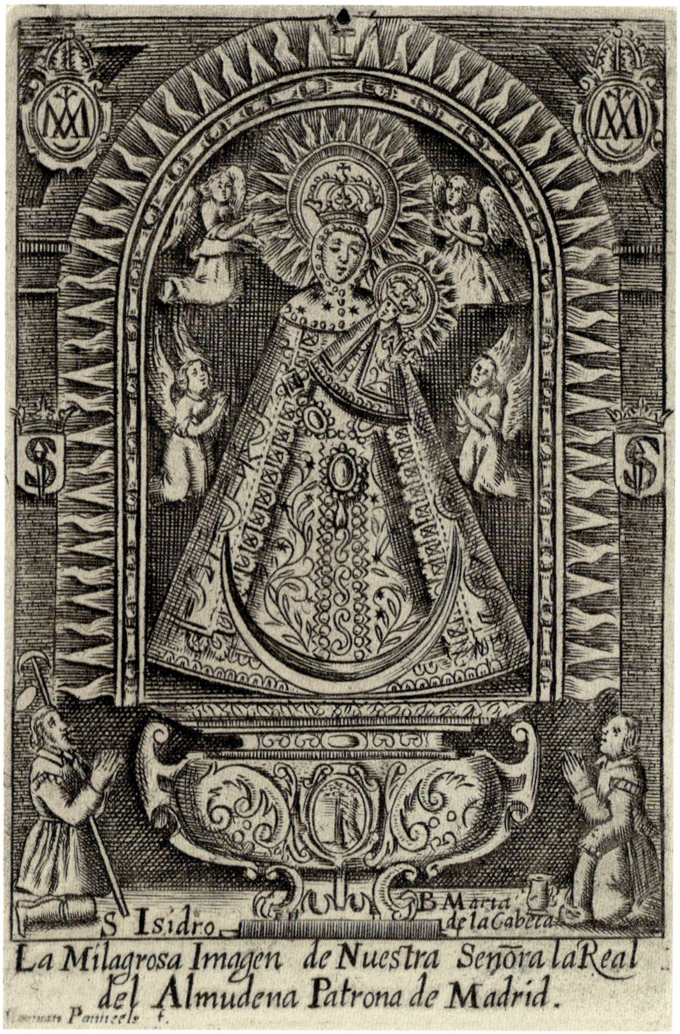

98. Herman Panneels, *The Miraculous Image of the Virgin of Almudena, Patroness of Madrid*, 1636–51. Engraving, 9.8 × 6.8 cm. Biblioteca Nacional de España, Madrid

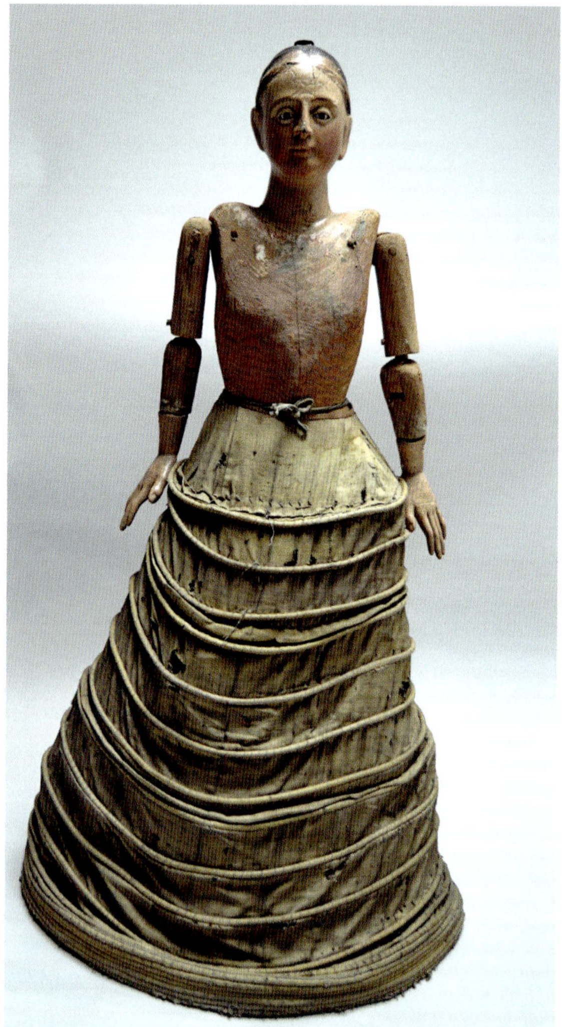

99. Devotional image wearing a *verdugado*, 16th–17th centuries. Polychromed wood, 102 cm tall. Museo Etnográfico de Castilla y León, Zamora

queen's farthingale-maker occasionally made miniature *verdugados* for sculptures of the Virgin, including one at the Church of San Gil, to give their skirts the conical shape that is represented in contemporary images (fig. 98).[50] Sculptures that were made in the later sixteenth and seventeenth centuries had articulated arms and cone-shaped lower bodies that made it easier to dress them in tailored garments (fig. 99, and see Chapter 5, fig. 127). For an image of the Virgin in Salamanca, Aguado made a complete *saya entera* with a skirt, a bodice with short skirts and shoulder-wings, and two sets of sleeves made from a "glittering fabric."[51]

In 1640 the queen commissioned Aguado to make new outfits for the Virgin of Almudena and Christ Child to wear in procession on the Virgin's November 9 feast day. Aguado made a dress-front and a floor-length mantle from white Chinese satin embroidered with gold and silver for the Virgin, and a matching dress with hanging sleeves and little shoulder-wings for the Christ Child.[52] An inventory recorded in 1693 claimed, perhaps fancifully, that the queen had embroidered the garments with her own hands.[53] Queen Isabel was especially devoted to the Virgin of Almudena, and she bequeathed one of her own richly embroidered doublets to the image in her will.[54] It was very difficult to dress the sculpture, however, since the Virgin and Child were joined together. In the early 1650s, an enterprising priest at the Church of Santa María solved this problem by having the figures surgically separated. At the same time, part of the Virgin's back was removed so that the clothed sculpture would fit inside the niche of its altarpiece.[55] The priest's actions, which were controversial at the time, sacrificed the integrity of Madrid's most ancient devotional image to the more urgent imperative to dress the sculpture in the silver-spangled dress and cape that had been made by the queen's tailor.

Royal Favors: Clothing the Queen's Household

Compared to the sumptuous dresses that Aguado made for sculpted images of the Virgin, clothing for the queen's household staff was relatively mundane. But this work, which occupied a large percentage of Aguado's workload, was of great importance to the men and women who received the gifts, and these clothes played a significant role in the palace economy. The clothing that Aguado made for the queen's staff was categorized as *mercedes*, that is, "favors" or "rewards." This included "ordinary" favors of clothing, which were contractually provided to an employee once a year, and "extraordinary" gifts that were given on special occasions. In the event of a royal birth, baptism, or death, Aguado made new clothing in bulk for members of the queen's household. Extraordinary gifts of clothing were also given to individual staff members when they married or, in the case of the queen's ladies, joined a convent. Whatever the occasion, a suit of clothes was a commodity that had intrinsic value, and these gifts of clothing were one of the greatest benefits of employment in the royal household.

Some staff members in the king's and queen's households received a new suit of clothes every year as a supplement to, or a substitute for, wages. This outfit could be worth more than an employee's salary: for example, one assistant in the king's wardrobe earned 429 *reales* per year in wages and a suit worth twice as much.[56] For employees who did not earn a salary, clothing could be their primary source of income; this was the case for an unsalaried stocking-maker in the queen's household who was compensated with an annual dress worth 1,650 *reales*.[57] Diego Velázquez was supposed to have a suit worth 990 *reales* made for him every year, but in 1634 the painter complained that he had not received a suit for four years and was owed 3,960 *reales*.[58] The ordinary favors that Aguado made included annual suits for the noble Keeper of the Queen's Wardrobe and his assistants, who were usually nine in number. The garments for the keeper and his assistants were identical—doublet, cassock, and cape—but the materials and decorations were carefully calibrated to the status of the offices they held. Their respective ranks were encoded in the trimmings on their cloaks: a junior assistant's cloak was decorated with three bands of plain satin, while the satin bands on the keeper's cloak were layered with narrow braided trim (*trencilla*) and velvet ribbon (*ribete*).[59]

A unique gift of clothing made with special attention by the royal tailor indicated that the recipient was held in exceptionally high favor. In the 1630s, Aguado made many garments for María Pope, called La Enana ("the Dwarf"), who had traveled with Isabel of Bourbon from France to Spain in 1615.[60] These gifts showed the queen's extraordinary regard for her longtime companion. Aguado was regularly paid to make drawings of the ornaments to decorate María Pope's dresses, which was a privilege that no other member of the queen's household received. In 1635, Aguado made María Pope a dress of blue and black velvet in the French style with a gathered skirt, which was an unusual item made specially for her.[61]

The aristocratic ladies who left the queen's household to "put on *chapines*"—that is, to get married—received a dowry and a dress made by Aguado. This favor was extended to lower-ranked female servants in the queen's household and also to the brides of her male employees. A bride's dress from the queen's tailor was a pragmatic all-occasion ensemble made from black fabric and trims of a quality and quantity that matched her station. Noblewomen received a *saya entera*, a formal dress with a train and round sleeves, made from plain black velvet and decorated with black velvet ribbons, satin edgings (*pestañas*), and silk trim woven by the orphan girls at the Royal College of Saint Isabel.[62] A dress of this style without color or gold decoration was considered to be "decent and honest."[63] A woman who married one of the senior assistants in the queen's wardrobe received a less formal and less expensive satin dress with a velvet over-gown lined in taffeta.[64] The girls who swept the queen's quarters were the lowest-ranking brides. They received dresses made of grosgrain that were lined in cotton (*fustán*) or linen (*holandilla*).[65] While Aguado's dresses for brides were made from black fabric with black decorations, much richer and flashier *sayas enteras* were given to ladies who left the court to enter a convent. Made from brocaded fabrics and decorated with silver and gold trimmings, those dresses could potentially be reused to dress the convent's devotional images or decorate its altars.[66]

Gifts of clothing to the artisans who were employed in the queen's household were extremely rare: only three are documented in Aguado's accounts. One of these favors was a doublet, cassock, and cloak given to the queen's shoemaker.[67] Another was a velvet dress for the wife of the *cordonero* who made silk cords for the queen's wardrobe.[68] And the third was a dress for Aguado's second wife, Bernarda Ruiz de Reinoso, which the tailor made for her as a gift from the queen in 1634.[69] His first wife, Alfonsa Martínez, had died less than a year after their marriage, and he had returned the dowry to her parents.[70] After waiting a year, in 1632 Aguado married Bernarda Ruiz, the 13-year-old daughter of the king's hatmaker, Gaspar Ruiz, and Juana Reinoso of Toledo.[71] While it was typical for brides to be younger than their husbands, Bernarda Ruiz was unusually young; perhaps the marriage agreement had something to do with a lawsuit between Aguado and Gaspar Ruiz.[72] Bernarda

Ruiz came to the marriage with a dowry of 22,000 *reales*, half of it in cash and the other half in household goods. This included clothing worth 1,114 *reales*.[73] The materials that went into the new dress that the queen commissioned Aguado to make for his wife in 1634 were worth 1,458 *reales*—more than the entire wardrobe that Bernarda Ruiz had brought to her marriage. The three-piece dress included a plain black velvet over-gown and a doublet and skirt made of black satin from Valencia, all lined with black taffeta, and decorated with 237 meters of *pasamanos de cristilla* (probably a woven silk trim decorated with pieces of glass).[74] Wearing this ensemble, the tailor's wife fit the social type of the "Spanish Gentlewoman" depicted in an etching by Wenceslaus Hollar of a woman wearing an over-gown with six rows of wide trim at the hem, its collar dramatically raised to frame her ruff collar (fig. 100). In addition to showing off social status, Bernarda Ruiz's dress demonstrated that her husband was held in great favor by the queen. The dress was also a very valuable asset for the recently wedded couple's household.

Having impressively dressed employees was a way for the royal family to publicly display its wealth and status, but sometimes corners were cut to give the impression of splendor without actually paying for it. Aguado's accounts of favors to the staff include the use of faux gold and silver trimmings, which he never used in his work for the queen or her children. In 1638, Aguado rushed to make a crimson wool coat decorated with a wide band of false gold trimming for Diego de Acedo, a dwarf man who held a position in the court bureaucracy.[75] The coat that Aguado made for Acedo was a *capote de campaña*, which was a simple outer garment with sleeves, cut close to the body at the shoulders and very wide at the hem to form a trapeze-line.[76] In 1644, Velázquez painted a portrait of a man with dwarfism

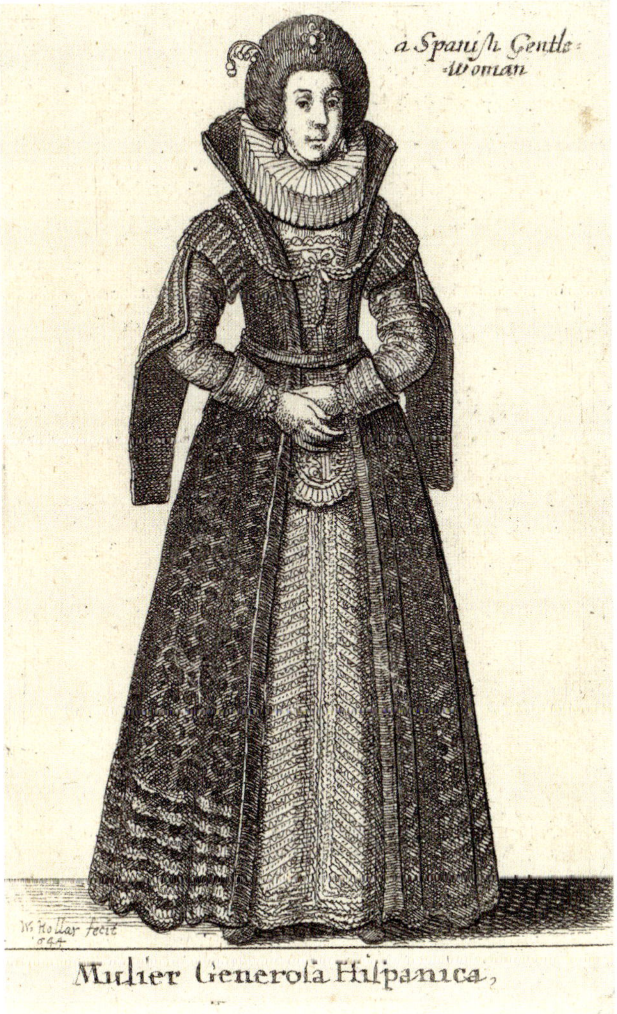

100. Wenceslaus Hollar, *Spanish Gentlewoman*, 1644. Etching, 9.3 × 5.9 cm. National Gallery of Art, Washington, DC

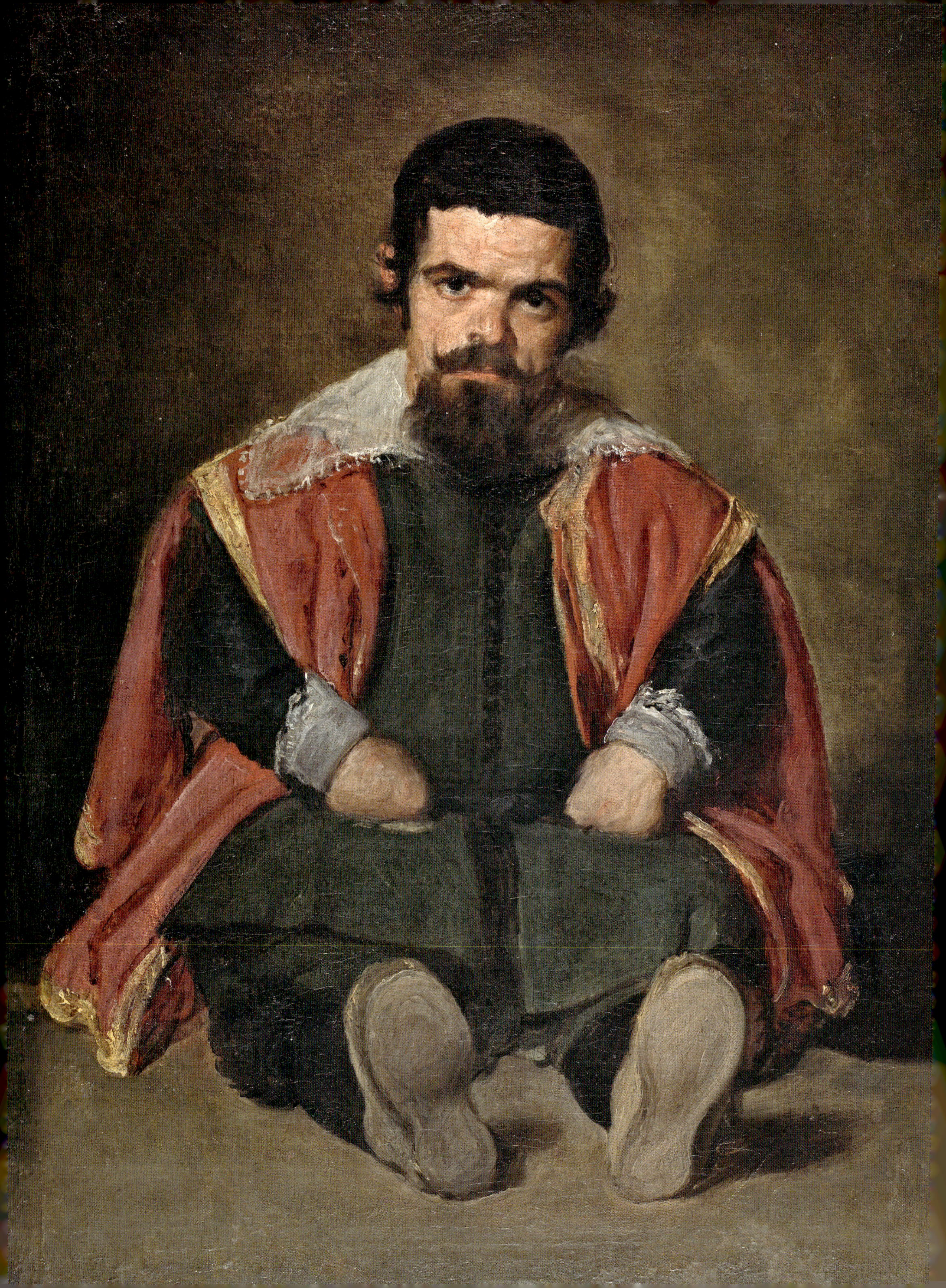

known as El Primo, "the Cousin," wearing a red *capote de campaña* trimmed with what appears to be gold (fig. 101). El Primo previously was assumed to be the nickname of Diego de Acedo, but this identification has been called into question.[77] Whoever the man in the painting is, his red and gold coat is just like the one that Aguado made for Diego de Acedo. The tailor's account reveals that all that glistens is not gold, and the rich-looking trim on El Primo's coat may well be a cheap imitation.

Wartime Cutbacks, Dress Laws, and Complaints

In 1637, while the court in Madrid was distracted by glamorous visitors from France, Spanish troops were suffering relentless defeats abroad.[78] The financial costs of the war with France, now in its second year, forced the Crown to rein in its expenses at home. On September 15, 1637, Philip IV's advisory committee, the *Cámara*, issued a memo recommending a reduction in spending on clothing for members of the king's household. Among other cutbacks, the memo recommended reducing the value of the suit that was given annually to Diego Velázquez from 990 to 880 *reales*.[79] This was a serious hardship for any palace employee, even one as well-compensated as Velázquez, who took pains to present himself as an elegant courtier in person and in his self-portraits, including the one that entered the collection of Duke Cosimo III de' Medici in 1689 (fig. 102).[80]

The queen's household began to economize on clothes expenditures in 1637. That year, for the first time, Aguado began to recycle the queen's clothes. He used her trains to make outfits for Baltasar Carlos and María Teresa, and he made alterations to the queen's dresses to fit the infanta's wet-nurses, who previously had received new dresses specially made for them. In 1640 the tailor made a dress for the Infanta María Teresa from the train of the dress that he had made for Queen Isabel the previous year with the brown and silver "fabric of memories" given to her by Prince Baltasar Carlos (see Chapter 2, p. 81).[81] When the infanta outgrew the dress, Aguado lengthened it and added longer skirts to the bodice. This was the third incarnation of the dress that Aguado made from the same piece of fabric.[82] Aguado's income declined substantially in the last years of the 1630s. In 1637 the amount that he earned for making the queen's clothes fell to 70 percent of the previous year's revenue.[83] Aguado's compensation for alms and favors declined in 1637 and dropped even more over the next two years.[84] He also stopped receiving extra payments for drawings.

As the decade came to an end, Philip IV sought to reset his reign by issuing a series of three proclamations on dress in the spring of 1639. These were the first major new laws on dress since the 1623 Articles of Reformation. But unlike that early reform effort, the laws of 1639 were less about luxury and more concerned with the "scandal" caused by men's and women's appearances. Men were forbidden from styling their hair in forelocks or lovelocks, and women could not go out covering their faces with their mantles.[85] All women, except for prostitutes, were banned from wearing *guardainfantes* and low-cut bodices.[86] In a dramatic display of royal authority, in July 1638 offending farthingales were confiscated and hung in shame from the gilded balconies of the Court Prison, which was an imposing new building off the southeast corner of the Plaza Mayor (see Chapter 7, fig. 169).[87] The public display of women's undergarments was an extraordinary spectacle—and a perfect distraction from Spain's military losses abroad and financial problems at home.

Aguado, for one, was not so easily distracted. In August 1639 the queen's tailor submitted a

101. *(facing page)* Diego Velázquez, *El Primo*, 1644. Oil on canvas, 106.5 × 82.5 cm. Museo Nacional del Prado, Madrid

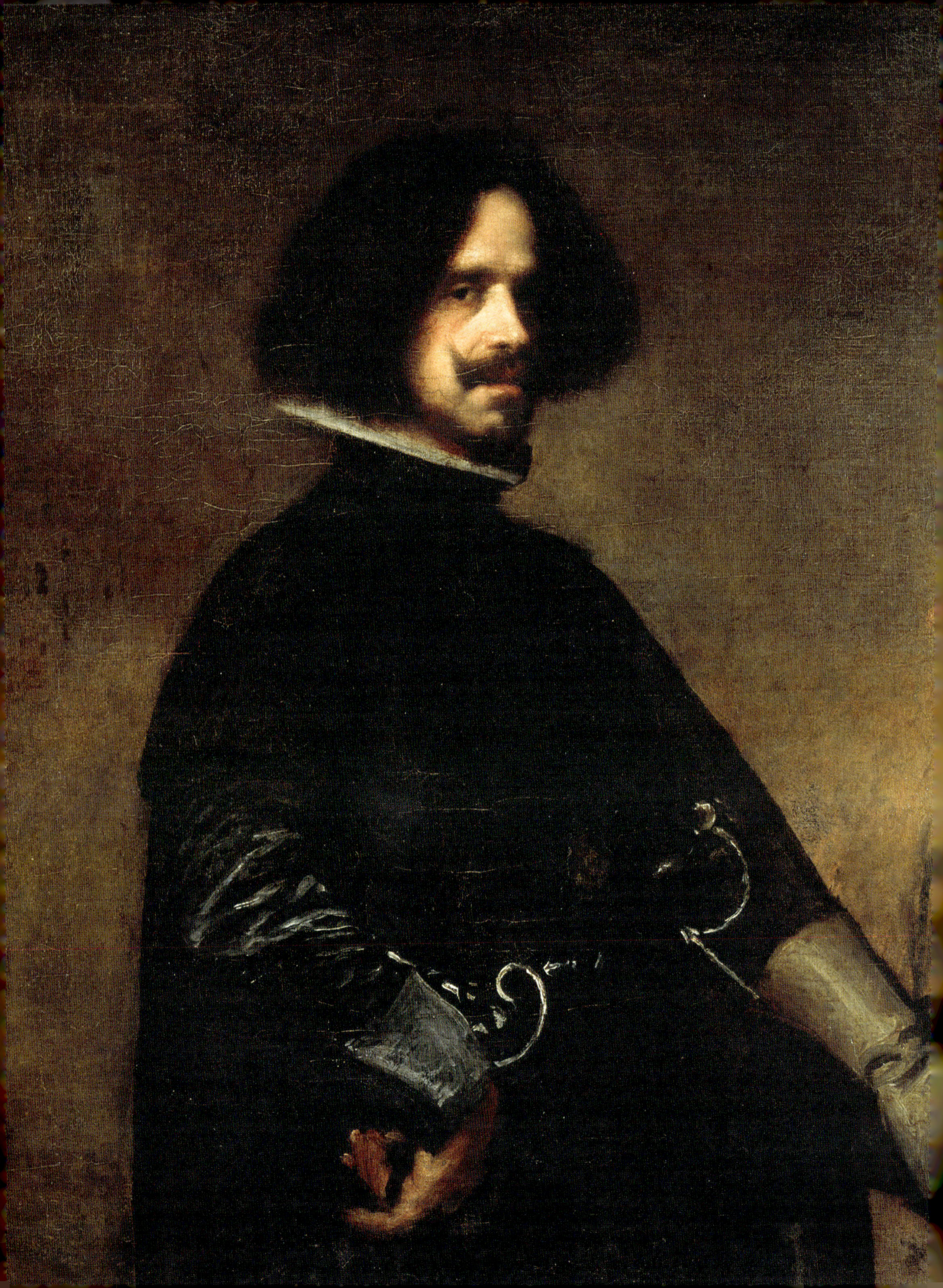

petition claiming his right to free lodging "such as his predecessors had and as some court artisans have today."[88] In theory, court employees were able to live rent-free in rooms that the Crown requisitioned in houses of a certain size, but the demand far exceeded the supply, and free housing was hard to come by. It is unclear whether or not Aguado's request was met. By 1640 the Crown had fallen so far behind in paying Aguado's salary that he was owed 36 months' worth of back pay.[89] That year, Spain's territorial integrity on the Iberian Peninsula splintered as the principality of Catalonia revolted against Castilian rule, and the Spanish viceroy was assassinated. Portugal, which had been part of the Spanish kingdoms since 1580, followed suit and deposed the Vicereine Margaret of Savoy, placing John, 8th Duke of Braganza on the throne as King John IV. "This year can undoubtedly be considered the most unfortunate that this Monarchy has ever experienced," the Count-Duke of Olivares wrote of 1640.[90]

The troubles of the Spanish monarchy reverberated throughout the Royal Palace. In 1640, staff in the king's household complained when they did not receive their annual suits of clothing for the second year in a row. But while cutbacks were affecting everyone else, Philip IV personally intervened to make sure that Miguel Soplillo, a longtime companion, received his annual allotment of clothes.[91] It was Soplillo who appeared so elegantly dressed in a richly decorated leather jerkin and wide ruff in the portrait of Philip that had been painted shortly before he ascended the throne (fig. 103). Soplillo was owed three suits—one each of velvet, grosgrain, and taffeta—and eight new shirts, all made to his measurements, every year.[92] In bad times, even more than in good ones, royal favor was displayed with gifts of clothing made by a royal tailor.

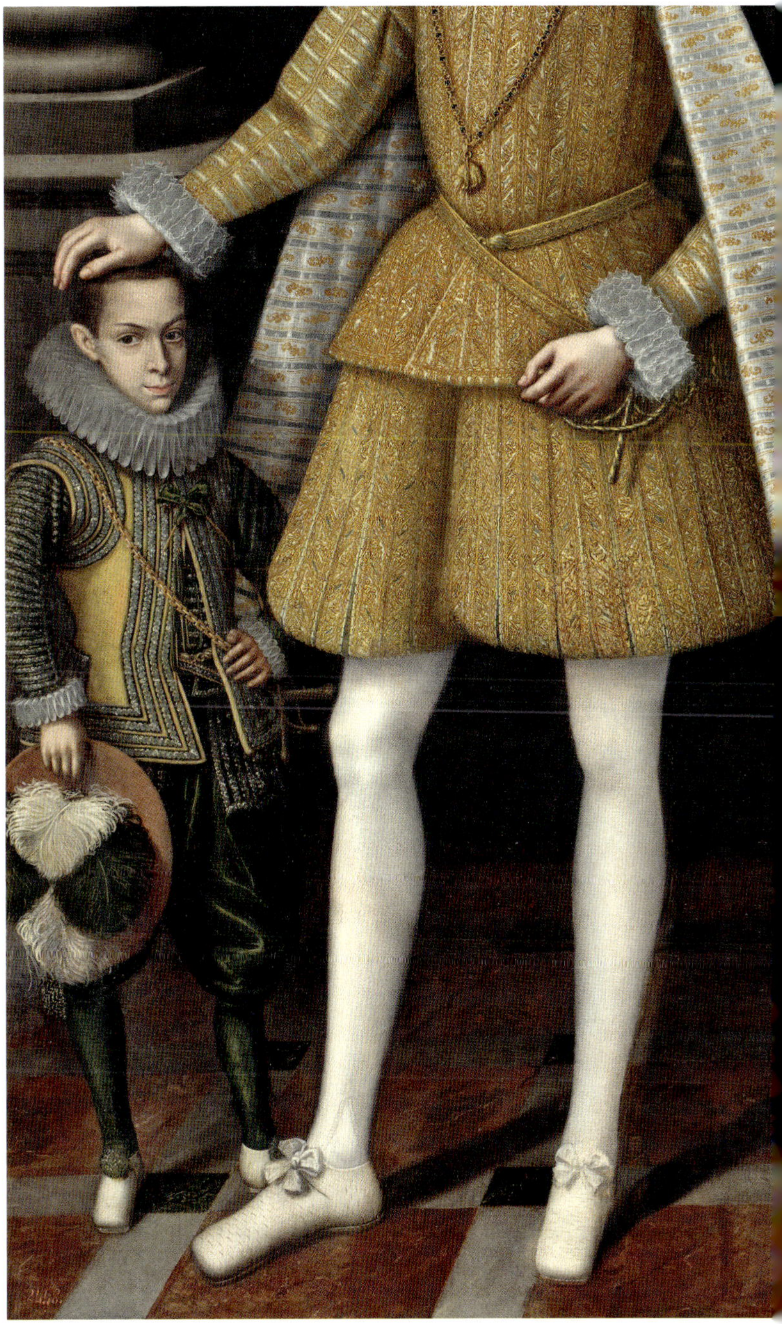

102. *(facing page)* After Diego Velázquez, *Self-Portrait*, c. 1645. Oil on canvas, 103.5 × 82.5 cm. Uffizi Gallery, Florence

103. *(above right)* Miguel Soplillo at the side of Prince Philip (detail of fig. 12)

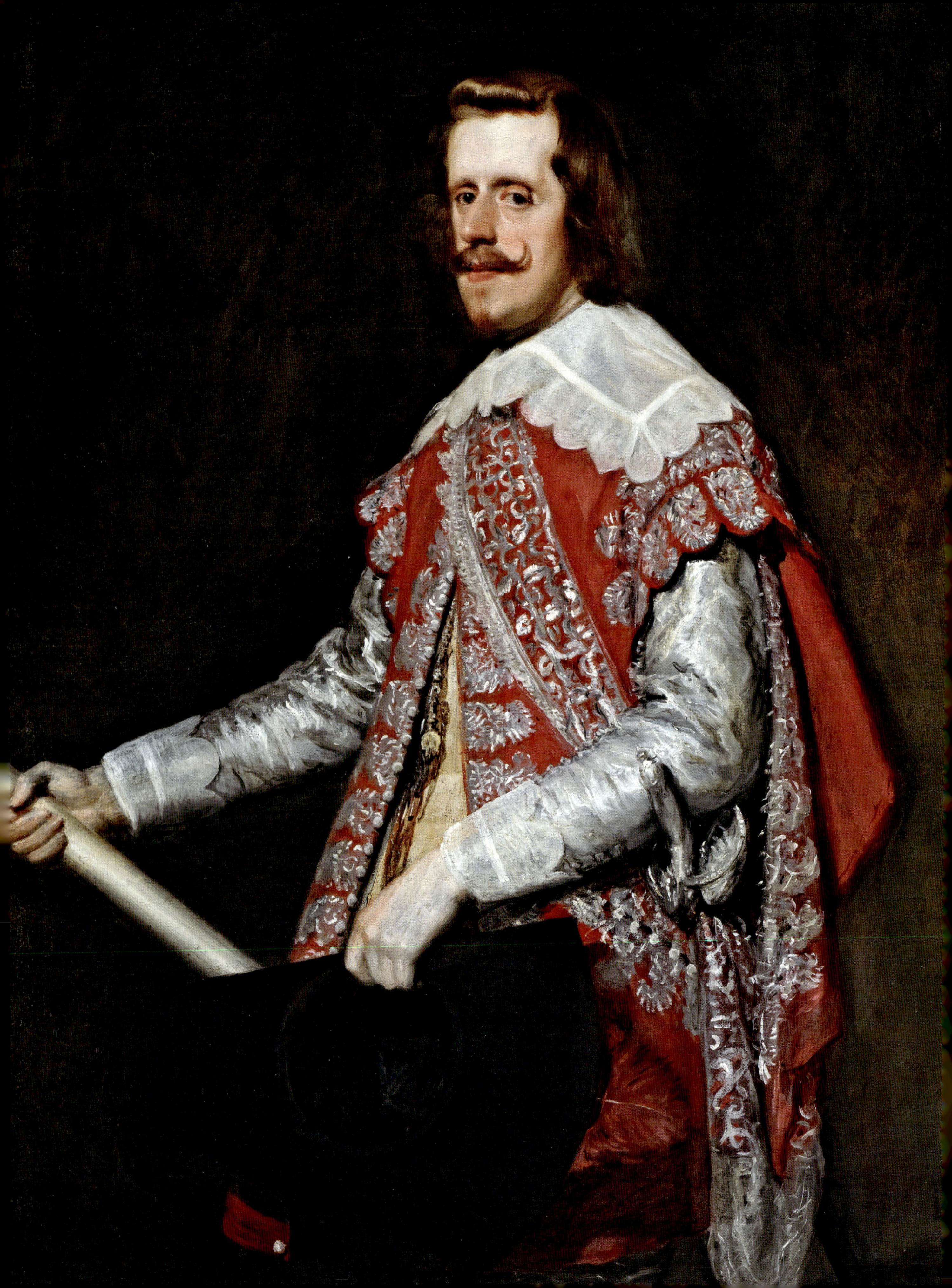

4. Interlude in Black

The Tumultuous 1640s

"It is imponderable just how good the King our Lord looked in a soldier's suit," fawned an anonymous admirer who saw Philip IV in person wearing the same red and silver campaign outfit that he modeled for Velázquez in 1644 (fig. 104).[1] This portrait of the king was painted in Fraga, on the border between Aragon and Catalonia, which had become the new front in Spain's war with France after the rebellious Catalans accepted French protection in January 1641 (see Map 1). The Catalan revolt gave Philip IV an opportunity to realize a long-held ambition to act—and dress—the part of commander in chief. In the Fraga portrait, the king wears a brilliant red cassock decorated with silver *alamares*.[2] The French-style cassock with long skirts is open beneath the sternum to reveal a yellow buff jerkin.[3] The king has abandoned his trademark *golilla* to wear a "campaign collar" (*valona de campaña*) trimmed with very fine Flemish lace.[4] Velázquez chose not to depict the details of Philip's collar, which was probably very similar to the one that King Christian IV of Denmark was wearing when he was wounded in a naval battle on July 1, 1644 (fig. 105).[5] As advertised by Philip IV's outfit in the Fraga painting, the Spanish king had joined the illustrious company of those monarchs who personally led their troops to war—although he remained on the Aragonese side of the border with Catalonia and never got too close to the fighting.

Philip IV was absent from Madrid during three campaigns in Aragon for a total of almost 22 months between April 1642 and October 1644. While the king was away, Queen Isabel was placed in charge of the government of Castile.[6] During the king's first campaign in 1642, the queen acquired a reputation for "great prudence, vigilance, and succor," in the words of the king's official chronicler, José Pellicer, who reported that Isabel had sold her own jewels in order to raise funds to form a new regiment in her name.[7] While the queen was winning plaudits at home, Philip IV's first military campaign ended in a disastrous defeat to French and Catalan troops outside of Lérida in October 1642.[8] The king returned to Madrid and forced his increasingly unpopular *privado*, the Count-Duke of Olivares, into retirement in January 1643, declaring that the queen was now his only advisor: "My *privado* is the Queen."[9] By this time, Mateo Aguado had served as the queen's *sastre de cámara* for over 12 years. Now he faced a new challenge: to dress a woman who held genuine power.[10]

104. *(facing page)* Diego Velázquez, *Philip IV in Fraga*, 1644. Oil on canvas, 129.9 × 99.4 cm. The Frick Collection, New York

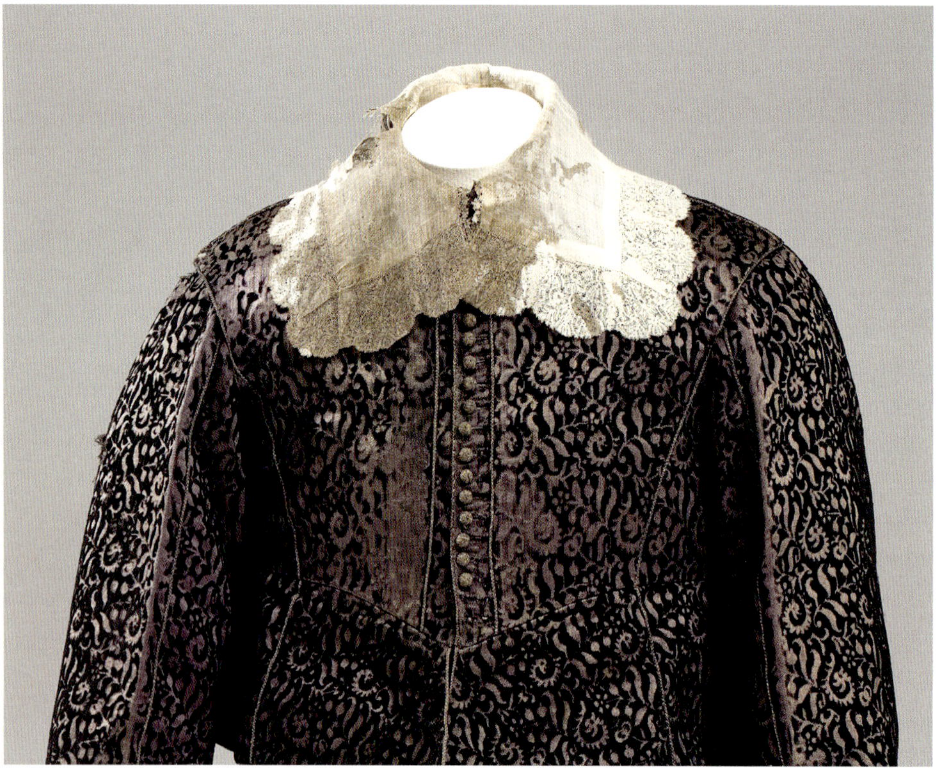

105. Christian IV's blood-stained collar, 1644. Falling collar in linen edged with bobbin lace. Rosenborg Castle, Copenhagen

Power Dressing

Aguado's accounts for the queen in the early 1640s have not been found, but the silk merchants' records provide enough information to reconstruct what Aguado made for her during these pivotal years. In keeping with her reputation for wartime austerity, Queen Isabel radically reduced spending on her wardrobe: the amount that she spent on materials from her silk merchants dropped more than 50 percent from 1642 to 1643.[11] In the later 1630s, Aguado had made the queen an average of 35 new dresses per year, but the silk merchants delivered materials for only 13 new dresses in 1643 (Table 1). That year, Isabel served as head of government during the king's absence between July 1 and mid-December.[12] The most notable feature of the queen's wardrobe during a year when she was governing is the predominance of black. The majority of her dresses in 1643 were made from black silk fabrics decorated exclusively with black trimmings. In previous years, Isabel had frequently worn black dresses, but they were usually decorated with silver or gold. The queen's monochrome black ensembles can be partially attributed to mourning for her brother, King Louis XIII of France, who died on May 14, 1643, but the silk merchant records reveal that the queen had been dressing all in black earlier in the year. Dressed entirely

Table 1: Dresses Made for Queen Isabel of Bourbon, 1643*	
Dress fabric and decoration	**Cost of materials**
Dress of black double borato from Valladolid, decorated with ribbons of black taffeta from Valencia	541 *reales*
Dress with a train of black wool-and-grass cloth (*herbax*) from Genoa decorated with taffeta edging	986 *reales*
Mourning dress of black wool	421 *reales*
Dress of black wool-and-grass cloth from Genoa with self-fabric decoration	699 *reales*
Dress of black patterned velvet with black satin from Florence for interlining, decoration, and buttons	463 *reales* [excludes the cost of the velvet, which was provided by the Keeper of the Jewels]
Dress of black ormuzine, embroidered in blue and silver	492 *reales* [excludes the cost of the embroidered silk, which was a gift from the Countess of Monterrey]
Dress of brown cloth of silver, decorated with silver lace and 40 dozen buttons made of black taffeta and silver; the doublet and sleeves embroidered with pieces of glass	760 *reales* [excludes the cost of the fabric, which was provided by the Keeper of the Jewels]
Dress and train of black veiling (*toca*) from Lyon, lined with black double taffeta from Valencia, decorated with trimmings made of black satin from Florence	2,403 *reales*
Over-gown and skirt of black baize from Seville with a doublet of black uncut velvet	633 *reales*
Dress of plain black velvet from Genoa with decorations made of black satin from Florence	1,362 *reales*
Dress of black and tan flowered satin, decorated with a border cut from voile	1,203 *reales*
Dress of silver and black plush, decorated with 349 meters of black, silver, and gold galloon; the doublet interlined with silver voile	2,886 *reales*
Dress of brown and black patterned velvet decorated with a border cut from heavy white voile	2,265 *reales*
* Source: AGP, AG, leg. 5253/1, silk merchants' accounts for Queen Isabel (1643)	

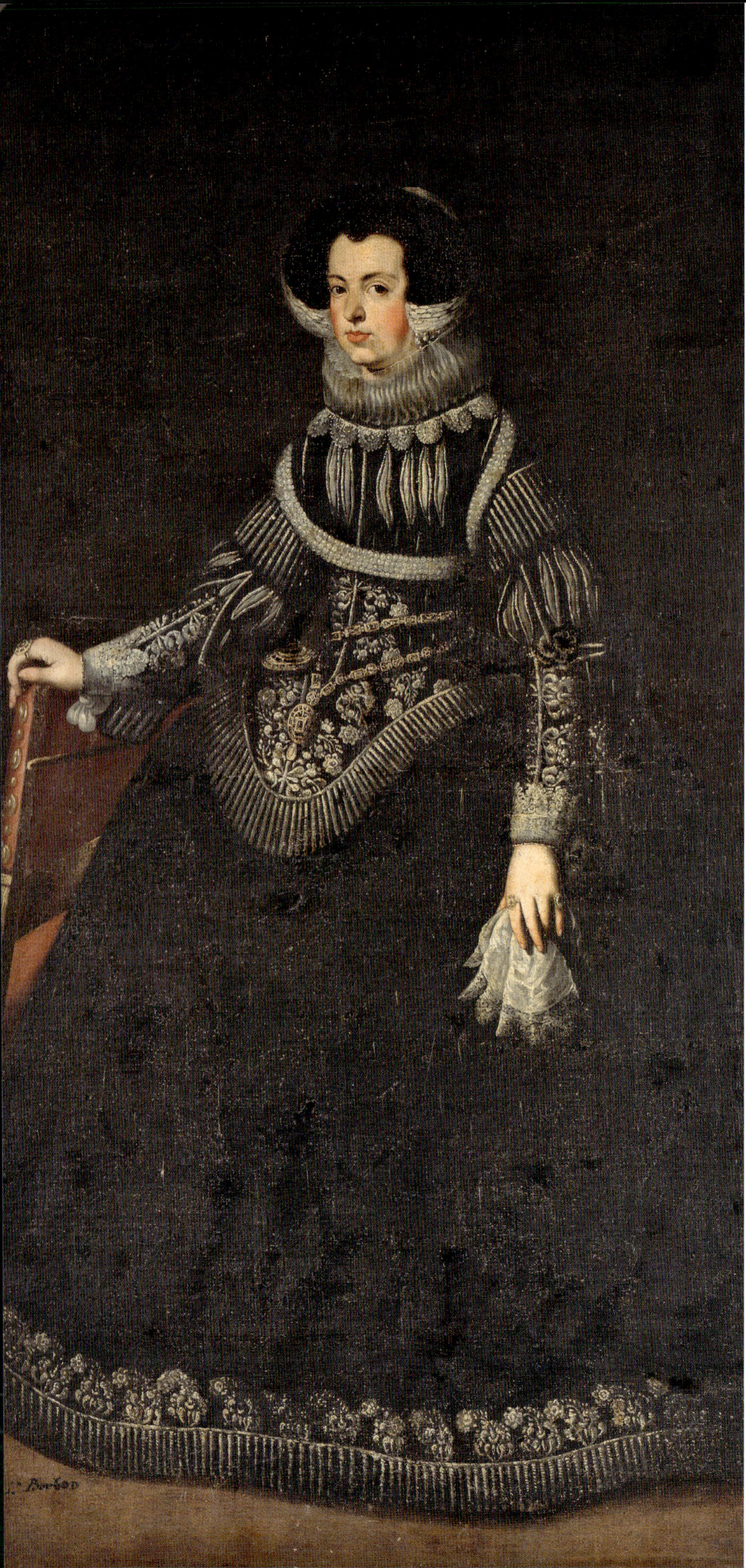

106. Unknown Spanish artist, *Queen Isabel of Bourbon in Black and Silver*, probably early 1640s. Oil on canvas, 210 × 108 cm. Museo Nacional del Prado, Madrid

107. *(facing page)* Attributed to Juan Bautista Martínez del Mazo, *Gathering of Gentlemen*, c. 1645–50. Oil on canvas, 47.2 × 77.9 cm. Musée du Louvre, Paris

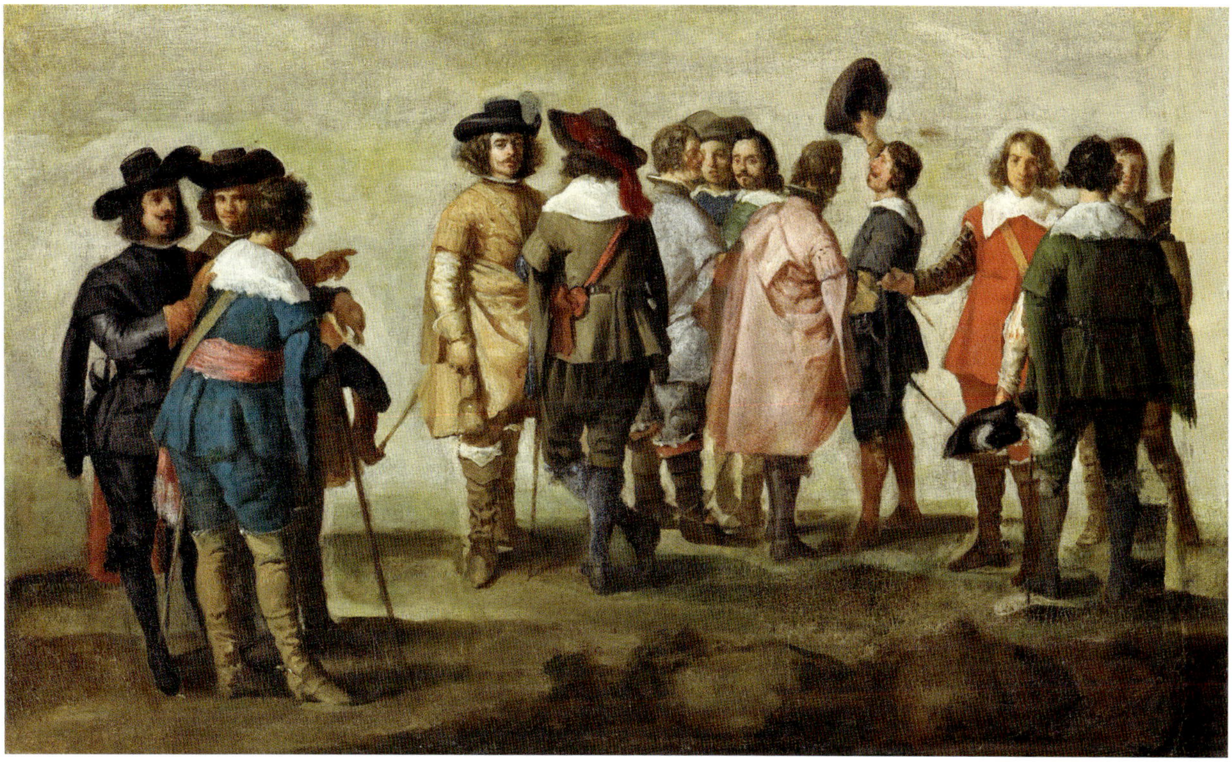

in black, Queen Isabel drew on a traditional association between black clothing and political power that dated back to the reign of Philip II and had been successfully appropriated by Philip IV at the start of his reign.[13] As head of government during a time of war, the queen demonstrated her seriousness, and her Spanishness, by wearing black dresses that projected power in the mold of the male rulers who came before her.

At the same time, Queen Isabel was using an exclusively feminine device to shape her new image: the *guardainfante*.[14] The ban on the *guardainfante*, which had been so dramatically enforced in the summer of 1639, had fallen by the wayside in the early 1640s. The first and only documented *guardainfante* that Diego López made for Queen Isabel was "a *guardainfante* of ribbons of crimson double taffeta" sometime between 1642 and 1644.[15] The silk merchant records for Isabel in the early 1640s reveal that the queen was still wearing old-fashioned *verdugados*, sometimes with "hips" and sometimes without. But portraits of the queen from this period invariably depict her with an exaggerated bell-shaped skirt that is clearly intended to suggest a *guardainfante* underneath. A portrait by an unknown artist depicts the queen with this dramatic silhouette in a dress that is an anthology of all of the military-style decorations that Aguado had incorporated into the queen's wardrobe in the 1630s (fig. 106). The embroidered bodice and sleeves are decorated with long vertical slashes with edges bound in silver and lined with white silk. Silver *alamares* with a floral design adorn the hem of her black skirt, which is decorated with subtle diagonal cuts all over its surface. The shoulder-wings have evolved into bona fide short sleeves, in keeping with trends in menswear (fig. 107).[16] Another portrait shows the queen

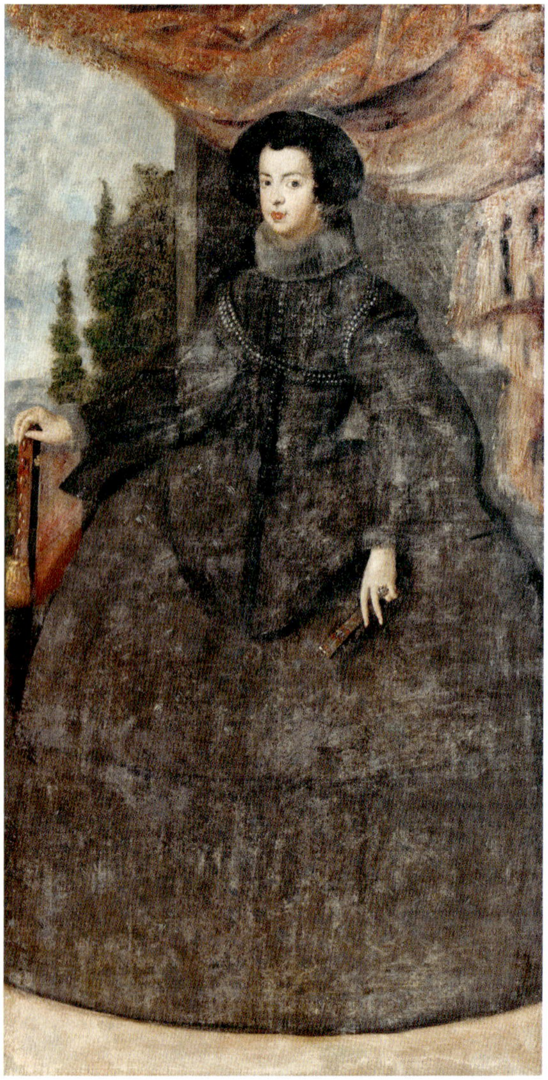

108. Unknown artist, *Queen Isabel of Bourbon*, probably early 1640s. Oil on canvas, 198.5 × 106 cm. Skokloster Castle, Sweden

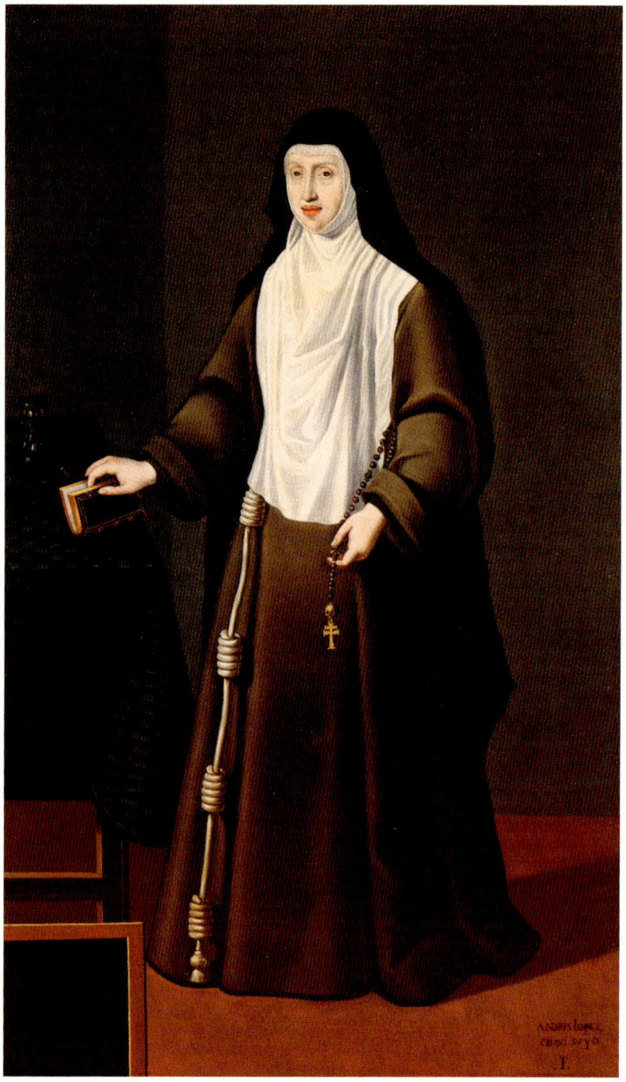

109. Andrés López Polanco, *Archduchess Margaret of Austria*, c. 1584. Oil on canvas, 163 × 91.5 cm. Kunsthistorisches Museum, Vienna

in a dark dress with an even more inflated hip (fig. 108). At the height of her power, Isabel of Bourbon was taking up more space than ever before.

There was a great celebration in Madrid on August 10, 1644, after the Spanish army recaptured Lérida from the French. Velázquez's lifelike portrait of Philip IV in his red and silver campaign outfit (see fig. 104) stood in as a substitute for the king during the festivities that took place at the Church of San Martín, where the painting was displayed beneath a rich canopy.[17] It was the last great celebration in Madrid for the next five years. The following month, Queen Isabel began to show the first signs of erysipelas, a skin infection that is also known as St. Anthony's Fire, named for the painful, fiery rash that it causes, which appeared on the queen's face, neck, and chest. She died on October 6, 1644, at age 41. The king, who had been at the front, was unable to make it back to Madrid to see the queen before she died. He described his grief in a letter to Sister María of Ágreda, the abbess of a convent he had visited during one of his journeys to Aragon, who had become a close spiritual advisor: "I lost in only one person everything that you can lose in this life."[18]

Isabel of Bourbon's wardrobe had changed with every milestone in her life, but one thing had remained constant, and that was the luxury of her clothes. After a lifetime of transitions, death brought the most radical clothing change of all. In keeping with Habsburg tradition, the queen was dressed for burial in the simple, ascetic habit of the Poor Clares, one of the Franciscan religious orders, whose nuns were known for their exceptional austerity. The habit of the Poor Clares was a long, loose dress of plain brown cloth that was worn with a coarse knotted rope around the waist and a white wimple around the face. This simple habit had been worn by the Archduchess Margaret of Austria after she took vows and joined the Poor Clares at the Convent of Las Descalzas Reales in 1584 (fig. 109).[19] Aguado's services were not required to make Isabel's burial habit, which was provided by the nuns at the royal convent.[20]

After Isabel was entombed in the Royal Pantheon of El Escorial, a great temporary monument called a catafalque was built in the Church of San Jerónimo to serve as the centerpiece of royal funeral rites that were held in her honor on November 17–18, 1644. Juan de Noort, a Flemish printmaker based in Madrid, preserved the memory of the painted wooden monument and its decorative program in a series of engravings that were included in a book describing the exequies at the Church of San Jerónimo (fig. 110). On the front of the monument, there was a painting of Philip IV and Isabel of Bourbon standing beneath the motto, "The Queen Stood at Your Right Hand" (fig. 111).[21] The king and queen appear in their respective wartime roles as military commander and head of government: he is dressed in half-armor accessorized with a sword, baton, and spurs, while she wears a *saya entera* with the elongated shoulder-wings and extended hip that characterized the queen's silhouette in the early 1640s. A printed portrait bust of the deceased queen, also by Noort, emphasizes the slashes on the breast of her bodice, which are meticulously detailed with the binding, decoration, and facing of each individual slash (fig. 112). The popular queen's funeral decorations, posthumous printed portraits, and published eulogies all presented her as a strong leader and a fierce defender of Spain.[22] These qualities had been projected by the clothing that Aguado designed for the queen while she lived and ruled, and they would be remembered through the details of her dress after her death.

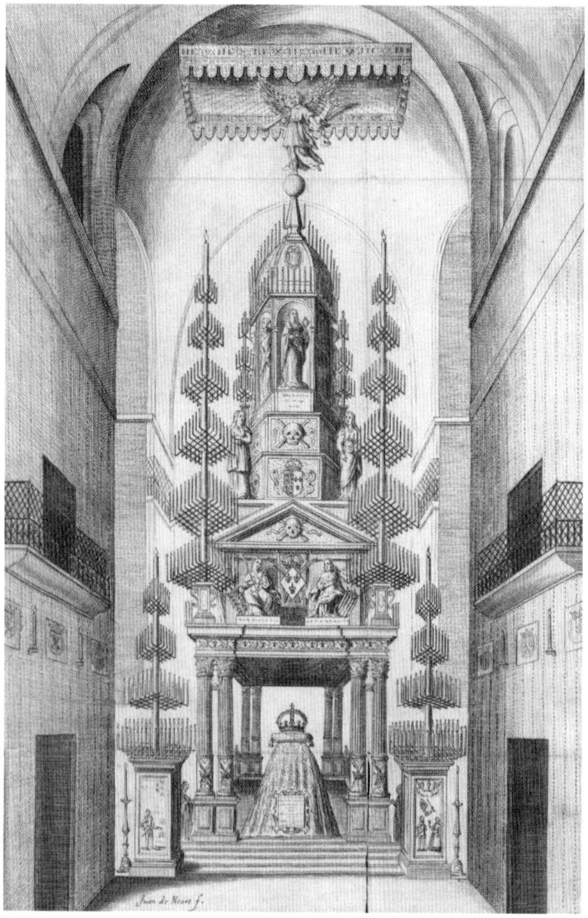

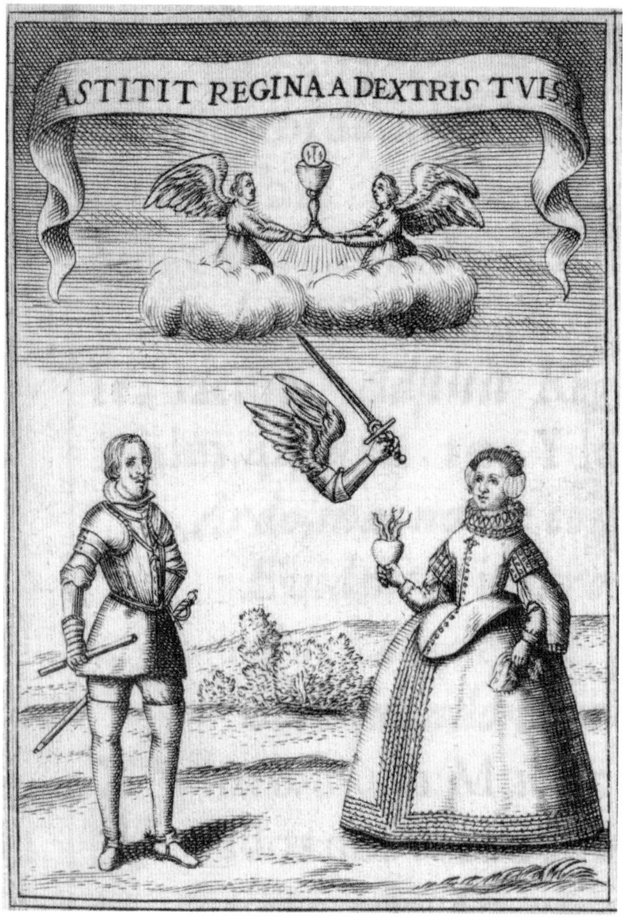

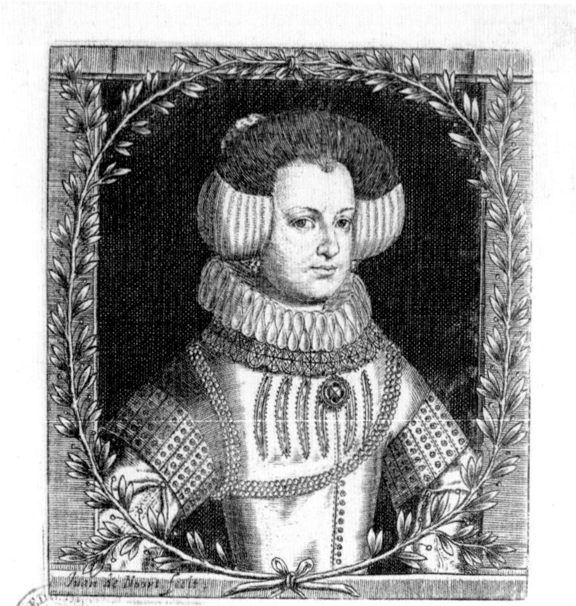

110. *(above left)* Juan de Noort, view of the catafalque for Isabel of Bourbon in the Church of San Jerónimo. *Pompa funeral…* (Madrid, 1645). Engraving, 35.5 × 23 cm. Biblioteca Nacional de España, Madrid

111. *(above right)* Attributed to Juan de Noort, "The Queen Stood at Your Right Hand." *Pompa funeral…* (Madrid, 1645). Engraving, 9 × 6.5 cm. Biblioteca Nacional de España, Madrid

112. *(left)* Juan de Noort, *Isabel of Bourbon*, c. 1644. Engraving, 9.9 × 8.9 cm. Biblioteca Nacional de España, Madrid

Madrid in Mourning

The local chronicler Gerónimo Gascón de Torquemada reported that the people of Madrid mourned Isabel of Bourbon in the streets by crying out and making great displays of grief for the queen whose talents for governing had been discovered in the king's absence.[23] For Aguado and his colleagues, there was no time to grieve: they were busy dressing the entire royal household in mourning (*luto*). Mourning dress had to be distinctive from everyday clothes in order to identify the bereaved and demonstrate their piety and grief.[24] At the Spanish court, mourning dress for men and women took the form of loose garments made from plain, dull black fabrics. These were usually woolens or wool-silk blends, such as baize and borato (*burato*), whose lack of luxury distinguished mourning from the usual dress of the court.

Aguado made a mourning dress called a *monjil* for the Infanta María Teresa, who had turned six just a few weeks before her mother's death. This was a loose-fitting, one-piece dress that typically was worn by widows and nuns.[25] The infanta's mourning dress was made from a lightweight wool blend called *filelí* and had long pointed sleeves, like a *saya entera*. Aguado also made the infanta a veil (*manto*) from very fine Neapolitan silk and a cloak decorated with silk galloon and lined with plush, everything in black.[26] Gaspar de Frutos, the long-serving tailor of the queen's stables, quickly produced mourning attire for the queen's footmen, coachmen, and their assistants, who were 40 in number. Those mourning outfits consisted of a doublet and breeches worn with a cloak and a *sotanilla*, which was a loose, calf-length soutane that buttoned down the front.[27] The mourning outfits for the queen's employees were made from black cloth lined with baize, and they lacked any decoration except for functional buttons.[28]

When a member of the general public died, there were laws that limited the kind of mourning dress that could be worn, who could wear it, and for how long.[29] These rules did not apply to deaths in the royal family, and the books of etiquette that governed the king's and queen's households were silent on the matter. When Queen Margaret of Austria had died in 1611, King Philip III and his children wore mourning dress for a year, although they made exceptions for special occasions (for example, they changed out of mourning dress to honor the French ambassador who came to Madrid to finalize the marriage between Louis XIII and Anne of Austria).[30] To mark the one-year anniversary of Queen Isabel's death on October 6, 1645, Aguado made new mourning suits for the king and for Prince Baltasar Carlos as a gift from the infanta. For the king, Aguado made a cloak and *sotanilla* of black baize with sleeves of uncut black velvet and breeches of the same, and a jerkin (*coleto*) of cordovan leather embroidered with gray silk and silver. The outfit that he made for the prince was identical, except that the jerkin was embroidered with silver and blue silk.[31] The use of decorative embroidery, metal thread, and colors other than black marked the end of deep mourning, but the loose *sotanillas* distinguished these outfits from the fitted black clothes that the king and prince—now all grown up—usually wore (fig. 113).

The Infanta María Teresa dressed exclusively in black until mid-March 1645, when Aguado began to incorporate some subdued color and sparkle into her wardrobe (see the 1640s in the Chronology of Women's Dress, pp. 216–17). He made her two striped dresses, one black and silver and the other black and tan, and a blue silk dress with black and blue trimming.[32] During this less austere phase of mourning, Juan Bautista Martínez del Mazo painted a portrait of the infanta wearing a black and silver dress (fig. 114). This may be the dress

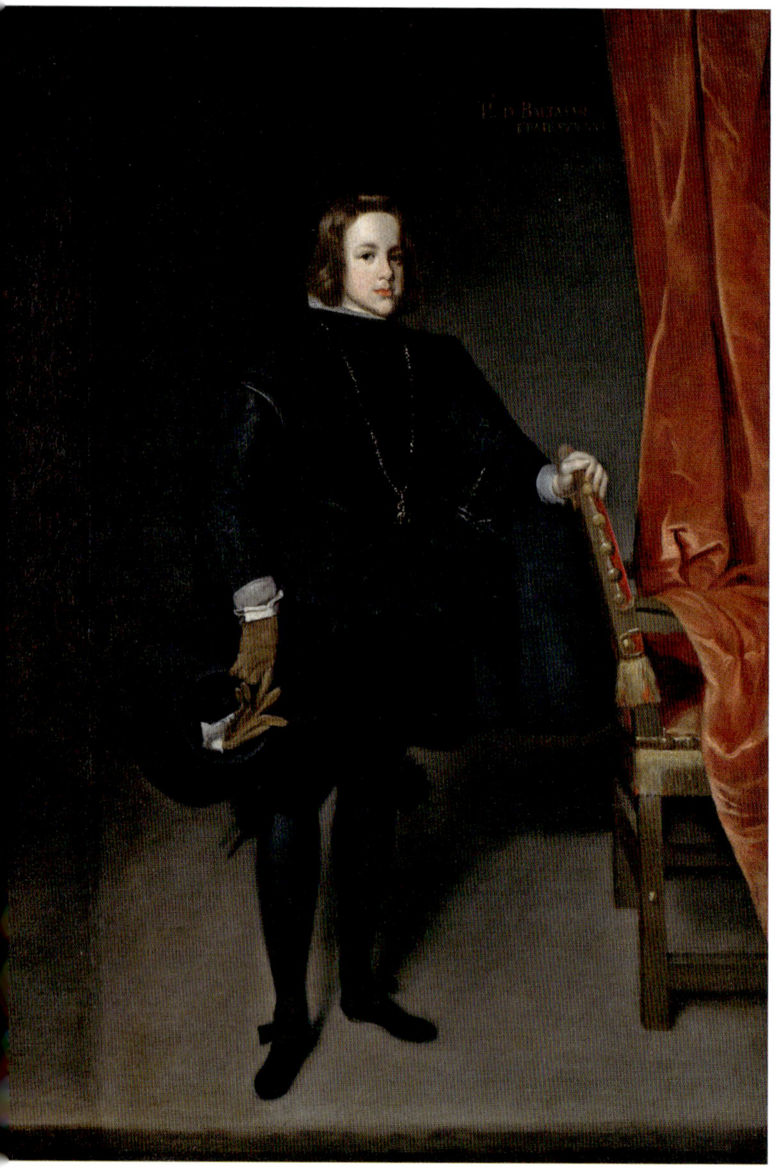

113. Juan Bautista Martínez del Mazo, *Prince Baltasar Carlos*, 1645. Oil on canvas, 209 × 144 cm. Museo Nacional del Prado, Madrid

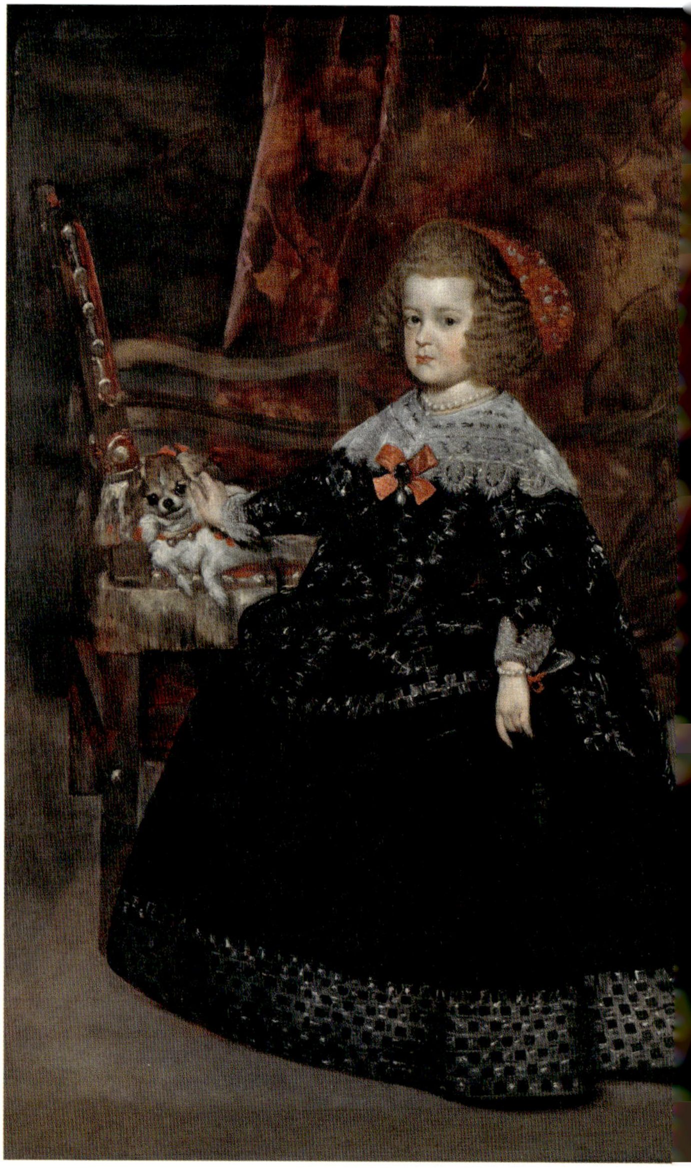

114. Juan Bautista Martínez del Mazo, *Infanta María Teresa*, c. 1645–6. Oil on canvas, 148 × 102.9 cm. The Metropolitan Museum of Art, New York

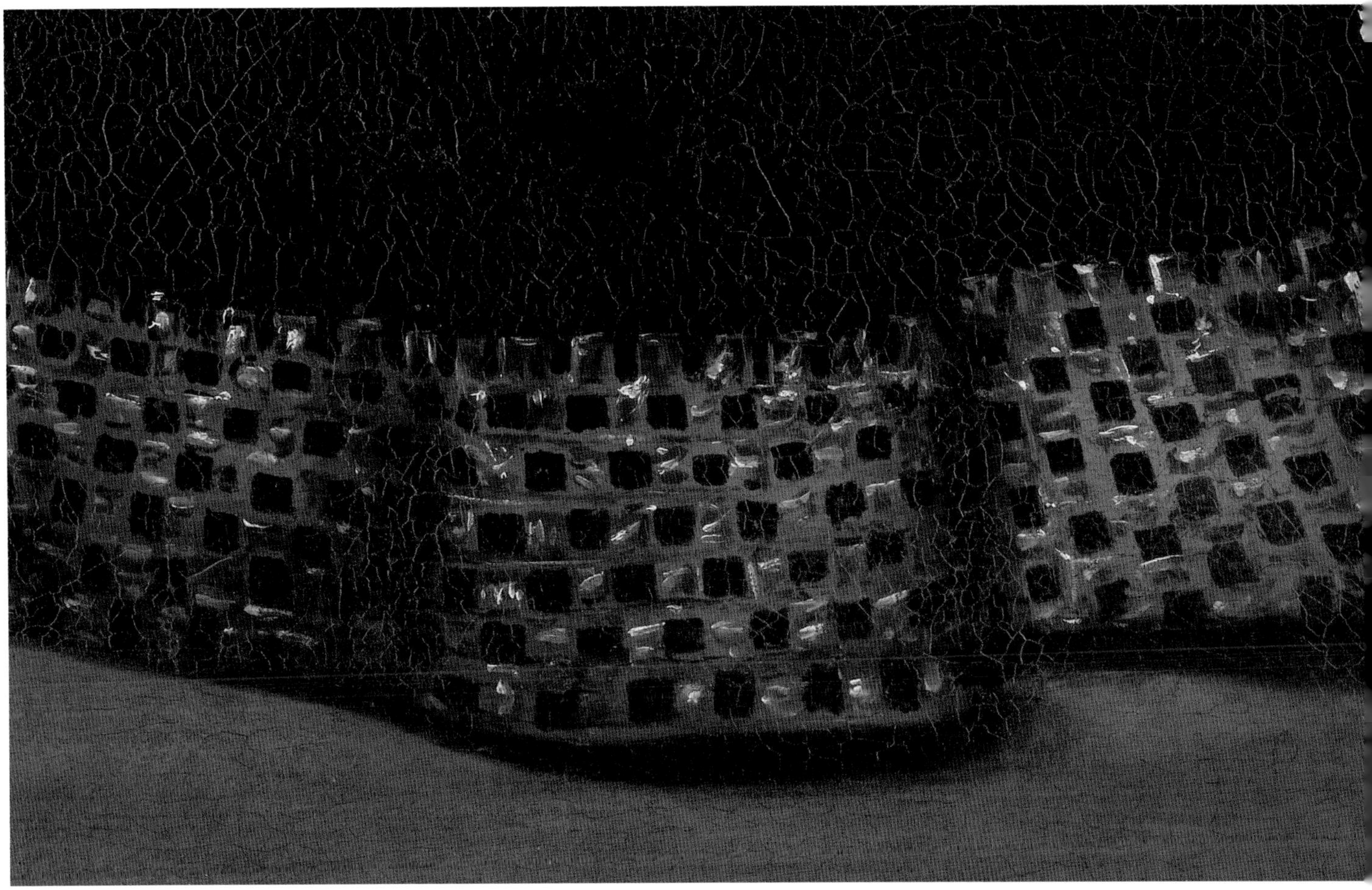

115. Detail of the infanta's skirt in fig. 114

that Aguado made in early January 1646 with "plain black velvet embroidered with silver in squares" that was given to the infanta by Inés de Zúñiga y Velasco, Countess of Olivares.[33] The infanta's former governess had retired to a convent following the death of her disgraced husband, the Count-Duke of Olivares, in the summer of 1645. Fabric embroidered with silver squares was unusual; there is nothing like it anywhere else in Aguado's accounts. In the portrait of the infanta, silver squares form a deep border at the hem of her skirt (fig. 115). They also outline the contours of her bodice and its skirts to create the illusion of a narrow waist and wide hips—womanly curves far beyond the infanta's years. Now age seven, with her mother gone, the Infanta María Teresa had become the head of her own household and Aguado's primary patron.

Dressing the Queenless Court

After the queen's death, Aguado remained on the payroll as *sastre de cámara* to the Infanta María Teresa. There were 41 *oficiales de manos* in the infanta's household, among them the hatmaker Gaspar Ruiz (Aguado's father-in-law), the farthingale-maker Diego López, and the embroiderer Jerónimo de Negrilla.[34] Aguado was also *sastre de cámara* to Prince Baltasar Carlos, who had established his own household in June 1643, but this position did not come with annual wages.[35] Before her death, the queen had favored Aguado with an additional appointment as a mounted palace guard. He began to occupy this position in early 1645.[36] Presumably this was a purely honorary post—the busy royal tailor surely had no time to fulfill its duties. It came with a monthly stipend of 60 *reales* and, perhaps even more importantly, a suit of yellow livery, which was an exceptional honor for an artisan.[37] For Aguado, who had been given multiple positions at court as a sign of the queen's favor, Isabel of Bourbon's death proved to be financially devastating.

At the time of her death, the queen owed Aguado close to 65,000 *reales*. In September 1645 the queen's treasurer paid Aguado approximately 3,000 *reales* in cash and the remainder of the debt in jewelry, loose diamonds and pearls of varying size and quality, and silverwork from the queen's collection.[38] The queen's *oficiales de manos* collectively complained that the items they received had been grossly overvalued, and they were subsequently given additional goods to compensate for the debts owed to them. In this second round of payments, Aguado received, among other things, three gilded silver figures of men with arquebuses on enameled pedestals.[39] These objets d'art were not sentimental gifts. Aguado likely sold the gilded arquebusiers, which were not among the possessions that were inventoried after his death in 1672.[40]

Aguado's workload declined precipitously after the queen's death, and so did his income. In June 1646 he unsuccessfully petitioned to be released from his long-standing obligation to pay an annual stipend to Francisco de Soria's widow, Mariana Núñez, whom he pointedly noted was "very wealthy and without children."[41] Aguado's financial situation became even more precarious that fall when the Crown, in an attempt to reduce its household expenses, issued a new rule forbidding employees from drawing more than one salary.[42] Aguado received two salaries—one as tailor to the Infanta María Teresa and another as a mounted guard—and was supposed to give up one of them. He tried to get around this by asking to have his tailor's salary given to Soria's widow so that he could keep the second salary.[43] In the end, Aguado was permitted to keep both salaries, but his obligation to pay Mariana Núñez proved to be a lengthy commitment, since she lived until 1671.[44]

Queen Isabel's death destabilized the entire fashion system, which depended on a royal role model for other women to follow. Influential figures who had the king's ear seized upon the sudden vacuum in women's fashion as an opportunity to enact major dress reforms. One was Sister María of Ágreda, the Franciscan abbess who served as the king's spiritual advisor. Famous for "bilocating" and converting indigenous communities in North America without ever leaving her convent in Spain, Sister María of Ágreda was recognized by the brilliant blue cloak of her Conceptionist Order. Time has turned Sister María of Ágreda's blue cloak black in a portrait at the Convent of Las Descalzas Reales, but the image clearly shows the rest of her habit, which consisted of a white wool tunic belted with a rustic rope and worn with a long rectangular scapular (*escapulario*) (fig. 116). Ever since her correspondence with Philip IV began in 1643, the nun had been pressing the king to reform women's dress.[45] When the king turned to Sister María of Ágreda for consolation after his wife's death, she responded by writing him a letter recounting a vision in which the queen had appeared to her from the fiery cavern of purgatory "dressed with the courtly finery and *guardainfantes* that ladies wear, but all of it was a flame of fire." Skirts ablaze, the queen begged the nun to convince the king to use all his power to stop "such profane dresses" in his kingdoms, the nun told him.[46]

The king was also being urged to reform women's dress by Juan Chumacero, president of the Council of Castile, who had been advocating dress reform ever since he took office in March 1643. While the queen was still alive, Chumacero entreated Philip IV to eliminate "foreign and enemy" influences (by which he meant all things French) and return to a native Spanish style. He argued that this would only be possible if the queen and her ladies set an example at the Royal Palace.[47] After the queen's death in October 1644, Chumacero stepped up his campaign. Before the year was over, he wrote to the king imploring him to crack down on low-cut bodices that were "revealing to everyone that which used to be left to the husbands."[48] Unhappy with his lack of progress with the king, in March 1645 Chumacero wrote to the superiors of all the religious orders in Spain instructing them to denounce the low-cut bodice (*escotado*) from the pulpit.[49] Following instructions, one Jesuit priest exhorted the women of Zaragoza to renounce "scandalous nudity" and to dress instead like a local devotional image of the Virgin Mary known as Our Lady of the Pillar, "with a dress buttoned up to her neck." "Who in their right mind would rather imitate the dress of some crazy actress than that of the most holy Virgin?" the preacher asked.[50]

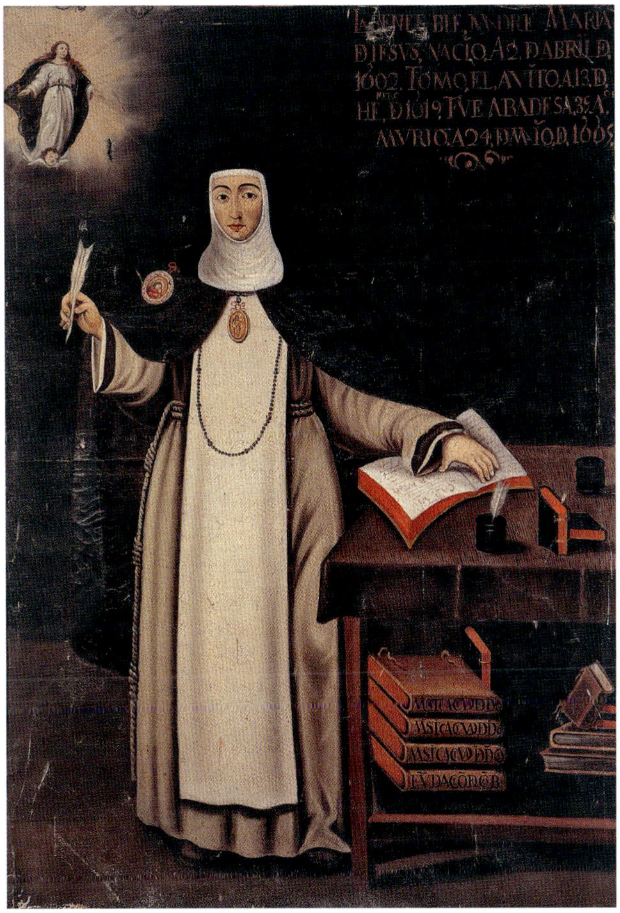

116. Unknown Spanish artist, *Venerable Mother Maria Jesus de Ágreda*, second half of 17th century. Oil on canvas, 202 × 142 cm. Convent of Las Descalzas Reales, Madrid

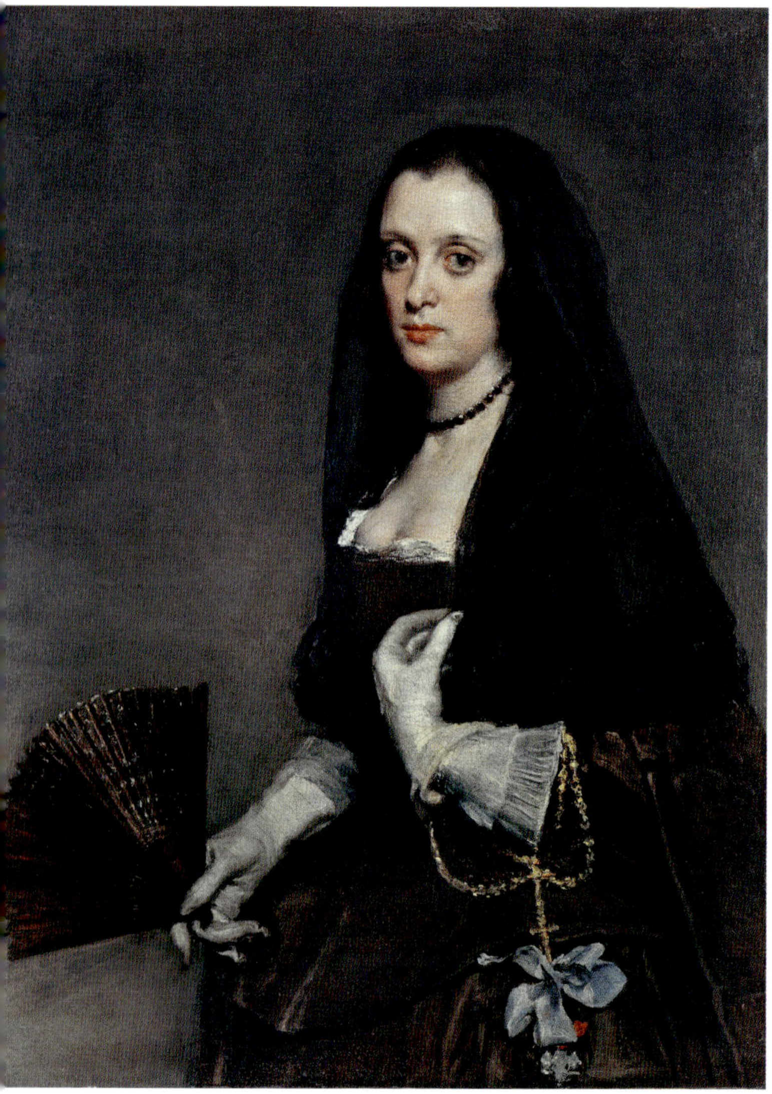

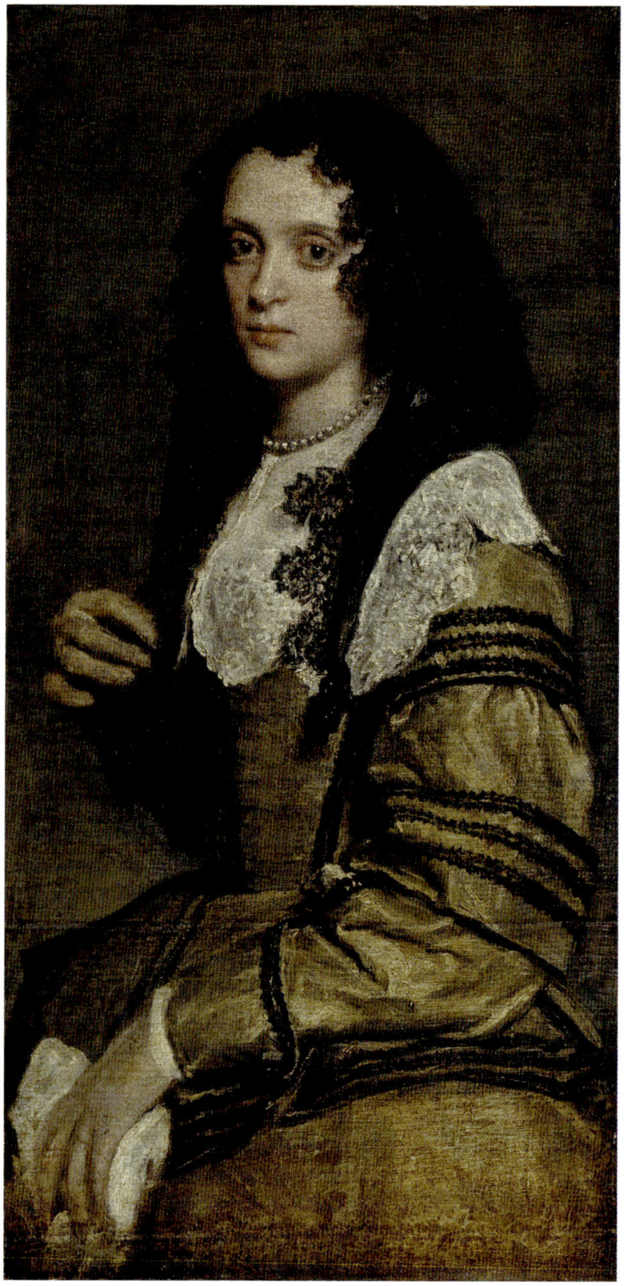

117. Diego Velázquez, *The Lady with a Fan*, probably 1640s. Oil on canvas, 95 × 70 cm. Wallace Collection, London

118. *(right)* Attributed to Diego Velázquez, *Lady in a Mantilla*, probably 1640s. Oil on canvas, 97.8 × 48 cm. Chatsworth House, Derbyshire

The contrast that the Jesuit preacher in Zaragoza described is well-illustrated by a pair of paintings with an ambiguous relationship to one another: Velázquez's *Lady with a Fan* (fig. 117), who wears a bodice with very deep décolletage, and her modestly covered-up counterpart, the *Lady in a Mantilla* (fig. 118), whose white linen and lace collar goes up to the base of her neck.[51] While these two well-known paintings represent the extremes of scandalous nudity and virginal decorum, other images from the 1640s depict Spanish women wearing necklines that fall somewhere in between. The wife of Juan González Barrio, a resident of Salamanca who commissioned an illuminated family portrait in his 1648 letters patent of nobility, wears a lace collar with a neckline just at or below her clavicle (fig. 119). According to an Italian Jesuit named Alberto Alberti, a neckline one finger-width below the throat was not sinful, but two or three fingers below was very dangerous.[52]

The efforts to reform women's dress bore fruit in the spring of 1646 with a royal decree that banned low-cut bodices. The delicate raw silk stockings (*medias de pelo*) that were popular among men at court were also outlawed. On April 9 the elected officials of the relevant guilds—tailors, doublet-makers, and clothing merchants—were instructed to ensure that all their members complied with the law by making women's bodices "up to the throat, in front as well as in the back." Anyone caught making or selling *escotados* or *medias de pelo* faced a harsh punishment: he would be sent off to serve two campaigns in one of the wars that Spain was fighting.[53] Also that spring, the public theaters of Madrid—which had reopened only recently after closing in mourning for Queen Isabel—were permanently shut down. Chumacero had been pressing Philip IV for years to close the theaters, which he argued contributed to the "invention and profanity of apparel."[54]

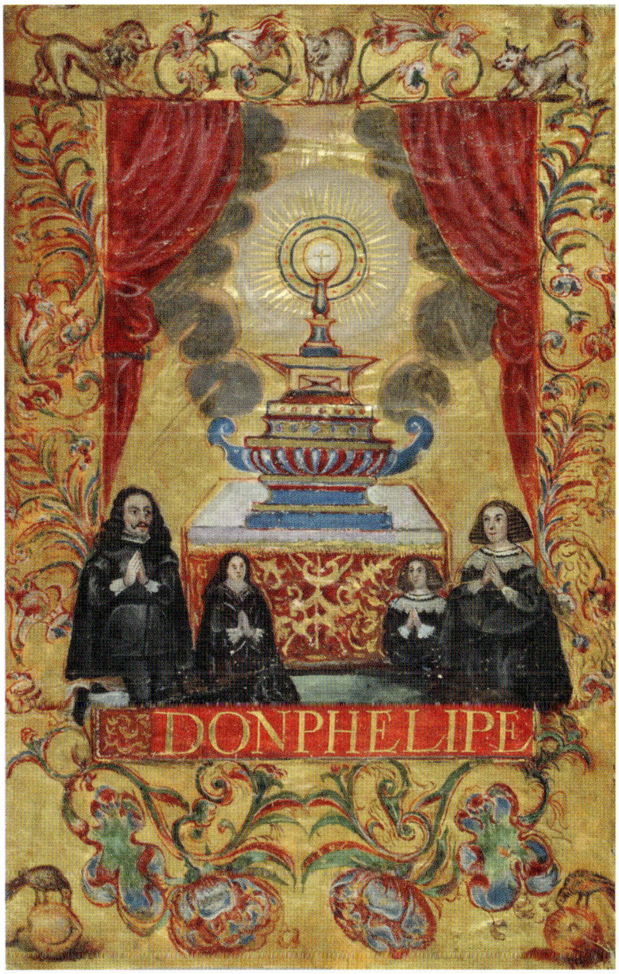

119. *Letters Patent of Nobility of Juan González Barrio, Resident of Salamanca*, Valladolid, 1648. Illumination on parchment, 33 × 23 cm. Museo Lázaro Galdiano, Madrid

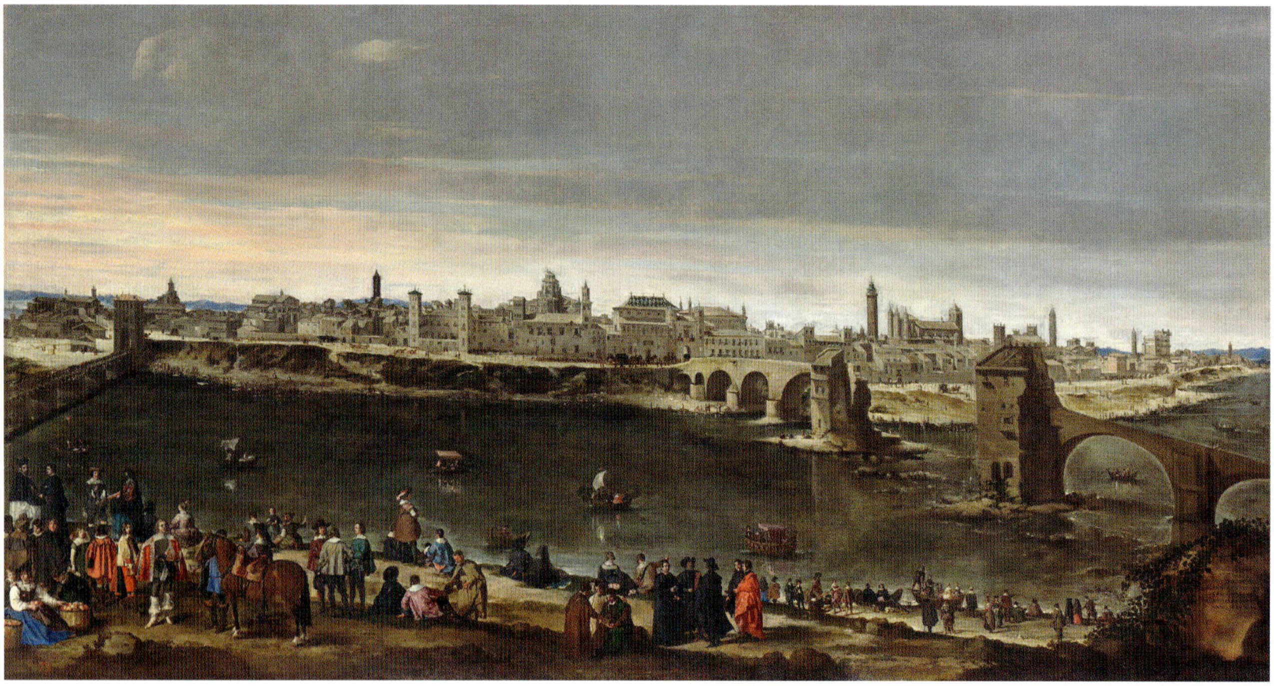

120. Juan Bautista Martínez del Mazo, *View of Zaragoza*, 1647. Oil on canvas, 181 × 331 cm. Museo Nacional del Prado, Madrid

The king was ambivalent about this, since he believed that the theater served a useful purpose by distracting the people during troubled times. Nonetheless, he conceded victory to the "zealous persons," as he called them.[55]

While dress reform was being implemented in Madrid in mid-April 1646, the king set off on his fifth journey to Aragon. This time he took Prince Baltasar Carlos with him. The 16-year-old prince commissioned Juan Bautista Martínez del Mazo to paint a view of Zaragoza, which had become like a second Spanish capital thanks to the king's frequent presence there in the 1640s (fig. 120). On the left-hand side of the view, a dashing gentleman wearing an eye-catching crimson cloak trimmed with silver stands out from the multitudes on the riverbank. This is thought to be the prince himself who, like his father, dressed in military style while on campaign.[56] Before the painting was finished, the prince fell ill with smallpox and died on October 9, 1646.[57] The weapons and clothing that the prince had taken on the journey were packed into chests and sent back to Madrid. The inventory includes a doublet made from walnut-brown silk embroidered with silver memory rings—perhaps a reminder of his mother and her dress made from the brown and silver brocaded fabric that he had given her (see Chapter 2, pp. 81–2).

The prince's trunks also contained several suits that had been cut out of fine English wool but had not been finished before their owner's life was unexpectedly cut short.[58] The death of Baltasar Carlos threw the future of the Spanish monarchy into question. The Infanta María Teresa became heir to the throne, and the widower King Philip IV now needed to remarry in order to produce another son (preferably more than one). The king's plans to marry again sounded the death knell for dress reform and unexpectedly revived Aguado's career.

The Return of Gala Dress

Shortly before his death, Baltasar Carlos had been engaged to his first cousin, the Archduchess Mariana of Austria. She was the daughter of Philip IV's sister María Ana, who had become Holy Roman Empress in 1637. After the empress died at age 39 on May 13, 1646, her daughter's marriage to Baltasar Carlos was arranged to maintain strong ties between the Spanish and Austrian branches of the House of Habsburg.[59] During their short-lived engagement, Aguado made a dress and petticoats for the 11-year-old archduchess and a garment bag (*tafetán*) in which to transport them to Austria. Shortly after, when Baltasar Carlos died, Aguado made a black *monjil* and a veil of very fine, deep black silk (*manto de humo*) for Mariana to mourn her fiancé.[60] Mariana's father, the Emperor Ferdinand III, offered her hand in marriage to her 41-year-old uncle Philip IV in his condolence letter to the Spanish king after the death of his son. Full-length portraits of Mariana, including one of her dressed in mourning, were sent to Madrid in order to calm concerns at the court that the very young and physically slight archduchess might not be able to produce an heir to the Spanish throne (fig. 121).[61] After

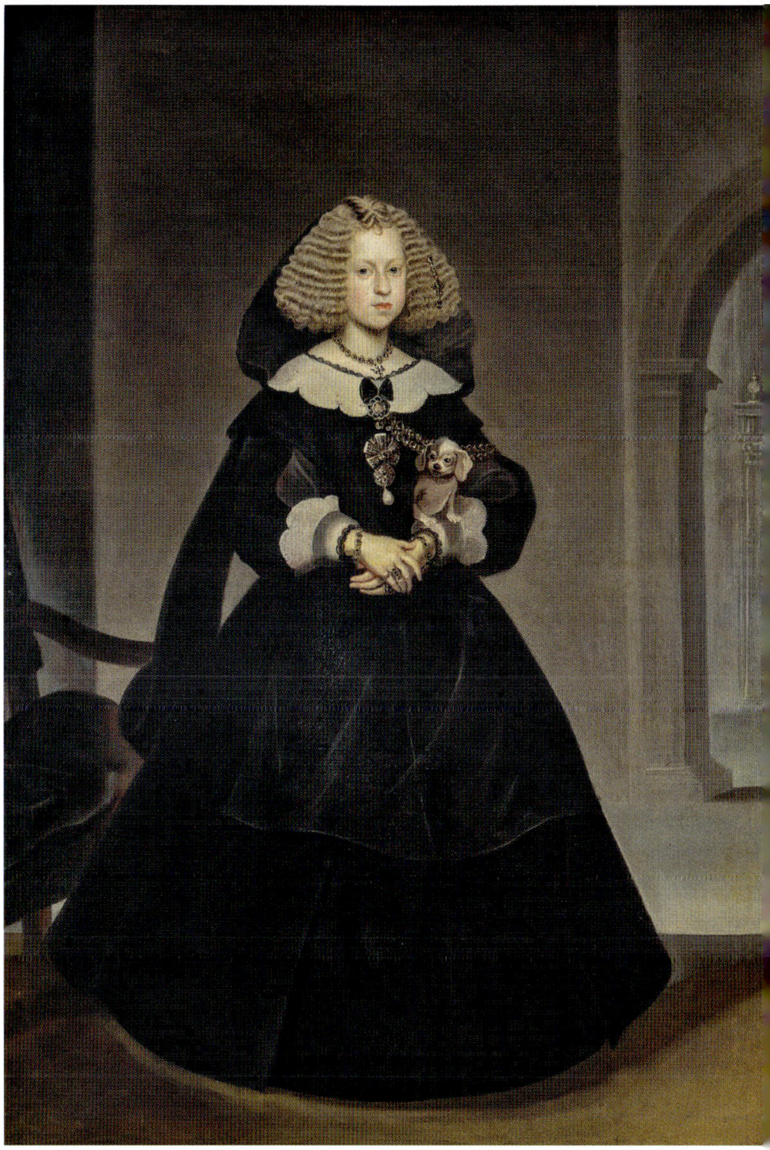

121. Frans Luyckx, *Archduchess Mariana of Austria*, mid-17th century. Oil on canvas, 174 × 126 cm. Museo Nacional del Prado, Madrid

so much death and mourning, the king's engagement was a cause for celebration, which launched a cautious return to the splendid festive attire that was known as "gala" dress.

Philip IV typically dressed for special events in black or walnut-brown silk encrusted with silver or gold decoration, of which Velázquez's *Philip IV in Brown and Silver* is the most famous representation (see fig. 25). A lesser and less well-known portrait of 1634, which was made for a series of paintings of the kings of Aragon for the Buen Retiro Palace, meticulously represents the decorations of another gala suit embroidered all over with black glass and gold (fig. 122).[62] The king renounced gala dress as inappropriate following the deaths of his wife and son. When the Infanta María Teresa gave him a "very splendid suit" with a doublet adorned with gold and steel sequins for his forty-second birthday in April 1647, the king refused to wear it "because it seemed to him that it was more elegant than the mourning for his son and wife demanded," according to a Jesuit at court.[63] The king sought a middle ground of finery "with great restraint" when the Spanish court celebrated his engagement to Mariana on August 3, 1647. Mourning was lifted for the occasion, but only modest colors like walnut- or chestnut-brown could be worn. Gold decorations and embroidery were forbidden, which meant that the Marquess of Aguilar was unable to wear his famous suit so heavy with embroidery that two men could not lift it off the floor. The king himself appeared at the engagement celebration as a paragon of restrained gala in black taffeta that was slashed to reveal dark brown taffeta underneath.[64]

In the months that followed the celebration of the king's engagement, Sister María of Ágreda continued to write to Philip IV encouraging him to curb "profanity" in dress.[65] But the king, who had never been fully committed to the cause, brought a definitive end to dress reform in July 1648. After the signing of the Treaty of Münster, all Madrid celebrated the end of the Thirty Years' War and peace with the Dutch Republic with three days of public festivities. There was a bullfight on July 4 at the Plaza Mayor, where titled noblemen mounted on horseback were each accompanied by a hundred lackeys dressed in brilliant livery.[66] Later that month, Philip IV dismissed Juan Chumacero from his position as president of Castile. Around the same time, Sister María of Ágreda retreated from political topics to focus on things spiritual in her correspondence with the king.[67]

Full gala dress resumed at the court in the final month of 1648. On December 15, news reached Madrid that Philip IV's marriage to Mariana had been carried out by proxy on November 8 at the imperial court. "All the court was filled with joy" to see the king celebrating, "dressed in a fabric from Italy, all embroidered with gold and steel," according to a printed *relación*.[68] Mariana had begun her journey "from the nest in Vienna," as Spanish court poet Gabriel Bocángel y Unzueta put it, "to the sun of Castile."[69] Awaiting the new queen's arrival, the Spanish court celebrated Mariana's fourteenth birthday on December 24 with a performance at the Royal Palace of a new play by Bocángel y Unzueta, even though the ban on the theater had not yet been lifted. The Infanta María Teresa, now ten years old, took center stage dressed in a costume of white voile decorated with gold flowers and embroidered with diamonds and pearls, while her ladies shone in metallic silks of pink, blue, orange, and red.[70] The sea of black had parted and color returned to the court. The years after the death of Queen Isabel had been a bleak interlude in Mateo Aguado's career, but with a new queen on her way to Spain, the curtain was raised for the tailor to begin his next act.

122. *(facing page)* Unknown artist, *Philip IV in Gala Dress*, 1634. Oil on canvas, 224 × 127 cm. Museo Nacional del Prado, Madrid

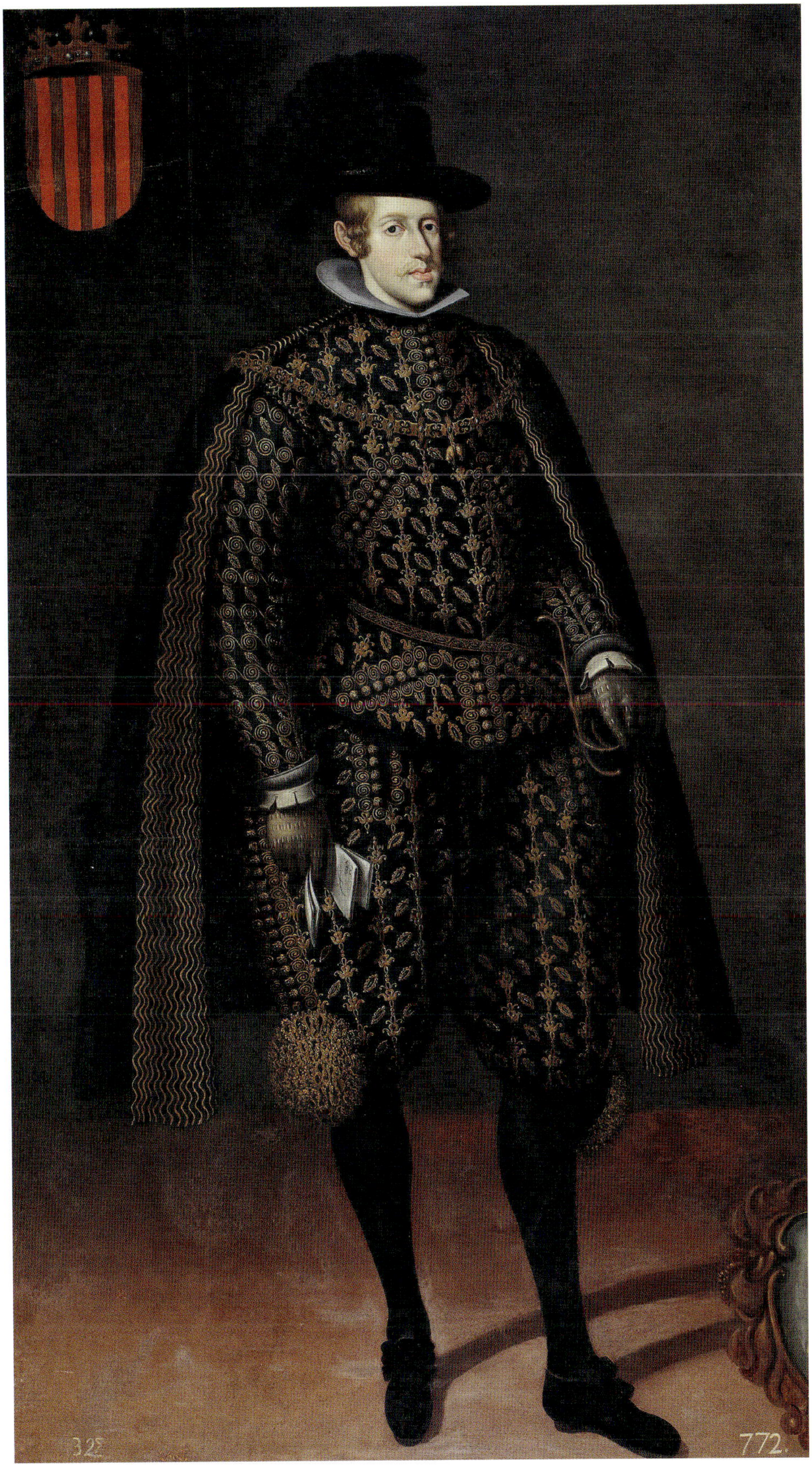

32
772.

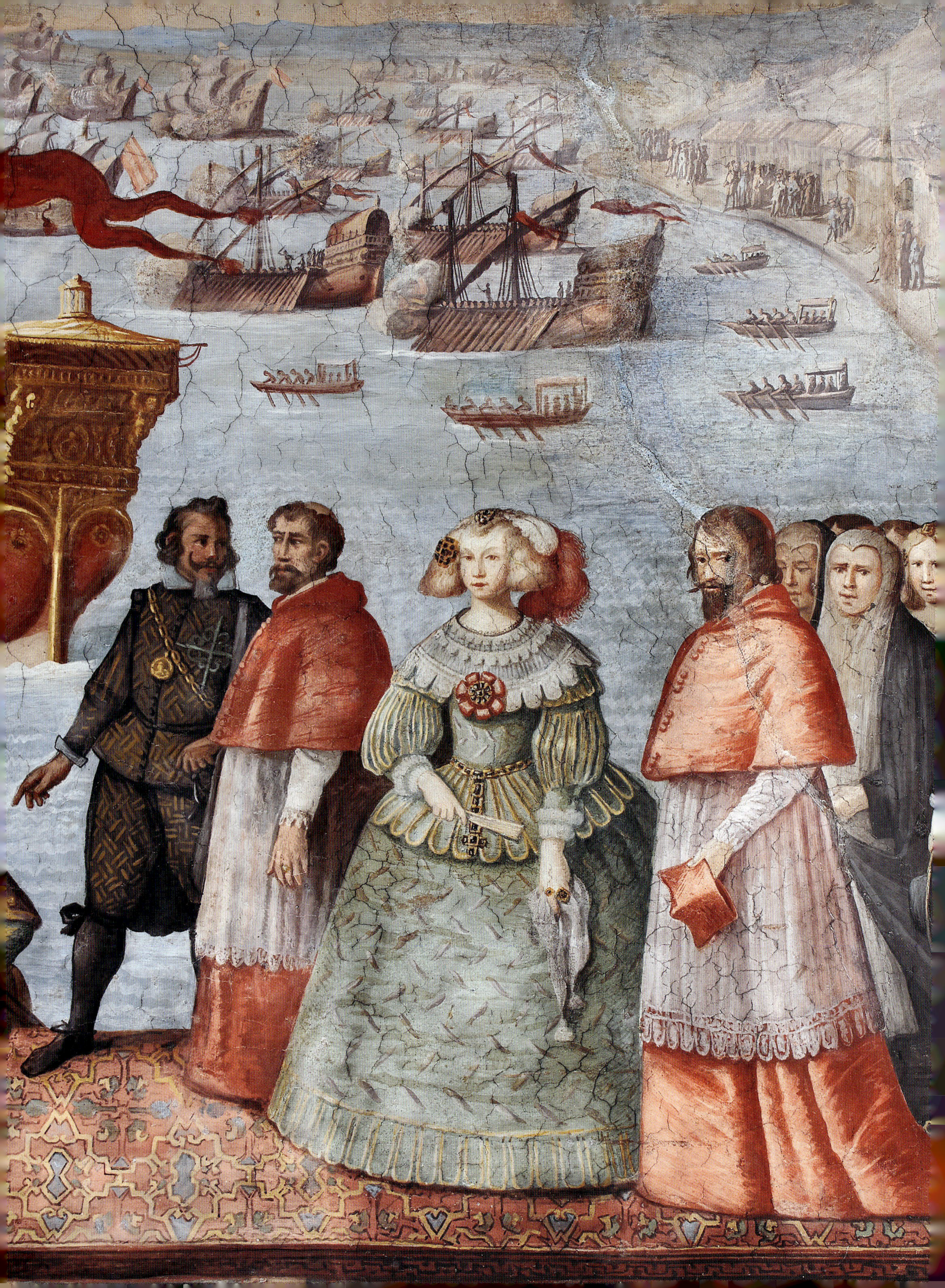

5. Aguado's Second Act

Novelties for a New Queen, Early 1650s

Mateo Aguado rarely, if ever, left Madrid. But in the summer of 1649 he traveled to the port town of Denia, in the province of Valencia on Spain's Mediterranean coast (see Map 1). The tailor went there to meet Mariana of Austria, who was due to arrive by boat from the Ligurian port of Finale (fig. 123). Aguado was accompanied by two tailors from his workshop whom he paid out of his own pocket. Years later the queen's tailor complained that this trip had cost him over 11,100 *reales*.[1] Aguado took with him a taffeta garment bag containing a green silk dress and matching traveling cloak decorated with gold bows, plumes, and roses.[2] With Aguado's dress and the new farthingales that Diego López had made for her over the summer, Mariana had everything that she needed to be dressed as queen of Spain when she first set foot on Spanish soil. The previous year, López had made a *verdugado* with a *cadera cariñana* (Carignano hip) that was sent to her at the imperial court, perhaps for her to practice wearing in preparation for this moment.[3]

Spanish fashion was not unfamiliar to Mariana of Austria. Her mother, María Ana, had taken a Spanish tailor with her when she moved from Madrid to Vienna in 1631, and she had continued to dress in the Spanish style at the imperial court—something that a queen could do when she left home to join the court of a friendly nation.[4] As mentioned in previous chapters, Aguado occasionally made luxurious new dresses that were sent to the Empress María Ana, and he also made several garments for the Archduchess Mariana during her brief, ill-fated engagement to Prince Baltasar Carlos in 1646. During that engagement, the Spanish court had received a briefing from the imperial court that described the archduchess as "the living portrait of her Spanish mother" who "was so familiar with the virtues, manners and customs of Castile, as well as its language, that she could almost be mistaken for being Spanish."[5]

When he met his new queen at Denia, Aguado was in a very different position than he had been when he was first appointed *sastre de cámara* almost 19 years earlier. Aguado had been 25 years old when he joined the household staff of Isabel of Bourbon, a queen who was firmly established in her position after having given birth to a male heir. Now Aguado was about 45 years old—the same age as the king—to the new queen's 15. It was conventional wisdom that an old tailor could not learn new tricks, but Mariana's arrival launched the most creative decade of Aguado's career.[6] In the early 1650s, the queen's tailor retired some of the most traditional features of formal courtly dress, and the female silhouette reached a new extreme with understructures built by Aguado and his colleague

123. *(facing page)* Unknown artist, *Mariana of Austria Departing for Spain from the Port of Finale, Liguria*, 1650–70. Detail; fresco, 300 × 430 cm. Royal Palace, Naples

Diego López. Aguado used the silhouette of the 1650s as a blank canvas onto which he applied a constant stream of new colors and decorations. Novelties were introduced only to disappear and be replaced by new ones. The accelerated pace of change was certainly assisted by the revival of the theaters, which reopened in 1651 and resumed their place at the center of Madrid's fashion world. Aguado's work in the early 1650s was part of a general cultural revival at the Spanish court that followed the dour 1640s. The philosopher Baltasar Gracián had forecast the mood of the new decade in a maxim on novelty in his *Art of Worldly Wisdom* (1647): "Dare to renew your brilliance," he wrote, "dawning many times like the sun ... renew it and make them applaud."[7]

First Impressions

When the ship carrying Mariana arrived at Denia on September 4, 1649, three artillery salutes were fired from the medieval cliffside castle overlooking the Mediterranean Sea.[8] For the next 12 days the new queen remained in Denia receiving well-wishers, and then she began the journey to Madrid. Working on the road, Aguado and his journeymen made and decorated the dresses that she wore along the way. The queen's first weeks in Spain were filled with important events as she was introduced to her husband, his court, and the people of Madrid. Aguado was responsible for ensuring that the new queen made a good first impression. The tailor needed to make a good impression too, for he faced some new competition: a tailor named Juan Cadenas, who had served the Empress María Ana at the imperial court for many years, had accompanied Mariana and served as her tailor on the way to Denia, and he was also moving to the Spanish court.[9]

The first stop on Mariana's Spanish itinerary was the town of Navalcarnero, about 35 kilometers southwest of Madrid. On October 7, 1649, the Archbishop of Toledo performed the *velaciones* ceremony, which was the official blessing of the royal marriage between Philip IV and Mariana that had taken place by proxy the previous year. This was one of three moments in Mariana's journey to Madrid that were represented in a fresco cycle at the Royal Palace in Naples, home of the Spanish viceroy (fig. 124).[10] The frescoes, which do not appear to have been based on eyewitness descriptions, capture the spirit of the events but are unreliable when it comes to the details of dress. A printed *relación* reports that the king appeared at the *velaciones* ceremony in gala dress of walnut-brown and silver but does not describe the bride's attire.[11] According to Aguado's charges for 1649, Mariana wore a dress of lustrous silk (*tercianela*) in a bright tan color with silver and blue embroidery, which she had acquired during her travels through Northern Italy en route to Spain. Aguado made a new over-gown to go with the dress and redecorated the doublet.[12] After the ceremony at Navalcarnero, the royal couple stopped at El Escorial before arriving in Madrid, where they stayed at the Buen Retiro Palace for ten days while preparations for Mariana's entry into Madrid were completed.

On November 15, 1649, Mariana made her grand entry into Madrid in a procession that traveled from the Buen Retiro through the center of town to her permanent new home at the Royal Palace. The dress that Aguado made for this climactic event was a traditional *saya entera* of mother-of-pearl satin embroidered in silver, with round sleeves worn over fitted sleeves of embroidered white satin.[13] A lifelike sculpture of the queen dressed in an identical outfit was displayed on the steps of the Monastery of San Felipe el Real, at the Puerta del Sol.[14] The official published account of the entry emphasized that Mariana was wearing a Castilian dress: "Venia *Su* MAGESTAD en *Trage* CASTELLANO."[15] It was an old-fashioned style that linked Mariana to the Spanish queens who had come before her, whose portraits by Velázquez hung on the facade of the Church of San Salvador along the parade route.[16] Mariana wore her traditional Castilian dress with "jewels of inestimable value" and an "elegant hat with white plumes" as she rode across Madrid on a white horse called Cisne (Swan).[17]

A fresco at the Royal Palace in Naples depicts Mariana on a white horse processing through the street as people watch from their windows, which have panels of fabric in various colors waving from their balconies (fig. 125). This was how the people of Madrid marked festive occasions, including the procession of their new queen. A prose pamphlet relating Mariana's entry begins by describing the "streets and balconies hung with brocades and fabrics," which were a "fine demonstration" of the joy of the occasion.[18] The queen was going to see Madrid for the first time, and the town strove to create a good first impression. The craft guilds played a significant role in financing and organizing the decorations, which included triumphal arches that the silk merchants, silversmiths, and furriers decorated with their wares—the furriers made lifelike animals from real pelts to decorate theirs. The tailors' and shoemakers' guilds sponsored decorated stages where dances were performed along the parade route.[19]

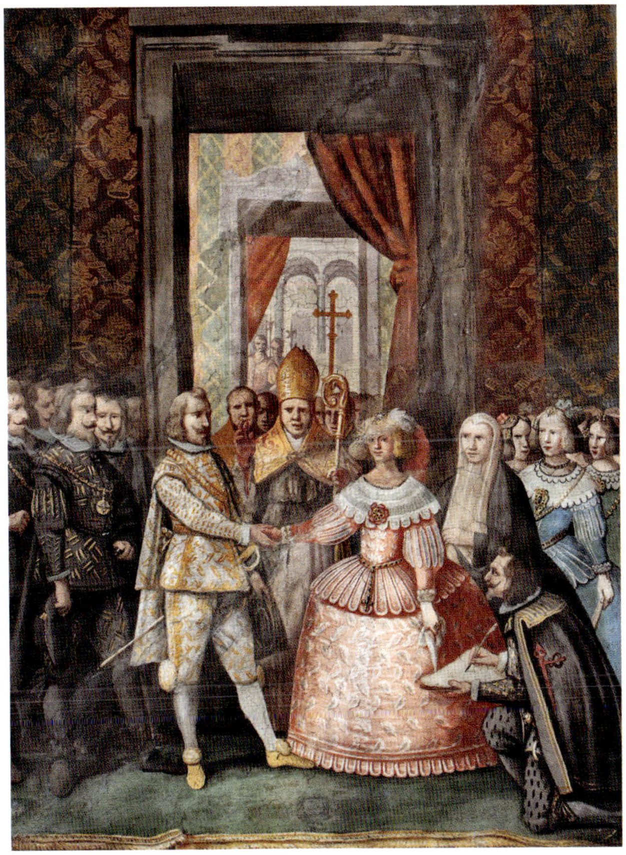

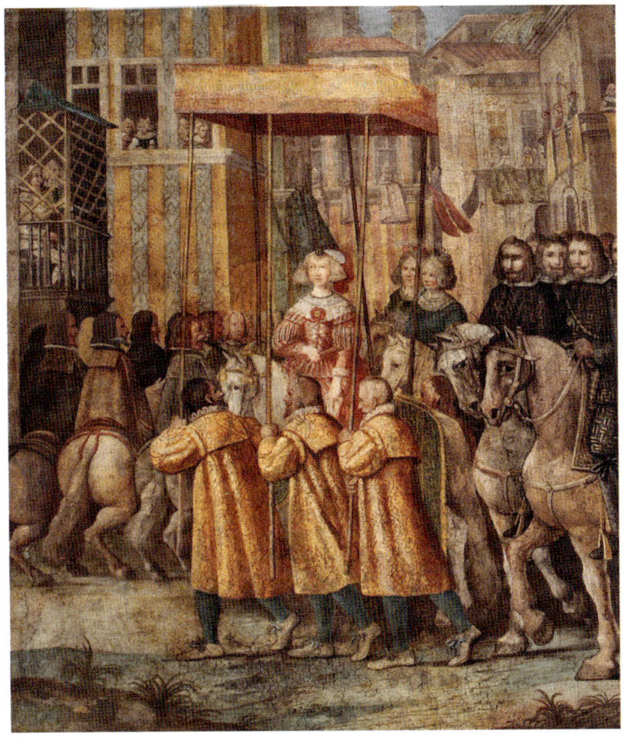

124. *(above right)* Unknown artist, *Blessing of the Nuptials of Philip IV and Mariana of Austria in Navalcarnero*, 1650–70. Detail; fresco, 430 × 230 cm. Royal Palace, Naples

125. *(right)* Unknown artist, *Mariana of Austria's Entry into Madrid*, 1650–70. Detail; fresco, 300 × 230 cm. Royal Palace, Naples

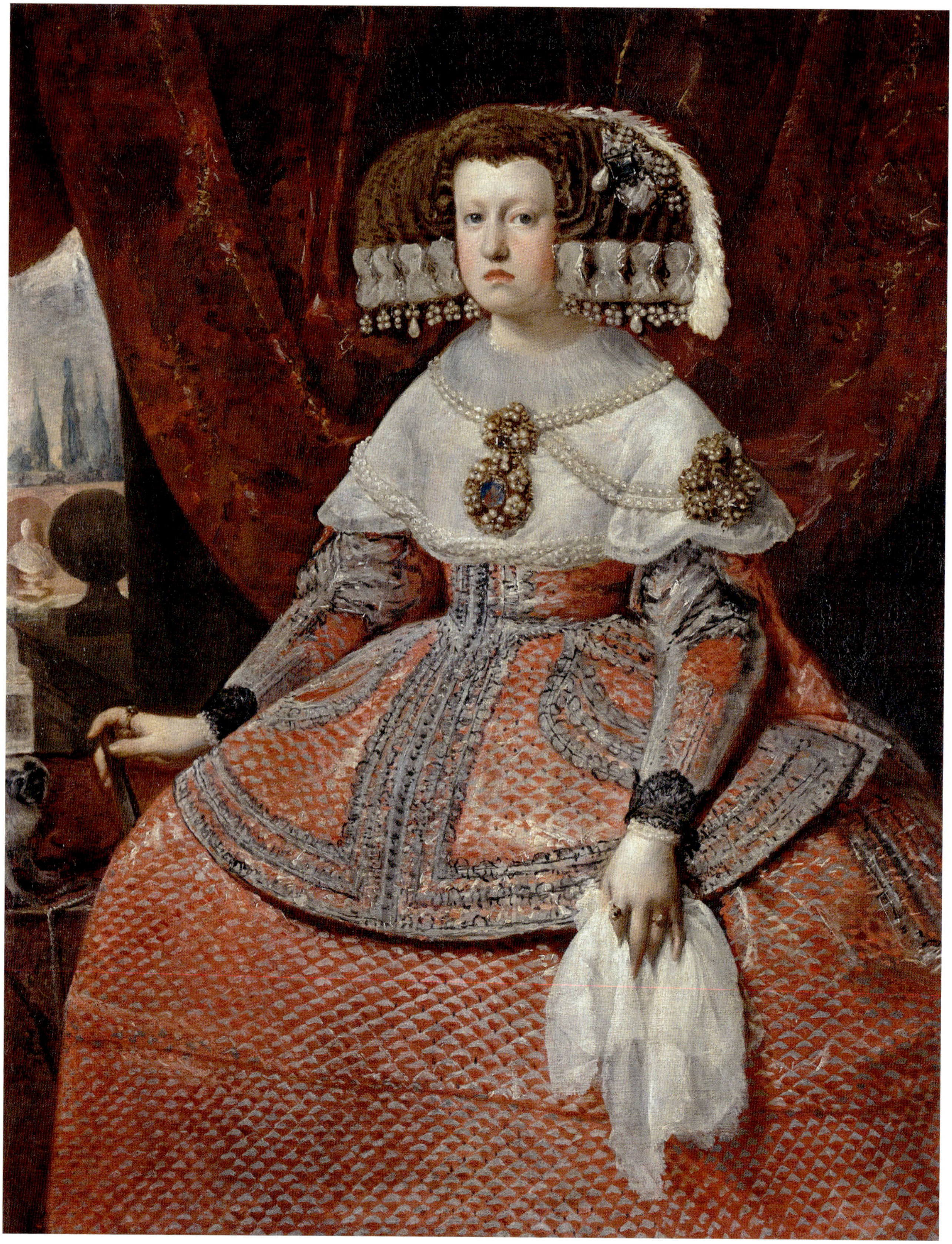

Before the procession concluded at the Royal Palace, Mariana stopped at the Church of Santa María to visit the Virgin of Almudena. Mariana later donated the "very rich dress" that she was wearing to the Virgin of Almudena, along with other jewels and rich gifts.[20] The old-fashioned dress that Aguado designed for Mariana to wear during her introduction to Madrid, and her donation of that dress to the Virgin of Almudena, drew upon traditions that were associated with her beloved predecessor, Isabel of Bourbon. There was no one better situated to help Mariana craft her image for this critical first public appearance than Aguado, who had dressed the previous queen for almost 15 years. The traditional dress that Aguado made for Mariana's entry was the last of its kind, as the decade of novelties began.

Dressing the New Queen

Aguado's work for Mariana in the 1650s is recorded in *cargos* (charges), which do not include the kinds of details about their working relationship that could be found in the tailor's accounts for Isabel of Bourbon. Nonetheless, Mariana's influence can be read in the descriptions of the garments that the tailor made for her. The young queen had a reputation for being fun-loving and deeply pious, and both of these sides of her personality are reflected in her wardrobe of colorful, feminine dresses interspersed with solemn religious habits.[21] Aguado's work for Mariana included much more variety in the kinds of garments he made and the colors he used than his work for her predecessor. Each dress was different and new. Mariana appeared frequently in public during her first year in Madrid, which gave the people many opportunities to study the tailor's creations.

The staple of the queen's wardrobe continued to be the standard three-piece dress (doublet, skirt, and over-gown), with two or three formal gowns per year for major religious holidays. Aguado also made a matched set (*juego*), which probably served as an informal dress, with a "little doublet" (*justillo*) that had eyelets (*ojetes*), presumably around the waist, to attach it with laces to a matching petticoat. In 1650, Aguado began to make half-moon-shaped hand-openings (*golpes*) in the front quadrants of the skirts attached to the queen's bodices. These novelties appear in a portrait of Mariana that was sent to Vienna, in which she wears a formal dress made from a rich fabric that looks like salmon-pink velvet pile on a silver ground (fig. 126). Formal gowns now had tubular sleeves (*mangas de casaca*) instead of round or pointed sleeves, which disappeared after 1650. "Fitted sleeves" (*mangas justas*) in the 1650s bore little resemblance to their name: they were constructed from three to five strips of fabric that were held together at the wrist. The gaps in between the strips revealed undersleeves made of heavy silk voile (*velo de peso*). The ubiquitous over-gown that was worn with everyday dresses diminished in scale and importance. The once-modest garment was now reduced to "a little triangle at the back, a ribbon for a train, two little circles for shoulder-wings, and two chestnuts for sleeves," as the Madrid-based writer Juan de Zabaleta described it in the mid-1650s.[22]

In September 1650, Aguado made the queen a "habit of Saint Francis of Paola." This *hábito* was quite different from the habit of the Poor Clares in which Queen Isabel had been buried. Mariana's habit consisted of a boned bodice (*cotilla*) with sleeves and little skirts, and a matching petticoat (*brial*) made from fine dark-brown wool (*lanilla*) decorated with white lace at the seams.[23] Descriptions of Aguado's habits for Mariana closely resemble the painted garments on the Virgin of

126. *(facing page)* Workshop of Velázquez, *Queen Mariana of Austria*, 1650s. Oil on canvas, 128.5 × 99 cm. Kunsthistorisches Museum, Vienna

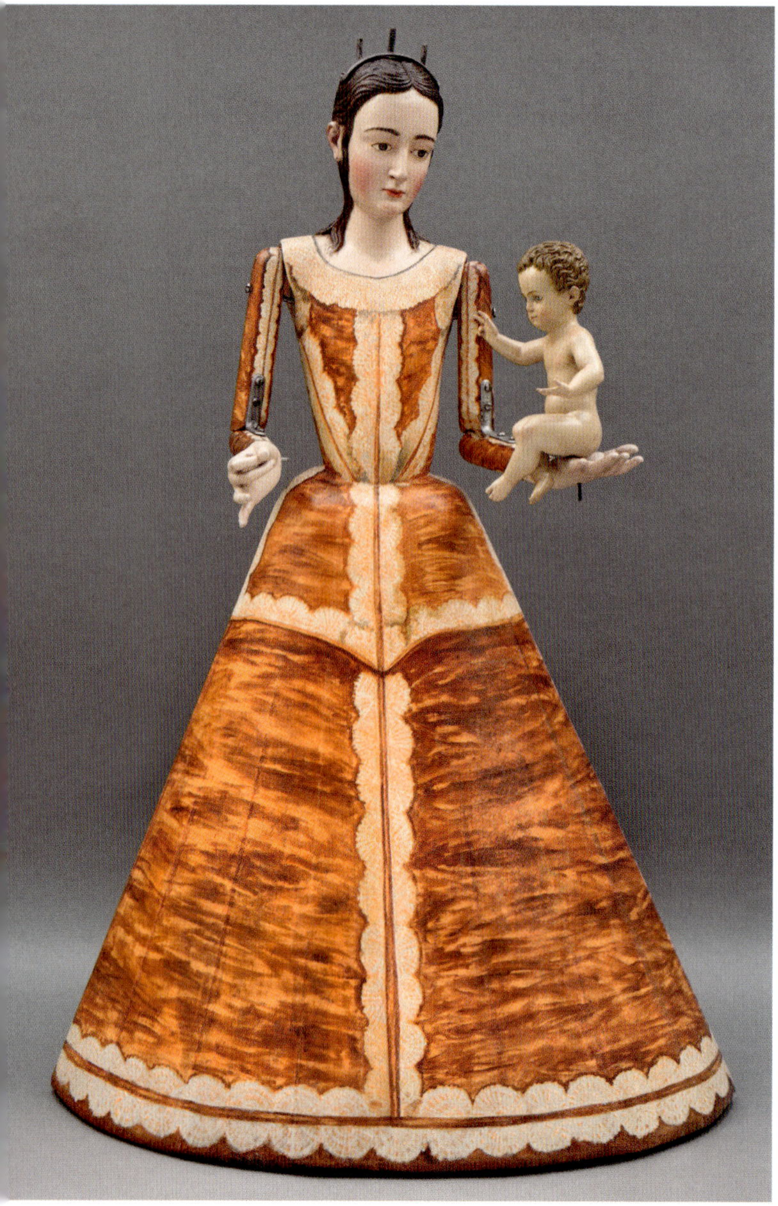

127. *Virgin of Patrocinio*, mid-17th century. Polychromed wood, 130 cm tall. Monastery of San Lorenzo de El Escorial, San Lorenzo

Patrocinio, a devotional sculpture with articulated arms and a built-in farthingale that was made to be dressed (fig. 127). Mariana was exceptionally devoted to this image of the Virgin, which was located at the Monastery of San Lorenzo de El Escorial in a chapel with portraits of Philip IV and Mariana of Austria kneeling in prayer (see fig. 136).[24] Mariana wore her brown wool boned bodice and petticoat beneath a pair of scapulars, a secular variation of the garment worn by members of religious orders, such as Sister María de Ágreda (see fig. 116). Aguado made habits like this for the queen regularly, approximately one to three per year in the 1650s.

Mariana's walnut-brown habits were unusual in a wardrobe that was otherwise bright and varied, with colors that included sky blue, olive- and grass-green, lemon-yellow, sand, and pearl gray. Unlike Queen Isabel, who had worn sober shades after her elevation to queen consort in 1621, Mariana did not give up the pleasures of color after she became queen. Aguado used twice as many colors in Mariana's wardrobe as he had for Isabel, and new colors were introduced almost every year. These fabrics included shot silks woven with more than one color to create complex shades like *colombino*, which was pink and white, like a radish flower, and *aire*, a pale apricot color that resembled the sky at dawn.[25] Black was used only for solemn occasions, such as mourning and Palm Sunday. The only color in Mariana's wardrobe that could be considered sober was musk-brown (*musco*, or *amusco*), which was usually combined with silver. Almost 40 percent of Mariana's dresses in the 1650s were made from silks interwoven with silver that likely resembled a piece of light green silk shot with silver threads that has survived in the form of a chalice veil (fig. 128).

The military-style dress decorations that had characterized Aguado's work for Queen Isabel were replaced with markedly feminine ornaments. *Alamares* became quite rare, while bows became ubiquitous. Gold buttons were out, and sparkling diamond buttons were in—but only for a brief time. Black and gold dress decorations disappeared, replaced by everything silver (see the 1650s in the Chronology of Women's Dress, pp. 217–18). Silver bobbin lace was immensely popular at the Spanish court, and across Europe, in the second half of the seventeenth century, but very little of it has survived.[26] A woman's cap made of brocaded silk and decorated with metal lace is one of the exceptions (fig. 129).

Aguado used various silver trimmings to create decorations that included bows, waves, whorls, half-pipes, diamond tips, and rows of scales called "goshawk breast" (*pecho de azor*). One of the new designs that Aguado introduced at the beginning of Mariana's reign was a latticework pattern called *celosía*. It is no coincidence that the Spanish word for "lattice" is connected to the word *celos*—"jealous"—for lattices were installed on windows, doors, and balconies so that women could look outside without being seen themselves.[27] In a portrait of Mariana from the later 1650s, she wears a brown dress (probably musk) decorated with wide bands of silver *celosía* that run vertically up her dress and hanging sleeves (fig. 130). The decorative latticework on Mariana's dresses evoked the ideal of female enclosure—but the queen who wore it was required to put herself on display to the public.

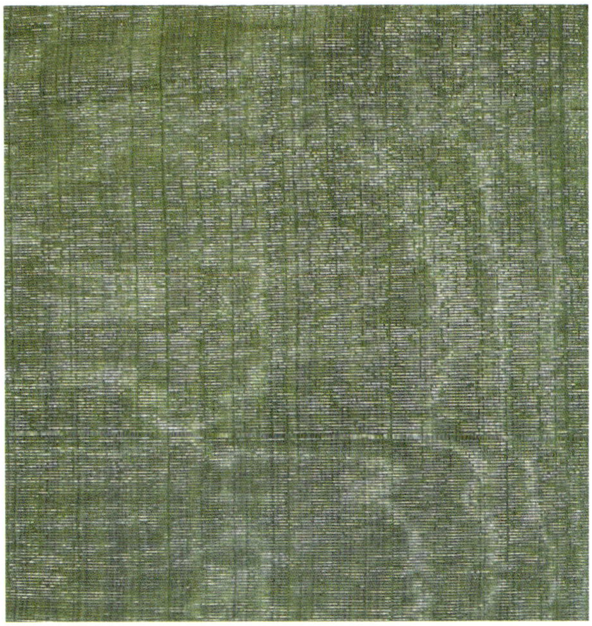

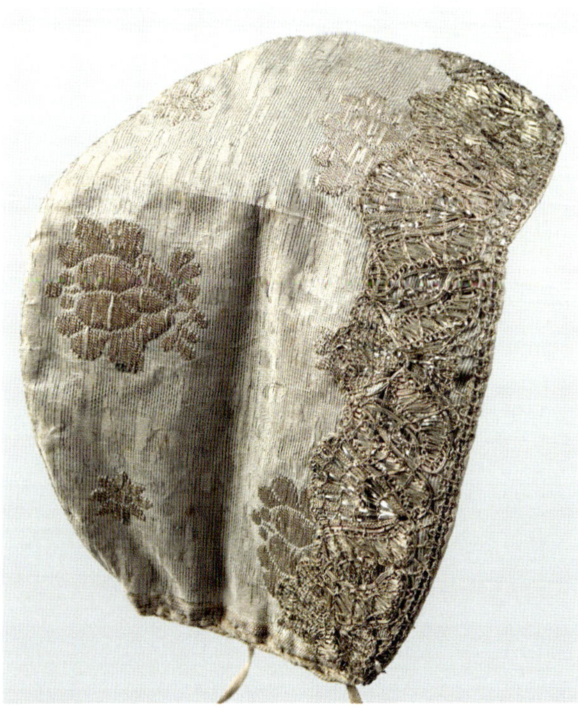

128. *(above right)* Green watered silk shot with silver. Chalice veil (detail), possibly Italian, 1600s–1700s. Victoria and Albert Museum, London

129. *(right)* Woman's cap (side view), Spanish, 17th century. Silver lamé brocaded with metal thread and decorated with silver bobbin lace. Museu Tèxtil, Terrassa

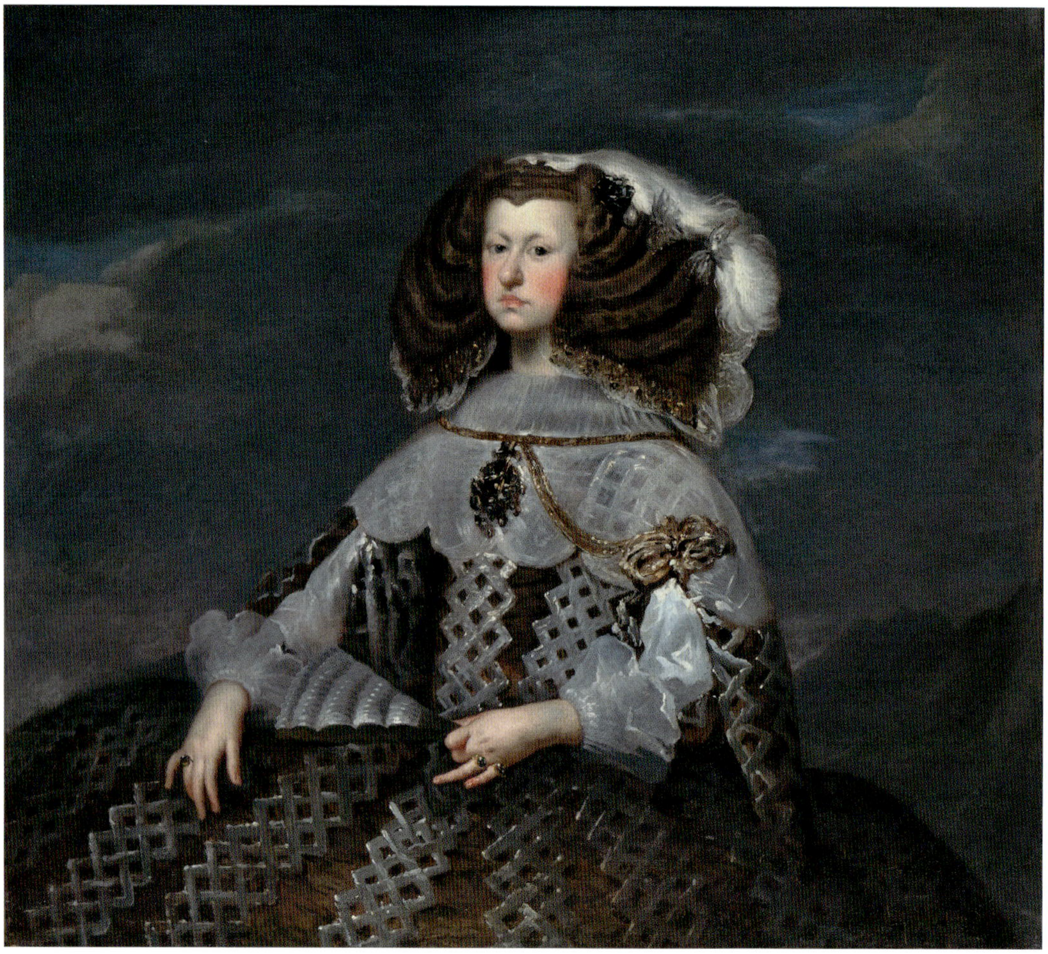

130. After Diego Velázquez, *Queen Mariana of Austria*, late 1650s. Oil on canvas, 109 × 122 cm. Palace of Versailles

Mariana's first year in Madrid was packed with events, each of which required a new outfit by her tailor. In 1650, Aguado made dresses for the queen to wear on 16 special occasions (Table 2). The most extravagant dress of the year was a *saya entera* for Candlemas, the feast day that marked the end of the Christmas season, when the king and queen went in procession to the Royal Palace chapel to receive a gilded, blessed candle.[28] The queen's Candlemas *saya* was made from 21 meters of sky-blue cloth of silver decorated with silver galloon from Milan and bordered with white rabbit fur. There were also special dresses for the queen to wear on the religious holidays of Palm Sunday and Corpus Christi, to visit royal residences outside of Madrid, to celebrate family birthdays, and to mark memorial days for royal ancestors. Each of the dresses that Aguado made for the queen was different from the rest, with its colors and decorations carefully calibrated to suit the occasion.

Table 2: Special-Occasion Dresses Made by Aguado for Queen Mariana of Austria, 1650*			
Month	**Occasion**	**Dress fabric and decoration**	**Cost of materials**
January	Visit to El Pardo	Dress of lemon-colored lightweight serge from Segovia with waves of gold and silver trimming	3,625 *reales*
February	Candlemas	*Saya entera* with pointed sleeves of blue cloth of silver with silver galloon and a border of white rabbit fur	9,665 *reales*
March	Palm Sunday	*Saya entera* with pointed sleeves of voided velvet from Genoa (presumably black) with borders embroidered with glass	2,607 *reales*
April	Birthday of Philip IV	Dress of yellow and silver camlet embroidered with black silk and silver	2,361 *reales*
	Visit to Aranjuez	Two dresses made from watered silk from France: one of black and silver camlet bordered with black lace, the other of musk-colored camlet with silver latticework	6,160 *reales* [for the two dresses]
May	Corpus Christi	Dress of white double taffeta from Valencia embroidered with gold esses	1,674 *reales*
	Octave of Corpus Christi	*Saya entera* with hanging sleeves, made from mother-of-pearl and white double taffeta, decorated with silver buttons-and-loops	1,114 *reales*
July	Birthday of Emperor Ferdinand III	Dress of green ormuzine, decorated with bows and very wide waves made from silver galloon	1,031 *reales*
August	Bullfight at the Plaza Mayor	Dress of silver, light green, and black camlet from Holland with white lace from Flanders	2,969 *reales*
	Feast of the Assumption of the Virgin	Dress of pearl-colored watered ormuzine embroidered with snail shapes made from silver plate and black silk	1,582 *reales*
September	Birthday of Infanta María Teresa	Dress of walnut-brown camlet from Holland decorated with silver lace	4,428 *reales*
October	Memorial Day for Queen Margaret of Austria	Doublet and skirt of plain black ormuzine with an over-gown of black borato	625 *reales*
	Visit to El Escorial	Dress of brown and black silk, decorated with diamond shapes made from black and silver trimming	2,099 *reales*
December	Feast of the Immaculate Conception	Dress of mother-of-pearl, black, and silver cloth of silver from Venice with twisted cords of black and silver	5,305 *reales*
	Feast of Our Lady of Expectation	Dress of apricot-colored short-haired plush from Genoa, decorated with silver lace	4,083 *reales*
	New Year's Eve	Dress of green plush velvet, decorated with wide bobbin lace of gold and silver	4,265 *reales*

*Sources: AGP, AG, leg. 904, Aguado's charges for Queen Mariana (1650); and leg. 5253/2, silk merchants' accounts for the queen (1650)

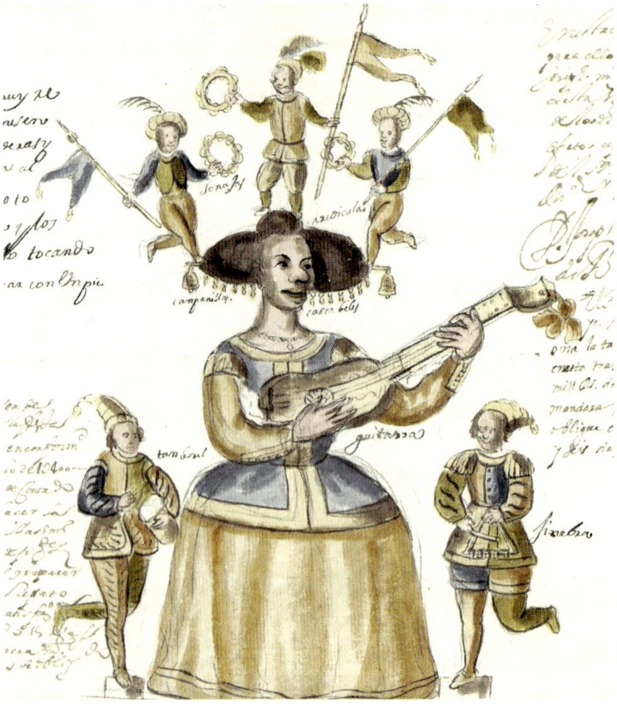

131. Design for figures atop a Corpus Christi *tarasca*, 1657. Detail; ink drawing and watercolor with traces of charcoal, 28 × 20.5 cm. Archivo de la Villa, Madrid

For her first Corpus Christi in Madrid, Mariana wore a dress of white double taffeta from Valencia embroidered with gold designs in the shape of the letter "S." During the festival, a full-length portrait of Mariana by Juan Bautista Martínez del Mazo hung at the Puerta de Guadalajara, where it was admired "as much for being among the first to be seen of Her Majesty in this court as for the amazing artistry," according to Lázaro Díaz del Valle, a chronicler who was living in Madrid at the time.[29] Unfortunately, he did not describe the dress in that painting, which is now lost. Corpus Christi had been an important fashion event during the reign of Queen Isabel, but the holiday came to play an even greater role in disseminating fashion trends in the 1650s. A figure of a fashionably dressed woman was mounted on the back of the *tarasca*, a gigantic papier-mâché dragon that represented vice in the Corpus Christi procession. The woman was dressed in the latest fashions, which could be real clothing or made from painted paper.[30] A drawing survives of a "very ridiculous woman" and five Harlequins playing music that were mounted on the *tarasca* for the Madrid parade in 1657 (fig. 131). The intention was to present the fashionably dressed woman as ugly and vain, but the actual outcome was that the woman atop the *tarasca* became a fashion icon that attracted stylish women and their tailors to come view the float as a fount of inspiration.[31]

Aguado made a dress of silver, black, and *verdegay*—a pale green color that was considered to be especially happy and pleasing—for the queen to wear to her first bullfight at the Plaza Mayor in August 1650.[32] The royal family watched bullfights from a balcony with a gilded balustrade and canopy on the front of the Casa de la Panadería, the twin-towered building on the northern end of the plaza (see Map 2). A view of such an event from the 1650s shows two royal women—presumably Mariana and her stepdaughter the Infanta María Teresa—seated on the royal balcony, while their ladies, all dressed in different colors, occupy the balcony to their right (viewer's left) (fig. 132).[33] Mariana reportedly thought that the Spanish tradition of women appearing on balconies was in poor taste: "she says that it looks bad to see women in festivals on balconies, saying that they go, not to see, but rather to be seen," wrote the chronicler Jerónimo de Barrionuevo, author of a series of letters to a dean at the Cathedral of Zaragoza between 1654 and 1658.[34] Nonetheless, in 1654 the king had the

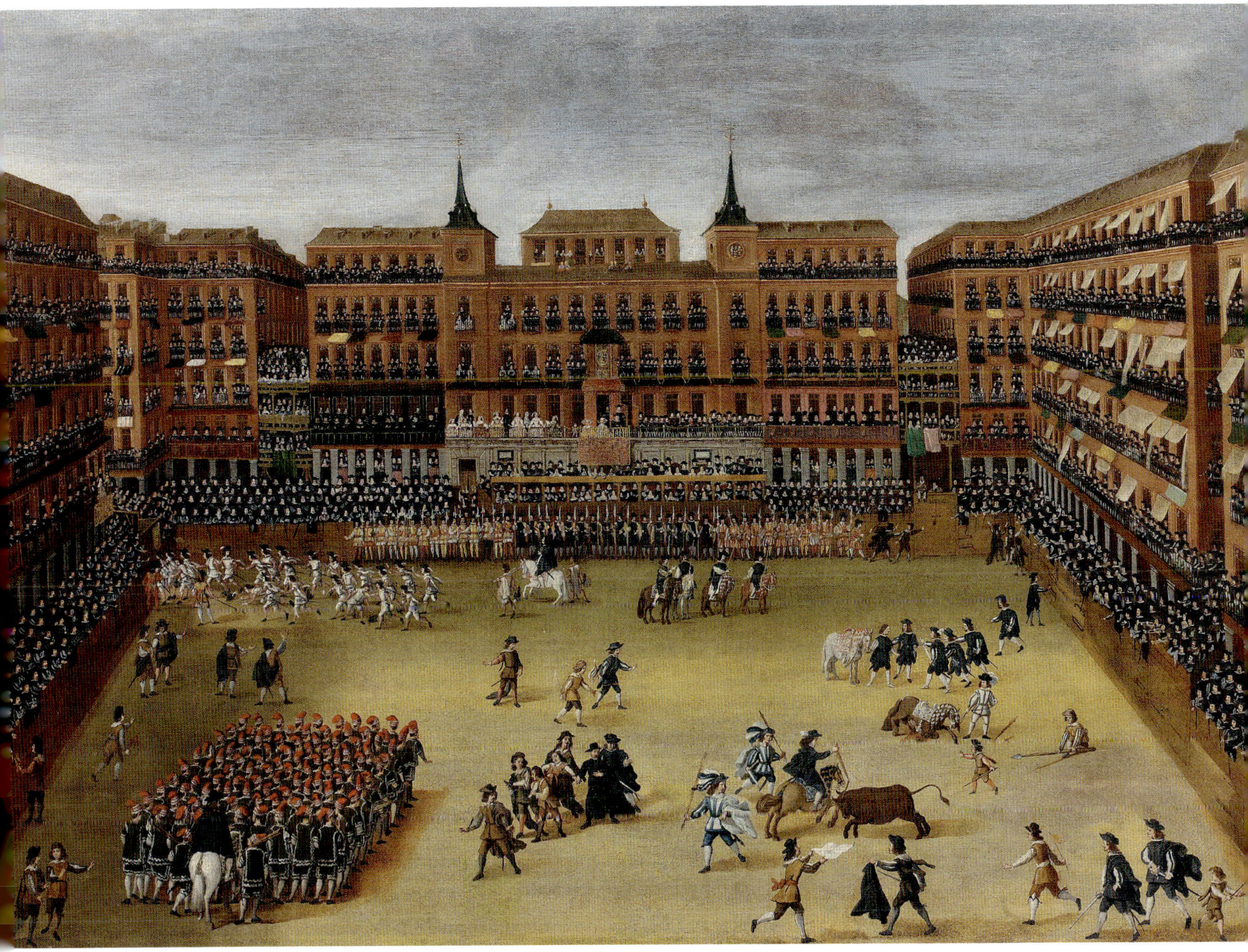

132. Unknown Madrid artist, *Bullfight at the Plaza Mayor of Madrid*, mid-1650s. Oil on canvas, 135 × 200 cm. Pérez Simón Collection, Mexico City

staircase to the balcony of the Panadería renovated, its steps made wider and shallower to accommodate the bulky skirts worn by the queen and her ladies with comfort and decency.[35]

To cap off Mariana's first full year as queen of Spain, at the end of 1650 Aguado made her a New Year's Eve dress of warm green plush. At the time, the queen was pregnant with her first child. She was not showing much, though, which worried the king: "I do not see the signs that I used to see in the queen who is in heaven," he wrote, referring to Isabel of Bourbon, "nor does her belly correspond to being five months along."[36] The king was writing to Luisa Enríquez Manrique de Lara, 9th Countess of Paredes de Nava, who had served as governess to the Infanta María Teresa after Isabel of Bourbon's death and then left the court to join a convent in 1648. On July 12, 1651 the 16-year-old queen gave birth to her first child, a girl who was named Margarita. It was a very difficult birth: the king wrote to the countess that he had feared his wife would die in his arms. Mariana survived, but the ordeal left her very thin, and her recovery took time.[37] This must have come as a fright to her tailor, who had experienced such a decline in his own fortunes following the death of Queen Isabel. By this time Aguado had successfully established a monopoly over the new queen's wardrobe. In August 1651 the tailor Juan Cadenas, who had come to Madrid with Mariana from the imperial court, requested permission to retire to the mountains, since he could not earn enough money to support himself and his family at the Spanish court. There was no work for Cadenas "because Mateo Aguado does the job," he explained.[38] Cadenas was granted permission to take his leave.

Constructing Mariana in Black and Silver

After Mariana of Austria recovered from giving birth, in late 1652 Velázquez painted his first portrait of the queen (fig. 133).[39] *Mariana in Black and Silver* marks a new era in the shape of Spanish women's courtly dress. The queen's skirt was so wide that the painter had to add a strip of fabric to the left-hand side of the canvas, on which he had previously painted a portrait of Philip IV.[40] Like the painter's early full-length portrait of Philip IV in black (see fig. 13), this is an image of a royal at work. Ambassadors who came to the Spanish court encountered the queen similarly posed: in the early 1660s, the Dutch ambassador Lodewijck Huygens reported seeing the queen wearing "a farthingale with a diameter of six feet and a dark gray dress decorated with silver lace" and holding a white handkerchief.[41] The formality of this state portrait is expressed by the fact that the queen is dressed in black, which was a rarity in her wardrobe. Since black was associated with melancholy, the bright red bows at the queen's wrists may have had a therapeutic function, for the cochineal grains that were used to make red dye were also used medicinally as a cure for heartache.[42] Thick rows of sparkling silver trim outline the elements of the queen's dress and draw attention to the construction lines of her garments. The detailed records kept by Mariana's silk merchants make it possible to go beneath the surface and uncover how the queen's dresses were made.

Beneath the silk fabrics and silver trimmings on the surface of Mariana's dresses, less glamorous materials gave the garments their structure and character. A typical dress used eight different kinds of fabric in its construction. Unseen interfacings and interlinings made from linen, wool, and flax reinforced stress points in the garments and gave the exterior a smooth appearance. In 1650, Aguado made Mariana a dress using 16.4 meters

133. *(facing page)* Diego Velázquez, *Mariana in Black and Silver* (detail of fig. 27)

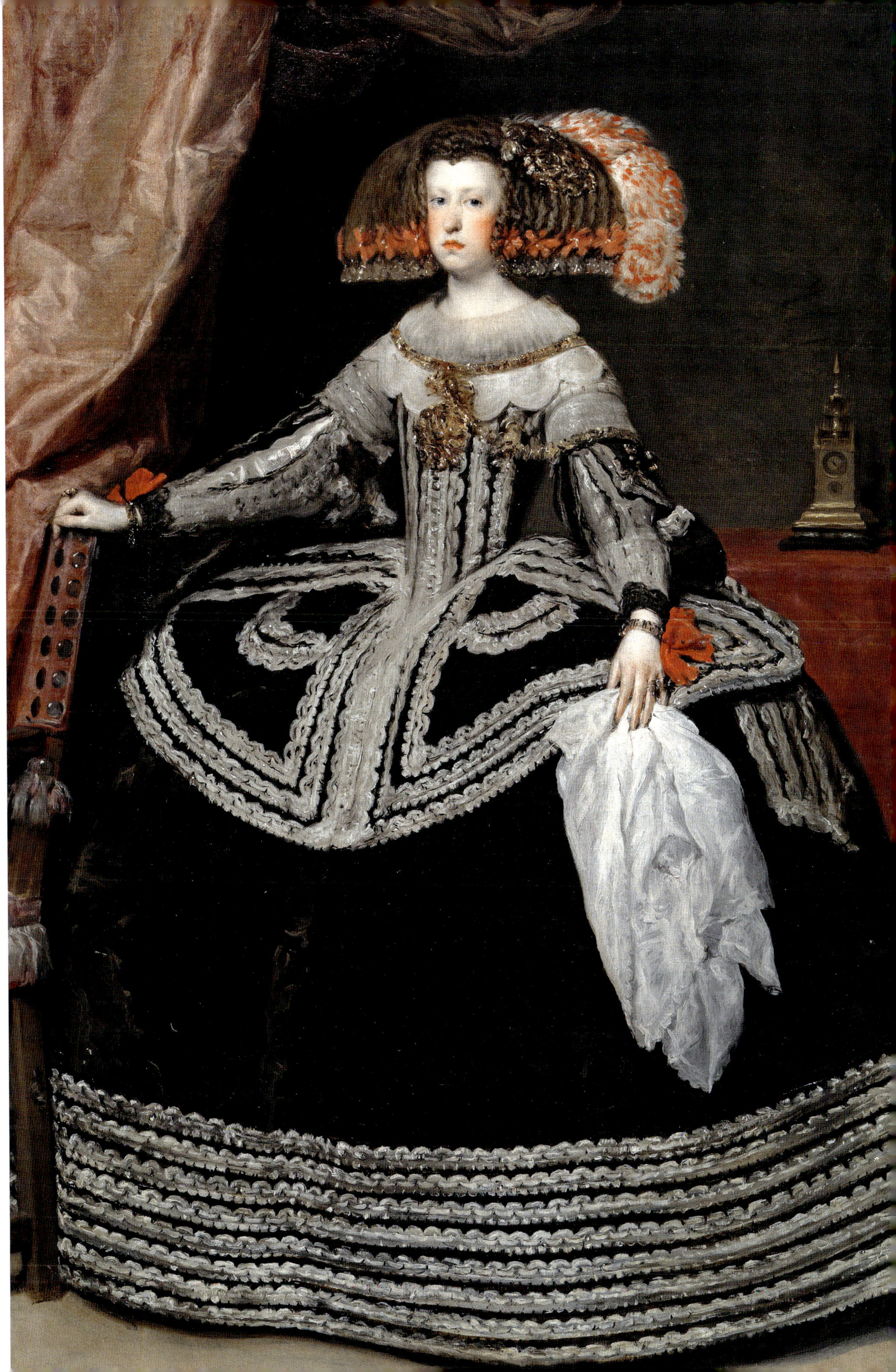

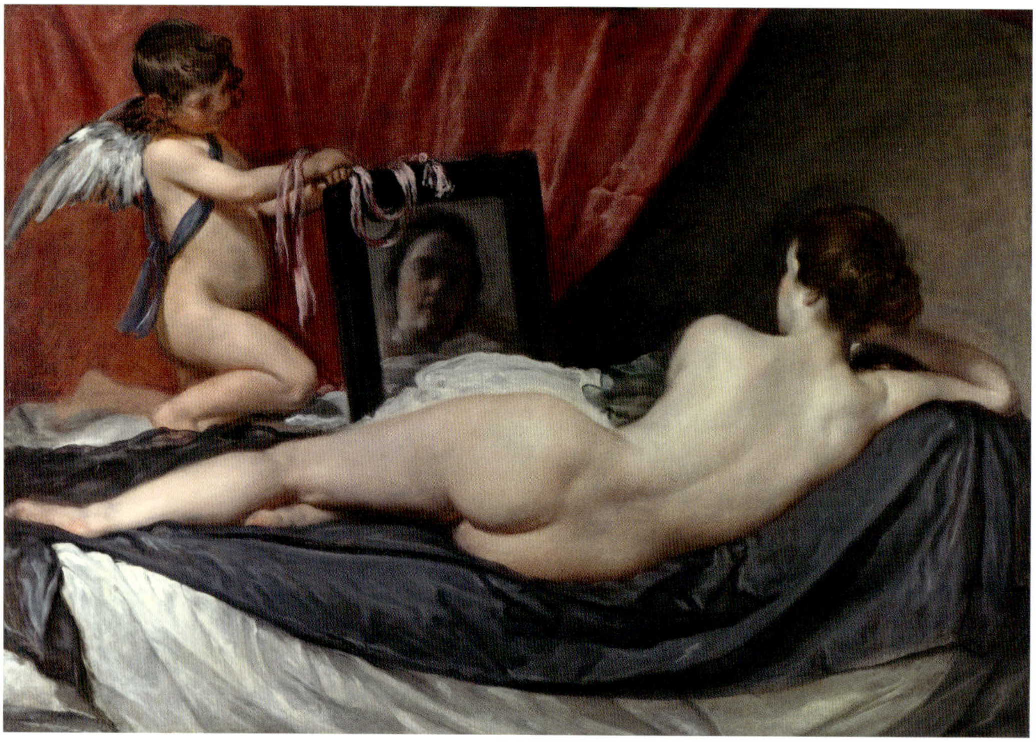

134. Diego Velázquez, *The Toilet of Venus ("The Rokeby Venus")*, c. 1647–51. Oil on canvas, 122.5 × 177 cm. National Gallery, London

of silver and black velvet from Holland that hid over 8 meters combined of buckram (*bocací*), canvas (*anjeo*), fustian (*fustán*), and baize (*bayeta*).[43] Much of that material was used to stiffen the doublet. Skirt hems were reinforced with canvas and covered with silk damask matching the dress fabric. Most of the queen's dresses were lined with taffeta, a crisp silk that contributed additional body to the fashion fabric. Even with all of this built-in structure, the queen's dresses required a stiff scaffolding underneath to achieve the radical silhouette of *Mariana in Black and Silver*.

In Velázquez's only known female nude, *The Rokeby Venus*, the ideal woman has long legs, rounded hips and buttocks, and a very narrow waist (fig. 134).[44] This is the shape of *Mariana in Black and Silver*, although the queen did not come by it naturally. Shaping garments hidden under Mariana's dress—a boned corset, a farthingale covered with multiple layers of stiff skirts, and platform shoes—molded the queen's body to conform to her dresses. Mariana's corsets were made by her tailor: Aguado had begun to fill this role when she arrived in Spain, and in 1654 he successfully defended his right to continue the

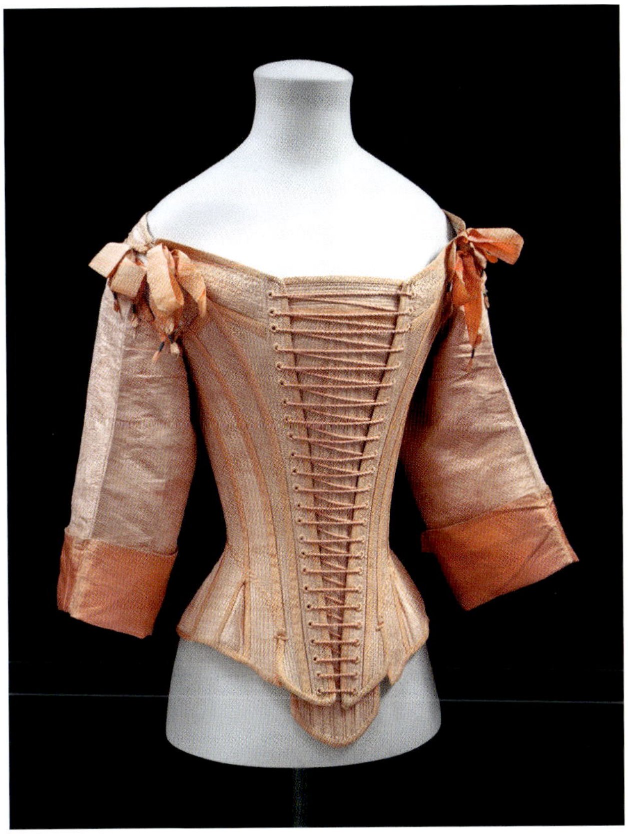

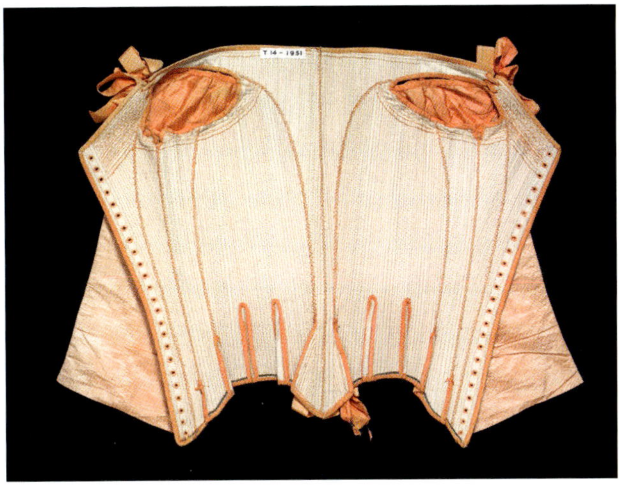

135. Front (*left*) and interior (*above*) of a woman's boned corset with sleeves and stomacher, probably Dutch, 1660–80. Pink watered silk with edges bound in grosgrain ribbon, fully boned and backstitched, lined in linen. Victoria and Albert Museum, London

work and officially hold the office of royal corset-maker.[45] The boned and backstitched corsets that Aguado made for Mariana were very similar to the *corpiños* that Isabel of Bourbon had worn, except now they were called *cotillas*. In the 1650s, Aguado made Mariana four to ten *cotillas* per year from double taffeta in shades of pink and red: crimson, mother-of-pearl, and incarnadine (*encarnado*, an ambiguous color that usually refers to carnation pink but could also be blood-red). A salmon-pink watered-silk corset made around the same time in Northern Europe reveals what a backstitched boned corset looked like, inside and out (fig. 135).[46] Mariana's corsets usually had fitted sleeves, and their skirt extensions were large enough to have pocket openings (*golpes*) in them. They were decorated with 15 meters of silver galloon.

Portraits of Mariana from the 1650s show the queen with skirts of different shapes, with *Mariana in Black and Silver* being the most extreme. The queen's farthingale-maker made three different structures to shape her skirts: *verdugados*, *caderas*, and *guardainfantes*. The *verdugado* was the classic funnel-shaped farthingale with hoops sewn into a floor-length skirt, which could

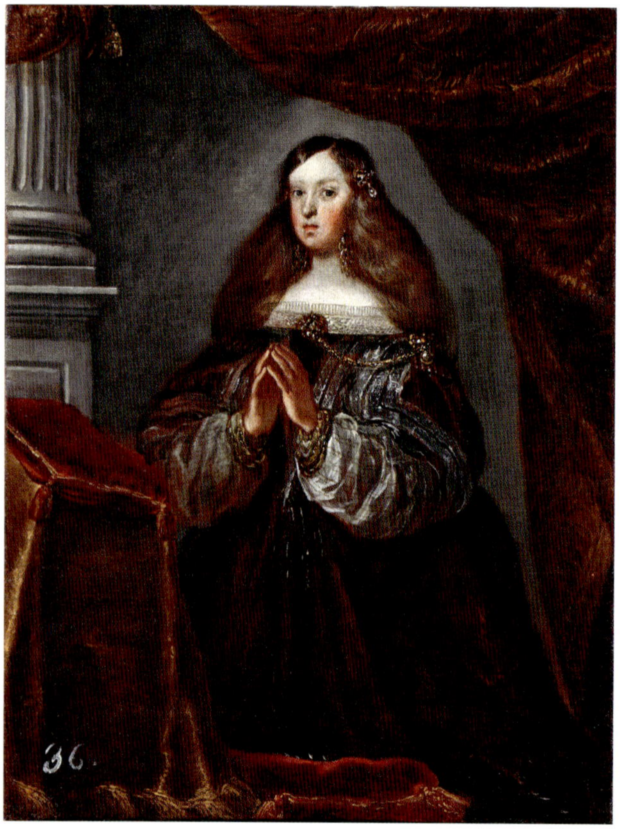

136. Circle of Velázquez, *Mariana of Austria in Prayer*, c. 1658–60. Oil on canvas, 53 × 41.5 cm. Monastery of San Lorenzo de El Escorial, San Lorenzo

137. *(facing page)* Spanish Royal Workshop, *Queen Mariana of Austria Dressed for the Hunt*, c. 1656. Oil on canvas, 206 × 108 cm. Dorotheum, Vienna

be worn alone or supplemented with a Carignano hip. Sometime between 1650 and 1659, the traditional Spanish farthingale disappeared, and the *guardainfante* reigned supreme.[47] Mariana's *guardainfantes* were constructed from hoops of wire or whalebone that were suspended from one another with ribbons (usually crimson in color); a *guardainfante* also called for a small yardage of double taffeta that was probably used to make a deep hem at the bottom. A *guardainfante* could be supplemented with a "little hip" (*caderilla*). Diego López made "small" and "large" *guardainfantes*, the size apparently referring to length rather than width; the larger version was made "in the style of a *verdugado*," which seems to mean floor-length.[48] In a portrait of Mariana in prayer, she appears to be wearing the shorter version of the *guardainfante*, which allows her to kneel (fig. 136). This is an unusually informal portrait of the queen, who wears her hair long and loose instead of a wig. *Mariana in Black and Silver* represents the more formal, full-length version of the farthingale. In a private letter of 1663, Mariana revealed that she chose not to wear a farthingale at all when she did not have to appear in public.[49]

A portrait of Mariana dressed for the hunt and holding an arquebus suggests that a dress could be worn with a variety of different farthingales depending on the occasion (fig. 137).[50] The queen has a relatively modest-sized hip with her hunting dress. The skirts of her bodice are divided into triangular quadrants, with one of the front pieces overlapping the other. If this same dress were worn over a farthingale with a wider hip, the bodice skirts could be extended to their full proportions. Mariana likely chose to wear a less restrictive farthingale for hunting—and she really did hunt. The Infanta María Teresa wrote a letter to her former governess in February 1650 describing a hunting trip at El Pardo during which the queen killed a wild boar.[51]

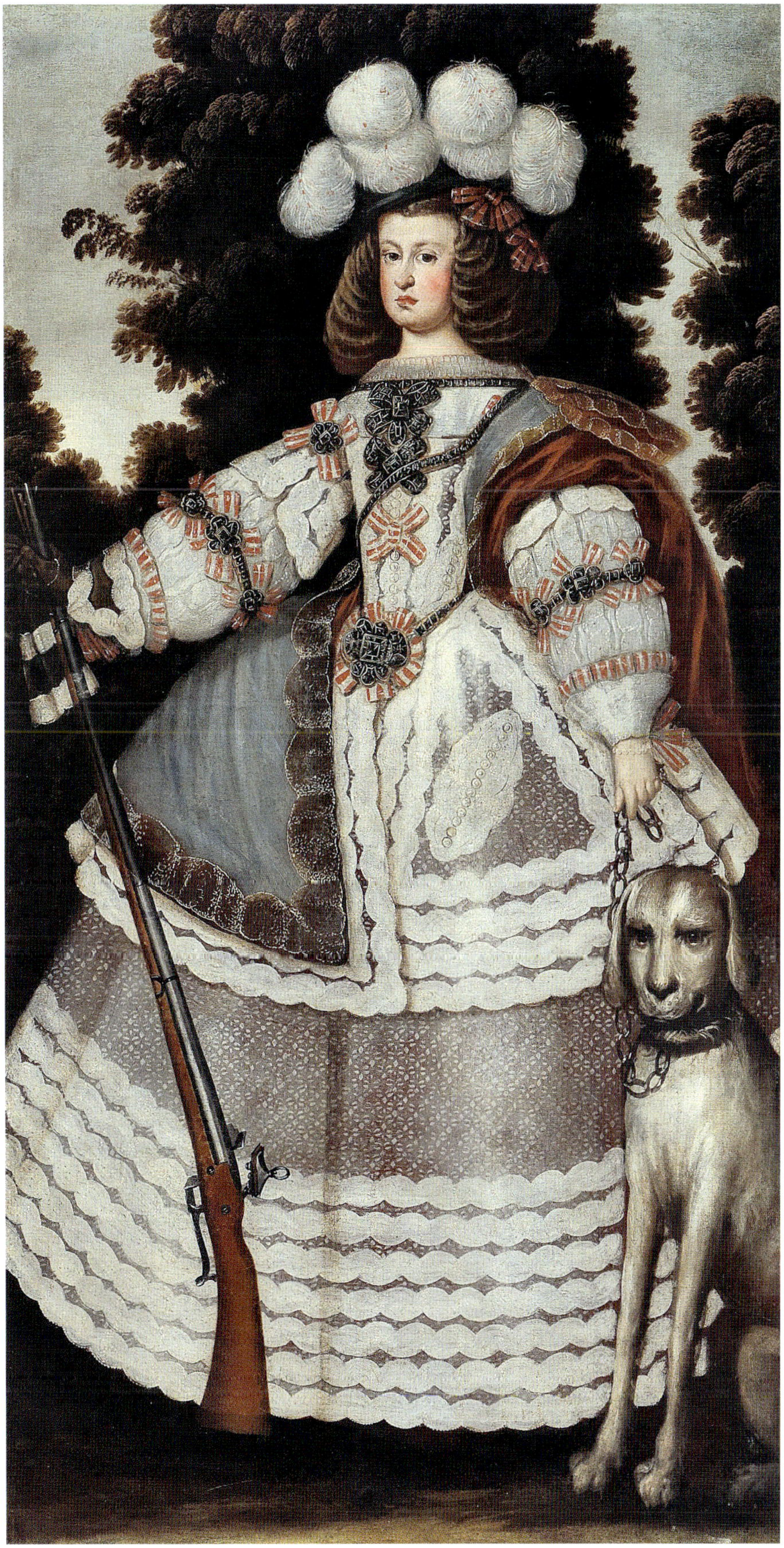

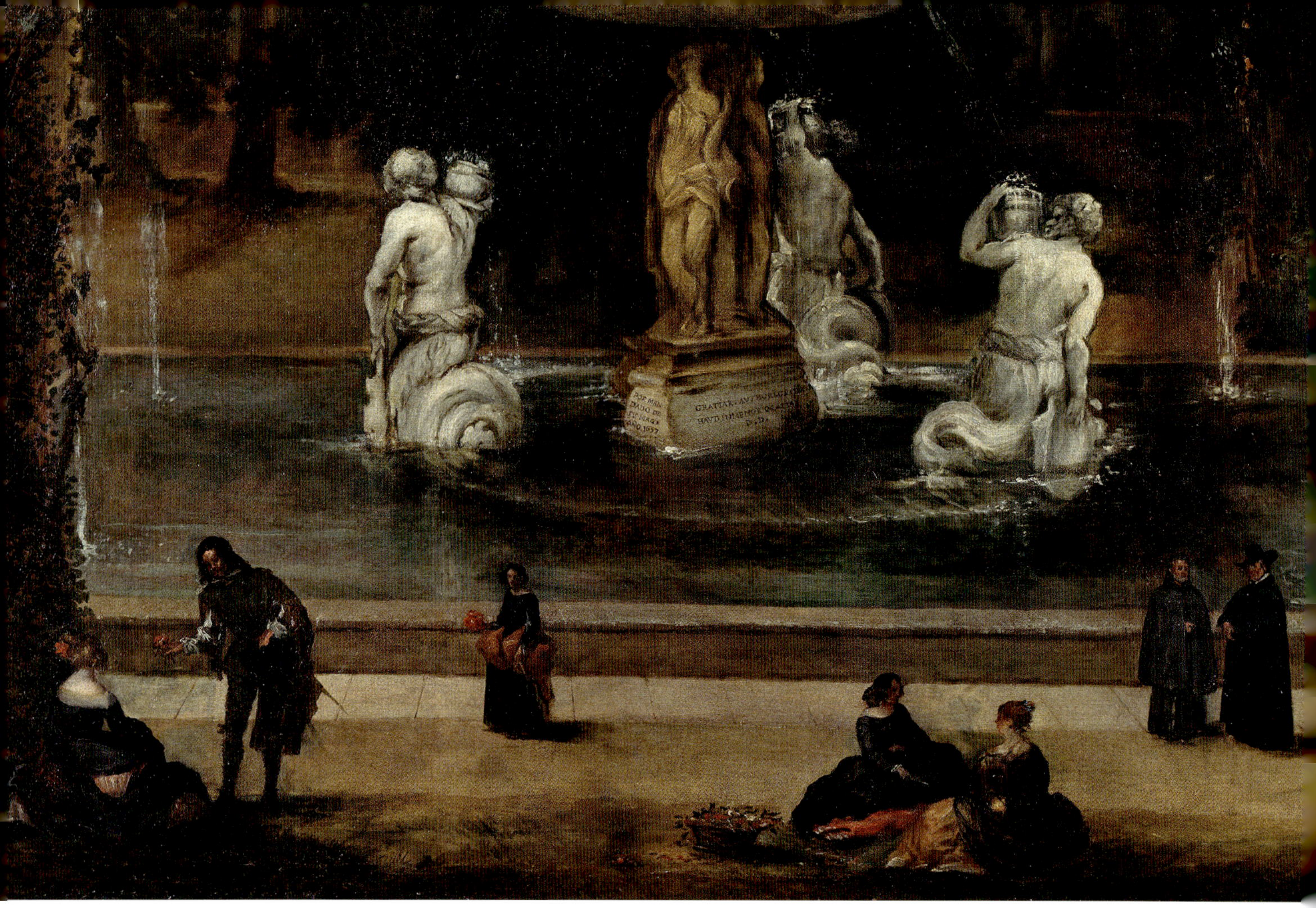

138. Workshop of Velázquez, *The Fountain of the Tritons in the Island Garden, Aranjuez*, 1657. Detail; oil on canvas, 248 × 223 cm. Museo Nacional del Prado, Madrid

Three or more silk petticoats were layered over a *guardainfante* to add even more volume to the queen's skirts. The uppermost petticoat, and the most richly decorated one, was the *pollera* (named for the baskets in which baby chickens were kept).[52] The *pollera* was made to be seen.[53] In a view of the grounds of the Royal Palace at Aranjuez, a seated woman in a black dress has arranged her skirts to reveal a bright red *pollera* with rows of glittering metal trimming (fig. 138). The queen's *polleras* were made from rich silks, including silver lamé and plush (for winter months), in a wide range of colors. The pinks and reds that were typically used for undergarments were most common, but there were also *polleras* in pale yellows and oranges, blue, and green. They were sometimes decorated with embroidery, but more often they were trimmed with silver lace. The Portuguese princess Catherine of Braganza modeled a silver *pollera* with wide scallop-edged silver lace around its vertical pocket openings (fig. 139). A *pollera* was worn over a *brial* or *guardapiés* and a *manteo*, which were made from the same materials but did not have pockets and were decorated with fewer rows of expensive trimming.

The majestic proportions of *Mariana in Black and Silver* were partially indebted to the high-soled cork shoes called *chapines* that elongated her legs beneath her skirt. Unmarried *meninas* such as Isabel de Velasco wore low-heeled shoes instead of *chapines* beneath their *guardainfantes*, which gave their skirts a horizontal, rectangular shape (fig. 140).[54] The Dutch diplomat Lodewijck Huygens reported that the petite Queen Mariana was still "more short than tall," even with her *chapines*.[55] Mariana's *chapines* were covered with rich cloth of silver imported from Italy, decorated with silver galloons, and adorned with rosettes made from silk ribbons trimmed with silver. She wore them with silk stockings and taffeta garters (*ligas*) trimmed with black or silver lace, which were made from silk of all colors to match her outfits from the inside out.[56]

While the archival evidence reveals what was going on beneath Aguado's dresses for the queen, Velázquez's portraits demonstrate how those dresses could be styled and accessorized. There was much room for creativity in the realm of accessories, which included lace collars and cuffs, large brooches and chains, ribbons worn on the wrists and in the hair, watches at the waist, muffs and gloves. Hairpieces were made from a wire framework, on which the queen's real hair was interwoven with false hair and a panoply of decorations.[57] In *Mariana in Black and Silver*, the queen wears a wig that echoes the shape of her *guardainfante*. The queen's wig is decorated with red bows, dangling gold ornaments, red and white plumes, and a large golden brooch. The wife of Antonio de

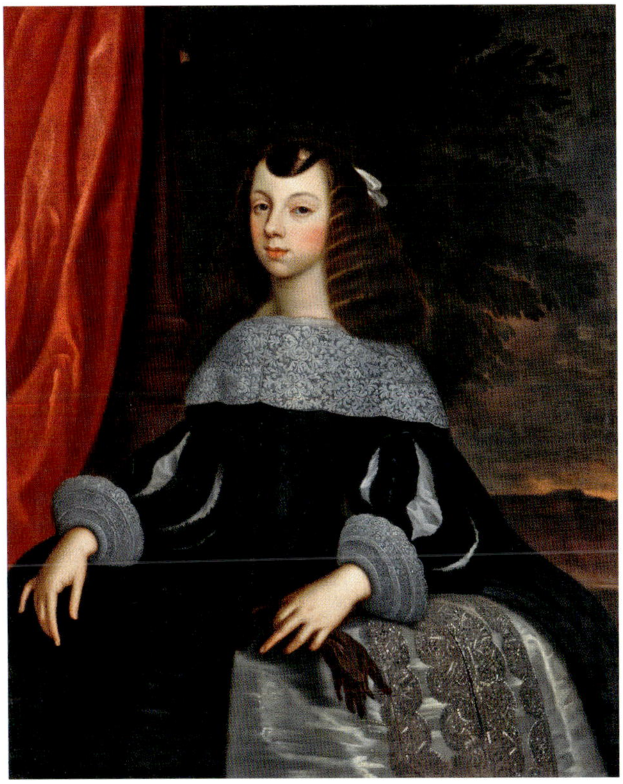

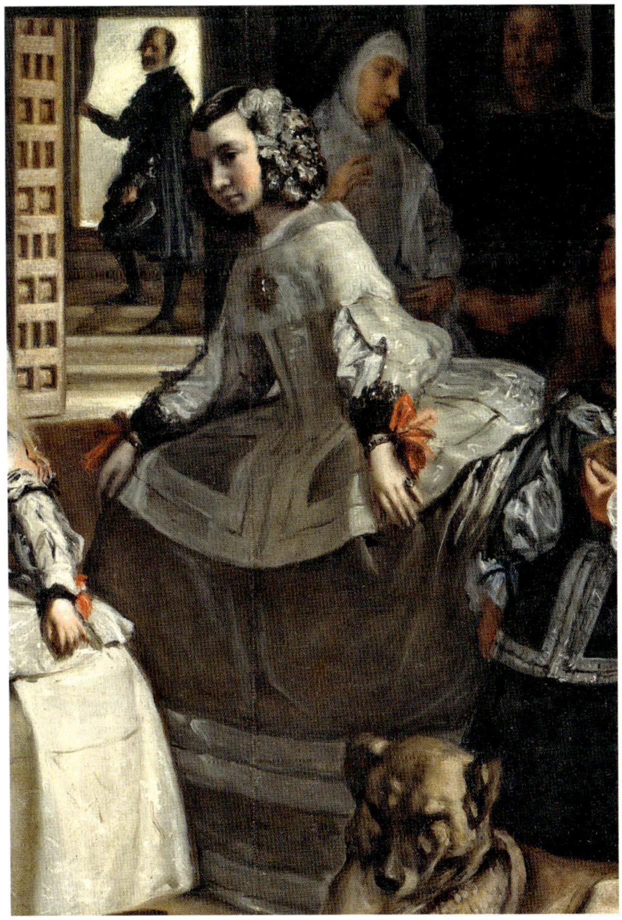

139. *(above right)* By or after Dirck Stoop, *Catherine of Braganza*, c. 1660–61. Oil on canvas, 123.2 × 100.3 cm. National Portrait Gallery, London

140. *(right)* The *menina* Isabel de Velasco. Diego Velázquez, *Las Meninas* (detail of fig. 2)

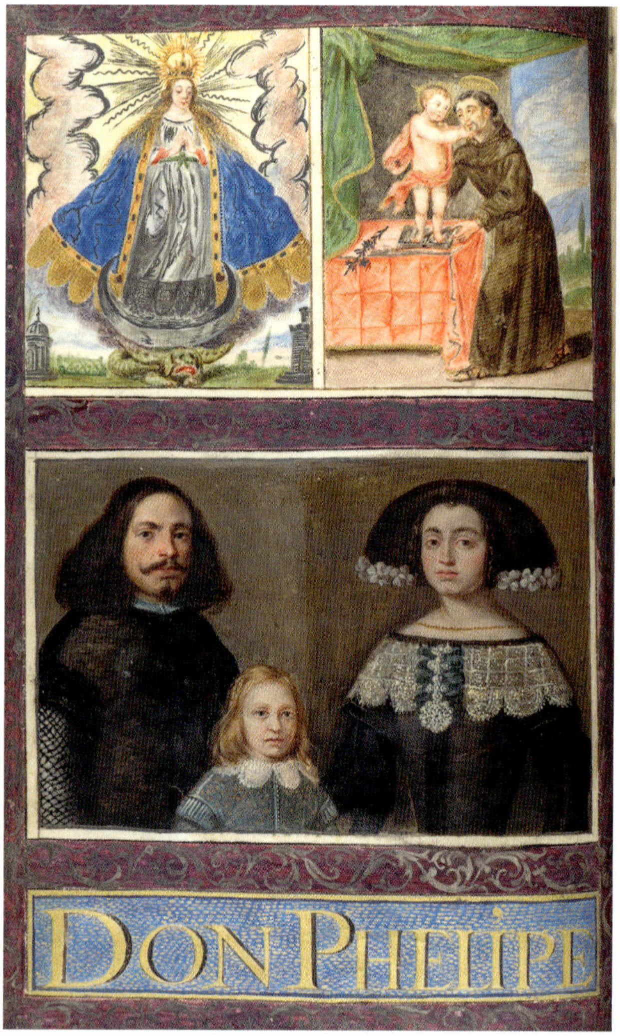

141. *Letters Patent of Nobility of Antonio de Contreras y Unçueta, Resident of Barajas*, Valladolid, 1651. Illumination on parchment, 31 × 19.2 cm. Hispanic Society of America, New York

Contreras wears a similarly shaped but less elaborately decorated hairpiece in an illuminated manuscript of 1651 (fig. 141). In this half-length portrait, the wig may serve as a proxy for the woman's unseen *guardainfante*.[58] Symmetrical *guardainfante*-shaped wigs fell out of favor shortly after *Mariana in Black and Silver* was painted and were replaced by an asymmetrical style that was equally embellished (see fig. 130).[59] The artificial hair of *Mariana in Black and Silver* matches the heavily made-up face, with whitened skin and brightly rouged cheeks and lips. Velázquez ignored what he had learned from Francisco Pacheco, who quoted Lodovico Dolce's caution against painting "flaming cheeks and coral lips, because they can look like masks" in his *Art of Painting*, completed in 1638 and posthumously published in 1649.[60] Pacheco's advice was ill-matched to the ethos of the court when Velázquez painted the queen's portrait in 1652. The same year saw the first performance of Pedro Calderón de la Barca's *Weapons of Beauty*, a play that revindicated the right of women to alter their appearances with clothing that changed their shape, false hair, and makeup.[61] In Mariana's Madrid, fashion, portraiture, and the theater were all connected in the celebration of artifice and the pursuit of novelty.[62]

The Return of the Theater

Queen Mariana delighted in the theater, which reclaimed its place as one of Madrid's most important venues for the dissemination of fashion in the early years of her reign.[63] The public playhouses that had been shut down by zealous reformers in 1646 officially reopened their doors in 1651. The Coliseo—the royal theater at the Buen Retiro—which had been completed in 1640 only to close a few years later, was restored and opened to the public. This was a state-of-the-art theater specially built for stage machinery and special effects, which were designed by a Florentine named Baccio del Bianco. "These Spaniards are desirous of novelties, of flying machines," Baccio wrote back home to the Grand Duke of Tuscany.[64] The audience that filled the royal theater could catch a glimpse of Aguado's latest dress designs worn by the queen, who viewed the extravagant performances from the royal balcony directly opposite the stage.[65] Underneath the royal balcony there was a seating section reserved for women called the *cazuela*—the "stewpot." Inside the theater, fashion information circulated in multiple directions, between the queen on her balcony, the actresses on the stage, and the women in the audience.

Queen Mariana commissioned Baccio del Bianco to make a set of drawings for her father, Emperor Ferdinand III, depicting the elaborate staging of Calderón's *Andromeda and Perseus*, which was performed at the Coliseo in the spring of 1653.[66] In Baccio's drawing of the final scene of the play, Perseus appears in Roman military dress, while Andromeda and the other women who decorate the stage wear the latest Spanish court fashions (fig. 142). Andromeda's dress, with its large bodice skirts and thick rows of trimming, resembles the dress in *Mariana in Black and Silver*, which had been painted only a few months earlier. The actress playing Andromeda wears her courtly dress over a wide farthingale that keeps Perseus at a distance; the shape of her skirt suggests that she is wearing flat shoes rather than high-soled *chapines*, which could have impeded her performance. Unlike the queen in her formal state portrait, the actress on stage wears her hair long and loose, and she goes without a modest collar, so that the tops of her shoulders are exposed. A French visitor who attended the royal theater in Madrid in 1655 was unimpressed by the costumes, which he described as "neither rich, nor appropriate to their subject." He denounced the use of anachronistic costumes, complaining that "the Spanish habit" was worn on stage even "where the scene is Greece or Rome."[67] As Baccio del Bianco's drawing shows, period-appropriate costumes were in fact worn by actors, but actresses dressed in the latest fashions were one of the great attractions of the theater. Perseus could wear antique garb because contemporary menswear was less changeable than women's fashions, and therefore much less interesting.

The Coliseo was open to the general public, and the women who flocked to attend its performances went dressed in the latest courtly fashions. A woman who did not own suitable attire could rent a dress from one of the licensed dress rental shops that specialized in fashionable finery for festivals, plays, and dances at the court.[68] The feminine ritual of getting dressed for a day at the theater was described in rich detail, with moralizing asides, in Juan de Zabaleta's *Holiday in the Morning* (1654). A lady's time-consuming toilette began with putting on her makeup and doing her hair up with ribbons (presumably she was already wearing her chemise at this point). Then the process of getting dressed began with putting on a *guardainfante* ("the stupidest nonsense to which the desire to look good has fallen"), followed by a petticoat "with rivers of gold for decoration," and then a "skirt with such a huge hem that it could serve as a pavilion." Once her lower half was dressed, Zabaleta's imaginary lady put on a boned bodice with skirts that were large enough to be worn as mantles, a flimsy over-gown, and a Carignano collar "with more needlework than if it were made in China."[69] An outfit was not complete without gold and pearl necklaces, a veil of transparent silk, gloves, and a muff in winter or a fan in summer. But a woman going to the theater left her apron behind, for

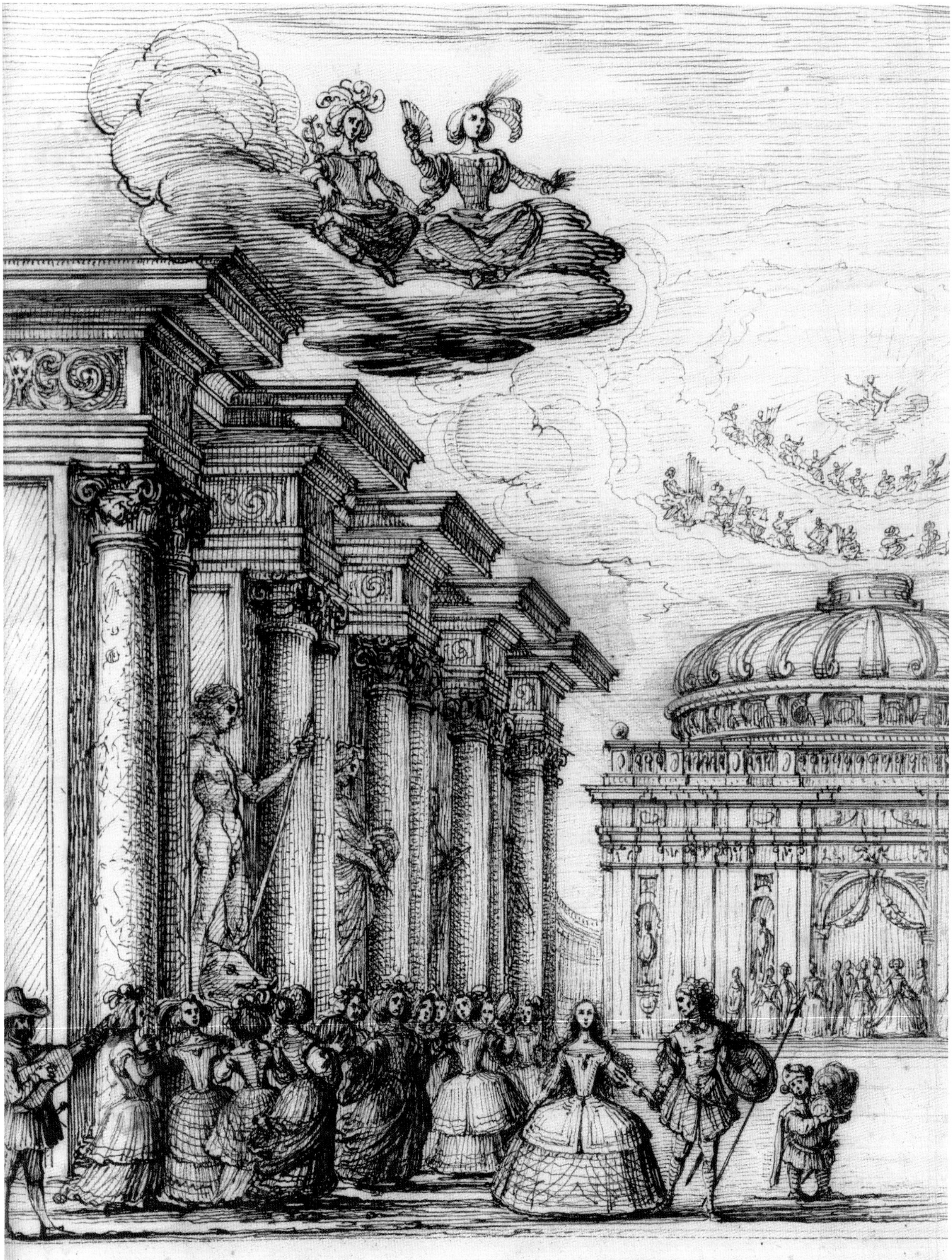

"this is the place of those who are going to see, and to be seen," as Zabaleta explained in *Holiday in the Afternoon* (1660).[70] The court chronicler Jerónimo de Barrionuevo recounted that the Coliseo was so overcrowded for one performance in June 1658 that women who arrived wearing *guardainfantes* were required to check in their farthingales at the cloakroom or turn around and go home.[71]

"Something Special"

From the actresses on the stage to the women watching the production from the "stewpot," all of the women at the Coliseo dressed in variations of the style that Aguado made for the queen. But they did not copy the queen exactly: each woman sought to wear something distinctive. Alonso Núñez de Castro, Philip IV's royal chronicler, articulated the philosophy that governed the Spanish court in his book *Only Madrid is Court, and the Courtier in Madrid* (1658). He advised the courtier to be neither the first nor the last to adopt the latest novelties in dress. It was best, he wrote, to follow the majority in dress and to seek singularity only in those garments that could not be easily imitated.[72] The Dutch ambassador Lodewijck Huygens described how Mariana's ladies distinguished themselves through dress while dining with the queen in public in 1660. All of the queen's ladies wore very wide *guardainfantes*, he noted, but "not all the women are dressed in the same way." Huygens noticed that their dresses were made from various kinds of fabrics in different colors, some with gold or silver lace and others with embroidery, and that there were differences in their sleeves and hair ornaments. "Almost every woman wears something special," he wrote.[73] When he traveled with the court to the Royal Palace of El Pardo, Huygens observed that the queen's ladies wore different kinds of head-coverings—some a small hat, others a cap or feathers—"almost all of them with a distinctive touch."[74] The novelties of the early 1650s had given rise to a new era of individuality in women's fashions at the Spanish court.

The dresses that Aguado made for Mariana provided the template for all other women to follow, the foundation onto which they could add their special something. What better, then, than to have a dress made by the queen's own tailor? This was a privilege that only Madrid's most elite families enjoyed. Beginning in the mid-1650s, Aguado began to work for high-ranking aristocrats who wanted their daughters to be dressed by the royal tailor. His exclusive clientele included Juana de Rojas y Córdoba, Marchioness of Leganés y Poza, who commissioned Aguado to make clothes for herself, her children and grandchildren, and liveries for her household staff between 1655 and 1657.[75] Another client, Mariana Engracia de Toledo y Portugal, Marchioness of Los Vélez, hired Aguado to make dresses for her daughter, María Teresa Fajardo, who was received as a lady-in-waiting by Queen Mariana in 1659.[76] Few details about Aguado's work outside of the court are documented, except for the fact that his aristocratic clients were negligent in paying for his services. Even so, working for the high nobility paid handsomely in terms of social status.[77] Aguado won an even more tangible sign of his standing in 1654, when he was granted the honor of hanging the royal coat of arms above his front door.[78] As Baltasar Gracián had promised, the inventor of novelties was richly rewarded.

142. *(facing page)* Baccio del Bianco, set design for Pedro Calderón de la Barca's *Andrómeda y Perseo*, 1653. Detail; pen and ink on paper, 39.5 × 30 cm. Houghton Library, Harvard University, Cambridge, MA

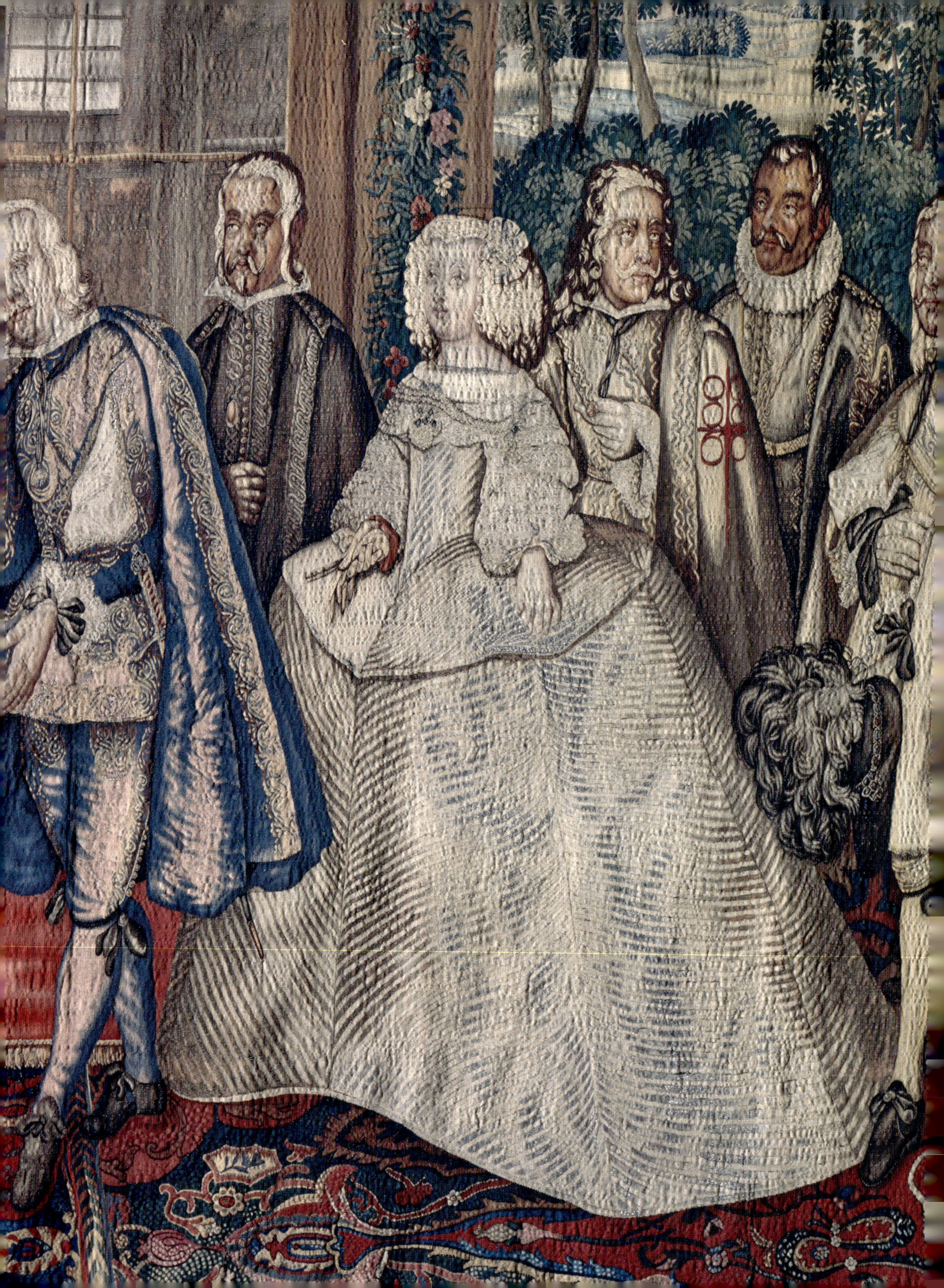

6. Royal Matchmaking

Dressing the Infantas, Later 1650s

"Famous" was the king's favorite adjective to describe his two daughters, María Teresa and her younger half-sister Margarita. "*Mis muchachas famosas*"—"my famous girls"—he called them.[1] The king wrote affectionately of his daughters and recounted their development in a series of personal letters to María Teresa's former governess, the Countess of Paredes de Nava. In 1652 the king wrote that María Teresa—just turned 14 "is famous and very much grown," while one-year-old Margarita "is a famous little bug [*savandija*], and although she doesn't talk, there is nothing that she does not understand, nor anyone she does not know."[2] By "famous," the king meant that his girls were perfect in every way.[3] They were of course also famous in the sense of being very well-known, thanks to their lineage. They remained famous centuries after their deaths, in large part because of Velázquez's portraits of them—and the extraordinary dresses that they wear in those paintings—with Margarita being the most famous of all thanks to her starring role in *Las Meninas*.

Making marriage matches for the infantas was one of the most important political issues at the Spanish court in the 1650s, second only to the related question of when or whether Queen Mariana would give birth to a male heir. With two daughters to marry off, Philip IV had two opportunities to strengthen an alliance or negotiate peace with an enemy. María Teresa's hand in marriage was so desirable that there had been a rumor in 1648 of a plot to kidnap the 10-year-old infanta and marry her to King Louis XIV of France or the Infante Teodósio of Portugal, two countries with which Spain was at war.[4] In the 1650s, the serious contenders for marriage to the Spanish infantas included Holy Roman Emperor Ferdinand III's two sons and his brother, Archduke Leopold Wilhelm, who was Governor of the Spanish Netherlands. A marriage between María Teresa and her cousin Louis XIV of France was considered to be the best possible match for Spain, as an honorable way to conclude the war that had begun before the potential bride or groom had been born. But the possibilities were limited as long as Philip IV lacked a male heir, since María Teresa was next in line for the throne. This meant that she could not leave Spain, and whomever she married would have to move to Madrid as her consort. The matchmaking map was scrambled in 1657 when the auspiciously named Felipe Próspero—Philip Prosper—was born. In the end, María Teresa married Louis XIV of France, and Margarita married Leopold I, who had replaced his father as Holy Roman Emperor. Thus one of the king's famous girls became Queen of France, the other Holy Roman Empress.

143. *(facing page)* Infanta María Teresa at Pheasant Island. Charles Le Brun, *Meeting between Louis XIV and Philip IV* (detail of fig. 162)

Throughout the complex and drawn-out negotiations that led to these unions, the infantas' appearances were closely scrutinized by royal wooers and their representatives. The Spanish court communicated through the dresses of the infantas, who had no public voice in these matters themselves; more than one foreign commentator noted how quiet María Teresa was, even when spoken to directly. Mateo Aguado, who dressed the Infantas María Teresa and Margarita from the day they were born until the day they left Madrid to marry abroad, designed the dresses that they wore at every phase of the matchmaking process. His dresses for the infantas in the 1650s were widely seen by an international audience, whether witnessed in person by diplomats visiting the Spanish court, viewed through portraits, or described in printed *relaciones*. The tailor's work culminated in the dresses that he made for María Teresa's trousseau, which is reconstructed here for the first time. Dress historian Diana de Marly called the meeting of the Spanish and French at the border in June 1660, which was commemorated in a tapestry designed by Charles Le Brun, "the most famous costume clash of the century" (fig. 143).[5] This famous event resulted from the well-known diplomatic efforts of the towering political figures of the age—and the work of Aguado and his colleagues who were dressing the infanta behind the scenes.

The Infantas, Aguado, and Velázquez

Diego Velázquez painted numerous portraits of the infantas in the 1650s, which were sent to the Holy Roman Emperor at the imperial court and remain in Vienna at the Kunsthistorisches Museum. The painter, who had ignored María Teresa in her younger years while he was focused on her older brother Baltasar Carlos, painted a full-length portrait of the king's elder daughter as she approached age 15 and her marriage became a matter of greater urgency. He also painted three portraits of the Infanta Margarita between ages three and eight, which documented her development and the evolution of her dresses at different stages of childhood. These four portraits provide an exceptionally rich visual record of Aguado's work for the king's daughters in this decade, while the tailor's documentation offers insights into the material reality of the infantas' famous dresses.

The Spanish court sent full-length portraits of the Infanta María Teresa—"promotional" portraits, as they have been aptly called—to potential suitors at the courts of Vienna, Brussels, and Paris in late 1653.[6] The best of the three paintings, which is thought to be the only one by the hand of Velázquez, was sent to the imperial court in Vienna, so that the potential Austrian bridegrooms could assess the infanta's beauty and suitability as a bride (fig. 144).[7] María Teresa, now about 15 years old, wears a formal dress with hanging sleeves (*mangas de casaca*) made from a pearlescent patterned silk fabric and decorated with crisscrosses of silver on the bodice that hint at a lattice design (*celosía*). The stiff, flat front of her bodice was undergirded by a boned corset; Aguado had begun to make corsets for the infanta in 1649, when she was about 11 years old.[8] María Teresa's development was a subject of great concern to her father. In April 1653, Philip IV wrote to the Countess of Paredes de Nava that his elder daughter had "grown and softened" but had not yet become a woman, which he hoped would happen soon.[9]

In addition to showing María Teresa's maturity to her prospective bridegrooms, Velázquez's portrait also communicated her Spanishness through her dress and

144. *(facing page)* Diego Velázquez, *Infanta María Teresa*, 1653. Oil on canvas, 127 × 98.5 cm. Kunsthistorisches Museum, Vienna

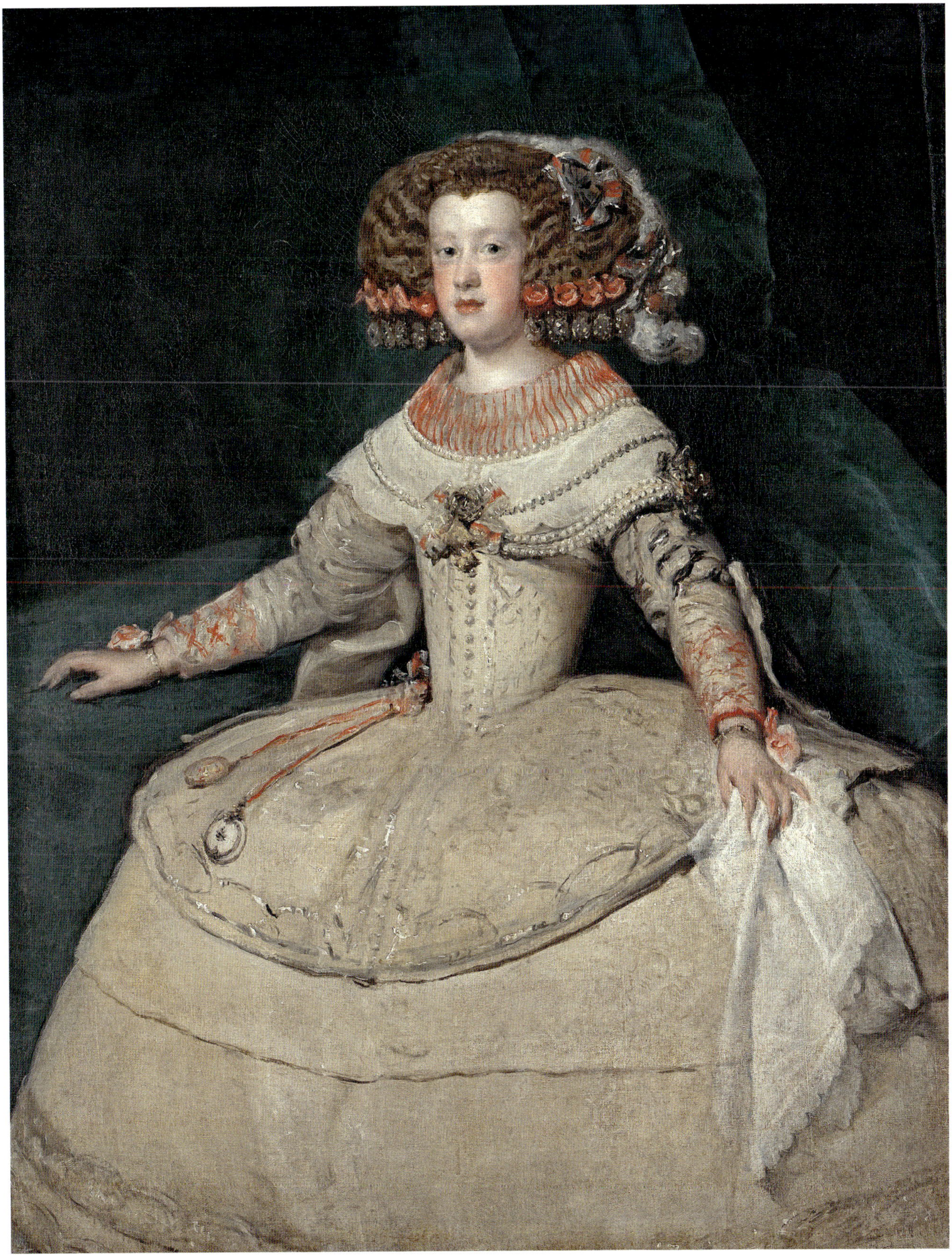

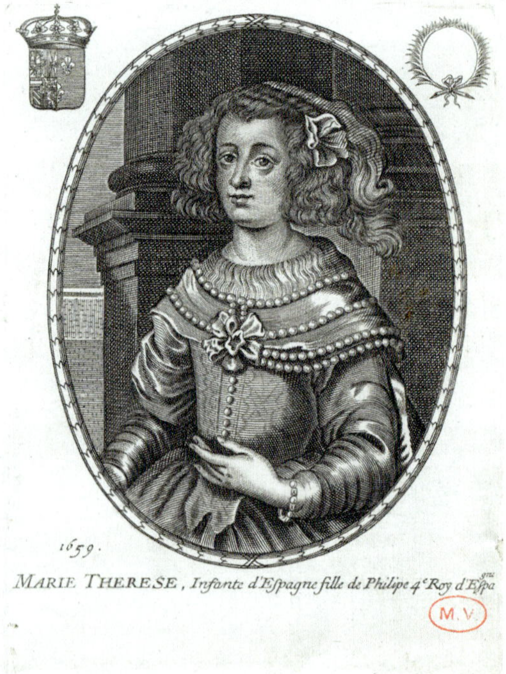

145. Unknown printmaker after Velázquez, *María Teresa, Infanta of Spain, Daughter of Philip IV, King of Spain*, 1659. Etching and engraving, 18.3 × 13.7 cm. Palace of Versailles

grooming. The most obvious sign of her nationality is the large *guardainfante*, which would have appeared even more imposing before the painting was cut down at the bottom and sides.[10] The infanta's elaborately decorated wig and heavy makeup were also features of the Spanish style that foreign observers tended to fixate upon. One Frenchman visiting the Spanish court in 1655 caught a glimpse of the Infanta María Teresa and wrote approvingly of her "sprightly mean and quick eye." But he thought it "a pity the custom of the country obliges her to paint, for with less red she would certainly appear more lovely," and he disparagingly described her hair as "thick and knotty elflocks" that looked like "hempen stuffing broke out of an old pack-saddle."[11] A print made in France edited Velázquez's promotional portrait, presumably to appeal to a French audience, by replacing her heavily decorated wig with natural hair and eliminating the *guardainfante* (fig. 145).

Velázquez's first portrait of the Infanta Margarita, painted in 1654 when she was about three years old, was made for Emperor Ferdinand III so that he could see his granddaughter (fig. 146). Margarita wears a rich floral-patterned silk in salmon pink and silver that is decorated with thick rows of wavy silver trimming. The dress in the portrait represents the kinds of luxurious materials that Aguado was using to make the infanta's dresses that year, which included flowered satin in white and incarnadine, silver satin, blue watered silk, cloth of silver, and embroidered mother-of-pearl plush. At this age, the Infanta Margarita had graduated from wearing leading strings, but she was still wearing a young child's "little sack" (*saquito*) over a floor-length skirt. A double layer of petticoats (*enaguas*) made from camlet or double taffeta added volume to her skirt, since she was not yet wearing a farthingale.[12] At the Spanish court, a girl's transition to a farthingale was equivalent to the masculine ritual of breeching. In April 1655, Margarita's governess wrote to the king that the infanta was amusing herself by playing dress-up with a *guardainfante*.[13] The next year, she began to wear a farthingale for real, as Aguado's charges reveal.

Margarita made the transition from a toddler's "little sack" to a mature doublet and began to wear a *guardainfante* and *pollera* beneath her skirt sometime between January and April 1656, when she was about four-and-a-half-years old. The infanta did not begin wearing over-gowns until the next year, so her earliest doublets had their own shoulder-wings and hanging sleeves. The first mature dress listed in Aguado's charges was a skirt and doublet with fitted sleeves and hanging sleeves made from an exceptionally rich silk fabric embroidered with silver and steel that was decorated along the edges with "little silver points" alternating up and down (*almenillas*).[14] This was one of three dresses that the infanta received as a gift from García de Haro Sotomayor y Guzmán, 2nd Count of Castrillo, who was serving as the Spanish viceroy in Naples—an Italian city known for its silks made with silver and gold.[15] The viceroy's gift also included outfits for the king and queen, María Teresa, and other favored members of the court. Jerónimo de Barrionuevo reported on March 25, 1656, that the garments made from Neapolitan silks were "priceless in their richness, expense, and fineness of the work."[16] The royal clothes made in Naples were likely cut from patterns sent from Madrid, as they had been in 1638, when buckram patterns were sent to the viceroy in Naples to have garments made for the king, queen, and prince.[17] The dresses that the Count of Castrillo sent to Queen Mariana and the Infantas María Teresa and Margarita are described in Aguado's charges, and this indicates that the queen's tailor worked on the garments after they reached the Spanish court.[18]

Velázquez painted a portrait of Margarita wearing a silvery-white dress with silver zigzag trimming that could be the dress decorated with "little silver points" that the Count of Castrillo had sent from Naples (fig. 147). The infanta wears the same dress in *Las Meninas*, which Velázquez painted in 1656 to hang in Philip IV's private quarters (fig. 148). The portraits for the king and emperor, Margarita's father and grandfather, depicted her at a crucial moment of her development shortly after she had made the transition to adult dress.[19] Until this time, the infanta had led a very cloistered life at the palace, with her interactions limited to the royal family and their closest household members. Now that she was old enough to dress in mature clothes and manipulate a *guardainfante*, the Infanta Margarita held her first public audience at the end of April 1656.[20]

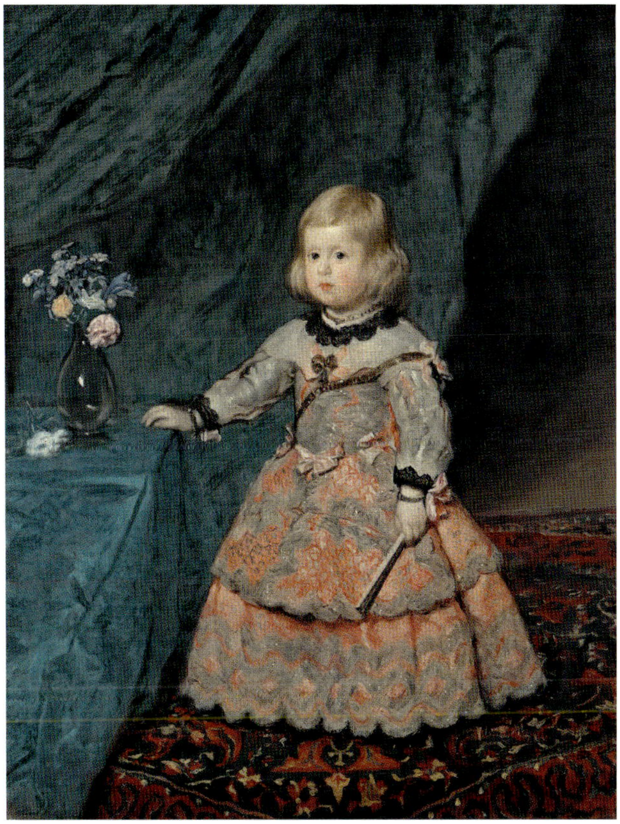

146. Diego Velázquez, *Infanta Margarita in Pink*, 1654. Oil on canvas, 128 × 99.6 cm. Kunsthistorisches Museum, Vienna

On September 11, 1657, Philip IV imposed a new sumptuary law—the first in almost a quarter century—forbidding the use of any fabrics or trims made from precious metals. This included brocaded silks, cloth of silver or gold, embroidery, lace, and galloon made with silver or gold. Only gold or silver buttons were exempt from the ban.[21] The purpose of the law was to support an earlier ban on luxury imports from enemy nations—France, Portugal, and England—by quashing demand for the forbidden items. The Council of Castile had advised the king on August 18, 1657, that the only way to successfully implement the law was for the queen and her household to observe it, and the evidence shows that they actually did.[22] In 1657, Aguado abruptly stopped using the silver decorations that had featured so prominently in his work for the queen and infantas the previous year. In place of silver trim, the tailor used ornaments cut from satin or kidskin (*cabritilla*), black and white silk *pasamanos*, and white openwork (*enrejado*) to decorate their dresses. In an anonymous portrait of Margarita from the collection of King James II of England, which was likely painted after the sumptuary law, the infanta wears a dress decorated with wide scallops of white bobbin lace in place of the silver trimmings that she had worn prior to 1657 (fig. 149).[23] The new laws were assiduously followed by the royal family, with one notable exception: after Mariana gave birth to Philip Prosper on November 28, 1657, the king celebrated the arrival of a male heir by wearing gala dress with diamond buttons.[24]

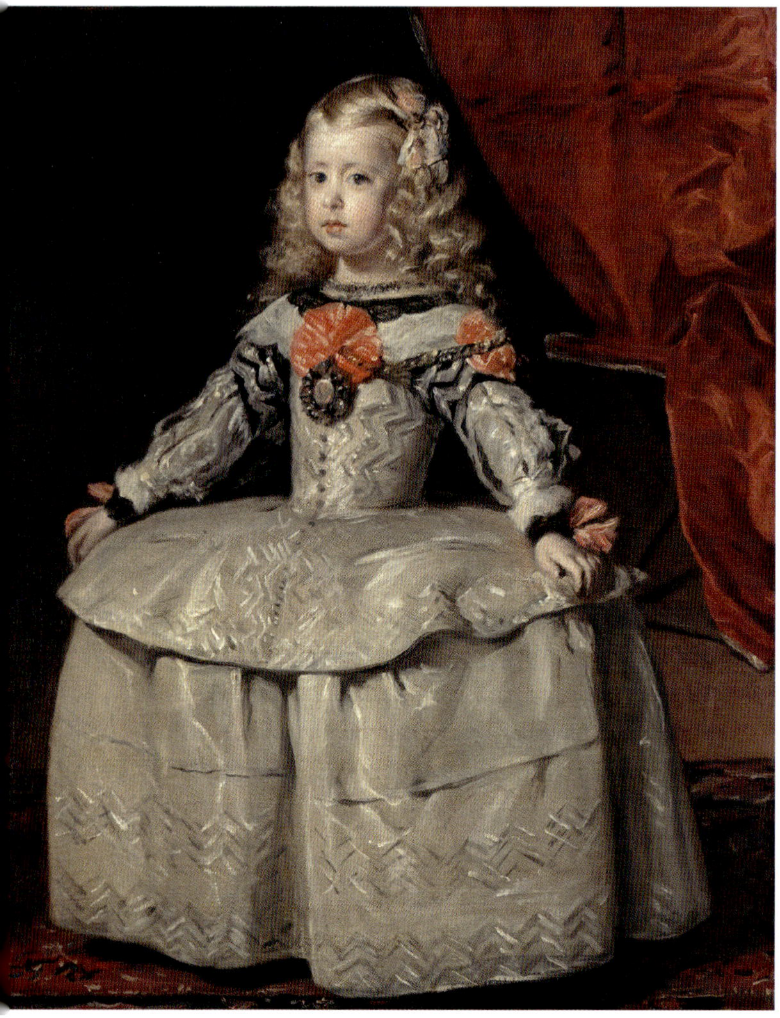

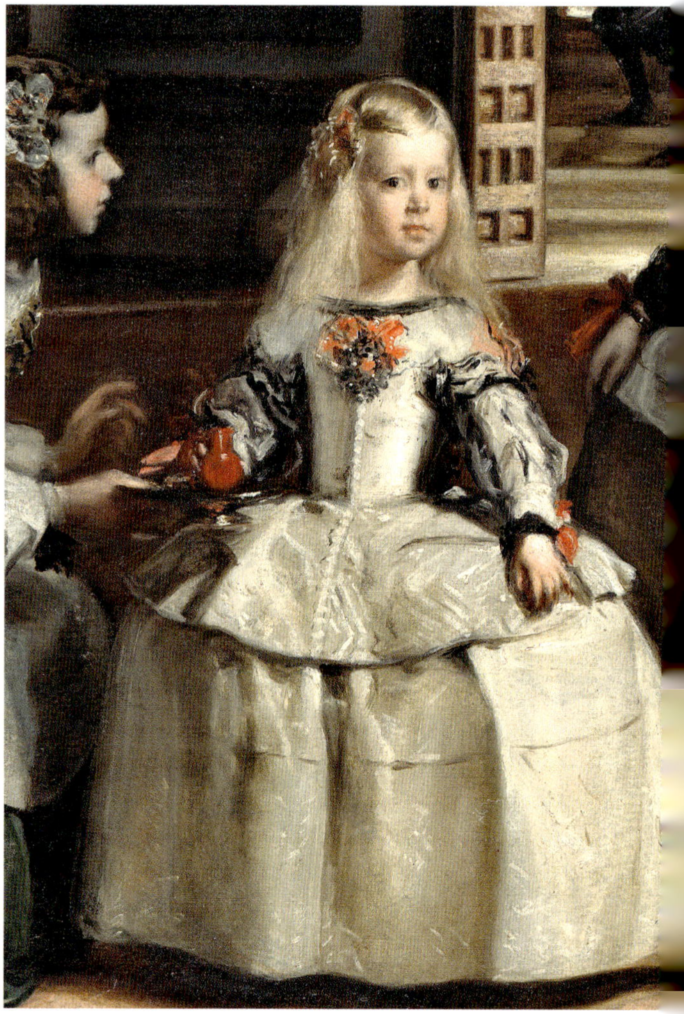

Velázquez painted a portrait of Philip Prosper wearing the skirts of early childhood in health-giving red, with a belt of protective amulets around his waist (fig. 150). This portrait was sent to the imperial court with Velázquez's final portrait of the Infanta Margarita, painted in 1659. Margarita, now about eight years old, wears a dress of silk plush in a brilliant blue color known as *celeste* (fig. 151).[25] The clothes worn by both of the king's children are richly decorated with silver trim (the metallic trimming on the infanta's dress has a warm, golden tone, but it was probably intended to read as silver). Aguado's charges show that the tailor was still following the sumptuary law of 1657 when these portraits were

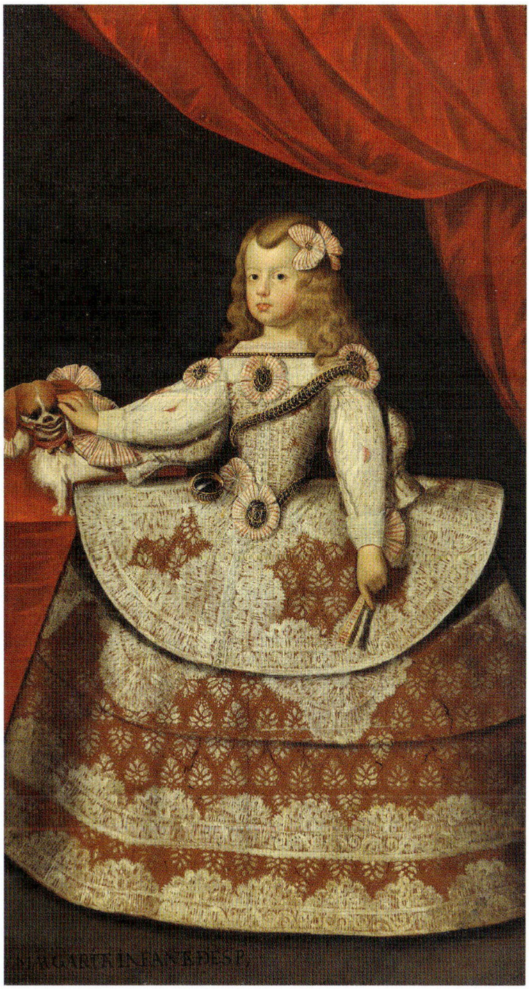

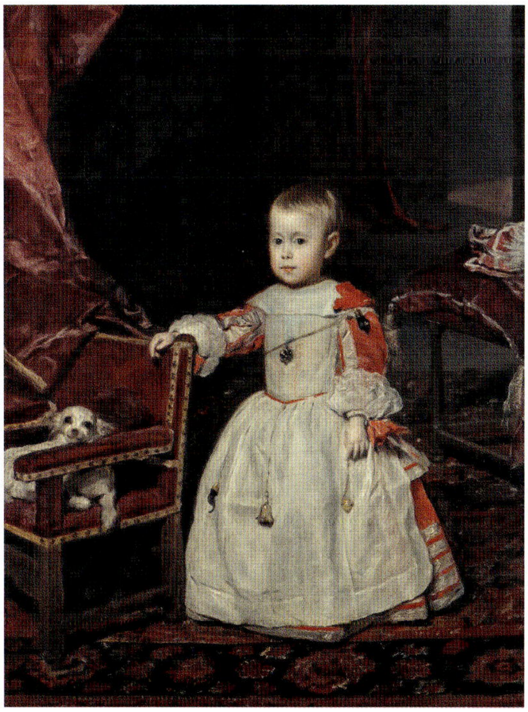

147. *(facing page, left)* Diego Velázquez, *Infanta Margarita in White*, c. 1656. Oil on canvas, 105 × 88 cm. Kunsthistorisches Museum, Vienna

148. *(facing page, right)* Infanta Margarita in *Las Meninas* (detail of fig. 2)

149. *(above right)* Workshop of Velázquez, *Infanta Margarita*, c. 1658–62. Oil on canvas, 186.5 × 103 cm. Royal Collection Trust, UK

150. *(right)* Diego Velázquez, *Prince Philip Prosper*, 1659. Oil on canvas, 129 × 100 cm. Kunsthistorisches Museum, Vienna

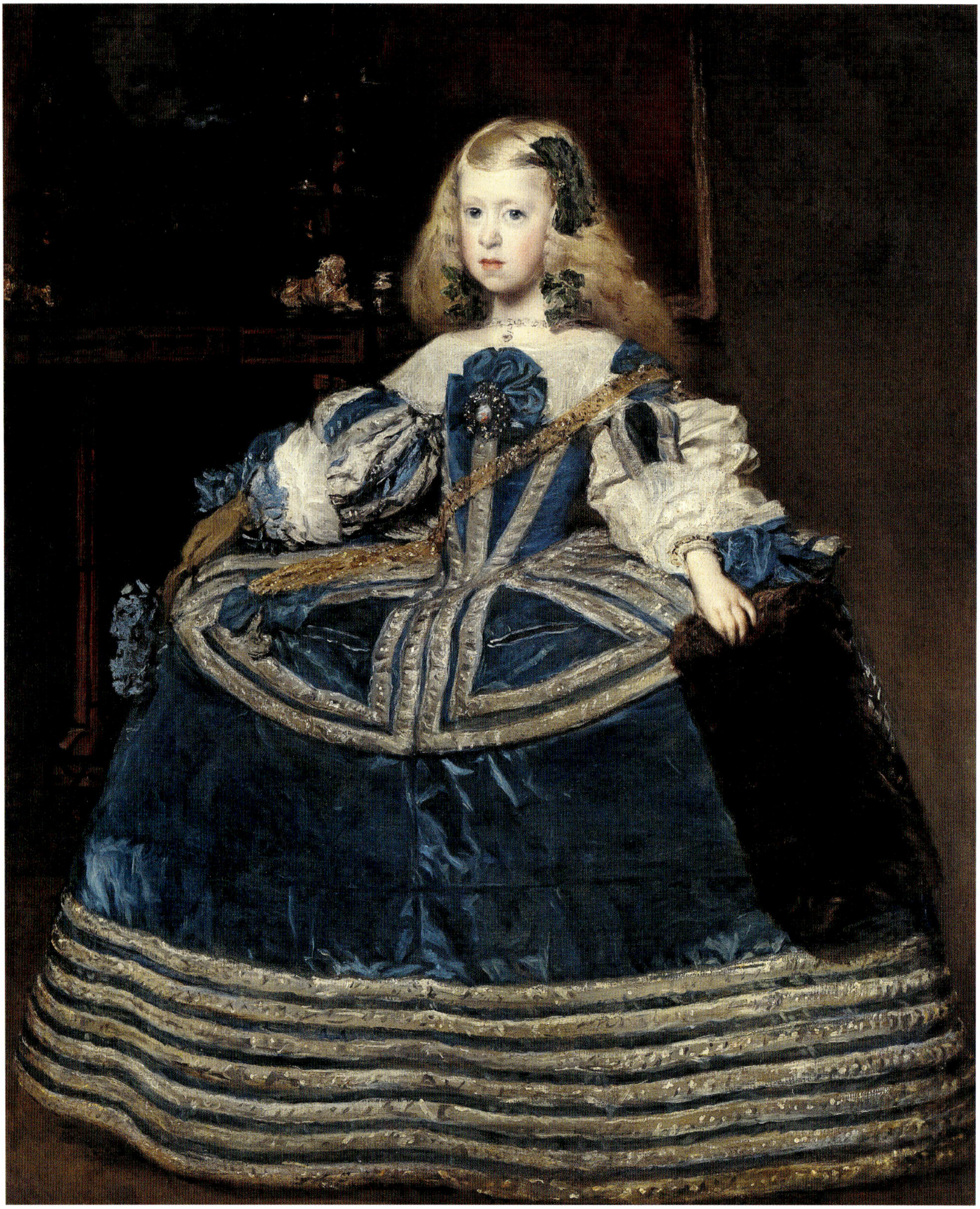

151. Diego Velázquez, *Infanta Margarita in Blue*, 1659. Oil on canvas, 125.5 × 106 cm. Kunsthistorisches Museum, Vienna

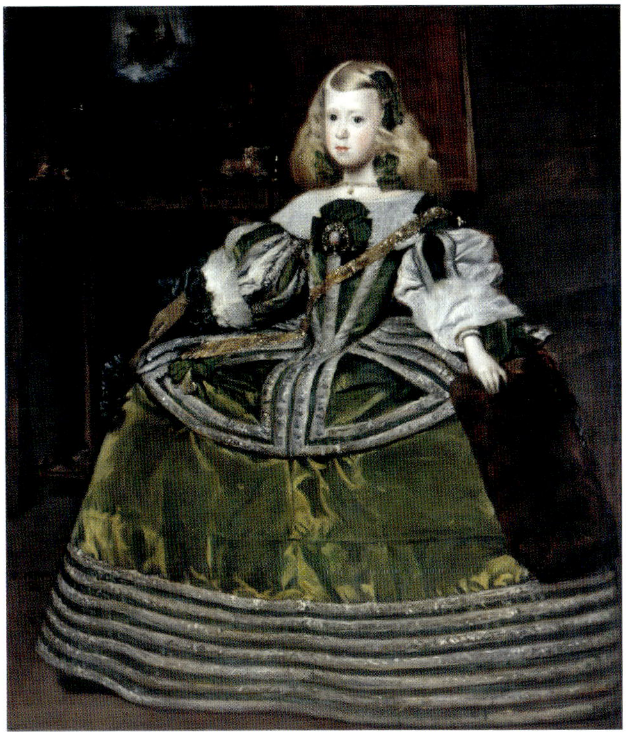

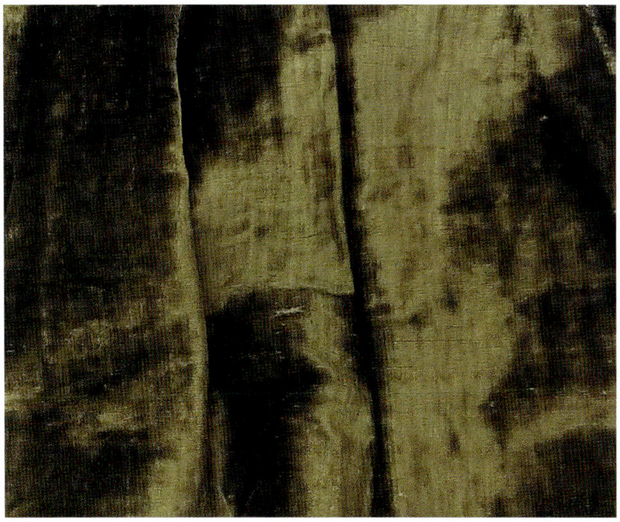

152. *(left)* Juan Bautista Martínez del Mazo, *Infanta Margarita in Green*, c. 1659. Oil on canvas, 121 × 107 cm. Szépművészeti Múzeum/Museum of Fine Arts, Budapest

153. *(above)* Olive-green silk plush girl's gown (detail), British, 1610–20. Victoria and Albert Museum, London

painted, and he made no dresses for the infanta with silver trimming in 1659. If Velázquez was working with an actual dress in his studio, he could have used an older dress that Aguado had made before the law was implemented. There was, for example, a skirt and doublet with fitted and hanging sleeves made in 1656 from blue *felpa* and decorated with six rows of silver trimming on the skirt.[26] Of course, Margarita had to have outgrown that dress by 1659, but a younger child could have modeled it for the painter, or he could have used a studio mannequin.

Another version of this portrait raises the question of whether Velázquez was actually working from a blue dress. In a painting that is attributed to Juan Bautista Martínez del Mazo, Margarita wears the same dress, except in green (fig. 152). Margarita wore green often, and in 1659, Aguado made her dresses of plush in two different shades of green: one was *verde* (grass-green) and the other was *olivo* (olive-green).[27] Plush has a deep pile that creates striking tonal variations in its color, a quality that can be appreciated in an early-seventeenth-century girl's gown made from olive-green plush (fig. 153). The highlights and shadows are almost identical in Mazo's green dress and Velázquez's version in blue. In both paintings, the ribbons adorning the infanta's wrists, brooch, and gloves match the color of her dress, with one exception: *Infanta Margarita in Blue* wears green ribbons in her hair. This is unexpected, since it was typical to match ribbons to a dress (except when that dress was black); the observant Dutch ambassador Lodewijck Huygens noticed that Queen Mariana wore green and silver ribbons in her hair and at her wrists that matched her green and silver dress.[28] Considering all the evidence, the most likely scenario is that both artists were working from a green dress, which Velázquez's junior colleague reproduced faithfully, while the master chose instead to dip his brush into the azurite on his palette and transform the bilious green into a showstopping blue. Velázquez also brightened the blue of the infanta's eyes—which appear grayer in the *Infanta Margarita in Pink* (see fig. 146)—to match her brilliant blue dress.[29]

The changes that Velázquez made to Margarita's dress and appearance created a realistic fiction that showed the infanta and the Spanish court to their best advantage. This was especially important when Velázquez painted *Infanta Margarita in Blue*, which had a different purpose from the earlier portraits of the infanta that had been sent to Vienna. While portraits of Margarita as a young child had been family portraits intended for her grandfather, *Infanta Margarita in Blue* was meant for the eyes of a potential suitor.[30] The portrait was sent to Margarita's cousin, Leopold I, who had been elected Holy Roman Emperor after the death of Emperor Ferdinand III. Previously, Leopold had been seen as a likely match for María Teresa, but this had changed after the birth of Philip Prosper. When Velázquez painted *Infanta Margarita in Blue*, negotiations were underway to marry the elder infanta to Louis XIV and bring about an honorable peace with France.[31]

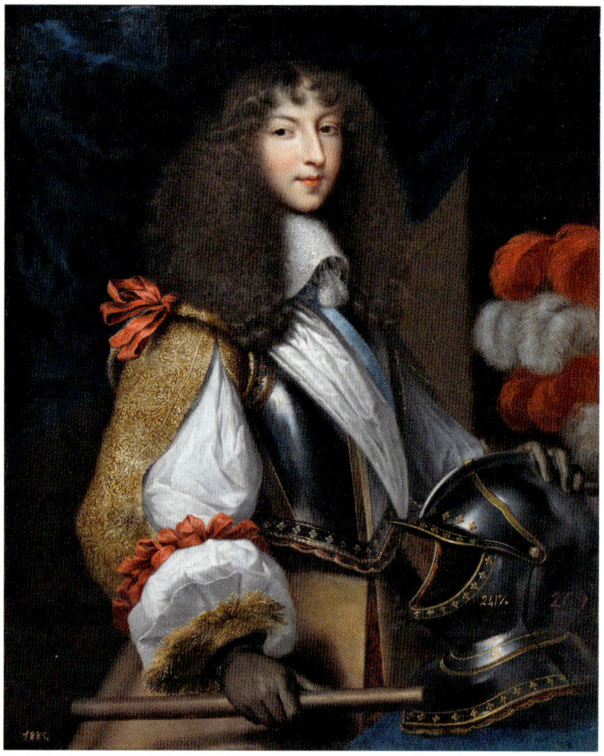

154. Attributed to Jean Nocret, *Young Louis XIV*, 1655. Oil on canvas, 108.5 × 89 cm. Museo Nacional del Prado, Madrid

Dress Diplomacy

In 1655, Anne of Austria, queen mother of France, sent her brother Philip IV a series of royal portraits, which included a portrait of her son, Louis XIV (fig. 154). The young King of France is dashing in a breastplate worn with full sleeves cinched below the elbow with the flame-colored ribbons that were popular at the French court.[32] A Venetian ambassador at the Spanish court reported that the Infanta María Teresa made every excuse possible to visit the portrait of her cousin and called him her *novio*, her "bridegroom."[33] Years later, when the two were married, María Teresa reportedly confided to Françoise Bertaut de Motteville that she had fallen in love with Louis XIV's portraits.[34] The possibility that María Teresa would marry Louis XIV grew much stronger in 1657 when Philip Prosper was born. Now that María Teresa was no longer first in line for the throne, she was free to marry and move abroad. At Philip Prosper's

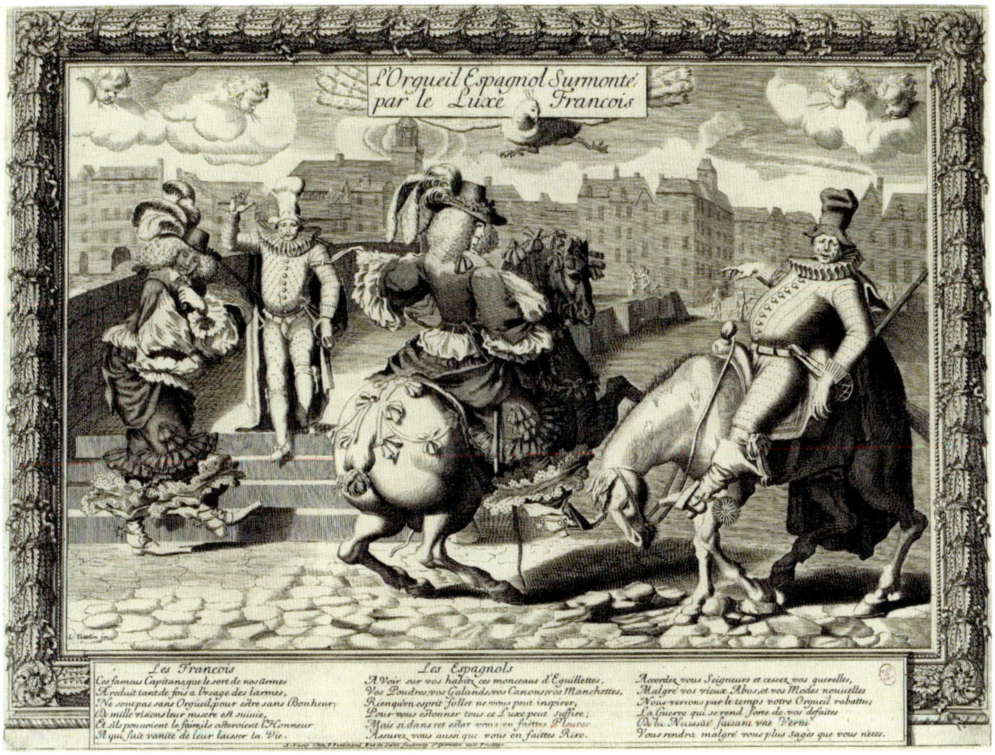

155. Anonymous engraver after a drawing by Louis Testelin, *French Luxury Victorious over Spanish Pride*, mid-17th century. Etching, 39 × 52.5 cm. Musée Carnavalet–Histoire de Paris

baptism on December 13, 1657, the elder infanta served as godmother. For the occasion, Aguado made María Teresa a *saya entera* of gauze with white and incarnadine stripes.[35] A printed *relación* describing the baptism explained that this "new and curious fabric" contained a coded message in its stripes, which symbolized "the blood-red rose of Castile on one side, and on the other the French fleur-de-lis."[36] Aguado's dress communicated the infanta's availability to the French, and the *relación* spread the news far and wide.[37]

Negotiations for a marriage between the Infanta María Teresa and Louis XIV began in earnest after Mariana gave birth to a second healthy boy, named Ferdinand Thomas, on December 23, 1658. With an heir and a spare, it seemed safe to marry Philip IV's elder daughter abroad. In August 1659, Philip IV's royal favorite, Luis Méndez de Haro (who replaced the Count-Duke of Olivares after his fall from grace), and Louis XIV's chief minister, Cardinal Mazarin, met at Pheasant Island, on the border between the two nations (see Map 1),

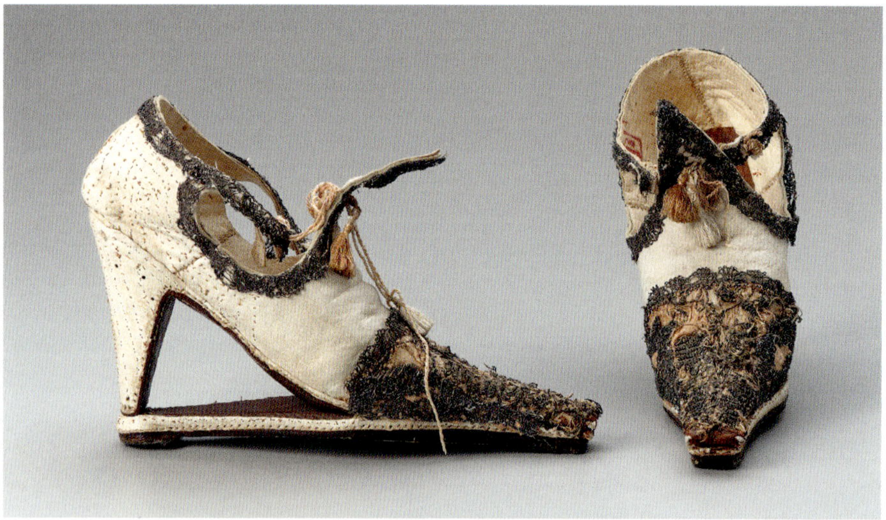

156. Pair of woman's "slap-sole" shoes, Italian, 1660s. Leather and silk brocade embroidered with gold and silver metal threads, applied metallic bobbin lace, silk lacing and tassels, and leather lining and sole, each 15.9 × 9.5 × 22.5 cm. Museum of Fine Arts, Boston

to negotiate a peace settlement that would be sealed by marriage. The amount of María Teresa's dowry was settled, her rights to the Spanish crown renounced.[38] The negotiations were a success, but Cardinal Mazarin portentously wrote, "I do not expect, given the differences between these two nations, that whatever agreement we may come to, we shall be able to meet each other dressed in the same manner."[39] Mazarin was drawing upon the tradition of juxtaposing French and Spanish dress to express the cultural differences between the neighboring nations. A 1617 book by Spanish author Carlos García on the "antipathy" between the French and the Spanish dedicated an entire chapter to the topic of differences in their dress, which the author described as being opposite in every way: for example, a Frenchman buttoned his doublet starting at the neck and ending at the waist, while a Spaniard buttoned his from the bottom up.[40] A French print produced around the time of the 1659 engagement illustrates the opposition between "French luxury" and "Spanish pride" with vain beribboned Frenchmen claiming victory over clownishly old-fashioned Spaniards wearing cartwheel ruffs and skintight suits (fig. 155).

María Teresa's wardrobe needed to reflect her new role as the fiancée of Louis XIV and the future Queen of France, which meant that she began to wear the *chapines* that indicated a married woman's status. Until this time, María Teresa had been wearing Carignano shoes, the slap-sole shoes that were named for her French godmother. The leather *zapatos cariñanos* lined with incarnadine taffeta that the royal shoemaker Andrés de Bustamante made for the infanta probably resembled a pointy-toed pair made in Italy in the 1660s (fig. 156).[41] After María Teresa's engagement, Bustamante instead began to make fine slippers (*zapatillas*) for the infanta to wear on her feet inside *chapines*. The infanta's new *chapines* were covered with rich silks imported from Venice and Milan (silver combined with mother-of-pearl, green, incarnadine, or blue) and decorated with silver galloon—the sumptuary law banning silver that was being applied to dresses was ignored for the shoes hidden beneath them.[42] In August 1659, Aguado began to make longer dresses for María Teresa to wear over her *chapines*. He added fabric to the bottoms of two dresses that had been cut out but had not yet been sewn together, and he altered several existing dresses and petticoats in her wardrobe.[43] Philip IV proudly reported to the Countess of Paredes de Nava that María Teresa was wearing *chapines* and "they suit her famously."[44]

In October 1659, Louis XIV dispatched a Spanish-speaking representative, the genteel Antoine III, Duke of Gramont, to the Spanish court to formally ask Philip IV for María Teresa's hand.[45] Gramont was "well known for the antiquity and grandeur of his family," according to one of the *relaciones* describing his visit to Madrid.[46] He was also known for his dazzling appearance, which was commemorated in a print depicting him in Roman costume on a beribboned horse for festivities at the Tuileries (fig. 157). A printed pamphlet described the Frenchman as "gallant, without ceasing to be grave; rich, without ceasing to be gallant," even in his travel clothes, as he appeared during his entry into Madrid on October 16. "This success in dress is something that you certainly cannot deny the French nation," the Spanish author acknowledged.[47] As Gramont and his suite of more than two dozen high-ranking French noblemen (plus their secretaries, stable boys, pages, cooks, and other attendants) traveled in procession on horseback across Madrid from the Puerta de Alcalá to the Royal Palace, they were reportedly met by throngs of cheering locals who grabbed at the plumes and ribbons decorating their clothes.[48] The stylish ambassador proceeded directly to his audience with Philip IV without changing his clothes—apparently exempt from the usual requirement to dress in a black Spanish suit.

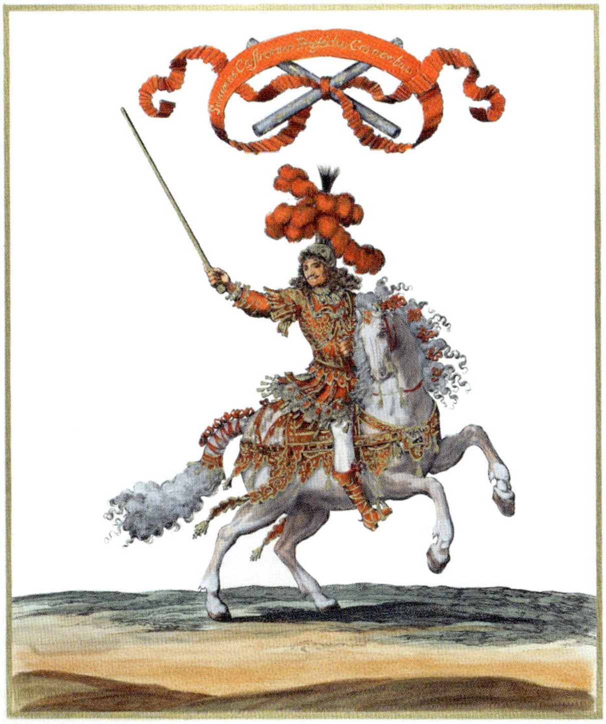

157. François Chauveau, *Antoine de Gramont in Field Marshal Costume*, c. 1670. Etching, 31 × 28.5 cm. Ateliers d'art des musées nationaux, moulages et chalcographies, Saint-Denis

After his audience with the king, Gramont and his retinue proceeded to the queen's quarters, where Queen Mariana, the Infanta María Teresa, and the Infanta Margarita were posed on a carpet-covered dais behind a latticework screen.[49] All three were wearing coordinating dresses that Aguado had made for the occasion from satin damask, with decorations cut from satin pricked in an olive-leaf pattern, symbol of peace and friendship.[50] The French delegates jockeying for position in the crowd to see their future queen included François Bertaut, who described the infanta's appearance in a letter to his sister, Françoise Bertaut de Motteville. Despite having seen María Teresa's portrait before coming to Madrid, Bertaut was flabbergasted by the size and scale of her *guardainfante*, which was "a thousand times larger than you can imagine." The skirts worn by the Infanta María Teresa and Queen Mariana were so large, Bertaut said, that they pushed the little Infanta Margarita to the very edge of the platform. He also reported that the Duke of Gramont tried to engage María Teresa in conversation but was only able to elicit a few words from her.[51]

One of Gramont's primary tasks in Madrid was to report back to Louis XIV on María Teresa's physical qualities—a topic of serious concern, since it related to her potential for childbearing. According to a letter that Gramont wrote to Cardinal Mazarin, he had pressed the infanta to speak so that he could get a good look at her teeth. Gramont told Mazarin that he had been unable to assess the quality of her body accurately, thwarted by her *chapines* and *guardainfante*.[52] François Bertaut reported back to his sister that the infanta was not very tall, "but she appears to have a good figure, as far as one can tell with her strange dress."[53] The wife of one of the French diplomats who traveled to Madrid with Gramont had her tailor in France make a copy of the dress that the infanta had worn at the reception with fabric that she brought back from Spain.[54] The Frenchwoman, who was the same size as María Teresa, modeled the dress for Louis XIV to give him a better sense of his future wife's appearance. The French king was reportedly displeased by her small stature.[55]

The Duke of Gramont was still in Madrid when the Spanish court suffered a terrible loss: the ten-month-old Infante Ferdinand died on October 22, 1659.[56] Nonetheless, the marriage agreement between María Teresa and Louis XIV was finalized, and Haro and Mazarin signed the Treaty of the Pyrenees on November 7.[57] The news arrived in Madrid on November 11, and, at nine o'clock that night, Aguado and a team of 50 journeymen began to make dresses for the queen and infantas to wear the next day in a public celebration of the peace. All three dresses were made from plush imported from the Netherlands—mother-of-pearl for María Teresa, incarnadine for Mariana and Margarita—and were decorated with undulating rows of trim cut from white satin.[58] The queen and infantas wore their peace-day dresses in a visit of thanksgiving to the chapel of the Virgin of Atocha, a miraculous thirteenth-century image to which the monarchy had a special devotion. According to a *relación* describing the celebrations, the matching dresses worn by Mariana, María Teresa, and Margarita showed "their equal desire and happiness for such a happy event."[59] Now that the peace was settled, the Spanish court began to prepare for María Teresa's journey to France, which was planned for April 1660. Aguado's workshop went into a frenzy of activity to prepare the infanta's trousseau.

María Teresa's Trousseau

Mateo Aguado made 22 dresses for María Teresa between January and April 1660: 6 *sayas enteras* with hanging sleeves and 16 three-piece dresses with an overgown, skirt, and doublet. The dresses came in many different hues, including sky-blue and grass-green; the colors of musk, antelope, and deer fur; shimmering shades of pearl, mother-of-pearl, and silver; and black, white, and incarnadine. Eight of the dresses were made from ormuzine, six from plush or uncut velvet, five from satin, two from cloth of silver, and one from camlet.[60] Fourteen of those dresses were embroidered by Juan

Table 3: Embroidered Dresses for the Infanta María Teresa's Journey to France, 1660*	
Decoration	Embroiderer's fee
Saya entera of white satin with life-size roses and carnations cut from silvered mica and stitched with white and incarnadine silk from Italy	52,800 *reales*
Saya entera of white satin with very small memory rings and bows with six loops (three on each side) embroidered in silvered mica stitched with white silk	45,600 *reales*
Saya entera of pale-yellow satin, decorated with bands (3.5 cm tall) cut from white taffeta and embroidered in a spiral pattern with black silk braid and strips of silvered mica	5,400 *reales*
Saya entera of mother-of-pearl cloth of silver embroidered with silver wire and silver plate in a design of bows, branches and leaves, and little square diamonds	4,488 *reales*
Dress of musk-brown satin with rows of alternating scales embroidered in white silk and mica, with a Hungarian coat of scarlet wool decorated to match	21,862 *reales*
Dress of musk- and pearl-colored ormuzine with "a meticulous design" of heads filled with five seeds and double half-moons embroidered with white silk braid on silk voile	9,680 *reales*
Dress of green and white ormuzine with a design of "great novelty" with tulips of varying sizes cut from amber-colored kidskin and stitched with fine white silk	14,250 *reales*
Dress of pearl-colored ormuzine with fleurs-de-lis in silvered mica stitched with white silk between chevrons in groups of three on white taffeta	11,506 *reales*
Dress of sky-blue ormuzine with branches, olive leaves, and flowers (Alexandria roses, tulips, and jasmine), an arrangement of "great novelty" embroidered with black silk braid on silk voile	14,657 *reales*
Dress of deer-colored ormuzine with roses, tulips, and a great variety of leaves on branches embroidered in musk-brown silk braid	11,494 *reales*
Dress of incarnadine ormuzine with large clouds with roses cut from silvered mica stitched with white silk on white taffeta	11,594 *reales*
Dress of pearl and black silk with a variety of flowers embroidered with black silk braid on white taffeta	6,504 *reales*
Dress of green ormuzine with half-moons embroidered with green silk braid on musk-brown silk	9,757 *reales*
Dress of incarnadine camlet with a design 15.75 cm tall of roses, fleurs-de-lis, tulips, and olive leaves cut out of cambric, overlaid with white silk gauze, and outlined with white silk thread	10,620 *reales*
*Sources: AGP, AG, leg. 5215/1, García de la Fuente's *Cuenta de la jornada* (1660); and leg. 904, Aguado's charges for the Infanta María Teresa (1660)	

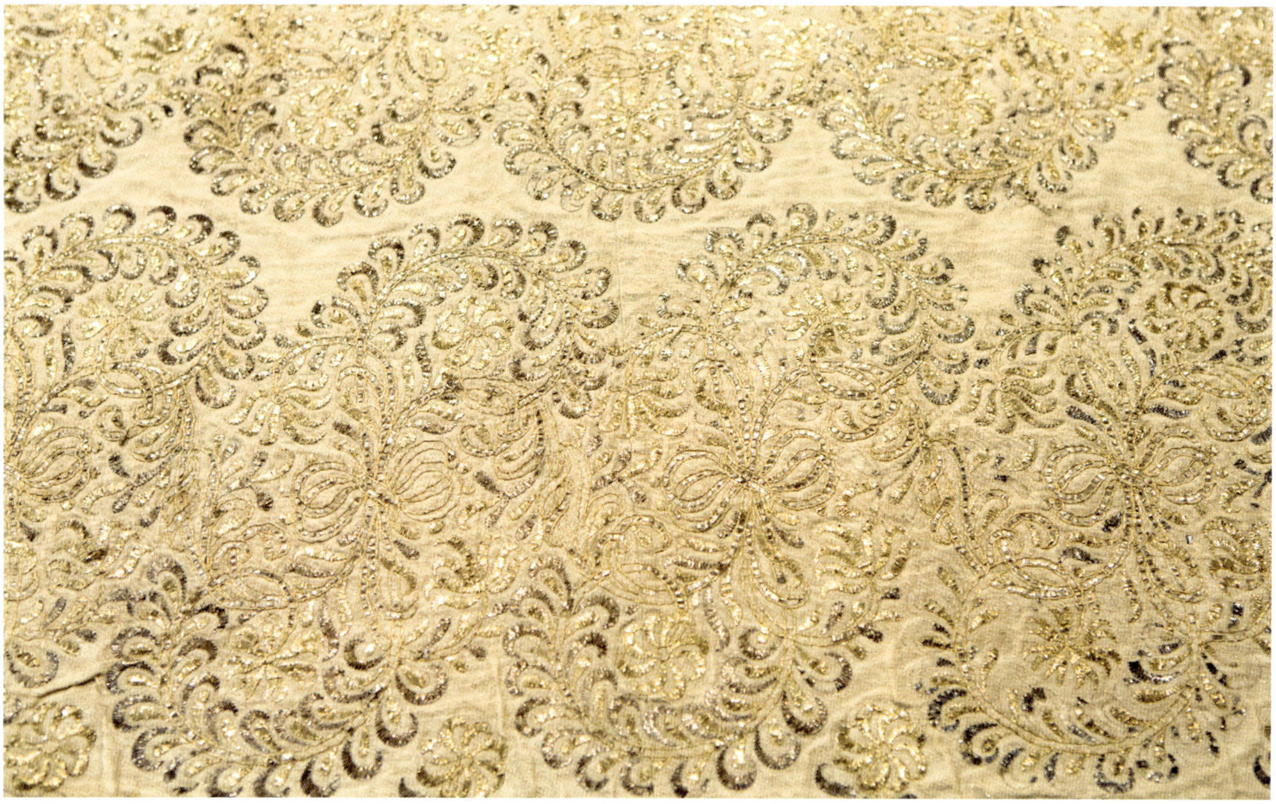

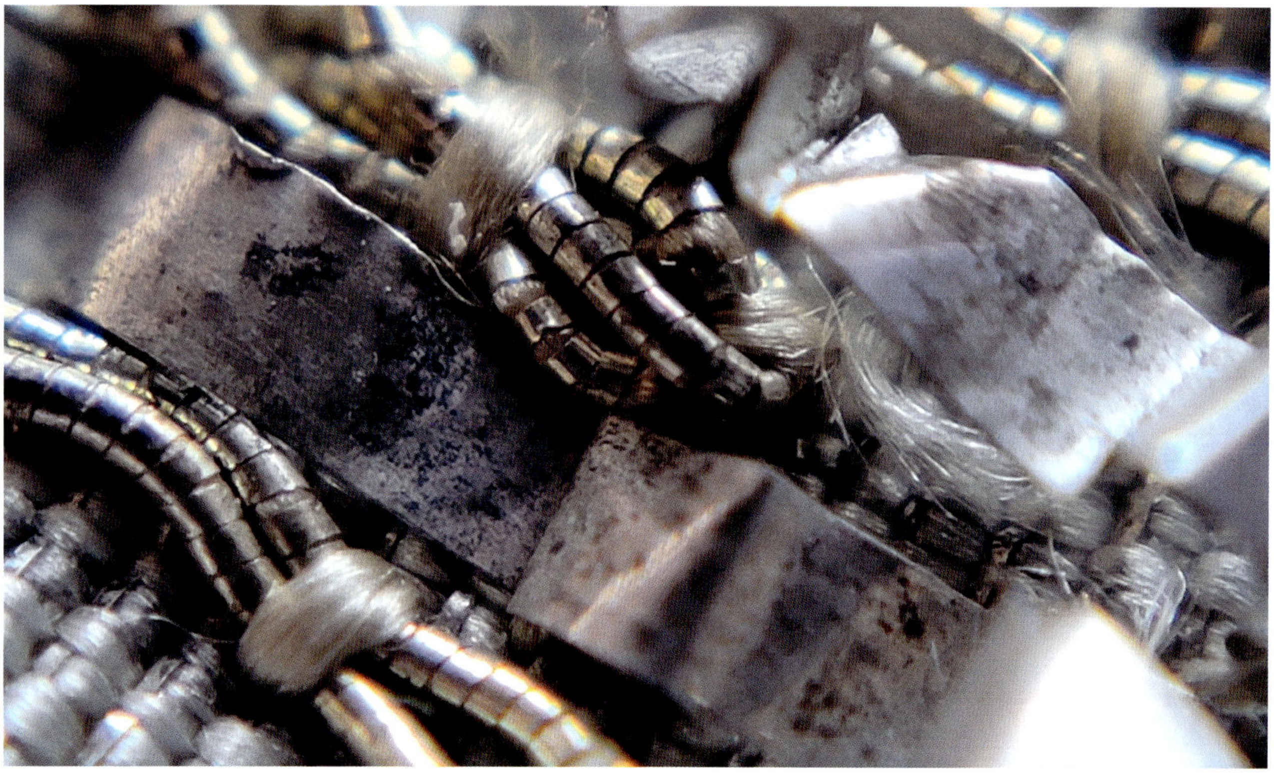

García de la Fuente, who was serving as interim embroiderer to the queen after the death of her long-standing embroiderer Jerónimo de Negrilla, until his son came of age to fill the office.[61] The embroiderer left a minutely detailed 40-page account of his work on the infanta's trousseau that describes the dress decorations with unusual precision (Table 3). García de la Fuente's embroidery designs included a variety of flowers, including the French lily and the Castilian rose, as well as loops and bows, spirals and interlocking circles. The embroiderer noted that his designs for two of the dresses were especially innovative (*"haciendo grande novedad"*).[62]

The 1657 law forbidding silver and gold decoration was observed, for the most part, in the dresses that were made for the infanta in 1660. Instead of silver, García de la Fuente used mica treated with quicksilver (*talco azogado*) to decorate most of the dresses that he embroidered for María Teresa's trousseau. A translucent and shiny mineral that flakes easily into very fine sheets, mica was also used frequently in English embroidery in the later seventeenth century. García de la Fuente used pieces of mica to create life-size roses and carnations on a white satin gown. Another dress of musk-brown satin had mica "scales" alternating with scales embroidered with white silk thread to create a "goshawk breast" pattern. García de la Fuente embroidered only one dress using real silver. This was the most extravagant gown in the infanta's trousseau, made from a silver and mother-of-pearl silk so valuable that the fabric was kept in the Jewel House at the Royal Palace. García de la Fuente used silver wire and silver plate from Milan and Madrid to embroider a design of bows, branches, and diamonds. Similar materials and motifs adorn a very rare dress of embroidered silver lamé that was probably made at the Spanish court in the later 1660s (fig. 158). A microphotograph of the embroidery on that dress shows how the metal threads were stitched in place using a white silk couching thread (fig. 159). In this surviving example, the designs were embroidered directly onto the dress fabric, but in the case of María Teresa's cloth-of-silver *saya entera*, a strip of white taffeta was embroidered and applied to the dress. The embroidered border, which measured approximately 10.5 centimeters wide and 20 meters long, was completed in just half a day and one night on the very eve of María Teresa's departure for France.[63]

The total value of García de la Fuente's embroidery for the infanta's trousseau—which included a set of 24 embroidered banners as well as 14 dresses—was appraised at 278,212 *reales*.[64] This was more than ten times as much as the embroiderer earned in a typical year's work for María Teresa.[65] Aguado also produced many more garments for the infanta's journey to France than he did in a normal year. He made undergarments in bulk: 24 linen waistcoats trimmed with black lace, 16 boned corsets with skirts and sleeves, and 8 sets of matching petticoats in every color. The tailor also made traveling cloaks (*ferreruelos* and *gabanes*) in various colors and an embroidered scarlet coat (*tomasina*) lined in white satin.[66] Aguado's charges for the infanta in 1660 do not reveal how much he earned for all of this work.

When it was time for the king and his famous elder daughter to depart Madrid, María Teresa's trousseau was packed in a set of custom-made luggage that was

158. *(facing page, above)* Woman's court ensemble (skirt detail), probably Spanish, c. 1665–70. Silk and silver lamé with a watered effect, embroidered in silver. FIDM Museum at the Fashion Institute of Design & Merchandising, Los Angeles

159. *(facing page, below)* Microphotograph of the embroidery on the woman's court ensemble in fig. 158. Couched silver-gilt smooth passing thread, crinkled silver plate, and silver-gilt plate

a sight to behold in and of itself. A printed *relación*, the first of four chronicling every step of the journey, describes the infanta's luggage and its contents in detail.[67] Over a hundred coffers and trunks of different shapes and sizes, covered with leather and adorned with gold, were filled with the infanta's personal and household linens, silverwork, brocade hangings and tapestries, and gifts of jewels and scented leather goods for the French delegation that would be at the border.[68] Twelve large chests that were lined inside and out with crimson velvet and decorated with silver were packed with the infanta's dresses, 23 altogether, "of different colors and embroideries, each one in itself with much to see and admire." This published description of María Teresa's dresses very closely matches the palace artisans' accounts (although García de la Fuente did not decorate any dresses with gold embroidery):

> Two of them were of cloth of silver with embroidery in silver and gold, and the others, although their embroideries were not gold or silver, were embroidered with mica and of extraordinary craftsmanship, all in good taste. Each dress had its matching petticoats, short cloak, and coat of rich silks of gold and silver wire, with the most splendid needlework and very expensive decorations, with traveling hats adorned with beautiful plumes. And as the entire collection was so brilliant and of such diverse colors, it fashioned a pleasant and delightful spring.[69]

On April 15, 1660, eight mounted trumpeters dressed in the king's yellow and red velvet livery led the procession of coaches, litters, and cargo mules—5,400 mounts altogether—that departed the Royal Palace to take María Teresa and her new dresses to the border with France.[70]

Spanish Dresses on the French Border

It took six weeks for Philip IV, María Teresa, and their luggage to reach Fuenterrabía, their destination in the Basque Provinces on the Spanish side of the border with France, on June 2, 1660 (see Map 1).[71] María Teresa was going to make the same border-crossing that her mother, Isabel of Bourbon, had made 45 years earlier, only going in the opposite direction. During the course of six event-packed days, the Spanish infanta wore the dresses that Aguado and García de la Fuente had prepared for her. Those dresses, which had been celebrated in Madrid for their novelty and variety, received a very different reception from the French in the Basque country. Two French noblewomen, Madame de Motteville and the Duchess of Montpensier, wrote memoirs that offer their reactions to María Teresa's appearance at various events.[72] Although the two women were usually together at these events, their descriptions of María Teresa's dresses do not always coincide, and they do not perfectly align with the documentation of the dresses in the artisans' accounts.[73] It is impossible to match the dresses in the infanta's trousseau with certainty to the dresses that the Frenchwomen describe, but their accounts offer eyewitness testimony to the performance of Aguado's dresses at the border, as they were seen through French eyes.

Madame de Motteville, whose given name was Françoise Bertaut, was the sister of François Bertaut, who had accompanied the Duke of Gramont to Madrid the previous year. Of Spanish and French descent, Madame de Motteville spoke Spanish and was a close confidante of Anne of Austria. She considered herself to be an astute and impartial judge of fashion, and she was in fact equally vicious in her criticisms of French and Spanish styles.[74] In a portrait that was painted a

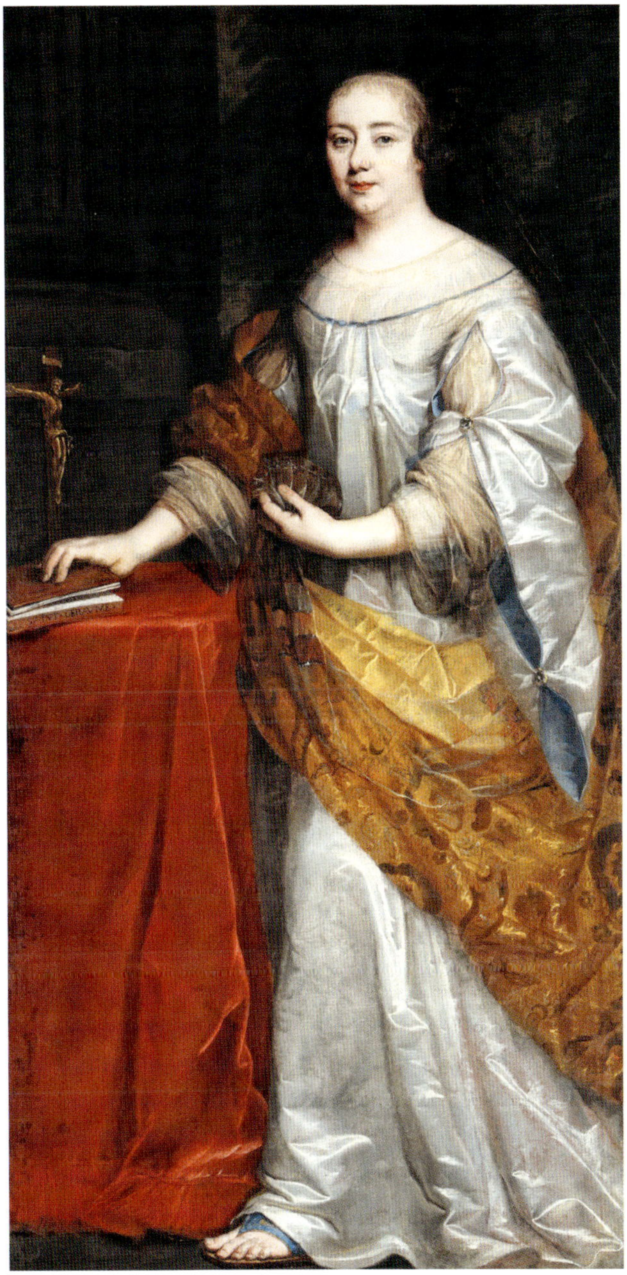

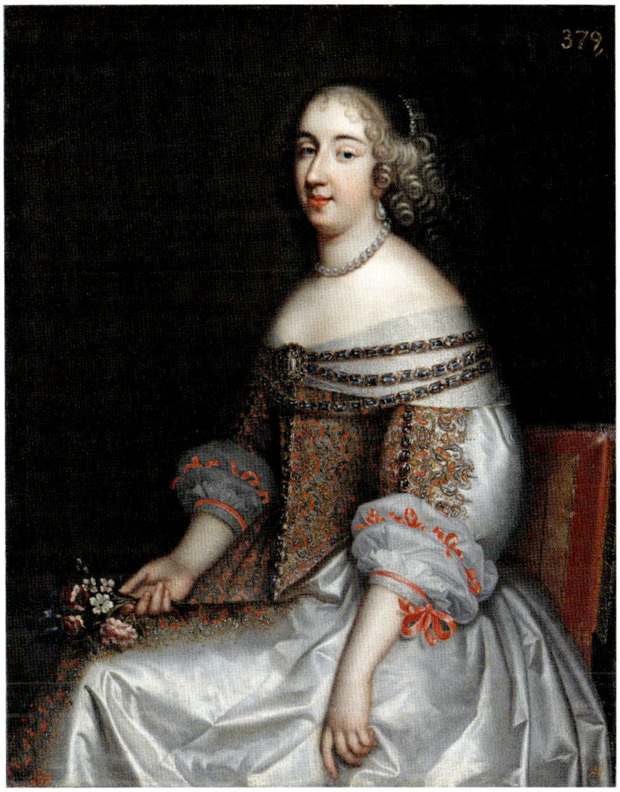

160. *(left)* Louis Ferdinand Elle the Elder, *Françoise Bertaut, Madame de Motteville*, 1664. Oil on canvas, 175.9 × 87.9 cm. Haggerty Museum of Art, Marquette University, Milwaukee

161. *(above)* Charles Beaubrun, *Anne-Marie-Louise d'Orléans, Duchess of Montpensier ("la Grande Mademoiselle")*, 1655. Oil on canvas, 108 × 88 cm. Museo Nacional del Prado, Madrid

few years after she witnessed the marriage of María Teresa and Louis XIV, Madame de Motteville is dressed very informally in a plain, loose gown and sandals, perhaps in the guise of a saint (fig. 160).[75] The Duchess of Montpensier (Anne-Marie-Louise d'Orléans), also known as "*la Grande Mademoiselle*," was a close relative of the French royal family and an heiress of extraordinary wealth. She was a person of such importance that her portrait had been sent to the Spanish court along with those of Louis XIV and his parents in 1655 (fig. 161).[76] In that portrait, the Duchess of Montpensier models the French style against which she and her compatriots judged María Teresa's Spanish dresses. Her white dress, richly embroidered in red and gold, features a low neckline, boned bodice, three-quarter sleeves, and a skirt without a farthingale. She wears minimal makeup and natural hair, which is done in curls. For the meeting with the Spanish, however, the duchess wore her hair uncurled and dressed all in black since she was in mourning for her recently deceased father.[77]

Madame de Motteville and the Duchess of Montpensier attended the June 3 wedding in Fuenterrabía, where María Teresa appeared in person and the bridegroom was represented by Philip IV's royal favorite, Luis Méndez de Haro. Both Frenchwomen reported that María Teresa was so soft-spoken during the ceremony that her "I do" was barely audible.[78] Their descriptions of the infanta's wedding dress differ somewhat but indicate that she was most likely wearing the white satin *saya entera* that García de la Fuente had embroidered in silvered mica with memory rings and bows—symbols for "tying the knot" that spoke more intelligibly than the bride herself (see Table 3). The Duchess of Montpensier described the profusion of decoration on the dress as characteristically Spanish.[79] Madame de Motteville judged the fabric to be "rather ugly stuff embroidered with talc [i.e., mica], silver being forbidden in Spain." She thought that the Spanish infanta's clothing was "horrible" but "nevertheless, in spite of her garments, we perceived her beauty—an infallible mark of its greatness."[80] In Madame de Motteville's narrative, María Teresa's true beauty could only be revealed once her Spanish garments had been removed and replaced with French dress.

On Sunday, June 6, the kings of France and Spain met in person to swear an oath to uphold the Treaty of the Pyrenees at a lavishly decorated pavilion on Pheasant Island. María Teresa had no speaking role in this event—once again her dress spoke for her. According to the Duchess of Montpensier, María Teresa appeared at the peace conference in white satin with fleurs-de-lis, the symbol of France, embroidered with jet on her Spanish-style dress.[81] There were two dresses in the infanta's trousseau that were embroidered with fleurs-de-lis—one of pearl-colored ormuzine embroidered in silvered mica and another of incarnadine camlet with cambric cut-outs—neither of which matches the duchess's description (see Table 3). Diplomatic fleurs-de-lis are absent from the famous image of María Teresa's conference dress in Le Brun's tapestry, which emphasizes the distinctive shape of the infanta's Spanish *guardainfante* rather than the details of her dress decoration (fig. 162). The meeting of Louis XIV and Philip IV was one of 14 key events from the French king's life that were commemorated in a series of tapestries. Le Brun, who had not attended the conference himself, based his design for the tapestry on written descriptions of the event.[82] In Le Brun's imagined version of the scene, María Teresa stands behind her father wearing an enormous *guardainfante* that physically isolates her from the men who have negotiated her fate.

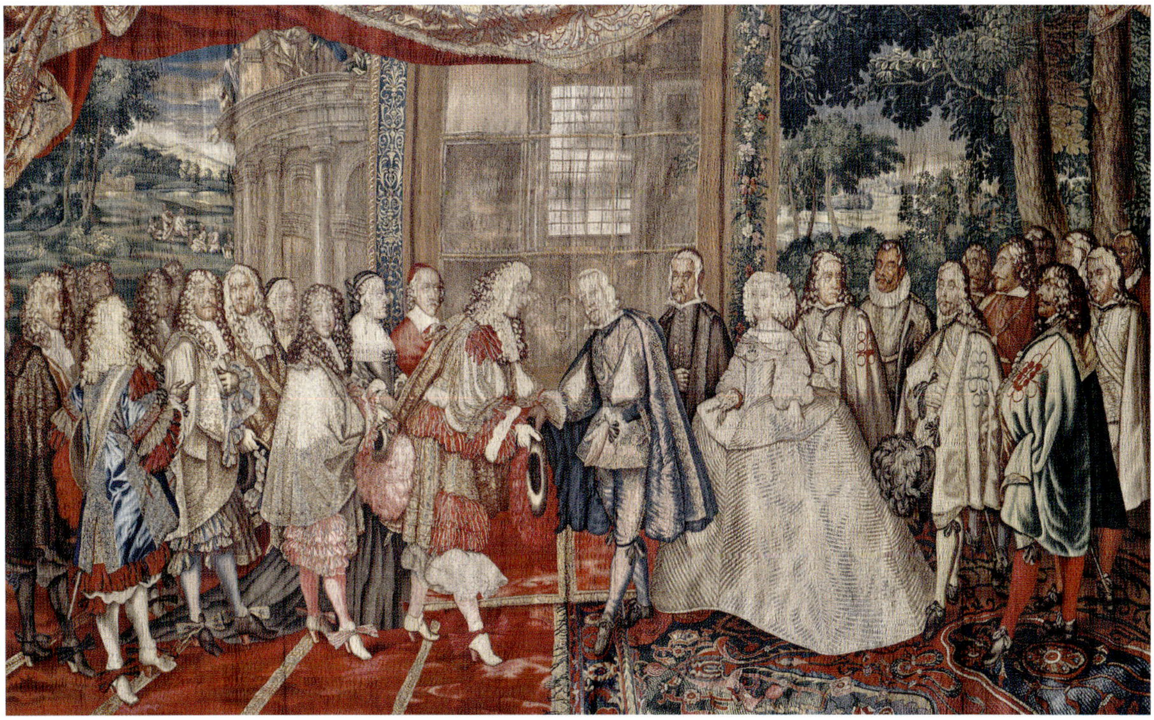

162. *Meeting between Louis XIV and Philip IV*. Tapestry design by Charles Le Brun, woven in the Manufacture Royale des Gobelins, Paris, 1665–80. Detail; tapestry, wool, silk, and gilt-metal-wrapped thread, 378 × 559 cm. Embassy of France in Madrid

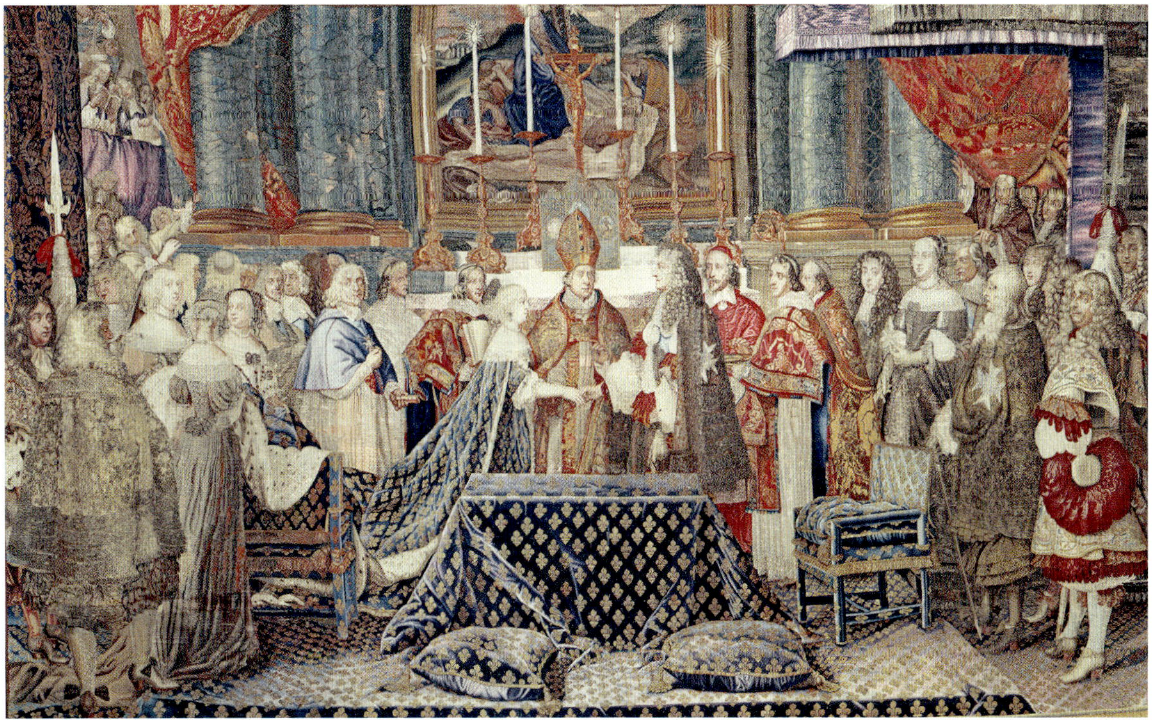

163. *Marriage of Louis XIV and María Teresa*. Tapestry design by Charles Le Brun, woven in the Manufacture Royale des Gobelins, Paris, 1665–80. Detail; tapestry, wool, silk, and gilt-metal-wrapped thread, 383 × 576 cm. Palace of Versailles

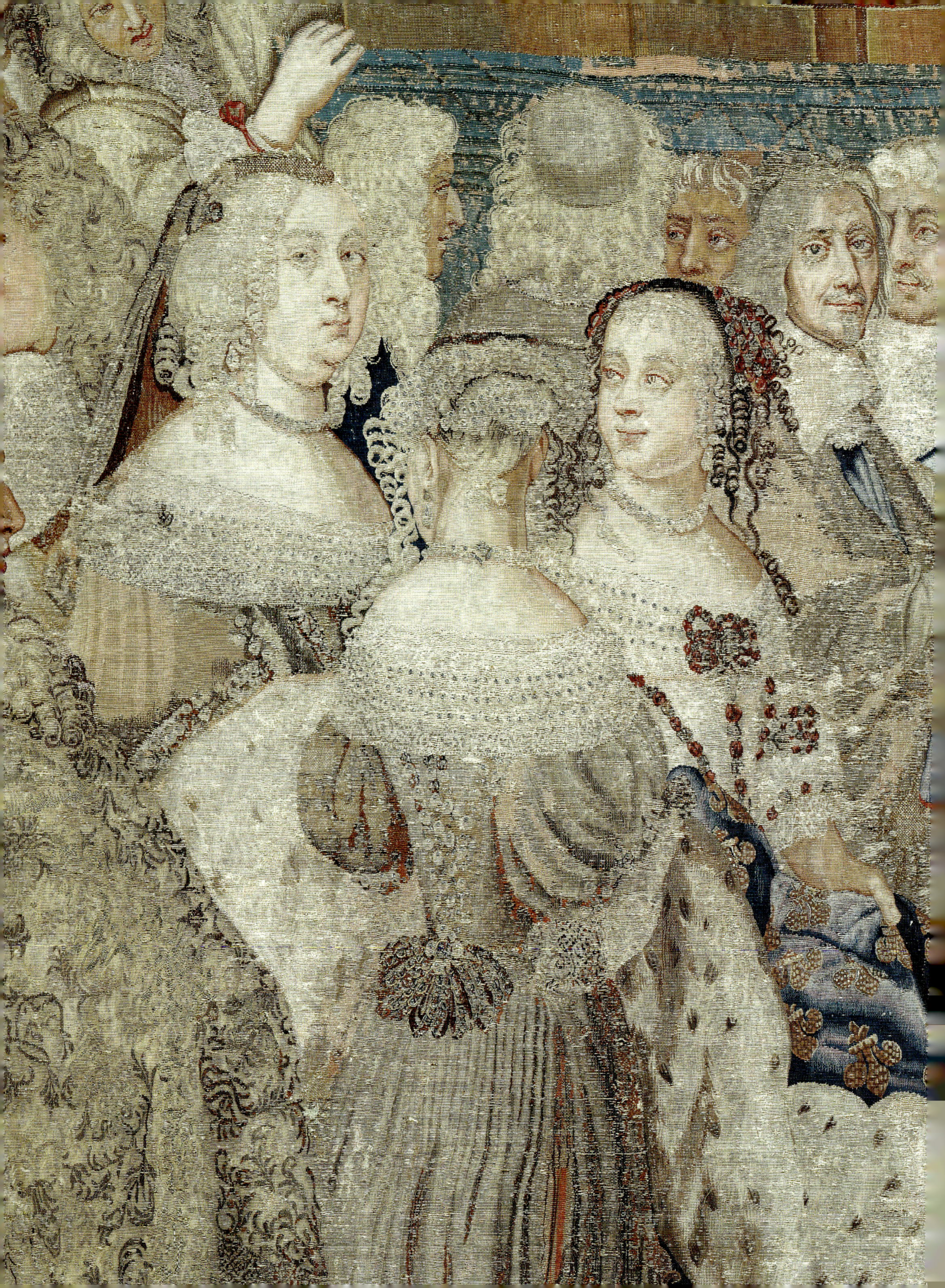

Her white and silver dress sparkles with real gilt-metal-wrapped threads that are woven into the tapestry (see the detail in fig. 143).[83]

The day after the meeting of Philip IV and Louis XIV on Pheasant Island, María Teresa parted from her father and crossed the border to Saint-Jean-de-Luz in France. Madame de Motteville and the Duchess of Montpensier both reported that María Teresa retired to the queen mother's apartment after the border-crossing and removed her *guardainfante*.[84] Always the more pointed of the two women in matters of dress, Madame de Motteville opined that "the infanta-queen was charming thus in half-dress; for the *Gard-Infante* [as she called it] was so monstrous a thing that when the Spanish women did not wear it they looked far better."[85] She wrote that the next evening María Teresa tried on her new French clothes and put on a French-style corset—the *corps de jupe*—for the first time. Unlike the Spanish *cotilla*, which was worn beneath the clothes, this was an external bodice with boning.[86] "At first she found it uncomfortable," the Frenchwoman said of María Teresa, "but she bore it with sweetness and patience."[87] In this telling of her story, María Teresa was liberated of the Spanish farthingale only to be subjugated by the French corset.

For her wedding to Louis XIV on the French side of the border—this time with the bridegroom appearing in person—María Teresa appeared without a farthingale in a white brocade French dress with a low neckline. The dress was largely hidden beneath a long, heavy royal robe in violet-colored velvet strewn with gold fleurs-de-lis and trimmed with ermine (fig. 163). Her train was carried by the Duchess of Montpensier's two half-sisters, with the point held by none other than the Princess of Carignano, María Teresa's godmother.[88] In Le Brun's tapestry depicting the wedding, however, it is the Grande Mademoiselle—the Duchess of Montpensier, no longer dressed in mourning—who carries the train and looks directly out at the viewer (fig. 164).[89]

After the wedding, the Infanta María Teresa—now known as Queen Marie-Thérèse—dressed exclusively in French clothing. It is uncertain what became of the dresses in her trousseau. Perhaps they were dispersed among the Spanish ladies who accompanied her on the journey, or maybe the embroidered fabric of the skirts and trains was reused for other purposes. If any of María Teresa's dresses were taken to the French court, they have not survived to this day, but few garments from the period escaped the ravages of the French Revolution.[90] Whatever their fate may have been, the embroidered dresses that Mateo Aguado and Juan García de la Fuente made for the infanta's trousseau were not intended to be preserved for future generations. The dresses spoke for the infanta during crucial diplomatic moments, and the language that they spoke was unmistakably Spanish. After appearing in distinctively Spanish dress at the border, María Teresa's transition to the French style of dress for her wedding was all the more dramatic. Like her mother before her, María Teresa took part in the ritual of a royal marriage in which she gave up her own nationality—made visible in her clothes—to assume that of her husband. The last dresses that Mateo Aguado made for María Teresa won no plaudits from French commentators, but they had been made to serve a higher purpose: there was peace between Spain and France at last.

164. *(facing page)* The Duchess of Montpensier carries the queen's train (detail of fig. 163)

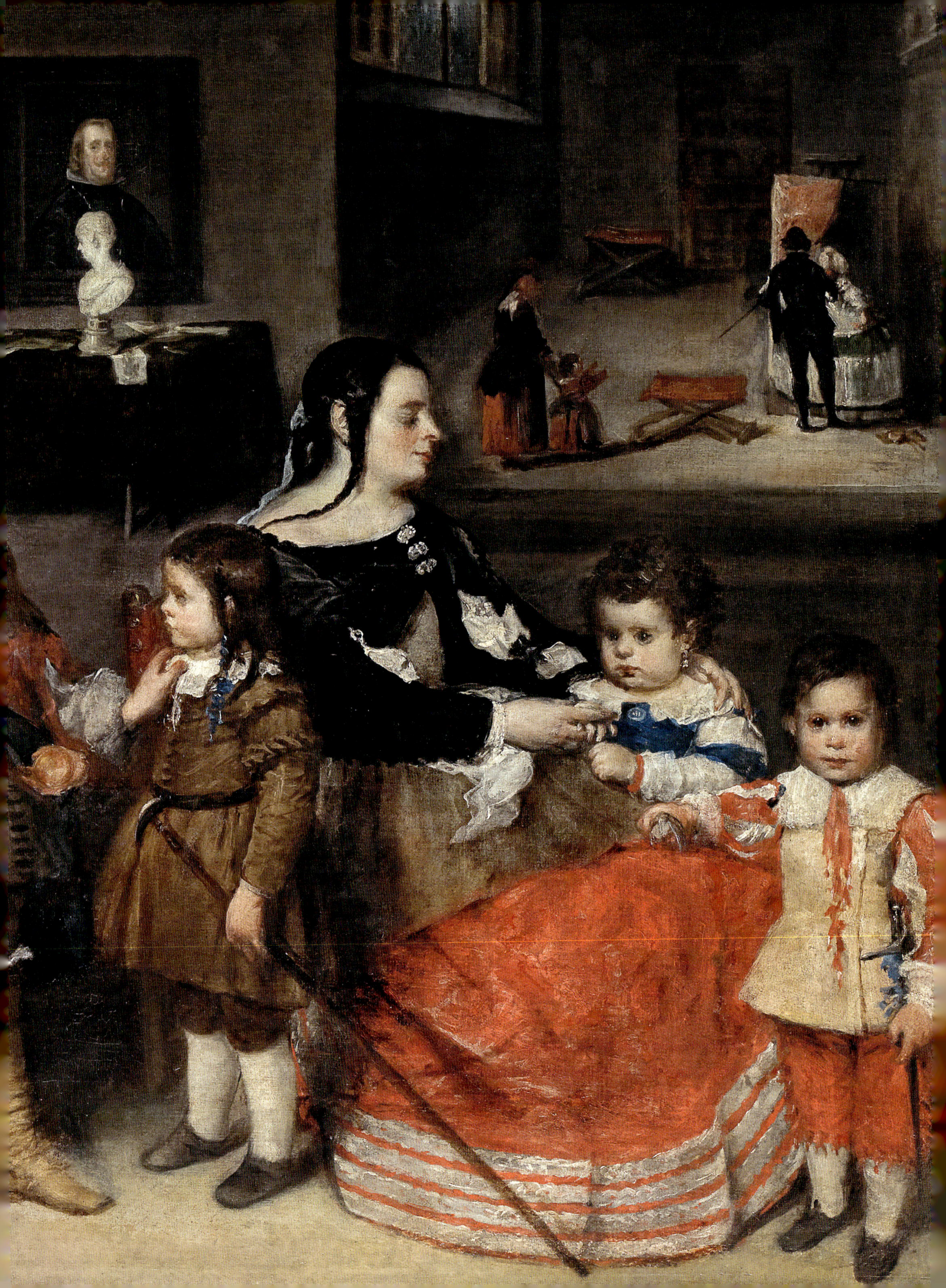

7. Paterfamilias

An Artisan Family's Fortunes, 1660–1724

Mateo Aguado engaged a notary public to write his last will and testament in December 1660, at the end of a busy and eventful year that had brought peace to Spain and France with the marriage of the Infanta María Teresa and Louis XIV. Now about 55 years old, the queen's tailor declared himself to be in good health. He expressed "great satisfaction" with his second wife, Bernarda Ruiz de Reinoso, to whom he had been married for over 28 years. Praising "her great Christianity, truth and judgment, and intelligence," Aguado named her the guardian of their two young daughters, María and Mónica, who were about six and three years old. Their eldest child and only son, 25-year-old Nicolás, had recently married, and Aguado made arrangements to finish paying the 77,000 *reales* that he had promised the newlyweds as a wedding gift. He also bequeathed money to his sister, Ana Aguado, to various nieces and nephews, and to Juan Martínez, a journeyman tailor who had been in Aguado's workshop for 25 years, "as a sign of the love and affection that I have had and have for him." The tailor left funds for a thousand masses to be said for his soul and more for those family members who had predeceased him: his parents, his brother Antonio, and his first wife Alfonsa Martínez. Aguado expressed his wish to be buried in the crypt of the Church of San Ginés, his parish church since boyhood, "on the day when it serves Our Lord to take me from this present life."[1]

In his later years, Aguado worked to ensure that his family would be well provided for after his death. Work and family were indivisibly intertwined in a royal artisan household such as Mateo Aguado's. His wife, Bernarda Ruiz, had grown up in a royal artisan family and almost certainly contributed in some capacity to Aguado's tailoring workshop, although this kind of labor is not acknowledged in the archival records.[2] Aguado worked with his brother, Antonio, who was an assistant in the queen's wardrobe with special privileges to work as a tailor.[3] After Antonio died in 1647, his daughter Ana inherited his position at court, which would go to her husband when she married.[4] Antonio's widow married Gaspar Ruiz—father of Bernarda—and thus Mateo Aguado's sister-in-law became his mother-in-law.[5] Mateo Aguado prospered and made a very comfortable urban life for his wife, children, and grandchildren, who used the honorific "doña" or "don" before their names. They were attended by two servants, one male and one female, in a spacious home that was filled with all of the material objects that communicated wealth and status in an aristocratic home in late-seventeenth-century Madrid: tapestries and rugs, paintings and books, silver and jewelry, wooden furniture, and silk curtains and bed-hangings.[6]

165. *(facing page)* Family of a royal artisan. Juan Bautista Martínez del Mazo, *The Family of the Artist* (detail of fig. 167)

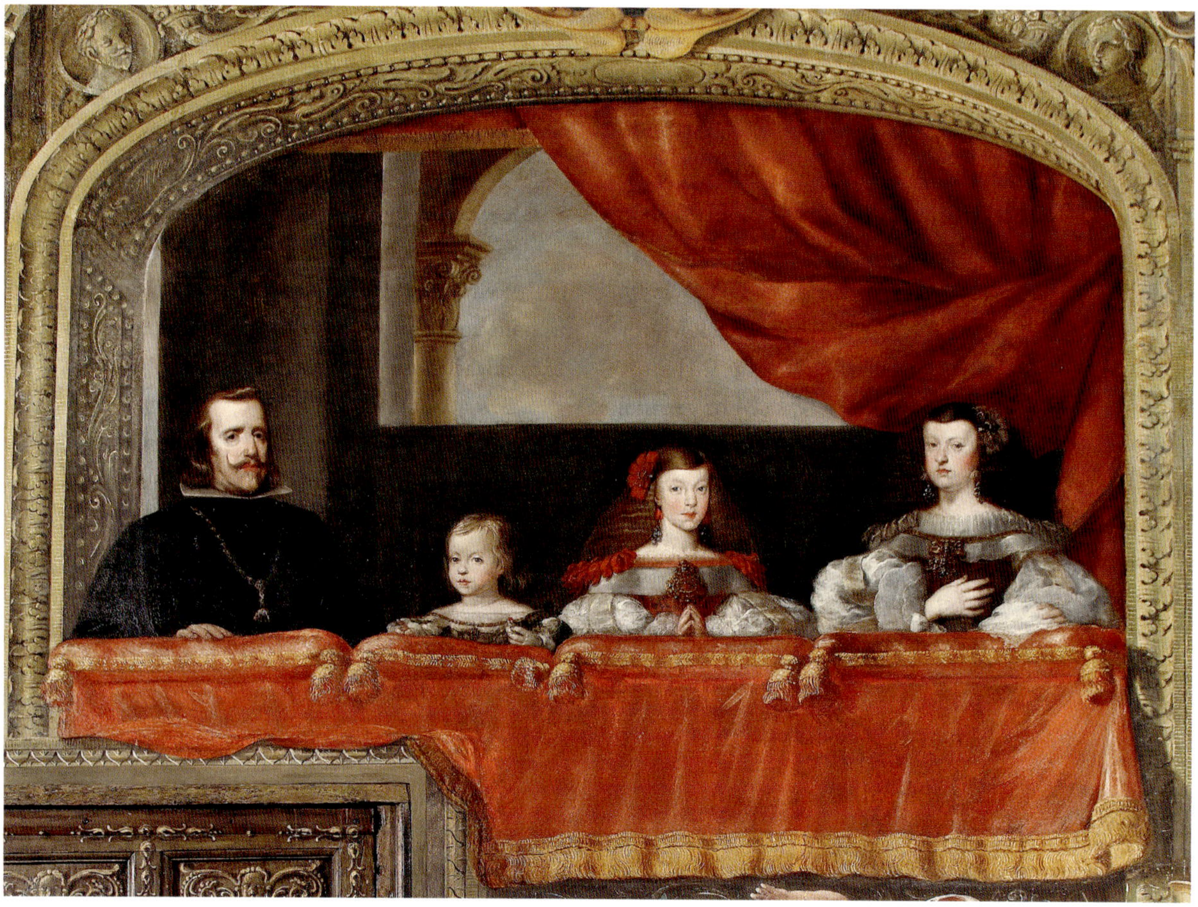

166. Unknown Madrid artist, *The Royal Balcony: Philip IV, Prince Philip Prosper, Infanta Margarita, and Mariana of Austria*, c. 1661. Mural painting in oil. Main staircase, Convent of Las Descalzas Reales, Madrid

As the year 1660 came to an end, Aguado no longer had to put in so many long nights now that work on the Infanta María Teresa's trousseau was finished, but he still had plenty of work to do for Queen Mariana, the Infanta Margarita, and Prince Philip Prosper.[7] The entire court breathed more easily now that there was a male heir to the throne. The royal family was complete, as they were portrayed around this time in a family portrait on a trompe l'oeil balcony on the wall of the staircase at the Convent of Las Descalzas Reales (fig. 166).[8] In the early 1660s, Aguado continued to innovate in his dress designs, which appear in court portraits by Juan Bautista Martínez del Mazo, who had been promoted to the king's Painter of the Chamber after Velázquez died on August 6, 1660. Mazo had been married to Velázquez's daughter, Francisca, with whom he had at least seven children; after her death in 1653, he remarried and had four more.[9] Mazo portrayed himself in his dual role as painter and paterfamilias in a unique group portrait of a royal artisan family that was inspired by Velázquez's composition in *Las Meninas* (fig. 167).[10]

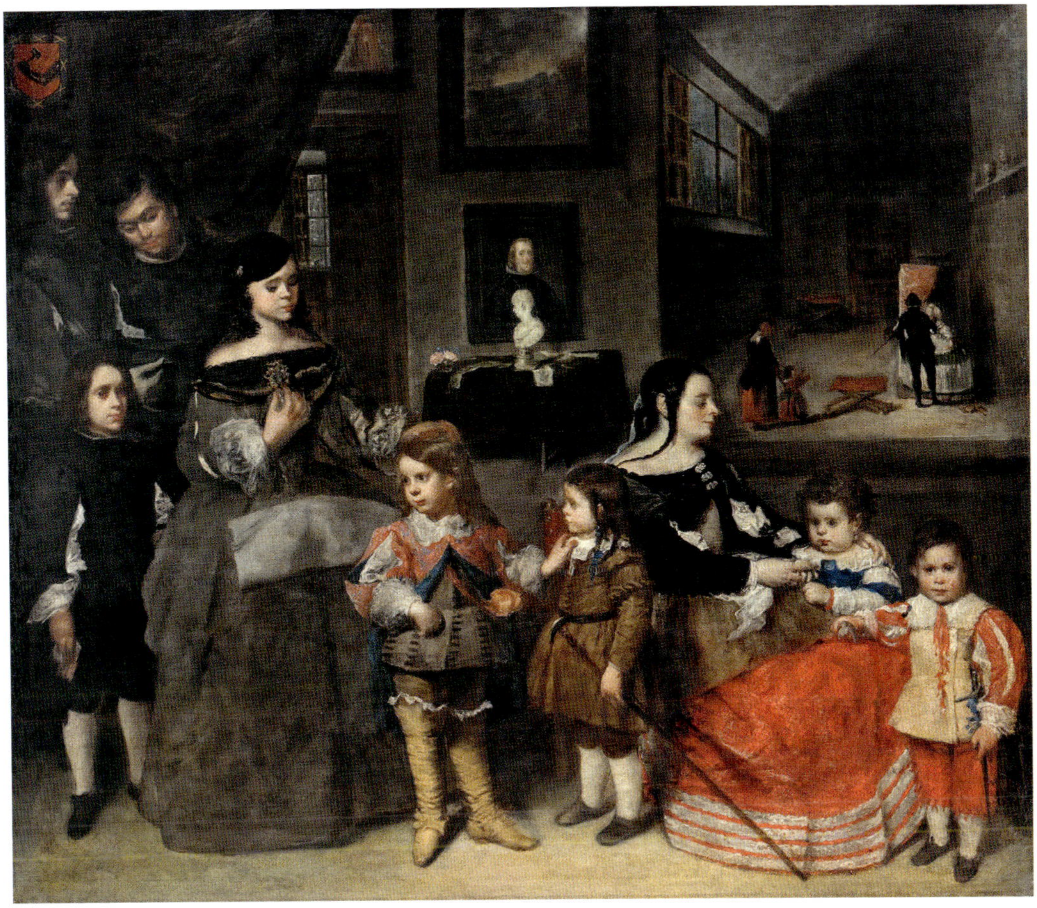

167. Juan Bautista Martínez del Mazo, *The Family of the Artist*, c. 1664–5. Oil on canvas, 149.5 × 174.5 cm. Kunsthistorisches Museum, Vienna

The artist appears in the background facing away from the viewer, painting a portrait of the Infanta Margarita. Mazo's large family occupies the foreground. The elder children—Velázquez's grandchildren—are dressed in sober courtly garb, while the younger ones by Mazo's second wife wear playful costumes. The little boy on the far right is dressed as a bullfighter, with a *muleta*—a bright red cloth mounted on a rod—in his right hand and a dagger in his left.[11] Aguado's family was smaller but similar in composition, with an elder son employed at the court and two much younger daughters at home. In addition to these three, Mateo Aguado and Bernarda Ruiz had a dozen other children who did not live to adulthood.[12] Aguado had every reason to be optimistic about his family's future when he signed his last will and testament in front of five witnesses on December 20, 1660. He had his health, a good marriage, a lucrative court appointment, and a son who was poised to start the next generation of the Aguado-Ruiz clan. Eighteen days later, everything began to fall apart.

"Great Difficulties"

Mateo Aguado and Bernarda Ruiz suffered a devastating blow when their son Nicolás died on January 7, 1661.[13] Nicolás Aguado was a *contador*, an accountant, in the king's household, a position that promised to elevate the Aguado family to a higher level of service at court with a corresponding rise in social status. Aguado and his wife always referred to their son by his title, "the accountant Nicolás Aguado, our son," with apparent pride.[14] Six months and one week after Nicolás Aguado's death, his widow Paula María Torrejón gave birth to their son, named Nicolás Tomás, who was baptized at the Church of San Ginés on July 14. The mother died five days later.[15] Mateo Aguado became the legal guardian of his orphaned grandson and was responsible for the child's education, food, clothing, and medical care for his "many considerable illnesses."[16] When the tailor and his wife wrote a new joint testament in February 1665, they changed their plan to be buried in their own parish church of San Ginés and expressed their wishes to be buried in the same tomb as their son, the accountant, at the Church of El Carmen near the Puerta del Sol.[17]

During the year in which he was grieving his son, Mateo Aguado made a grave error on the job. On October 1, 1661, the queen's majordomo, Gaspar de Moscoso Osorio, 6th Count of Altamira, issued an order for Aguado to be arrested because he "lacked the obedience and submission that he owes to don Francisco Gaztelu y Gamboa, Keeper of the Queen's Wardrobe, under whose orders he should always be."[18] Gaztelu y Gamboa, who had held the position of Keeper of the Wardrobe since 1634, was a high-ranking aristocrat and knight in the Order of Alcántara, an elite military order like the Order of Santiago that Velázquez had joined.[19] It is unclear exactly what the tailor said or did to offend

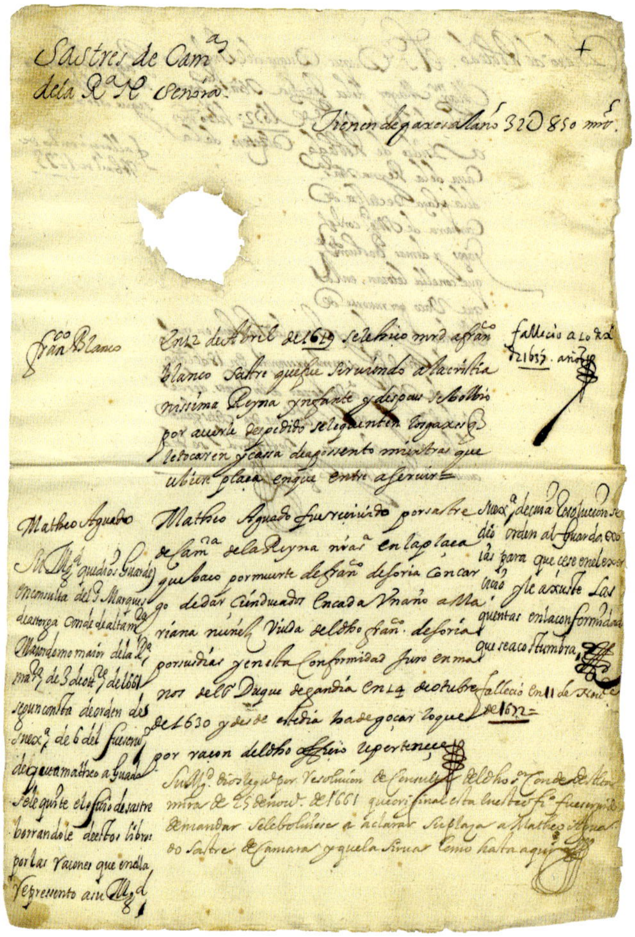

168. "Tailors of the Chamber of Our Lady the Queen." Archivo General de Palacio, Madrid

169. *(facing page)* Unknown Madrid artist, *The Court Prison, Madrid*, 17th century. Oil on canvas, 108 × 164.5 cm. Ministry of Foreign Affairs, Madrid

his superior; the word used to describe his offense is *desatención*, which means inattention or rashness, discourtesy or lack of respect.[20] The written rules that governed the queen's household required all *oficiales de manos* to "obey, respect, and comply with" the aristocrats who ran the household.[21] Violations of rules of etiquette were strictly enforced at Philip IV's court, and even high-ranking noblemen were imprisoned for seemingly minor offenses.[22] Thus it is not at all surprising that a tailor was jailed for his *desatención*. On October 3, the Count of Altamira ordered the tailor's name to be erased from the royal payroll. A list of the queen's tailors was updated with a note in the margin stating that "on October 6, 1661, the office of tailor was to be taken from Mateo Aguado, erasing him from these books" (fig. 168).[23] After more than three decades of service, Aguado had been fired.

Aguado was held at the Court Prison, which was located just off the southeast corner of the Plaza Mayor (see Map 2). The building was, incongruously, one of the most impressive works of architecture in Madrid and a favorite among tourists (fig. 169). A French visitor to the Spanish capital in 1655 wrote that he had mistaken the Court Prison for "the habitation of some grandee of Spain" thanks to the gilded iron bars on its windows.[24] The exterior of the Court Prison was splendid, but the prisoners' cells inside were dark and dungeon-like.[25] Nearly two months after Aguado's firing, on November 25, the queen's majordomo wrote a letter to the king advocating for the queen's tailor to be reinstated. He wrote that the Keeper of the Queen's Wardrobe had assured him that "Mateo Aguado has recognized his error" and that other court artisans had learnt from his

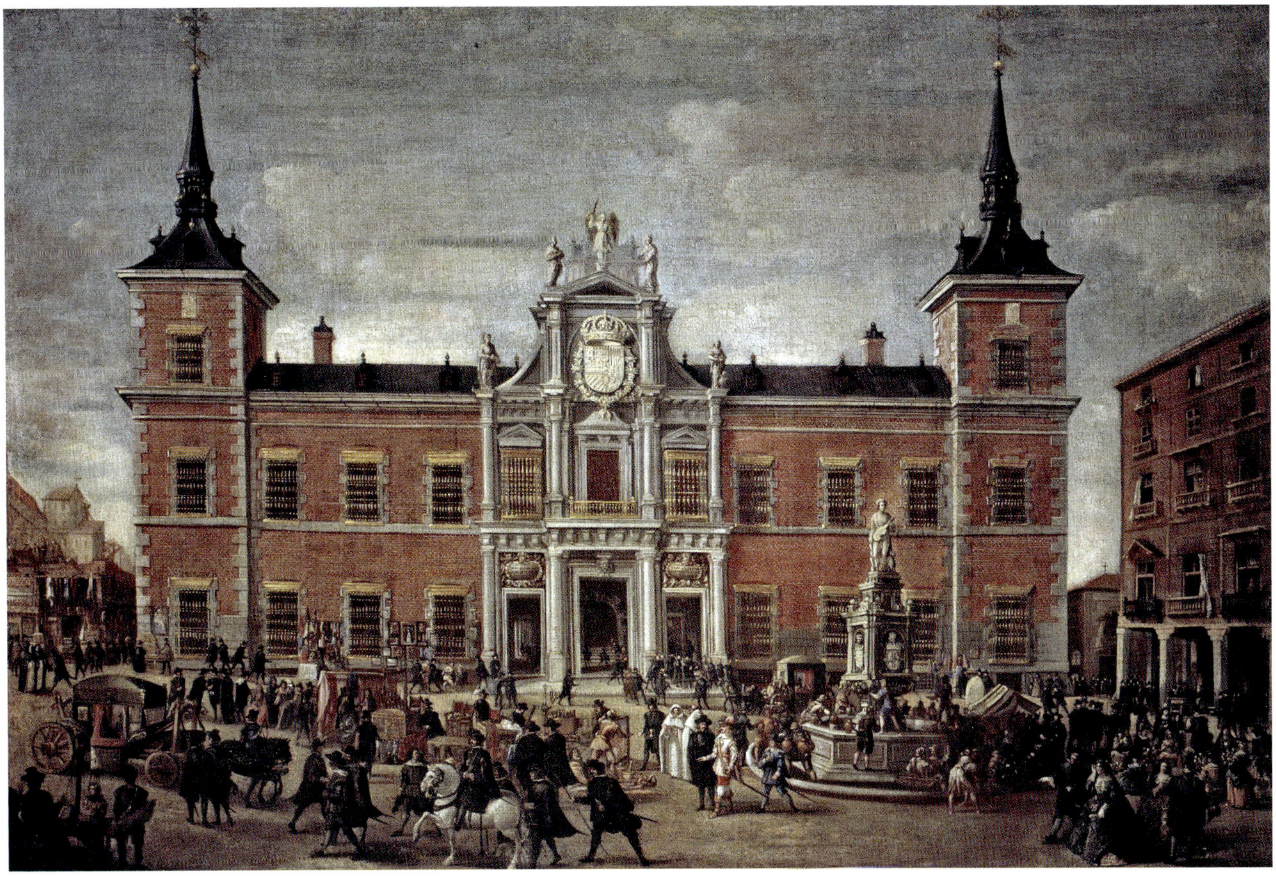

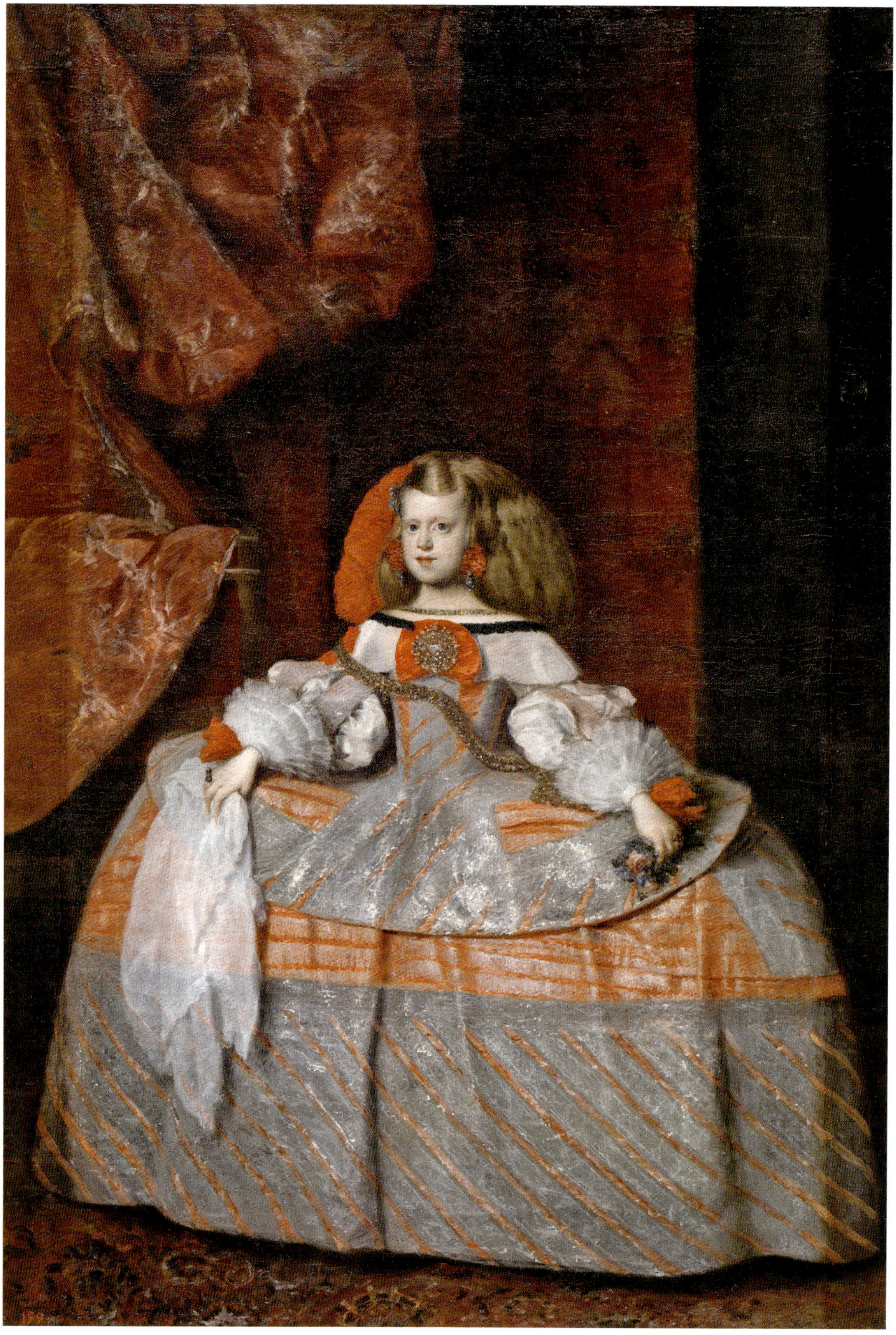

example "to fulfill their duty without lack of respect to their superiors." Philip IV laconically acceded: "*Está bien*"—"That's fine"—he wrote on the majordomo's petition.[26] A disobedient tailor was the least of the king's worries in the fall of 1661: his son and heir, three-year-old Philip Prosper, had died on November 1, and the queen had given birth to another son, the future Charles II, five days later. During this tumultuous time, Aguado's jailing had led to an interruption in service in the queen's household. The queen's tailor was needed back at court.

With his name returned to the payroll after his brief fall from grace, Aguado resumed dressing Queen Mariana and the Infanta Margarita. Aguado developed a new style of dress decoration in the early 1660s by applying French lace and other trims to an ever more exaggerated feminine silhouette (see the early 1660s in the Chronology of Women's Dress, p. 218). Skirts in this decade were extremely wide at the sides and flattened in the front. The *guardainfantes* that shaped Aguado's dresses were made by Francisco Antonio Salinas, who was appointed farthingale-maker to the queen after the death of Diego López in 1660.[27] In order to fill the vast space of his royal patrons' skirts, Aguado cut wide bands out of silk fabric and applied them to the dresses in horizontal or diagonal rows. In a portrait of the Infanta Margarita by Juan Bautista Martínez del Mazo, she wears a pink dress that is almost completely covered by bands of silver decoration, probably silver lamé layered with white lace (fig. 170). Silver decorations and imported French lace were permitted now that Spain and France were at peace. As Mazo's painting illustrates, bodices were cut off-the-shoulder and worn with a Carignano collar. Sleeves made from decorated strips of fabric, worn over voluminous white silk undersleeves, show the continuing influence of French fashions from earlier in the century (fig. 171). A version of *Infanta Margarita in Pink and Silver*, with the infanta wearing a brooch with the double-headed eagle of the Habsburg empire on her bodice, was sent to Vienna at the request of Leopold I, to whom Margarita had become engaged.[28] The emperor also asked his ambassador in Madrid to supply the infanta's measurements "without padding."[29]

Even though Aguado had resumed his work for the queen's household, the tailor was "suffering very great difficulties with his creditors," according to a petition that he wrote in 1663. In light of his long record of service "with the exactness and assistance that is well known," he asked the Crown to give one of his

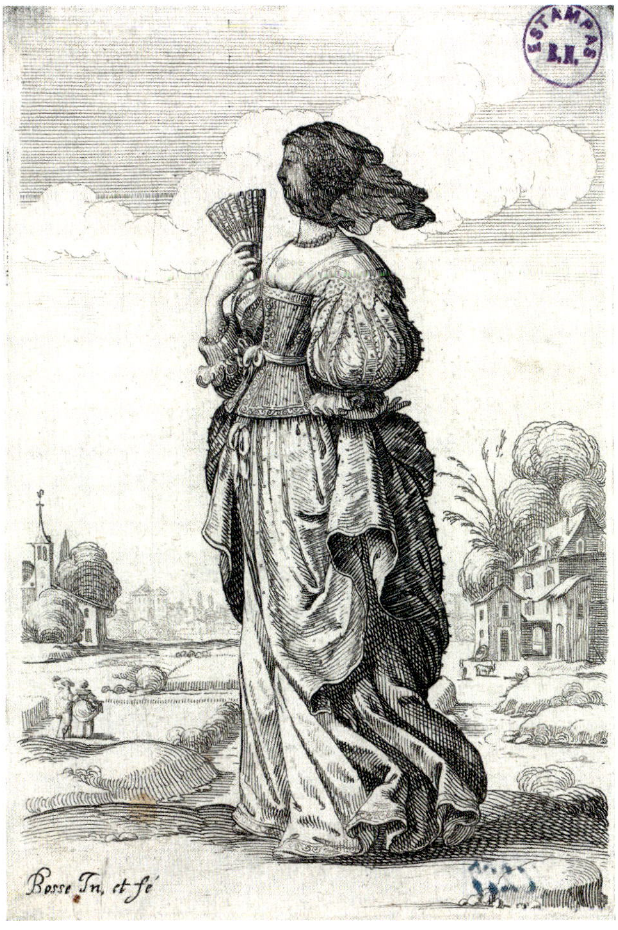

170. *(facing page)* Juan Bautista Martínez del Mazo, *Infanta Margarita in Pink and Silver*, c. 1665. Oil on canvas, 212 × 147 cm. Museo Nacional del Prado, Madrid

171. *(right)* Abraham Bosse, *Sanguine*, from *The Four Complexions* series, 1629. Etching, engraving, and stippling, 14 × 9.6 cm. Biblioteca Nacional de España, Madrid

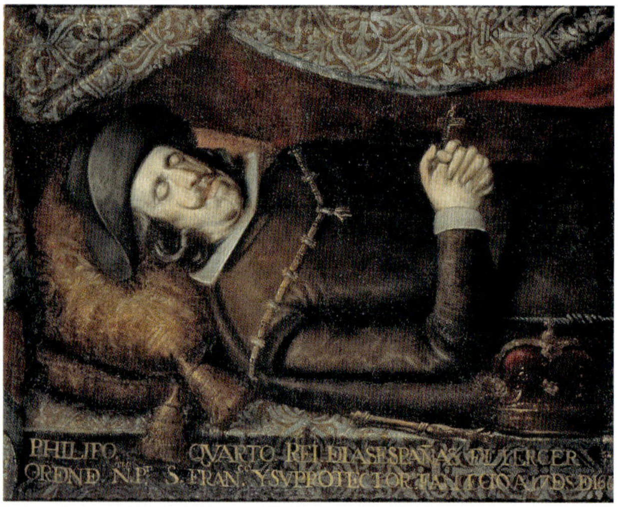

172. Unknown artist, *Philip IV Deceased*, 1665. Oil on canvas, 82 × 104 cm. Real Academia de la Historia, Madrid

daughters a position in the queen's private chamber or a post as an assistant to the harbinger—that is, the court official in charge of furnishing the queen's quarters.[30] Such a position, which came with annual wages and free housing, would augment his daughter's dowry and eventually be filled by her future husband. Until then, Aguado suggested that he could perform the duties himself, even while he fulfilled his responsibilities as the queen's *sastre de cámara*. Aguado's attempt to take on extra work indicates the extent to which he was struggling financially, especially since he had begun to suffer from an unspecified illness around this time.[31]

King Philip IV, who was the same age as Mateo Aguado, was also experiencing a decline in his health. When the king died on September 17, 1665, at age 60, his body was embalmed and laid in state at the Royal Palace.[32] Eyewitnesses offer conflicting descriptions of the king's burial attire. According to Lady Ann Fanshawe, wife of the English ambassador to Spain, the deceased king was dressed in gala attire with a "musk-colored silk suit, embroidered with gold, a *golilla* about his neck" and accessories—hat, stockings, and shoes—all in white.[33] Contradicting Lady Fanshawe, an anonymous *relación* claims that the king's brown silk suit was decorated with silver lace.[34] A death portrait depicts the king in more sober dress, with a plain brown suit, black hat, and a Franciscan rope belt (fig. 172).[35] One thing that all accounts agree upon is that the king was buried wearing a *valona* and *golilla*, the austere standing collar that had defined Philip IV's 44-year reign. The king's death was described by one *relación* as an eclipse of the sun. This was certainly true for Aguado, whose final years were cast in shadow after the king's passing.[36]

Widow's Weeds

The death of the king brought Aguado's long run of inventive court confections to an end. The 30-year-old widow Mariana of Austria exchanged her richly decorated dresses for plain black and white widow's weeds. In the first portrait of Mariana that was painted after the king's death, she wears a floor-length loose black gown (*monjil*) with a long white wimple (*toca*) that envelops her face, and a black mantle draped over her head (fig. 173).[37] With this dramatic change of dress, Mariana marked her transition from wife to widow—and her rise to political power. Now the queen mother, Mariana was appointed regent to govern until the three-year-old Charles II was old enough to rule. The Infanta Margarita's mourning dress was less austere than her mother's widow's weeds and included some black decorations: a wide black band around the hem of

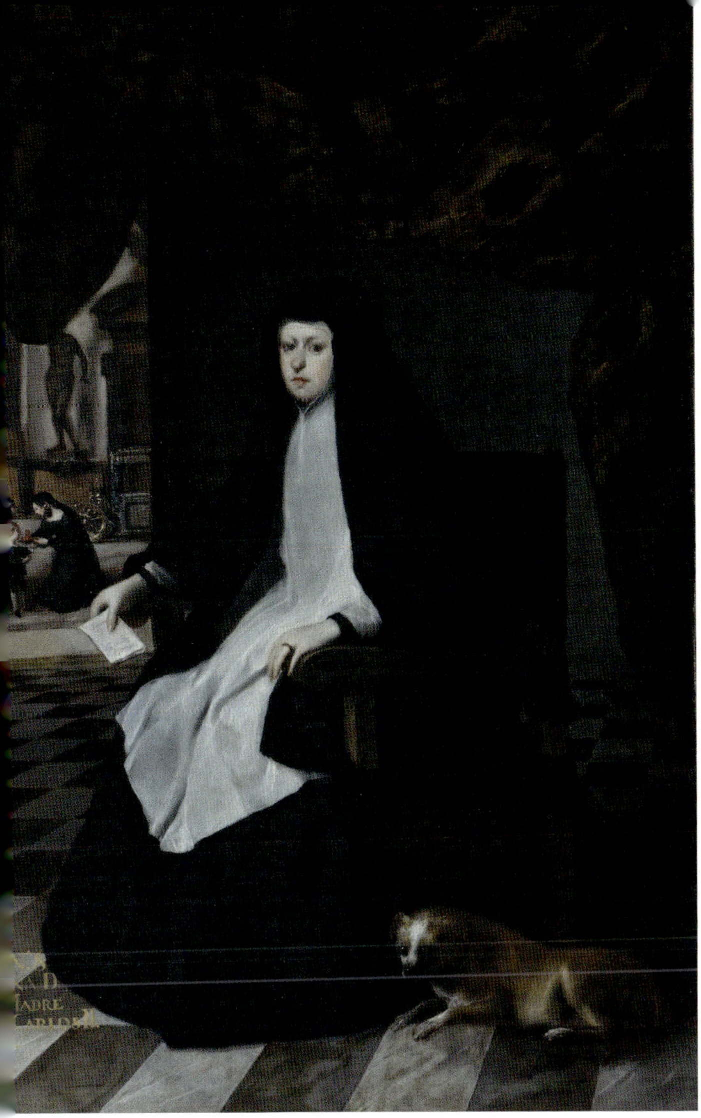

173. Mariana of Austria in widow's weeds. Juan Bautista Martínez del Mazo, *Queen Mariana of Spain in Mourning*, 1666. Oil on canvas, 196.8 × 146 cm. National Gallery, London

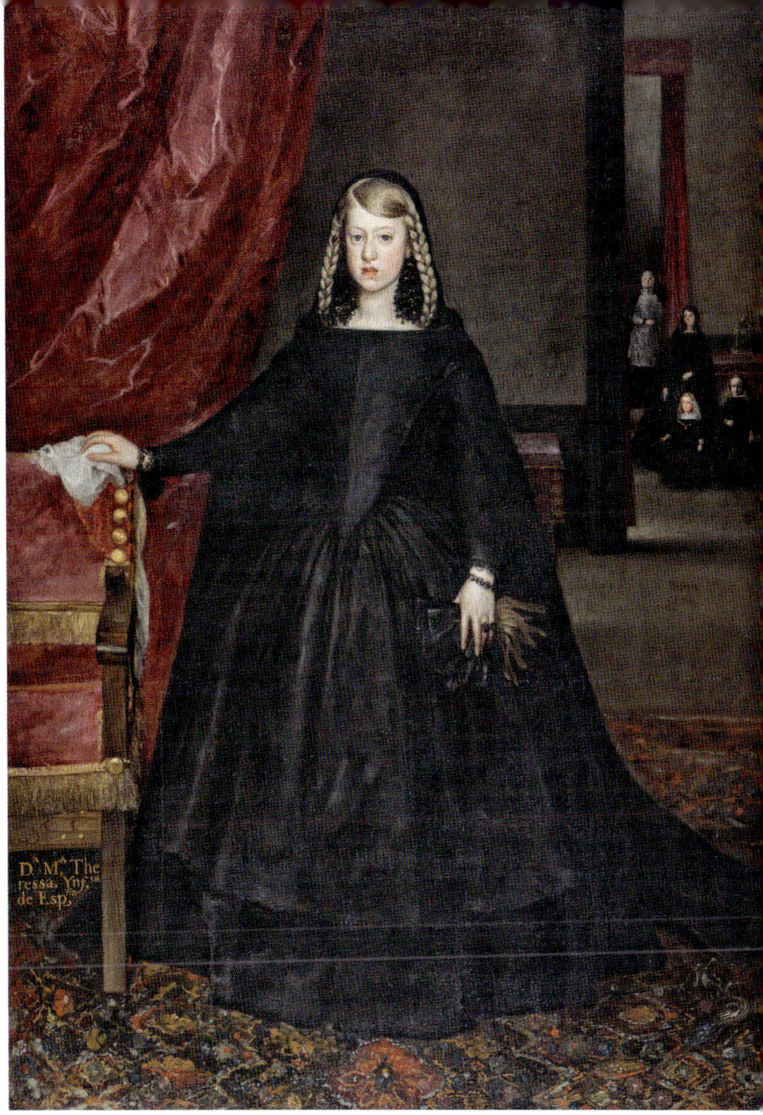

174. Juan Bautista Martínez del Mazo, *Infanta Margarita in Mourning Dress*, 1665–6. Oil on canvas, 205 × 144 cm. Museo Nacional del Prado, Madrid

her skirt and narrow black lace at her wrists (fig. 174). After half a year of mourning, the infanta followed her portraits to Vienna, where she married the emperor in April 1666. A German printed sheet advertising Margarita as an imperial bride depicts her in a richly decorated dress with wide bands of lace forming a chevron on the bodice, one of the last illustrations of Aguado's style at the end of his career (fig. 175).

With Mariana dressed as a widow and Margarita gone to Vienna, Madrid again lacked a royal role model for feminine fashions. A new generation of zealous persons seized the opportunity to press for the reform of women's dress, just as they had in the aftermath of Isabel of Bourbon's death some 20 years earlier. The late 1660s and early 1670s saw a proliferation of printed polemics denouncing women's profane dress and calling for the reform of low-cut bodices. At the time of Philip IV's death, women's bodices had become lower-cut than ever and exposed the top of the shoulders, as worn by the women who appear in Antonio Sáenz de Herquiñigo y Vergara's 1665 illuminated letters patent of nobility (fig. 176).[38] One printed petition called directly upon Mariana, in her powerful role as regent, to exile "profane dresses" like these from the Spanish kingdoms.[39] In 1668 the Archbishop of Zaragoza banned women from attending church wearing bodices "that expose any part of the back, shoulders, and breasts" and ordered the priests in his archbishopric to refuse those women communion.[40] In a lengthy treatise published in 1673 arguing against the *escotado*, the theologian Tirso González de Santalla acknowledged that the most effective way to eliminate the low-cut bodice was not through the church but rather through the example set at the court: "with only reforming [the dress of] the ladies of the palace, and not allowing any lady to appear [at court] who was not with a high bodice, and with the modesty with which her Majesty dresses, in two days everything would be reformed."[41] The polemics trailed off once a new queen, Marie Louise d'Orléans, arrived from France to marry Charles II in 1679. Off-the-shoulder bodices remained popular. A black taffeta doublet made in the later seventeenth century is cut straight across the top to reveal the entire shoulder (fig. 177). The zealous persons had lost yet again.

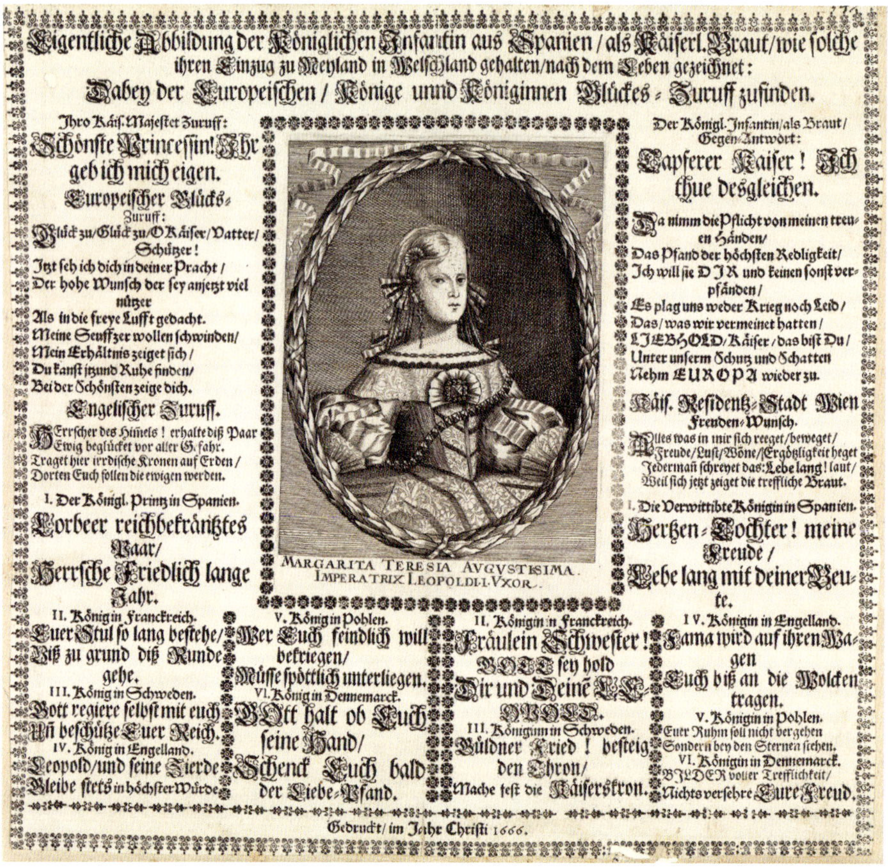

175. Unknown German artist, *True Portrait of the Spanish Infanta Margarita*, 1666. Engraving and woodcut, 29.5 × 30.8 cm. Germanisches Nationalmuseum, Nuremberg

176. *(facing page, above) Letters Patent of Nobility of Antonio Sáenz de Herquiñigo y Vergara, Resident of Madrid and Arcicóllar*, Valladolid, 1665. Illumination on parchment, 34.8 × 22.9 cm. Hispanic Society of America, New York

177. *(facing page, below)* Woman's doublet, Spanish, c. 1670–95. Black silk taffeta with white silk appliqués. Museo del Traje, Madrid

In 1667, Aguado wrote a letter to Queen Mother Mariana complaining that he had been unable to provide for his family ever since the king's death. He had three daughters who needed to be married or placed in a convent, he explained, referring to María and Mónica and probably to a ward who was taken in by the family sometime in the later 1660s.[42] Aguado was paying high interest to his creditors, while the Crown owed him 154,000 *reales* for accounts past due in addition to unpaid wages dating back decades. The tailor declared that he was "in the greater years of his age" and had been sick for the last four years.[43] In light of these hardships, and considering his 37 years of loyal service, Aguado asked to keep his deceased son's position of court accountant in the family, so that the wages could be used as a dowry for one of his daughters. Aguado's request was granted, and the wages of the court accountant were given to his elder daughter, María.[44] His younger daughter, Mónica, had been granted the wages of a maidservant in the queen's private chamber in January 1665.[45] That post, valued at 44,000 *reales*, was included in Mónica's dowry when her marriage was arranged in 1669.[46] Mónica was only 12 years old at the time, which could indicate that Aguado felt a sense of urgency to place his daughter, although marriage at a young age was at this point a family tradition: Bernarda Ruiz had been only 13 when she married Mateo Aguado. Mónica Aguado's husband, Juan de Castillo de la Concha, was an official who worked for the king's Secretary of State for Italy. It was a marriage that promised to give the Aguado family a new foothold in the court's white-collar bureaucracy.

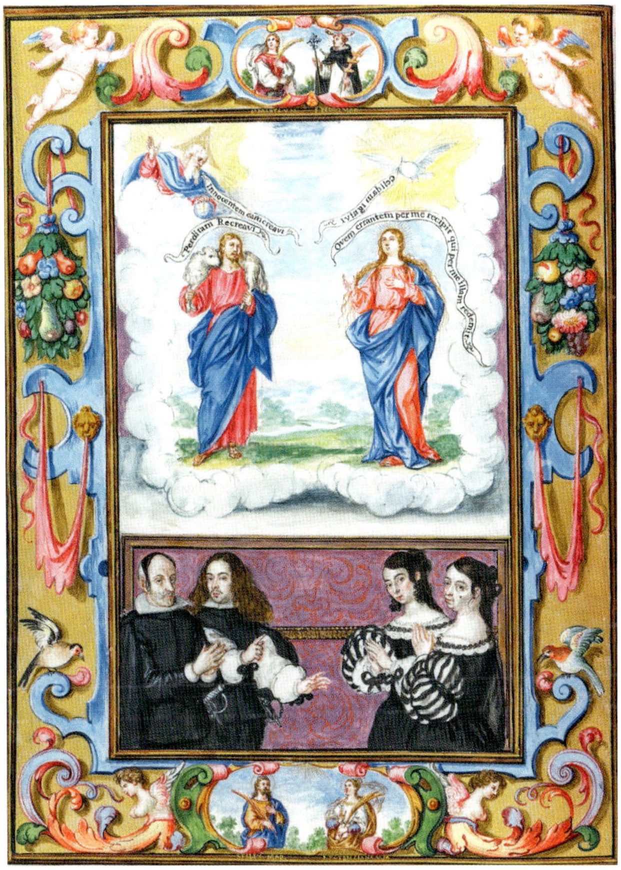

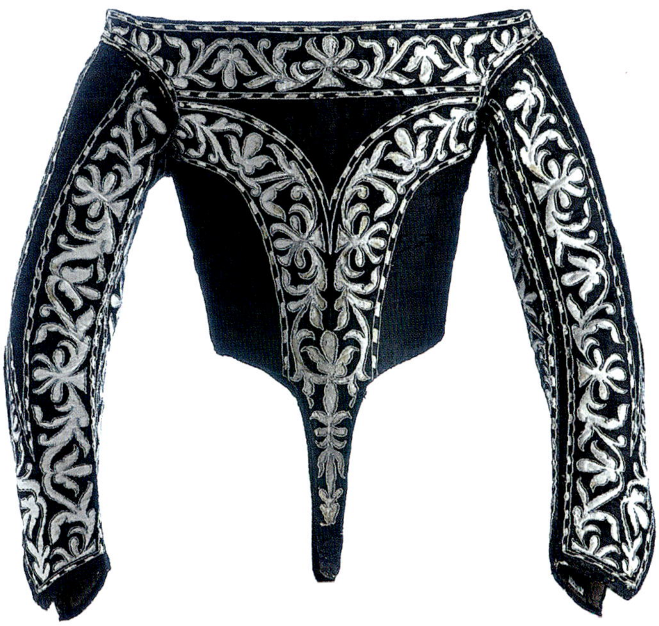

On November 5, 1672, Mateo Aguado was sick in bed when he revised his will for the last time. The queen's tailor died six days later on November 11. According to his final wishes, Aguado's body was to be dressed for burial in a Franciscan habit. Aguado and his wife were both *terceros*—secular members—of the Franciscan Order. The tailor also had been an active member of five religious confraternities, in which he held leadership roles that included treasurer and head brother.[47] His confraternities were based at the Churches of San Ginés and San Felipe, but Aguado repeated his wishes to be buried next to his son at the Church of El Carmen. The tailor wanted his body to be carried, uncovered, to the church with an accompaniment of 50 poor mourners holding candles, who were to be dressed in gray wool clothes that were given to them as a charitable bequest.[48] After burying her husband, Bernarda Ruiz set about the task of executing Mateo Aguado's estate.

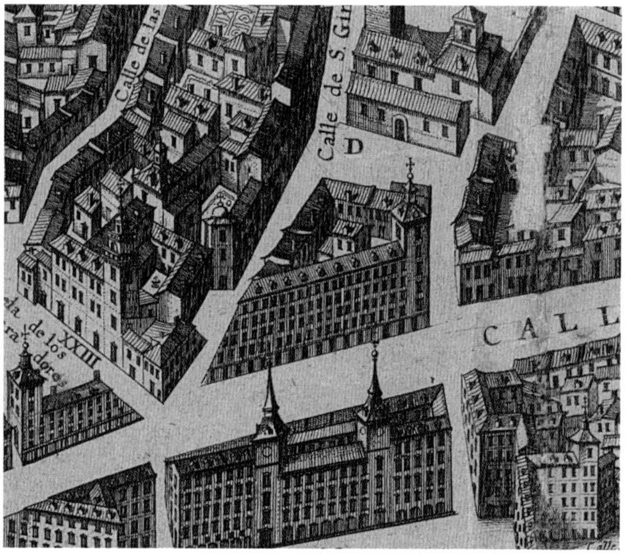

178. Mateo Aguado's block on the Calle Mayor. Pedro Teixeira, *Topographia de la Villa de Madrid* (detail of fig. 31)

179. *(facing page, left)* Corner of the Calle Mayor and Calle de Bordadores, Madrid

180. *(facing page, right)* Bell tower of the Church of San Ginés, 1645

The Royal Tailor's Estate

Bernarda Ruiz and her son-in-law, Juan de Castillo de la Concha, were joint executors of Mateo Aguado's estate.[49] They spent two months between November 14, 1672, and January 14, 1673, inventorying the royal tailor's possessions. The resulting 20-page document was organized into 10 categories: real estate, cash, wooden furniture, household linens, silver and jewelry, tapestries and rugs, kitchenware, clothes and domestic textiles, paintings, and books.[50] After the inventory had been drawn up, each category was professionally appraised—the wood furniture was assessed by a joiner, the books by a bookseller, the paintings by a painter, and so on. Tools and supplies related to the tailoring profession are notably absent, with the exception of a few lengths of fabric. This may be because the costly fabrics and trims that Aguado worked with belonged to his clients, while the professional tools that he owned were not very valuable: a tailor's scissors were worth about 10 *reales*, his thimbles and needles much less.[51] Even with these lacunae, Aguado's postmortem inventory paints a vivid portrait of the material world of a successful royal artisan in late-seventeenth-century Madrid.

Aguado's most valuable possession was his home in the parish of San Ginés. The tailor owned three conjoined houses plus additional space above a neighbor's shop in a five-story building on the Calle Mayor where it meets Calle de Bordadores at an acute angle.[52] On Pedro Teixeira's 1656 map of Madrid, the left-hand corner of

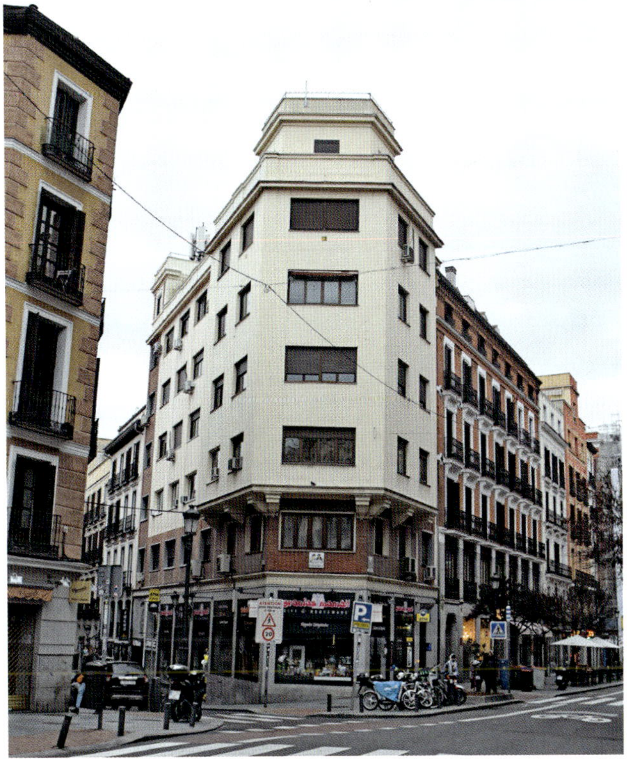

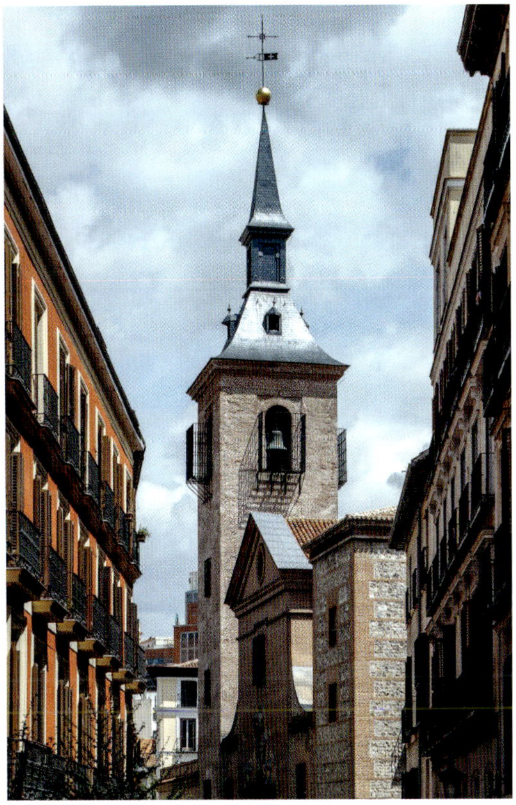

Aguado's building has been cut off in order to better show the layout of the streets (fig. 178). A wedge-shaped building occupies the space today (fig. 179). Aguado's home was in a prime location between the Plaza Mayor and the Church of San Ginés (see Map 2). The church had been demolished in the 1640s and rebuilt with an impressive new bell tower on Calle de Bordadores, just down the street from Aguado's home (fig. 180). According to a 1756 survey of domestic architecture in Madrid, Aguado acquired these properties *sin carga*—that is, tax-free—on March 1, 1662.[53] This was a special privilege granted by the king that exempted the owner from the obligation to give half of his living space for use by the Crown or to pay the equivalent in taxes.[54] When Madrid's master builder Joseph de Pineda appraised the Aguado properties, he calculated 286 square meters after adjusting for the building's extreme angles.[55] By comparison, the celebrated playwright Pedro Calderón de la Barca lived in a home with only 66.5 square meters on the Calle Mayor, just a few blocks west of Aguado.[56] Made of red brick with iron window grilles and balconies and a tile roof, Aguado's building was typical of Madrid. What set the tailor's home apart was the royal coat of arms that hung above the door by permission of the Crown, which probably resembled the carved royal arms that were installed above the nearby Casa de la Villa in 1691 (fig. 181).

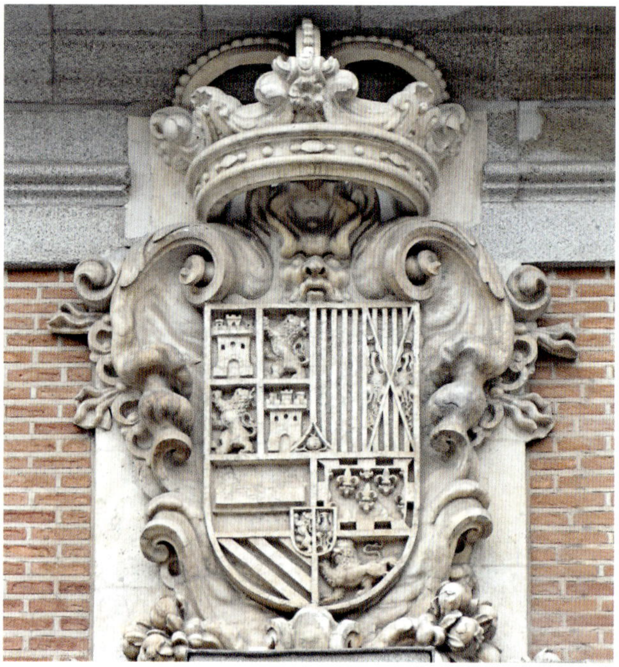

181. Royal coat of arms, Casa de la Villa, Madrid, installed in 1691

Aguado's inventory does not describe the layout of his home, which almost certainly included a spacious workshop on the ground floor.[57] There was probably an entrance hall for receiving guests at the front of the house, which Aguado could have furnished like the reception room that is represented in a late-seventeenth-century etching by the Madrid-based artist José García Hidalgo (fig. 182). The tailor owned crimson taffeta curtains and velvet valances decorated with gold buttons-and-loops (*alamares*) to hang in the doorways, and he had a set of six chairs upholstered in crimson velvet to line along the wall for guests. There was a pair of glass mirrors in ebony frames, which could have been hung at an angle to show off decorative objects placed atop a pair of matching desks. Intricately carved desks were a quintessential furnishing in upper-class Spanish homes, and Aguado owned five of them. Among Aguado's desks there was a matching pair made from fragrant *palo santo* wood imported from the Indies, inlaid with turtle shell, with bronze fittings and walnut-wood feet (for a comparable example, see fig. 183).[58]

Tapestries were the traditional form of wall decoration in noble households, but painting collections had become even more fashionable during the reign of Philip IV. Aguado owned two sets of valuable tapestries, including a set of five woodland scenes that had been woven in Antwerp. He also owned 59 paintings, a collection comparable in size to those of other high-ranking royal artisans such as the silversmiths Andrés de Villarroel and Luis de Zabalza.[59] Aguado owned paintings of every shape and size in black or gold frames.[60] There was a set of four oblong canvases (each measuring 28 × 126 cm) called *sobreventanas* that were specially designed to hang over windows. The subject matter of Aguado's *sobreventanas* is unidentified, but they could very well have represented royal sites, such as the garden view of the Buen Retiro Palace populated with a variety of social types, which hung above one of the windows in the great hall of the Royal Palace at Aranjuez (fig. 184).[61] Aguado also owned landscapes, a few floral still lifes, and one mythological scene (*Danaë and the Shower of Gold*—perhaps a copy after the painting by Titian that was in the Spanish royal collection, sent by the artist to Philip II). There were four full-length portraits (each 210 × 105 cm) of King Philip IV, Queen Isabel of Bourbon, Prince Baltasar Carlos, and the Infanta María Teresa. Such royal portraits, copied after official images by Velázquez, were commonplace in upper-class households as a visible display of status and loyalty.[62] Hanging in Aguado's home, these royal

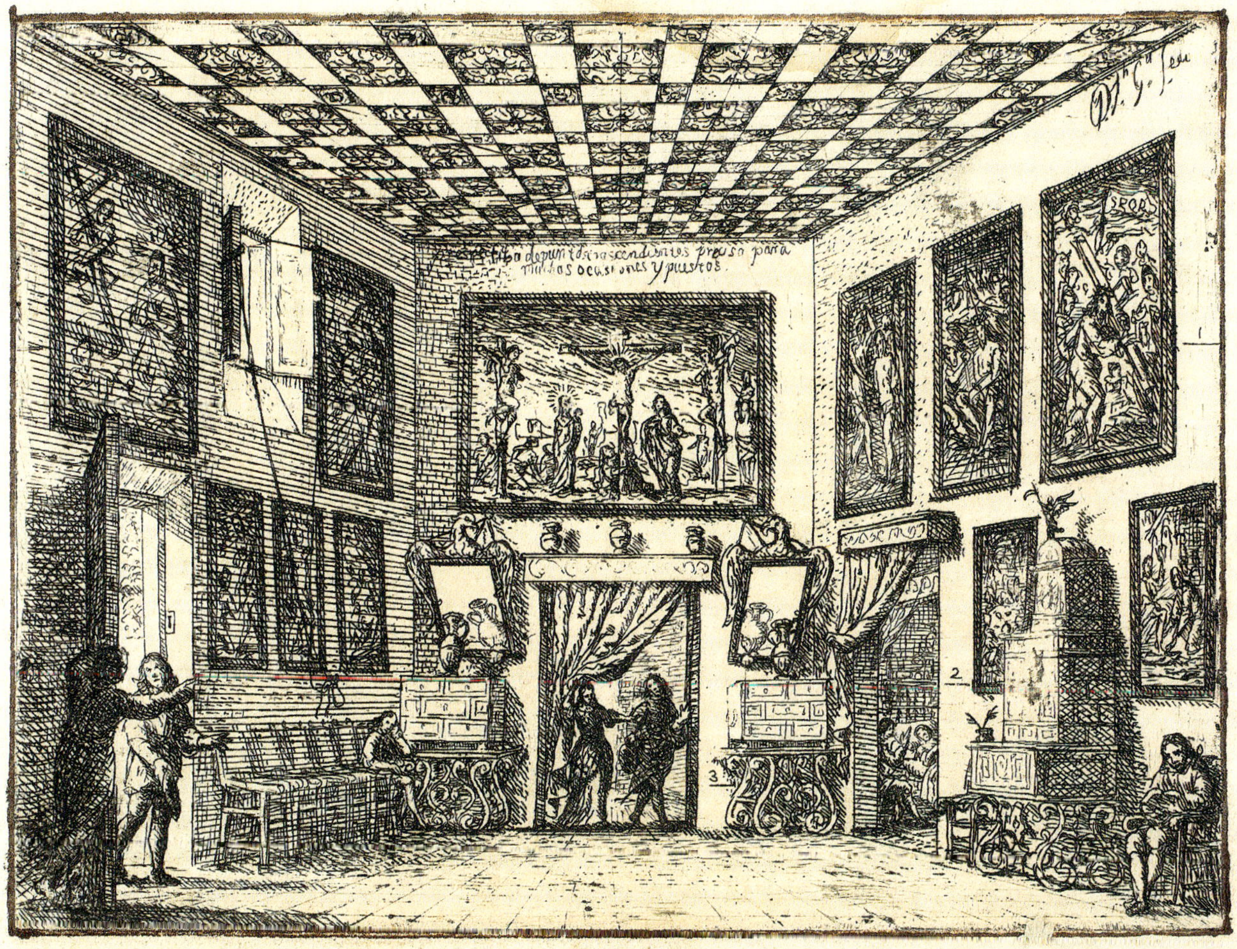

182. Vestibule decorated with paintings and furnishings. José García Hidalgo, *Principios para estudiar el nobilissimo, y real arte de la pintura* (Madrid, [1691]). Etching, 20.5 × 28.9 cm. Museo Nacional del Prado, Madrid

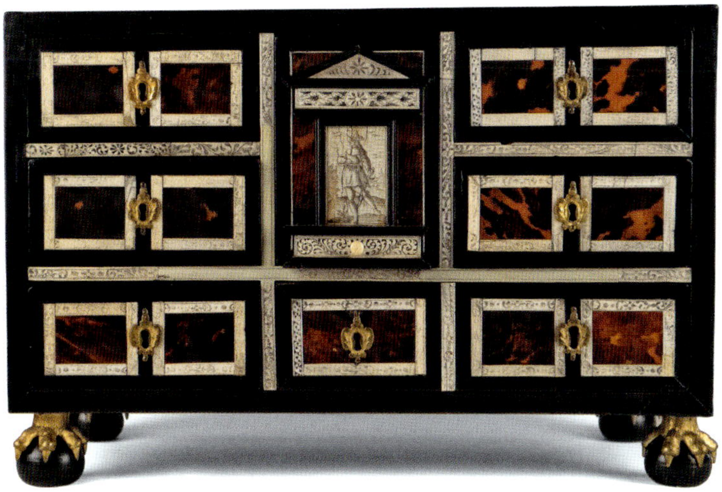

183. *(right)* Desk, Spanish or Italian, second half of the 17th century. Walnut and pine wood with *palo santo* and ebony wood marquetry, turtleshell and bone veneers, and gilded bronze claws, 41.2 × 62.6 × 29 cm. Museo Nacional de Artes Decorativas, Madrid

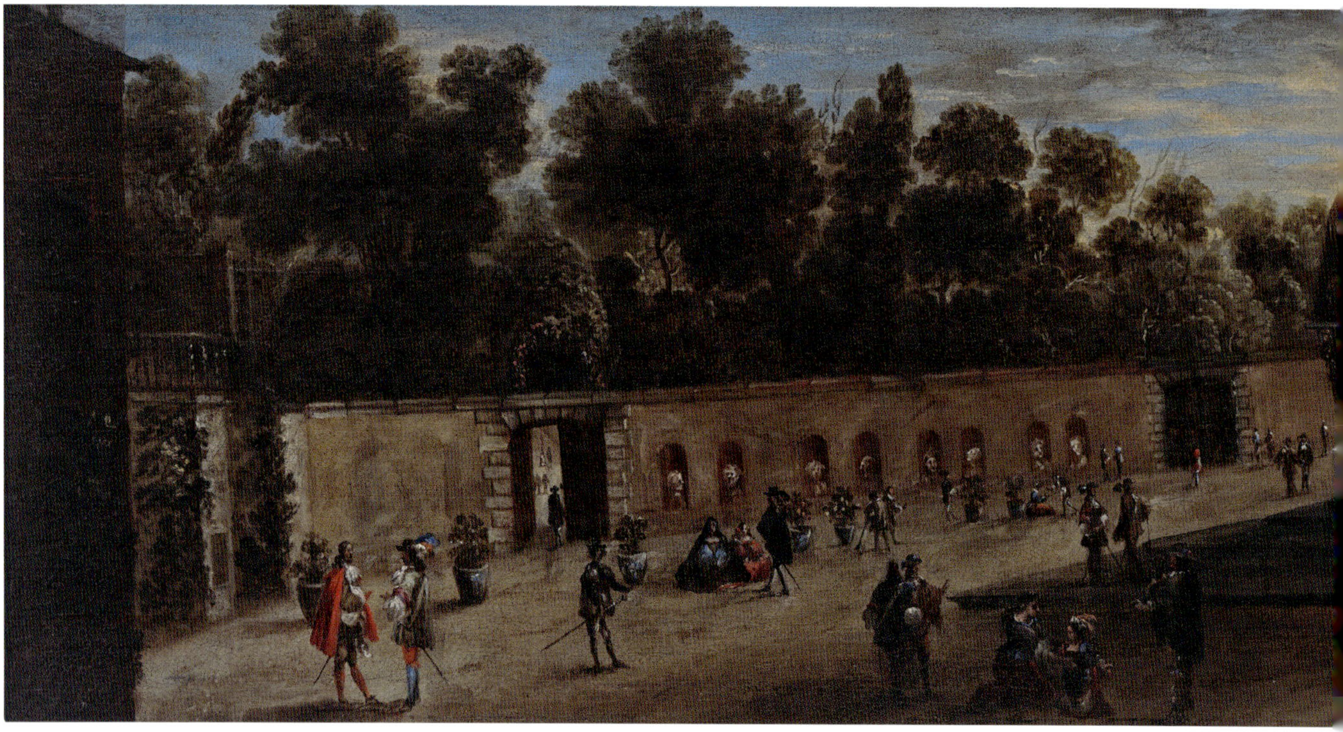

184. Benito Manuel Agüero, *View of the Queen's Garden, Buen Retiro Palace*, c. 1660. Oil on canvas, 47.5 × 190 cm. Private Collection, Philadelphia

portraits may have meant something even more personal: he had dressed each of the sitters, all of them now dead or gone, and Aguado's own dress designs may have been featured in the paintings. Curiously, Aguado did not own portraits of Queen Mariana and her children at the time of his death.

Aguado's art collection included 19 religious paintings. Some of them were quite large, like the framed paintings seen decorating the vestibule in García Hidalgo's etching (see fig. 182). Aguado's most valuable painting, a large *Saint John the Evangelist* in a black frame (210 × 147 cm), was valued at 1,000 *reales*. His taste in religious art was very typical of a late-seventeenth-century Madrid picture collector: he owned images of Christ on the Cross, the Immaculate Conception, Saint Peter, Mary Magdalene, and the grieving Virgin known as Our Lady of Solitude.[63] In addition to religious works on canvas, he also owned a Veronica painted on leather, a "Trinity of the Earth" (Mary, Joseph, and Jesus) painted on a mirror, an embroidered head of the Virgin, framed prints of Mary Magdalene, and boxes with wax figures of religious subjects. The most valuable of all was a painted wooden sculpture of the Baby Jesus mounted on a gilded pedestal (valued at 1,600 *reales*), which was displayed in a case of crystal, ebony, and mahogany (worth 600 *reales*) (for a similar display, see fig. 185).[64] Aguado also owned a silver basin with a figure of the Ecce Homo for holy water, and silver cruets called *vinajeras* to hold water and wine for Mass.[65] He probably had an oratory where he could hear Mass in the privacy of his own home, a privilege that was supposed to be reserved for the nobility.[66]

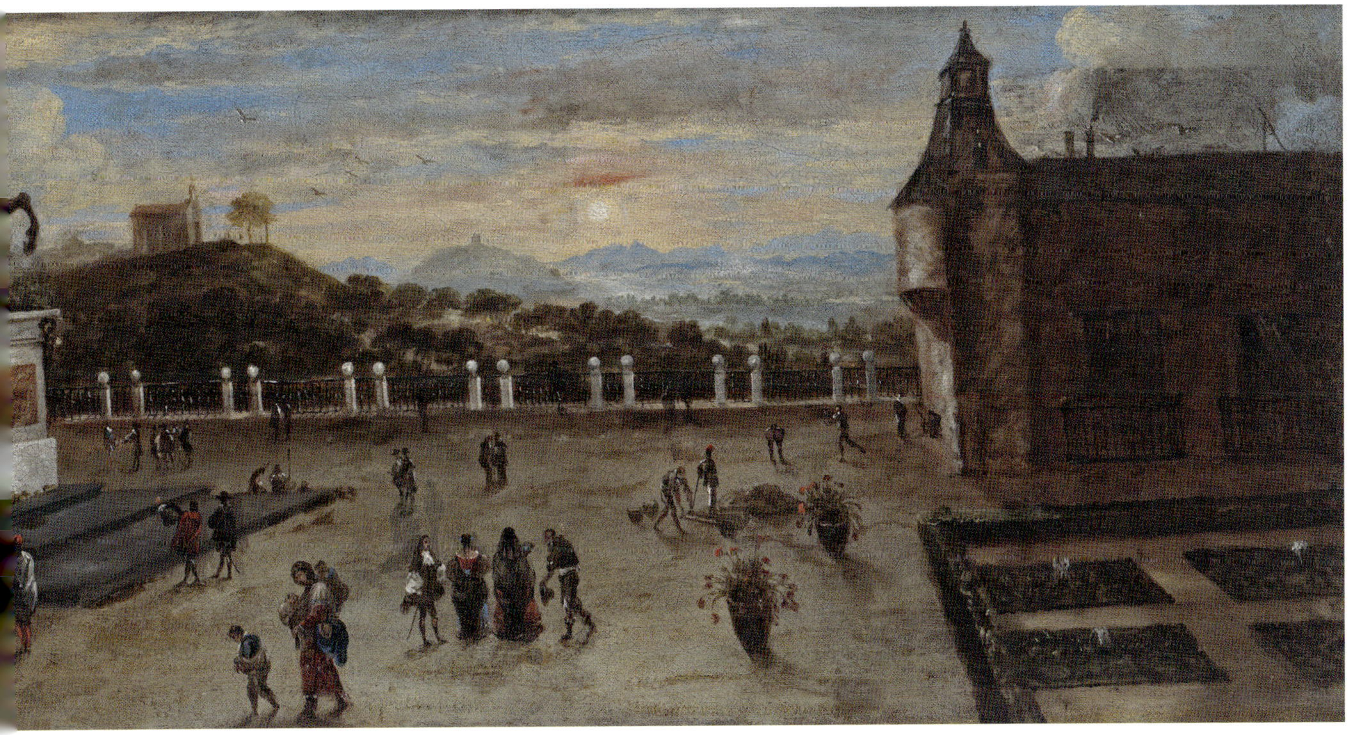

Aguado owned a library of 60 books, all of them written in Spanish.[67] This was a relatively small collection; Velázquez, in comparison, possessed 154 titles, while some other seventeenth-century Spanish artists and architects owned more than 300 or even 650 books.[68] Nonetheless, it is significant that Aguado owned any books at all: there were none listed in the posthumous inventory of his predecessor Francisco de Soria.[69] Like Aguado's paintings, his books were a mix of religious and secular works. His library was very different from that of Velázquez, who collected books relevant to his art, including many of Italian origin.[70] Aguado's books, in contrast, focused on Spanish authors and subjects, and included a large number of spiritual works and contemporary literature, two genres that were absent from the painter's library. Aguado did not own any books related to the tailoring profession. Instead, the tailor owned mystical works by Teresa of Ávila and Luis de Granada, novels by Miguel de Cervantes (the second book of *Don Quixote* and *The Travails of Persiles and Sigismunda*), and five books by Francisco de Quevedo. He also owned books about Spanish history from the time of the Gothic kings to the expulsion of the Moriscos, festival books, anti-French polemical works published in the 1630s, and an expensive six-volume history of the popes—the *Pontifical History* by Gonzalo de Illescas. In sum, the titles in Aguado's library suggest that the tailor read for spiritual edification and for personal pleasure, and they indicate an interest in Spanish history and politics but show no curiosity about the wider world beyond the Spanish court.

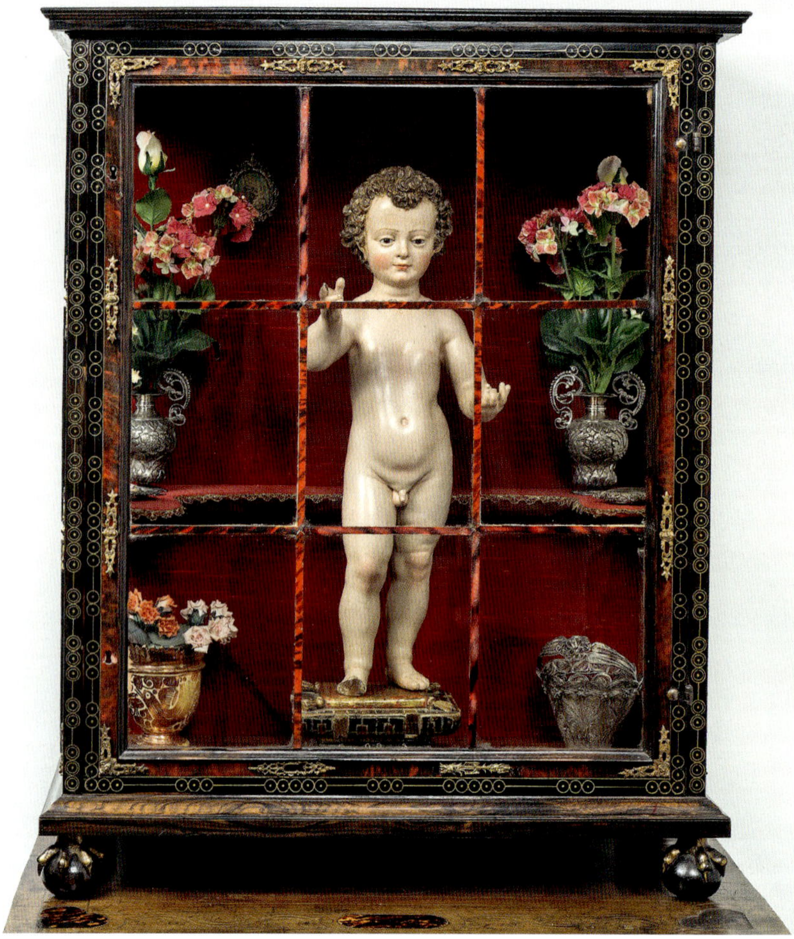

185. Polychromed wooden sculpture of the Baby Jesus (Seville, late 17th or early 18th century, 58.5 cm tall) in a glass display case of ebonized wood decorated with mollusk shell and bronze, and lined in red velvet (Madrid, second half of the 17th century, 91 cm tall). Museo Nacional de Artes Decorativas, Madrid

186. *(facing page, above left)* Wool rug with yellow ground and blue and green designs. Spanish (Alcaraz?), 17th century. 227.3 × 208.3 cm. The Textile Museum Collection, Washington, DC

187. *(facing page, above right)* Juan de Pareja, *The Calling of Saint Matthew*, 1661. Oil on canvas, 225 × 325 cm. Museo Nacional del Prado, Madrid

188. *(facing page, below)* Recreation of an *estrado* in a noble 17th-century home. Museo Nacional de Artes Decorativas, Madrid

Aguado's inventory included three rugs: one large "Turkish" rug (420 × 210 cm) and two "Alcaraz rugs," which were highly prized carpets woven in the town of that name in southeastern Spain.[71] One of Aguado's Alcaraz rugs was blue and gold, like a seventeenth-century Spanish carpet in the Textile Museum Collection in Washington, DC (fig. 186). Aguado could have used his rugs as table-covers, as seen in Juan de Pareja's *Calling of Saint Matthew*, a biblical scene that the artist set in a contemporary late-seventeenth-century Spanish interior (fig. 187). The large "Turkish" rug may have served in wintertime to cover an *estrado*, which was a platform of the kind seen in Velázquez's *Infanta Margarita in Pink* (see fig. 146). *Estrados* were features of well-off households where women received guests, sewed, and performed other leisure activities.[72] Women sat on cushions, while men were seated on short-legged armless chairs called *taburetes*, like the one covered with blue velvet at the National Museum of Decorative Arts in Madrid (fig. 188). Aguado owned enough cushions and chairs to furnish more than one *estrado*: there were 22 cushions upholstered in crimson velvet, black damask, and embossed leather, and 10 *taburetes*, 8 of which were upholstered in cowhide

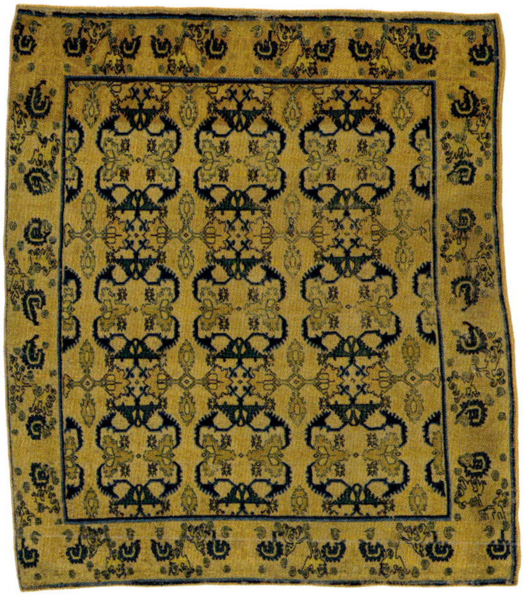

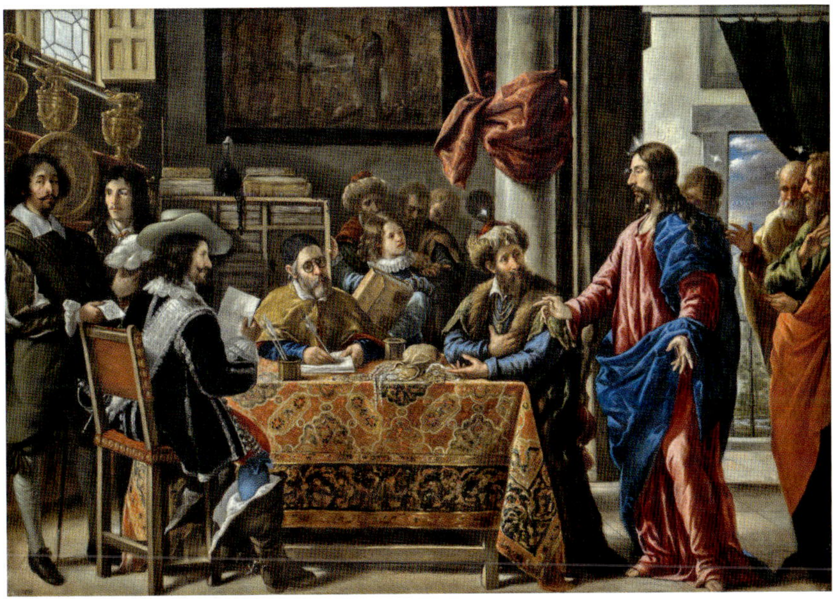

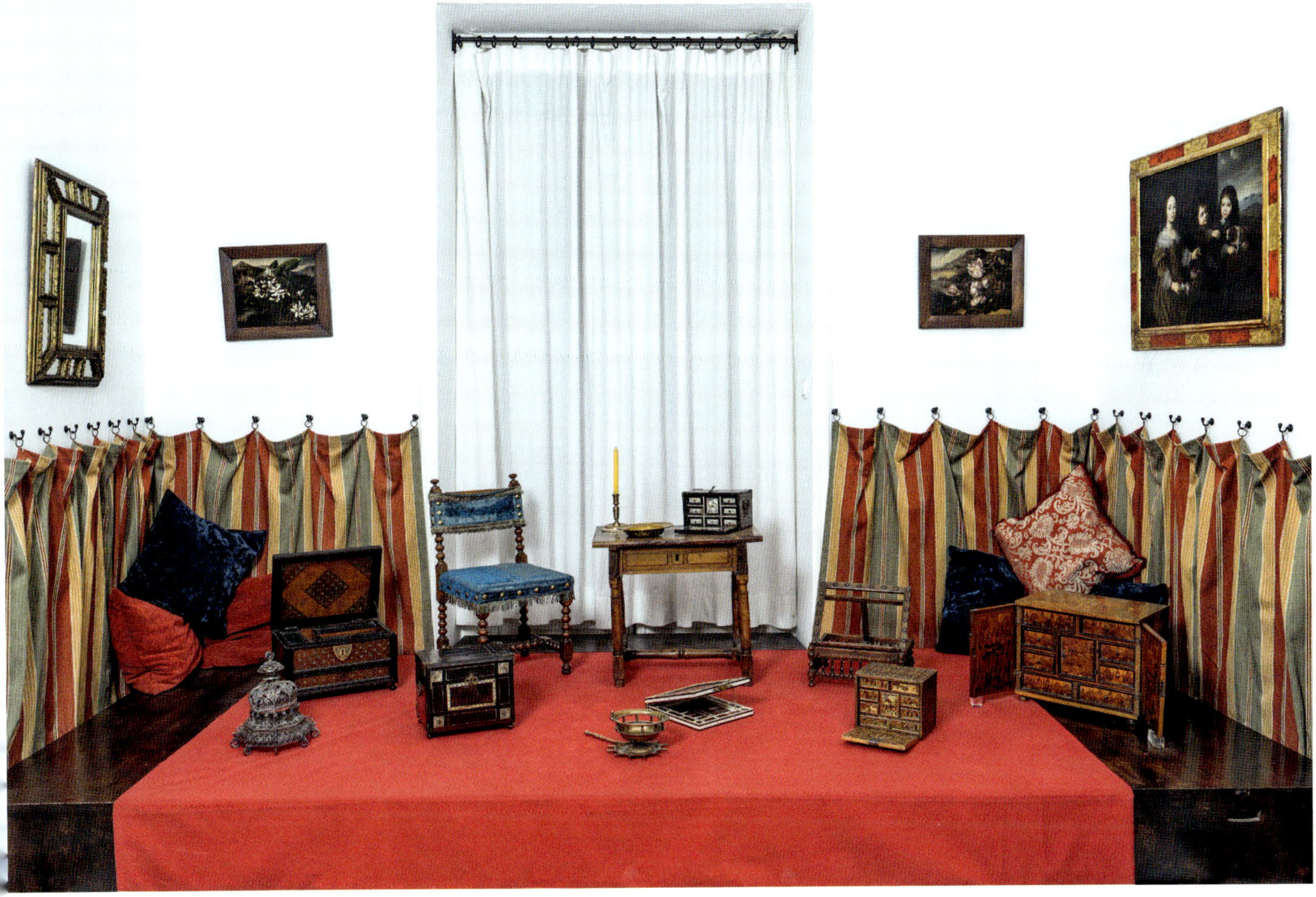

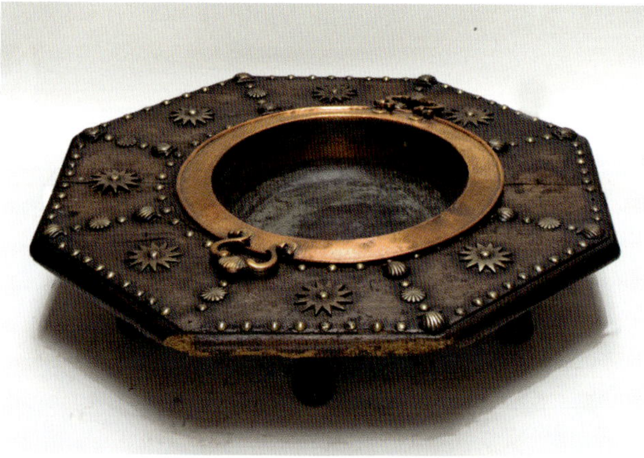

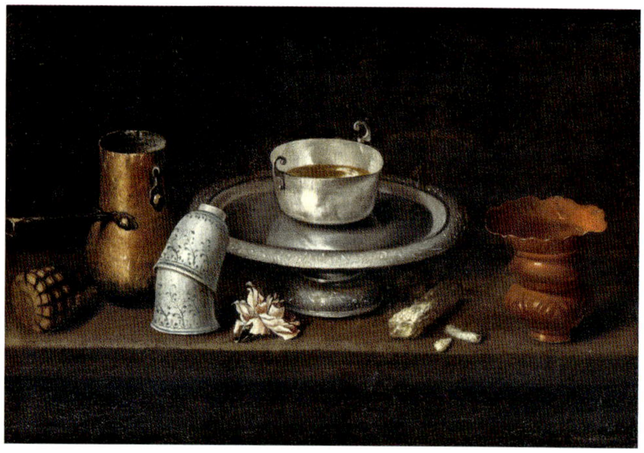

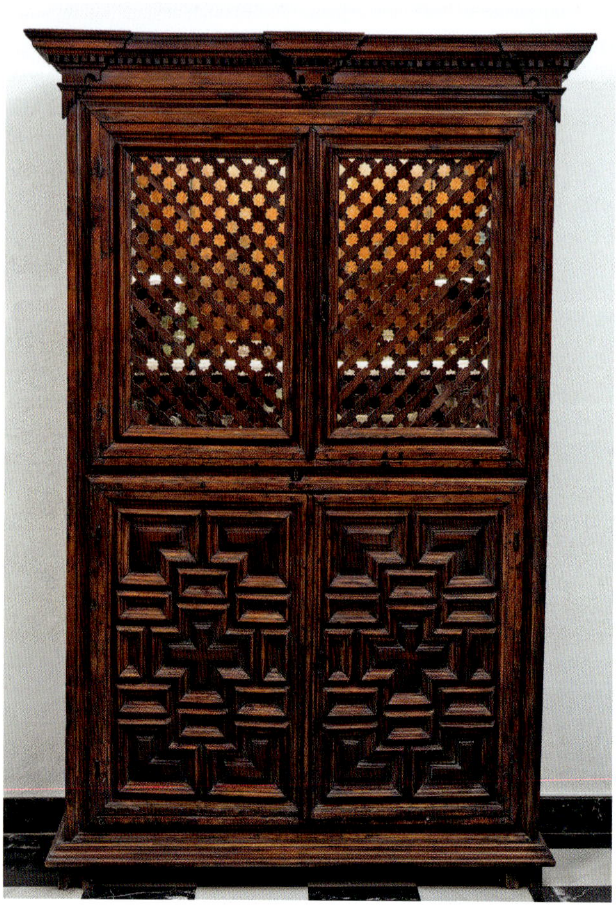

189. *(above left)* Octagonal brazier with gilded studs, stars, and conch shells, 17th century. Walnut wood and copper, 16 cm tall, 88 cm diameter. Museo Nacional de Artes Decorativas, Madrid

190. *(above right)* Juan de Zurbarán, *Still Life with a Bowl of Chocolate*, c. 1640. Oil on canvas, 52 × 74.5 cm. Musée des Beaux-Arts et d'Archéologie, Besançon

191. *(left)* Armoire, Spanish, last quarter 17th century. Walnut and pine wood with iron hinges, 220 × 137 × 55 cm. Museo Nacional de Artes Decorativas, Madrid

and 2 in plush.[73] In wintertime, Bernarda Ruiz and her guests could warm themselves on the *estrado* with a brazier made from walnut wood with a copper interior (as in fig. 189), while enjoying hot chocolate prepared in a pear-shaped copper pot and served on a silver platter (as illustrated in fig. 190).[74]

The bedrooms in the Aguado house were furnished with Italian-style canopied beds made from walnut wood and hung with rich silks, including one set of heavy green taffeta bed curtains with blue silk fringe and another set in crimson damask.[75] For storing clothing, bed linens, and other items, there were over a dozen large wooden chests, most of them covered with fine black leather studded with gold tacks.[76] There was also a large, expensive armoire made of pine and walnut wood with decorative and functional latticework that allowed air to circulate inside (as in fig. 191).[77]

A leather-covered dressing table listed in Aguado's inventory may have been stocked with small-scale luxuries like the ones represented in *Still Life with a Lady's Dressing Table*, including a small writing desk made of ebony and ivory (fig. 192).[78] Aguado owned items of jewelry similar to those in the painting, including a gilded silver pomander, a coral rosary, expensive strands of pearls, and devotional images of Saints Dominic and Francis enameled on an octagonal piece of gold jewelry encircled with rock crystal.[79] The tailor also owned several protective amulets, including a crystal fist called a *higa* and a preserved badger claw in a silver setting, which were believed to ward off the evil eye.[80] These amulets had probably been attached to a belt and worn by Aguado's children while they were still nursing (like the example in fig. 193; see the portraits of royal children wearing amulet belts in figs. 83 and 150).

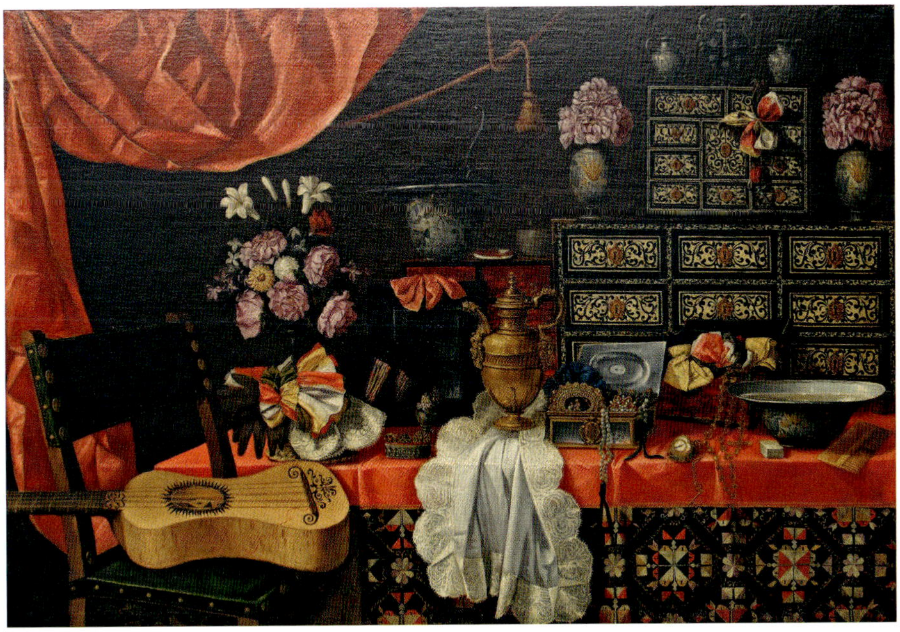

192. Circle of Tomás Yepes, *Still Life with a Lady's Dressing Table*, c. 1650–80. Oil on canvas, 111 × 165 cm. Museo Nacional de Artes Decorativas, Madrid

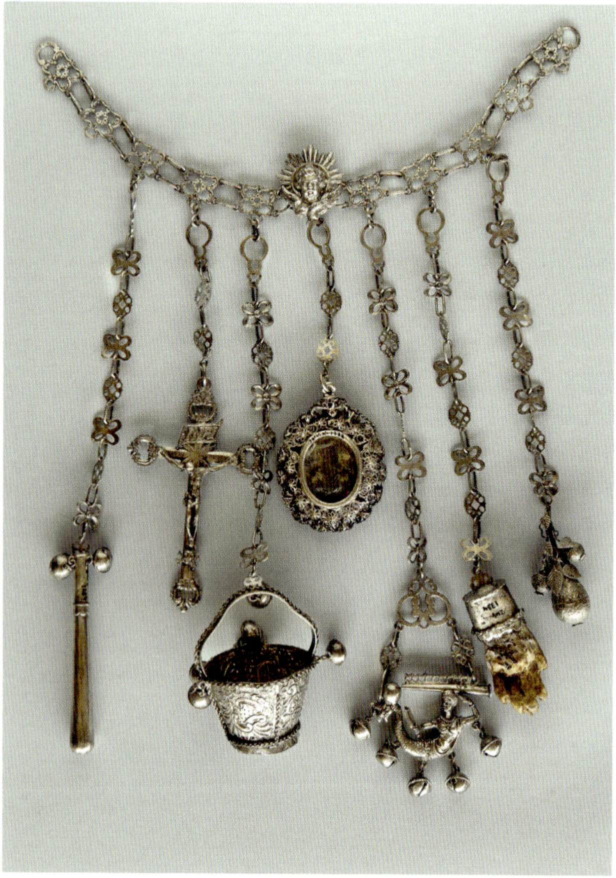

193. Silver belt with amulets, c. 1650–1700. Museo Nacional de Artes Decorativas, Madrid

All of Aguado's books, paintings, furniture, silver and jewelry, and cookware combined were not worth as much as the tailor's clothing and domestic textiles. Master tailor Francisco Fernández appraised 75 men's and women's garments worth a total of 20,523 *reales*.[81] The owners of the garments are not identified, but they presumably belonged to Aguado, Bernarda Ruiz, and their elder daughter María, who was still unmarried and living at home. In keeping with the style of the early 1670s, Aguado's clothes were made predominantly from floral-patterned silks and decorated with lace. The most valuable item was the yellow livery, valued at 600 *reales*, that Aguado had been given by the king with his post as a mounted palace guard. There was a large collection of expensive men's doublets—22 of them—made from velvet, cloth of silver, and other silks that were decorated with silver and black lace. One of the most expensive women's dresses was made of buff-colored brocaded silk decorated with plumes almost half a meter high. Another expensive dress was made from black and brown flowered silk trimmed with French lace.

After her husband's death, Bernarda Ruiz had no use for such finery now that she was dressing as a widow. The finest dresses in the Aguado estate were among the movable goods that were put up for sale at a public auction over a period of ten days in April 1673.[82] The first buyer chose two of Aguado's doublets, one of his rugs, some pillows, and a set of satin bed-hangings. Aguado's brother-in-law, Gaspar Ruiz de Obregón, purchased a large number of the tailor's paintings. Juan Martínez, the journeyman who had worked for Aguado for decades, bought two paintings of Mary Magdalene. Other buyers purchased Aguado's suits and doublets, and the best women's dresses and skirts, including the brocaded silk dress adorned with feathers and the flowered silk dress with French lace. The clothes lost much of their value in the sale, with the best and newest garments selling for only 30 to 60 percent of their appraised value. Even garments that were worn or very worn were snapped up by buyers. After his death, the tailor's clothes were worn by others until they could be worn no more.

The End of the Line

Just as Aguado's material possessions were sold to outsiders, the position of *sastre de cámara* also left the family. On November 17, 1672, six days after Aguado's death, Isidro de Robledo was sworn in as his successor. Robledo had served for more than a decade as the king's hosier, a position that he had acquired thanks to his wife, who came from a long line of royal *calceteros* dating back to the era of Philip II. Aguado knew Robledo, to whom he owed a small debt when he died.[83] Robledo's contract as the queen's tailor granted him annual wages plus a holiday bonus of almost two kilograms of Christmas candies. Unlike Aguado, he did not have to pay a yearly stipend to his predecessor's widow.[84] When Robledo died in 1693, his son Francisco de Robledo inherited the job "pursuant to the many years that his father Isidro de Robledo served in this same office, and because he has the combination of talents and ability required to execute this position."[85]

The valuable office of *sastre de cámara* had been Mateo Aguado's to lose. He could have founded a dynasty of royal tailors, but his son had trained to be an accountant, and his daughter had married a bureaucrat instead of an artisan. If the Aguado family had followed tradition, then Bernarda Ruiz likely would have retained her husband's position of *sastre de cámara*. Aguado's widow could have done the job herself or subcontracted the work out to a male tailor until a grandson or son-in-law was ready to continue the family line of work. Artisanry had been the foundation of Aguado's success. In the end, the royal tailor's efforts to maneuver his children into the court bureaucracy failed to pay off for the family that he left behind.

Widowhood was not easy for Bernarda Ruiz. In March 1676, just over three years after her husband's death, Bernarda Ruiz wrote a petition to Queen Mother Mariana—widow to widow—in which she described the hard times that had befallen her family. Her younger daughter Mónica had died in childbirth and left a second grandson in her care. She had to feed her elder daughter María, who had not yet married. Aguado's widow complained that she was being harassed and extorted by creditors. She requested the 198,000 *reales* that the Crown owed her husband, who, she reminded the queen mother, had served the court for over four decades "with well-known reliability." She also requested an allowance (*ración*), since she had not been given her husband's office or a pension like her predecessors had received.[86] The Crown slowly paid off its debt to Aguado's heirs over the years to come. In January 1704, the final payment was made on wages owed to Aguado dating back to his first month on the job in October 1630.[87]

It is unclear what became of Aguado's widow. His elder daughter, María, eventually married, was widowed, and died in 1681.[88] His grandson Nicolás Tomás, who had been a sickly child, lived to adulthood and held an unsalaried position in the palace larder. He married the daughter of a royal wetnurse but struggled to feed and clothe their two daughters after his wife's death.[89] One of those daughters, Bernarda Eugenia Aguado, died in poverty in 1700.[90] That year, Nicolás Tomás Aguado finally received a salaried position in the palace larder.[91] He supplemented his income by renting out property on the Calle Mayor to a painter.[92] After remarrying and having three sons with his second wife, Nicolás Tomás Aguado died in 1724 at the home he had inherited from his grandfather.[93] By the mid-eighteenth century, the Aguado property had been purchased by the Marquess of Navahermosa.[94] This was a relatively new title created by Charles II in 1683.[95] The home where the royal tailor and his family had lived nobly in all but name was occupied by an aristocrat of the blood.

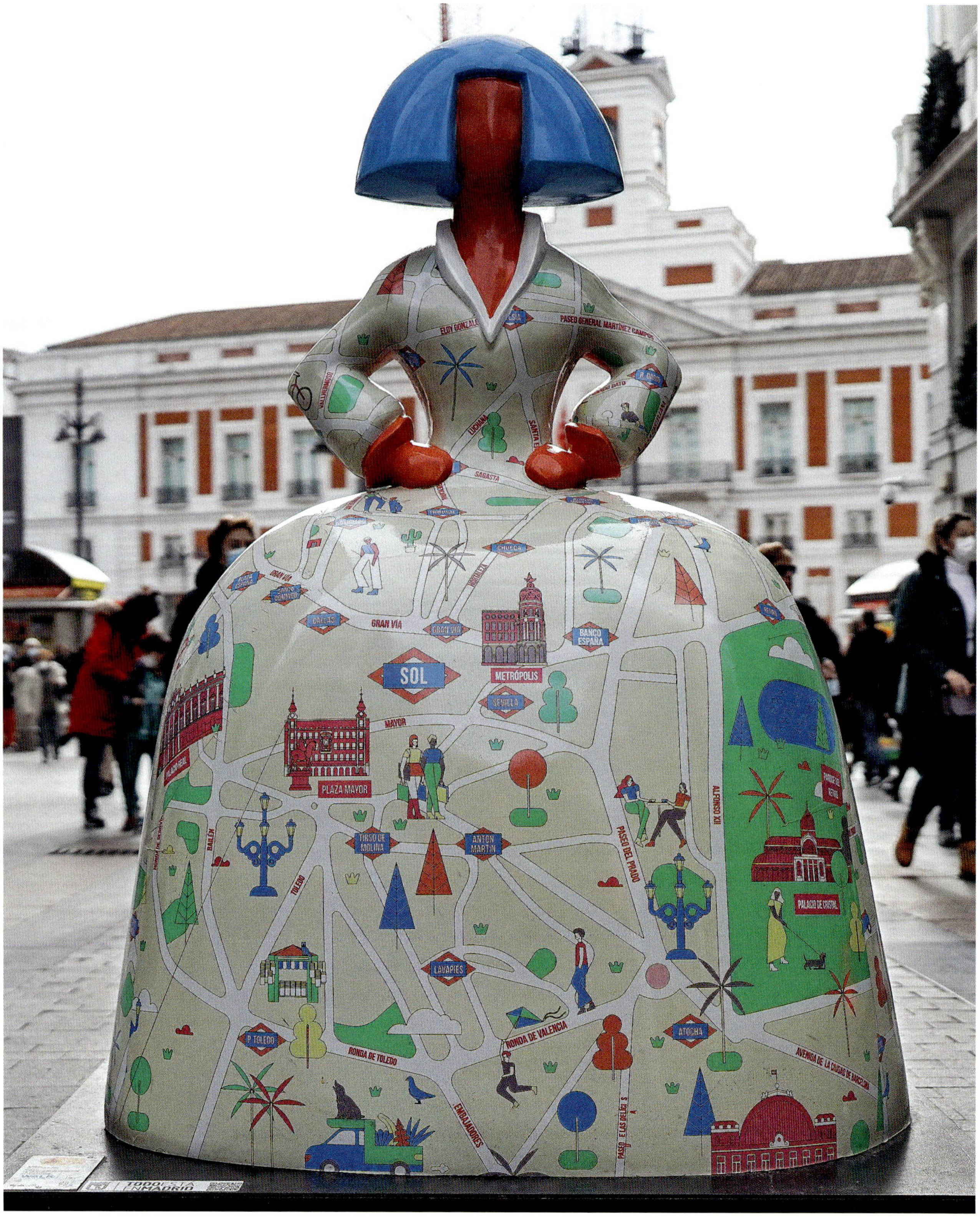

PASEO GENERAL MARTÍNEZ CAMPOS
SAGASTA
CHUECA
GRAN VÍA
CALLAO
BANCO ESPAÑA
SOL
METRÓPOLIS
SEVILLA
MAYOR
PLAZA MAYOR
TIRSO DE MOLINA
ANTÓN MARTÍN
PASEO DEL PRADO
ALFONSO XII
TOLEDO
PALACIO DE CRISTAL
LAVAPIÉS
ATOCHA
P. TOLEDO
RONDA DE TOLEDO
RONDA DE VALENCIA
AVENIDA DE LA CIUDAD DE BARCELONA
EMBAJADORES

Conclusion

Redressing Las Meninas

In Mateo Aguado's old neighborhood around the Church of San Ginés, and all around central Madrid, larger-than-life sculptures with the distinctive silhouette of mid-seventeenth-century Spanish court dresses appeared in 2018 and subsequent years in an annual public art installation project called the "Meninas Madrid Gallery." Each *menina* is different: there have been *meninas* covered with clouds, polka dots, stars, herbage, and graffiti. A *menina* installed at the Puerta del Sol in 2021 wore a dress made from a tourist map of Madrid (fig. 194). These sculptures belong to a long and thriving tradition of artistic interpretations of Velázquez's *Las Meninas* that essentialize the female figures through the silhouette of their dress.[1] The meaning of the word "*menina*" has expanded beyond its original definition of an unmarried lady-in-waiting at court to signify any female figure with the shape created by a *guardainfante* and matching wig like Velázquez's *Mariana in Black and Silver* (see fig. 27). Redressed in eye-catching designs for the twenty-first-century consumer, the *menina* has become the unofficial mascot of Madrid, available for purchase as a figurine or on a coffee mug or T-shirt (fig. 195). The purpose of this book has been to redress *Las Meninas* in a different sense, by restoring credit to Mateo Aguado as the dress designer whose original work is the foundation for all of these later interpretations.

The anonymous artisan does not have to remain unknown. It has proven possible to do much more than name the tailor behind the famous dresses in Velázquez's portraits. We have gotten to know Mateo Aguado well, although much remains to be learned, especially about his early life and apprenticeship. No doubt there are more archival documents waiting to be found, and maybe there is a drawing by Aguado tucked away somewhere. If his apprenticeship or guild exam surfaces in the notarial archives, we might even learn something about Aguado's physical appearance—Francisco de la Rocha Burguen's court guild exam certificate reveals that he was missing an upper tooth and had markings on two fingers of his left hand, which were probably the result of working for years with needle, thread, and thimble.[2] The information available in Aguado's accounts paints a vivid portrait of the life of a royal artisan with its relentless cycle of work, its rewards and punishments. Aguado's career at court suggests that the role of the *sastre de cámara* was evolving by the 1630s into that of a dress designer who was remunerated for his original designs. Aguado's end-of-life documents have revealed the material comforts and signs of social status that a top-ranking court artisan could accrue, but the travails of his final years indicate the limits of an artisan's advancement. Aguado's story somewhat resembles that of the court

194. *(facing page)* Antonio Azzato, *Connecting Travelers to Madrid*, 2021. Painted fiberglass, 180 × 130 × 85 cm. "Meninas Madrid Gallery," Puerta del Sol, Madrid

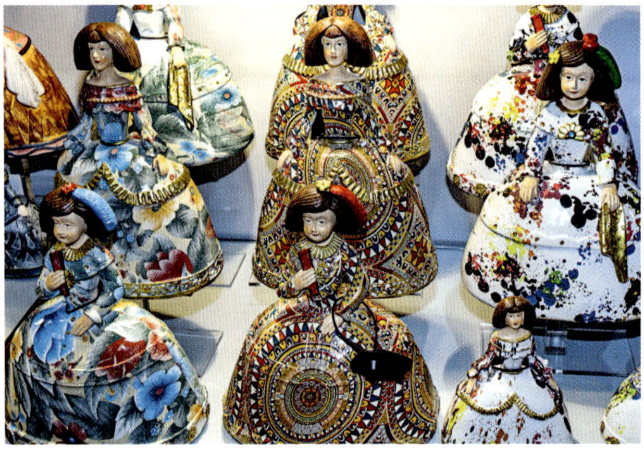

195. Figurines in the Objetos de Arte Toledano souvenir shop on the Paseo del Prado, Madrid

poet Gabriel Bocángel y Unzueta, author of printed poetic descriptions of court festivities in the late 1640s and early 1650s, who complained about his financial struggles and strove to leave his family financially secure.[3] For all the privileges that came with an appointment as a royal artisan, the extraordinary social success that the painter Velázquez achieved was out of reach for a practitioner of a "mechanical art" like tailoring.[4]

The study of Mateo Aguado's life has opened the door to enter the world of Madrid's *oficiales de manos*, the artisans who dressed the court of Philip IV. Aguado's own family illustrates well the endogamous nature of court artisan society, in which professional connections forged at court were sealed with marriages between families who were fortunate enough to hold heritable posts at the court. The youthfulness of the brides in Aguado's family comes as a surprise. The wives of favored artisans could receive gifts of clothing made by the queen's tailor, which had great monetary value and brought honor and prestige to the husbands. The large amount of work that Aguado devoted to royal favors foregrounds the important role that clothing played within the court economy and society, and the almost incomprehensible value that textiles and clothing had at this time, so different from our own. Since the tailor Mateo Aguado has been the focus of this book, the lives of his colleagues in related crafts have by necessity been relegated to the sidelines, but there are many more stories to be told and no shortage of documentation about the *oficiales de manos* at court.[5] There are only the merest hints in Aguado's documents about the craftsmen and craftswomen who worked for him—the journeymen, seamstresses, quilters, and pressers. Artisans below the rank of *oficial de manos* have remained largely anonymous, and their world of work is much more challenging to penetrate.

Examining Aguado's work for the queen's household has also brought to light new information about the lives of the queens and infantas who were his primary patrons. It is well known that royal women in general changed their clothes to reflect transitions in their lives, and there is a substantial body of scholarship on the specific cases of the Spanish infantas and queens at the court of Philip IV.[6] The tailor's accounts and charges analyzed in this book have provided concrete evidence about the changes of clothing that marked transitional moments in these royal girls' and women's lives, such as the dresses that Aguado made for María Teresa to wear with *chapines* after her engagement and the alterations that he made to Queen Isabel's wardrobe when she was pregnant. These changes certainly were noticed by the seventeenth-century public, which was well-trained to read such sartorial clues, none more so than the chroniclers who carefully documented and publicized the details of royal women's public appearances. Aguado's records have also documented the strong role that Queen

Isabel of Bourbon played in having her wardrobe made to her own taste. The documents of Aguado and his colleagues, especially the silk merchants and farthingale-makers, have supplied concrete information about the structural underpinnings that supported the Spanish style of female courtly dress in the seventeenth century. Queens were not just made from velvet and damask (as the peasant Casilda expressed in Lope de Vega's *Peribáñez*)—they were also constructed out of wire and whalebone and pasteboard and gummed canvas.[7] Knowing what went into their dresses gives us a better sense about these women's physical experiences with the garments that transformed their bodies into the shapes that we see in the paintings.

In the course of tracing Aguado's career over four decades, the fashion system of the Spanish court has come into sharper focus. Radical change was rare, with the revolution in menswear at the start of Philip IV's reign in the early 1620s being the single great exception. More often than not, change came slowly to Spanish court fashions, which were inherently conservative. The queens' tailors made the same garments decade after decade. The fundamental structure of Spanish women's courtly dress retained its core elements of a stiff bodice over a corset and a long skirt over a farthingale, even as novelties were introduced to the smaller pieces, such as sleeves, bodice skirts, and collars. When a new style of farthingale—the *guardainfante*—took the Spanish capital by storm in the mid-1630s, it was not immediately incorporated into the queen's wardrobe. Even when the queen's silhouette began to evolve in the late 1630s, the traditional *verdugado* remained in use for another two decades. Diego Velázquez made two lengthy trips to Italy that had a strong influence on his painting style, but Mateo Aguado stayed in Madrid—so new ideas had to come to him. Many of the novelties that Aguado introduced to the royal wardrobe came from France. The Princess of Carignano's visit to the Spanish court is an interesting lesson about the influence that one individual could exert over fashion trends, with widespread and long-lasting impact.

Once the royal wardrobe incorporated novelties, there were many mechanisms in place for their dissemination. In Madrid, the public viewed the queen and her clothes—always from below—when she appeared in person on a balcony during Corpus Christi processions, bullfights at the Plaza Mayor, and performances at the theater. For those who did not see the queen in person, there were portraits hanging outdoors on building facades, and there was one documented case of a sculpture dressed in the same clothes that Queen Mariana wore during her entry into Madrid in 1649. *Relaciones* published immediately after an event reported what everyone had worn and presented that information to shape public opinion. It has been beyond the scope of this book to explore the dissemination of Aguado's work beyond Madrid to the courts of the Spanish viceroys, where women adapted the style to different environments.[8] Women wearing dresses made after Aguado's designs for Isabel of Bourbon at the height of her power stroll in the gardens in front of the Viceroy's Palace in Mexico City, in a view painted on a *biombo*, a luxurious folding screen (fig. 196, detail in fig. 197).[9] The influence did not only flow in one direction: this study has shown that Naples played an important role in the making of Spanish court fashion, as a source of treasured dress fabrics and a place where clothes were made and sent back to the capital.

A pattern has emerged connecting royal deaths to reform efforts. Like clockwork, "zealous persons"—as Philip IV called them—raised their voices crying out for the reform of women's fashions in the wake of a

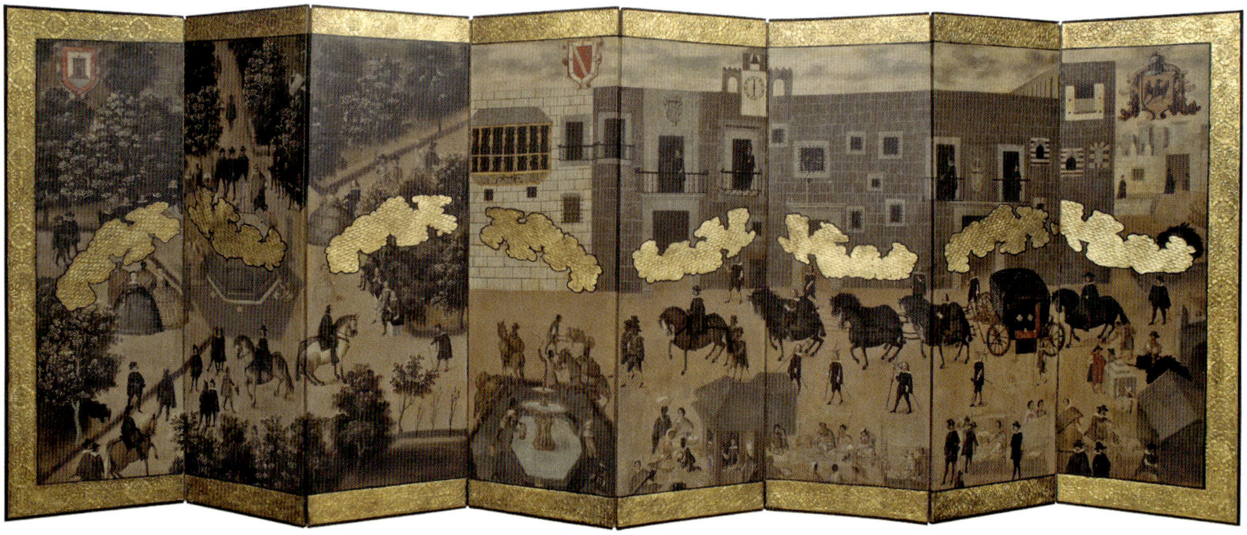

196. Unknown Mexican artist, *Biombo with a View of the Palace of the Viceroy in Mexico City*, probably 1640s. Oil on canvas, 184 × 488 cm. Museo de América, Madrid

197. *(facing page)* Women in Mexico City dressed in Spanish court style (detail of fig. 196)

major royal death. Just as predictably, the pious efforts to reform women's dress ended as soon as a new queen took the throne. The story of the Virgin of Almudena—the venerated wooden sculpture that was mutilated so it could be dressed in gifts of clothes from the queen—graphically illustrates the triumph of courtly fashion over religion. Royal proclamations could be an effective way to reform dress, but only when the court followed its own laws. While the 1623 Articles of Reformation that banned men's ruffs is the best-known example, a lesser-known 1657 law forbidding the wearing of precious metals was also quite effective. Aguado's accounts clearly show that the queen's tailor followed the 1657 law and offer interesting information about the way he adapted to the ban on silver by decorating dresses with mica, which remained popular even after the restrictions were lifted.

Aguado's records offer many clues to explain why none of his work survives (as far as we know). Court fashion was made at a frenetic pace, often at the very last minute. The tailor's work could be compared to that of the playwrights who worked with similar urgency: Francisco de Quevedo and Antonio Hurtado de Mendoza reportedly wrote an entire play for a festival in a single day.[10] This was a fashion system that was responsive to the politics of the moment. A dress could be made overnight to convey a particular message at an event taking place the next day, such as the red and white dress that the Infanta María Teresa wore to

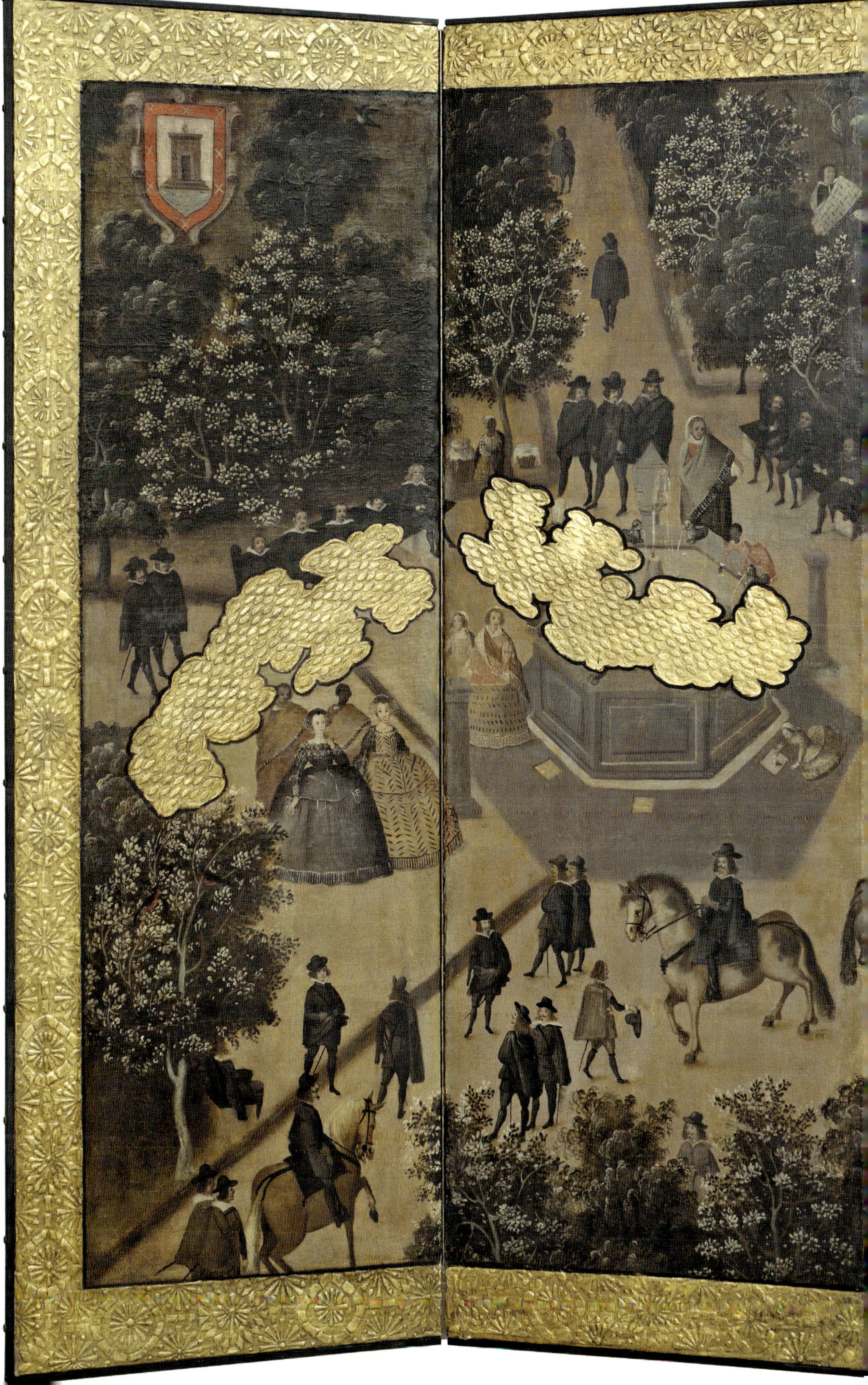

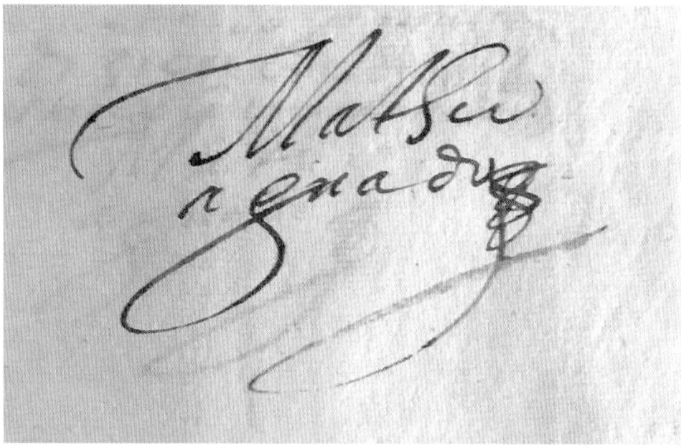

198. Signature of Mateo Aguado, *sastre de cámara de la reina*, November 1, 1631. Archivo Histórico de Protocolos de Madrid

Philip Prosper's baptism in 1657. Once its purpose had been achieved, such a dress was of little use for other occasions. The hastily constructed dress could then be taken apart and its valuable decorations applied to another garment. Everyday clothes, such as the pragmatic black three-piece dresses that were given as wedding presents to women in the queen's household, were probably made more slowly and carefully; garments like those must have been worn to pieces. Royal clothes were regularly taken apart, remade, and redecorated for queens whose bodies were constantly changing with back-to-back pregnancies, and for royal children who were outgrowing and staining their clothes, and graduating to adult garments. Some of the queen's dresses were altered to give as gifts to other women or to devotional images, but Aguado's records indicate that this was a rare occurrence and was probably not a significant factor in the disappearance of seventeenth-century court clothes. They have not survived because they were never meant to last.

Lacking surviving garments, this book has relied on written records to reconstruct Mateo Aguado's work. Formulaic and repetitive, the accounts and charges itemizing Aguado's work make it possible to track expenses, trace changes in dress fabrics and colors, and delve into the construction details of garments and undergarments. Descriptions of the queen's clothes by her own tailor provide a working terminology for writing more accurately about the features of dress seen in portraits, using the period vocabulary described in this book's Glossary. There are differences between the language used in court documents and contemporary literature. For example, in a short story by María de Zayas published in 1647, a woman's life is saved by the boning of her *justillo* ("little doublet") when she is stabbed in the chest.[11] Yet the *justillos* that Aguado made at court were never boned; the tailor was very consistent in calling boned bodices *corpiños* or *cotillas*. The precise language of tailoring that was used at the court seems to have been more flexible in the wider world.

The language of Aguado's documents offers insights into the cultural concepts that certain garments and materials conveyed to their seventeenth-century makers, wearers, and viewers. A dress decorated with *celosía* surely summoned images of women jealously hidden behind latticed balcony railings or screens. The "little breastplates"—*petillos*—worn with a formal dress evoked miniature pieces of armor. The language of color spoke to an audience that knew the difference between the browns of deer, musk, and hair (*ciervo*, *musco*, and *cabellado*). Learning about the fabrics that were used to make women's undergarments has uncovered the association between incarnadine and crimson—the colors of flesh and blood—and female health. Some language has remained elusive, especially the vocabulary of dress decorations. A thorough study of the accounts kept by the royal *pasamaneros* and *cordoneros* would provide the kind of granular information that is needed to understand the decorative details of dress in documents and portraits.

When it comes to court portraiture, some general conclusions can be drawn from this study about Velázquez's approach to representing dress. Velázquez elided and eliminated decorative details, and he may have changed the colors of dress fabrics, but he did not make things up. In his portraits of Philip IV's wives and daughters, the painter represented the garments that Aguado was making, and the same colors, fabrics, and trimmings that he was using. The dresses that Velázquez painted never present a perfect match to the garments described in Aguado's accounts, but they are true to the styles that the tailor was making at a particular moment in time. The clothes that we see in a Velázquez portrait may have been his invention to some degree, but they were firmly grounded in the reality of the royal wardrobe. An intriguing possibility has emerged from this research that some portraits by Velázquez may feature special gifts of exceptional fabrics, such as the brown silk with silver memory rings that Prince Baltasar Carlos gave Isabel of Bourbon (see fig. 75), the black velvet embroidered with silver squares that was given to the Infanta María Teresa by the Countess of Olivares (see fig. 114), and the dress of silver-embroidered fabric that the Viceroy of Naples sent to the Infanta Margarita (see fig. 147). It makes sense that gifts of fabric would have been commemorated in paintings, considering the value that textiles held at this time. Finally, studying Velázquez's portraits in conjunction with Aguado's accounts raises challenging questions about style and mutual influence. To what degree did Velázquez's evolving style of depicting dress reflect or influence contemporaneous developments in dress design? This remains an open question, but one thing is certain: Velázquez's portraits of his female sitters would not be the same without those dresses.

Aguado was responsible more than any other individual for the signature style of feminine dress that defined—and continues to define—the Spain of Philip IV. Iconic images such as Queen Mariana in her black and silver dress and the Infanta Margarita in *Las Meninas* were not the creations of Velázquez alone. Credit is also due to Mateo Aguado, whose name, life, and work were long buried in the archives (fig. 198). Velázquez's portraits of Philip IV's family bear witness to the hidden hand of the tailor who stayed up all night making their clothes.

Chronology of Women's Dress: 1620s–1660s

The primary garments that the royal tailors made for women remained the same throughout this period, although the female silhouette changed significantly. A skirt, doublet, and over-gown were worn as an everyday dress. The formal *saya entera* consisted of a skirt with a train and a bodice called a *cuera* that had a pair of hanging sleeves worn over fitted sleeves. The construction details provided here have been extracted from descriptive lists of dresses made by the tailors Francisco de Soria (1620s) and Mateo Aguado (1630s–60s) (AGP, AG, legs. 5272/2, 5272/3, and 904). Occasionally, court portraits are used to fill in details left out of the tailors' records, as noted. Comparative information by decade is not always available (for example, measurements for skirt hems appear in documents for the 1620s and 1630s but not in later decades). Terms in italics are defined in the Glossary.

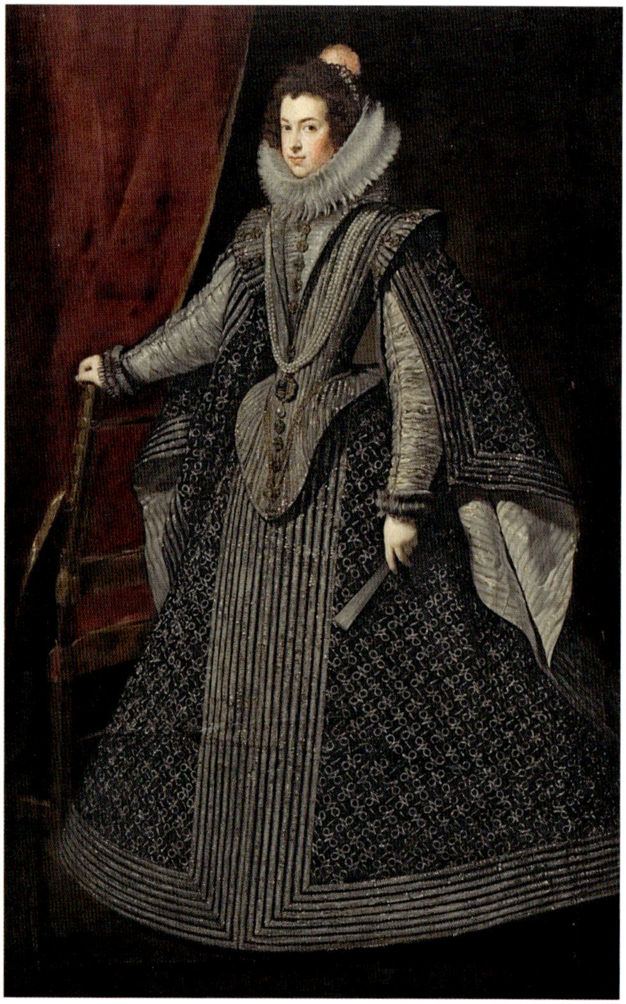

Queen Isabel of Bourbon in the 1620s (detail of fig. 65)

1620s

Tailor to the Queen: Francisco de Soria, dressing Queen Isabel of Bourbon (becomes queen consort in 1621) and Infanta María Ana (departs for the imperial court in Vienna in 1629)

Bodices: Around 1620, the point at the bodice front is elongated and its short skirts become longer. The *cuera* opens at the front and can be worn with accessory pieces—front facings, collars, chest-coverings, and fitted sleeves—that are made from rich materials and often embroidered.

Sleeves: *Cueras* have shoulder-wings and pointed or round sleeves (often slashed "in the German style") or tubular hanging sleeves trimmed in chevron stripes. Over-gowns have round sleeves and shoulder-wings. Portraits show that shoulder-wings are flared; documents reveal that they grew larger in the early 1620s and were stiffened with pasteboard (*cartón*).

Skirts: Skirts have a bottom circumference (*ruedo*) of 3.9 meters; the hem is reinforced with canvas that is covered with a band of silk. The skirt is worn over a cone-shaped farthingale and a petticoat (*manteo* or variation) whose hem may be reinforced with whalebone.

Dress fabrics: Taffeta (single or double) is most common, followed by satin, camlet, and ormuzine. Floral-patterned silks are used for dresses; striped silks to make fitted sleeves and to line pointed sleeves. Plain fabrics are pressed with designs, pricked, or embroidered. Dark colors—black, gray, and walnut-brown—become increasingly dominant in the queen's wardrobe over the decade. Fabrics often combine black with other colors, including silver and gold. Blue and green are also popular, but decreasingly so.

Decorations: Embroidery, sometimes with sequins and black or white glass (*vidrios*), is used to decorate the entire surface of the dress fabric or bands that are applied to the garment. Narrow pointed lace in silver and/or gold and plume-shaped buttons-and-loops (*alamares de penacho*) are common. Various types of trimmings (*caracolillos, espiguillas, fluecos, galones, pasamanos, puntillas, sevillanejas, soguillas*) in silver, gold, and black are layered on top of one another. Court portraits show trimmings applied in straight rows; the documents indicate that they could also be applied in waves.

1630s

Tailors to the Queen: Francisco de Soria (d. October 10, 1630), followed by Mateo Aguado (sworn in October 14, 1630), dressing Queen Isabel of Bourbon and Infanta María Teresa (b. 1638)

Bodices: Bodices are stiffened with pasteboard. The breast of the bodice is slashed in the later 1630s. Visual evidence shows that the bodice remains pointed at the front, and its short skirts may be crenellated at the edges. Decorative chest-coverings continue to be worn with *cueras*.

Sleeves: Fitted and hanging sleeves are both slashed. Round sleeves are used on over-gowns, pointed sleeves on formal gowns; tubular hanging sleeves disappear. Portraits show that shoulder-wings are no longer flared by the end of the decade.

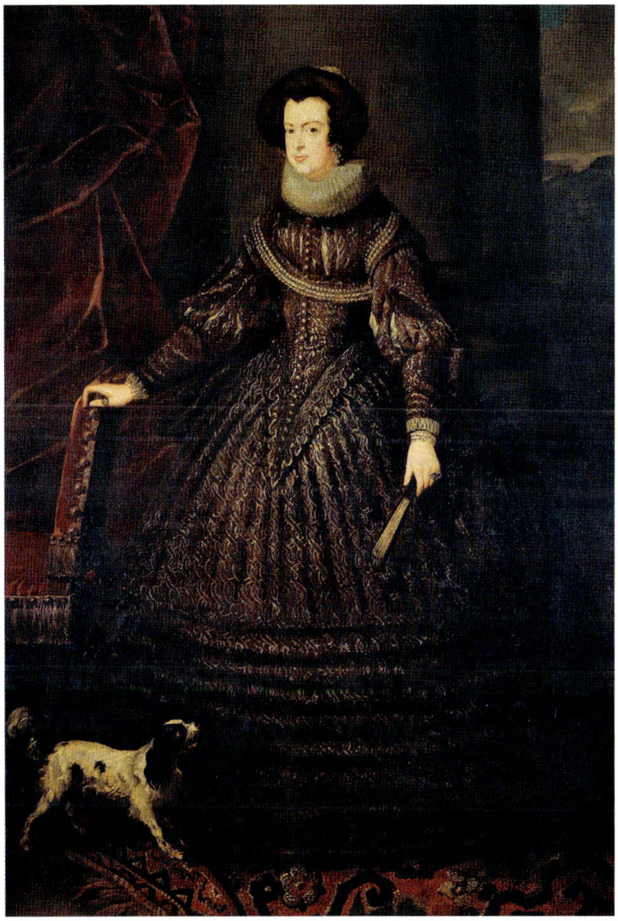

Queen Isabel of Bourbon in the 1630s (detail of fig. 74)

Skirts: The skirt grows wider at the hip and hem in the later 1630s, and hand-openings are added at the sides. In the later 1630s, hip padding is added to the farthingale, which is now shaped by wire in addition to esparto grass. At mid-decade, the bottom circumference of the queen's farthingales is 4.2 meters and petticoats measure 4.8–5 meters around the hem.

Dress fabrics: Patterned velvet (*terciopelado*) is more common than before. Ormuzine, taffeta, satin, damask, and camlet are frequently used. Rich fabrics imported from Naples become prominent at the end of the decade. Plain black predominates, followed by floral-patterned silks with black and one or two other colors, frequently silver; also walnut-brown, gray, and pearl. Dress fabrics are pricked to show a contrasting underlining, especially in the later years of the decade.

Decorations: Decorations are almost exclusively gold, silver, and black. Black Flemish lace, black ribbons and gold galloons of different widths, and gold fringe are common. Designs include *almenillas*, whorls (*caracoles*), eyeglasses (*anteojos*), carnations and other flowers, and *alamares* in many new shapes; these are made from a wide variety of woven and braided trimmings in black silk and/or metal threads: *caracolillos*, *entorchados*, *galones*, *pasamanos*, *pestañas*, *puntillas*, *sevillanejas*, *soguillas*, *torzales*, and *trencillas*. Buttons made of gold or silk thread are prominent and abundant. Embroidery incorporates gold twist, silver drawn wire, colored glass beads (*abalorios*) and pieces of glass, sequins, and occasionally false gems.

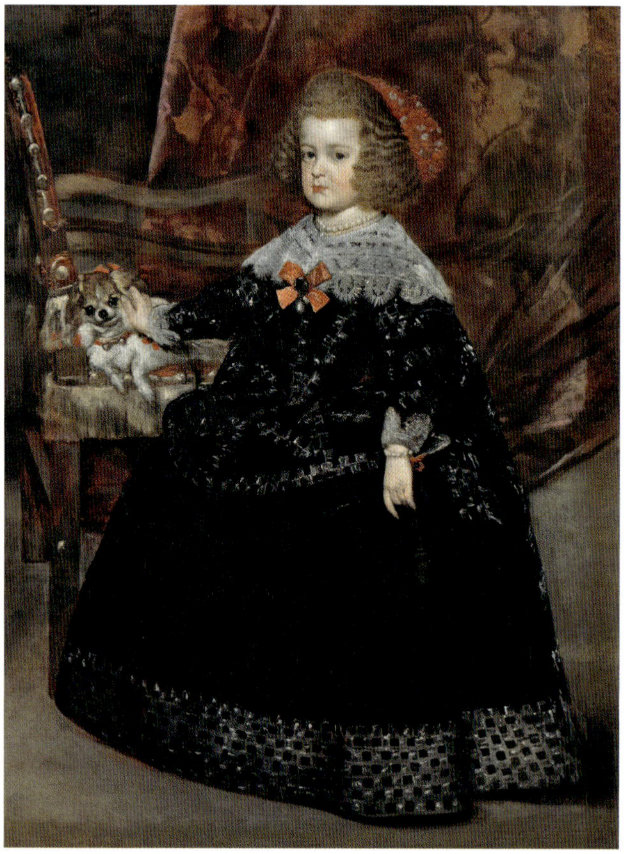

Infanta María Teresa in the 1640s (detail of fig. 114)

1640s

Tailor to the Queen: Mateo Aguado, dressing Queen Isabel of Bourbon (d. 1644) and Infanta María Teresa

Bodices: Visual evidence shows that the point at the front of the bodice is no longer as pronounced and has been subsumed by the bodice skirts, which have grown much larger. Decorative chest-coverings are still worn with *cueras*.

Sleeves: Fitted sleeves are slashed in the upper third. Round sleeves disappear, replaced by tubular hanging sleeves. Wide guitar-shaped sleeves are a short-lived novelty in María Teresa's wardrobe. Portraits show that shoulder-wings are long and straight.

Skirts: Skirts have side hand-openings and are worn over a farthingale, either a *verdugado* or a *guardainfante*, with or without a supplementary "hip" (*cadera*). Between the farthingale and skirt there are several layers of petticoats (*manteos*, *polleras*, and *briales*).

Dress fabrics: In a decade marked by frequent periods of mourning at the court, fabrics are predominantly black and include baize, borato, *herbax*, and various velvets (plain, patterned, and uncut). Other fabrics used include taffeta and ormuzine, and flowered camlets and satins. Infanta María Teresa transitions from all-black mourning dress by March 1645 and wears fabrics combining black with another color (silver, green, hair-colored). Fabrics become much lighter in color starting in 1646, with silks combining silver with green, white, and mother-of-pearl.

Decorations: Silver or silver and black trimmings prevail over gold; buttons-and-loops are still in use. Black and silver embroidery and black diamond buttons are characteristic of the decade. The little skirts of the bodice may be decorated in "Caños de Carmona" (the name of a famous Roman aqueduct in Seville).

1650s

Tailor to the Queen: Mateo Aguado, dressing Queen Mariana of Austria, Infanta María Teresa, and Infanta Margarita (b. 1651)

Bodices: Bodices no longer use pasteboard. Bodice skirts—now very long—are divided into quadrants. Decorative half-moon-shaped pocket openings are used on the bodice skirt fronts between 1650 and 1654. *Cueras* no longer have contrasting chest-coverings.

Sleeves: The slashed sleeve has been replaced by sleeves made from three to five strips of fabric that are worn over a white silk voile undersleeve. *Cueras* have shoulder-wings and tubular hanging sleeves; round and pointed sleeves are no longer worn. Over-gowns still have shoulder-wings but do not seem to have hanging sleeves of any kind.

Skirts: Skirts have hand-openings in the sides and are worn over multiple petticoats (a *pollera*, a *brial* or *guardapiés*, and a *manteo*). *Polleras* are richly decorated and have four pockets (*faltriqueras*). *Verdugados* are still being worn at court in 1650 but disappear by 1659; they are replaced by *guardainfantes* made of ribbon, baleen, and wire, which could be supplemented with a "little hip" (*caderilla*).

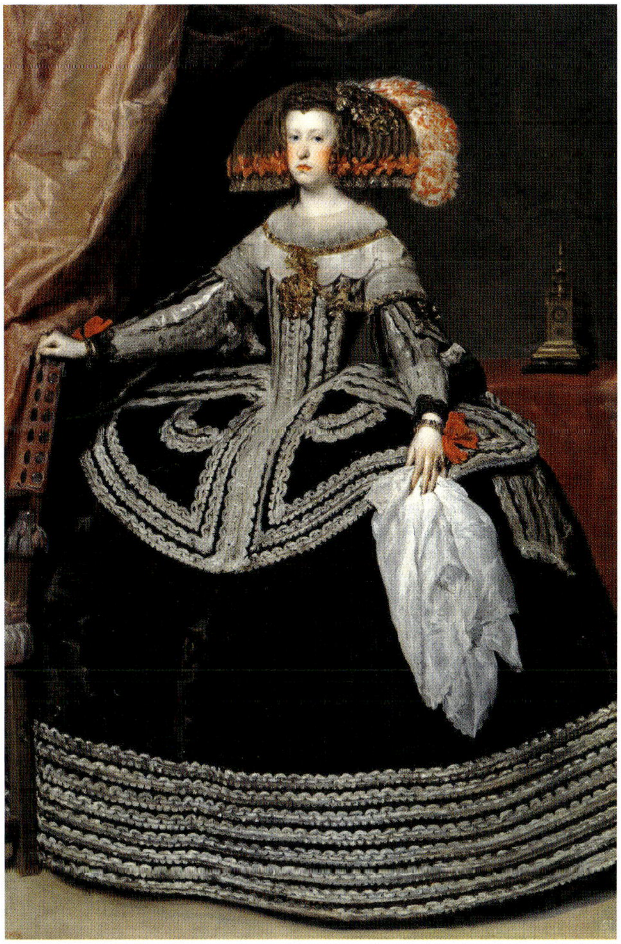

Queen Mariana of Austria in the 1650s (detail of fig. 27)

Dress fabrics: A lighter and brighter palette of colors is used in a rainbow of hues, often mixed with silver. Black is infrequent, only used for mourning and solemn religious holidays. Dark gray disappears, and walnut-brown recedes; musk-brown is the only dark color in vogue. Camlet is the most common fabric in the queen's wardrobe. Moiré silks are especially popular 1650–56; some floral-patterned and striped silks are used. More fabrics are imported from Venice.

Decorations: Diamond buttons are used 1650–53. Silver dress trimmings are very popular: *caracolillos, galoncicos, pasamanos, peinecillos, pestañas, punticas*, and silver plate (*hojuela de plata*). When silver decorations are banned by royal proclamation in 1657, they are replaced by embroidery with silvered mica (*talco azogado*), white or black openwork (*enrejados*), white bobbin lace (*encajes*), and borders cut from kidskin or white, black, or colored satin. Designs include latticework (*celosía*), rows of scales resembling the pattern of a goshawk breast (*pecho de azor*), and large esses. Bows are used abundantly.

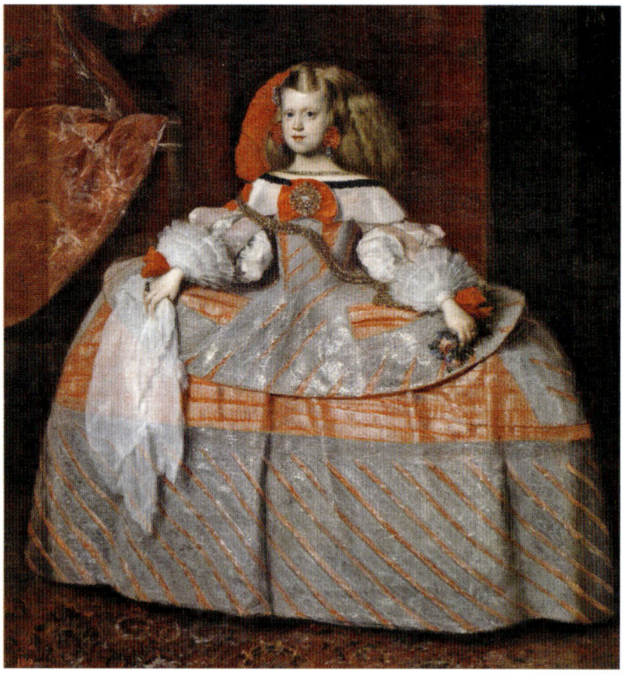

Infanta Margarita in the 1660s (detail of fig. 170)

Early 1660s

Note: Archival documentation of Aguado's work ends in 1663.

Tailor to the Queen: Mateo Aguado, dressing Queen Mariana of Austria (widowed 1665) and Infanta Margarita (departs Madrid for the imperial court in Vienna in 1666)

Bodices: Visual evidence shows that bodices are cut off-the-shoulder.

Sleeves: Paned sleeves of four or six decorated strips of fabric attached at the wrist are worn over voluminous white silk undersleeves decorated with white and/or black lace. *Cueras* have tubular hanging sleeves trimmed in chevron stripes.

Skirts: The skirt, which is almost completely covered by decoration, is worn over a *guardainfante* and three layers of petticoats (*pollera, guardapiés*, and *manteo de vuelta*). Court portraits show that the farthingale is now very wide at the sides and flat in the front.

Dress fabrics: Floral-patterned silks become very common starting in 1660. In wintertime, plush is favored; plain and patterned velvets are also used; for the rest of the year, camlet and satin are the primary fabrics. Ormuzine is less prominent than before. Musk is the most popular color, plain or in combination with silver, black, pearl, white, or green. Other leading colors are green, blue, black, pearl, silver, and chamois.

Decorations: Dresses are decorated with bands made from white voile (or, less often, from kidskin or lamé) measuring 9 to 14 centimeters wide, which are applied in horizontal rows or on a diagonal. Decoration of skirts is 1 to 1.4 meters deep. These bands are overlaid with wide lace, much of it imported from France, mostly black but also silver, porcelain, and the color *aire*. Embroidery with mica continues even though the 1657 law banning silver is no longer followed.

Dress Patterns

Valuable information about the women's garments that Aguado made most frequently—the three-piece dress (*vestido*) and the formal dress with a train (*saya entera*)—is provided by pattern layouts in Martín de Andújar's 1640 tailoring manual, *Geometry and Patterns Pertaining to the Tailoring Profession* (*Geometria y trazas pertenecientes al oficio de sastres*). Andújar's primary purpose was to illustrate how to lay out the pieces of a garment to minimize fabric waste, not to provide the reader with detailed patterns. Large pattern pieces, such as a skirt front or back, have to be pieced together; Andújar's diagrams use dotted lines to indicate where an extension needs to be attached to the main pattern piece. The fabric is folded in half lengthwise or widthwise, so that each piece is cut out twice (once if placed on the fold). Uppercase and lowercase letters on the diagrams refer to measurements based on the *vara*.

Key:
b = 1 *bara*, or *vara* (84 cm)
d = *dozavo* = 1⁄12 *vara*
i = 1 *dedo* (1.75 cm)
m = *media* = ½ *vara*
o = *ochavo* = ⅛ *vara*
q = *quarta* = ¼ *vara*
s = *sesma* = ⅙ *vara*
t = *tercia* = ⅓ *vara*
v = 5 *varas*
x = 10 *varas*

A digital copy of Andújar's book is available through the Biblioteca Digital Hispánica (the digital library of the Biblioteca Nacional de España): <bdh-rd.bne.es/viewer.vm?id=0000178274&page=1>.

PATTERN 1: WOMAN'S OVER-GOWN WITH ROUND SLEEVES

(Andújar 1640, fol. 47v)
Fabric: 7.56 m of silk (fabric 56 cm wide)

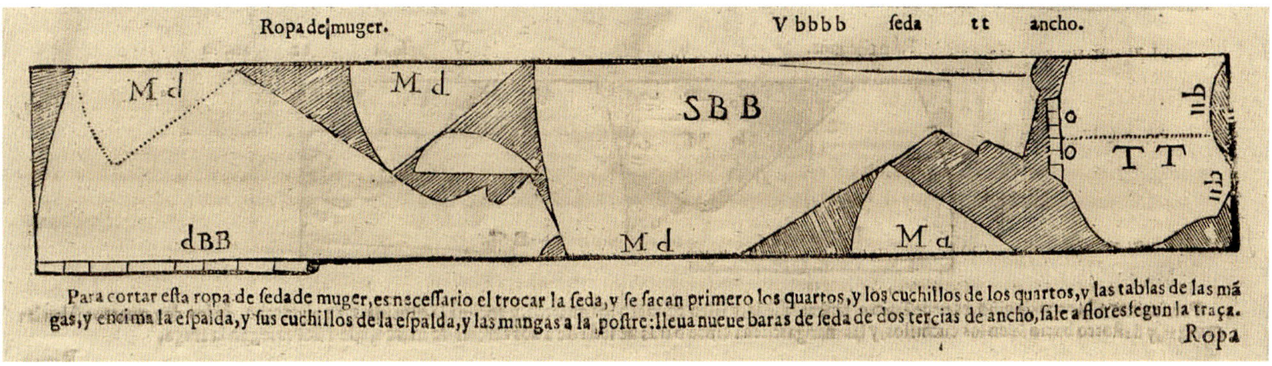

The main pieces of the over-gown—front, back, and round sleeve—have to be pieced together with extensions. These three main pieces and their extensions are laid out from left to right: gown front (hem at the left edge of the fabric), a wedge-shaped skirt extension for the front and a half-moon-shaped extension for the sleeve, the gown back and its wedge-shaped skirt extension, and the round sleeve with the shoulder cap at the right-hand edge of the fabric. Shoulder-wings, which could be cut from the fabric scraps, are not included in the layout. Neither are front facings and a collar, which would be cut from a contrasting fabric.

PATTERN 2: SKIRT (*BASQUIÑA*) AND DOUBLET WITH ROUNDED SHORT SKIRTS (*FALDILLAS*)

(Andújar 1640, fol. 43v)
Fabric: 10.5 m of silk (fabric 56 cm wide)

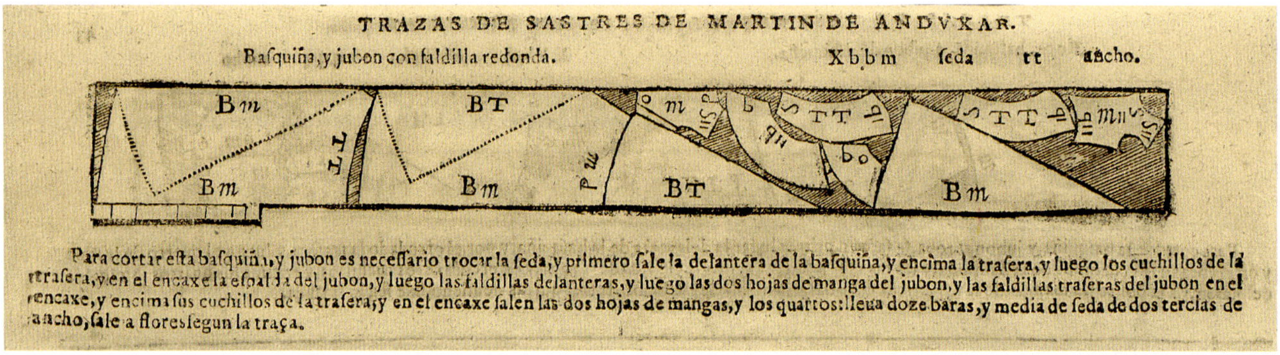
TRAZAS DE SASTRES DE MARTIN DE ANDVXAR.

Baſquiña, y jubon con faldilla redonda. Xbbm ſeda tt ancho.

Para cortar eſta baſquiña, y jubon es neceſſario trocar la ſeda, y primero ſale la delantera de la baſquiña, y encima la traſera, y luego los cuchillos de la traſera, y en el encaxe la eſpalda del jubon, y luego las faldillas delanteras, y luego las dos hojas de manga del jubon, y las faldillas traſeras del jubon en el encaxe, y encima ſus cuchillos de la traſera; y en el encaxe ſalen las dos hojas de mangas, y los quartos: lleua doze baras, y media de ſeda de dos tercias de ancho, ſale a flores ſegun la traça.

All of the pieces are cut on the grainline, except for the short skirts of the doublet (*faldillas*), which are cut on the bias. This layout is appropriate for a fabric with a one-way woven pattern or nap. The skirt has to be pieced together, with triangle-shaped extensions sewn to each side of the center-front and center-back pieces. The pattern pieces are laid out from left to right: skirt front, skirt back, skirt back extension, doublet back, front *faldillas*, first sleeve half, back *faldillas*, skirt front extension, second sleeve half, and doublet front.

PATTERN 3: FORMAL DRESS WITH FITTED SLEEVES AND POINTED SLEEVES

(Andújar 1640, fol. 51)
Fabric: 5.88 m of baize (fabric 1.68 m wide)

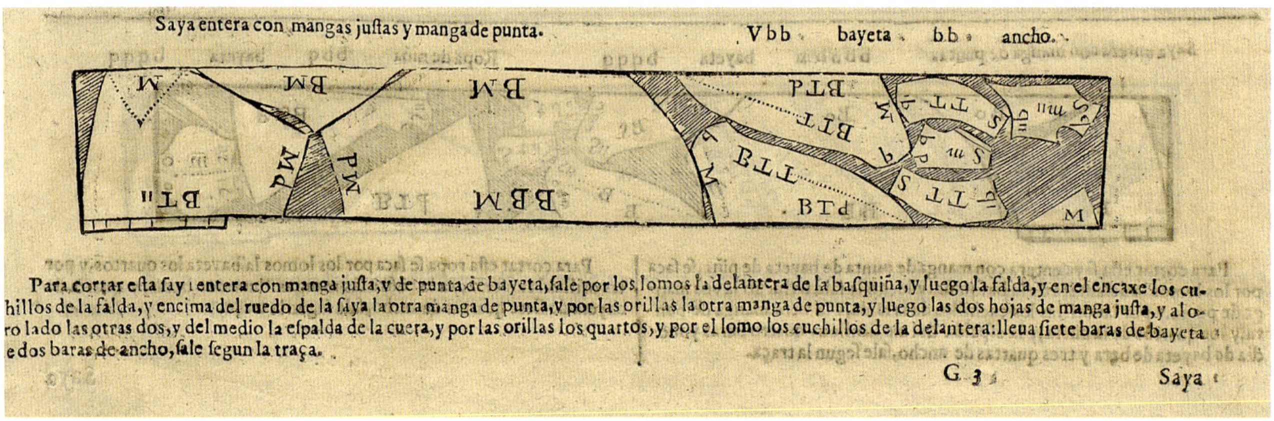
Saya entera con mangas juſtas y manga de punta. Vbb bayeta bb ancho.

Para cortar eſta ſaya entera con manga juſta, y de punta de bayeta, ſale por los lomos la delantera de la baſquiña, y luego la falda, y en el encaxe los cuchillos de la falda, y encima del ruedo de la ſaya la otra manga de punta, y por las orillas la otra manga de punta, y luego las dos hojas de manga juſta, y al otro lado las otras dos, y del medio la eſpalda de la cuera, y por las orillas los quartos, y por el lomo los cuchillos de la delantera: lleua ſiete baras de bayeta e dos baras de ancho, ſale ſegun la traça.

G 3 Saya

This *saya entera* is made from baize, which was used for mourning at the court. Wool fabrics like baize were woven on wider looms than silk, so this dress requires less piecing and significantly less fabric than one made from silk. With the pieces facing in different directions, this layout is not suitable for fabrics with a nap or one-way design. The center of the skirt front is placed along the fold (hem at the left-hand side), followed by the skirt back. Between the skirt front and back, at the top of the fabric, is the extension for the skirt back. The back of the skirt, which has a rounded hem, is significantly longer than the front to create a train. Next come two pointed sleeves (oriented in different directions), followed by the two pieces of the fitted sleeves with the back of the bodice between them (the bodice waist at the right-hand side). The piece in the upper-right corner is the bodice front, which has a pronounced point at its bottom center; the triangular piece at the bottom-right corner is the extension for the skirt front.

Glossary

This glossary includes terms for garments, textiles and other dressmaking materials, colors, and decorations that were worn at the court of Philip IV. Garments for men and children are included, but women's dress is the primary focus here, as it is in this book. Terms are listed first in modern Spanish (in plural when they usually appear this way in the documents), sometimes followed by square brackets with spelling variations that are used frequently in court artisans' accounts; additional variations can be found in the documents, in which the following letters are used interchangeably: i and y; g and x (in place of the modern j); b, u, and v; ç and z. Literal translations appear in quotation marks, followed by English equivalents and definitions. The information in this glossary is primarily based on the context in which the terms were used by Mateo Aguado and his closest colleagues (silk merchants, farthingale-makers, and embroiderers) at the Royal Palace. The documents consulted in the Archivo General de Palacio are listed in the Bibliography. Other sources used in the compilation of this glossary include:

Garments: Andújar 1640; Bernis 2001; Herrero García 2014a; Rocha Burguen 1618

Textiles: Burnham 1981; Dávila Corona, Durán Pujol, and García Fernández 2004; Herrero García 2014b; Monnas 2008; Phipps 2011; *SILKNOW*, "Silk Heritage Thesaurus" online; "Tassa general de los precios" 1627; Thornton 1965

Colors: Buss 2017; Fernández 1778; Linthicum 1936

Decorations (lace, embroidery, trimmings): González Mena 1974 and 1976; Levey 1983; May 1980; Westman 2019

Spanish dictionaries: Covarrubias Orozco 1995; *Diccionario de autoridades* 1726–39; Terreros y Pando 1786–9

Spanish–English dictionaries: Howell 1660; Minsheu 1599; Stevens 1726

abalorios colored glass beads, used in embroidery.

acuchillado/a "knifed"; slashed. Long decorative slashes in the sleeves or bodice of a garment, often described as *acuchillado a lo tudesco*, "slashed in the German style." Cf. *picado*.

aguas, de watered; *moiré*. A ribbed fabric such as ormuzine or camlet with a rippled effect created by folding the fabric in half lengthwise and pressing it under a wooden roller to crush the ribs so that flattened and unflattened ribs reflect light in different directions.

aire "air," referring to the color of the sky at dawn. A delicate apricot color created by weaving an apricot-colored weft on an ivory warp.

alamares buttons-and-loops. Called "lace buttons" or "tufted buttons" in 17th-century English, *alamares* were made in a variety of shapes from narrow plaited or woven trimmings and were used on garments and furnishings. They could be functional closures or purely ornamental.

alamares de penacho buttons-and-loops in the shape of a plume.

almenillas "little battlements." Decoration of alternating heights made from any kind of trimming and applied to the seams and hems of a garment.

almilla waistcoat. An upper-body garment for men and women. A woman's *almilla*, which could be used as nightwear, had sleeves, skirts, and shoulder-wings; most often made from fine white linen and decorated with black lace, but they could also be made from silk.

ámbar amber. (1) Perfume of ambergris (a secretion of the sperm whale) used to scent leather gloves and garments. (2) Yellow amber (tree resin) used to make beads for jewelry and embroidery.

amusco/a See *musco*.

andador de tirantes harness with leading strings attached to the garment of a toddler who is learning to walk.

anjeo [angeo] canvas. Coarse fabric made from flax or hemp, used to stiffen and shape women's bodices and skirt hems.

arpón [harpón], en "in harpoon"; chevron stripes. Diagonal stripes that meet at an angle to form a V-shape, made by applying trimmings or by cutting out the pieces of a garment on the bias of striped fabric. Decoration used especially on shoulder-wings, sleeves, and the front facings of over-gowns.

avantal apron. The queens' aprons were made from silk (*lama, ormesí, tafetán doble*) and usually decorated with silver lace; also called a *delantal*.

barba de ballena baleen; whalebone. Stiffening material used in corsets, farthingales, and the hems of petticoats.

basquiña skirt. A woman's outermost skirt, which was worn over a farthingale and several layers of petticoats.

***bayeta* [*baieta*]** baize. A thin, lightweight woolen fabric, used especially for mourning garments.

bebederos "troughs"; facings. Pieces of decorative contrasting fabric applied to the interior front edges of a garment, such as a *ropa* or *cuera*, which were visible when the garment was worn open with the edges turned back.

bocací buckram. Thick, coarse linen stiffened with gum; used as an interfacing.

bordado/a embroidered. Embellishment with a needle and thread; may also incorporate narrow cording, ribbon, beads, sequins, etc. Fabric to be embroidered could be stretched on a frame (*bastidor*) or worked freehand (*a la mano*).

bordado/a de matices embroidered with shading using colored silk threads.

botones de muletilla large buttons made from silk thread by a cordmaker.

***brahones* [*braones*]** shoulder-wings. Pieces projecting from the top of a garment's shoulders where the sleeves are set into the armholes. Used on outer garments such as a man's *ropilla* and a woman's *almilla, cuera, gabán*, and *ropa*.

brial petticoat. Decorated underskirt worn in a matching set with a *pollera, manteo*, or both; synonymous with *guardapiés*.

burato borato. A very thin fabric made of wool, silk, or a combination of the two, used to make summer mourning clothes, women's veils, and men's cloaks.

cabellado/a hair-colored. A light tan color.

cabritilla kidskin. Used to make gloves and sometimes women's bodices; also cut into decorative trims and applied to garments.

cadera*; diminutive *caderilla "hip" or "little hip." Hip padding worn with a farthingale (*verdugado* or *guardainfante*).

cadera cariñana Carignano hip. Hip padding named for the Princess of Carignano.

calzones breeches. A man's lower-body garment, extending from the waist to the back of the knee, usually made by a specialist hosier.

***camelote* [*chamelote*]** camlet. A term usually used to describe fabric made of silk mixed with camel or goat hair, here *camelote* refers to a silk taffeta dress fabric that could be pressed with patterns of waves (*camelote de aguas*) or flowers (*camelote de flores*).

camisa shirt; smock. Long white linen undergarment worn between the skin and outer garments.

capote de campaña "campaign coat." A man's short, loose-fitting coat open at the front.

caracoles "snails"; whorls. Spiral shapes made from any kind of trimming to decorate a garment.

caracolillos "little snails." A plaited trimming made from gold, silver, or black thread, or a combination of those colors.

cariñano adjective applied to various accessories named for Marie de Bourbon, Princess of Carignano, who was at the Spanish court from November 1636 until June 1644.

carmesí crimson. Considered to be a healthy color, crimson was used often in women's farthingales, corsets, and gowns for childbirth.

cartón pasteboard. Made by pasting together layers of paper; used to stiffen women's shoulder-wings and doublets in the first half of the 17th century.

celeste sky-blue color.

celosía latticework. Dress decoration made by interlacing lengths of trimming and leaving open spaces in between, like the decorative pattern used in window screens.

chapines clogs. Cork-soled platform shoes covered with rich silk fabric or leather, worn by married women.

cola train. Elongated skirt back cut longer than the front. Cf. *cota*.

coleto leather jerkin. A man's sleeveless upper-body garment that was worn over a doublet. Closely fitted to the torso, with short skirts and shoulder-wings, *coletos* were made from lined leather (buff, cordovan, or chamois), sometimes perfumed, slashed, and decorated with silver or gold trimming. Synonymous with *cuera*.

colombino a variegated pink color created by weaving alternating weft threads of white and pale pink on a purplish pink warp.

colonias broad silk ribbons.

corpiño corset (era of Isabel of Bourbon). Boned and back-stitched bodice with short skirts, with or without sleeves and a stomacher (*petillo*). Usually made from crimson double taffeta, lined, and decorated with gold or silver trimming (*galón* or *caracolillos*). Also the unboned sleeveless bodice of a *manteo francés*.

cota train. A separate garment worn with the skirt of a three-piece dress on special occasions. Cf. *cola*.

cotilla "little coat of mail"; corset (era of Mariana of Austria). Boned and backstitched bodice with sleeves and skirts that were long enough to have pocket openings. Most often made from double taffeta in mother-of-pearl, crimson, or incarnadine; decorated with silver galloon up to 1657, thereafter with white lace.

cuera an upper-body garment. In women's wear, the bodice of a formal gown, which had shoulder-wings and hanging sleeves; see *saya entera*. In menswear, a leather jerkin; synonymous with *coleto*.

damasco damask. A rich silk fabric with a reversible woven pattern. Used to make dresses and petticoats; also used for pockets and to cover skirt hems and *chapines*.

doble double weave. See *tafetán doble*.

enaguas voluminous skirt worn by women in multiples as underskirts or as a top skirt with a *justillo*. Also a skirt worn by a toddler, together with a *saquito*.

encaje [***encaxe***] bobbin lace. Trimming with decorative designs created by intertwining many bobbins wound with threads of white, black, silver, or gold, or a combination of silver and gold.

encarnado/a [***incarnato/a, incarnado/a***] "made flesh"; incarnadine. An ambiguous color, usually carnation pink but sometimes also blood-red. The term was sometimes used interchangeably with *nácar*.

enrejado openwork. Lattice-like trimmings applied to garments, usually made from white silk thread but sometimes made from black or metal thread, using any of a variety of techniques (such as reticella, macramé, embroidered net, or drawn work) to produce a decorative pattern of holes.

entorchados twisted cords, usually black silk thread with silver or gold, used in embroidery.

escapulario(s) scapular(s). Long rectangular piece or pieces of fabric hanging down the front and back of the body, worn over a religious habit or secular dress. Patterns in Andújar 1640 show that an *escapulario* made for a religious habit had a hole cut in the center to fit over the head, while those for secular dress were made in pairs and cut straight across the short edges, presumably attached to each other by strings to hang over the shoulders. See *hábito*.

escotado low-cut bodice. Used to describe a woman's bodice cut below the base of the neck, whether it revealed the shoulders, cleavage, or just a bit of the chest around the clavicle.

esparto a stiff grass used to form the hoops of cone-shaped farthingales (*verdugado*) and sometimes the hems of petticoats.

espiguillas narrow ribbon made from black silk used to trim the seams and edges of garments.

espolín [***espulín, espulino***] brocaded silk fabric woven with a raised pattern of flowers.

faja [***faxa***] band. A wide decorative band made from a contrasting fabric or embellished with embroidery, pinking, lace, etc., used to decorate the bottom of a skirt or over-gown.

faldillas "little skirts." Short skirts attached to the waist of upper-body garments for men and women. The diminutive form was used regardless of the size of these skirts, which started off as short tabs and grew much longer over the decades.

faltriqueras [***fratriqueras***] pockets. Pockets in women's skirts were made from damask in a color matching the dress fabric.

felpa plush. Long-haired cut velvet; a sumptuous silk fabric with a long, soft pile that was used to make winter garments and to line dressing gowns and cloaks.

ferreruelo [***herreruelo***] cloak with a collar, worn by men and women.

filelí [***fileyle***] a very lightweight fabric of wool mixed with silk or plant fibers, used at the court to make women's mourning dresses.

flueco*; diminutives *flequillo* and *fluecuecillo fringe. Narrow band of woven trimming, usually made from black silk or metallic threads, with the selvedge cut along one side to create a fringe.

fustán fustian. Cotton fabric used as an interlining for royal garments and as a garment lining for lower-class court employees.

gabán [*gauán*] cloak. A loose-fitting outer garment for a man or woman. Women's versions had shoulder-wings and wide sleeves called "friar's sleeves" (*mangas de fraile*); often made from warm velvet or plush, they could be used as nightwear.

galón (plural *galones*); diminutives *galoncico* and *galoncito* galloon. Narrow woven trimming with even edges, with or without a woven design in relief, made from silk, silver, or gold thread.

gamuzado/a chamois-colored; "isabella" in 17th-century English. A pale yellow color.

gasa [*gassa*] gauze. A very fine net-like fabric, often embroidered. Used to make sleeves and dresses (in which case it was underlined).

golilla man's collar supporter, worn around the neck under the chin, with a *valona* on top of it.

golpes openings for the hands in cloaks and in the short skirts attached to a woman's doublet or corset. Cf. *maneras*.

gorgorán [*gorguerán*] grosgrain. A ribbed silk used as a dress fabric.

grana scarlet. Fine fabric dyed a deep red color, used to make baby-blankets at court. Term also applied to the kermes and cochineal used to make red dye.

guardainfante a farthingale with hoops extending the hips at the sides. In contrast to the *verdugado*, in which hoops were sewn into a petticoat, the hoops of a *guardainfante* were suspended from one other by ribbons.

guardapiés petticoat. Decorated underskirt worn in a matching set with a *pollera*, *manteo*, or both; synonymous with *brial*.

hábito habit. Any set of garments worn as religious apparel by a man, woman, or child, with various cuts and colors signifying different religious orders. Worn by men and women who had taken vows, habits were also made frequently for queens and royal children to demonstrate their piety. See *monjil* and *escapulario*.

herbax [*herbaje*] wool-and-grass cloth. Fabric of wool mixed with plant fiber, with a rough surface, used most often to make cloaks and habits.

hilo de oro/plata thread of gold/silver; passing thread, also called filé. Metal-wrapped thread made by wrapping narrow strips of gilded silver or silver around a core fiber. Cf. *hojuela de plata* and *plata pasada*.

hojuela [*ojuela*] *de plata* silver plate. Narrow strips of silver or a silvered substrate. Cf. *hilo de oro/plata* and *plata pasada*.

holanda [*olanda*] Holland cloth. Very fine linen fabric used to make undergarments.

holandilla (diminutive of *holanda*) lightweight linen used in garment linings.

humo "smoke". A very fine, deep black silk used to make women's veils.

jerga; diminutive *jerguilla* a fabric like serge made from silk, wool, or a mixture.

jubón doublet. Man's or woman's upper-body garment with short skirts and fitted sleeves.

juego matching set of garments to be worn together.

justillo a woman's fitted upper-body garment with sleeves and short skirts that could have eyelets to attach it to a petticoat; usually made as part of a set with one to three matching petticoats.

lama lamé. Lustrous silk fabric interwoven with flat metallic threads (silver or gold), without floral patterning. Cf. *tela de plata*.

lanilla fine, lightweight woolen fabric.

lentejuelas "little lentils"; sequins. Thin round pieces of metal (usually silver) with holes in the center, used in embroidery.

ligas garters. Silk bands used by women and men to hold up their stockings.

luto mourning apparel. For men, a black wool doublet and breeches, short soutane (*sotanilla*), and cloak. Women wore a regular three-piece dress or formal dress made from a dull black fabric such as baize until the 1640s, when the *monjil* was adopted as mourning attire; worn with a dark veil, such as a *manto de humo*.

maneras vertical openings for the hands in the sides of women's skirts at the hip, which began to appear with the use of *caderas* in the late 1630s. Cf. *golpes*.

mangas sleeves. Sleeves were made separate from the upper-body garment and were often worn in multiples, with a functional fitted sleeve combined with a decorative hanging sleeve.

mangas de casaca hanging sleeves. Decorative tubular sleeves used in men's, women's, and children's clothes.

mangas de punta pointed sleeves. Long hanging sleeves with a contrasting lining on a woman's *saya entera* or *monjil*, worn over fitted sleeves.

mangas justas fitted sleeves. In the 1620s–40s, these were narrow, closely fitted sleeves that completely covered the arms; starting in the early 1650s, the same term was applied to paned sleeves made from strips of fabric joined at the wrist, which were worn over a voluminous silk voile undersleeve.

mangas redondas round sleeves. Loose sleeves rounded on one side that encased the upper arm and hung freely below the elbow, worn over a pair of fitted sleeves; used on a woman's *ropa* and the *cuera* of a formal dress.

manguillas "little sleeves." Richly decorated fitted sleeves in a contrasting fabric worn with a formal dress. See *saya entera*.

manteo petticoat. The innermost underskirt worn over a woman's chemise; cut in the shape of a semicircle, it wrapped at the waist and was open at center front. Cf. *manteo de vuelta* and *manteo francés*. Also a circular skirt worn by toddlers, priests, and scholars.

manteo de vuelta wrap-around petticoat. An underskirt cut from a full circle of fabric that wrapped around itself completely.

manteo francés French petticoat. A woman's underdress consisting of a sleeveless bodice (*corpiño*) attached to a skirt.

manto mantle; veil. Woman's garment that covered the head and body, usually made from fine black silk or wool and trimmed with pointed lace.

manto de humo "mantle of smoke." A woman's veil made from a very fine, thin, transparent black silk.

medias de pelo "hair stockings." Delicate stockings made from raw silk that were so fine as to be almost transparent.

memorias memory rings. Interlaced rings embroidered or brocaded on dress fabric, worn by women and men.

monjil [mongil] long, loose-fitting mourning dress made from a dull black fabric such as baize with fitted and pointed sleeves. See *luto*.

muestra fabric sample, often prepared with decorations.

musco/a [amusco/a] musk-brown; filemot, the color of a dead leaf.

nácar mother-of-pearl. A pale carnation color. The term was sometimes used interchangeably with *encarnado*.

noguerado/a walnut-brown. A dark brown color.

ojales buttonholes.

ojetes eyelets. Small holes pierced in a garment and reinforced with stitching, through which laces or ribbons with metal points could be threaded to attach one garment half to the other or to another garment.

ormesí ormuzine. A silk taffeta, similar to camlet but finer, that could have a watered effect (*ormesí de aguas*). See *camelote*.

oro de Milán "Milanese gold." Drawn gold thread.

paño wool cloth.

pardo/a gray. A dark color, considered to be grave but less severe than black (Cordato 1639).

pasamanos woven or plaited trimmings made from silk or metal thread to decorate the edges of garments. Translated into English as "lace" in early modern dictionaries, but the term is avoided here to avoid confusion with bobbin and needle lace.

pecho de azor "goshawk breast." Dress decoration in rows of scales.

peinecillos "little combs." Decorative trimming, usually silver, used, for example, to make *celosía* and *pecho de azor* patterns.

pel de rata [pelderata] "rat fur." A dark gray, almost black, color used to dye silk and wool.

pespuntado/a [pespunteado/a] backstitched. Layers of fabric, for example in a boned corset, stitched together with rows of small, continuous stitches.

pestañas "eyelashes." Decorative edging, often made from satin, applied to a garment.

petos;* diminutive *petillos "little breastplates"; chest-coverings. A pair of decorative pieces of rich fabric, reinforced with canvas and lined in taffeta, that attached with hooks and eyes to the *cuera* of a formal gown. Translated as "stomacher" in Arnold, Tiramani, and Costigliolo 2018 (p. 159). See *saya entera*.

picado/a pricked; pinked. Garment fabric decorated all over with a pattern of small cuts or perforations to show an interlining fabric in a contrasting color. Cf. *acuchillado*.

plata pasada silver wire, used in embroidery. Cf. *hilo de plata* and *hojuela de plata*.

pollera a large petticoat named for the baskets in which chickens were kept. Worn over a *guardainfante*, the *pollera* was the topmost petticoat directly beneath the outer skirt; it had pockets and was richly trimmed.

puntas "points." (1) border decoration; a very broad term used to describe any trimming (including woven trims, decorations cut from fabric, and bobbin lace) that was applied in rows on the edges of a garment. (2) aglets. Pointed metal toggles attached to ribbons that were used as a garment closure and decoration.

puntillas narrow bobbin lace edging with points or scallops on one edge, typically made with gold thread.

raso satin. A lustrous, smooth silk dress fabric.

ribete ribbon. Narrow strips of fabric such as velvet, taffeta, or lamé, used to decorate the borders of a garment and bind the edges of slashes.

ropa over-gown. Loose, open, floor-length woman's garment without a waist seam, worn over a *basquiña* and *jubón*.

ropa de levantar dressing gown. A morning- or night-gown for a man or woman, usually lined with fur or plush.

ropilla cassock. Unlike a long clerical cassock, this short secular masculine garment was a jacket with little skirts, shoulder-wings, and sleeves that could be worn over the arms or left hanging. Worn by men over a doublet, often with matching breeches; worn with a skirt (*manteo*) by young boys before breeching.

ruedo bottom edge of a garment, such as a skirt, petticoat, or over-gown.

saquito "little sack." A young girl's upper-body garment with short skirts and sleeves, worn until about age five.

saya entera*; also *saya grande*, or simply *saya formal gown consisting of a skirt cut long in the back to form a train and a bodice (*cuera*) with short skirts, shoulder-wings, hanging sleeves (*mangas redondas, mangas de punta,* or *mangas de casaca*) and contrasting fitted sleeves (*manguillas*).

seda silk thread. Sewing thread made from silk in black or in colors, sold by the ounce.

sempiterna perpetuana. A very durable woolen fabric used to clothe the poor.

sevillanejas diminutive of "Sevillian," ribbons made from black silk, sometimes also with silver or gold thread, used to make decorations such as *alamares* and *almenillas*.

soguilla "little rope." Narrow cord used as a dress trimming.

sotanilla "little soutane." A loose, calf-length garment that buttoned down the front, worn by men as a mourning garment.

tafetán taffeta. (1) A tightly-woven silk with ribs across the width of the fabric; crisp and lustrous, taffeta was a lightweight fabric that was favored for summer garments. The name *tafetán* was said to come from the "*tif-taf*" sound that was made by a person wearing the fabric (Covarrubias Orozco 1995, p. 908). (2) A garment bag made from this fabric.

tafetán doble*, or simply *doble double taffeta. A heavy-bodied taffeta with two sets of warps and two sets of wefts.

talco azogado silvered mica. Mica tempered with quicksilver, used as a substitute for silver in dress decorations.

tela de oro/plata*, or simply *tela cloth of gold/silver. While *tela* is a broad term that can refer to any kind of fabric, in the courtly context it was an expensive silk fabric with metal threads woven selvedge to selvedge, with a floral pattern. Cf. *lama*.

tercianela a plain-weave silk fabric similar to taffeta but heavier and more lustrous.

terciopelado patterned velvet. A rich velvet fabric with a design created by contrasting areas of cut pile on a background of uncut pile or satin weave.

terciopelo velvet. A silk fabric with a pile produced by raised loops that can be cut, uncut, or a combination of cut and uncut to create a pattern. Used for winter garments.

terciopelo liso plain velvet. Velvet with cut loops covering the entire surface of the fabric.

terciopelo rizo/rizado uncut velvet. Velvet fabric whose pile loops are left uncut, creating a curly effect.

toca (1) a woman's headcovering, worn by all married women up through the first decade of the seventeenth century but thereafter exclusively by widows; (2) veiling; the very fine linen or silk fabric used to make *tocas*.

tomasina a woman's coat, probably the same or similar to a Hungarian coat. See *ungarina*.

torzales narrow cording made from twisted silk threads.

trencilla narrow trimming made from plaited silk, silver, or gold thread, used as a garment decoration.

ungarina Hungerlin; Hungarian coat. Outer garment with shoulder-wings and sleeves. See also *tomasina*.

valona flat linen collar, usually worn by Spanish men atop a supporter called a *golilla*.

valona cariñana Carignano collar. A wide band of lace or fabric worn by women around the shoulders that was named for the Princess of Carignano. See *cariñano*.

valona de campaña "campaign collar"; falling collar. A lace-trimmed linen collar worn by men that draped over the shoulders and was associated with military dress.

vaquero coat with long skirts and a fitted waist worn by men, women, and children. Women's *vaqueros* had hanging tubular sleeves (*mangas de casaca*) and long fitted sleeves or elbow-length sleeves, and were worn with a matching skirt (*basquiña*) as a two-piece dress.

velo voile. A very thin, transparent silk fabric, sometimes interwoven with silver. Used primarily for making undersleeves, interlinings, and dress decorations.

velo de peso "weighty voile"; presumably a more substantial variation of voile; often used to make sleeves.

venturina goldstone. Used as a substitute for gold in embroidery.

verdegay "happy green." A light green color.

verdugado floor-length farthingale in the shape of an inverted funnel that was made by sewing hoops into a petticoat, with the hoops starting smaller at the top and growing larger and larger to reach the maximum circumference at the hem.

vestido dress or suit of clothes. Term used to refer to a matching set of clothes for any age or gender. A woman's *vestido* was usually composed of a *ropa*, *basquiña*, and *jubón*; a man's *vestido* included breeches, doublet, cassock, and cloak.

vidrios [***vidros***] glass pieces, usually black or white, used in embroidery and trimmings.

zapatillas slippers made from silk or cordovan leather and lined with taffeta, worn inside *chapines*.

zapatos cariñanos Carignano shoes; known in English as "slap-sole shoes." Leather shoes with the ball and heel attached to a flat sole, named for the Princess of Carignano. See *cariñano*.

Notes

KEY FOR ARCHIVAL CITATIONS

The primary sources cited most frequently in the notes are the artisan accounts (*cuentas de artesanos*) at the Archivo General de Palacio in Madrid. These documents, which are almost never numbered or foliated, are collected in bundles called *legajos*. In order to identify specific documents within these *legajos*, the notes include the artisan's last name followed by the name of the royal patron and the date(s). For example, the citation AGP, AG, leg. 5272/2, Aguado/Isabel (1631) refers to Mateo Aguado's account for Queen Isabel of Bourbon for the year 1631, which is in bundle 5272/2 in the Administración General section of the Archivo General de Palacio.

AG	Administración General (section of the AGP)
AGP	Archivo General de Palacio, Madrid
AGS	Archivo General de Simancas
AHDM	Archivo Histórico Diocesano de Madrid
AHN	Archivo Histórico Nacional, Madrid
AHPC	Archivo Histórico Provincial de Cuenca
AHPM	Archivo Histórico de Protocolos de Madrid
AMF	Archivo Municipal de Fuenlabrada
APSG	Archivo de la Parroquia de San Ginés, Madrid
BL	British Library, London
BMNP	Biblioteca del Museo Nacional del Prado, Madrid
BNE	Biblioteca Nacional de España, Madrid
caja/cajas	box/boxes
CCG	Contadurías Generales (section of the AGS)
CMC	Contaduría Mayor de Cuentas (section of the AGS)
doc./docs.	*documento/s* (document/s)
exp./exps.	*expediente/s* (file/s)
leg./legs.	*legajo/s* (bundle/s)
lib./libs.	*libro/s* (book/s)
ms./mss.	*manuscrito/s* (manuscript/s)
Per.	Personal (section of the AGP)
Prot./Prots.	Protocolo/s (notarized protocol/s at the AHPM)

INTRODUCTION

1 Technical information about *Las Meninas* is based on Brown and Garrido 2003, pp. 191–4.

2 See the classic interpretation of the composition in Brown 2008a.

3 Palomino de Castro y Velasco 1987, p. 166.

4 On the clothing in *Las Meninas*, see Bernis 1994, pp. 281, 298–9; Bandrés Oto 2002, pp. 353–63; and Bullón 2021.

5 Palomino de Castro y Velasco 1987, p. 165.

6 Brown 1986, pp. 267–9.

7 Aguado has been mentioned in a few academic publications; most notably, the inventory of Aguado's library was published in Barrio Moya 2008. Aguado is also briefly mentioned in Zofío Llorente 2005, p. 214; García Sierra 2014, p. 117; Novo Zaballos and Pizarro Llorente 2015, p. 2600; Oliván Santaliestra 2021, p. 279; and Romero González 2021a, p. 638. Two doctoral dissertations about court artisans, including Aguado, were being finished just as this book was going into publication: Fernández Fernández 2022 and Romero González 2022.

8 Steele 2017, p. 120.

9 Magidson 2013, pp. 115–16.

10 On Madrid's tailors, see especially Zofío Llorente 2005 and Nieto Sánchez 2006. Studies of tailors elsewhere in late medieval and early modern Europe include Puerta Escribano 1997, Frick 2002, Pitman 2017, and Tosi Brandi 2017.

11 Carmen Bernis's magisterial *El traje y los tipos sociales en "El Quijote"* (2001) covers Spanish fashion between 1590 and 1617. Objects from the same time period are the subject of two important exhibition catalogues: Pereda de Castro and Rodríguez Bernis 2005, and García Serrano 2015.

12 Arnold 1988, pp. 177–80. Also see Hayward 2007, pp. 317–43, on royal artificers at the court of Henry VIII.

13 See Hamann's important contribution to *Las Meninas*

studies, which brings anonymous indigenous New World laborers into the picture through the objects that they made (Hamann 2010).

14 *"Sastre"* in Covarrubias Orozco 1995, p. 886.

15 Pitman 2017, p. 51.

16 On Moroni's tailor and his shears, see Ng, Facchinetti, and Galansino 2019, pp. 144–50. Curator Anne-Katrin Rossberg provided the weight of the shears in the MAK collection.

17 Cervantes 2010, p. 138.

18 On Spanish tailoring treatises, see Puerta Escribano 2001.

19 Alcega 1580 and 1589; English translation, Alcega 1999.

20 Segovia 1617.

21 *Pregón* 1626, fol. [2r].

22 Gállego 1995, p. 64.

23 Gutiérrez de los Ríos 1600, pp. 25–7, 56. On Velázquez and ingenuity, see Marcaida 2022.

24 Gutiérrez de los Ríos 1600, pp. 111–12.

25 Quevedo 1635, fol. 75r.

26 García 1619, pp. 156–7.

27 Cervantes 1998, p. 153.

28 Pitman 2017, pp. 67–71.

29 Search results for *"sastre"* in Real Academia Española, *CORDE*.

30 Freyle 1588, fol. 1r.

31 Ibid., fols. 5r–v.

32 Suárez de Figueroa 2006, vol. 2, p. 655.

33 Currie 2006.

34 Suárez de Figueroa 2006, vol. 2, p. 655.

35 Quoted in Schroth 2008, p. 78.

36 *Capitulos de reformacion* ... 1623; translated into English as *A Proclamation for Reformation* [1623].

37 Anderson 1969; Wunder 2017b, pp. 113–23.

38 Tiffany 2012, pp. 125–8.

39 Portús 2012, p. 22.

40 See the overview of the Spanish style from 1550 to 1660 in Reade 1951.

41 On Spanish Habsburg men's and women's dress, see Bernis and Descalzo 2014 and Descalzo 2014.

42 Casanova 1650, fols. 8r–v.

43 Winkel 2006, p. 300, n. 181. On the contrasts between French and Spanish dress, see Miller 2019.

44 Quoted in Rangström 2002, p. 364.

45 On the dissemination of Spanish court fashion beyond Madrid, see Colomer and Descalzo 2014.

46 Ribeiro 2014; McDonald 2017, pp. 484–7.

47 Boucher 1987, p. 278.

48 See McKendrick 2009, ch. 7 on the *corrales* and ch. 8 on theater at court.

49 Bertaut 1664, pp. 125–6.

50 Ruano de la Haza 2007, p. 44.

51 AGP, AG, leg. 5272/2, Soria/Isabel (1630), "gorgorán negro, noguerado, y plateado que llaman cisma de Inglaterra."

52 Castillo Solórzano 2016, pp. 99–100.

53 For illuminated *cartas ejecutorias*, see Codding and O'Neill 2021, pp. 72–107.

54 Quoted in Ribeiro 2003, p. 30.

55 Valdivieso 2002, pp. 54–64.

56 The concept of "divine methods" is explored in Wunder 2017a, pp. 1–3.

57 On sumptuary laws in the early modern world, see Riello and Rublack 2019; on the case of Spain, see Wunder 2019.

58 Sempere y Guarinos 2000, p. 301.

59 Elliott 1997a and 1997b.

60 On the Royal Palace, known as the Real Alcázar de Madrid, see Checa 1994.

61 BNE, Mss/1007, fol. 1v.

62 Núñez de Castro 1658, fol. 14v; translated in Elliott 1997a, p. 144.

63 Vega 1990, p. 121.

64 On royal female representation and gender, see Oliván Santaliestra 2006, pp. 181–2, 274–5.

65 Griffey 2019.

66 BNE, Mss/1007, fol. 53v. On the Jewel House, see Martínez Leiva and Rodríguez Rebollo 2015, p. 107.

67 Gascón de Torquemada 1991, pp. 266, 282.

68 Trewinnard 1991, pp. 333–46.

69 AGP, Per., cajas 781/4 and 1065/15.

70 AGP, Per., caja 682/27.

71 Pellicer de Tovar 2002, p. 28.

72 AGP, Per., caja 1067/11, unnumbered doc. (December 12, 1647).

73 AGP, AG, leg. 5278/1.

74 BNE, Mss/1007, fols. 2r–v.

75 AGP, AG, legs. 5272/2 and 5272/3.

76 AGP, AG, leg. 904.

77 AGP, AG, legs. 5251/2, 5252/1, 5252/2, 5253/1, 5253/2, 5255/1.

78 For the purposes of this book, the most essential studies of Velázquez's portraits have been López-Rey 1996; Portús (ed.) 2012 and 2014; and Haag 2014. Other works frequently consulted include Brown 1986; Domínguez Ortiz, Pérez Sánchez, and Gállego 1989; Carr et al. 2006; Checa 2008; Cruz Valdovinos 2011; and Kientz 2015a and 2015b.

79 Brown 2008c, p. 152.

80 On Velázquez's technique in *Philip IV in Brown and Silver*, see Keith 2006, pp. 80–81.

81 On Velázquez's workshop, see Doval Trueba 2003.

82 Gabriele Finaldi in Carr et al. 2006, p. 172.

83 Ribeiro 2017, p. 88.

84 Palomino de Castro y Velasco 1987, p. 176.

85 Sánchez Cantón 1942; *Corpus velazqueño* 2000, pp. 473–6.

86 On decorum in Spanish royal portraiture, see Jasienski 2021.

87 Winkel 2006, ch. 4; Gordenker 2001, p. 15.

88 *Corpus velazqueño* 2000, pp. 95–6.

89 On Velázquez as court portraitist, see Portús 2012, 2014, and 2015.

90 McKim-Smith, Andersen-Bergdoll, and Newman 1988, pp. 51–2.

91 Quoted in Ettinghausen 2014, p. 434.

92 For example, the subject of fashion is entirely absent from the monumental multi-volume *La Corte de Felipe IV* (Martínez Millán 2015–18), even though it contains much valuable information about court artisans. Earlier works by José Deleito y Piñuela, most notably *La mujer, la casa y la moda (en la España del rey poeta)* (1946), were exceptional in the author's attention to the importance of fashion.

93 Also called Jusepe Nieto Velázquez; see his brief biography in Novo Zaballos and Pizarro Llorente 2015, p. 2816.

CHAPTER I

1 Gómez Ruiz 1999, p. 139.

2 AHPM, Prot. 5684, fol. 681r. Aguado testified to being "33 years of age, a little more or less" on January 28, 1638.

3 AMF, Caja s. XVII, C-O-20, C-O-25, and C-O-45.

4 Cabrero Garrido 2004, p. 398.

5 AMF, Caja s. XVII, C-O-20.

6 This profile of Fuenlabrada is based on Philip II's survey of Castile, known as the *Relaciones topográficas*; see the modern edition: Alvar Ezquerra, García Guerra, and Vicioso Rodríguez 1993, pp. 339–45.

7 AHDM, Exp. matrimonial, 2733/71. Aguado testified on October 19, 1630, that he had been a parishioner of San Ginés for 19 years.

8 Translated in Escobar 2014, p. 55.

9 Pinto Crespo and Madrazo Madrazo 1995, pp. 42, 141.

10 Funes de Villalpando 2013, p. 142.

11 Irigoyen-García 2017, p. 8. On the Plaza Mayor as a festival space, see Blasco Esquivias 2018.

12 López Barahona and Nieto Sánchez 2011, p. 121.

13 Braun et al. 2016, pp. 14–19.

14 "Tassa general de los precios" 1627, fols. 16r–17r, on the fees that tailors could charge for garments; and fol. 1v on wool prices. A man's cloak required 3 *varas* of wool (Andújar 1640, fol. 9r).

15 López Barahona and Nieto Sánchez 2011.

16 Bass and Wunder 2014, pp. 368–71.

17 The names of Madrid's *toqueros* and other artisans, and the streets on which they lived, were compiled in 1625 and are organized in lists according to their craft guilds in AGS, CCG, libs. de donativos, 59 and 86.

18 AHN, Consejos, lib. 1221, fols. 386r–v (*zapateros de viejo*); lib. 1225, fols. 347r–v (*calceteros*); and lib. 1218, fols. 88r–93v (*sombrereros de viejo*).

19 Suárez de Figueroa 2006, vol. 2, p. 638.

20 *Ordenanzas*… [1754]. These revised bylaws of 1754 are based on the tailors' *ordenanzas* of 1598, of which there are no known copies.

21 López Castán 1986, p. 211.

22 Capella Martínez 1962, pp. 448–9, cites a census of 1611 at the Archivo de la Villa with the names and addresses of 418 members of the tailors' guild, but that document cannot be located.

23 AGS, CCG, lib. de donativos, 86, fols. 140r–178r.

24 AHN, Consejos, 25498, exp. 7, fols. 41r–45r.

25 On the parish of San Ginés, see Larquié 1966.

26 The doublet-making Aguados are listed in AHN, Consejos, 25498, exp. 7, fols. 41r–44r; and in AGS, CCG, lib. de donativos, 86, fols. 181r–184r.

27 Pinto Crespo and Madrazo Madrazo 1995, p. 157.

28 Capmani y Montpalau 1863, p. 54.
29 AHN, Consejos, lib. 1206, fols. 95r–96v (*mercaderes de paños*).
30 Chesterton 1924, pp. 55–8.
31 "Tassa general de los precios" 1627, fols. 1r–2v.
32 AGS, CCG, lib. de donativos, 86, fols. 379r–381r; Suárez de Figueroa 2006, vol. 2, pp. 1009–11.
33 Nieto Sánchez 2017, pp. 259–65.
34 "Tassa general de los precios" 1627, fols. 2v–6r.
35 AHN, Consejos, lib. 1207, fols. 77r, 80r (*joyeros*).
36 AHN, Consejos, lib. 1200, fols. 63r–v; and lib. 1240, fols. 525r–526r (*roperos*).
37 AHN, Consejos, lib. 1200, fols. 612r–617r (*roperos de viejo*).
38 AHDM, Exp. matrimonial, 2733/71.
39 Zofío Llorente 2000, p. 528.
40 AGS, CCG, lib. de donativos, 86, fol. 142v; Nieto Sánchez 2006, p. 155.
41 AHPM, Prot. 5300, fols. 214r–v; Prot. 5556, fols. 147v–148r; and Prot. 5622, fols. 470r–v.
42 Zofío Llorente 2005, p. 447.
43 Suárez de Figueroa 2006, vol. 2, p. 649.
44 Zofío Llorente 2000, p. 528.
45 *Ordenanzas*... [1754], pp. 25–6.
46 Nieto Sánchez 1995.
47 "Tassa general de los precios" 1627, fols. 15r–v.
48 *Pregón* 1613, fol. [2v].
49 Rocha Burguen 1618, unpag., "Carta del examen de la Corte" and "Carte del examen de la Villa de Madrid."
50 AHN, Consejos, 25498, exp. 7, fols. 37r, 75r, 77r; Bouza 2015, p. 26.
51 Zofío Llorente 2005, p. 535.
52 *Cartas jesuitas* 1865, vol. 7, p. 156.
53 *Ordenanzas*... [1754], pp. 18–20.
54 Zofío Llorente 2011, p. 97; López Barahona and Nieto Sánchez 2010, pp. 150–51.
55 AHN, Consejos, 25498, exp. 7, fol. 41r.
56 AHPM, Prot. 5684, fols. 363r–v. In the paperwork settling Soria's estate after his death in 1630, he owed a small debt of 350 *reales* to Mateo Aguado for unpaid work "from the time that he worked in his house until he died."
57 Ibid., fol. 681. In January 1638, Aguado testified in a case on behalf of Soria's widow and stated under oath that he had met Francisco de Soria 15 years earlier.
58 AGP, AG, leg. 658, "Sastres de cámara de la Reina nuestra señora."
59 AGP, AG, legs. 5272/1 and 5272/2 include Soria's accounts of his work for Queen Margaret of Austria and her children.
60 On Isabel of Bourbon's Hispanicization, see Oliván Santaliestra 2013, pp. 225–36.
61 BNE, Mss/2348, fol. 228v; Río Barredo 2008.
62 Elisabeth of Bourbon's French tailor Luis Guillén was briefly given a salaried post at the Spanish court before he returned to France in August 1616 (AGP, AG, leg. 658, "Sastres de cámara de la Reina nuestra señora"). Two other French tailors who accompanied Elisabeth remained at the Spanish court, married Spanish women, and worked as tailors for the queen's ladies (AGP, Per., caja 828/11).
63 AGP, AG, leg. 5272/2, Soria/Isabel (1616), "gorgorán color de yema de huevo rayadillo."
64 Gascón de Torquemada 1991, p. 81. AGP, AG, leg. 5272/2, Soria/Isabel (1620), "un vestido para [llevar] con chapines que es el primero."
65 Abad Zardoya 2016, p. 39.
66 Gallagher 2010, p. 187.
67 AGP, AG, leg. 5272/2, Soria/Isabel (1624), "ropa y basquiña de tafetán negro doble." Soria was paid 500 *reales* for the over-gown and skirt, 55 *reales* for the doublet, and 4 *reales* for buttonholes.
68 There are multiple versions of Rubens's portrait of Queen Isabel; see Jaffé 1992, p. 12. On Rubens and fashion, see Thépaut-Cabasset 2013.
69 Moulinier and Vesin 2015, pp. 62–5.
70 On the Pollok House painting, see Macartney 2002, p. 349; Rodríguez Moya and Mínguez Cornelles 2014.
71 Rocha Burguen 1618, unfol. end pages, "Saya grande de terciopelo, o damasco, de manga redonda."
72 AGP, AG, leg. 5272/2, Soria/Isabel (1627), "hice para los años del Rey y puse para bordar un vestido de raso blanco de la China."
73 There are also fragments at the Museo Poldi Pezzoli, Milan (inv. 2649; Museo Poldi Pezzoli 1999, p. 126) and the Museo del Tessuto, Prato (inv. 75.01.187).
74 María Dolores Vila Tejero in García Serrano 2015, p. 222.
75 BMNP, SG Pra.Gen (55), vol. 2, inventory of the Alcázar de Madrid (1636), no. 2445.

76 When the Crown collected donations in 1625, Soria gave 2,200 *reales*—more than any other tailor and 20 times the average master tailor's donation (AGS, CCG, lib. de donativos, 86, fol. 157r).
77 AHPM, Prot. 5684, fols. 394r–405r.
78 Ibid., fols. 334r–335v.
79 AGP, AG, leg. 5272/2, Soria/Isabel (1630), "una almilla que se le dio juntada de encajes blancos y colonias encarnadas."
80 Zofío Llorente 2005, pp. 214–15.
81 AGP, AG, leg. 5648/2ª/14, "Mateo Aguado: Su cuenta de gajes desde 14 de octubre de 1630 que juró en plaza de sastre de cámara."

CHAPTER 2

1 AHDM, Exp. matrimonial, 2733/71. Aguado and Alfonsa Martínez wed on December 1, 1630 (APSG, Matrimonios, lib. 5, fol.111r).
2 AGP, AG, leg. 658, "Los sastres de las damas que han de tener entrada en la portería adentro" (November 18, 1664).
3 Wilkinson Zerner 1994; Rodríguez G. de Ceballos 1997.
4 BNE, Mss/1007, fol. 1v.
5 AGP, Per., caja 16/10, doc. 4 (June 8, 1646).
6 AGP, AG, leg. 5272/2, Aguado/Isabel (1631), "Sumario de esta cuenta."
7 *Ordenanzas*... [1754], p. 4.
8 AHPM, Prot. 10097, fol. 396v.
9 AHPM, Prot. 6514, fol. 95r.
10 AGP, AG, leg. 5272/2. The first payment for a drawing appears in Aguado's accounts for Prince Baltasar Carlos in October 1631. Aguado's accounts for 1634–6 include 35 drawings for the prince and 18 for the queen.
11 Currie 2006, p. 164.
12 On various classes of drawings, see McDonald 2012, pp. 26–32.
13 On the Corpus Christi procession during the reign of Philip IV, see Río Barredo 2000, pp. 223–33.
14 Gascón de Torquemada 1991, p. 244.
15 AGP, AG, leg. 5252/2, Criales & Porras/Isabel (1639), "vestido de ormesí negro."
16 AGP, AG, leg. 5252/1, Criales & Porras/Isabel (1635), "media vara de terciopelo azul y oro que se hizo en esta corte."
17 Portús 2012, p. 26.
18 *Cartas jesuitas* 1865, vol. 7, pp. 69–70.
19 Cordato 1639, fols. [2r–v].
20 AGP, AG, leg. 5272/3, Aguado/Isabel (1639), "se llevó el vestido ... a quitar los botones ..."
21 AGP, AG, leg. 5272/2, Aguado/Isabel (1631), "Cortó una ropa de levantar de felpa de nácar corta ... casi acabado mandó su Majestad se hiciese un gabán ..."
22 Brown and Elliott 2003, pp. 149–202.
23 García Martín 2004, p. 170.
24 Oliván Santaliestra 2012a, p. 16.
25 López-Rey 1996, vol. 2, pp. 128–31; Pérez Sánchez and Spinosa 2005, p. 93. Diverging from most scholars, Jordan 2006 (p. 214) dated the portrait of Isabel in black and gold for the Buen Retiro Palace prior to Velázquez's 1629 departure for Italy.
26 Crombie 1958, p. 238.
27 AGS, CMC, 3ª *época*, leg. 2286, exp. 2, fol. 1bis.
28 Oliván Santaliestra 2011.
29 AGP, AG, leg. 5251/2, Criales & Porras/Isabel (1634), "unos petillos y puntas bordados de estrellas de vidrios y torzales de oro."
30 AGP, AG, leg. 5252/1, Criales & Porras/Isabel (1635), "dos gruesas de diamantillos que se pusieron en unos petillos usados que se habían caído."
31 Letter from Francisco de Quevedo to don Sancho de Sandoval, March 13, 1635, in Quevedo 1946, pp. 286–7; cited in Brown and Elliott 2003, p. 279, n. 11.
32 Gascón de Torquemada 1991, p. 398.
33 Oliván Santaliestra 2012b, pp. 201–15; Franganillo Álvarez 2020, pp. 196–205.
34 The Spanish term *picado* encompasses the English terms for "pinking" (small cuts) and "snipping" (medium cuts) as defined in Arnold 1975.
35 AGP, AG, leg. 5272/2, Aguado/Isabel (1636), "después de acabado mandó su Majestad echar entretelas de tela brillante."
36 Patterson 2009, pp. 37–8.
37 Other portraits of Isabel of Bourbon in brown and silver include a study of the head of the queen (Garrido 2014); a portrait at the Art Institute of Chicago that combines elements of the versions in Vienna and Hampton Court; and an image of the queen in the background of Velázquez's

Prince Baltasar Carlos in the Riding School (Grosvenor Estate, London).

38 Brown and Elliott 2002, pp. 57–8.

39 Zayas y Sotomayor 2009, p. 148, n. 5.

40 AGP, AG, leg. 5272/3, Aguado/Isabel (1639), "ropa, basquiña, jubón, y cota de espolín noguerado y plata de memorias que dio el Príncipe nuestro señor a su Majestad guarnecido con una faja de doble noguerado bordado de plata pasada de memorias."

41 Portraits of Queen Isabel were sent to Vienna in 1632 and in 1639 (Giulietta Beaufort in Haag 2014, pp. 303–4); the portrait of the queen in brown and silver is usually dated 1632, but the later date of 1639 is more likely based on the descriptions of the queen's wardrobe in Aguado's accounts. However, accounts for 1632 and 1633, which could contain relevant information, have not been found.

42 Vega 1970, p. 93.

43 Sorapán de Rieros 1616, pp. 205–6.

44 Pitman 2017, p. 296.

45 Bernis 2001, pp. 215–16; Anderson 1979, pp. 208–9.

46 *Verdugado* in Stevens 1726.

47 AGP, AG, leg. 5278/9, López/Isabel (1635–6 and 1636–7).

48 Rodríguez Bernis 2014, p. 145.

49 AGP, AG, leg. 5272/2, Aguado/Isabel (1634), "un manteo francés ... [con] dos ballenas, una en ruedo y otra en la alforza"; and Aguado/Isabel (1636), "un manteo francés ... [con] un esparto colteado para que hiciese ruedo."

50 Carranza 1636, fol. 20v.

51 Bernis 2001, pp. 211–14, 302.

52 Wunder 2015, pp. 143–5.

53 Carranza 1636, fol. 22r.

54 Blum 1951, p. 7.

55 Bernis 1991, p. 54.

56 Jiménez Patón 1638, fol. 42r.

57 Quiñones de Benavente 1991; on the dating of Quiñones de Benavente's *El guarda-infante* (parts I and II), see Bergman 1965, p. 182.

58 AGP, AG, leg. 5278/9, López/Isabel (1635–6), "para el ama ... un guardainfante de cuatro órdenes."

59 Arnold, Tiramani, and Costigliolo 2018, p. 26.

60 AGP, AG, leg. 5278/9, López/Isabel (1638–40). Between 1638 and 1640, López made three *verdugados* "con sus caderas y con sus alambres."

61 Jiménez Patón 1638, fol. 4v.

62 Carlos Varona 2018, p. 234.

63 Queen Isabel, who gave birth to María Antonia on January 17, 1635, was pregnant for most of the year 1634, when Velázquez was commissioned to paint her equestrian portrait for the Hall of Realms (see Brown 2008c, p. 154).

64 Hearn 2020, pp. 32–50.

65 Bernis 2001, p. 229.

66 AGP, AG, leg. 5272/2, Soria/Isabel (1623). Soria added canvas to Queen Isabel's skirts when she was pregnant: "A cinco basquiñas les hecho anjeos por estar su Majestad preñada."

67 "*Cinta*" in Covarrubias Orozco 1995, p. 314.

68 Carranza 1636, fols. 20v–21r.

69 AGP, AG, leg. 5272/3, Aguado/Isabel (1638), "por estar su Majestad preñada y no traer verdugado." The silk merchants' records confirm that the queen's garments were altered during her pregnancy in 1638 so she could go without a farthingale; see AGP, AG, leg. 5252/2, Criales & Porras/Isabel (1638).

70 Arnold, Tiramani, and Costigliolo 2018, pp. 68–9.

71 AGP, AG, leg. 5272/3, Aguado/Isabel (1638), "una ropa de damasco carmesí guarnecida con dos pasamanos de oro y plata"; and leg. 5252/2, Criales & Porras/Isabel (1638), "vestido para parir."

CHAPTER 3

1 AGP, AG, leg. 5272/2, Aguado/Isabel (1635), "ropa, basquiña, y jubón, y bebederos de lama parda y oro para enviar a la serenísima Reina de Hungria."

2 AGP, AG, leg. 5272/2, Aguado/*mercedes* (1634), "un muchacho que se ha criado por cuenta de su Majestad"; and leg. 5272/3, Aguado/*mercedes* (1636), "un turco que se volvió cristiano."

3 AGP, AG, leg. 5272/2. The summaries (*sumarios*) at the end of Aguado's accounts for 1631 show that he was paid 8,078.50 *reales* for favors; 6,595 *reales* for Queen Isabel; and 2,427 *reales* for Baltasar Carlos.

4 AGP, AG, leg. 5272/3, Aguado/Baltasar Carlos (1635), "llevó un vestido de terciopelado negro de su Alteza a pegar treinta docenas de botones de plata y seda negra a media noche."

5 Llorente 2011, pp. 39–47.

6 AGP, AG, leg. 5272/3, Aguado/María Teresa (1638–40), "seis vestidos de holanda coleados para sacar las manos de su Alteza."

7 AGP, AG, legs. 5272/2 and 5272/3. Aguado's accounts for the prince in 1631, 1634, 1635, and 1636 include 36 payments for drawings.

8 Hurtado de Mendoza 1632, fol. 15v.

9 Aguado's accounts for 1632 are missing, but multiple eyewitnesses provide consistent descriptions of the prince's ceremonial dress: Hurtado de Mendoza 1632, fol. 15v; Gómez de Mora 1632, fol. 11v; and León Pinelo 1971, p. 287.

10 Hurtado de Mendoza 1632, fols. 16r–v.

11 AGP, AG, leg. 5272/2. Aguado's accounts for the prince include many *manteos* in 1631 but none in 1634 (1632–3 accounts are missing).

12 H. Wunder 2002, pp. 25–6.

13 AGP, AG, leg. 5272/3, Aguado/Baltasar Carlos (1639), "Botarga"; and leg. 5272/2, Aguado/Baltasar Carlos (1634), "Arlequín."

14 AGP, AG, leg. 5272/2, Aguado/Baltasar Carlos (1634), "cuatro archeros, cuatro españoles, y cinco tudescos muñecos."

15 AGP, AG, leg. 5272/3, Aguado/Baltasar Carlos (1638–9) and Aguado/María Teresa (1638–40). Aguado was paid 8,029 *reales* for work for the prince over 24 months in 1638–9 and 4,129 *reales* for work for the infanta over 28 months in 1638–40.

16 Oliván Santaliestra 2014, p. 168.

17 AGP, AG, leg. 5272/3, Aguado/María Teresa (1638–40), "seis vestidos de holanda para poner a andar su Alteza … por no contar a mi señora la Condesa se deshicieron."

18 Ibid. For example: "vestido de doble noguerado guarnecido con un galón de plata … las [mangas] justas acuchilladas a lo tudesco."

19 Carmen Bernis dated *The Royal Family in the Gardens of the Casa de Campo* to 1641–2 based on the infanta's age; see Bernis 1994, p. 294.

20 Méndez Silva 1637, fol. 12r.

21 Blum 1951, p. 7; Goldstein 1998, p. 21.

22 AGP, AG, leg. 5252/1, Criales & Porras/Isabel (1636).

23 Bernis 2001, pp. 245–6.

24 AGP, AG, leg. 5272/2, Aguado/Isabel (1636), "hizo y puso para bordar una ropa de levantar que su Majestad presentó a la señora Princesa de Cariñan … y se hizo en tres horas de hechura."

25 Reported in a 1623 account of the Prince of Wales's entry into Madrid by palace quartermaster Diego de Soto y Aguilar (Soto y Aguilar 1863, p. 491).

26 Sánchez de Espejo 1637, fol. 9r.

27 See, for example, royal chronicler José Pellicer de Tovar's *Avisos* describing life at court between 1639 and 1644 (Pellicer de Tovar 2002, pp. 9, 58) and the gossip-filled Jesuit correspondence in the *Cartas jesuitas* 1862, vol. 2, pp. 302, 322, 328–9.

28 Quoting Juan Francisco Ayala Manrique, author of the manuscript *Noticias de Madrid* (1636–7), published without attribution by Antonio Rodríguez Villa: see [Ayala Manrique] 1886, p. 233. On the Duchess of Chevreuse and the dissemination of the low-cut bodice in Spain, see Harris 2006, p. 118.

29 Reported in a letter dated February 16, 1638, in the *Cartas jesuitas* 1862, vol. 2, pp. 328–30.

30 [Ayala Manrique] 1886, p. 245.

31 See the analysis of the dress in *Lady with a Fan* by fashion historians Bernis 1994, p. 296, and Descalzo Lorenzo 2007; the identification of the sitter with the Duchess of Chevreuse was popularized by Veliz 2004.

32 Peña 1623, fol. [iv]. On the Prince of Wales's attire during his visit to Madrid, see Miller 2014.

33 *Relación* 1638, fol. [2r].

34 [Ayala Manrique] 1886, p. 122.

35 AGP, AG, leg. 5252/1, Criales & Porras/Isabel (1637), fol. 15.

36 AGP, AG, leg. 5252/2, Criales & Porras/Isabel (1640), fol. 6bis verso, "vestido de camelote plateado y plata."

37 AGP, AG, leg. 5253/1, Criales & Porras/Isabel (1641), fol. 3v, "Aderezo de vestido de camelote plateado y negro que se cubrió con gasa negra."

38 Franganillo Álvarez 2017b, p. 100.

39 Varela Merino 2009, p. 793.

40 Semmelhack 2009, pp. 92–3.

41 Bernis 1994, p. 294; Varela Merino 2009, p. 796.

42 AGP, AG, leg. 5278/9, López/Isabel (1648–50). In November 1648, López made "un verdugado de tafetán doble carmesí con cuatro guarniciones de oro y su cadera

cariñana de por sí" to send to Mariana of Austria at the imperial court.

43 Gascón de Torquemada 1991, p. 232.

44 The Church of Santa María was demolished in 1865; today the Virgin of Almudena is housed at the modern cathedral named for the image. A painting (c. 1640) at the Cathedral of La Almudena in Madrid depicts the procession of 1636; see the catalogue entry by Ángel Aterido in Quesada Valera 2015, pp. 176–80.

45 Gascón de Torquemada 1991, p. 399.

46 Vera Tassis y Villarroel 1692, p. 413.

47 Gascón de Torquemada 1991, p. 186.

48 Carlos Varona 2018, pp. 184–6.

49 Tarrero Alcón 2017, p. 51.

50 For example: AGP, AG, leg. 5278/9, López/Isabel (1629–30), "hizo un verdugadito para una imagen de Nuestra Señora del Convento de San Gil."

51 AGP, AG, leg. 5272/2, Aguado/*mercedes* (1634), "a una imagen de Nuestra Señora que está en Salamanca una saya de tela brillante."

52 AGP, AG, leg. 5272/3, Aguado/*mercedes* (1640), "un manto y delantera de saya y vestido de Niño Jesús con sus mangas de casaca y brahoncillos de raso blanco de la China bordado de oro y casquillos de plata, forrado."

53 AHDM, Fábrica, 2561, *Inventario general* (1693), fol. 173r.

54 Vera Tassis y Villarroel 1692, p. 445.

55 Ibid., pp. 485–6; Gómez Menéndez 2019, pp. 544–5.

56 Francisco Esteban in AGP, Per., caja 16878/11, unnumbered doc. (June 23, 1642).

57 Josefa de Gamboa in AGP, Per., caja 389/10, unnumbered doc. (April 20, 1663).

58 *Corpus velazqueño* 2000, p. 114.

59 AGP, AG, leg. 5272/2, Aguado/*mercedes* (1634). Aguado was paid 216 *reales* for one outfit for the keeper (*guardajoyas y ropa*), 610 *reales* for outfits for three assistants (*ayudas*), and 342 *reales* for six outfits for junior assistants (*mozos*).

60 Ravenscroft 2014, pp. 153–4.

61 AGP, AG, leg. 5272/3, Aguado/*mercedes* (1635), "para la Enana un vestido a lo francés, que es faldón fruncido y jubón con faldillas a lo francés."

62 For example: AGP, AG, leg. 5272/3, Aguado/*mercedes* (1635), "para doña Catalina de Guevara de la cámara de su Majestad para casarse una saya entera."

63 BNE, Mss/18196, fols. 141r–v.

64 For example: AGP, AG, leg. 5272/3, Aguado/*mercedes* (1636), dresses for the wives of don Diego Sarmiento and Tomás Ruiz de Zurbano, *ayudas de guardajoyas*.

65 For example: AGP, AG, leg. 5272/3, Aguado/*mercedes* (1638–40), dress for "una barrendera del cuarto de las damas para casarse."

66 For example: ibid., *saya entera* for doña Francisca de Somoza to enter the Convent of La Encarnación.

67 AGP, AG, leg. 5272/3, Aguado/*mercedes* (1635), "para Dionisio [Andino], zapatero de la Reina nuestra señora."

68 AGP, AG, leg. 5272/3, Aguado/*mercedes* (1636), "para la mujer de Francisco de Arboleda, cordonero."

69 AGP, AG, leg. 5272/2, Aguado/*mercedes* (1634), "para la mujer de Mateo Aguado, sastre de la Reina nuestra señora."

70 AHPM, Prot. 6514, fol. 95r.

71 Gaspar Ruiz and Juana Reinoso married in 1617 (AHDM, Exp. matrimonial, 2654/43) and their daughter Bernarda Ruiz de Reinoso was baptized at the Church of San Ginés on August 28, 1618 (APSG, Bautismos, lib. 18, fol. 340v). Gaspar Ruiz was appointed hatmaker to the king in 1628 (AGP, Per., caja 928/22). Mateo Aguado and Bernarda Ruiz married on May 20, 1632 (APSG, Matrimonios, lib. 5, fol. 169r).

72 In a study of bridal ages in the parish of San Ginés in the second half of the seventeenth century, the 12 brides with known birth dates ranged in age from 15 to 28 years old; see Larquié 1988, pp. 142–3. "Pleitos y litigios" between Aguado and Ruiz are cited in documents dated 1638 in AGP, AG, leg. 658; and in AHPM, Prot. 8166, fol. 757v.

73 AHPM, Prot. 8166, fols. 814r–818v.

74 AGP, AG, leg. 5251/2, Criales & Porras/*mercedes* (1634), "A la mujer de Mateo Aguado."

75 AGP, AG, leg. 5272/3, Aguado/*mercedes* (1638), "para el enano don Diego de Acedo para venir de correo un capote de campaña guarnecido con un pasamano ancho de oro falso cosido a tres puntos con sus mangas y portezuelas con dicho pasamano por de dentro." Cf. AGP, AG, leg. 5252/2, Criales & Porras/*mercedes* (1638). The silk merchants' account specifies that the fabric for Acedo's coat was crimson baize and describes the trim as false silver, not gold.

76 See the pattern for a *capote de campaña* in Andújar 1640, fol. 20r.

77 Pérez D'Ors, Johnson, and Johnson 2012.
78 Elliott 1986, pp. 523–4.
79 *Corpus velazqueño* 2000, p. 118.
80 Brown (ed.) 1999, pp. 112–14.
81 AGP, AG, leg. 5272/3, Aguado/María Teresa (1638–40), "vestido ... de una tercianela noguerada con memorias de plata que se hizo de una cota de su Majestad."
82 Ibid., "se le llevaron los dos hábitos, el uno de memorias que se hizo de la cota de su Majestad."
83 AGP, AG, leg. 5272/2, Aguado/Isabel (1635–7), "Sumarios." Aguado's earnings dropped from 11,936 *reales* in 1636 to 8,308 *reales* in 1637.
84 AGP, AG, leg. 5272/3, Aguado/*mercedes* (1636, 1637, 1638–40), "Sumarios."
85 *Pregón* 1639b and *Premática* 1639; Bass and Wunder 2009.
86 *Pregón* 1639a.
87 Wunder 2015, pp. 133–4.
88 AGP, AG, leg. 658, doc. no. 36 (August 16, 1639).
89 AGP, AG, leg. 5648/2ª/14, "Mateo Aguado: Su cuenta de gajes ..."
90 Quoted in Elliott 2002, p. 347.
91 Stradling 1988, p. 324.
92 *Corpus velazqueño* 2000, p. 119.

CHAPTER 4

1 "Campañas de Cataluña ..." 1890, p. 369; Pérez D'Ors and Gallagher 2010, p. 652. On this phase of the Catalan revolt, see Elliott 1963, pp. 521–2.
2 Pellicer de Tovar 2002, p. 508.
3 Bernis 1982b, p. 204.
4 Philip IV's *valona de campaña* is itemized in his campaign expense accounts in AGP, AG, leg. 911, "Cuenta de los gastos." On Flemish lace, see Levey 1983, pp. 22–3.
5 King Christian IV's collar was published in Arnold, Tiramani, and Levey 2008, p. 42. During the campaign in Aragon, Velázquez painted a portrait of a nobleman's daughter that was rejected because the client was unhappy with the painter's treatment of the sitter's expensive Flemish lace collar; the incident was described by the Aragonese painter Jusepe Martínez at whose home Velázquez completed the portrait (Martínez 1988, p. 212).
6 Franganillo Álvarez 2017a, pp. 33–45.
7 Pellicer de Tovar 2002, p. 376.
8 Elliott 1986, pp. 637–9.
9 *Cartas jesuitas* 1863, vol. 5, p. 18.
10 Sicard 2015; Pizarro Llorente 2019.
11 AGP, AG, leg. 5253/1, Criales & Porras/Isabel (1642–4). The silk merchant accounts totaled 219,699 *reales* in 1642; 105,807 *reales* in 1643; and 89,073 *reales* in 1644.
12 Stradling 1988, p. 216, n. 25.
13 Colomer 2014, pp. 89–90.
14 Oliván Santaliestra 2016.
15 AGP, AG, leg. 5278/9, López/Isabel (1642–4), "un guarda-infante de colonias y tafetán doble carmesí."
16 On the *Gathering of Gentlemen* attributed to Mazo, see Kientz 2015a, pp. 328–9.
17 Bodart 2011, p. 267.
18 Ágreda 1991, pp. 68–9.
19 Van Wyhe 2014, pp. 256–66.
20 *Pompa funeral* ... 1645, fol. 7r.
21 Ibid., fols. 23v–24r; translated in Orso 1990, p. 68.
22 Vincent-Cassy 2013.
23 Gascón de Torquemada 1991, p. 414.
24 Taylor 1983, p. 65.
25 Bernis 2001, pp. 298–301.
26 AGP, AG, leg. 904, Aguado/María Teresa (1644), "Monjiles" and "Capa de burato negro."
27 Bernis 2001, pp. 109, 113–14.
28 AGP, AG, leg. 5272/3, Gaspar de Frutos, "Memoria de los lutos" (1644).
29 *Premática* 1588; Martínez Bonanad 2019.
30 Hoffman 2011, p. 19.
31 AGP, AG, leg. 904, Aguado/María Teresa (1645), "Luto para el Rey nuestro señor" and "Luto para el Príncipe nuestro señor."
32 Ibid., "Vestido de rayadillo plateado y negro"; "Otro de rayadillo cabellado y negro"; and "Vestido de ormesí de aguas azul."
33 AGP, AG, leg. 904, Aguado/María Teresa (1646), "un saquito con faldillas y mangas de casaca [y] justas de terciopelo liso negro bordado de plata en cuadros, que dio a su Alteza para un vestido la señora Duquesa de Sanlúcar."
34 AGP, Per., caja 16/10, doc. 6 (December 19, 1646).
35 AGP, Per., caja 16/10, doc. 1 (November 26, 1644).

36 Hortal Muñoz 2015, p. 790.
37 Rodríguez Villa 1913, pp. 58–9.
38 AHPM, Prot. 5412, fols. 97r–99v.
39 Ibid., fols. 146r–147v.
40 AHPM, Prot. 8166, inventory on fols. 761r–776v.
41 AGP, Per., caja 16/10, doc. 4 (June 8, 1646).
42 Jurado Sánchez 2005, pp. 58, 138.
43 AGP, Per., caja 16/10, doc. 10 (May 20, 1647).
44 APSG, Difuntos, lib. 10, fols. 544r–v.
45 Ágreda 1885, vol. 1, pp. 1, 413–14.
46 Ágreda 1991, pp. 92–3.
47 BL, Add. Ms. 24947, fol. 9r, Chumacero to the king (March 25, 1643); BNE Mss/13163, fol. 77r, Chumacero to the king (May 18, 1643).
48 BL, Add. Ms. 24947, fol. 45r.
49 *Cartas jesuitas* 1864, vol. 6, p. 38.
50 Jerónimo López quoted in González de Santalla 1673, p. 292.
51 If Velázquez's *Lady with a Fan* dates to the advanced 1640s, as proposed by Carmen Bernis (Bernis 1994, p. 296), and *Lady in a Mantilla* was made around the same time, then the relationship between the two pictures could be explained as a commentary on the *escotado* controversy—although the message of that commentary remains to be explored.
52 Alberti dedicated his treatise on women's dress to Mariana of Austria; see Alberti 1650, p. 293.
53 AHN, Consejos, lib. 1231, fols. 60r, 62r, 74r.
54 BL, Add. Ms. 24947, fol. 56r.
55 Malcolm 2006, pp. 104–5.
56 Andrés de Uztárroz 1646, pp. 107–11; Portús, García-Máiquez, and Álvarez-Garcillán 2015.
57 Andrés de Uztárroz 1646, p. 111.
58 AGP, AG, leg. 911, "Memoria de los vestidos y demás cosas que vinieron en los cofres de la Guardaropa del Príncipe … de Zaragoza a Madrid" (n.d.).
59 Mitchell 2021, pp. 24–9.
60 AGP, AG, leg. 904, Aguado/María Teresa (1646), "Lutos para su Alteza y la señora doña Mariana por el Príncipe nuestro señor."
61 Cobo Delgado 2016, pp. 156–8; Llorente 2019, pp. 163–4.
62 On the portrait series, see Morte García 1990–91, esp. Pt. 2 (1991), pp. 25–6.
63 *Cartas jesuitas* 1864, vol. 6, pp. 477–8.
64 *Cartas jesuitas* 1865, vol. 7, pp. 69, 72–4.
65 Ágreda 1885, vol. 1, pp. 241, 260.
66 Gascón de Torquemada 1991, p. 419.
67 Sánchez Hernández and Baranda Leturio 2018, p. 96.
68 Dávila [1648], fol. 1v.
69 Bocángel y Unzueta 1648, fol. 1r.
70 Bocángel y Unzueta [1649], "Relación," fols. [6r–8r].

CHAPTER 5

1 AGP, Per., caja 16/10, doc. 24 (1667).
2 AGP, AG, leg. 904, Aguado/Mariana (1649), "Vestido de camelote verde" and "Ferreruelo de herbax verde."
3 AGP, AG, leg. 5278/9, López/Mariana (1648–50).
4 Bastl and Colomer 2014, pp. 143–7.
5 Quoted in Cobo Delgado 2016, p. 155.
6 Currie 2006, p. 154.
7 Gracián 1991, p. 46.
8 Mascareñas 1650, p. 280.
9 AGP, Per., caja 16708/21.
10 Palos 2010, pp. 249–84.
11 *Relación* 1649, fol. [1r].
12 AGP, AG, leg. 904, Aguado/Mariana (1649), "Vestido de tercianela cabellada bordado de plata."
13 Ibid., "Saya entera para el día de la entrada de raso nácar bordada de plata, con mangas redondas y justas, las redondas acuchilladas a lo tudesco y las justas de raso blanco bordadas."
14 *Noticia del recibimiento* … [1650], p. 67.
15 Ibid., p. 104.
16 Varey 1972, p. 60.
17 *Noticia del recibimiento* … [1650], p. 104.
18 Villaverde Prado y Salazar 1650, fol. [1v].
19 Zapata Fernández de la Hoz 2017, pp. 106, 371–2, 379.
20 Vera Tassis y Villarroel 1692, p. 471.
21 Malcolm 2005, pp. 174–5.
22 *El día de fiesta, primera parte* (1654) in Zabaleta 1667, p. 189.
23 AGP, AG, leg. 904, Aguado/Mariana (1650), "Vestido de lanilla noguerada que es hábito de San Francisco de Paula."
24 Campos y Fernández de Sevilla 2012, pp. 707–9.
25 Buss 2017, pp. 192–4.

26 Levey 1983, pp. 37–9.
27 *"Celosía"* in Covarrubias Orozco 1995, pp. 294–5.
28 Rodríguez Villa 1913, pp. 93–4.
29 Díaz del Valle 1991, p. 470; López-Rey 1996, vol. 1, p. 207.
30 Portús 1993, pp. 115–18, 123.
31 Varey and Shergold 1953, p. 22.
32 *"Verdegay"* in *Diccionario de autoridades* 1739, vol. 6.
33 Escobar 2003, p. 3.
34 Barrionuevo 1969, vol. 2, p. 58.
35 Escobar 2003, pp. 250–51.
36 Pérez Villanueva 1986, p. 136.
37 Ibid., pp. 155, 158.
38 AGP, Per., caja 16708/21, unnumbered doc. (August 31, 1651).
39 Portús (ed.) 2014, pp. 108–10; Llorente 2019, pp. 168–72.
40 Brown and Garrido 2003, pp. 174–6.
41 Dutch edition Huygens 2005, p. 223; Spanish edition Huygens 2010, pp. 176–7.
42 On black, Cordato 1639, fol. [iv]; on cochineal, Sorapán de Rieros 1616, pp. 203–4.
43 AGP, AG, leg. 5253/2, Porras/Mariana (1650), "Vestido de terciopelo de Holanda."
44 On the relationship between the nude and the clothed portrait, see Hollander 1993, p. xiii.
45 AGP, AG, leg. 629, "Cotilleros"; AGP, Per., caja 16/10, doc. 12 (June 27, 1654).
46 North and Tiramani 2012, pp. 80–97.
47 The farthingale-maker records end in 1650, and silk merchant records for 1650 and 1659 are the only years that have been found.
48 AGP, AG, leg. 5278/9, López/Mariana (1648–50).
49 Oliván Santaliestra 2019, pp. 218–19.
50 *Queen Mariana of Austria Dressed for the Hunt* belongs to a series, with portraits of Philip IV and the Infantas María Teresa and Margarita all dressed for the hunt. Dorotheum, Vienna, Old Master Paintings auction, October 18, 2016, lot nos. 237–40 <dorotheum.com/en/a/5951/>.
51 Travesedo and Martín de Sandoval 1977, p. 426.
52 *"Pollera"* in *Diccionario de autoridades* 1737, vol. 5.
53 Herrero García 2014a, p. 257.
54 Bertaut 1664, pp. 45–6.
55 Huygens 2005, p. 238; Huygens 2010, pp. 188–90.
56 The silk merchant accounts are filled with details of Mariana's accessories: AGP, AG, leg. 5253/2, Porras/Mariana (1650); and leg. 5255/1, Ximénez/Mariana (1659).
57 Bandrés Oto 2002, p. 69.
58 Patrick Lenaghan in Codding 2017, p. 192.
59 Portús (ed.) 2014, p. 106.
60 Pacheco 2001, p. 399.
61 Calderón de la Barca 2019.
62 The culture of novelty and artifice is provocatively explored in Maravall 1986, see esp. pp. 225–47.
63 Malcolm 2005, pp. 175–7.
64 Bacci 1963, p. 73.
65 Shergold 1967, pp. 298–305; plan of the Coliseo in fig. 3.
66 Massar 1977, p. 367.
67 [Brunel] 1670, p. 20. This anonymous account of a traveler's experiences at the Spanish court, first published in French in 1665, is attributed to a French Protestant named Antoine de Brunel.
68 Dress-rental shops are documented in 1628 in AHN, Consejos, lib. 1213, fols. 559r–v, "Alquiladores de vestidos para danzas"; additional documents from 1658 and 1661 are catalogued in Archivo Histórico Nacional 1925, p. 57.
69 Zabaleta 1667, pp. 187–92.
70 Ibid., pp. 308–9.
71 Barrionuevo 1969, vol. 2, p. 194.
72 Núñez de Castro 1658, fol. 93r.
73 Huygens 2005, p. 235; Huygens 2010, pp. 185–7.
74 Huygens 2005, p. 258; Huygens 2010, p. 200.
75 AHPM, Prot. 8166, fols. 808v–809r.
76 Ibid., fol. 809r; Novo Zaballos and Pizarro Llorente 2015, p. 2692.
77 Zofío Llorente 2005, p. 214.
78 AGP, Per., caja 16/10, doc. 13 (June 28, 1654).

CHAPTER 6

1 Pérez Villanueva 1986, p. 244.
2 Ibid., p. 186.
3 *"Famoso"* in *Diccionario de autoridades* 1732, vol. 3.
4 Valladares 1998, pp. 98–9.
5 Marly 1987, p. 22. On the tapestry, see Meyer 1980, pp. 22–6.
6 Quoting Sommer-Mathis 2014, p. 65. On the various versions of Velázquez's *María Teresa*, see Gudrun Swoboda

in Haag 2014, pp. 316–17; on the version at the Louvre, see Kientz 2015a, p. 286.

7 On the marriage negotiations between Madrid and Vienna, see Höbelt 2011.

8 AGP, AG, leg. 904, Aguado/María Teresa (1649). María Teresa's first documented corset was a "cotilla de camelote nácar pespuntada y embutida guarnecida con galón de plata."

9 Pérez Villanueva 1986, p. 197.

10 Wolfgang Prohaska in Carr et al. 2006, pp. 230–32.

11 [Brunel] 1670, pp. 67–8.

12 AGP, AG, leg. 904, Aguado/Margarita (1654), multiple entries for "Enaguas."

13 Oliván Santaliestra 2014, p. 178.

14 AGP, AG, leg. 904, Aguado/Margarita (1656), "Basquiña, jubón, y mangas justas y de casaca bordado de plata y acero (que envió el Conde de Castrillo) vaciados los cantos en almenillas guarnecidas con punticas de plata y pequeñas y el jubón por delante calados y faldillas y golpes y dos pares de mangas y la basquiña de órdenes en ribetón."

15 Ragosta 2009, pp. 105–6.

16 Barrionuevo 1968, vol. 1, p. 259.

17 AGP, AG, leg. 5252/2, Criales & Porras/Isabel (1638). The silk merchants supplied 51 *varas* (42.84 meters) of *bocací* for the patterns.

18 AGP, AG, leg. 904. Aguado's charges for 1656 include gifts from the Count of Castrillo for Mariana (4 pairs of sleeves and 3 dresses); María Teresa (6 pairs of sleeves, 2 dresses, and a *justillo* with two matching petticoats); and Margarita (3 dresses, one with a matching set of petticoats, including a *pollera* to wear over a *guardainfante*).

19 Llorente 2011, p. 42.

20 Oliván Santaliestra 2014, pp. 178–9.

21 *Premática* 1657.

22 AHN, Consejos, leg. 7137, letter from the *Consejo* to the king (August 18, 1657).

23 "The Infanta Margarita of Spain (1651–1673), c. 1658–62," Royal Collection Trust <rct.uk/collection/403016/the-infanta-margarita-of-spain-1651-1673>.

24 Barrionuevo 1969, vol. 2, p. 121.

25 On the color *celeste*, see Buss 2017, p. 176.

26 AGP, AG, leg. 904, Aguado/Margarita (1656), "Basquiña, jubón, y mangas justas y de casaca de felpa celeste, la basquiña guarnecida con seis puntas de plata, el jubón dos por delante y calados y faldillas con dicha guarnición, mangas de casaca cuajadas en arpón, las justas en pie, y otras de tela para debajo."

27 AGP, AG, leg. 904, Aguado/Margarita (1659), "Ropa, basquiña, y jubón de felpa color de olivo, guarnecida la ropa con una faja de raso color de caña y encima un pasamano negro"; "Ropa, basquiña, y jubón de felpa verde, guarnecida la ropa con una faja ancha de raso blanco."

28 Huygens 2005, p. 238; Huygens 2010, pp. 188–90.

29 Oberthaler and Strolz 2014, pp. 286–7.

30 Gudrun Swoboda in Haag 2014, p. 320.

31 Martínez López 2015, p. 99.

32 Marly 1987, p. 23.

33 Baticle 1960, p. 198.

34 Motteville 1902, pp. 216–17.

35 AGP, AG, leg. 904, Aguado/María Teresa (1657), "Saya entera de gasa listada encarnada y blanca bordada en guarnición de unas puntas de talco sobre venturina y otras mangas de tafetán bordadas debajo."

36 Méndez Silva 1658, fol. 20v.

37 Menéndez de Luarca 2015, p. 50.

38 Malcolm 2017, pp. 228–9.

39 Quoted in Zanger 1997, p. 39.

40 García 1642, ch. 12, unpag.

41 AGP, AG, leg. 5278/1, Bustamante (1659), "zapatos cariñanos forrados en tafetán encarnado."

42 AGP, AG, leg. 5255/1, Ximénez/María Teresa (1659). Materials for *chapines* appear throughout the silk merchant's 1659 account for María Teresa.

43 For example: AGP, AG, leg. 5272/3, Aguado/María Teresa (1659), "ropa, basquiña, y jubón de camelote nácar que estaba cortado para zapatos y se añadió por haberse su Majestad puesto chapines."

44 Pérez Villanueva 1986, p. 322.

45 Haan 2020, p. 151.

46 BNE, Mss/2387, fol. 1v.

47 Cubillo de Aragón 1659, fol. [2v].

48 Ibid.; Bertaut 1669, p. 26.

49 Bertaut 1669, p. 28.

50 AGP, AG, leg. 5272/3, Aguado/Mariana (1659). Mariana's dress was a "ropa, basquiña, y jubón de raso de puntas plateado y negro, guarnecida la ropa con dos fajas de raso negro picadas en hojas de oliva."

51 Bertaut 1669, pp. 28, 35.
52 Gramont 1717, pp. 217–18.
53 Bertaut 1669, p. 29.
54 The original dress that Aguado made for María Teresa was a "ropa, basquiña, y jubón de raso de puntas de tártaro, guarnecida la ropa con una punta que se cortó de un raso plateado y negro en almenillas." The color of the fabric, *tártaro*, may have been a pale yellow (see "*tártaro*" in Sanz and Gallego 2001, pp. 884–5).
55 Zanger 1997, p. 40.
56 Bertaut 1669, p. 37.
57 *Tratado de paz* ... 1660.
58 AGP, AG, leg. 5272/3, Aguado/Mariana (1659). María Teresa's peace-day dress was a "ropa, basquiña, y jubón de felpa nácar, la basquiña con siete dozavos de guarnición de unas puntas cortadas de raso blanco y fundadas sobre velo." On plush (*felp*) weaving in the Netherlands, see Colenbrander 2013, p. 85.
59 *Relación* 1659, fol. [2r].
60 AGP, AG, leg. 904, Aguado/María Teresa (1660).
61 AGP, Per., caja 407/31. The younger Jerónimo de Negrilla never did take office, and when he died in 1679 the position was given to Juan García de la Fuente, who had been serving as interim embroiderer for many years; Novo Zaballos and Pizarro Llorente 2015, p. 2815.
62 AGP, AG, leg. 5215/1, García de la Fuente, *Cuenta de la jornada* (1660), "vestido de ormesí verde" and "vestido de ormesí azul celeste."
63 Ibid., "Bordáronse veinte y cuatro varas de guarnición de puntas sobre tafetán blanco para el cumplimiento de una saya de tela nácar."
64 Ibid., "Sumario general de esta cuenta."
65 AGP, AG, leg. 5215/1, García de la Fuente/María Teresa (1656). The embroiderer was paid 26,174 *reales* for his work for María Teresa in 1656.
66 AGP, AG, leg. 904, Aguado/María Teresa (1660), "una tomasina de escarlata." The embroiderer called this same garment a "Hungarian coat" (*ungarina*); see AGP, AG, leg. 5215/1, García de la Fuente, *Cuenta de la jornada* (1660), "una ungarina de escarlata." Philip IV wore a masculine version of the Hungarian coat; see Giorgi 2016, pp. 88–9.
67 *Relación* 1660a, 1660b, 1660c, and 1660d.
68 *Relación* 1660a, fols. 2r–v.
69 Ibid., fol. 2r.
70 Ibid., fol. 3v.
71 *Relación* 1660b.
72 English editions of the memoirs (Motteville 1902 and Montpensier 1848) are cited below, except when my translations differ, in which case the original French editions are cited (Motteville 1723 and Montpensier 1735).
73 The French accounts are analyzed in Zanger 1997. See the extensive bibliography of Spanish and French accounts in Colomer 2003, pp. 81–3.
74 Motteville 1902, p. 201.
75 Haggerty Museum of Art 1984, pp. 29–31.
76 Baticle 1960.
77 Montpensier 1848, p. 180.
78 Ibid., p. 184; Motteville 1902, p. 200.
79 Montpensier 1848, p. 182.
80 Motteville 1902, pp. 201–02.
81 Montpensier 1735, p. 109, "une robe de satin blanc en broderie de geais, dans les lisiéres étoient des fleurs de lis."
82 Campbell 2007, p. 375.
83 Ibid., p. 348.
84 Montpensier 1848, p. 199; Motteville 1902, p. 211.
85 Motteville 1723, pp. 106–7; Motteville 1902, p. 211.
86 Roche 1994, pp. 122–3.
87 Motteville 1723, p. 109.
88 Montpensier 1848, pp. 205–6; *La pompe* ... 1660, pp. 10–11.
89 Stein 1985, p. 32; Vittet 2015, p. 90.
90 Pascale Gorguet Ballesteros, "Avant-propos," in Arizzoli-Clémentel and Gorguet Ballesteros 2009, pp. 18–19.

CHAPTER 7

1 AHPM, Prot. 6514, fols. 92r–97v.
2 López Barahona and Nieto Sánchez 2010, pp. 160–61.
3 AGP, Per., caja 16878/11, undated document in which Francisco Esteban, *mozo de guardaropa*, requests to fill an interim position as tailor, citing Antonio Aguado as precedent.
4 AGP, Per., caja 14/13.
5 AHPM, Prot. 6514, fol. 95r.
6 Art historians have identified these luxuries as signifiers of artists' rising status in seventeenth-century Spain; see

Martín González 1993, pp. 290–91. Aguado's servants are named in AHPM, Prot. 10097, fol. 397v.

7 AGP, AG, leg. 904, Aguado/Mariana and Margarita (1660–63); no charges after 1663 have been found. Aguado almost certainly dressed Philip Prosper, although no records of this work have surfaced.

8 On the attribution of the mural painting, see Morán Turina 2010, pp. 53–4.

9 López Navío 1960, pp. 405–8.

10 Swoboda 2014.

11 The child's bullfighting costume was identified as such by Fernanda Sepúlveda at the Kunsthistorisches Museum.

12 Thirteen babies born to Mateo Aguado and Bernarda Ruiz between 1637 and 1659, including María and Mónica, were baptized at the Church of San Ginés (APSG, Bautismos, lib. 24, fols. 71v, 199v, 302v; lib. 25, fols. 38r, 143r, 317v, 427v; lib. 26, fols. 29r, 155v, 279v, 359v, 436v; lib. 27, fol. 84r). The deaths registered at the church include at least one additional Aguado Ruiz child (APSG, Difuntos, lib. 6, fol. 185r; lib. 7, fols. 134v, 190v–191r, 299v, 337v).

13 APSG, Difuntos, lib. 10, fol. 240v.

14 AHPM, Prot. 8166, fol. 748r.

15 APSG, Bautismos, lib. 28, fol. 2v; and Difuntos, lib. 10, fol. 252v.

16 AHPM, Prot. 8166, fol. 754r.

17 AHPM, Prot. 10097, fol. 393v.

18 AGP, Per., caja 16/10, doc. 14 (October 1, 1661).

19 Novo Zaballos and Pizarro Llorente 2015, p. 2720.

20 AGP, Per., caja 16/10, doc. 17 (November 25, 1661); "*desatención*" in *Diccionario de autoridades* 1732, vol. 3.

21 BNE, Mss/1007, fol. 67v.

22 Stradling 1988, p. 324.

23 AGP, AG, leg. 658, "Sastres de cámara de la Reina nuestra señora."

24 [Brunel] 1670, p. 19.

25 Escobar 2022, p. 124.

26 AGP, Per., caja 16/10, doc. 17 (November 25, 1661).

27 AGP, Per., caja 950/29.

28 Gudrun Swoboda in Haag 2014, p. 323.

29 Quoted in Sommer-Mathis 2014, p. 73, n. 48.

30 AGP, Per., caja 16/10, doc. 23 (1663).

31 AGP, Per., caja 16/10, doc. 24 (1667).

32 Orso 1989, p. 5.

33 Fanshawe 1907, pp. 176–7.

34 *Eclipsòse el Sol* ... [1665], fol. [1r].

35 González Zymla 2003, pp. 245–7.

36 *Eclipsòse el Sol* ... [1665], fol. [1r].

37 Bernis 1982a; Llorente 2006.

38 Patrick Lenaghan in Codding 2017, pp. 193–4.

39 Villalba [c. 1666–77].

40 Romeo 1671, pp. 1–2.

41 González de Santalla 1673, p. 286.

42 AHPM, Prot. 8166, fol. 756v. Aguado's ward was named Francisca Velázquez (not to be confused with the painter Diego Velázquez's daughter of the same name).

43 AGP, Per., caja 16/10, doc. 24 (1667).

44 AHPM, Prot. 8166, fol. 754v.

45 AGP, Per., caja 16/10, doc. 29 (February 9, 1665).

46 AHPM, Prot. 8166, fols. 755r, 821r–825r; APSG, Matrimonios, lib. 9, fol. 37v.

47 AHPM, Prot. 6514, fols. 92v–93r.

48 AHPM, Prot. 10097, fols. 394r–v; and Prot. 8166, fol. 747v.

49 AHPM, Prot. 8166, fol. 761r.

50 Ibid., fols. 762r–763v, 767r–776v.

51 AHPC, Jud-62/15, [fol. 3r]. The value of a new pair of large tailor's shears is recorded in the inventory of Pedro Rodríguez de Baldivieso (1631).

52 AHPM, Prot. 8166, fols. 758r, 792r–793r, 812r–813v.

53 BNE, Mss/1674, fol. 167r. See the plan of the city block with Aguado's houses in BNE, Mss/1668, plan no. 388.

54 On the *carga de aposento*, see Marín Perellón 1988, esp. p. 85.

55 AHPM, Prot. 8166, fols. 792r–793r.

56 Mesonero Romanos 1861, p. 80.

57 Cámara Muñoz 2006 and Blasco Esquivias 2017 were especially helpful for this reconstruction of Aguado's home.

58 AHPM, Prot. 8166, fols. 778r–v.

59 Inventories in Burke and Cherry 1997, vol. 1, pp. 533–4, 680–84.

60 AHPM, Prot. 8166, inventory of paintings on fols. 767r–769v.

61 Kagan and Simpson 2018.

62 Cherry 1997, pp. 88–90.

63 Ibid., pp. 75–8.

64 AHPM, Prot. 8166, fols. 779r, 783v.

65 Ibid., fols. 794v–795r. The same objects appear in inventories of domestic oratories studied by Vinuesa Herrera 2016.

66 González Heras 2015, pp. 88–90.
67 AHPM, Prot. 8166, fols. 774v–776r, 806r–807r; Barrio Moya 2008.
68 Martín González 1993, pp. 224–9.
69 AHPM, Prot. 5684, inventory on fols. 324r–345v.
70 Ruiz Pérez 1999.
71 Arraiza and Partearroyo 1999, p. 245.
72 Cámara Muñoz 2006, pp. 147–50.
73 AHPM, Prot. 8166, fol. 778r (*taburetes*) and fol. 788v (*almohadas*). A well-furnished *estrado* had a dozen cushions according to Río Barredo 2018, p. 800.
74 AHPM, Prot. 8166, fols. 779v–780r, 791r, 794r.
75 Ibid., bed hangings appraised on fol. 788r.
76 On storage furniture for clothing, see Rodríguez Bernis 2014.
77 AHPM, Prot. 8166, furniture appraisal on fols. 778r–780r.
78 Ibid., fol. 778v.
79 Ibid., jewelry appraised on fols. 795v–797v. On jewelry, see Muller 1972, esp. pp. 124–9 on pendants with religious images.
80 AHPM, Prot. 8166, fol. 795v. On *higas*, see Muller 1972, p. 24.
81 AHPM, Prot. 8166, fols. 784r–788v.
82 Ibid., fols. 798r–805v.
83 Ibid., fol. 808r–v.
84 AGP, Per., caja 888/12, unnumbered docs. (November 17, 1672, and August 21, 1686).
85 AGP, AG, leg. 658, "Sastres de cámara de la Reina nuestra señora."
86 AGP, AG, leg. 658, "Señora doña Bernarda Ruiz de Reinoso viuda de Mateo Aguado."
87 AGP, AG, leg. 5648/2ª/14, "Mateo Aguado: Su cuenta de gajes ..."
88 APSG, Difuntos, lib. 11, fol. 276r.
89 AGP, Per., caja 11935/2.
90 APSG, Difuntos, lib. 13, fol. 170r.
91 AGP, Per., caja 11935/2.
92 Agulló y Cobo 1994, p. 66.
93 APSG, Difuntos, lib. 14, fol. 451r.
94 BNE, Mss/1674, vol. 10, fol. 167r.
95 Berni y Català 1769, p. 381.

CONCLUSION

1 Portús 2018.
2 Rocha Burguen 1618, unpag., "Carta del examen de la Corte." Thanks to Francisco Javier Moreno Díaz del Campo for sharing his expertise on the physical descriptions of persons in archival documents.
3 Dadson 1983, p. 75.
4 Warnke 1993, p. 120.
5 See, for example, the study of court embroiderers in Romero González 2021b.
6 See especially the works by Laura Oliván Santaliestra and Mercedes Llorente in the Bibliography.
7 Vega 1990, p. 121.
8 Solé Peñalosa 2009.
9 Aguilar Ochoa 2017.
10 Hume 1911, p. 339.
11 "Desengaño décimo" in Zayas y Sotomayor 2021, p. 648; English translation ("Tenth Tale of Disillusion") in Zayas y Sotomayor 2009, pp. 285–326.

Bibliography

ARCHIVAL SOURCES

Note on Archival Sources for the Life of Mateo Aguado
Documentation of Mateo Aguado's personal and professional life begins in 1630, the year he was sworn in as *sastre de cámara*. Information about his early years, including the date of his birth in Fuenlabrada around 1605 and his move to Madrid around 1611, is derived from later documents. Aguado's father and other likely relatives appear in tax records at the Municipal Archive of Fuenlabrada. There are 84 tax documents from the years 1603–15, which also provide valuable bits of information about life in the village where Aguado spent the first years of his life (AMF, Caja s. XVII). The main documents for Aguado's personal life are three notarized wills and testaments written in 1660, 1665, and 1672, and postmortem paperwork that includes an inventory of the tailor's possessions, all at Madrid's Historic Archive of Protocols (AHPM, Prots. 6514, 10097, and 8166). Aguado is also mentioned in the paperwork executing the estate of Francisco de Soria, the previous tailor to the queen (AHPM, Prot. 5684). Additional information about Aguado's personal life comes from the registers of baptisms and deaths at the Archive of the Parish of San Ginés (APSG) and marriage records at the Historic Diocesan Archive of Madrid (AHDM).

Aguado's work life is thoroughly documented at the General Archive of the Palace in Madrid. There is a robust personnel file on Aguado, with 30 documents from 1644–68 that detail the highs and lows of his career at court (AGP, Per., caja 16/10). Further details about Aguado's career can be found in other bundles (*legajos*) related to court artisans (AGP, AG, legs. 629, 658, and 5648/2ª/14). There are over 870 pages of documents—accounts (*cuentas*) with financial information and less-detailed charges (*cargos*)—recording the work that Aguado did for Philip IV's queens, their children, and charity and favors between 1630 and 1663. The 1630s are especially well-documented, with *cuentas* that include financial information for every year except 1632–3 (AGP, AG, legs. 5272/2 and 5272/3). There are only a few *cuentas* for the 1640s–1650s; fortunately, these include the eventful year 1659, when María Teresa's marriage to Louis XIV was being arranged (AGP, AG, leg. 5272/3). *Cargos* have been found for 1641–6 and 1649–63 (AGP, AG, leg. 904). The royal silk merchants' records provide an enormous amount of information about the materials that they provided to Aguado; here again, the era of Isabel of Bourbon is better-documented than that of Mariana (the 1630s are in AGP, AG, legs. 5251/2, 5252/1, and 5252/2; the years 1641–4 in 5253/1; 1650 in 5253/2; and 1659 in 5255/1). Payments owed to Aguado are recorded in the account records of the Keeper of the Queen's Wardrobe at the General Archive of Simancas (AGS), but I only scratched the surface of these records, and more remains to be found there.

Archivo General de Palacio, Madrid (AGP)
Administración General (AG):
- legs. 629, 658, 911, 5648/2ª/14: Various documents on royal artisan appointments, wages, etc.
- leg. 904: Mateo Aguado's charges and other documents related to the royal wardrobe
- leg. 5215/1: Accounts of the embroiderers
- leg. 5219/6: Accounts of the *chapines*-makers
- legs. 5251/2, 5252/1, 5252/2, 5253/1, 5253/2, 5255/1: Accounts of the silk merchants
- legs. 5272/1, 5272/2, 5272/3: Accounts of the tailors
- leg. 5278/1: Accounts of the shoemakers
- leg. 5278/9: Accounts of the farthingale-makers

Personal (Per.):
- caja 14/13: Antonio Aguado, assistant in the queen's wardrobe
- caja 16/10: Mateo Aguado, tailor of the chamber of the queen
- caja 389/10: Josefa de Gamboa, stocking-maker of the queen
- caja 407/31: Juan García de la Fuente, embroiderer of the queen
- caja 682/27: Manuel Milor, furrier of the queen
- caja 781/4: Sebastiana de Palacios, embroiderer of the king

caja 828/11: Juan Petil and Jiraldo de Urice, French tailors
caja 888/12: Isidro Robledo, tailor of the chamber of the queen
caja 928/22: Gaspar Ruiz, hatmaker of the king
caja 950/29: Francisco Antonio Salinas, farthingale-maker of the queen
caja 1065/15: Catalina de Vallejo, gold-wire drawer of the royal house
caja 1067/11: Juan Varela, tailor of the chamber of the king and doorman
caja 11935/2: Nicolás Tomás Aguado, assistant in the palace larder
caja 16708/21: Juan Cadenas, former tailor of the chamber of the Empress María Ana
caja 16878/11: Francisco Esteban, wardrobe assistant and tailor of the chamber of the king

Archivo General de Simancas (AGS)
Contaduría Mayor de Cuentas (CMC):
3ª *época*, leg. 2286, exp. 2
Contadurías Generales (CCG):
libs. de donativos, 59 and 86

Archivo Histórico Diocesano de Madrid (AHDM)
Expedientes matrimoniales:
2654/43: Gaspar Ruiz and Juana Reinoso (1617)
2733/71: Mateo Aguado and Alfonsa Martínez (1630)
Fábrica:
2561: *Inventario general de todas las alhajas y bienes desta iglesia de Santa María la Real de Almudena según el auto de visita de 1693*

Archivo Histórico Nacional, Madrid (AHN)
Consejos:
25498, exp. 7: *Pleito de Jerónimo de Arce, Lucas de Riaño y otros maestros sastres contra Francisco de Soria, Blas Muñoz y consortes, veedores y examinadores de dicho gremio sobre las condiciones para ser elegidos en estos oficios* (1624; includes docs. from 1618 to 1629)
leg. 7137: *Sobre reformación de todo género de abusos y excesos* (1621–68)
libs. 1200, 1206, 1207, 1213, 1214, 1218, 1221, 1225, 1231, 1240: Various documents regulating the making and selling of clothes and accessories in Madrid

Archivo Histórico de Protocolos de Madrid (AHPM)
Prot. 5300: Francisco de Medinilla, tailor apprentice contract (1624), fols. 214r–v, transcribed by José A. Nieto Sánchez
Prot. 5412: Queen Isabel of Bourbon, posthumous inventory and estate appraisal (1645)
Prot. 5556: Bartolomé Hernández, tailor apprentice contract (1627), fols. 147v–148r, transcribed by José A. Nieto Sánchez
Prot. 5622: Eugenio de la Cruz, tailor apprentice contract (1624), fols. 470r–v, transcribed by José A. Nieto Sánchez
Prot. 5684: Francisco de Soria, posthumous inventory and estate appraisal (1636)
Prot. 6514: Mateo Aguado, testament (1660), fols. 92r–97r
Prot. 8166: Mateo Aguado, final testament, posthumous inventory, and estate appraisal (1672–4), fols. 746r–827r
Prot. 10097: Mateo Aguado, testament (1665), fols. 393r–398v

Archivo Histórico Provincial de Cuenca (AHPC)
Jud-62/15: *Inventario de bienes de Pedro Rodríguez de Baldivieso* (1631), transcribed by Elena Morejón Burón for the *Corpus Léxico de Inventarios* <web.frl.es/CORLEXIN.html>

Archivo Municipal de Fuenlabrada (AMF)
Caja s. XVII:
C-O-20: *Repartimiento del salario del médico* (1601)
C-O-25: *Repartimiento del salario del médico* (1596)
C-O-45: *Repartimiento del salario de las guardas* (1607)

Archivo de la Parroquia de San Ginés, Madrid (APSG)
Bautismos: libs. 18, 24, 25, 26, 27, 28
Difuntos: libs. 6, 7, 10, 11, 13, 14
Matrimonios: libs. 5, 9

MANUSCRIPT SOURCES

Biblioteca del Museo Nacional del Prado, Madrid (BMNP)
SG Pra.Gen (55): *Inventarios Reales*, 12 vols., (n.d.)

British Library, London (BL)
Add. Ms. 24947: *Consultas hechas al Rey Phelipe 4 con las resoluciones de su propio puño*, 1643–8

Biblioteca Nacional de España, Madrid (BNE)

Mss/1007: *Etiquetas de Palacio: Cédulas reales sobre el gobierno y etiqueta de la Casa de la Reina y oficios que en ella había, con las obligaciones de cada uno y sus gajes*, 1603/40

Mss/1668: Antonio de las Ribas, *Planimetría general de Madrid*, 1749–74, vol. 4

Mss/1674: Antonio de las Ribas, *Planimetría general de Madrid*, 1749–74, vol. 10

Mss/2348: "Relación de la jornada de las entregas de las Serenísimas Señoras Doña Ana, Reina de Francia, y Doña Isabel, Princesa de España, hechas en los meses de octubre y noviembre de este año de 1615," in *Sucesos del año 1611 al de 1617*, 17th-century ms., fols. 219r–232r

Mss/2387: "Relación de la venida y entrada en Madrid del Duque de Agramont," in *Sucesos de los años 1659 y 1660*, 17th-century ms., fols. 1r–3r

Mss/13163: *Papeles de D. Juan Chumacero y Carrillo, referentes a su presidencia de Consejo de Castilla en los años 1643–1648*, 18th-century ms., vol. 1

Mss/18196: "Observación sobre lo que deben hacer y guardar las mozas de cámara de la Reina nuestra señora" (1621), in *Papeles varios del reinado de Felipe IV*, 17th-century ms., fols. 140r–142r

PRINTED SOURCES

Note on Early-Modern Titles

Spelling, accents, capitalization, and punctuation are erratic in the titles of early-modern printed books. In order to help the reader locate these works, this bibliography generally follows the transcriptions of titles of seventeenth-century Spanish sources in the general catalogue of the Biblioteca Nacional de España <catalogo.bne.es/>.

Abad Zardoya, Carmen, 2016, "Ratas, cenizas y perlas: El vocabulario del color en los interiores del siglo XVIII," *Res mobilis*, 5:5, pp. 21–46

Ágreda, María de Jesús, 1885–86, *Cartas de la venerable madre Sor María de Ágreda y del Señor Rey don Felipe IV*, ed. Francisco Silvela, 2 vols. (Madrid: Sucesores de Rivadeneyra)

———, 1991, *Correspondencia con Felipe IV: Religión y razón de estado*, ed. Consolación Baranda (Madrid: Castalia)

Aguilar Ochoa, Arturo, 2017, "La indumentaria novohispana del siglo XVII y su uso para la datación de tres biombos virreinales," *Anales del Museo de América*, 25, pp. 94–108

Agulló y Cobo, Mercedes, 1994, *Documentos para la historia de la pintura española*, vol. 1 (Madrid: Museo Nacional del Prado)

Alberti, Alberto, 1650, *Paradoxa moralia de ornatu mulierum* (Milan: Francisco Mognagae)

Alcega, Juan de, 1580 and 1589, *Libro de geometria, practica, y traça: El qual trata de lo tocante al officio de sastre* [...] (Madrid: Guillermo Drouy)

———, 1999, *Tailor's Pattern Book, 1589*, facsimile edn, trans. Jean Pain and Cecilia Bainton, intro. and notes J. L. Nevinson (New York: Costume & Fashion Press)

Alvar Ezquerra, Alfredo, María Elena García Guerra, and María de los Ángeles Vicioso Rodríguez, 1993, *Relaciones topográficas de Felipe II: Madrid*, vol. 1 (Madrid: Comunidad de Madrid and CSIC)

Anderson, Ruth, 1969, *The Golilla: A Spanish Collar of the 17th Century* (New York: Hispanic Society of America)

———, 1979, *Hispanic Costume, 1480–1530* (New York: Hispanic Society of America)

Andrés de Uztárroz, Juan Francisco, 1646, *Obelisco historico i honorario que la imperial ciudad de Zaragoza erigio a la immortal memoria del señor don Balthasar Carlos de Austria* [...] (Zaragoza: Hospital R. i G. de Nuestra Señora de Gracia)

Andújar, Martín de, 1640, *Geometria y trazas pertenecientes al oficio de sastres* [...] (Madrid: Imprenta del Reino)

Archivo Histórico Nacional, 1925, *Consejo de Castilla: Sala de Alcaldes de Casa y Corte: Catálogo por materias* (Cuenca: Imprenta del Seminario Conciliar)

Arizzoli-Clémentel, Pierre, and Pascale Gorguet Ballesteros (eds.), 2009, *Fastes de cour et cérémonies royales: Le costume de cour en Europe, 1650–1800*, exh. cat. (Paris: Réunion des Musées Nationaux)

Arnold, Janet, 1975, "Decorative Features: Pinking, Snipping and Slashing," *Costume*, 9:1, pp. 22–6

———, 1988, *Queen Elizabeth's Wardrobe Unlock'd* (Leeds: Maney)

Arnold, Janet, Jenny Tiramani, and Luca Costigliolo, 2018, *The Content, Cut, Construction and Context of Bodies, Stays, Hoops and Rumps c. 1595–1795*, Patterns of Fashion 5 (London: The School of Historical Dress)

Arnold, Janet, Jenny Tiramani, and Santina Levey, 2008, *The Cut and Construction of Linen Shirts, Smocks, Neckwear, Headwear and Accessories for Men and Women c. 1540–1660*, Patterns of Fashion 4 (London: Macmillan)

Arraiza, Alberto Bartolomé, and Cristina Partearroyo, 1999, "Alfombras," in *Summa Artis*, vol. 45, *Artes Decorativas II* (Madrid: Espasa Calpe), pp. 203–56

[Ayala Manrique, Juan Francisco], 1886, *La corte y monarquía de España en los años de 1636 y 37*, ed. Antonio Rodríguez Villa (Madrid: Luis Navarro)

Bacci, Mina, 1963, "Lettere inedite di Baccio del Bianco," *Paragone*, 14:157, pp. 68–77

Bandrés Oto, Maribel, 2002, *La moda en la pintura: Velázquez: Usos y costumbres del siglo 17* (Pamplona: EUNSA)

Barrio Moya, José Luis, 2008, "La biblioteca del fuenlabreño Mateo Aguado, sastre de cámara de las reinas Isabel de Borbón y Mariana de Austria (1672)," *Anales del Instituto de Estudios Históricos del Sur de Madrid "Jiménez de Gregorio"*, 8, pp. 139–65

Barrionuevo, Jerónimo de, 1968–9, *Avisos (1654–1658)*, 2 vols., ed. A. Paz y Meliá, Biblioteca de autores españoles, vols. 221–2 (Madrid: Atlas)

Bass, Laura R., and Amanda Wunder, 2009, "The Veiled Ladies of the Early Modern Spanish World: Seduction and Scandal in Seville, Madrid, and Lima," *Hispanic Review*, 77:1, pp. 97–144

———, 2014, "Fashion and Urban Views in Seventeenth-Century Madrid," in José Luis Colomer and Amalia Descalzo (eds.), *Spanish Fashion at the Courts of Early Modern Europe*, vol. 1 (Madrid: CEEH), pp. 363–84

Bastl, Beatrix, and José Luis Colomer, 2014, "Two Spanish Infantas at the Imperial Court," in José Luis Colomer and Amalia Descalzo (eds.), *Spanish Fashion at the Courts of Early Modern Europe*, vol. 2 (Madrid: CEEH), pp. 137–72

Baticle, Jeannine, 1960, "Note sur les portraits de la Maison de Bourbon envoyés en Espagne au XVIIe siècle," *La revue des arts*, 10:4-5, pp. 195–200

Bergman, Hannah E., 1965, *Luis Quiñones de Benavente y sus entremeses* (Madrid: Castalia)

Berni y Català, Joseph, 1769, *Creación, antigüedad, y privilegios de los títulos de Castilla* (Valencia: The Author)

Bernis, Carmen, 1982a, "El traje de viudas y dueñas en los cuadros de Velázquez y su escuela," *Miscelánea de arte* (Madrid: Instituto Diego Velázquez, CSIC), pp. 145–54

———, 1982b, "El vestido francés en la España de Felipe IV," *Archivo español de arte*, 55:218, pp. 201–8

———, 1991, "Velázquez y el guardainfante," in *Velázquez y el arte de su tiempo*, V Jornadas de Arte (Madrid: Alpuerto), pp. 49–60

———, 1994, "La moda en los retratos de Velázquez," in *El retrato en el Museo del Prado* (Madrid: Anaya), pp. 271–301

———, 2001, *El traje y los tipos sociales en "El Quijote"* (Madrid: Ediciones El Viso)

Bernis, Carmen, and Amalia Descalzo, 2014, "Spanish Female Dress in the Habsburg Period," in José Luis Colomer and Amalia Descalzo (eds.), *Spanish Fashion at the Courts of Early Modern Europe*, vol. 1 (Madrid: CEEH), pp. 39–75

Bertaut, François, 1664, *Relation d'un voyage d'Espagne, où est exactement décrit l'estat de la Cour de ce royaume, & de son gouvernement* (Paris: Claude Barbin)

———, 1669, *Journal du voyage d'Espagne, contenant une description fort exacte de ses royaumes et de ses principales villes, avec l'estat du gouvernement* […] (Paris: Claude Barbin)

Blasco Esquivias, Beatriz, 2017, "Vivir y convivir: Familia y espacio doméstico en la Edad Moderna," in Margarita María Birriel Salcedo (ed.), *La(s) casa(s) en la Edad Moderna* (Zaragoza: Instituto "Fernando el Católico"), pp. 65–92

———, 2018, "La plaza en fiestas (1617–2017)," in Beatriz Blasco Esquivias (ed.), *La Plaza Mayor, 400 años: Retrato y máscara de Madrid*, exh. cat. (Madrid: Museo de Historia de Madrid), pp. 75–103

Blum, André, 1951, *Early Bourbon, 1590–1643*, Costume of the Western World (London: George G. Harrap)

Bocángel y Unzueta, Gabriel, 1648, *Piedra candida con que en real, y festiua mascara numera los felicissimos años de* […] *Maria Ana de Austria* […] *el rey N.S. don Felipe IIII* (Madrid: Diego Díaz de la Carrera)

———, [1649], *El nueuo olimpo: Representacion real, y festiua mascara que a los felicissimos años de la Reyna* […] *celebraron la atencion amante del rey* […] *y el obsequio y cariño de la Serenissima Señora Infante, damas y meninas del Real Palacio* (Madrid: Diego Díaz de la Carrera)

Bodart, Diane, 2011, *Pouvoirs du portrait sous les Habsbourg d'Espagne* (Paris: CTHS-INHA)

Boucher, François, 1987, *20,000 Years of Fashion: The History of Costume and Personal Adornment* [1965], exp. edn (New

York: Harry N. Abrams)
Bouza, Fernando, 2015, "Vivir en hábito de: La Cultura de la indumentaria en el Siglo de Oro," in Rafael García Serrano (ed.), *La moda española en el Siglo de Oro*, exh. cat. (Toledo: Junta de Comunidades de Castilla La Mancha), pp. 21–32
Braun, Melanie, Luca Costigliolo, Susan North, Claire Thornton, and Jenny Tiramani, 2016, *17th-Century Men's Dress Patterns: 1600–1630* (London: Thames and Hudson)
Brown, Jonathan, 1986, *Velázquez: Painter and Courtier* (New Haven and London: Yale University Press)
———, 2008a, "On the Meaning of *Las Meninas* (1978)," in *Collected Essays on Velázquez* (Madrid: CEEH), pp. 47–75
———, 2008b, "Enemies of Flattery: Velázquez's Portraits of Philip IV (1986)," in *Collected Essays on Velázquez* (Madrid: CEEH), pp. 103–15
———, 2008c, "Velázquez in the 1630s and 1640s (1999)," in *Collected Essays on Velázquez* (Madrid: CEEH), pp. 151–63
Brown, Jonathan (ed.), 1999, *Velázquez, Rubens y Van Dyck: Pintores cortesanos del siglo XVII*, exh. cat. (Madrid: Museo Nacional del Prado and Ediciones El Viso)
Brown, Jonathan, and John H. Elliott, 2002, *The Sale of the Century: Artistic Relations between Spain and Great Britain, 1604–1655* (New Haven and London: Yale University Press)
———, 2003, *A Palace for a King: The Buen Retiro and the Court of Philip IV* [1980], rev. and exp. edn (New Haven and London: Yale University Press)
Brown, Jonathan, and Carmen Garrido, 2003, *Velázquez: The Technique of Genius* (New Haven and London: Yale University Press)
[Brunel, Antoine de], 1670, *A Journey into Spain* (London: Henry Herringman)
Bullón, José María, 2021, "Las Meninas: Una indumentaria familiar," *Además de: Revista on line de artes decorativas y diseño*, 7, pp. 9–40
Burke, Marcus, and Peter Cherry, 1997, *Collections of Paintings in Madrid, 1601–1755*, 2 vols. (Los Angeles: The Provenance Index of The Getty Information Institute)
Burnham, Dorothy K., 1981, *Warp & Weft: A Dictionary of Textile Terms* [1980] (New York: Scribner)
Buss, Chiara, 2017, "Half-Tints in Italy in 1628: An Unusual Book of Samples from the Milan State Archives," in Thomas Ertl and Barbara Karl (eds.), *Inventories of Textiles, Textiles in Inventories: Studies on Late Medieval and Early Modern Material Culture* (Göttingen: Vienna University Press), pp. 165–200
Cabrero Garrido, Félix, 2004, "Fuenlabrada," in Andrés Pérez Tirado et al. (eds.), *Arquitectura y desarrollo urbano: Comunidad de Madrid*, vol. II (Madrid: Dirección General de Arquitectura), pp. 382–587
Calderón de la Barca, Pedro, 2019, *Las armas de la hermosura*, ed. Laura Hernández González (Valladolid: Universidad de Valladolid)
Cámara Muñoz, Alicia, 2006, "La dimensión social de la casa," in Beatriz Blasco Esquivias (ed.), *La casa: Evolución del espacio doméstico en España*, vol. I (Madrid: Ediciones El Viso), pp. 125–99
"Campañas de Cataluña y Extremadura del año de 1644," in José Sancho Rayón and Francisco de Zabálburu (eds.), 1890, *Colección de documentos inéditos para la historia de España*, vol. 95 (Madrid: Rafael Marco y Viñas), pp. 361–465
Campbell, Thomas P. (ed.), 2007, *Tapestry in the Baroque: Threads of Splendor*, exh. cat. (New York: Metropolitan Museum of Art)
Campos y Fernández de Sevilla, Francisco Javier, 2012, "La Virgen del Patrocinio y el Monasterio del Escorial," in *Advocaciones Marianas de Gloria*, Simposium XXa Edición (San Lorenzo de El Escorial: Ediciones Escurialensis), pp. 699–732
Capella Martínez, Miguel, 1962, *La industria en Madrid: Ensayo histórico-crítico de la fabricación y artesanía madrileñas*, vol. I (Madrid: n.p.)
Capitulos de reformacion, que Su Magestad se sirue de mandar guardar por esta ley, para el gouierno del Reyno, 1623 (Madrid: Tomas Junta)
Capmani y Montpalau, Antonio de, 1863, *Origen histórico y etimológico de las calles de Madrid* (Madrid: Manuel B. de Quirós)
Carlos Varona, María Cruz de, 2018, *Nacer en palacio: El ritual del nacimiento en la corte de los Austrias* (Madrid: CEEH)
Carr, Dawson, et al., 2006, *Velázquez*, exh. cat. (London: National Gallery)
Carranza, Alonso, 1636, *Discurso contra los malos trajes y adornos lascivos* (Madrid: María de Quiñones)
Cartas jesuitas, 1861–5, Pascual de Gayangos (ed.), *Cartas de algunas PP. de la Compañía de Jesús*, 7 vols. Memorial

histórico español, vols. 13–19 (Madrid: Imprenta Nacional)
Casanova, José de, 1650, *Primera parte del Arte de escrivir todas formas de letras* (Madrid: Diego Díaz de la Carrera)
Castillo Solórzano, Alonso de, 2016, *La niña de los embustes, Teresa de Manzanares*, ed. María Soledad Arredondo (Barcelona: Penguin Clásicos)
Cervantes, Miguel de, 1998, "The Jealous Old Man from Extremadura," in *Exemplary Stories*, ed. and trans. Lesley Lipson (Oxford: Oxford University Press), pp. 150–84
———, 2010, *"The Bagnios of Algiers" and "The Great Sultana": Two Plays of Captivity*, ed. and trans. Barbara Fuchs and Aaron J. Ilika (Philadelphia: University of Pennsylvania Press)
Checa, Fernando, 1994, "El Real Alcázar de Madrid," in Fernando Checa (ed.), *El Real Alcázar de Madrid: Dos siglos de arquitectura y coleccionismo en la corte de los reyes de España*, exh. cat. (Madrid: Nerea), pp. 16–35
———, 2008, *Velázquez: The Complete Paintings* (New York: Harry N. Abrams)
Cherry, Peter, 1997, "Seventeenth-Century Spanish Taste," in Marcus Burke and Peter Cherry, *Collections of Paintings in Madrid, 1601–1755*, vol. 1 (Los Angeles: The Provenance Index of The Getty Information Institute), pp. 1–107
Chesterton, Gilbert K., 1924, *St. Francis of Assisi* (New York: George H. Doran Company)
Cobo Delgado, Gemma, 2016, "Intercambios de retratos en la familia Habsburgo durante el siglo XVII: Entre Viena y Madrid," *Boletín del Seminario de Estudios de Arte y Arqueología*, 82, pp. 143–66
Codding, Mitchell A. (ed.), 2017, *Tesoros de la Hispanic Society of America: Visiones del mundo hispánico*, exh. cat. (Madrid: Museo Nacional del Prado; New York: Hispanic Society of America)
Codding, Mitchell A., and John O'Neill, 2021, *Treasures from the Hispanic Society Library*, exh. cat. (New York: The Hispanic Museum & Library)
Colenbrander, Sjoukje, 2013, *When Weaving Flourished: The Silk Industry in Amsterdam and Haarlem, 1585–1750*, trans. Peggy Birch (Amsterdam: Aronson Publishers)
Colomer, José Luis, 2003, "Paz política, rivalidad suntuaria: Francia y España en la Isla de Los Faisanes," in José Luis Colomer (ed.), *Arte y diplomacia de la Monarquía Hispánica en el siglo XVII* (Madrid: CEEH), pp. 61–88
———, 2014, "Black and the Royal Image," in José Luis Colomer and Amalia Descalzo (eds.), *Spanish Fashion at the Courts of Early Modern Europe*, vol. 1 (Madrid: CEEH), pp. 77–112
Colomer, José Luis, and Amalia Descalzo (eds.), 2014, *Spanish Fashion at the Courts of Early Modern Europe*, 2 vols. (Madrid: CEEH)
Cordato, Fabio Virgilio, 1639, *Grandezas del color pardo* (Orihuela: Juan Vicente Franco)
Corpus velazqueño, 2000, ed. Ángel Aterido Fernández, vol. 1 (Madrid: Ministerio de Educación, Cultura y Deporte)
Covarrubias Orozco, Sebastián de, 1995, *Tesoro de la lengua castellana o española*, ed. Felipe C. Maldonado, rev. Manuel Camarero, 2nd corr. edn (Madrid: Castalia)
Crombie, Theodore, 1958, "Isabella of Bourbon by Velázquez," *The Connoisseur*, 141:570, pp. 238–44
Cruz Valdovinos, José Manuel, 2011, *Velázquez: Vida y obra de un pintor cortesano* (Zaragoza: Caja Inmaculada)
Cubillo de Aragón, Álvaro, 1659, *Relacion breue, de la solemnissima entrada que hizo en la Villa de Madrid* [...] *al Excelentissimo Señor Duque de Agramont* [...] (Madrid: Andrés García de la Iglesia)
Currie, Elizabeth, 2006, "Diversity and Design in the Florentine Tailoring Trade, 1550–1620," in Michelle O'Malley and Evelyn Welch (eds.), *The Material Renaissance* (Manchester: Manchester University Press), pp. 154–73
Dadson, Trevor J., 1983, *The Genoese in Spain: Gabriel Bocángel y Unzueta (1603–58): A Biography* (London: Tamesis)
Dávila, Juan Francisco, [1648], *Relacion de los festivos aplausos con que celebrò esta Corte Catolica las alegres nuevas del feliz Desposorio del Rey* [...] *Don Felipe Quarto* [...] *y el cumplimiento de años de la Reyna* (Madrid: Domingo García y Morrás)
Dávila Corona, Rosa María, Montserrat Durán Pujol, and Máximo García Fernández, 2004, *Diccionario histórico de telas y tejidos: Castellano-catalán* (Salamanca: Junta de Castilla y León, Consejería de Cultura y Turismo)
Deleito y Piñuela, José, 1946, *La mujer, la casa y la moda (en la España del rey poeta)* (Madrid: Espasa-Calpe)
Descalzo, Amalia, 2014, "Spanish Male Costume in the Habsburg Period," in José Luis Colomer and Amalia Descalzo (eds.), *Spanish Fashion at the Courts of Early Modern Europe*, vol. 1 (Madrid: CEEH), pp. 15–38

Descalzo Lorenzo, Amalia, 2007, "Velázquez y la moda: Aproximación a la identidad de *La dama del abanico*," in *In sapientia libertas: Escritos en homenaje al profesor Alfonso E. Pérez Sánchez* (Madrid: Museo Nacional del Prado), pp. 435–40

Díaz del Valle, Lázaro, 1991, "Origen yllustración del nobilíssimo y real arte de la pintura," in Francisco Calvo Serraller (ed.), *La teoría de la pintura en el Siglo de Oro* [1981], 2nd edn (Madrid: Cátedra), pp. 461–78

Diccionario de autoridades, 1726–39, Real Academia Española, *Diccionario de la lengua castellana* [...], 6 vols. (Madrid: Francisco del Hierro) <apps2.rae.es/DA.html>

Domínguez Ortiz, Antonio, Alfonso E. Pérez Sánchez, and Julián Gállego, 1989, *Velázquez*, exh. cat. (New York: Metropolitan Museum of Art)

Doval Trueba, María del Mar, 2003, *Los "Velazqueños": Pintores que trabajaron en el taller de Velázquez*, PhD dissertation (Universidad Complutense de Madrid)

Eclipsòse el Sol de España, el mayor Monarca [...] *el Rey Felipe Quarto el Grande* [1665] (n.p.)

Elliott, John H., 1963, *The Revolt of the Catalans: A Study in the Decline of Spain (1598–1640)* (Cambridge: Cambridge University Press)

———, 1986, *The Count-Duke of Olivares: The Statesman in an Age of Decline* (New Haven and London: Yale University Press)

———, 1997a, "The Court of the Spanish Habsburgs: A Peculiar Institution?" [1987], in *Spain and Its World: 1500–1700* (New Haven and London: Yale University Press), pp. 142–61

———, 1997b, "Philip IV of Spain: Prisoner of Ceremony," in Arthur Geoffrey Dickens (ed.), *The Courts of Europe: Politics, Patronage and Royalty 1400–1800* (London: Thames and Hudson), pp. 169–89

———, 2002, *Imperial Spain, 1469–1716* [1963], rev. edn (London: Penguin Books)

Escobar, Jesús, 2003, *The Plaza Mayor and the Shaping of Baroque Madrid* (Cambridge: Cambridge University Press)

———, 2014, "Map as Tapestry: Science and Art in Pedro Teixeira's 1656 Representation of Madrid," *Art Bulletin*, 96:1, pp. 50–69

———, 2022, *Habsburg Madrid: Architecture and the Spanish Monarchy* (University Park: Pennsylvania State University Press)

Ettinghausen, Henry, 2014, "Fashion Reporting in Early Seventeenth-Century Spain: Andrés de Almansa y Mendoza and Prince Charles's Spanish Trip," in José Luis Colomer and Amalia Descalzo (eds.), *Spanish Fashion at the Courts of Early Modern Europe*, vol. 1 (Madrid: CEEH), pp. 419–45

Fanshawe, Ann, 1907, *The Memoirs of Ann, Lady Fanshawe* (London: John Lane)

Fernández, Luis, 1778, *Tratado instructivo, y práctico sobre el arte de la tintura: Reglas experimentadas y metódicas para tintar sedas, lanas, hilos de todas clases, y esparto en rama* (Madrid: Blas Román)

Fernández Fernández, José Antonio, 2022, *La indumentaria infantil en la corte española de los Habsburgo (1556–1621)*, PhD dissertation (Universidad Politécnica de Madrid)

Franganillo Álvarez, Alejandra, 2017a, "Isabel de Borbón and the Governance of the Spanish Monarchy," *Early Modern Women*, 12:1, pp. 25–47

———, 2017b, "Servicio y deservicio a Felipe IV: Los Príncipes de Carignano, entre Francia y la Monarquía Hispánica (1634–1644)," *Hispania: Revista española de historia*, 77:255, pp. 91–115

———, 2020, *A la sombra de la reina: Poder, patronazgo y servicio en la corte de la Monarquía Hispánica (1615–1644)* (Madrid: CSIC)

Freyle, Diego de, 1588, *Geometria y traça para el oficio de los sastres* [...] (Seville: Fernando Díaz)

Frick, Carole Collier, 2002, *Dressing Renaissance Florence: Families, Fortunes, and Fine Clothing* (Baltimore: The Johns Hopkins University Press)

Funes de Villalpando, Francisco Jacinto (Marquess of Osera), 2013, *Escribir la corte de Felipe IV: El diario del Marqués de Osera, 1657–1659*, ed. Santiago Martínez Hernández (Madrid: CEEH and Doce Calles)

Gallagher, Michael, 2010, "Velázquez's *Philip IV* in the Metropolitan Museum," *Metropolitan Museum Journal*, 45, pp. 187–98

Gállego, Julián, 1995, *El pintor, de artesano a artista* (Granada: Diputación Provincial de Granada)

García, Carlos, 1619, *Desordenada codicia de los bienes agenos* (Paris: Adrian Tiffeno)

———, 1642, *The Antipathy betweene the French and Spaniard*, trans. Robert Gentilys (London: Humphrey Moseley)

García Martín, Pedro, 2004, "De estética barroca: Vestido y belleza en la España del Siglo de Oro," *Ludica: Annali di storia e civiltà del gioco*, 10, pp. 165–78

García Serrano, Rafael (ed.), 2015, *La moda española en el Siglo de Oro*, exh. cat. (Toledo: Junta de Comunidades de Castilla La Mancha)

García Sierra, María José, 2014, "Who Dressed Kings and Queens? Royal Wardrobe and Court Tailors," in José Luis Colomer and Amalia Descalzo (eds.), *Spanish Fashion at the Courts of Early Modern Europe*, vol. 1 (Madrid: CEEH), pp. 113–35

Garrido, Carmen, 2014, "Diego Velázquez: Un retrato del natural de la Reina Isabel de Borbón," *Ge-conservación*, 6, pp. 83–100

Gascón de Torquemada, Gerónimo, 1991, *Gaçeta y nuevas de la corte de España desde el año 1600 en adelante*, ed. Alfonso de Ceballos-Escalera y Gila (Madrid: Real Academia Matritense de Heráldica y Genealogía)

Giorgi, Arianna, 2016, *España viste e la francesa: La historia de un traje de moda de la segunda mitad del siglo XVII* (Murcia: Editum Artes)

Goldstein, Carl, 1998, "Looking in the Mirror of Abraham Bosse," in Sue Welsh Reed (ed.), *French Prints from the Age of the Musketeers*, exh. cat. (Boston: Museum of Fine Arts), pp. 21–7

Gómez de Mora, Juan, 1632, *Relacion del iuramento que hizieron los Reinos de Castilla i Leon al Ser[enísi]mo don Baltasar Carlos* [...] (Madrid: Francisco Martínez)

Gómez Menéndez, Mercedes, 2019, "La Virgen de la Almudena: Historia, leyendas y representaciones de la imagen venerada en la Catedral de Madrid," in Francisco Javier Campos y Fernández de Sevilla (ed.), *El mundo de las catedrales (España e Hispanoamérica)* (San Lorenzo de El Escorial: Instituto Escurialense de Investigaciones Históricas y Artísticas), pp. 533–52

Gómez Ruiz, Adriano, 1999, *Fuenlabrada: Cinco siglos de historia* (Fuenlabrada: Ayuntamiento de Fuenlabrada)

González de Santalla, Tirso, 1673, *Respuesta theologica acerca del abuso de los escotados dada al señor Andres Giron, arçobispo de Santiago* (Santiago: Antonio Fraiz Pineiro)

González Heras, Natalia, 2015, "La religiosidad doméstica de las elites al servicio de la Monarquía en el siglo XVIII: Reflejos materiales de actitudes piadosas," *Cuadernos de Historia Moderna*, 14, pp. 85–106

González Mena, María Angeles, 1974, *Catálogo de bordados* (Madrid: Instituto Valencia de Don Juan)

———, 1976, *Catálogo de encajes: Con una adición al catálogo de bordados* (Madrid: Instituto Valencia de Don Juan)

González Zymla, Herbert, 2003, *Catálogo de pinturas de la Real Academia de la Historia* (Madrid: Real Academia de la Historia)

Gordenker, Emilie E. S., 2001, *Anthony Van Dyck (1599–1641) and the Representation of Dress in Seventeenth-Century Portraiture* (Turnhout: Brepols)

Gracián, Baltasar, 1991, *The Art of Worldly Wisdom*, trans. Christopher Maurer (New York: Doubleday)

Gramont, Antoine de, 1717, *Mémoires du Marechal de Gramont, duc et pair de France* [...], vol. 2 (Amsterdam: La Compagnie)

Griffey, Erin (ed.), 2019, *Sartorial Politics in Early Modern Europe: Fashioning Women* (Amsterdam: Amsterdam University Press)

Gutiérrez de los Ríos, Gaspar, 1600, *Noticia general para la estimacion de las artes y de la manera en que se conocen las liberales de las que son mecanicas y seruiles* [...] (Madrid: Pedro Madrigal)

Haag, Sabine (ed.), 2014, *Velázquez*, exh. cat. (Munich: Hirmer)

Haan, Bertrand, 2020, "Diplomatic Stagecraft at the Court of Spain: The 1659 Reception for Louis XIV's Ambassador Antoine Gramont," in José Luis Colomer and Jorge Fernández-Santos (eds.), *Ambassadors in Golden-Age Madrid: The Court of Philip IV through Foreign Eyes* (Madrid: CEEH), pp. 147–71

Haggerty Museum of Art, 1984, *Selected Works: Patrick and Beatrice Haggerty Museum of Art, Marquette University* (New York: Pelion Press)

Hamann, Byron Ellsworth, 2010, "The Mirrors of *Las Meninas*: Cochineal, Silver, and Clay," *Art Bulletin* 92:1–2, pp. 6–35

Harris, Enriqueta, 2006, "The Cleaning of Velázquez's *Lady with a Fan* (1975)," in *Complete Studies on Velázquez* (Madrid: CEEH), pp. 113–18

Hayward, Maria, 2007, *Dress at the Court of King Henry VIII* (Leeds: Maney)

Hearn, Karen, 2020, *Portraying Pregnancy: From Holbein to Social Media* (London: Paul Holberton)

Herrero García, Miguel, 2014a, *Estudios sobre indumentaria española en la época de los Austrias* (Madrid: CEEH)

———, 2014b, *Los tejidos en la España de los Austrias: Fragmentos de un diccionario* (Madrid: CEEH)

Höbelt, Lothar, 2011, "'Madrid vaut bien une guerre?': Marriage Negotiations between the Habsburg Courts, 1653–1657," in José Martínez Millán and R. González Cuerva (eds.), *La dinastia de los Austria: Las relaciones entre la Monarquía Católica y el Imperio*, vol. 3 (Madrid: Polifemo), pp. 1421–36

Hoffman, Martha K., 2011, *Raised to Rule: Educating Royalty at the Court of the Spanish Habsburgs, 1601–1634* (Baton Rouge: Louisiana State University Press)

Hollander, Anne, 1993, *Seeing Through Clothes* [1978], reprint (Berkeley: University of California Press)

Hortal Muñoz, José Eloy, 2015, "La casa del rey," Appendix I in José Martínez Millán and José Eloy Hortal Muñoz (eds.), *La Corte de Felipe IV (1621–1665): Reconfiguración de la Monarquía católica* (Madrid: Polifemo), tome II: CD, pp. 741–2543

Howell, James, 1660, *Lexicon Tetraglotton: An English–French–Italian–Spanish Dictionary* (London: Samuel Thomson)

Hume, Martin Andrew Sharp, 1911, *Queens of Old Spain* (London: Grant Richards)

Hurtado de Mendoza, Antonio, 1632, *Convocacion de las Cortes de Castilla, y Iuramento del Principe* [...] *Don Baltasar Carlos* [...] (Madrid: Imprenta del Reino)

Huygens, Lodewijck, 2005, *Lodewijck Huygens' Spaans journaal: Reis naar het hof van de koning van Spanje, 1660–1661*, ed. Maurits Alexander Ebben (Zutphen: Walburg Pers)

———, 2010, *Un holandés en la España de Felipe IV: Diario del viaje de Lodewijck Huygens (1660–1661)*, ed. Maurits Alexander Ebben, trans. Goedele de Sterck (Madrid: Doce Calles and Fundación Carlos de Amberes)

Irigoyen-García, Javier, 2017, *"Moors Dressed as Moors": Clothing, Social Distinction and Ethnicity in Early Modern Iberia* (Toronto: University of Toronto Press)

Jaffé, Michael, 1992, "Rubens's *Portrait of Isabella de Bourbon, Queen of Spain*," *Artibus et Historiae*, 13:26, pp. 9–14

Jasienski, Adam, 2021, "Velázquez and the Fragile Portrait of the King," *Art History*, 44:5, pp. 922–47

Jiménez Patón, Bartolomé, 1638, *Reforma de trages* (Baeza: Juan de la Cuesta)

Jordan, William B., 2006, *Juan van der Hamen y León and the Court of Madrid*, exh. cat. (New Haven and London: Yale University Press)

Jurado Sánchez, José, 2005, *La economía de la corte: El gasto de la Casa Real en la Edad Moderna (1561–1808)* (Madrid: Instituto de Estudios Fiscales)

Kagan, Richard L., and Marianna S. Simpson, 2018, "Two Seventeenth-Century Garden Views from the Royal Palace of Aranjuez," *Boletín del Museo del Prado*, 36:54, pp. 110–17

Keith, Larry, 2006, "Velázquez's Painting Technique," in Dawson Carr et al., *Velázquez*, exh. cat. (London: National Gallery), pp. 70–89

Kientz, Guillaume, 2015a, *Velázquez*, exh. cat. (Paris: Réunion des Musées Nationaux-Grand Palais)

———, 2015b, *Velázquez: L'affrontement de la peinture* (Paris: Cohen & Cohen)

La pompe et magnificence faite au mariage du roy et de l'infante d'Espagne, 1660 (Paris: Jean Promé)

Larquié, Claude, 1966, "Étude de démographie madrilène: La paroisse de San Ginés de 1650 à 1700," *Mélanges de la Casa de Velázquez*, 2, pp. 225–58

———, 1988, "La famille madrilène du XVIIe siècle," *Mélanges de la Casa de Velázquez*, 24, pp. 139–52

León Pinelo, Antonio de, 1971, *Anales de Madrid (desde el año 447 al de 1658)*, ed. Pedro Fernández Martín (Madrid: Instituto de Estudios Madrileños)

Levey, Santina M., 1983, *Lace: A History* (London: Victoria and Albert Museum, and Maney)

Linthicum, M. Channing, 1936, *Costume in the Drama of Shakespeare and His Contemporaries* (Oxford: Clarendon)

Llorente, Mercedes, 2006, "Imagen y autoridad en una regencia: Los retratos de Mariana de Austria y los límites del poder," *Studia historica: Historia moderna*, 28, pp. 211–38

———, 2011, "Portraits of Children at the Spanish Court in the Seventeenth Century: The Infanta Margarita and the Young King Carlos II," *Bulletin for Spanish and Portuguese Historical Studies*, 35:1, pp. 30–47

———, 2019, "La representación de dos reinas ibéricas: Luisa de Guzmán y Mariana de Austria," in Gonzalo del Puerto y Gil, Mercedes Llorente, and Renato Epifânio (eds.), *Mulheres da realeza ibérica mediadoras políticas e culturais* (Lisbon: Instituto Cervantes), pp. 159–88

López Barahona, Victoria, and José A. Nieto Sánchez, 2010, "La formación de un mercado de trabajo: Las industrias del vestido en el Madrid de la edad moderna," *Sociología del trabajo*, 68, pp. 147–69

———, 2011, "La ropa estandarizada: Innovaciones en la producción, comercio y consumo de vestuario en el Madrid del

Siglo XVII," *Sociología del trabajo*, 71, pp. 118–36
López Castán, Ángel, 1986, "El gremio de pasamaneros de Madrid en los siglos XVII y XVIII: Estudio histórico artístico y jurídico de su organización corporativa," *Anales del Instituto de Estudios Madrileños*, 23, pp. 207–25
López Navío, José, 1960, "Matrimonio de Juan B. del Mazo con la hija de Velázquez," *Archivo español de arte*, 33:129, pp. 387–420
López-Rey, José, 1996, *Velázquez*, 2 vols. (Cologne: Taschen)
Macartney, Hilary, 2002, "La Colección Stirling Maxwell en Pollok House, Glasgow," *Goya: Revista de Arte*, 291, pp. 345–56
Magidson, Phyllis, 2013, "A Fashionable Equation: Maison Worth and the Clothes of the Gilded Age," in Donald Albrecht and Jeannine Falino (eds.), *Gilded New York: Design, Fashion, and Society* (New York: Museum of the City of New York and Monacelli Press), pp. 107–30
Malcolm, Alistair, 2005, "Spanish Queens and Aristocratic Women at the Court of Madrid, 1598–1665," in Christine Meek and Catherine Lawless (eds.), *Victims or Viragos?*, Studies on Medieval and Early Modern Women 4 (Dublin: Four Courts Press), pp. 160–80
———, 2006, "Public Morality and the Closure of the Theatres in the Mid-Seventeenth Century: Philip IV, the Council of Castile and the Arrival of Mariana of Austria," in Richard J. Pym (ed.), *Rhetoric and Reality in Early Modern Spain* (London: Tamesis), pp. 92–112
———, 2017, *Royal Favouritism and the Governing Elite of the Spanish Monarchy, 1640–1665* (Oxford: Oxford University Press)
Maravall, José Antonio, 1986, *Culture of the Baroque: Analysis of a Historical Structure* [original Spanish edn 1975], trans. Terry Cochran (Minneapolis: University of Minnesota Press)
Marcaida, José Ramón, 2022, "Velázquez, *ingenioso*: Intertextuality and Biographical Artifice in Early Modern Spanish Artistic Writing," *Bulletin of Spanish Visual Studies*, 6:1, pp. 73–103
Marín Perellón, Francisco J., 1988, "Planimetría general de Madrid y regalía de aposento," in Jesús Campos (ed.), *Planimetría general de Madrid*, vol. 2 (Madrid: Tabacalera), pp. 81–111
Marly, Diana de, 1987, *Louis XIV & Versailles* (London: Batsford)
Martín González, Juan José, 1993, *El artista en la sociedad española del siglo XVII* [1984], 2nd edn (Madrid: Cátedra)
Martínez, Jusepe, 1988, *Discursos practicables del nobilísimo arte de la pintura*, ed. Julián Gállego (Madrid: Akal)
Martínez Bonanad, David, 2019, "Costumbres, usos y representaciones del luto durante el gobierno de la Casa de Austria. El caso de las estancias reales durante la viudedad de Mariana de Austria," in *Vestir la arquitectura: XXII Congreso Nacional de Historia del Arte*, vol. 1 (Burgos: Universidad de Burgos), pp. 931–35
Martínez Leiva, Gloria, and Ángel Rodríguez Rebollo, 2015, *El inventario del Alcázar de Madrid de 1666: Felipe IV y su colección artística* (Madrid: Polifemo)
Martínez López, Rocío, 2015, "'La infanta se ha de casar con quien facilite la paz o disponga los medios para la guerra': Las negociaciones para la realización del matrimonio entre la infanta María Teresa y Leopoldo I (1654–1657)," *Revista de historia moderna: Anales de la Universidad de Alicante*, 33, pp. 79–99
Martínez Millán, José (ed.), 2015–18, *La Corte de Felipe IV (1621–1665): Reconfiguración de la Monarquía católica*, 4 tomes in 11 vols. and 1 CD-ROM (Madrid: Polifemo)
Mascareñas, Jerónimo, 1650, *Viage de la serenissima reyna doña Maria Ana de Austria segunda muger de don Phelipe Quarto [...] hasta la real corte de Madrid desde la imperial de Viena* (Madrid: Diego Díaz de la Carrera)
Massar, Phyllis Dearborn, 1977, "Scenes for a Calderón Play by Baccio del Bianco," *Master Drawings*, 15:4, pp. 365–75, 445–55
May, Florence Lewis, 1980, *Hispanic Lace and Lacemaking* (New York: Hispanic Society of America)
McDonald, Mark P., 2012, *Renaissance to Goya: Prints and Drawings from Spain*, exh. cat. (London: British Museum Press)
———, 2017, *The Paper Museum of Cassiano dal Pozzo*, Series C, Part I, *Ceremonies, Costumes, Portraits and Genre*, vol. 2 (London: Royal Collection Trust and The British Library)
McKendrick, Melveena, 2009, *Theatre in Spain, 1490–1700* [1989] (Cambridge: Cambridge University Press)
McKim-Smith, Gridley, Greta Andersen-Bergdoll, and Richard Newman, 1988, *Examining Velázquez* (New Haven and London: Yale University Press)
Méndez Silva, Rodrigo, 1637, *Dialogo compendioso [...] de Madrid, y recibimiento que en ella hizo su Magestad catolica*

con la grandeza de su Corte a la princesa de Cariñan [...] (Madrid: Viuda de Alonso Martín)

———, 1658, *Gloriosa celebridad de España en el feliz nacimiento, y solemnissimo bautismo de su deseado principe D. Felipe Prospero* [...] (Madrid: Francisco Nieto Salcedo)

Menéndez de Luarca, José Ramón, 2015, "Retratos de la infanta María Teresa por Velázquez y Martínez del Mazo," *Locus amoenus*, 13, pp. 43–56

Mesonero Romanos, Ramón de, 1861, *El antiguo Madrid: Paseos histórico-anecdóticos por las calles y casas de esta villa* (Madrid: F. de P. Mellado)

Meyer, Daniel, 1980, *L'Histoire du Roy* (Paris: Réunion des Musées Nationaux)

Miller, Lesley Ellis, 2014, "An Illustrious English Gentleman Dressed the Spanish Way: The Visit of the Prince of Wales to Madrid in 1623," in José Luis Colomer and Amalia Descalzo (eds.), *Spanish Fashion at the Courts of Early Modern Europe*, vol. 2 (Madrid: CEEH), pp. 293–315

———, 2019, "Surface and Substance: Baroque Dress in Spain and France, 1600–1720," in John D. Lyons (ed.), *The Oxford Handbook of the Baroque* (New York: Oxford University Press), pp. 238–63

Minsheu, John, 1599, *A Dictionarie in Spanish and English* (London: Edmund Bollifant) <ems.kcl.ac.uk/content/proj/anglo/dict/pro-anglo-dict-main.html>

Mitchell, Silvia Z., 2021, *Queen, Mother, and Stateswoman: Mariana of Austria and the Government of Spain* (University Park: Pennsylvania State University Press)

Monnas, Lisa, 2008, *Merchants, Princes and Painters: Silk Fabrics in Italian and Northern Paintings, 1300–1550* (New Haven and London: Yale University Press)

Montpensier, Anne-Marie-Louise d'Orléans, 1735, *Mémoires de Mademoiselle de Montpensier, fille de Gaston d'Orléans, frère de Louis XIII roi de France*, vol. 5 (Amsterdam: Wetstein & Smith)

———, 1848, *Memoirs of Mademoiselle de Montpensier, Grand-Daughter of Henri Quatre, and Niece of Queen Henrietta-Maria*, vol. 2 (London: H. Colburn)

Morán Turina, Miguel, 2010, "La escalera del convento de las Descalzas Reales de Madrid," in Ana García Sanz (ed.), *Pinturas murales de la escalera principal: Monasterio de las Descalzas Reales de Madrid* (Madrid: Patrimonio Nacional), pp. 39–54

Morte García, M. Carmen, 1990–91, "Pintura y política en la época de los Austrias: Los retratos de los reyes de Aragón para la Diputación de Zaragoza (1586), y las copias de 1634 para el Buen Retiro de Madrid," in 2 parts, *Boletín del Museo del Prado*, 11:29 (1990), pp. 19–36 and 12:30 (1991), pp. 13–28

Motteville, Françoise Bertaut de, 1723, *Mémoires pour servir à l'histoire d'Anne d'Autriche, épouse de Louis XIII, roi de France*, vol. 5 (Amsterdam: François Changuion)

———, 1902, *Memoirs of Madame de Motteville: On Anne of Austria and Her Court*, trans. Katherine P. Wormeley, vol. 3 (London: Heinemann)

Moulinier, Axel, and Sophie Vesin, 2015, "Women's Undergarments and the Submission of the Body in the Sixteenth Century," in Denis Bruna (ed.), *Fashioning the Body: An Intimate History of the Silhouette*, exh. cat. (New Haven and London: Yale University Press), pp. 57–65

Muller, Priscilla E., 1972, *Jewels in Spain: 1500–1800* (New York: Hispanic Society of America)

Museo Poldi Pezzoli, 1999, *Velluti e moda tra XV e XVII secolo* (Milan: Skira)

Ng, Aimee, Simone Facchinetti, and Arturo Galansino, 2019, *Moroni: The Riches of Renaissance Portraiture*, exh. cat. (New York: The Frick Collection)

Nieto Sánchez, José A., 1995, "La conflictividad laboral en Madrid durante el siglo XVII: El gremio de sastres," in *Actas del I Congreso de Jóvenes Geógrafos e Historiadores* (Seville: Escuela Libre de Historiadores), pp. 283–89

———, 2006, *Artesanos y mercaderes: Una historia social y económica de Madrid, 1450–1850* (Madrid: Fundamentos)

———, 2017, "Madrid como centro consumidor, productor y redistribuidor de tejidos de seda en la Edad Moderna," in Ricardo Franch Benavent and Germán Navarro Espinach (eds.), *Las rutas de la seda en la historia de España y Portugal* (Valencia: Universitat de València), pp. 245–74

North, Susan, and Jenny Tiramani (eds.), 2012, *Seventeenth-Century Women's Dress Patterns*, Book Two (London: V&A Publishing)

Noticia del recibimiento i entrada de la reyna nuestra señora doña Maria-Ana de Austria en la muy noble i leal coronada villa de Madrid, [1650] ([Madrid]: n.p.)

Novo Zaballos, José Rufino, and Henar Pizarro Llorente, 2015, "La casa de las reinas," Appendix II in José Martínez Millán and José Eloy Hortal Muñoz (eds.), *La Corte de*

Felipe IV (1621–1665): Reconfiguración de la Monarquía católica (Madrid: Polifemo), tome II: CD, pp. 2545–3087

Núñez de Castro, Alonso, 1658, *Libro historico politico: Solo Madrid es corte, y el Cortesano en Madrid* (Madrid: Andrés García de la Iglesia)

Oberthaler, Elke, and Monika Strolz, 2014, "On Velázquez's Late Painting Technique," in Sabine Haag (ed.), *Velázquez*, exh. cat. (Munich: Hirmer), pp. 284–9

Oliván Santaliestra, Laura, 2006, *Mariana de Austria: Imagen, poder y diplomacia de una reina cortesana* (Madrid: Editorial Complutense)

———, 2011, "Minerva, Hispania y Bellona: Cuerpo e imagen de Isabel de Borbón en el Salón de Reinos," *Chronica nova: Revista de historia moderna de la Universidad de Granada*, 37, pp. 271–300

———, 2012a, "'Decía que no se dejaba retratar de buena gana': Modestia e invisibilidad de la reina Isabel de Borbón (1635–1644)," *Goya: Revista de Arte*, 338, pp. 16–35

———, 2012b, "Isabel de Borbón, 'paloma medianera de la paz': Políticas y culturas de pacificación de una reina consorte en el siglo XVII," in Juan Manuel Jiménez Arenas and Francisco A. Muñoz Muñoz (eds.), *La Paz, partera de la historia* (Granada: Universidad de Granada), pp. 191–220

———, 2013, "Isabel of Borbón's Sartorial Politics: From French Princess to Habsburg Regent," in Anne J. Cruz and Maria Galli Stampino (eds.), *Early Modern Habsburg Women: Transnational Contexts, Cultural Conflicts, Dynastic Continuities* (Farnham: Ashgate), pp. 225–42

———, 2014, "'My Sister Is Growing up Very Healthy and Beautiful, She Loves Me': The Childhood of the *Infantas* María Teresa and Margarita María at Court," in Grace E. Coolidge (ed.), *The Formation of the Child in Early Modern Spain* (Farnham: Ashgate), pp. 165–87

———, 2016, "The Representational Strategies of the Count-Duke of Olivares and Elisabeth of France: Equestrian Portraits, *Guardainfantes* and Miniatures (1628–1644)," in Luc Duerloo and R. Malcolm Smuts (eds.), *The Age of Rubens: Diplomacy, Dynastic Politics and the Visual Arts in Early Seventeenth-Century Europe* (Turnhout: Brepols), pp. 213–34

———, 2019, "Clothes Make the Queen: Mariana of Austria's Style of Dress, from Archduchess to Queen Consort (1634–1665)," in Erin Griffey (ed.), *Sartorial Politics in Early Modern Europe: Fashioning Women* (Amsterdam: Amsterdam University Press), pp. 207–26

———, 2021, "Dresses, Portraits and Spaces: Female Identities at the Royal Alcázar (1621–1665)," in Jeremy Roe and Jean Andrews (eds.), *Representing Women's Political Identity in the Early Modern Iberian World* (New York: Routledge), pp. 274–92

Ordenanzas para oficiales maniobreros del Gremio de Sastres [...], [1754] (Madrid: n.p.)

Orso, Steven N., 1989, *Art and Death at the Spanish Habsburg Court: The Royal Exequies for Philip IV* (Columbia: University of Missouri Press)

———, 1990, "Praising the Queen: The Decorations at the Royal Exequies for Isabella of Bourbon," *Art Bulletin*, 72:1, pp. 51–73

Pacheco, Francisco, 2001, *Arte de la pintura*, ed. Bonaventura Bassegoda i Hugas (Madrid: Cátedra)

Palomino de Castro y Velasco, Antonio, 1987, *Lives of the Eminent Spanish Painters and Sculptors*, ed. and trans. Nina Ayala Mallory (Cambridge: Cambridge University Press)

Palos, Joan Lluís, 2010, *La mirada italiana: Un relato visual del imperio español en la corte de sus virreyes en Nápoles (1600–1700)* (Valencia: Universitat de València)

Patterson, Angus, 2009, *Fashion and Armour in Renaissance Europe: Proud Lookes and Brave Attire* (London: V&A Publishing)

Pellicer de Tovar, José, 2002, *Avisos: 17 de mayo de 1639–29 de noviembre de 1644*, ed. Jean-Claude Chevalier and Lucien Clare, vol. 1 (Paris: Éditions Hispaniques)

Peña, Juan Antonio de la, 1623, *Relacion de las fiestas reales y iuego de cañas, que la Magestad Catolica del Rey nuestro señor hizo a los veinte y vno de Agosto deste presente año para honrar y festejar los tratados desposorios del serenissimo Principe de Galès, con la señora Infanta doña Maria de Austria* (Madrid: Juan González)

Pereda de Castro, Rosa, and Sofía Rodríguez Bernis, 2005, *El Quijote en sus trajes*, exh. cat. (Madrid: Ministerio de Cultura, Secretaría General Técnica)

Pérez D'Ors, Pablo, and Michael Gallagher, 2010, "New Information on Velázquez's Portrait of Philip IV at Fraga in The Frick Collection, New York," *The Burlington Magazine*, 152: 1291, pp. 652–9

Pérez D'Ors, Pablo, Richard Johnson, and Don Johnson,

2012, "Velázquez in Fraga: A New Hypothesis about the Portraits of El Primo and Philip IV," *The Burlington Magazine*, 154:1314, pp. 620–25

Pérez Sánchez, Alfonso E., and Nicola Spinosa, 2005, *Velázquez a Capodimonte*, exh. cat. (Naples: Electa Napoli)

Pérez Villanueva, Joaquín (ed.), 1986, *Felipe IV y Luisa Enríquez Manrique de Lara, Condesa de Paredes de Nava: Un epistolario inédito* (Salamanca: Caja de Ahorros y Monte de Piedad)

Phipps, Elena, 2011, *Looking at Textiles: A Guide to Technical Terms* (Los Angeles: J. Paul Getty Museum)

Pinto Crespo, Virgilio, and Santos Madrazo Madrazo (eds.), 1995, *Madrid: Atlas histórico de la ciudad* (Madrid: Lunwerg)

Pitman, Sophie, 2017, *The Making of Clothing and the Making of London, 1560–1660*, PhD dissertation (University of Cambridge)

Pizarro Llorente, Henar, 2019, "Isabel de Borbón (1621–1644): Una reina con poder," in María Leticia Sánchez Hernández (ed.), *Mujeres en la Corte de los Austrias: Una red social, cultural, religiosa y política* (Madrid: Polifemo), pp. 361–90

Pompa funeral, honras y exequias en la muerte de [...] Isabel de Borbon [...] que se celebraron en el Real Convento de S. Geronimo de Madrid, 1645 (Madrid: Diego Díaz de la Carrera)

Portús, Javier, 1993, *La antigua procesión del Corpus Christi en Madrid* (Madrid: Centro de Estudios y Actividades Culturales)

———, 2012, "Velázquez in Gray: Decorum and Representation," in *Diego Velázquez: The Early Court Portraits*, exh. cat. (Madrid: Museo Nacional del Prado), pp. 17–35

———, 2014, "Diego Velázquez, 1650–60: Portraiture and Court Culture," in *Velázquez: Las Meninas and the Late Royal Portraits*, exh. cat. (New York: Thames and Hudson), pp. 17–59

———, 2015, "Control e imagen real en la corte de Felipe IV (1621–1626)," *Studia Aurea: Revista de Literatura Española y Teoría Literaria del Renacimiento y Siglo de Oro*, 9, pp. 245–64

———, 2018, "Meninas e infantas: Historia de una seducción (1656–1901) (2008)," in *Velázquez: Su mundo y el nuestro* (Madrid: CEEH), pp. 353–78

Portús, Javier (ed.), 2012, *Diego Velázquez: The Early Court Portraits*, exh. cat. (Madrid: Museo Nacional del Prado)

———, 2014, *Velázquez: Las Meninas and the Late Royal Portraits*, exh. cat. (New York: Thames and Hudson)

Portús, Javier, Jaime García-Máiquez, and María Álvarez-Garcillán, 2015, "La *Vista de Zaragoza*, de Juan Bautista Martínez del Mazo: Notas al hilo de su restauración," *Boletín del Museo del Prado*, 33:51, pp. 60–77

Pregón, 1613. *Pregon general mandado guardar por los señores alcaldes de la casa, y corte de su Magestad, para el buen gouierno della, publicado en esta villa de Madrid* (Madrid: Cosme Delgado)

———, 1626. *Pregon en que su Magestad manda, que las mercaderias [...] no se puedan vender ni vendan a mas subidos precios [...]* (Granada: Francisco Heylan)

———, 1639a. *Pregon en que su Magestad manda, que ninguna muger de qualquier estado y calidad que sea pueda traer, ni traiga guardainfante, ò otro instrumēto, ò trage semejante, excepto las mugeres que con licencia de las justicias publicamente son malas de sus personas* (Madrid: Francisco Martínez)

———, 1639b. *Pregon en que su Magestad manda, que por quanto el abuso de las guedejas y copetes con que andan algunos hombres, y los rizos con que componen el cabello ha llegado à hazer escandalo, en estos Reynos, ningun hombre pueda traer guedejas ni copete* (Madrid: Francisco Martínez)

Premática, 1588. *Prematica, en que se da la orden que se ha de tener en el traer de los lutos en estos Reynos* (Madrid: Pedro Madrigal)

———, 1639. *Prematica en que su Magestad manda, que ninguna muger ande tapada, sino descubierta el rostro, de manera que pueda ser vista, y conocida [...]* (Madrid: Pedro Tazo)

———, 1657. *Prematica que su Magestad manda publicar sobre conseruacion del contrauando, reuocacion de las permissiones, prohibicion del vso de las mercaderias, y frutos de los Reynos de Francia, Inglaterra, Portugal, y reformacion de trajes, y vestidos [...]* (Madrid: Pablo de Val)

A Proclamation for Reformation, [1623] (London: Printed for Nathaniell Butter, Nicholas Bourne, and Thomas Archer)

Puerta Escribano, Ruth de la, 1997, *Historia del gremio de sastres y modistas de Valencia: Del siglo XIII al siglo XX* (Valencia: Ayuntamiento de Valencia)

———, 2001, "Los tratados del arte del vestido en la España Moderna," *Archivo español de arte*, 74:293, pp. 45–66

Quesada Valera, José María (ed.), 2015, *El triunfo de la imagen: Tesoros del arte sacro restaurados por la Comunidad de Madrid*, exh. cat. (Madrid: Dirección General de Patrimonio Histórico)

Quevedo, Francisco de, 1635, *Iuguetes de la niñez, y trauesuras de el ingenio* (Barcelona: Pedro Lacavallería)

———, 1946, *Epistolario completo de D. Francisco de Quevedo Villegas*, ed. Luis Astrana Marin (Madrid: Instituto Editorial Reus)

Quiñones de Benavente, Luis, 1991, "*El guarda-infante* Primera Parte," in Christian Andrès (ed.), *Entremeses* (Madrid: Cátedra), pp. 141–54

Ragosta, Rosalba, 2009, *Napoli, città della seta: Produzione e mercato in età moderna* (Rome: Donzelli)

Rangström, Lena, 2002, *Lions of Fashion: Male Fashion of the 16th, 17th, 18th Centuries* (Stockholm: Livrustkammaren and Bokförlaget Atlantis)

Ravenscroft, Janet, 2014, "Dwarfs—and a Loca—as Ladies' Maids at the Spanish Habsburg Courts," in Nadine Akkerman and Birgit Houben (eds.), *The Politics of Female Households: Ladies-in-Waiting Across Early Modern Europe* (Leiden and Boston: Brill), pp. 147–77

Reade, Brian, 1951, *The Dominance of Spain, 1550–1660*, Costume of the Western World (London: George G. Harrap)

Real Academia Española, *CORDE: Corpus diacrónico del español* <rae.es/banco-de-datos/corde>

Relación, 1638. *Relacion verdadera de todo lo sucedido el dia del bautismo de la serenissima Infanta* (Barcelona: Sebastián y Jaime Matevad)

———, 1649. *Relacion verdadera de las fiestas que se hizieron a las velaciones del Rey nuestro Señor, que Dios guarde, en la Villa de Naualcarnero* [...] (Madrid: Viuda de Juan Sánchez)

———, 1659. *Relación de la felize nueva* [...] *de los casamientos de la Serenissima Infanta doña María Teresa de Austria y Boruon, con el Christianissimo Rey de Francia Luis Dezimoquarto, y de las pazes tan deseadas de las dos Coronas* [...] (Alcalá: María Fernández)

———, 1660a. *Primera parte de la Relacion de las Reales Disposiciones, y Magestuosos aparatos, co[n] que su Magestad* [...] *se ha seruido hazer jornada a la Prouincia de Guipuzcoa* [...] (Madrid: José Fernández de Buendía)

———, 1660b. *Segunda parte de la relacion diaria del itinerario, que su Magestad* [...] *ha seguido desde que saliò de Madrid, hasta llegar a Fuenterrabia y forma de los desposorios* [...] (Madrid: José Fernández de Buendía)

———, 1660c. *Tercera parte de la relacion de las vistas de los dos poderosos monarcas de la Europa, entregas de la señora reyna de Francia* [...] (Madrid: José Fernández de Buendía)

———, 1660d. *Quarta parte de la relacion de las fiestas que se hizieron al Rey nuestro señor en la ciudad de Valladolid y llegada de su Magestad a la Villa de Madrid* (Madrid: José Fernández de Buendía)

Ribeiro, Aileen, 2003, *Dress and Morality* [1986] (Oxford: Berg)

———, 2014, "A Story of Pride and Prejudice: Perceptions of Spain and Spanish Dress in Seventeenth-Century England," in José Luis Colomer and Amalia Descalzo (eds.), *Spanish Fashion at the Courts of Early Modern Europe*, vol. 2 (Madrid: CEEH), pp. 317–39

———, 2017, *Clothing Art: The Visual Culture of Fashion, 1600–1914* (New Haven and London: Yale University Press)

Riello, Giorgio, and Ulinka Rublack, 2019, "Introduction," in *The Right to Dress: Sumptuary Laws in a Global Perspective, c. 1200–1800* (Cambridge: Cambridge University Press), pp. 1–33

Río Barredo, María José del, 2000, *Madrid, urbs regia: La capital ceremonial de la Monarquía Católica* (Madrid: Marcial Pons)

———, 2008, "Imágenes para una ceremonia de frontera: El intercambio de las princesas entre las cortes de Francia y España en 1615," in Joan Lluís Palos and Diana Carrió-Invernizzi (eds.), *La historia imaginada: Construcciones visuales del pasado en la Época Moderna* (Madrid: CEEH), pp. 153–84

———, 2018, "Espacios de mujeres en el Madrid del siglo XVII: El estrado, entre la casa y la calle," in James Amelang et al. (eds.), *Palacios, plazas, patíbulos: La sociedad española moderna entre el cambio y las resistencias* (Valencia: Tirant Humanidades), pp. 789–800

Rocha Burguen, Francisco de la, 1618, *Geometria y traça perteneciente al oficio de sastres* [...] (Valencia: Pedro Patricio Mey)

Roche, Daniel, 1994, *The Culture of Clothing: Dress and Fashion in the "Ancien Régime"* [original French edn 1989], trans. Jean Birrell (Cambridge: Cambridge University Press)

Rodríguez Bernis, Sofía, 2014, "Where Clothing Was Kept," in José Luis Colomer and Amalia Descalzo (eds.), *Spanish*

Fashion at the Courts of Early Modern Europe, vol. 1 (Madrid: CEEH), pp. 137–64

Rodríguez G. de Ceballos, Alfonso, 1997, "El cuarto de la Reina en el Alcázar y otros sitios reales," in *La mujer en el arte español*, VIII Jornadas de Arte (Madrid: Alpuerto), pp. 203–16

Rodríguez Moya, María Inmaculada, and Víctor Manuel Mínguez Cornelles, 2014, "Olivares y la escenificación del poder a través de la arquitectura: Un lienzo de Juan de la Corte en Pollock House (h. 1635)," *Potestas*, 7, pp. 159–77

Rodríguez Villa, Antonio, 1913, *Etiquetas de la Casa de Austria* (Madrid: Jaime Ratés)

Romeo, Lázaro, 1671, *Por la iustificacion del edicto, que el ilustrissimo Señor Don Fray Francisco de Gamboa mando publicar, acerca de los Escotes de las Subditas de el Arçobispado* (Zaragoza: n.p.)

Romero González, Álvaro, 2021a, "Los sastres de Felipe IV: Modos de vida en la corte madrileña del siglo XVII," in Cristina Borreguero Beltrán et al. (eds.), *A la sombra de las catedrales: Cultura, poder y guerra en la Edad Moderna* (Burgos: Universidad de Burgos), pp. 633–47

———, 2021b, "Los bordadores en la Corte de la monarquía hispánica: Trayectorías profesionales y familiares (1578–1700)," *Magallánica: Revista de Historia Moderna*, 7:14, pp. 268–98

———, 2022, *Vistiendo al Rey: Artesanado, familia y trayectorias sociales en la Corte de los Austrias (1598–1700)*, PhD dissertation (Universidad de Castilla-La Mancha)

Ruano de la Haza, José María, 2007, "El vestuario en el teatro de corral," in Mercedes de los Reyes Peña (ed.), *El vestuario en el teatro español del Siglo de Oro* [2000], Cuadernos de Teatro Clásico 13–14, 2nd edn (Madrid: Compañía Nacional de Teatro Clásico), pp. 43–62

Ruiz Pérez, Pedro, 1999, *La biblioteca de Velázquez: De la pintura y las letras*, exh. cat. (Seville: Consejería de Cultura)

Sánchez Cantón, Francisco Javier, 1942, "Cómo vivía Velázquez: Inventario descubierto por D. F. Rodríguez Marín," *Archivo español de arte*, 15:50, pp. 69–91

Sánchez de Espejo, Andrés, 1637, *Relacion aiustada* […] *de la entrada en estos Reynos de Madama Maria de Borbon, Princesa de Cariñan* […] (Madrid: María de Quiñones)

Sánchez Hernández, María Leticia, and Nieves Baranda Leturio, 2018, "Conventual Correspondence," in Nieves Baranda and Anne J. Cruz (eds.), *The Routledge Research Companion to Early Modern Spanish Women Writers* (Abingdon and New York: Routledge), pp. 87–102

Sanz, Carlos, and Rosa Gallego, 2001, *Diccionario del color* (Madrid: Akal)

Schroth, Sarah, 2008, "A New Style of Grandeur: Politics and Patronage at the Court of Philip III," in Sarah Schroth and Ronni Baer (eds.), *El Greco to Velázquez: Art During the Reign of Philip III*, exh. cat. (Boston: Museum of Fine Arts), pp. 77–120

Segovia, Baltazar, 1617, *Llibre de geometria del offici de sastre* (Barcelona: Esteve Liberos)

Semmelhack, Elizabeth, 2009, *On a Pedestal: From Renaissance Chopines to Baroque Heels*, exh. cat. (Toronto: Bata Shoe Museum)

Sempere y Guarinos, Juan, 2000, *Historia del luxo y de las leyes suntuarias de España*, ed. Juan Rico Giménez (Valencia: Institució Alfons el Magnànim)

Shergold, N. D., 1967, *A History of the Spanish Stage: From Medieval Times until the End of the Seventeenth Century* (Oxford: Clarendon Press)

Sicard, Frédérique, 2015, "Regencia e imagen de la reina Isabel de Borbón," in José Martínez Millán and José Eloy Hortal Muñoz (eds.), *La Corte de Felipe IV (1621–1665): Reconfiguración de la Monarquía católica*, tome I, vol. 2 (Madrid: Polifemo), pp. 1458–1500

SILKNOW, "Silk Heritage Thesaurus," <skosmos.silknow.org/thesaurus/es/>

Solé Peñalosa, Guillermina, 2009, *Verdugados, guardainfantes, valonas y sacristanes: La indumentaria, joyería y arreglo personal en el siglo XVII novohispano*, PhD dissertation (Universidad Nacional Autónoma de México)

Sommer-Mathis, Andrea, 2014, "Dynastic and Cultural Relations between the Two Lines of the Habsburg Dynasty and Their Effect on Velázquez's Work," in Javier Portús (ed.), *Velázquez: Las Meninas and the Late Royal Portraits* (New York: Thames and Hudson), pp. 61–73

Sorapán de Rieros, Juan, 1616, *Medicina española* (Granada: Martín Fernández Zambrano)

Soto y Aguilar, Diego de, 1863, "Festejos hechos en Madrid para la recepción del Príncipe de Gales," in José Amador de los Ríos, *Historia de la Villa y Corte de Madrid* (Madrid: M. López de la Moya), vol. 3, pp. 489–91

Steele, Valerie, 2017, *Paris Fashion: A Cultural History* (London: Bloomsbury)

Stein, Fabian, 1985, *Charles Le Brun: La tenture de l'Histoire du Roy* (Worms: Wernersche Verlagsgesellschaft)

Stevens, John, 1726, *A New Dictionary, Spanish and English, and English and Spanish, Much more Copious than any other hitherto Extant* [1706] (London: Printed for J. Darby et al.)

Stradling, R. A., 1988, *Philip IV and the Government of Spain, 1621–1665* (Cambridge: Cambridge University Press)

Suárez de Figueroa, Cristóbal, 2006, *Plaza universal de todas ciencias y artes*, ed. Mauricio Jalón Calvo, 2 vols. (Valladolid: Junta de Castilla y León, Consejería de Cultura y Turismo)

Swoboda, Gudrun, 2014, "Juan Bautista Martínez del Mazo *The Artist's Family* – the First Variation on Velázquez' *Las Meninas*," in Sabine Haag (ed.), *Velázquez*, exh. cat. (Munich: Hirmer), pp. 277–83

Tarrero Alcón, María Cristina, 2017, *La Iglesia de Santa María de la Almudena y la Real Esclavitud* (Madrid: Cabildo Catedral de Madrid)

"Tassa general de los precios," 1627, in *Prematica que su Magestad mando publicar sobre la reformacion de las causas de la carestia general en estos Reynos y moderacion en los precios [...]* (Madrid: Viuda de Luis Sánchez)

Taylor, Lou, 1983, *Mourning Dress: A Costume and Social History* (Boston: G. Allen and Unwin)

Terreros y Pando, Esteban, 1786–9, *Diccionario castellano con las voces de ciencias y artes y sus correspondientes en las tres lenguas, francesa, latina é italiana*, 4 vols. (Madrid: Viuda de Ibarra, Hijos y Compañía)

Thépaut-Cabasset, Corinne, 2013, "La mode dans les portraits de Rubens," in Blaise Ducos (ed.), *L'Europe de Rubens*, exh. cat. (Paris: Hazan; Lens: Musée du Louvre-Lens), pp. 143–59

Thornton, Peter, 1965, *Baroque and Rococo Silks* (New York: Taplinger)

Tiffany, Tanya, 2012, *Diego Velázquez's Early Paintings and the Culture of Seventeenth-Century Seville* (University Park: Pennsylvania State University Press)

Tosi Brandi, Elisa, 2017, *L'arte del sarto nel Medioevo: Quando la moda diventa un mestiere* (Bologna: Società editrice Il mulino)

Tratado de paz entre esta corona, y la de Francia, aiustado por el Excel[entisi]mo señor D. Luis Mendez de Haro y Guzman [...] Y por el Emin[entisi]mo señor Cardenal Iulio Mazarini, 1660 (Madrid: Domingo García Morrás)

Travesedo, Carmen de, and Evaristo Martín de Sandoval (eds.), 1977, "Cartas de la infanta doña María Teresa [...] a la condesa de Paredes de Nava (1648–1660)," in Jorge Guillén (ed.), *Homenaje a Emilio Gómez Orbaneja* (Madrid: Editorial Moneda y Crédito), pp. 417–37

Trewinnard, Richard Giles, 1991, *The Household of the Spanish Monarch: Structure, Cost and Personnel, 1606–65*, PhD dissertation (University of Wales)

Valdivieso, Enrique, 2002, *Vanidades y desengaños en la pintura española del Siglo de Oro* (Madrid: Fundación de Apoyo a la Historia del Arte Hispánico)

Valladares, Rafael, 1998, *La rebelión de Portugal: Guerra, conflicto y poderes en la monarquía Hispánica, 1640–1680* (Valladolid: Consejería de Educación y Cultura)

Van Wyhe, Cordula, 2014, "The Making and Meaning of the Monastic Habit at Spanish Habsburg Courts," in José Luis Colomer and Amalia Descalzo (eds.), *Spanish Fashion at the Courts of Early Modern Europe*, vol. 1 (Madrid: CEEH), pp. 251–89

Varela Merino, Elena, 2009, *Los galicismos en el español de los siglos XVI y XVII*, vol. 1 (Madrid: CSIC)

Varey, J. E., 1972, "Notas velazqueñas," *Archivo español de arte*, 45:177, pp. 58–60

Varey, J. E., and N. D. Shergold, 1953, "La *tarasca* de Madrid," *Clavileño*, 4:20, pp. 18–26

Vega, Lope de, 1970, *El perro del hortelano; El castigo sin venganza*, ed. A. David Kossoff (Madrid: Castalia)

———, 1990, *Peribáñez and the Comendador of Ocaña*, ed. and trans. James Lloyd (Warminster: Aris & Phillips)

Veliz, Zahira, 2004, "Signs of Identity in *Lady with a Fan* by Diego Velázquez: Costume and Likeness Reconsidered," *Art Bulletin*, 86:1, pp. 75–95

Vera Tassis y Villarroel, Juan de, 1692, *Historia del origen, invención y milagros de la sagrada imagen de nuestra señora de la Almudena: Antiguedades y excelencias de Madrid* (Madrid: Francisco Sanz)

Villalba, José de, [c. 1666–77], *Memorial contra los profanos trages que se usan en estos tiempos en los Reynos de España, que propone á la catolica consideracion de la Reyna nuestra señora, para que se sirua mandar se destierren dichos profanos trages de su Reino Catolico* (n.p.)

Villaverde Prado y Salazar, Manuel, 1650, *Relación de la entrada que su Magestad la Reina N.S.D. Mariana de Austria hizo desde el Retiro a su Real Palacio de Madrid* (Madrid: Domingo García y Morras)

Vincent-Cassy, Cécile, 2013, "La reina en majestad: Imagen política póstuma de Isabel de Borbón," *Tiempos Modernos: Revista Electrónica de la Historia Moderna*, 7:26 <www.tiemposmodernos.org/tm3/index.php/tm/article/view/338/369>

Vinuesa Herrera, Rosalía María, 2016, *Estudio de los oratorios domésticos y capillas privadas en los siglos XVII y XVIII a través de la documentación conservada en el Archivo General del Arzobispado de Sevilla*, PhD dissertation (Universidad de Sevilla)

Vittet, Jean, 2015, "La tenture de l'Histoire du roi de Charles Le Brun: Le portrait entre vérité et propagande," in Philippe Bordes and Pascal-François Bertrand (eds.), *Portrait et tapisserie* (Turnhout: Brepols), pp. 87–95

Warnke, Martin, 1993, *The Court Artist: On the Ancestry of the Modern Artist* (Cambridge: Cambridge University Press)

Westman, Annabel, 2019, *Fringe, Frog & Tassel: The Art of the Trimmings-Maker in Interior Decoration in Britain and Ireland* (London: Philip Wilson Publishers)

Wilkinson Zerner, Catherine, 1994, "Women's Quarters in Spanish Royal Palaces," in Jean Guillaume (ed.), *Architecture et vie sociale: L'organisation intérieure des grandes demeures à la fin du Moyen Âge et à la Renaissance* (Paris: Picard), pp. 127–36

Winkel, Marieke de, 2006, *Fashion and Fancy: Dress and Meaning in Rembrandt's Paintings* (Amsterdam: Amsterdam University Press)

Wunder, Amanda, 2015, "Women's Fashions and Politics in Seventeenth-Century Spain: The Rise and Fall of the *Guardainfante*," *Renaissance Quarterly*, 68:1, pp. 133–86

———, 2017a, *Baroque Seville: Sacred Art in a Century of Crisis* (University Park: Pennsylvania State University Press)

———, 2017b, "Innovation and Tradition at the Court of Philip IV of Spain (1621–1665): The Invention of the *Golilla* and the *Guardainfante*," in Evelyn Welch (ed.), *Fashioning the Early Modern: Dress, Textiles and Innovation in Europe, 1500–1800* (Oxford: Oxford University Press), pp. 111–33

———, 2019, "Spanish Fashion and Sumptuary Legislation from the Thirteenth to the Eighteenth Century," in Giorgio Riello and Ulinka Rublack (eds.), *The Right to Dress: Sumptuary Laws in a Global Perspective, c. 1200–1800* (Cambridge: Cambridge University Press), pp. 243–72

Wunder, Heide, 2002, "What Made a Man a Man? Sixteenth- and Seventeenth-Century Findings," in Ulinka Rublack (ed.), *Gender in Early Modern German History* (Cambridge: Cambridge University Press), pp. 21–48

Zabaleta, Juan de, 1667, *Obras en prosa de don Ivan de Zaualeta, coronista del rey nuestro señor, por él mismo añadidas* (Madrid: Andrés García de la Iglesia)

Zanger, Abby E., 1997, *Scenes from the Marriage of Louis XIV: Nuptial Fictions and the Making of Absolutist Power* (Stanford: Stanford University Press)

Zapata Fernández de la Hoz, Teresa, 2017, *La corte de Felipe IV se viste de fiesta: La entrada de Mariana de Austria (1649)* (Valencia: Universitat de València)

Zayas y Sotomayor, María de, 2009, *Exemplary Tales of Love and Tales of Disillusion*, ed. and trans. Margaret Rich Greer and Elizabeth Rhodes (Chicago: University of Chicago Press)

———, 2021, *Parte segunda del sarao y entretenimiento honesto* [*Desengaños amorosos*], ed. Alicia Yllera (Madrid: Cátedra)

Zofío Llorente, Juan Carlos, 2000, "Trabajo y socialización: Los aprendices en Madrid durante la segunda mitad del siglo XVI," in Enrique Martínez Ruiz (ed.), *Madrid, Felipe II y las ciudades de la monarquia*, vol. 2 (Madrid: Editorial Actas), pp. 521–35

———, 2005, *Gremios y artesanos en Madrid, 1550–1650: La sociedad del trabajo en una ciudad cortesana preindustrial* (Madrid: CSIC)

———, 2011, "Reproducción social y artesanos: Sastres, curtidores y artesanos de la madera madrileños en el siglo XVII," *Hispania: Revista española de historia*, 71:237, pp. 87–120

Acknowledgments

This book was shaped by two pivotal fellowships, first at New York's Metropolitan Museum of Art and then, 12 years later, across Central Park at the Bard Graduate Center. At the Met, I gained my first experience with early modern textiles at the Antonio Ratti Textile Center and broadened my approach from a study of fashion based on textual and visual representations to one that focused on materials and objects as well. A sprawling project came into focus at the Bard Graduate Center thanks to conversations with faculty, graduate students, visiting scholars, and my fellow fellows. A Faculty Fellowship Award from Lehman College made it possible for me to take a year of leave from teaching, and additional support came from a City University of New York Office of Research Book Completion Award. The research for this book in Spain and elsewhere was supported by the Renaissance Society of America, the National Endowment for the Humanities, the American Philosophical Society, Lehman College, and the Professional Staff Congress-City University of New York. The publication of this book with its many images was made possible by Princeton University's Barr Ferree Publication Fund, and I am very grateful to the Princeton Department of Art & Archaeology managers, first Susan Lehre and then Maureen Killeen, who administered the grant. Publication subventions were provided by the Newberry Library and the Custard Institute for Spanish Art and Culture at the Meadows Museum, SMU. I am very grateful to the institutions and private collectors who contributed images free of charge.

The bulk of the archival documentation for this book is at the Archivo General de Palacio in Madrid, and I appreciate the staff there who made it such a pleasurable place to work. I am particularly indebted to palace archivist Javier Fernández Fernández and his colleagues in document reproduction who provided me with scans of documents when it was impossible for me to visit the archive in person during the Covid-19 pandemic. Staff at the Archivo Histórico Nacional, the Biblioteca Nacional de España, and the British Library also supplied scans of key documents during that difficult time. For their invaluable assistance, I thank archivists Óscar Castañón at the Archivo de la Parroquia de San Ginés, Emilia Suárez Juega at the Archivo Histórico Diocesano de Madrid, Beatriz García Gómez at the Archivo Histórico de Protocolos de Madrid, Isabel Aguirre Landa at the Archivo General de Simancas, and Luisa Cano Moya at the Archivo Municipal de Fuenlabrada. I also thank Mayor Francisco Javier Ayala Ortega for welcoming me to Fuenlabrada, Mateo Aguado's home town, which is a village no more.

I owe a special debt of gratitude to the museum curators, conservators, and staff members who made their collections accessible and shared their knowledge about textiles, garments, paintings, and sundry objects. First and foremost, heartfelt thanks go to everyone at the Met Museum's Antonio Ratti Textile Center (from 2005 to the present), with special appreciation to Eva Labson and Eva Holiday DeAngelis-Glasser. Also at the Met, I would like to express my gratitude to Janina Poskrobko, Cristina Carr, and Giulia Chiostrini in

Textile Conservation; Michael Gallagher in Paintings Conservation; Stephan Wolohojian and David Pullins in European Paintings; Elizabeth Cleland and Wolf Burchard in European Sculpture and Decorative Arts; and Mark McDonald in Drawings and Prints. I am also grateful to Hispanic Society of America curators Constancio del Álamo, Marcus Burke, Noemí Espinosa, Patrick Lenaghan, and John O'Neill, and director Guillaume Kientz; Xavier Salomon and Aimee Ng at the Frick Collection; Kimberly Randall at Cooper Hewitt, Smithsonian Design Museum; and Kevin Jones at the Fashion Institute of Design & Merchandising Museum, who brought the splendid embroidered dress illustrated in Chapter 6 to my attention. In Spain, very special thanks go to Sofía Rodríguez Bernis, director of the Museo Nacional de Artes Decorativas, and Pilar Benito García and María Barrigón Montañés of the Patrimonio Nacional, for countless kindnesses; thanks also to Javier Portús and Ana González Mozo (Museo Nacional del Prado), Elvira González (Museo del Traje), Almudena Pérez de Tudela (El Escorial), Isabel Tuda Rodríguez (Museo de Historia de Madrid), María Cristina Tarrero Alcón (Museo Catedral de la Almudena), Ana García Sanz and Lorena Robredo García (Patrimonio Nacional), Sílvia Saladrigas Cheng (Centre de Documentació i Museu Tèxtil, Terrassa), Cristina Partearroyo Lacaba (Instituto Valencia de Don Juan), Germán Dueñas Beraiz (Museo del Ejército, Toledo), and Marta Negro Cobo (Museo de Burgos). Gudrun Swoboda at the Kunsthistorisches Museum in Vienna and Letizia Treves at the National Gallery in London have been exceptionally helpful by sharing access and information about their collections of Spanish court portraits. Daniela Degl'Innocenti at the Museo del Tessuto in Prato expertly matched several textile fragments to patterned fabrics in seventeenth-century portraits. Additional help was provided by Maria Matilde Simari at the Uffizi Gallery, Lelia Packer at the Wallace Collection, and Inger Olovsson at Skokloster Castle in Sweden. Staff at the Victoria and Albert Museum's Clothworkers' Centre, then located in Blythe House, facilitated a unique opportunity to study seventeenth-century garments and accessories under ideal conditions. Finally, Elizabeth Semmelhack has responded to many email queries about historic footwear and offered a memorable tour of the Bata Shoe Museum's extraordinary collection in Toronto.

I am immensely grateful to dear friends who read all or part of this book in draft form: Jesús Escobar, Richard Kagan, Patrick Lenaghan, Mark McDonald, and Silvia Mitchell. While the generous souls named above have helped me avoid many mistakes, the errors that undoubtedly remain are entirely my own. It was such a treat to work with Maura Whang, who drew the maps that appear in this book; Antonio Urquízar Herrera, who photographed Mateo Aguado's Madrid; Marina Cotugno, who tracked down the most elusive images; and Gilad BenDavid, who assisted with research queries. At Lehman College, I received unwavering moral and professional support for this project from dean James Mahon, history chair Marie Marianetti, and department administrator Laura Guerrero, while José Torres provided essential technical support. At the Graduate Center of the City University of New York, I thank Stephen Klein, Silvia Cho, and the Inter-Library Loan staff at the Mina Rees Library, and director of public safety John Flaherty and the security guards who made it possible for me to work in my office throughout the pandemic. At Yale University Press, I am grateful to Mark Eastment for taking this book on board when it was still just a twinkle in the eye and for sending the first draft of the manuscript to two exceptionally qualified and magnanimous anonymous readers, who wrote the most thorough, detailed, and helpful reader reports that any author could hope to receive. This book is infinitely better than it would have been without them. I was very fortunate to work with editor Julie Hrischeva, copyeditor Lise Connellan, and Catherine Bankhurst, who designed the book and guided it through publication as project manager. Also at the Press, Sophie Neve and Rachel Hughes were unfailingly helpful.

Many individuals have contributed to this project over the years. First and foremost, Melinda Watt has been my good-humored guide to all things related to textiles, and she made a crucial contribution to this book by deciphering many of the textiles depicted in the paintings that illustrate its pages. José Nieto Sánchez generously shared his expertise on early modern tailors in Madrid and provided transcriptions of apprentice contracts. Sofía Rodríguez Bernis and María Dolores Vila Tejero valiantly helped decode terms for dress trimmings, while Elena Kanagy-Loux graciously imparted her knowledge on the infinitely complicated subject of lace. Expert assistance on many different topics was kindly provided by Jim Amelang, Laura Bass, Cristian Berco, María Caba, Javier Castro, Amalia Descalzo Lorenzo, Borja Franco, John Gagné, Guy Geltner, Arianna Giorgi, Anthony Grafton, Marina Hays, Paula Erichsen Hohti, Hilary Macartney, Michele Majer, Alistair Malcolm, José Martínez Torrejón, Timothy McCall, Mariola Merino, Lesley Miller, Benito Navarrete, Laura Oliván Santaliestra, Sophie Pitman, Allyson Poska, Lena Rangström, Mariña Regueiro, Giorgio Riello, María José del Río, Carmen Ripollés, Carmen Saen de Casas, Danielle Peterson Searls, Shreve Simpson, Corinne Thépaut-Cabasset, Tanya Tiffany, Harriet Turner, Cordula van Wyhe, Evelyn Welch, and Betsy Wright. I am especially indebted to Edward Sullivan, Andrew Morrall, and Deborah Krohn, whose feedback led me to focus this book on Mateo Aguado. The ideas in this book took shape and found their place on the page thanks to conversations with Abigail Balbale, Peter Miller, Laurie Nussdorfer, Katrina Olds, Robyn Spencer, Zach Stewart, Chuck Wooldridge, and the graduate students in my classes on early modern fashion at the Graduate Center of the City University of New York.

For their friendship and support throughout the process of writing this book, I am grateful to Jessica Benjamin, Sandra Goldmark, and Kristin Roth-Ey. Most of all, thank you to Shamus Adams and Anders Wunder Adams. There is no one I would rather live with during a pandemic lockdown, and this book is finished thanks to the two of you. I could not have written a book about a tailor if my mom had not taught me how to sew my own clothes when I was a teenager. While my mom taught me how to read patterns, lay out the fabric, and use the sewing machine, my dad reveled in the flurry of activity that took over the dining-room table. This book is dedicated to my parents, Susan and John Wunder, with love.

Picture Credits

Abelló Collection, photo © Joaquín Cortés: fig. 15 (and back cover)
Alamy Stock Photos: figs. 83 [Archivart], 97 [Godong], 180 [KarSol], 194 [Sipa USA], 195 [Jeffrey Isaac Greenberg 8+]
Album/Art Resource, NY: figs. 33 and 86
Archivio di Stato di Firenze, by permission of the Ministero della Cultura: fig. 58 [Guardaroba Medicea 143, c. 418r]
Archivo General de Palacio/Patrimonio Nacional, Madrid: figs. 24 [Administración general, Legajo 5272 expediente 2] and 168 [Administración general, Legajo 658]
Archivo Histórico de Protocolos, Madrid: fig. 198 [T.5684, f. 271r]
The Art Institute of Chicago/Art Resource, NY: fig. 53 [Purchase Fund, 1907.356]
Ayuntamiento de Madrid, Archivo de la Villa: fig. 131 [2-197-16]
Ayuntamiento de Madrid, Museo de Historia de Madrid: fig. 22
© Besançon, Musée des Beaux-Arts et d'Archéologie, Photo C. Choffet: fig. 190
Biblioteca Nacional de España, Madrid: figs. 10, 18, 31, 50, 57, 77, 98, 110–12, 171, 178; pp. 219–20
Bibliothèque nationale de France: figs. 9 and 79
bpk Bildagentur/Gemäldegalerie, Staatliche Museen, Berlin/ photo Jorg P. Anders/Art Resource, NY: fig. 60
British Library, London, UK © British Library Board. All Rights Reserved/Bridgeman Images: fig. 78 [Egerton Ms 1269]
Cooper Hewitt, Smithsonian Design Museum: figs. 38 [1905-2-16-b; 1905-2-18; 1905-2-35; 1905-2-112] and 71 [1962-56-8]
The Devonshire Collections, Chatsworth. Reproduced by permission of Chatsworth Settlement Trustees/Bridgeman Images: fig. 118
Dorotheum Vienna, auction catalogue 18.10.2016: figs. 26 and 137
FIDM Museum Collection: Funds donated by Linda & Steven Plochocki / Fashion Institute of Design & Merchandising, Los Angeles / 2020.5.35A-E: figs. 158 [Photo Brian Davis] and 159 [Photo Andreana Langston]
Used by permission of the Folger Shakespeare Library: fig. 40 [TT575.F8 1588 Cage, leaf A2r]
© The Frick Collection: fig. 104
Fundación Álvaro de Bazán: fig. 34
Fundación Casa Ducal de Medinaceli: fig. 67
Galleria Palatina & Appartamenti Reali di Palazzo Pitti, Florence, Tuscany, Italy/Bridgeman Images: fig. 43
© MiC–Musei Reali, Galleria Sabauda: fig. 96
Germanisches Nationalmuseum: fig. 175
Glasgow Life Photo Library © CSG CIC Glasgow Museums and Libraries Collections: fig. 49
Courtesy of the Haggerty Museum of Art, Marquette University: fig. 160
Courtesy of the Hispanic Society of America, New York: figs. 62, 84, 141, 176
Houghton Library, Harvard University: fig. 142 [MS Typ 258]
KHM–Museumsverband: figs. 42, 75, 80, 88, 109, 126, 144, 146–7, 150, 151 (and frontispiece), 165, 167
© MAK/Hanady Mustafa: fig. 7 (and jacket flap)
Image copyright © The Metropolitan Museum of Art. Image source: Art Resource, NY: figs. 61 (and endpapers) and 114–15; p. 216
The Metropolitan Museum of Art, New York, public-domain artworks: figs. 8, 13–14, 45, 72, 91, 94–5
Ministry of Foreign Affairs, Madrid, Spain/Index Fototeca/ Bridgeman Images: fig. 169
Musée Carnavalet–Histoire de Paris: fig. 155
Musée des Arts Décoratifs © MAD, Paris/Jean Tholance: fig. 48
Museo Arqueológico Nacional, photo Ángel Martínez Levas: fig. 54 [72048]
Museo de América, Madrid. Photo Joaquín Otero: figs. 196–7
Museo de Getafe (virtual)/Asociación Amigos del Museo de Getafe, photo Pablo Cabellos del Sol, Getafe (Madrid, Spain): fig. 92
Museo del Ejército, Toledo: fig. 68 [34999.02]
Museo del Traje, Centro de Investigación del Patrimonio Etnológico, Madrid: figs. 73 [MTCE080289_002, photo Lucia Ibarra Zubiaga] and 177 [MTCE001019, photo David Serrano Pascual]

Museo Etnográfico de Castilla y León, Zamora: fig. 99
© Museo Lázaro Galdiano, Madrid: figs. 37 and 119
Museo Nacional de Artes Decorativas, Madrid: figs. 35, 183, 185, 188–9, 191–3
© Photographic Archive Museo Nacional del Prado: figs. 1–4, 11–12, 27 (and front cover), 28–30, 41, 52, 55–6, 64, 69–70, 76, 82, 87, 101, 103, 106, 113, 120–22, 133, 138, 140, 148, 154, 161, 170, 174, 182, 187; pp. 217–18
© Museu Tèxtil de Terrassa/Quico Ortega: figs. 51 [21654] and 129 [18960]
Museum of the City of New York: fig. 5 [42.146.8AB]
© 2023 Museum of Fine Arts, Boston: figs. 85 (and detail fig. 81) [Henry Lillie Pierce Fund, 01.104] and 156 [The Elizabeth Day McCormick Collection, 44.521a-b]
© National Gallery, London/Art Resource, NY: figs. 6, 25, 134, 173
Courtesy National Gallery of Art, Washington, DC: figs. 46 and 100
National Heritage Institute Funds, Sychrov Castle, Czech Republic: fig. 93 [S-00043]
© National Portrait Gallery, London: fig. 139
Oronoz: figs. 19–21, 89–90
Palazzo Reale di Napoli, Ministero della Cultura: figs. 123–5
Patrimonio Nacional, Monasterio de las Descalzas Reales: figs. 39 (and detail facing Measurements and Prices) [00612179], 116 [00615657], 166 [00612384]
Patrimonio Nacional, Real Monasterio de San Lorenzo de El Escorial: figs. 59 [10051472], 127 [10034968], 136 [10014297]
Pérez Simón Collection, Mexico © Studio Sébert Photographes: fig. 132
Private Collection, Philadelphia: fig. 184
Real Biblioteca de Palacio, Madrid/Patrimonio Nacional: figs. 32 and 63 [ROLL/109]
© Real Academia de la Historia, Spain: fig. 172
© RMN-Grand Palais/Art Resource, NY: figs. 107, 130, 143, 145, 157, 162–4
Royal Collection Trust/© His Majesty King Charles III 2023: figs. 74, 149; p. 215
The Royal Danish Collection, Rosenborg: fig. 105
Scala/Art Resource, NY: fig. 102
Skokloster Castle/SHM: figs. 16–17 [photo Göran Schmidt], 108 [photo Jens Mohr]
© The State Hermitage Museum. Photo Vladimir Terebenin, Leonard Kheifets: fig. 44
Statens Museum for Kunst/National Gallery of Denmark, Copenhagen: figs. 47, 65; p. 214
Szépművészeti Múzeum/Museum of Fine Arts, Budapest, 2021: fig. 152
The Textile Museum Collection, Washington, DC: fig. 186 [R44.00.1, Acquired by George Hewitt Myers in 1940]
Antonio Urquízar Herrera photos: figs. 179 and 181
© Victoria and Albert Museum, London: figs. 23, 36, 128, 135, 153
By kind permission of the Trustees of the Wallace Collection, London/Art Resource, NY: fig. 117
Drawings by Maura Whang: Maps 1 and 2
Wikimedia Commons: fig. 66

Index

Numbers in *italic* denote pages with figures.